# The Rise of Political
# Economy as a Science

# The Rise of Political Economy as a Science

Methodology and the
Classical Economists

Deborah A. Redman

The MIT Press
Cambridge, Massachusetts
London, England

This book was set in Palatino using Ventura Publisher under Windows 95 by Wellington Graphics.

Printed and bound in the United States of America.

Library of Congress Cataloging-in-Publications Data

Redman, Deborah A.
  The rise of political economy as a science : methodology and the
  classical economists / Deborah A. Redman.
    p.  cm.
  Includes bibliographical references and index.
  ISBN 0-262-18179-7 (alk. paper)
  1. Economics. 2. Economics—History. 3. Economics—Philosophy.
I. Title.
HB171.R415  1997
330'.09—dc21                                                      97-22275
                                                                       CIP

# Contents

# Illustrations

# Preface

Because so much has been written about the first serious attempts to formulate the methods of the natural sciences, I was surprised to discover that a book like this one—the counterpart for the social sciences—has never been written. James Bonar published *Philosophy and Political Economy* in 1893, but it focuses primarily on tracing political economy's link with political philosophy, not the philosophy of science. And the ambitious time frame of Horst Wagenführ's survey of economic methodology from the Greeks to 1930 in *Systemgedanke in Nationalökonomie. Eine methodologische Betrachtung* (1933)[1] precludes detailed analyses of either individual thinkers or philosophical problems. In terms of detail, analysis, and historical depth, the present volume is unquestionably more ambitious than Wagenführ's. Not only does it document the development of classical methodology up to John Stuart Mill, it also chronicles and analyzes the theories of scientific method that laid the foundations of social science in general.[2]

The subject matter of this book, then, falls squarely into that broadly interdisciplinary area designated as the history and philosophy of science. The lack of attention accorded economics as a science no doubt helps explain why a book like this one has never been written before. After all, no formal subdiscipline such as "the history and philosophy of economics" is fully

---

1. "A Methodological Consideration of the Idea of Systems in Economics." Works cited in parentheses are included in "Sources Cited," at the end of this volume.

2. It may be added that this book represents the third volume of a series of works on economic methodology aimed at providing readers with a broader understanding of economics as a science and the history of economic methodology (see Redman 1989 and 1991).

established in any area of inquiry. Although it could be a
subfield of the history of science, history of economic thought,
history of philosophy, or history of ideas, the subject matter of
the present volume does not fit comfortably in these fields as
they are presently defined. Historians of science, or at least the
editors of such journals as the *History of Science, Isis,* and *Studies
in History and Philosophy of Science* apparently do not even view
economics as a science, for one can search in vain there for
contributions on economics. Economic methodologists show little interest in the history of methodology, preferring instead to
put current methodological arguments to ideological use.[3] This
puts economics in an unusual position, for most philosophers of
science nowadays seek evidence for their theories of science in
the facts of history.[4] It may be added that at most economic
departments since the 1960s, the history of economic thought
has gained the reputation as "a slightly depraved entertainment" (Boulding 1971: 232).[5] No wonder, then, that so few
scholars have ventured into such uneasy territory.[6]

The present work offers no novelties for scholars of the classical period: the information contained in this volume can be
found in published sources. It is nonetheless unique in three
respects. First, as already mentioned, it is, to my knowledge, the
first work solely devoted to the methodological heritage and
methods of the major classical thinkers in economics: surely, a
reliable, systematic history and analysis of the philosophies of
science of Smith, Malthus, Ricardo, and Mill and their epistemo-

---

3. This is equally true of the journals *Economics and Philosophy, Philosophy of
the Social Sciences,* and the *Journal of Economic Methodology* (known from 1989
to June 1993 as *Methodus*), as well as the annual *Research in the History of
Economic Thought and Methodology,* (Warren J. Samuels, ed.).
4. The disinterest in the history of economic methodology may explain why
economic methodology is in such wild and woolly shape these days. I am
assuming, of course, that the facts of the history of methodology are just as
important as those of the history of economic thought.
5. Recently even the continued maintenance of Harvard's Kress Library for
the history of economic thought has been challenged ("Editorial," 1993: 1).
Neither the *History of Political Economy* nor the *Journal of the History of Economic
Thought* publishes much about the history of economics as a science. Perhaps
the two new journals, the *European Journal of the History of Economic Thought*
and the *History of Economic Ideas,* will devote more space to the subject.
6. See Schabas (1992) on the history of economics as the history of science and
the comments on her article in the spring 1992 issue of the *History of Political
Economy.*

logical heritage is wanting and long overdue. Second, I have neither a preference for any particular classical author nor any axes to grind; thus, I hope that this volume will be a special contribution to a literature that is all too often partisan in outlook and consequently of limited scientific value. Last, and for purely pedagogical purposes, I have marshalled the literature on the methodology of the classical economists with the research interests of future generations in mind: It is arranged both by topic, for the reader interested in learning more about a particular subject/thinker, and alphabetically, to help the reader quickly find the source of a citation embedded in the text (in the final section, "Sources Cited").[7] Rarely have scholars writing on the classical period collected and absorbed the literature on classical economic methodology or classical philosophy of science; they, ostensibly, seem to prefer writing in a virtual vacuum or from a knowledge of the present position only. The consequence of this self-imposed ignorance is a trail of errors in the literature.

For readers who are unfamiliar with the literature on classical economics, the historical research has burgeoned since the 1960s, although the revolutionary additions to the primary literature may very well be behind us. The most significant development has been the appearance of definitive scholarly editions of most of the economics classics, some containing new primary materials. The Glasgow edition of Smith's works was published in the late 1970s and mid-1980s. Between 1951 and 1973 eleven volumes of Ricardo's works and correspondence, edited by Piero Sraffa and M. H. Dobb, appeared. E. A. Wrigley and David Souden brought out the first collection of Malthus's writings in 1986. Finally, the 33-volume University of Toronto edition of John Stuart Mill's collected works was issued between 1960 and 1991. In addition to the emergence of scholarly editions, the task of assembling the secondary literature on each thinker has been greatly facilitated by John C. Wood's collections of articles on great economic thinkers (Routledge's "Critical Assessments"

---

7. I am acutely aware that my *Economic Methodology: A Bibliography with References to Works in the Philosophy of Science (1860–1988)* fails to provide either a section on classical economic methodology or on the methodology of the various classical economists, even though a sizable literature exists in this area (expositions on Malthus and Ricardo are the major exceptions). The selected bibliography by topic appearing at the end of this study is aimed at remedying that deficiency.

series). The four-volume collections on each of the classical economists figuring in this volume became available in the 1980s and are being expanded.

This encouraging state of affairs in economics does not, unfortunately, extend to the philosophy of science. The works and correspondence of Bacon, Descartes, Newton, and the other philosophers discussed in part I of this volume are still being discovered and collected. Only now are scholarly editions of the works of such major sixteenth- and seventeenth-century figures as Bacon, Hobbes, Locke, and Leibniz being prepared. To date no one has collected the works of Herschel, Hume, Newton, or Whewell. The available primary sources on these great philosophers of the sixteenth and seventeenth centuries are, consequently, still strikingly deficient. In the 1990s, however, the Routledge four-volume "Critical Assessments" series appeared for Descartes, Hobbes, Hume, and Locke, providing scholars with a handy vade mecum of the secondary literature on these thinkers.

In the course of my research, two things greatly enhanced my understanding of the classical era: first, familiarizing myself with the background materials absorbed by Smith, Hume, Malthus, Mill, and their contemporaries; and, second, delving freely into interdisciplinary sources—sources often neglected by economists and philosophers alike. To get a feel for the science of the day I combed, page by page, the *Gentleman's Magazine* for the years 1731–1759 (the results are reported in the appendix); the *Edinburgh Review* and the *Quarterly Review* from the time they started up their presses in 1802 and 1809, respectively, to 1845; and the *Westminster Review* from its founding in 1824 to 1850. Having noticed that even the most meticulous check of bibliographic indexes in both economics and philosophy misses some useful sources on classical methodology, I scoured, again page by page, every volume of the *History of Science*, the *Journal of the History of Ideas*, the *Journal of the History of Philosophy*, the *Journal of the History of the Behavioral Sciences*, *Philosophy of the Social Sciences*, *Studies in Eighteenth-Century Culture*, and *Studies in History and Philosophy of Science* for information on classical economics and classical philosophy of science.

Owing to special exegetical and interpretative problems that I deal with in greater detail later, this book cannot be considered a definitive work on classical methodology. For one thing, the classical economists wrote too little and too ambiguously on the subject to allow for a definitive treatment.[8] Add to this the problem of breadth, which obviously has a decisive impact on the quality of any scholarly work. The reader who gets the feeling after a glance at the table of contents that I have bitten off more than I can chew may well be right. I certainly could have limited myself, for instance, to the methods and epistemological heritage of Adam Smith rather than taking on the entire classical era. The decision to trace the development of methodology from, essentially, Francis Bacon to J. S. Mill involved weighing costs and benefits: Should I delimit a topic and risk a horse-with-blinders effect on history and philosophy[9] or capture the sweep of time and ideas while tolerating a loss of detail and the disadvantages of simplification? I chose the latter course because it allowed me to depict the methodological developments associated with the rise of political economy as a science.

In spite of the drawbacks and the bold breadth of this work, my intention is to provide readers with a lucid account of (1) the body of methodological doctrines passed down to the classical economists and (2) the methods and methodologies of Smith, Malthus, Ricardo, and Mill—while providing insights into the modern significance of their ideas. In short, I hope the reader will find in this volume a reliable reference—one that is well documented, well reasoned, and tuned in to the historical, philosophical, and economic subtleties of eighteenth- and nineteenth-century Britain. Echoing James Bonar a century ago, I implore the reader to understand the shortcomings of this volume as due, in part, to "the absence of guiding models" (1893: 7).

Deborah A. Redman, Tübingen

---

8. Only one of the major figures in the classical period examined in this work, John Stuart Mill, wrote a systematic treatise on economic methodology.
9. When the time frame is limited, it becomes difficult, if not impossible, to distinguish between novel or old ideas.

# Acknowledgments

I am indebted to a number of persons and institutions for their assistance in bringing about a finished manuscript. A warm thanks goes to the librarians at the main library of Tübingen University, in particular to Heike Bauer, Elke Bidell, Regina Keinath, Brigitte Koppo, Sibylle Ruf, and Monica Theurer for their cheerful, generous support in obtaining the materials I needed to complete this study. Jack Sulzer, head of the general reference section at the Pennsylvania State University library (State College); Donald A. Walker, editor of the *Journal of the History of Economic Thought;* and Tsutomu Hashimoto, a doctoral student at Tokyo University in Japan, all deserve special mention for helping me secure materials not available in Germany.

I would also like to extend my gratitude to those who took the time to make helpful comments on various chapters of the manuscript while they were in rather primitive form: in particular, Sergio Cremaschi (Ferrara, Italy), Terence W. Hutchison (Birmingham, England), J. Ralph Lindgren (Bethlehem, Pennsylvania), John M. Pullen (Armidale, Australia), and Andrew Skinner (Glasgow, Scotland). Neil De Marchi (Durham, North Carolina) was kind enough to read the entire manuscript and make suggestions for its improvement and deserves special acknowledgment.

The final credit goes to the *Deutsche Forschungsgemeinschaft,* whose generous funding made the completion of the manuscript possible.

I would also like to take this opportunity to thank the University of California Press, which granted permission to reproduce pages 122 and 123 of volume 1 of Isaac Newton's *Principia,* translated by Andrew Motte in 1729 and revised and edited by

Florian Cajori in 1934 (reprinted in 1962). Chapter 5, on Adam Smith, is a greatly revised version of my article "Adam Smith and Isaac Newton," which appeared in the *Scottish Journal of Political Economy* 40, no. 2, (May 1993): 210–30: Incorporation of this previously published material was made possible through the courtesy of the Scottish Economic Society.

# I    The Heritage

# 1

# Introduction: Scope, Purpose, and Limitations of this Study

The subtitle, *Methodology and the Classical Economists*, is somewhat misleading, for I make no attempt to offer a comprehensive analysis of the methodological positions of the British classical economists.[1] Instead I focus solely on the work and methodological heritage of the economist-philosophers Adam Smith, Thomas Robert Malthus, David Ricardo, and John Stuart Mill. An acquaintance with the ideas handed down to these classical economists, the task of Part I, is crucial, for the bequest is awesome. Not by chance has the seventeenth century become known as the "age of genius" and the eighteenth as the "enlightened" or "philosophical age." While political economy was emerging as a science, the philosophical foundations upon which modern culture has been built were being laid. Such a wealth of ideas on epistemology and science was available to

---

1. Although few writers are able to agree on which economists fall under the rubric *English classical economists*, the term, even when employed in its narrowest sense to include Smith, Malthus, Ricardo, and J. S. Mill, is a misnomer because Smith was a Scot. If we use the term more loosely, we must take account of several more Scots (James Mill, James Anderson, James Lauderdale, and John Rae), a number of Irishmen (J. E. Cairnes, Robert Torrens, Samuel M. Longfield, and John R. McCulloch), a Russian (Thomas Tooke), and a German (Karl Marx). Consequently, the English—Malthus, Ricardo, and J. S. Mill, plus Richard Whately, William F. Lloyd, Henry Thornton, Nassau Senior, and Edward West—are clearly in a minority. For this reason, I use the more appropriate appellation *British classical economists*. If we use even broader definitions of the term *classical*, at least one French and Swiss economist, Jean-Baptiste Say and Sismondi, who, unlike Tooke and Marx, did not make their home in Great Britain, would have to be added to the list. For more on the meaning of the term *classical*, see Sowell (1974: 4–8) and Blaug (1987: 434–35).

the classical economists that the classical period in economics is, epistemologically speaking, backward-looking.[2]

Part I, then, combines the great-man and philosophical-problem approaches. First, in chapter 2, I discuss great thinkers whose philosophies of science were available to the classical economists. Because most mistaken notions about classical methodology have their roots in a misunderstanding of science in the age, the substance of chapter 3 focuses on the meaning of science in the eighteenth and nineteenth centuries: on moral philosophy and social engineering, on scientific analogies such as the clock metaphor, and on the development of scientific methods such as analysis and synthesis and statistical techniques. In chapter 4, I present a history of the problem of induction.

Part II is dedicated to the methodology of selected major figures in classical economics. The focus of chapter 5 is Smith's appeal to the "Newtonian method"; I explore the methodological dialogue of Malthus and Ricardo in chapter 6; chapter 7 centers on Mill and the method of political economy. I selected these particular thinkers for their historical importance: not only are they the founders of economics and modern social science in general, they also share a common intellectual lineage, one that is firmly based in Scottish thought. Binding the eighteenth- and early nineteenth-century thinkers was a belief in a common method for the social sciences. This strand of thought stops, however, with J. S. Mill, who developed the idea of political economy as a separate science, a view that becomes a convenient endpoint for this volume. Needless to say, I also chose these four figures because I think that they still have something significant to say about economics, social science, and philosophy of science, without meaning to imply that those not included are insignificant.

Indeed, it is necessary to say something about those excluded, for they are not inconsiderable in number or inconsequential in their influence. Sir James Steuart, Jean-Baptiste Say, Sismondi, Nassau Senior, John E. Cairnes, Robert Torrens, John Ramsey McCulloch, John Rae, Richard Whately, and Karl Marx, among

---

2. I say this without wishing to give the impression that the classical era is not methodologically innovative in its own right.

others, certainly had interesting things to say about methodology. But in today's methodological discussions their names are dropped far less frequently than those of Smith, Ricardo, Malthus, and Mill. Marx, I admit, is an unfortunate exclusion, although as a transitional figure in the history of economics, he deviated greatly from the methodological course laid from Smith to Mill. Because of his reputation as a special figure in classical economics, I finally opted against inclusion, which would have placed demands upon space, organization, and flow that could not have been done justice to in this volume.

My original interest in this subject was spurred by the profusion of references to the methods of Smith, Ricardo, Malthus, and Mill in the contemporary literature. I could not help but notice that the overwhelming majority of these allusions were made to condemn or endorse a particular position; in other words, name-dropping was a mere ploy to boost or bust the credibility and authority of a particular scholar's work. Of course, the practice of quoting an authority's methodological predilection to legitimate one's own approach is an invalid means of making a point, for cogent arguments stand solely on their merits. While exploring the literature on methodology, I discovered an interesting byproduct of this practice of name-dropping: the method of the same thinker ends up providing support for almost every possible methodological position in economics! Under these circumstances, an authoritative text on matters methodological ought to be welcomed—both to winnow out the multifarious inaccurate versions from the reliable interpretations of classical methodology and to shed light on the methodological problems troubling today's economist.

A second reason for such a study: an understanding of these economists' methods is a prerequisite to forming a sound interpretation of their main arguments. The significance of this study, however, is not limited to historical concerns. Many of the methodological problems debated by the classical economists are still with us today: questions of scope; the realism of assumptions; the role and limits of history, mathematics, statistics, and theorizing in economics; semantics; testing; the conflict between facts and theory; and problems of causation and generalization all are issues addressed by the classical economists that each new generation of economists continues to debate. Once economists realize that their discipline has a long history of methodological problems—*a history of problem-solving and investigation into the limits of knowledge*—they will begin to appreciate how important it is to record, cultivate, and teach that history. At the very least, then, a history of methodological developments preserves an account of erroneous procedures, fallacies, and failures that will be instructive for future economists. But such a history is actually much more, for the rise of political economy as a science was tied to the struggle to demonstrate that economic phenomena, like natural phenomena, could be handled in a scientific way.

While researching this era I confronted several obstacles to writing a study of classical methodology. In 1959 Bela Balassa opened a paper on classical economics with this remark: "Our conception of classical doctrine still abounds in 'stereotypes.' In order to produce a neat classification, divergent views of economists belonging to the classical school have been overly simplified and presented as *the* classical theory" (263). It seems to me that this is still true and that these practices continue to hinder the historiography of the discipline. The prevailing tendency to generalize about the classical thinkers by lumping them together as a methodological unit, also mentioned with regret by Hutchison (1978: 56), begs for the individual treatments I attempt in Part II of this volume. A second, related problem, which reinforces old stereotypes and inaccuracies, is many scholars' willingness to accept the assertions of their intellectual predecessors and to take secondhand opinions on philosophical matters. Because it is time-consuming to consult and digest all of the original sources, many of which fall outside of the boundaries of economics, very few scholars do it. As a consequence, inaccuracies and misunderstandings, some appalling, persist and proliferate. Thus, the history of economics as a science is, in my view, still waiting to be properly written.

Efforts to appraise the methodological positions and methods of the classical thinkers are further thwarted by the various conflicting theoretical interpretations of their chief works. Never, for instance, has there been a consensus on Ricardo's contributions to economics or on his position in the history of economic thought. A number of radical interpretations of Smith, Malthus, and Mill have also appeared, some of which could, given the discovery of new information, later be dispelled. The evolution of each economist's thought further complicates the task of interpretation. Some classical writers completely reversed their views; for instance, Malthus changed his mind about the value of industry for society, Ricardo about the effects of machinery on labor. Because we need to ask how these authors reached their conclusions in order to analyze their methods and methodological positions, these changes of mind create special difficulties.

Rather than discouraging them, these obstacles, as well as those mentioned in the preface, will, I hope, invite future scholars to take the challenge to probe this era with greater care and diligence. For all its difficulties, the rise of political economy as a science is a seductive topic whose intricacies, surprises, disappointments, and challenges continue to entertain each generation.

# 2      The Philosophical Background: Thinkers Who Influenced the Classical Economists

In a work on the methodology of the classical economists compelling reasons necessitate a lengthy introduction to the philosophical ideas that buttressed the epistemological structure of classical theory. Except for the contributions made by Ricardo, who lacked a university education and was less well read than the other economists, the intellectual accomplishments of the classical economists were clearly the product of the great minds of preceding generations. The roots of their methodology, then, lie in the philosophical period preceding it, in a heritage rich in epistemological insights. The maxim that those inquiring into the contributions scientific methods make to human problems must first equip themselves with a broad knowledge of natural and social science and the philosophy of science has little practical relevance today—for no one can have such a broad command of knowledge. It, however, applies perfectly to the classical era. A polymathic approach was so pronounced in the classical era that I would venture to say that being an economist today (or being only an economist) might well be an impediment to understanding the classical economists, especially their reasoning on method. In this chapter, therefore, I provide a condensed introduction to the philosophies of science available to the classical thinkers. A sketch of the developments in induction—the backbone of the philosophy of science in the classical era—is so important that I consider it separately in chapter 4.

Undoubtedly the two most important influences on the methodological development of political economy were Sir Isaac Newton and Lord (Francis) Bacon. Other significant actors were David Hume, René Descartes, Thomas Hobbes, and John Locke; Dugald Stewart, John Herschel, and William Whewell are included because of their impact on John Stuart Mill. Regrettably, the need to be selective meant neglecting other important figures, such as Robert Boyle,[1] Galileo,[2] William Harvey, Johannes Kepler, Gottfried Wilhelm von Leibniz, and others.

This age witnessed a veritable boom in epistemology, the inquiry into the nature, origins, and limits of knowledge. The thinkers whose ideas are discussed in this chapter have in common a desire to establish a sound basis for the beliefs of their time—although they do not always agree on what constitutes soundness—and to separate certain from uncertain knowledge. In this period, the "recognition of a more fundamental and ineliminable uncertainty or hypothetical character in physical science was not an easy achievement" (D. Clarke 1982: 203). Philosophy was not yet distinct from religion, and most of these thinkers, notably Bacon, Hobbes, and Hume, were fighting the influence of theology on science. In *The Wealth of Nations* (1976a: 796) Adam Smith reminds us that "[s]cience is the great antidote to the poison of enthusiasm and superstition [i.e., religion]." The intellectual world of the seventeenth, and even to a certain extent the eighteenth, century was marked by contempt for the actual practice of the scientists of the day and by a dispute between the adherents of the ancients (i.e., the Schoolmen or Aristotelians) and the moderns. The latter criticized the ancients for being sterile while stressing the importance of experiment and observation and promoting a corpuscular (atomistic) theory of matter. One of the most conspicuous outgrowths of the anti-traditionalist epoch was the Royal Society of London.

The most important point gleaned from a systematic study of the epistemology and philosophy of science available to the political economists is the unnecessarily restrictive nature of the categories *empiricist* and *rationalist*, labels that have been adopted since the eighteenth century to designate two basic sorts of philosophers.[3] Differences among the early thinkers on methodology are often exaggerated, leaving us with a picture of

---

1. Boyle (1627–1691) dominated science in England during the third quarter of the seventeenth century. This propagandist for "experimental philosophy" put forward the results of his work in hopes of inspiring others to repeat them or devise their own experiments.
2. Smith, for instance, owned a copy of Galileo's complete works (Mizuta 1967: 96).
3. And with them the categories *inductive* and *deductive*. On this subject, see chapter 4.

Baconians who suppose that truth springs from a mass of facts and experiments and of Cartesians who believe scientific certainty can be deduced from a handful of first principles.[4] While standard interpretations of Bacon, Descartes, Newton, and Hume are slowly yielding to more balanced, richer representations of their philosophies of science, the ideas of such other philosophers as Stewart, Herschel, and Whewell are just starting to gain our attention.

## Francis Bacon (1561–1626) and the Philosophy of Science

### The Reformation of Science

Bacon, a reformer at heart and a constitutional lawyer by profession, was the first to insist that science and theology be held apart. This does not, however, mean that Bacon's philosophy was not influenced by religion.[5] Moreover, as Julian Martin (1992) points out, if we want to understand his natural philosophy we need to keep in mind that Bacon was first and foremost a statesman and councilor to the king. Martin suggests, more specifically, that Bacon's reform of natural philosophy "was always governed by his political perspective and his loyal ambition to create bureaucratic machinery with which his master could better govern and expand his kingdom," and that Bacon even patterned the process of discovering the laws of nature and its respective terminology on the English legal process (1992: 172; 1993: 85).

The dominant intellectual goal in Bacon's life was the complete reformation of learning. He alone would usher in a complete revolution in knowledge—new goals, new methods, and

---

4. "Unfortunately, it is still fashionable to divide seventeenth-century thinkers into empiricists and rationalists, and to spell out a theory of knowledge that Bacon, Gassendi, Locke and Newton shared, and a theory radically different that Descartes, Spinoza, Leibniz and Malebranche shared, and a muddled mix that Hobbes, Henry More, Ralph Cudworth, and other Cambridge Platonists accepted. However one defines 'empiricist' or 'rationalist,' scholars have found empirical elements in the theories of Descartes, Spinoza, Leibniz, Malebranche, and the Cambridge Platonists, and rationalist aspects in the thought of the so-called 'British empiricists'" (Popkin 1987: 41).

5. Religious metaphors abound in Bacon's works. For Bacon scientific laws were divine commandments (ordinances or decrees). The symbol of light is a favorite symbol and one associated with the attributes of God (consider his *experimenta lucifera*). And the end of science is moral—to fulfill the Christian obligation of charity.

a new scientist. Bacon planned a life work entitled *Instauratio Magna* (*The Great Instauration*), whose purpose was to replace the existing foundations of science with a new method that would move slowly from particulars to principles of greater and greater generality and then descend back to particulars by induction. The *Instauration* was to consist of six parts: the classification of the sciences, the new inductive logic, phenomena of the universe, applications of the inductive method, tentative generalizations, and an exposition of the new philosophy. Three of these parts were scarcely begun by the time of his death. The second part of the *Instauration*, Bacon's famous *Novum organum* (1620), contains the central ideas of his philosophy of science.

Part 1 of the *Novum organum*, the first book of aphorisms, is essentially an attack on received systems. Early in his life Bacon developed a distaste for Aristotelian philosophy that continued into old age. Insisting that no adequate method had yet been formulated to investigate nature, he argued that something completely new was needed to replace the false philosophy of his age. His purpose was twofold: he wanted to correct both the excessive rationalism of the ancient thinkers and the unregulated empiricism of contemporary alchemists. In the *Novum organum* he decries the "mischievous authorities of systems" that are embedded in three false philosophies: sophistry, empiricism, and superstition (1858: 66). While the sophistical or rational school of Aristotle had corrupted philosophy with its logic, the empirical school advocated scanty, unregulated experiment. Superstition (by which Bacon also means theology) had corrupted philosophy in the worst way. Men would be better scientists according to Bacon "if they could bind themselves to two rules,—the first, to lay aside received opinions and notions; and the second, to refrain the mind for a time from the highest generalizations" (115). These are Bacon's two negative methodological rules.

Bacon's attack on systems is of a generalized nature. He names several philosophers whose systems were fanciful abstractions, mere inventions whose only achievement was to corrupt natural philosophy.[6] "[O]n account of the pernicious and inveterate

6. Concerning systems, Bacon explains that "after the sciences had been in several parts perhaps cultivated and handled diligently, there has risen up some man of bold disposition, and famous for methods and short ways which

habit of dwelling on abstractions, it is safer to begin and raise the sciences from those foundations which have relation to practice, and to let the active part itself be a seal which prints and determines the contemplative counterpart" (1858: 120–21). In other words, logic had been divorced from the facts for so long that it was time to return to the facts. He tends to believe that the intellect is more subject to error than the senses, although the latter can also be deceptive (1858: 26, 112, 412). In no sense does Bacon simply favor empiricism and reject rationalism; he is for a sensible mingling of the two and for freeing men's minds from the stronghold of opinion and obsolete, fallacious systems. The "business of philosophy," then, "neither relies solely or chiefly on the powers of the mind, nor does it take the matter which it gathers from natural history and mechanical experiments and lay it up in the memory whole, as it finds it; but lays it up in the understanding altered and digested. Therefore from a closer and purer league between these two faculties, the experimental and the rational, (such as has never yet been made) much may be hoped" (1858: 93).

Bacon's attacks on the ancients were daring for his day, for as Anthony Quinton observes, philosophers then were preservers, not creators, of knowledge (1980: 29). The focus of his attacks was an uncritical acceptance of tales, myths, magic, dogma, and unfounded opinion as sources of knowledge. Quinton associates Bacon's emphasis on exposing scientific results to criticism and on the public nature of knowledge as a means of insuring the objectivity and soundness of scientific results with Karl Popper's philosophy of science (1980: 30–31). "As for Bacon's critique of the uncritical acceptance of individual reports of marvels or oddities," Quinton remarks, "it does not, in itself, amount to much. But it points the way to a familiar requirement of scientific method as it has developed since his time, that experiments and, where possible, observations should be *repeatable*" (32).

In the second book of the *Novum organum* Bacon propounds the doctrine of the *idols*, whose purpose is to explain why and how the human intellect succumbs to error (1858: 54ff.). He chose the term *idols* to designate the phantoms, false divinities,

---

people like, who has in appearance reduced them to an act, while he has in fact only spoiled all that the others had done" (1858: 15). Bacon probably has Aristotle in mind.

or images that capture the mind and must be rooted out before humanity can come to know the truths of nature. The idea of phantoms infecting the human mind continued to preoccupy the major figures of the Scottish Enlightenment in the eighteenth century.

According to Bacon, idols can be classified into four groups: idols of the tribe, of the cave, of the marketplace, and of the theater. They can be either adventitious, as are doctrines of certain sects of philosophers, or innate to the mind,[7] the former being easier to eliminate than the latter. This part of Bacon's method of inquiry, then, is centered on the task of eliminating prejudices. The ancient skeptics had analyzed defects in man's ability to learn and judge reality and come to the conclusion that nothing could be known. Bacon rejects total skepticism as a philosophy of knowledge, transforming it into a principle of method (Prior 1954: 350).

The *idols of the tribe* is a fallacy that occurs because of the human tendency to find too much regularity and order in nature. It is human nature to prefer order to disorder, even when the facts point to chaos. Bacon was aware that people may find similarities that do not exist, refusing to acknowledge negative instances that fail to fit the category.

The name of the second mental weakness, the *idols of the cave,* alludes to a certain narrowness that results from the tendency of humans to reside in their "caves." This potential source of human error illuminates the ways in which the environment can influence observation and interpretation. Some people see similarities, others differences; some scientists are analytically minded, others historically oriented. Researchers who have taken great pains to learn certain ideas may later have a predilection for those ideas.[8]

Bacon's *idols of the marketplace* involve language problems and are, he suggests, perhaps the most troublesome obstacle to learning. Underscoring the fact that no language conveys ideas with absolute precision, Bacon points out that the use of definitions

---

7. "Now the idols, or phantoms, by which the mind is occupied are either adventitious or innate" (Bacon 1858: 27).
8. In this case, examples from contemporary economics would be easy to find. Certainly economists trained in the Chicago tradition see phenomena differently from those trained at MIT or Yale.

does not resolve the problem because they consist of words that require yet further definitions.

The last fallacy, the *idols of the theater*, demonstrates how scientists can be duped by the dogmas of schools of thought. Here Bacon has the objectionable mix of theology and philosophy in mind.

Bacon viewed the problems of the natural philosophy of his time as so prodigious that the sciences would have to be reconstructed from the ground up. He believed that the axioms and principles handed down by past generations were worthless— rash generalizations of questionable reliability. For Bacon a great storehouse of facts and observations, what he called "Natural or Experimental History," was a precondition of science. This step, he rightly believed, must precede theorizing. A great organizer and synthesizer, Bacon saw that the investigator's first task was to divide work into manageable components. One of the essential tasks of scientific inquiry was, then, to redress the paucity of factual information. Once investigators had collected and ordered the facts, scientists could then derive the laws of nature by inductive reasoning from individual facts such as those recorded by the natural history.

Bacon believed in a universal science called the *philosophia prima*, primitive or summative philosophy, which he compared to the trunk of a tree with branches of specialist disciplines. He likens natural philosophy to a vast pyramid, with the history of nature as its base, moving upwards to physics, metaphysics, and finally to a perhaps unobtainable peak, the *Summary Law of Nature* (1857: 356–57).[9] For Bacon natural philosophy is the "the great mother of the sciences" and induction—his answer to eliminating the problems of the idols—must be patterned after natural history (1858: 78).[10] "Of this reconstruction the foundations must be laid in natural history, and that of a new kind and gathered on a new principle (1858: 28). From these

9. "For knowledges are as pyramides, whereof history is the basis: so of Natural Philosophy the basis is Natural History; the stage next the basis Physic; the stage next the vertical point is Metaphysic. As for the vertical point . . . the Summary Law of Nature, we know not whether man's inquiry can attain unto it" (1857: 356).
10. "The formation of ideas and axioms by true induction is no doubt the proper remedy to be applied for the keeping off and clearing away of idols" (1858: 54).

considerations emerge three positive methodological rules: (1) prepare a natural experimental history; (2) arrange the instances in natural order; and (3) use induction to deduce laws. As Bacon saw it, the new method of induction would have been the natural one had human thinking not been corrupted by the idols. Bacon's natural history and theory of induction will be handled extensively in chapter 4.

In the *Novum organum* Bacon clearly intends his ideas on method to apply equally to the sciences of nature and man:

It may also be asked . . . whether I speak of natural philosophy only, or whether I mean that the other sciences, logic, ethics, and politics, should be carried on by this method. Now I certainly mean what I have said to be understood of them all; and as the common logic, which governs by the syllogism, extends not only to natural but to all sciences; so does mine also, which proceeds by induction, embrace everything (1858: 112).

Quinton, however, calls attention to the fact that "although his general scheme of classification suggests that human and natural philosophy are on the same footing, in their concrete description the two very greatly diverge. . . . [I]t is only such theoretical sciences [as natural science] which can arise from Baconian induction. His account of the human sciences fails to connect them with the new method which alone makes what is claimed to be a science really scientific" (1980: 53–54). That did not stop Bacon—or those who followed him—from asserting that his method, once mastered, would allow anyone to practice good science.

The criticisms of Bacon's method found in standard interpretations (e.g., Hesse 1964) revolve around the fact that Bacon seemed not to recognize the usefulness of hypotheses, abstractions, and mathematics in scientific research. Positions attributing to Bacon no role for hypotheses have, however, been challenged and will be treated in chapter 4. Similarly, Peter Urbach finds no evidence that Bacon relegated mathematics to a subsidiary role in science (1982: 125). Quite to the contrary, Bacon insists that data should "set forth (as far as may be) numbered, weighed, measured, defined. . . . And when exact proportions cannot be obtained," he adds, "then we must have recourse to indefinite estimates and comparatives" (1858: 259). Elsewhere he argues that "many parts of nature can neither be

invented with sufficient subtlety, nor demonstrated with sufficient perspicuity, nor accommodated to use with sufficient
dexterity, without the aid and intervention of Mathematic"
(371). Yet, for all that, Bacon evenhandedly concludes that
mathematics is a tool "which ought only to give definiteness to
natural philosophy, not to generate or give it birth" (1858: 93).

Quinton, I think, rightly notes that the relatively minor role
that Bacon assigned to mathematics in science "stemmed largely
from the fact that he did not know much about mathematics,"
which is not surprising for a statesman and lawyer (1980: 83).
Equally important, Quinton reminds us of some of the shadier
associations the mathematics of Bacon's age conjured up, of "the
close association between mathematics and occultism, shown in
numerology, astrology, the measuring of pyramids and the calculating of millennia" (83).[11] These practices were, of course,
what Bacon was fighting. Finally, Bacon was a man of general
knowledge; specialization and with it the "fanciful systems"
invited by a mathematical treatment of a subject were for him
an impediment to its advancement.[12] In any case, Bacon has been
somewhat neglected by analytic philosophers, who, put off by
his lack of rigor, prefer to concentrate on probability inference,
a notion that plays no role in Bacon's writings or, for that matter,
in those of the classical economists.[13]

## "Bacon-Faced" Generations

After Bacon died in 1626, his name was promoted by individuals
whose interests were often quite different from, if not opposed
to, his own. Immediately he became associated with experimen-

---

11. Compare also Ashley's view that "[i]t is evident that Bacon left very little
room for hypotheses, and this in keeping with his aversion to anticipation of
nature by means of 'phantoms' of any sort. . . . Bacon gave no explanation of
the function of the hypothesis; in his opinion it had no lawful place in scientific
procedure and must be banished as a disturbing element. . . . So fearful is he
of the influence of pre-judgement, of prejudice, that he will have no judging
which depends upon ideas, since the idea involves anticipation of the fact"
(1903: 157–58).
12. He believed, for example, that there was no sense in limiting oneself to a
single pursuit "such as the nature of the magnet, the ebb and flow of the sea,
[or] the system of the heavens," which have been "handled without much
success" (1858: 87).
13. In economics, probability inference had to wait for W. S. Jevons in order
to catch on.

tal natural philosophy and eventually was characterized as the "Father of Experimental Philosophy" or the "Father of the Inductive Logic,"[14] misleading distinctions if they are used to portray Bacon as a mere collector of facts. Besides promoting the importance of experimentation, Bacon impressed on his followers an optimism about what science could achieve.

In 1645, only nineteen years after his death, the Philosophical or Invisible College was organized in London to discuss topics on natural philosophy; it held weekly meetings, often at the home of William Petty. In 1662 this informal group was transformed into the Royal Society of London. According to Macvey Napier, a student of Dugald Stewart and in 1829 successor to *Edinburgh Review* editor Francis Jeffrey, the "philosophical spirit" underlying both institutions "was chiefly owing to the effects produced by Bacon's writings" (1818: 398).[15] No doubt the early Royal Society was "Bacon-faced," to use the expression coined by Henry Stubbe;[16] the early fellows so fervently venerated Bacon that many of their works had an apologetic air to them.[17] When Thomas Sprat wrote the Royal Society's history, he announced that the institution had been formed in Bacon's image; Bacon became, so to speak, its patron saint, although not all historians of science have viewed the Royal Society as a truly Baconian institution (Martin 1992: 174). Both Robert Hooke and Robert Boyle praised him, and Leibniz referred to him as "the incomparable Lord Bacon" (Martin 1993: 72), mimicking pointedly the reference to "the incomparable Sir Isaac Newton."[18]

Sprat's *History of the Royal Society* (1959: 83–119) devotes considerable space to the Royal Society's method. There he argues that the extraordinary features of science are not the subject

---

14. See Napier (1818: 373, 383). It is worth noting that Hume refers to Lord Bacon as "the father of experimental physicks" (1965: 7).

15. Dugald Stewart had recommended Napier (1776–1847) for his chair at the University of Edinburgh when he resigned his professorship, but Napier declined. The article on Bacon is one of Napier's most famous.

16. The term was meant pejoratively. Stubbe, whose favorite pastime, according to Napier, was to "abuse Lord BACON, and to depreciate his philosophical character" (1818: 408), opposed the method of the Royal Society and made his sentiments on the "experimental method" known through the products of his prolific pen.

17. Hume remarked in his *History of England* that "national spirit" compelled the English to make "partial and excessive" claims for Bacon (n.d., 4: 115).

18. Although it is uncertain whether it originated with him, the phrase "the incomparable Sir Isaac Newton" is used frequently by John Clarke (1972: iii).

matter of the natural historian and that the method of recording extraordinary phenomena is "subject to much corruption" and does not yield results that accurately mirror the "true following of Nature" (1959: 90). All knowledge, he claims, "is to be got the same way that a Language is, by *Industry, Use,* and *Observation*" (1959: 97). The "highest pitch of *humane reason,*" writes Sprat, is "to follow all the links of this chain, till all their secrets are open to our minds; . . . to rank all the *varieties,* and *degrees* of things, so orderly one upon the other; that standing on the top of them, we may perfectly behold all that are below, and make them serviceable to the quiet, and peace, and plenty of Man's life" (1959: 110).

On matters of style, Sprat emphasizes that the goal is "to reject all the amplifications, digressions, and swellings, of style: to return back to the primitive purity, and shortness, when men deliver'd so many *things,* almost in an equal number of *words.*" The writer was to exact a "close, naked, natural way of speaking; positive expressions; clear senses; a native easiness bringing all things as near the Mathematical plainness, as they can: and preferring the language of Artizans, Countrymen, and Merchants, before that, of Wits, or Scholars" (1959: 113). It must be added that in view of the fact that the fellows of the Royal Society used diverse methods, Sprat's account of a Royal Society method should not necessarily be viewed as a reflection of actual practice.[19] J. R. Jacob sums up the Royal Society method this way: "Science promoted the virtues of moderation, exact and cautious inquiry, methodical and diligent labour, even a certain degree of doubt productive of the search for further truth, and these were the virtues of the latitudinarian Reformation and the Protestant work ethic for which the Royal Society stood" (1980: 33).

By the 1730s Bacon's works were an integral part of the curriculum at Scottish universities (P. Wood, 1989: 90). The second "Bacon-faced" generation, therefore, was the eighteenth-century Scottish philosophers, who quoted Bacon with approbation and were ostensibly guided by his statements on method. Both Hume and Smith[20] enlisted his support and lavished praise on him, as did most of the great figures of the French and Scottish

---

19. For details, see J. Jacob (1980).
20. We know, for instance, that Smith owned Bacon's complete works.

Enlightenments. Colin Maclaurin, the Scottish mathematician who refined Newton's work in calculus, geometry, and gravitation, claimed that Bacon "is justly held among the restorers of true learning, but more especially the founder of *experimental philosophy*" (1971: 56). Bacon's works "were as flexible and appealing as the Bible, and no author provided a more ready stock of quotations" (Webster 1967: 117). For the Scots, then, the methods of Bacon and Newton often became inextricable. "To begin with the examination and comparison of phenomena in order to rise to the knowledge of general truths, and to proceed gradually from truth to truth, till we reach the most general that can be discovered,—these are the principles of philosophizing which BACON unfolded, and which NEWTON has, in the most emphatic terms, embodied with his discoveries" (Napier 1818: 404–405). Napier captures the relationship even more clearly in this passage: "Such, indeed, was the connection between the logic of the *Novum organum,* and the philosophy of the *Principia,* that it was only where the one was followed, that the other prevailed" (1818: 405).

August Comte, too, found much to praise in Bacon. In his *System of Logic* J. S. Mill refers to him as the philosopher who "taught mankind to follow experience, and to ground their conclusions on facts instead of metaphysical dogmas" (*Works,* 8: 879). Mill, however, was most concerned to point out that his contemporaries were slow to realize that Bacon was passé, for "those who reason on political subjects . . . [are] entirely unaware that Bacon's conception of scientific inquiry has done its work, and that science has now advanced into a higher stage" (8: 886). That, nonetheless, did not stop Mill from treating Bacon's work as a landmark in science. In assessing Bentham's accomplishments, he wrote in the characteristic style of his age: "What Bacon did for physical knowledge, Mr. Bentham has done for philosophical legislation" (*Works,* 10: 9).[21] By Mill's time the reigning consensus on Bacon could be summed up in the conclusion Thomas Macaulay draws in his *Edinburgh Review* article on Bacon's complete works: "It was not by furnishing philosophers with rules for performing the inductive process well, but by furnishing them with a motive for performing it well, that

---

21. Nor did it stop him from borrowing Bacon's concept of an *instantia crucis* (a crucial experiment) in his *System of Logic,* although he prefers the terminology used by Hooke and Newton, *experimentum crucis.*

he conferred so vast a benefit on society" (1837: 94).[22] Bacon's greatest achievement, then, was not inventing induction, but possessing "a knowledge of the mutual relations of all departments of knowledge" (1837: 96).

Mill, Herschel, and Whewell would all go on to propose corrections to the logic of the *Novum organum*. As we will see later in the chapter, Whewell spurned the Baconian method in favor of Newton's. For Friedrich Engels Bacon was "the real progenitor of English materialism" (in Martin 1993: 73); for F. A. von Hayek (1991: 75), the "progenitor of scientism." Today, as Quinton so aptly notes, many treat Bacon as a propagandist for natural science who, nonetheless, had little real practical understanding of it (1980: 30). Martin sums up Bacon's legacy this way: "Bacon, then, has had many differing significances, . . . yet one can conclude generally that the historical figure Francis Bacon quickly disappeared, and that in his place was left the philosopher 'Bacon,' a name to conjure with, extremely useful for the business of constructing a reputable intellectual genealogy for one's own philosophical positions" (1993: 73).

## René Descartes (1596–1650): Mathematical Scientist

Recent insights into the problems of translation and semantics that involve key terms in Descartes's French and Latin works have greatly altered the orthodox view of his philosophy of science. In the following discussion I address the new consensus emerging on Descartes's methodology with a view to discerning how his views on universal method, mathematics, empiricism, and hypotheses have been misinterpreted by scholars.

### From Mathematics to a Method of General Science
Descartes is probably best known as the man who stated *cogito, ergo sum*—I am thinking, therefore I exist—the first principle of his metaphysics.[23] A mathematician of considerable stature,

---

22. In a similar fashion, Macaulay wrote that Bacon "was the person who first turned the minds of speculative men, long occupied in verbal disputes, to the discovery of new truth" (1837: 92).

23. Since Descartes begins his work by showing the necessity of doubting everything to obtain certain knowledge, he can contend that the maxim "*I am thinking, therefore I exist* . . . is the first and most certain of all [principles] to occur to anyone who philosophizes in an orderly way" (1985: 195).

Descartes made significant contributions to physics, mathematics, and optics. Unlike Bacon, Descartes was primarily a practicing scientist.[24] Like Bacon, Descartes sought to bring about a radical reform of the sciences. The disciplines that would assist him were the only ones which in his opinion provided knowledge—logic, geometry, and algebra. He advocated a method combining the advantages of the three and got such impressive results that not even Bacon or Galileo could always match him (Sorell 1987: 3). Descartes is also responsible for bringing to science numerous mathematical notational devices that in his day added to the clarity and unity of science and quickly became conventions: the representation of unknowns in equations by $x$, $y$, or $z$ and knowns by $a$, $b$, $c$; the standard notation for roots, cubes, and higher powers; and the representation of solutions to equations in geometrical form with the use of X and Y axes.[25]

In Descartes's time men of science believed, with Aristotle, that no scientific result could guarantee absolute certainty. Descartes was impressed with the method of using proofs to establish truth in mathematics and convinced that a discipline without demonstrably certain results was not entitled to the name of science. In November 1619, while in southern Germany, Descartes had a vision, followed that night by a dream he took for a divine revelation of his life's work—the discovery of a method that would unify the sciences, a master method applicable to all scientific questions (Descartes 1985: 4, 116). After this experience nine years would pass before his dream was realized.

Descartes's classic works on the philosophy of science are the *Regulae ad directionem ingenii* (*Rules for the Direction of the Mind*), written around 1628 but published posthumously in 1701, and the *Discourse on Method*, originally written in French and published in 1637. The *Discourse* is autobiographical and consists of

---

24. "Scientific rather than philosophical questions dominated Descartes's work" (Sorell 1987: 4).

25. Descartes explains that he employs mathematical symbols "in order to keep them [the relations or proportions] in mind or understand several together, I thought it necessary to designate them by the briefest possible symbols. In this way I would take over all that is best in geometrical analysis and in algebra, using the one to correct all the defects of the other" (1985: 121). He uses geometrical diagrams because it is "generally helpful if we draw these figures and display them before our external senses. In this way it will be easier for us to keep our mind alert" (1985: 65).

four treatises written between 1619 and 1633: the "Discourse on Method," the "Meteors," the "Optics," and "Geometry."[26] The *Regulae* was never finished; it was to consist of thirty-six rules divided into three groups of twelve, but Descartes completed only twenty-one rules, eighteen of which were supported with explanatory remarks. He never clarified the exact relationship between the two works, but simply commented that the *Discourse* was not his complete statement on method (Moyal 1991a: 4). Lacking an explanation from the author, most scholars believe the two works supplement each other. The *Discourse,* a popular writing, marked a turning point in European thought because it was composed in French rather than Latin and aimed at bringing a message to the common people.[27] Roth (1937) notes that the fundamental doctrine of both works is the same. The *Regulae,* however, clearly provides more details about method and its application than the *Discourse* does.

Descartes's method involves the unity of science, the geometrization of physics—to borrow Alexandre Koyré's expression —and the abolishment of occult influences on science. Descartes realized that a body of information needs a method by which to obtain knowledge that is systematic and coherent. He believed he had happened upon such a method while exploring mathematics and that it could be applied not only to mathematical sciences but to all domains of inquiry. Thus Descartes, like Bacon, believed in a universal method (Descartes 1985: 9); the basis of the unity of science rested, however, not in nature but in the mind. In his view the material from which knowledge is derived—ideas—is homogeneous: if ideas are appropriately categorized and ordered, differences between them dissolve. They therefore become epistemologically equal and can yield

---

26. The full title of the *Discourse on Method* was *Discourse on the Method of rightly conducting one's reason and seeking the truth in the sciences, and in addition the Optics, the Meteorology and the Geometry, which are essays in this Method* (*Discours de la méthode pour bien conduire sa raison, et chercher la vérité dans les sciences. Plus la Dioptrique, les Météores et la Géométrie qui sont les essais de cette Méthode*).

27. Descartes explained his use of French this way: "And if I am writing in French, my native language, rather than Latin, the language of my teachers, it is because I expect that those who use only their natural reason in all its purity will be better judges of my opinions than those who give credence only to the writings of the ancients" (1985: 151).

certain knowledge (Moyal 1991a: 1). Descartes's aim was to secure mathematical certainty for all areas of knowledge. If it could be shown that the sciences form a coherent system, that is, that the sciences could be unified, they would become equally reliable.

Like Bacon before him, Descartes likens the system of philosophy to a tree. "The whole of philosophy is like a tree. The roots are metaphysics, the trunk is physics, and the branches emerging from the trunk are all the other sciences, which may be reduced to three principal ones, namely medicine, mechanics and morals. By 'morals' I understand the highest and most perfect moral system, which presupposes a complete knowledge of the other sciences and is the ultimate level of wisdom" (1985: 186). This scheme reverses the Aristotelian and Baconian hierarchy with its ascent from physics to metaphysics. Descartes's reaction against the Scholastics, however, was not limited to the structure of philosophy. He also opposed Aristotle's view that different disciplines require different methods and that the degree of precision varies from discipline to discipline. Extremely objectionable were the syllogisms the ancients used, for they incorporated premises that were assumed but not proven to be true. Most irritating of all, however, was the disputatiousness that characterized their scripts. It was this uncertainty and sponginess that Descartes proposed to eliminate. The turnabout in method that Descartes so ardently desired made his method radical in the early seventeenth century.

By *method* Descartes means "reliable rules which are easy to apply, and such that if one follows them exactly, one will never take what is false to be true or fruitlessly expend one's mental efforts, but will gradually and constantly increase one's knowledge till one arrives at a true understanding of everything within one's capacity" (1985: 16).[28] He sums up his method in the *Discourse on Method* in four rules of thumb: (1) do not accept anything as true which is not clearly so; avoid rash and prejudiced judgments, (2) divide problems into as many parts as possible, (3) reflect in due order from the most simple to the

---

28. Descartes is optimistic but certainly not dogmatic: "My present aim, then, is not to teach the method which everyone must follow in order to direct his reason correctly, but only to reveal how I have tried to direct my own" (1985: 112).

most complex, and (4) generalize so comprehensively that seemingly nothing is omitted.[29] Rules 2 and 3—breaking up a problem into its constituent parts and arranging them in a natural order—form what Leon Roth calls the "distinctive conception of Cartesian logic" (1937: 71). Descartes's suggestion that we analyze a complex by breaking it down into its component parts was also the basis of the clock analogy and the method of analysis, which I discuss in chapter 3.

Practically speaking, the method Descartes used and knew best, at least in his youth, was the mathematical method. "We should attend only to those objects of which our minds seem capable of having certain and indubitable cognition," he argues, concluding that "out of all the sciences so far devised, we are restricted to just arithmetic and geometry" (1985: 10–11).[30] Descartes tried to prove that sound geometric properties—length, depth, and breadth (i.e., form and extension)—were essential to matter and, with motion, were the only properties needed to explain natural phenomena. Finding Galileo's approach to geometrical physics lacking in rigor (Sorell 1987: 2), Descartes resolved that his mathematics could be applied with rigor and certitude of results to all propositions under his consideration. All soluble problems, in his view, should be able to be expressed

---

29. Rephrased from Descartes:

The first was never to accept anything as true if I did not have evident knowledge of its truth: that is, carefully to avoid precipitate conclusions and preconceptions, and to include nothing more in my judgements than what presented itself to my mind so clearly and so distinctly that I had no occasion to doubt it.

The second, to divide each of the difficulties I examined into as many parts as possible and as may be required in order to resolve them better.

The third, to direct my thoughts in an orderly manner, by beginning with the simplest and most easily known objects in order to ascend little by little, step by step, to knowledge of the most complex, and by supposing some order even among objects that have no natural order of precedence.

And the last, throughout to make enumerations so complete, and reviews so comprehensive, that I could be sure of leaving nothing out (1985: 120).

30. He continues in the same vein: "Of all the sciences so far discovered, arithmetic and geometry alone are . . . free from any taint of falsity or uncertainty" because "they alone are concerned with an object so pure and simple that they make no assumptions that experience might render uncertain; they consist entirely in deducing conclusions by means of rational arguments" (1985: 12).

in equations between known and unknown quantities abstracted from relevant data. In other words, problems should be abstracted into forms involving certain magnitudes and relations between them that can be readily observed and calculated mechanically. Descartes saw that many problems once considered insoluble could be solved if they were formulated correctly.

Like Plato, Descartes was fascinated with the clearness and precision of geometry. As he saw it, geometrical propositions represented order, and method "consists entirely in the ordering and arranging of the objects on which we must concentrate our mind's eye if we are to discover some truth" (1985: 20). In his correspondence Descartes acknowledged that mathematics "accustoms us to the recognition of truth, because in mathematics we discover correct reasoning such as cannot be found elsewhere. Consequently, anyone who has once accustomed his mind to mathematical reasoning will keep it apt for the inquiry into other truths, for reasoning is everywhere identical" (in McRae 1957: 35). A science modeled on the analytic method of the ancient geometers, reasoned Descartes, is superior to all others because it possesses unity and the greatest simplicity. Nevertheless, he noted that mathematics is not infallible: "Even arithmetic and geometry lead us astray here in spite of their being the most certain of all the arts" (1985: 61).

If mathematics can be systematized and made coherent by focusing on order and measure, Descartes reasoned, then extending order and measure to other sciences will bring coherency to all sciences. This does not mean, however, that Descartes was advocating extending the mathematical method to all sciences, as many Descartes scholars have claimed. Frederick Van De Pitte has shown that Descartes's concept of a universal method, *mathesis universalis*, has been misunderstood by almost all scholars because it was inaccurately translated as *universal mathematics*. Three Latin words appear to be the culprits: *mathematica(e)*, *mathesis*, and *mathesis universalis*. Although all three terms have been translated as *mathematics*, Van De Pitte is correct in assuming that Descartes's use of three terms suggests three distinct meanings. *Mathematica* is correctly translated as the discipline of mathematics; *mathematicae*, the plural form, refers to the branches or fields of mathematics, such as geometry and algebra. The key word, *mathesis*, from the Greek, refers to the act or process of learning. When it was taken into Latin it came to be associated with the object of learning, science. In Descartes's time *mathesis* was often used to mean mathematical science, but it also had the meaning of a discipline of a universal or generalized mathematics. According to Van De Pitte, the term *mathesis universalis* was often employed to refer to all mathematical knowledge as well as to an ultimate foundation for all mathematical sciences based on a set of general principles. He notes that in his correspondence Descartes defines *mathesis* as "the ability to resolve all problems . . . to discover by one's own industry everything that can be discovered by the human mind in this science" (1991: 63, 64). *Mathesis* is thus a process of discovery and learning in mathematics. Descartes was intent on determining the prior principles required to ground mathematics as a scientific discipline—principles that necessarily fall outside the scope of mathematics. The principles that make mathematics scientific, he discovered, were those of order and measure. But instead of being unique to mathematics, they were, he asserted, common to all disciplines.

To become a science, he observed, all subject matter must be capable of being organized and systematized. Only after we find patterns and give structure and order to a body of material can we call it a science. Descartes was convinced that, once we grasp a science's principles, we can discover all its truths and extend its scope. What he learned in endeavoring to provide mathematics with a scientific foundation, then, was that the principles of a science are the principles of learning and discovery. The word *mathesis* therefore takes on two meanings: the underlying principles that make mathematics a science (method) and the principles of learning, both of which Descartes conflates. Thus, *mathesis universalis* refers both to the universal principles of learning and to a universal method. It follows, then, that *mathesis universalis* is not a science of quantification, as most Descartes scholars have mistakenly assumed. While *mathesis universalis* is the set of universal first principles of knowledge—a science of method or a methodology—it is also universal in the sense that all knowledge can be discovered by using it. It does not, however, contain the other sciences, for Descartes admits that each separate field of inquiry has its own methodological difficulties (Van De Pitte 1991: 70).

When the key passage from Rule 4 of the *Regulae*—perhaps the chief source of the confusion—is corrected to distinguish between *mathesis* and mathematics, we can easily see that Descartes's universal method is not quantification.

I began my investigation [of the method of mathematics] by inquiring what exactly is generally meant by the term 'mathematics' [*mathesis*] and why it is that, in addition to arithmetic and geometry, sciences such as astronomy, music, optics, mechanics, among others, are called branches of mathematics [*mathematicae*]. To answer this it is not enough just to look at the etymology of the word, for, since the word 'mathematics' [*mathesis*] has the same meaning as 'discipline' [*disciplina*], these subjects have as much right to be called 'mathematics' [*mathematicae*] as geometry has. Yet it is evident that almost anyone with the slightest education can easily tell the difference in any context between what relates to mathematics [*mathesis*] and what to the other disciplines. When I considered the matter more closely, I came to see that the exclusive concern of mathematics [*mathematica*] is with questions of order or measure and that it is irrelevant whether the measure in question involves numbers, shapes, stars, sounds, or any other object whatever. This made me realize that there must be a general science which explains all the points that can be raised concerning order and measure irrespective of the subject-matter, and that this science should be termed *mathesis universalis*—a venerable term with a well-established meaning—for it covers everything that entitles these other sciences to be called branches of mathematics [*mathematicae*] (Descartes 1985: 19).

Before summing up, it is well worth considering Descartes's use of several other terms, in particular *deduction* and *mathematical demonstration*. Desmond Clarke has found that in Descartes's day neither *demonstration* nor *deduction* had the precise sense it has since acquired; both must be understood in terms of the ordinary usage of the seventeenth century (1991b: 237). Descartes uses the Latin *demonstrare* and the French *démontrer* much like the English verb *to show*. *Demonstrate,* says Descartes, can mean either *to prove* or *to explain*.[31] Clarke explains that Descartes uses the word *induction*, or *enumeration*, to designate a number of scientific procedures, including a generalization based on a sample of a given class, arguments combining analogy and

---

31. In a letter to Morin in 1638, Descartes wrote: "There is a great difference between proving [*prouver*] and explaining [*expliquer*] . . . one can use the word demonstrate [*démontrer*] to signify one or the other, at least if one takes the word in its ordinary usage" (in D. Clarke 1991b: 238).

induction that Descartes called *enumeratio* (e.g., if you cannot obtain a representative sample, you compare instances of a similar type), and any deductive argument that involves a series of inductive stages made in drawing a conclusion (242). A wide variety of procedures—inferential procedures such as induction and arguments by analogy, deductive inference in formal disciplines such as logic or mathematics, and hypothetico-deductive explanations—are called *deduction* by Descartes. Clarke thus concludes that Descartes uses *deduction* to mean "any reasoning process by means of which we argue from whatever evidence is available for the credibility of a given conclusion" (241). Moreover, the reference to a scientific explanation as a *mathematical deduction,* explains Clarke, "can be translated as a physical theory with appropriate arguments and adequately assessed evidence" (245). Hence, when he insists "there are no paths to certain knowledge of the truth accessible to men save manifest intuition and necessary deduction," or concludes in the same vein that deduction "remains as our sole means of compounding things in a way that enables us to be certain of the truth," Descartes is simply making an argument for providing as much evidence as possible to support a conclusion (1985: 48).

It was, in fact, later generations who attributed to Descartes an infatuation with mathematics. The evidence, however, reveals that Descartes was interested in mathematics primarily for its applications to physics; he lost interest in pure mathematics once he began to practice as a physicist. Clarke notes that this disinterest is conspicuous in his private correspondence from 1630 on. The following admission of waning interest is just one of many examples Clarke cites: "I am so fed up with mathematics and I take such little account of it now that I could hardly take the trouble to resolve them [the problems] myself" (in Clarke 1991b: 243).

And so it is clear that Descartes's universal method was not an imposition of quantification upon other disciplines, but the imposition of order and coherence upon all subject matter to be made scientific. Similarly, the demonstrations that make all fields of inquiry scientific are not exclusively mathematical deductions, but any method of showing and explaining the evidence, including a wide variety of deductive and inductive procedures and analogy.

## The Myth of the Conflict Between Reason and Experience

Because for Descartes science encompasses only those propositions that we are certain of, one can find support in his writings
for the view that method is essentially a deductive one modeled
after geometry, that is, it entails deducing propositions of science from a few self-evident principles. Thus, we find Descartes
asserting, that "[t]he only principles which I accept, or require,
in physics are those of geometry and pure mathematics; these
principles explain all natural phenomena, and enable us to provide quite certain demonstrations regarding them" (1985: 247).
Yet this passage leaves the reader with a one-sided impression
and does not reflect Descartes's primary interest in advancing
physics as a practicing scientist.

Arithmetic and geometry owe their certainty to the fact that
experience does not enter into their determination, says Descartes.[32] But he knows physics cannot boast such certainty. A
careful reading of the *Regulae* shows that Descartes uses mathematics as a kind of "propaedeutic to the investigation of the
'loftier sciences'" (Gewirtz 1941: 187). In Rule 14 of the *Regulae*,
for instance, Descartes acknowledges that "these Rules are so
useful in the pursuit of deeper wisdom that I have no hesitation
in saying that this part of our method was designed not just for
the sake of mathematical problems; our intention was, rather,
that the mathematical problems should be studied almost exclusively for the sake of the excellent practice which they give us
in the method" (1985: 59).

Roth points out that "[t]he natural tendency of the mathematical bias of Cartesianism was to lead Descartes further and further into the realm of the possible" (1937: 80), but further and
further from actual scientific practice. The dilemma was grasped
by Descartes: if mathematical reasoning alone could lead to
incontrovertible knowledge, a reliance on extra-mathematical
assumptions would yield knowledge that is no longer beyond
dispute. Roth notes that in practice Descartes realized the need
for experience, an acknowledgement that is "almost Baconian in
its emphasis" (88). As a result, Descartes ends up qualifying his
theory of natural philosophy to such an extent that it brings

---

32. See note 30 above.

him somewhat closer to the Aristotelian position he was fighting.[33]

Although much has been written about how Descartes's scientific practice clashed with his doctrine of scientific method, the evidence also suggests that Descartes understood the role of experience—that it is the source of principles and basic concepts in physical science and that observation and experiment are the backbone of practical insights into nature. He acknowledged that "there are two ways of arriving at a knowledge of things— through experience and through deduction"[34] (1985: 12) and reportedly said that method "consists more in practice than in theory" (in Gewirtz 1941: 183). Moreover, in part 6 of the *Discourse on Method,* he finds the state of experimentation clearly lacking and, regretting that he does not have the time to perform all the experiments he needs, appeals to others for assistance:

I know no other means to discover this [an explanation for his system] than by seeking further observations whose outcomes vary according to which of these ways provides the correct explanation. Moreover, I have now reached a point where I think I can see quite clearly what line we should follow in making most of the observations which serve this purpose; but I see also that they are of such a kind and so numerous that neither my dexterity nor my income (were it even a thousand times greater than it is) could suffice for all of them. And so the advances I make in the knowledge of nature will depend henceforth on the opportunities I get to make more or fewer of these observations. I resolved to make this known in the treatise I had written, and to show clearly how the public could benefit from such knowledge. This would oblige all who desire the general well-being of mankind (1985: 144).

This passage has a distinctly Baconian ring to it. In fact, in his private correspondence Descartes describes Bacon's method as well suited to those interested in performing experiments (in

---

33. Cottingham explains that "what began as a seemingly straightforward exercise, that of supporting the trunk of his physics by unearthing its metaphysical roots, gradually overwhelmed Descartes by its complexity; and that in attempting to complete the task, he was drawn, little by little, to fall back on the very scholastic apparatus that he so derided in his scientific work" (1993: 150).

34. Consider also his discussion, in Rule 12 of the Regulae, of the way truth is found: "It is of course only the intellect that is capable of perceiving the truth, but it has to be assisted by imagination, sense-perception and memory" (1985: 39).

Napier 1818: 415). Alan Gewirtz observes that Descartes knows "the possibilities of experiment set the limits for human knowledge" (1941: 208), for he writes in Rule 8 of the *Regulae*: "As often as he [the scientist] applies his mind to acquire knowledge of something, either he will be entirely successful, or at least he will realize that success depends upon some observation which it is not within his power to make." And in Rule Thirteen he urges us to "take care not to assume more than the data, and not to take the data in too narrow a sense" (1985: 32, 54).

I should also add that in an early work entitled *Studium bonae mentis* (written between 1619 and 1621), Descartes divides the sciences into "cardinal," "experimental," and "historical" types. He defines the experimental sciences as "those sciences whose principles are not clear and certain to every sort of person, but only to those who have learned them by their experiments and observations" (in Gewirtz 1941: 208). As Desmond Clarke rightly notes, Descartes is not, as the orthodox view holds, engaged in a conflict of reason and experience that is resolved by his choosing rational arguments over empirical evidence (1991a: 470). Descartes instead argues that there are two types of empirical evidence: that which is reliable and that which is not. Keeping in mind his definition of the experimental sciences, we can see that Descartes's alleged choice of reason above empiricism is simply the preference for the findings of a seasoned scientist over those of a naive observer. "It is clear from this that when we say 'The reliability of the intellect is much greater than that of the senses,' this means merely that when we are grown up the judgements which we made as a result of various new observations are more reliable than those which we formed without any reflection in our own childhood; and this is undoubtedly true" (Descartes 1984: 295).

It should now be clear that for Descartes, "both reason and experience are important, though in different ways" (Garber 1993: 306).[35] Because of the semantic difficulties mentioned

---

35. Garber continues: "His genius was in seeing how experience and experiment might play a role in acquiring knowledge without undermining the commitment to a picture of knowledge that had motivated him since his youth, a picture of a grand system of certain knowledge, grounded in the intuitive apprehension of first principles" (306). To repeat, what Descartes opposed was a *naive* dependence on the senses (see, e.g., the first and fourth Meditations).

above, and a tendency among philosophers to ignore Descartes's contributions as a scientist of physics, many Descartes scholars have viewed his admission of the necessity of experience as an acknowledgement of failure; this has, in turn, generated a heated debate on the exact place of empiricism in his methodology. The inconsistencies in Descartes's methodology will likely allow the debate over this issue to persist.[36] Of this much, however, the philosophy and history of science is certain: The characterization of Descartes as an archrationalist who did not appreciate the experimental side of science is a false representation of Descartes as scientist and philosopher. This was still recognized in Newton's lifetime by his colleague Colin Maclaurin, who pithily sums up Descartes's position this way: "After all, *Des Cartes* saw the necessity of having recourse to observation, tho' unwillingly; and he appears to be at a loss how to acknowledge it, after having boasted so much of his principles" (1971: 73).

**Descartes and the Hypothetico-Deductive Method**
Because Descartes was interested in accepting into science only those propositions that are clearly true, it may be surprising to learn that Descartes wielded a considerable influence on the English hypothetico-deductivists (Buchdahl 1969: 88). (For this reason, he has been dubbed "the father of modern philosophy.") As Gerd Buchdahl points out, Descartes does not usually hold

---

36. Until recently, philosophers of science have treated Bacon and Descartes as poles to be contrasted. Descartes's approach to experience and experimentation has led various interpreters to perceive a discrepancy between his method and methodology. Some believe his method is based on an a priori justification of first principles (rationalism), which leaves no room for experience or experimental testing (empiricism). Randall (1962) falls into this category; D. Clarke mentions several other sources of this interpretation (1982, 15: n. 10). Roth (1937) and others assert his methodology is a priori, his method empiricist. No one argues that his methodology is empiricist and his method a priori.
   More recently, scholars taking into account his whole work recognize that there is an empiricist dimension involved in both his method and methodology (e.g., D. Clarke 1982: 15, n. 13). This view attributes the seeming conflict between his method and methodology, in part, to the varying nature of his scientific investigations. Some of Descartes's methodological writings, for instance, are rooted in his *Geometry,* where he asserts that the premises of scientific reasoning are true. The method of forming explanatory hypotheses, on the other hand, is anchored in his cosmological theories (see Buchdahl 1969: 119).

that scientific explanation requires the use of explanatory hypotheses whose deductive consequences describe observable natural phenomena (86). Although Descartes claimed he could deduce everything from first principles, as a practitioner of science he was forced to make additional assumptions about matter, which meant he had to rely on principles of lower generality. Certainly his use of hypotheses in practice made him famous, "so much so that when Newtonians came to react against the *physical content* of Cartesian theory they frequently did this by fastening on its purported *methodological* weaknesses instead . . . the condemnation of 'mechanical' hypotheses being reserved (among others) for the Cartesians" (124).

What is more, when Descartes discusses the use of *conjectures*, he admits to making "some assumptions which are agreed to be false" but which "must be retained to provide an explanation of the true natures of things" (Descartes 1985: 256, 267). It is quite clear that Descartes believes hypotheses are indispensable to method, even when they are false, for their falsity "does not prevent the consequences deduced from them [from] being true and certain" (257). He denies that the use of a hypothesis "really deceives us, so long as we judge it to be merely probable, and never assert it to be true" (48). He even distinguishes between epistemological certainty obtained from mathematical proofs, *absolute certainty*, and from the explanatory power of hypotheses, *moral certainty*.[37]

Larry Laudan notes that Descartes used the clock analogy, which I discuss in more detail in chapter 3, to express the method of hypotheses (1981: 31). The metaphor of the clock whose internal workings are unseen by the watchmaker was well suited because Descartes's philosophy was corpuscular and its object unobservable particles whose hypothetical character had to be postulated. The natural philosopher is thus likened to a skilled watchmaker who cannot see the internal mechanisms, but knows the general principles that govern the matter and can, consequently, offer only conjectures about its internal construction and workings. The natural philosopher, Descartes remarks, is on the right track as long as the proposed mechanisms are compatible with the phenomena.

---

37. See Descartes (1985: 289 ff.) and Buchdahl (1969: 120 ff.).

It may be retorted to this that, although I may have imagined causes capable of producing effects similar to those we see, we should not conclude for that reason that those we see are produced by these causes; for just as an industrious watch-maker may make two watches which keep time equally well and without any difference in their external appearance, yet without any similarity in the composition of their wheels, so it is certain that God works in an infinity of diverse ways <each of which enables Him to make everything appear in the world as it does, without making it possible for the human mind to know which of all these ways He has decided to use>. And I believe I shall have done enough if the causes that I have listed are such that the effects they may produce are similar to those we see in the world, without being informed whether there are other ways in which they are produced (1985: 289).[38]

Laudan comments that Descartes is confronting the "classic species of *empirical undeterminism* of theories" (1981: 30). In other words, indefinitely many inconsistent hypotheses cannot explain a phenomenon, which means that experience will not be useful in determining which hypothesis is correct.[39]

The clock analogy is, however, only valid as long as doubt exists about ability to perceive the "inner mechanisms" of nature. In time this doubt faded, and with it, Descartes's influence. Newton's invective against hypotheses (meaning unfounded speculation) contributed to its decline. As Laudan notes, "the method of hypothesis went into virtual eclipse after 1700 until its revival a century later" (1981: 48).

## Thomas Hobbes (1588–1679): Philosophizing vs. Experimentation

Hobbes is usually remembered as the first in the line of the famous British empiricists that continues with Locke, Berkeley, Bentham, James Mill, and John Stuart Mill—all of whom were "primarily moralists . . . anxious to apply the successful methods of the natural sciences to the field of human affairs, to render the conduct of men more enlightened, intelligent, and humane" (Randall 1962, 1: 596). Although Hobbes was a man of the

---

38. This passage, which is based on Adam and Tannery's edition of Descartes's *Oeuvres*, is Laudan's translation (1981: 30–31). The phrase in diamond brackets appears exclusively in the French edition.
39. Laudan observes that philosophers have overlooked this methodological ramification of the clock analogy (1981: 50, n. 17).

seventeenth century—1988 marked the four-hundredth anniversary of his birth—a number of hindrances still make it difficult for us today to assess Hobbes's philosophy of science. First, early Hobbes research has focused on his political theories to the exclusion of his philosophy of science. More important, we are still waiting for a modern scholarly edition of his complete works. Finally, Hobbes research was initially hindered by his controversial reputation: even in Smith and Hume's lifetime being put into a category with Hobbes was tantamount to being labeled an atheist.[40]

The upshot is that there is no agreement whatsoever on the nature of Hobbes's method. Wolfgang Röd (1970), for instance, argues that Hobbes developed a method applicable to every branch of science. Numerous scholars see him as an advocate of a geometrical method. According to Blake and associates (1960), Hobbes has no consistent method. Some authors have even compared Hobbes's state of nature to the prisoner's dilemma of modern game theorists (Zagorin 1990: 327). Because of the discord, Hobbes's method will probably attract more attention in the future, a welcomed consequence of disagreement. In the following discussion, I present the strands of Hobbes's method that seem to be undisputed: his corpuscular theory, the focus on deduction and demonstrability, and his lack of enthusiasm for experimentation.

Hobbes was Bacon's friend and, sporadically between 1622 and 1626, his amanuensis, assisting Bacon in the translation of his essays into Latin. Yet their views on methodology stand in sharp contrast, for Hobbes never came to appreciate the experimental method. On a journey to the Continent (1634–37) Hobbes met the then incarcerated Galileo and took away from their discussion the notion that an adequate explanation of the universe could be found in the concepts of body and motion. His contacts extended, in addition, from Descartes and the Cartesian circle in Paris to Boyle and the Royal Society, which declined Hobbes's bid for membership, in part because of his unpalatable methodological position.

What Galileo had done for physics, Hobbes wanted to do for politics. The project of the eighteenth century was to work out

---

40. According to historian Peter Gay, Hobbes was as notorious in his lifetime as it was possible to be, while still escaping hanging (in Russell 1985: 58).

a science of human nature, and in this respect Hobbes had a vision that would influence later thinkers trying to develop a science of man: the creation of a social physics that would make men's views of society scientific and break the authoritative tie with religion. As the "first major thinker to apply the intellectual methods and concepts of the new science to human affairs," John Randall notes, Hobbes applied the concept of Galilean bodies in motion to psychology, intending to make it a branch of mechanics dealing with matter moving in accordance with mechanical laws (1962, 1: 536).[41] Because "his is the first serious attempt at working out a mechanical science of society, a social physics founded on a mechanistic rendering of human nature," Hobbes is generally thought of as the founder of modern metaphysical materialism (1: 548). Although Galilean mechanics was the primary analogy he used to create his civil philosophy, Hobbes did not really understand the new physics: "He swallowed it whole, as he counseled men to take their religion, without chewing," Randall tells us (1: 536).

We find in Hobbes's recorded views on method that he, like Descartes, believed there can be no science without method. A method that is scientific demonstrates the connectedness of propositions and uses, he explains in *De corpore*, "the shortest way of finding out effects by their known causes, or of causes by their known effects" (*Works*, 1: 66).[42] "Philosophy is the knowledge we acquire, by true ratiocination," he notes, adding that "all true ratiocination, which taketh its beginning from true principles, produceth science, and is true demonstration" (1: 65, 86). Demonstration is very important to Hobbes because it illustrates the necessary connections between propositions. Because definitions explain how an object is caused for Hobbes, deduction must proceed from definitions. In his view geometry is a paradigm of both certainty and causal knowledge; the method of reasoning used by geometers is the proper scientific method to use when reasoning is from causes to effects. How are causes determined? Hobbes claims that there is "no method, by which

---

41. The novelty of Galileo's new science lay in its understanding of motion as the natural state of bodies, which undermined Aristotle's view that bodies at rest were in their natural state.
42. Hobbes used the word *methodus* to mean both a scientific method and a means of instruction.

we find out the causes of things, but is either *compositive* or
*resolutive*, or *partly compositive*, and *partly resolutive*. And the
resolutive is commonly called *analytical* method, as the compositive is called *synthetical*" (66). He stresses that the method of
demonstration is synthetical; synthesis is of primary importance
to science while analysis plays a secondary role (81).[43] I return
to the significance of these concepts below.

Demonstrability according to Hobbes is tied to the idea of
man-made creation. "Geometry therefore is demonstrable, for
the lines and figures from which we reason are drawn and
described by ourselves; and civil philosophy is demonstrable,
because we make the commonwealth ourselves" (*Works*, 7: 184).
Thus, applying the analogy of the geometrical method to the
philosophy of the state is valid because both disciplines are
produced by human design. Demonstrability also explains
Hobbes's idiosyncratic classification of sciences. He sees geometry and civil philosophy as true sciences because of their demonstrability; natural philosophy, on the other hand, which reasons
from effects to causes and thus arrives only at what may be, is
indemonstrable and for this reason necessarily hypothetical
(Seifert 1993: 306). This is, in a nutshell, the essence of Hobbes's
philosophy of science.

Yet his philosophy of science is part of a larger project: the
construction of a science of human nature and conduct.[44] Moral
and civil philosophy (the theory of government) could, according to Hobbes, be known by both ratiocination and observation:
"*Civil* and *moral philosophy* do not so adhere to one another, but
that they may be severed. For the causes of the motions of the
mind are known, not only by ratiocination, but also by the
experience of every man that takes the pains to observe those
motions within himself (*Works*, 1: 73). Hobbes's approach to civil
philosophy has been summarized by D. D. Raphael in the following way (1977: 20). An investigator observes unstable and
stable societies and explores the cause for each. The answer,
Hobbes reasons, lies in human nature. The investigator then sets
about determining the elements in human nature that might

43. Hobbes calls the combined process of analysis and synthesis *logistica*.
44. Phyllis Doyle's 1927 article in *Economica* remains one of the most informative discussions of Hobbes's views on human nature.

give rise to these effects, showing how both states come about (i.e., he determines the respective laws of nature). Assuming that a stable society is preferable to strife, a statement on how to maintain civil order is deduced. Hobbes shows, in conclusion, that stability can be attained under the protection of the state, which requires almost absolute authority to provide its subjects with that security.

Many scholars attribute Hobbes's misjudgments to his infatuation with geometry; but his appeals to the geometrical method have often been misunderstood. Hobbes's interest in science came late in life, at age 40 and after having read Euclid's *Elements*. He was so taken by the geometrical method, "whose conclusions have . . . been made indisputable" (*Works*, 3: 33), that he came to believe that true science could only result from demonstration via rigorous deduction.[45] It is worth noting, however, that the term *geometric* in the seventeenth and eighteenth centuries did not expressly refer to Euclidean geometry, but also to the method of mechanics and exact natural philosophy (Röd 1970: 10). This usage stems from Descartes and was reinforced by the physician William Harvey, who believed that the method of natural philosophy could be applied to physiology. As Röd explains, "[t]he geometrical method construed in a broad sense thus amounted to submitting an area of study to the methodological principles of the exact natural sciences" (1970: 10).[46] Hobbes does in fact imply that the methods of all sciences—ethics and politics included—should be based on the rationalist geometrical method, for geometry "is the only science that it hath pleased God hitherto to bestow on mankind" (*Works*, 3: 23–24). Understanding the geometrical method in this sense explains how Hobbes—who, unlike Descartes, possessed not the slightest talent for mathematics—could make geometrical

45. Despite a shared predilection for geometry, Descartes apparently did not care for Thomas Hobbes's ideas. Although he solicited Hobbes's comments on his *Meditations* and Hobbes supplied him with a set of objections, Descartes's replies were, as his modern editors so aptly characterize them, "curt and dismissive in the extreme" (in Descartes 1984: 64).
46. The passage from Röd that I took the liberty of translating reads: "Die Anwendung der geometrischen Methode im weiten Wortsinn war somit gleichbedeutend mit der Unterwerfung eines Gegenstandsbereichs unter die methodologischen Grundsätze der exakten Naturwissenschaften."

demonstration the source of reliable knowledge in his philosophical system. His statement simply means that demonstration from indisputably sound principles is the correct method to use in geometry, mathematics, mechanics, physics, ethics, and politics.[47]

For Hobbes, the key to finding the causes of things, as mentioned above, is the method of analysis and synthesis. By this method, a problem is first resolved into simple elements that can be quantified. Like so many of his contemporaries, Hobbes employs the clock analogy to illustrate the usefulness of analysis in the social world. In the preface to *De cive* he writes: "Concerning my method . . . everything is best understood by its constitutive causes. For as in a watch, or some such small engine, the matter, figure, and motion of the wheels cannot well be known, except it be taken insunder and viewed in parts" (*Works*, 2: xiv). The synthesis (composition), which follows analysis, is executed by starting from known causes and deducing effects from them. R. S. Peters comments that "[i]n Galileo's hands this method was highly successful because he tested such deductions by observation. In Hobbes's hands the method was not fruitful because it always remained an imaginary experiment" (1967: 35).

Until recently scholars believed that Hobbes's resolutive-compositive (analytic-synthetic) method was rooted in the school of philosophy already firmly established at the University of Padua. J. Prins, however, points out that Hobbes's method of analysis and synthesis is not located in the Paduan methodological tradition, but in that of the school of Philipp Melanchthon and the Ramists. Although the Hobbesian method superficially resembles the philosophy of the school of Padua, Prins shows that the similarity is spurious, that Hobbes's ideas on method diverge from the Paduans and the influence of the Philippo-Ramists dominates.[48] While the Paduans thought the natural philosopher could acquire absolute knowledge, Hobbes and the Philippo-Ramists considered natural science to be a purely

---

47. Röd points out that the geometrical method results in ambiguity when used in a theory of state as a mechanistic science of social bodies (a "physics of the state") and in an autonomous normative science [*Normwissenschaft*] (1970: 18).

48. Still very popular in the 1600s, the Philippo-Ramist approach to the problem of method was "richly represented in a long list of books compiled by Hobbes circa 1630" (Prins 1990: 44). Why Hobbes compiled the list is unknown, but his writings evidence his familiarity with the Philippo-Ramists.

hypothetical science.[49] The main Philippo-Ramist strain in Hobbes's thought, claims Prins, is

linked up with his conviction that we can only know something with absolute certainty when we know how it is generated. This implies that we can only have scientific knowledge of things we produce ourselves like, for example, geometrical figures or political structures. . . . Consequently the natural philosopher, as he does not himself generate the phenomena he investigates, will never get any further than probability. He does not start from self-made, and therefore absolutely certain definitions, like the geometer or political philosopher, but from presuppositions concerning the kind of movements by which the phenomenon he wants to explain might be generated. Therefore one cannot ask more from him than that he formulate hypotheses that at least are conceivable, that show the necessity of the phenomena at hand, and from which nothing can be inferred that is untrue (1990: 36).

That Hobbes unquestionably falls into the Ramist methodological tradition can be confirmed by perusing the works of Peter Ramus (1515–1572) and Philipp Melanchthon (1497–1560).[50]

Perhaps the most contentious aspect of Hobbes's methodology in his day was his challenge of the scientific findings on which Boyle's air pump rested—a challenge that took the form of a public attack on the experimental method. The position taken by Boyle and the Royal Society was that a philosophy of nature could not be sound unless grounded in experimentation. In the method of the Royal Society Hobbes saw his methodological adversaries as a collective, in the air pump their symbol. He was convinced experimental results could never produce truth, or even scientific knowledge. Hobbes responded to the Royal Society in a work called *Dialogus physicus de natura aeris*, which has only recently been translated into English by Simon Schaffer (in Shapin/Schaffer 1985). Baconian induction, then all the rage at the Royal Society, was dismissed scornfully by Hobbes: "For if experimentations of natural phenomena are to be called philosophy, then pharmacists are the greatest physicians of all."[51] In

49. In this respect, Hobbes also deviates from Galileo, who was convinced that the true causes of natural phenomena could be known with certainty.
50. On the Philippo-Ramist aspect of Hobbes's methodology, see Ong (1958: 245–69).
51. This is Blake and colleagues' translation of the Latin passage in *Dialogus* (1960: 109). Schaffer translates the same passage this way: "If the sciences were said to be experiments of natural things, then the best of all physicists are quacks" (in Shapin/Schaffer 1985: 128).

*Human Nature* Hobbes argues in addition that "experience concludeth nothing universally" (*Works*, 4: 18). For him, reasoning from cause to effect makes science universal and certain; empirical knowledge, on the other hand, reasons in the reverse direction, making it merely probable and hypothetical. At the bottom of the dispute between Hobbes and the Royal Society are divergent views of the role of the philosopher and the nature of intellectual work.

Both Hobbes and Boyle revered the scientist, but Hobbes refused to put a mechanic's approach to nature on an equal footing with that of a philosopher. Not just anyone, in his view, could be a philosopher—and then certainly not an exponent of "engine philosophy." Experimental philosophy that was not grounded in causal knowledge fell far from the true mark of science and was, therefore, only of peripheral importance.[52] In short, "empirical evidence, whether from observation or from experiment . . . serves to *illustrate* the conclusions reached by method, and not to determine belief" (Shapin/Schaffer 1985: 145). Hobbes's philosophical outlook was so out of tune with the time that it played a role in his exclusion from the Royal Society.[53] Experimentation in Hobbes's system is put into perspective by Shapin and Schaffer this way: "The point to be made is not that Hobbes 'despised' experiment, or that he argued that experiments ought not to be performed, or even that experiments had no significant place in a properly constituted philosophy of nature. What Hobbes was claiming, however, was that the systematic doing of experiments was not to be equated with philosophy: going on in the way Boyle recommended for experi-

---

52. Hobbes concedes this much to experimentation in his "Ten Dialogues of Natural Philosophy": "What I want of experiments you may supply out of your own store, or such natural history as you know to be true; though I can be well content with the knowledge of the causes of those things which everybody sees commonly produced" (*Works*, 7: 88).

53. In addition, his reputation as an atheist and his political principles, which some fellows rejected, did not help him win advocates. Nonetheless, Hobbes had a good relationship with King Charles II, the Royal Society's founder and patron. Q. Skinner suggests two related explanations for Hobbes's exclusion: he alienated two of the most influential founders of the Society (Wallis and Boyle), and he was excessively dogmatic. Even so, Skinner notes that Hobbes was so highly regarded that a portrait of him hung in the Society's meeting room, and Hobbes had a high opinion of the Society, a sentiment returned by most of its members (1993: 162–63, 170).

mentalists was not the same thing as philosophical practice" (1985: 129).

A more systematic treatment of Hobbes's methods will have to await a critical edition of his complete works. At this point, the historical significance of Hobbes's methodology is perhaps best expressed by Richard Tuck.

[I]n many ways Hobbes's philosophy is closer to the assumptions on which modern science rests than any of the competing philosophies on offer in the seventeenth century. It shared with Descartes's the stress on the need to think of the real world as essentially different from how we experience it, and this stress has been characteristic of the most important achievements of the physical sciences—beginning with Galileo pointing out that the experience of someone on the earth itself could not determine whether the earth was rotating, and ending with the utterly unimaginable postulates of modern theoretical physics about the objects which really make up the material universe. But, unlike Descartes, Hobbes was able to make sense of a material world outside our minds without bringing in elaborate theological postulates, which fits the secular cast of mind of many modern scientists (1989: 50).

## Isaac Newton (1642–1727): The Deductive-Mathematical Experimental Method

### The Method of the *Principia*

It is well known that the successful combination of two major streams of seventeenth-century thought—the mathematical rationalism of the Continent typified by Descartes's work and the mathematical-experimental method—is the hallmark of Newton's genius and the reason he has been dubbed "the first of the moderns." Yet a glance through his two masterpieces, the *Principia* and the *Opticks*, seems to suggest that Newton used two separate methods, relying heavily on mathematical deduction in the former and experimentation in the latter. Although the methodological schizophrenia is illusory, the differences between the two works nevertheless justify examining the method of each one separately. I will start with the *Principia*.

Newton opens the *Philosophiae naturalis principia mathematica* (the *Mathematical Principles of Natural Philosophy* (1686) or *Principia*, as it is almost always called), with the remark that since "the moderns, rejecting substantial forms and occult qualities, have endeavored to subject the phenomena of nature to the laws of mathematics, I have in this treatise cultivated mathematics as far as it relates to philosophy" (1962: xvii). Then he sets forth his aim: "I offer this work as the mathematical principles of philosophy, for the whole burden of philosophy seems to consist in this—from the phenomena of motions to investigate the forces of nature, and then from these forces to demonstrate the other phenomena" (1962: xvii-xviii). Newton's science is mechanical; its success made the negative association with mechanics and artisans that so irritated Hobbes a curiosity of the past.[54] In his philosophy, Newton assumes the idea of natural law as a regularity and takes gravitation as the law upon which all other laws are fashioned. He then explains nature in terms of attractions and repulsions in a vacuum.

A perusal of the *Principia* confirms that Newton was an astute mathematician and that he indeed "cultivated mathematics as far as it relates to philosophy" by patterning his magnum opus after a treatise on geometry.[55] Besides the infinitesimal calculus that he and Leibniz independently discovered, Newton's contributions to algebra, infinite series, cubic curves, dynamics, and coordinate geometry are impressive enough to guarantee him a place among renowned mathematicians. (See the facsimile pages from the *Principia* in figure 1.) The *Principia*, especially the first two books, is written in a strict "mathematical way," to borrow Newton's own expression.[56] "The mathematical way," which Newton exploits to its fullest in the *Principia*, would today be called *mathematical experimentalism*, a method that emphasizes

---

54. In 1730 John Clarke made this point about Newton's mechanics: "[T]hough it may be looked upon as a vulgar Term, because it is generally applied to the meanest trades and Artificers, yet if we duly consider the Nature of the Science, and examine what Opinion the antient Mathematicians had of it, we shall find that it is the Foundation of all true Philosophy" (1972: x).

55. Needless to say, the treatise, if written today, would look different. "Not only was this masterpiece written in an austere mathematical style, consisting largely of definitions, theorems, lemmas, scholia, and demonstrations," writes I. B. Cohen in his preface to the *Opticks*, "but it was in a definite sense written in an archaic mathematical language. Newton did not consistently apply his own discovery of the calculus, but preferred to use the geometrical style of Apollonious and Euclid" (in Newton 1952: xx-xxi).

56. In book 3 of the *Principia*, "The System of the World (in Mathematical Treatment)," Newton remarks several times that he chooses to reduce the substance of his work to "the form of Propositions . . . in the mathematical way" (1962: 397).

the role of measurement in experimental inquiry and mathematical demonstration (Strong 1951: 90–91). In Newton's system the language of mathematics is the language in which experiments are to be formulated, the conclusions drawn from observation and experiment are to be recorded, and the laws of nature are to be expressed. Once laws have been established, inferences can be drawn in precise language and, in turn, tested in precise terms.[57] The power of this method is its precision. The mathematical way, of course, dictated that certain aesthetic factors would be used to judge the question of the adequacy of his scientific explanation; the aesthetic virtues of Newton's system, as enumerated by Dale Jacquette, are simplicity, generality, universality, and fecundity of explanation (1990: 661). The key to the method of the *Principia* and its very novelty is, in fact, its mathematics or, as Koyré puts it, the "geometrization of nature," which is all the more impressive when one considers that the mathematics Newton encountered was not very old.[58]

The mathematical sophistication and rigor that so distinguishes the *Principia* were intentional. According to William Derham, a close acquaintance of Newton, it was written intentionally in a particularly rigorous mathematical fashion in order to evade both criticism and the competition. As Derham recalls, "mainly to avoid being baited by little Smatterers in Mathematicks, he [Newton] told me, he designedly made his *Principia* abstruse; yet so as to be understood by able Mathematicians, who he imagined, by comprehending his Demonstrations, would concurr with him in his Theory" (in Axtell 1965: 237).[59]

---

57. "What is ascertained in observation and experiment are measurements and relations between measurements, what is generalized by induction are mathematical relationships among the theoretic concepts, and what is shown by synthesis is that other phenomena will display certain measurable characteristics agreeing quantitatively with the results following from the principles" (Robert Black 1963: 6).

58. According to Westfall, the seventeenth century was the most creative age in mathematics since classical Greece (1987: 552).

59. Henry Pemberton starts his *View of Sir Isaac Newton's Philosophy* with these words: "The manner, in which Sir ISAAC NEWTON has published his philosophical discoveries, occasions them to lie very much concealed from all, who have not made the mathematics particularly their study" (1728: 1). His contemporary John Clarke writes in a similar vein: "To express the Proportions required in these Particulars, takes up a vast Compass of mathematical Knowledge, more than the Generality of Readers who have studied that Science are capable of understanding, or at least more than they would be willing to spend their Time in, before they come to the Application or Use of them" (1972: iv-v).

namely, if in the coalescence of the points D, $d$ the ultimate ratios of the lines are taken. Therefore,

$$AC : AO \text{ or } SK = CD \cdot Cc : SY \cdot Dd.$$

Further, the velocity of the descending body in C is to the velocity of a body describing a circle about the centre S, at the interval SC, as the square root of the ratio of AC to AO or SK (by Prop. xxxiii) ; and this velocity is to the velocity of a body describing the circle OK$k$ as the square root of the ratio of SK to SC (by Cor. vi, Prop. iv) ; and, consequently, the first velocity is to the last, that is, the little line C$c$ to the arc K$k$, as the square root of the ratio of AC to SC, that is, in the ratio of AC to CD. Therefore,

$$CD \cdot Cc = AC \cdot Kk,$$

hence,     $AC : SK = AC \cdot Kk : SY \cdot Dd,$

and         $SK \cdot Kk = SY \cdot Dd,$

and         $\tfrac{1}{2}SK \cdot Kk = \tfrac{1}{2}SY \cdot Dd,$

that is, the area KS$k$ is equal to the area SD$d$. Therefore in every moment of time two equal particles, KS$k$ and SD$d$, of areas are generated, which, if their magnitude is diminished, and their number increased *in infinitum,* obtain the ratio of equality, and consequently (by Cor., Lem. iv) the whole areas together generated are always equal. Q.E.D.

CASE 2. But if the figure DES is a parabola, we shall find, as above,

$$CD \cdot Cc : SY \cdot Dd = TC : TS,$$

that is, $= 2 : 1$; therefore,

$$\tfrac{1}{4} CD \cdot Cc = \tfrac{1}{2} SY \cdot Dd.$$

But the velocity of the falling body in C is equal to the velocity with which a circle may be uniformly described at the interval $\tfrac{1}{2}$ SC (by Prop. xxxiv). And this velocity to the velocity with which a circle may be described with the radius SK, that is, the little line C$c$ to the arc K$k$, is (by Cor. vi, Prop. iv) as the square root of the ratio of SK to $\tfrac{1}{2}$ SC; that is, in the ratio

**Figure 1**
Excerpt from Newton's *Principia,* book I on the "Motion of Bodies," reprinted, by permission of the University of California Press, from *Sir Isaac Newton's Mathematical Principles of Natural Philosophy and His System of the World* (Berkeley, 1962, pp. 122–23)

of SK to ½ CD. Therefore ½ SK · K*k* is equal to ¼ CD · C*c*, and therefore equal to ½ SY · D*d*; that is, the area KS*k* is equal to the area SD*d*, as above. Q.E.D.

### PROPOSITION XXXVI. PROBLEM XXV

*To determine the times of the descent of a body falling from a given place A.*

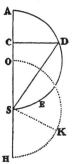

Upon the diameter AS, the distance of the body from the centre at the beginning, describe the semicircle ADS, as likewise the semicircle OKH equal thereto, about the centre S. From any place C of the body erect the ordinate CD. Join SD, and make the sector OSK equal to the area ASD. It is evident (by Prop. xxxv) that the body in falling will describe the space AC in the same time in which another body, uniformly revolving about the centre S, may describe the arc OK. Q.E.F.

### PROPOSITION XXXVII. PROBLEM XXVI

*To define the times of the ascent or descent of a body projected upwards or downwards from a given place.*

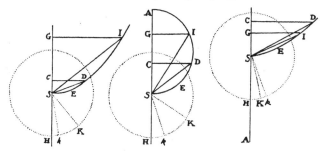

Suppose the body to go off from the given place G, in the direction of the line GS, with any velocity. Take GA to ½ AS as the square of the ratio of this velocity to the uniform velocity in a circle, with which the body may

Figure 1 (continued)

Newton's plan worked: the *Principia* was regarded as esoteric literature for the specialist and remains so to this day.

Newton is aware that, while mathematical conclusions correctly drawn yield certain knowledge, physics necessarily lacks such accuracy. He points out in the *Opticks* that "what is perfectly accurate is called geometrical; what is less so, is called mechanical" (1952: xvii). And he was aware that his physics was quite revolutionary. On the Continent the *Principia* was heralded as a brilliant display of mathematics but was not considered to be physics.[60] The mathematical way allowed him to base his system on a force—universal attraction or gravity—whose underlying causes could not really be explained or laid bare. Gravity was a mystery, or, as his opponents contended, even an occult cause like those so despised in Aristotelian physics. But it was not, in Newton's view, postulated hypothetically, for it was inferred from phenomena and explained the observed motions of celestial bodies. What Newton had introduced was a new philosophy of nature. In that age, scientists viewed nature as a vast machine whose inner springs and mechanisms were hidden from humans and thus incapable of being understood. Newton extended scientific investigation to the hidden mechanisms by inferring their laws and relationships from phenomena and substantiating them by observation and experiment.

Nonetheless, the extension, in Newton's view, had its limits. Later in the preface to the *Principia* Newton has this to say:

I deduce the motions of the planets, the comets, the moon, and the sea. *I wish I could derive the rest of the phenomena of Nature by the same kind of reasoning from mechanical principles,* for I am induced by many reasons to suspect that they may all depend upon certain forces by which the particles of bodies, by some causes hitherto unknown, are either mutually impelled towards one another, and cohere in regular figures, or are repelled and recede from one another [emphasis added] (1962: xviii).

The ambiguity of the italicized phrase has the potential to cause considerable misunderstanding. First, it could lead readers to believe that Newton was a mechanist. His critics generally objected to the mechanistic worldview that explains the entire

---

60. This, says Guerlac, was the reaction of Christiaan Huygens and an anonymous reviewer in the *Journal des sçavans* (1965: 329).

world (i.e., not just planetary movements) by classical mechanics. But although Newton invented classical mechanics, a physical discipline, the mechanistic property is a philosophical concept.[61] Horst Heino von Borzeszkowski and Renate Wahsner argue convincingly that Newton's work is not mechanistic. "Philosophie aber wie Physik betreiben zu wollen, führt stets zu einem mechanistischen Weltbild" [Doing philosophy like doing physics will always lead to a mechanistic worldview] (1980: 16). It was Voltaire, Newton's most famous interpreter, they claim, who initiated the mechanistic understanding of classical mechanics. Newton did not make the mistake of identifying life with mechanics or of arguing that gravitation can explain everything; the mechanistic worldviews are a part of the vulgarized interpretations of Newton's work, that is, of Newtonianism.

Second, the italicized statement may well have induced the Scottish moral philosophers to believe that by "the rest of the phenomena," Newton meant social phenomena even though he was concentrating solely on the physical world. Marie Boas and Rupert Hall explain that by "the rest of the phenomena" Newton means "all of physics apart from the celestial motions and those of the tides, whose theory he had in fact succeeded in deducing from 'mechanical principles'—the principles of the mechanical philosophy—by mathematical reasoning" (1959: 170).

Many historians of science have attempted to capture Newton's success in a nutshell. Koyré calls it a "synthesis" (1965), while I. Bernard Cohen refers to it as a "transformation" (1980). Stephen Toulmin and June Goodfield argue that his success is due to his "imaginative interpretation of many ideas into a single picture" (in Gjertsen 1988: 23). J. M. Keynes sums up Newton's achievement as follows:

I believe that the clue to his mind is to be found in his unusual powers of continuous concentrated introspection . . . His peculiar gift was the power of holding continuously in his mind a purely mental problem until he had seen straight through it. I fancy his pre-eminence is due

---

61. To drive the point home, note that the word *mechanical* means to act in accordance with the principles of mechanics or to be governed by the quantitative relations of force and matter (a purely physical as opposed to chemical property). *Mechanistic*, on the other hand, relates to a doctrine holding that all natural processes are mechanically determined and completely explainable by the laws of physics and chemistry.

to his muscles of intuition being the strongest and most enduring with which a man has ever been gifted. Anyone who has ever attempted pure scientific or philosophical thought knows how one can hold a problem momentarily in one's mind and apply all one's powers of concentration to piercing through it, and how it will dissolve and escape and you will find that what you are surveying is a blank. I believe that Newton could hold a problem in his mind for hours and days and weeks until it surrendered to him its secret. Then being a supreme mathematical technician he could dress it up, how you will, for purposes of exposition, but it was his intuition which was preeminently extraordinary (1973: 364–65).

Although a cursory understanding of Newton's work or a short summary of the key to his success cannot do him justice, Jacquette puts Newton's accomplishments into a broader perspective: "Newton universalized the piecemeal scientific findings of Galileo, Kepler, Descartes, Wallis, Huygens, Wren, and others, and wove them together into a single new organon with the power computationally to predict and explain nearly every known physical phenomenon with previously unmatched precision and rigor" (1990: 661).[62] Jacquette thus brings us to the second key to Newton's method—the demand that hypotheses be substantiated by experiment or observation. Cohen reminds us that Newton's requirement that every scientist be able to reproduce experiments and observational findings—a code of honesty—was a new feature of science (1980: 6). This code of honesty was probably as valuable to science as his astronomical and mathematical discoveries.

In summary, then, the heart of his method in his work on astronomy is (1) the formation of an intricate, mathematical system that seeks to discover the "hidden mechanisms" of nature and (2) experiments designed to check the mathematical relationships and predictions postulated in the system.[63]

---

62. John Wallis (1616–1703), natural scientist and enemy of Hobbes; Christiaan Huygens (1629–1695), Dutch mathematician, physicist, and astronomer; and Sir Christopher Wren (1632–1723), natural scientist.
63. Robert Black describes the distinguishing characteristics of Newton's method differently: (1) there is order in nature; (2) in nature there are isolable systems and subsystems; (3) the universal properties or elements of nature are atoms; (4) results are predominantly systematic, orderly, and harmonious; (5) order comes about through the operation of opposing forces or tendencies; (6) disturbing forces exist, but the system is self-adjusting (1963: 49–50). The problem with this description is that these properties were not, as this chapter so clearly shows, original with Newton.

## The Method of the *Opticks*

In contrast to the *Principia*, the *Opticks*, which was written in English instead of Latin, is "[o]ne of the most readable of all great books in the history of physical science" (Cohen in Newton 1952: ix). It held the attention of nonspecialists like Benjamin Franklin, who Cohen tells us, read and reread the *Opticks*, but could not manage the mathematics of the *Principia* (xxxviii). Because Newton held the mathematics to a minimum and took up broad questions about the nature of light, the *Opticks* "was a rich intellectual feast for philosophers as well as scientists, for poets as well as experimenters, for theologians as well as for painters, and for amateurs of the products of the human imagination at its highest degree of refinement" (Cohen in Newton 1952: xxxvi). Although the popularity of the *Opticks* far surpassed that of the *Principia* in Newton's day, today it stands in the shadow of the *Principia* chiefly because it set forth the wrong, corpuscular theory of light rather than the correct, wave theory.[64]

The difference in the methods of the two works is striking. In the *Opticks*, Cohen notes, Newton describes an abundance of experiments, whereas in the *Principia* he usually borrows data from others (1952: xxxviii). Moreover, the *Opticks* closes with thirty-one *Queries* cast in conjectural form. Cohen clarifies the difference between the two works this way. From the point of view of the 18th century, the *Principia* had settled the problem of planetary motions: the law of universal gravitation was held to be true. But the *Opticks* dwellt on newly discovered phenomena on colors and diffraction that "clearly marked the beginning of a new direction in physical inquiry" (xxxix). The queries, then, were questions for future generations.

Newton anchors his approach in *the method of analysis* and *the method of composition,* or *synthesis,* which, we will learn in chapter 3, had a long-standing tradition and would later capture the fancy of the moral philosophers and political economists. As Newton was not tacit about his choice of methods, we can turn

---

64. Newton embraced the corpuscular theory of light because atomism was taken for granted in his day (Cohen in Newton 1952: xliv-xlv). His sweeping influence and authority retarded the development of the correct theory for more than a century (xii). In a similar situation, Newton's fluxions initially prevailed over Leibnitz's calculus, which we use today.

to his own words, keeping in mind that the word *philosophy* during his lifetime was roughly analogous to *science* today. In a letter to Henry Oldenburg, secretary of the Royal Society, Newton argued that "the best and safest method of philosophizing seems to be, first, to inquire diligently into the properties of things and to establish those properties by experiments, and to proceed later to hypotheses for the explanation of things themselves" (in Thayer 1953: 5). In probably the most frequently cited passage in all of Newton's works, Query 31 of the *Opticks*, Newton set forth his methodological prescriptions.

As in Mathematicks, so in Natural Philosophy, the Investigation of difficult Things by the Method of Analysis, ought ever to precede the Method of Composition. This Analysis consists in making Experiments and Observations, and in drawing general Conclusions from them by Induction, and admitting of no Objections against the Conclusions but such as are taken from Experiments, or other certain Truths. For Hypotheses are not to be regarded in experimental Philosophy. And although the arguing from Experiments and Observations by Induction be no Demonstration of general Conclusions; yet it is the best way of arguing which the Nature of Things admits of, and may be looked upon as so much the stronger, by how much the Induction is more general . . . By this way of Analysis we may proceed from Compounds to Ingredients, and from Motions to the Forces producing them; and in general, from Effects to their Causes, and from particular Causes to more general ones, till the Argument end in the most general. This is the Method of Analysis: And the Synthesis consists in assuming the Causes discover'd, and establish'd as Principles, and by explaining the Phaenomena proceeding from them, and proving the Explanations (1952: 404; in Thayer 1953: 178–79).

In other words, the first task of philosophy is to discover fundamental or basic experiences by using the method of analysis; the second task, to extend this basic experience by synthesis to a wider range of phenomena.

There are several things to note about this famous passage. In it Newton distinguishes three levels of abstracting from the senses, two of which he names here. At one level, propositions are inferred or deduced from phenomena (*synthesis*). At another, propositions (mathematical formulas and mechanical principles) are rendered general by *induction*. The third level is first introduced in the General Scholium at the end of the *Principia* and at the conclusion of the *Opticks:* the order of nature is attributed to God as the first cause. The third level need not be taken very seriously, says Strong, because the Scholium was introduced twenty-six years after the first edition appeared at the urging of Cotes, who thought its inclusion was necessary to satisfy Leibniz's criticism of Newton's neglect of the role of God (1951: 101–102).

Jacko Hintikka and Unto Remes give the method Newton cites in the above passage greater precision (1974: 110). Their scheme is well worth adopting, for it extracts and isolates each step of his method, which, concisely put, comes down to the following:

1) an analysis of a situation into its various parts and factors (step one of the method of analysis),
2) an examination of interdependencies between parts and factors (step two of the method of analysis),
3) a generalization of the relationships discovered to all similar situations (the method of induction),
4) deductive applications of the general laws to explain and predict other phenomena (the method of synthesis).

The methods of analysis and synthesis, by the way, are old, having first been used by the Greeks—a topic that I take up in detail in chapter 3. I will return to Newton's use of analysis, synthesis, and induction later in this chapter.

The final point to note about this famous passage is that while Newton advocates his method as the "best way," he concedes that it cannot guarantee certain results. Although some scholars attribute to Newton the view that we can obtain absolute, certain knowledge, this interpretation does not withstand scrutiny. For as he explained in a letter to Oldenburg, "the absolute certainty of a science cannot exceed the certainty of its principles" (in Thayer 1953: 81).[65] Henry Pemberton, a close friend and expositor of Newton as well as editor of the third edition of the *Principia*, perhaps best sums up the significance of methodological certainty in Newton's system.

The proofs in natural philosophy cannot be so absolutely conclusive, as in mathematics. . . . But in natural knowledge the subject of our

65. A comment attributed to Newton shortly before his death substantiates his belief in the relative nature of knowledge: "I do not know what I may appear to the world; but to myself I seem to have been only like a boy playing on the sea-shore, and diverting myself in now and then finding a smoother pebble or a prettier shell than ordinary, whilst the great ocean of truth lay all undiscovered before me" (in Cassirer 1943: 380).

contemplation is without us, and not so compleatly to be known: therefore our method of arguing must fall a little short of absolute perfection. It is only here required to steer a just course between the conjectural method of proceeding, against which I have so largely spoke; and demanding so rigorous a proof, as will reduce all philosophy to mere scepticism, and exclude all prospect of making any progress in the knowledge of nature (1728: 23).

In the final paragraph of the *Opticks*, Newton takes up the subject of moral philosophy: "And if natural Philosophy in all its Parts, by pursuing this Method, shall at length be perfected," he conjectures, "the Bounds of Moral Philosophy will be also enlarged" (1952: 405). The impact of this single remark on future generations is immeasurable. Later it would become the shibboleth of the eighteenth-century Scottish philosophers.

## The Methodological Link Between the *Principia* and the *Opticks*

Because the conjectural character of the queries in the *Opticks* seems "totally alien to the mathematical rigor of the *Principia*," a closer look at the relationship between the two works is in order (Boas/Hall 1959: 167). Newton followed Descartes in seeing that the actual world may not be similar to the world we perceive through our senses—a view that is requisite to the mechanical philosophy. But, as Boas and Hall point out, that does not mean that Newton ever "supposed that a competent picture of the universe could be obtained by unwrapping the consequences of a mathematical equation; he was well aware that it was possible in mathematics to work out the detailed features of what might look like a physical system, but had in fact no relation to the actual world. And that was the kind of *a priori*, nonempirical system he did not intend to develop" (177). As Cohen mentions, it is rare for an experimenter and theoretician to be found in one person (in Newton 1952: xxxvii).

Although both works use hypotheses, the hypotheses of the *Principia* are formulated as exact mathematical expressions and checked by experiments referring back to nature, whereas the hypotheses of the *Opticks* are open-ended guesses. Boas and Hall explain why Newton used different methods: "Only part of his work was expounded on the higher, mathematical level; the rest remained in the state in which the theory of fluids had been before the second book of the *Principia* was written. But Newton clearly believed that *all* of natural philosophy could gradually be transferred to the higher level, that this mathematization of the whole of physics would be effected on the foundation of the mechanical philosophy, and that probably this could be done by developing the various hints he offered" (1959: 178). This reasoning is completely consistent with Newton's comment in the preface to the *Principia* about extending his method to "the rest of the phenomena." Boas and Hall thus conclude that the speculative science of Newton's *Opticks* "is merely Newtonian science incomplete" (178). To put it another way, the method Newton advocates does not vary from book to book: while the principles in the *Principia* are a polished product, the queries represent "bold conjectures"—to use Popper's terminology—that mark the beginning of science.[66]

## The Controversy over Hypotheses

After having learned that Newton used hypotheses in both of his great works, the reader may be surprised to learn, further, that it was Newton who made famous the maxim *hypotheses non fingo,* I feign no hypotheses.[67] As Richard Westfall notes in his succinct formulation of the paradox, "[t]he man who asserted 'hypotheses non fingo' was in fact the most daring speculator of the scientific revolution" (1987: 563). How this came about and how the paradox can be resolved is the task of this section.

No one hated controversy more than Newton. "He had a particular aversion to disputes, and was with difficulty induced to enter into any controversy," wrote his colleague and friend Colin Maclaurin. "Nor," noted Maclaurin, "did his aversion to disputes proceed from the love of quiet only" (1971: 13). Newton was also sensitive to the word *hypothesis,* which conjured up the illegitimate methods of Cartesian and Aristotelian philosophy that he so opposed.[68] One can then imagine Newton's reaction

66. "One can hardly doubt that Newton was both a speculative and an exact theorist, both an experimenter and a mathematician; but the very fact that the *Principia* does not exclude hypotheses reveals the absence of any sharp distinction between the two levels of his activity" (Boas/Hall 1959: 178).
67. "I feign no hypotheses," Koyré (1965) argues, is the correct translation of *hypotheses non fingo* because *feign* implies falsehood. The phrase was originally mistakenly translated as "I frame no hypotheses."
68. The word *hypothesis* "was forever corrupted by its association with the 'fantastic vortices' of Descartes" (Bryson 1968: 17).

upon learning that his colleagues on the Continent had objected
to his concept of gravity on the grounds that his inability to
explain its cause made it a mere hypothesis that deserved to be
relegated to the occult causes of the Scholastics. Newton wrote
many of the passages on hypotheses in the midst of this
controversy.

The famous remark *hypotheses non fingo* can only be understood within the context of this dispute; and, it must be stressed,
it was intended to be applied *only* to the principle of gravity. It
was not, as many of Newton's followers believed, a guiding
principle for all of science. The passage in which this remark
first appeared is located in the General Scholium appended to
book 3 of the second edition of the *Principia*.

But hitherto I have not been able to discover the cause of those
properties of gravity from phenomena, and I frame [i.e., feign] no
hypotheses; for whatever is not deduced from the phenomena is to be
a hypothesis; and hypotheses, whether metaphysical or physical,
whether of occult qualities or mechanical, have no place in experimental philosophy . . . And to us it is enough that gravity does really exist
and act according to the laws which we have explained, and abundantly serves to account for all the motions of the celestial bodies and
of our sea (1962: 547; Thayer 1953: 45).

Still, no explanation for the cause of gravity could be found—a
circumstance that ate away at Newton.

So that "the argument of induction may not be evaded by
hypotheses," Newton formulated the fourth of his famous four
Rules of Reasoning in Philosophy, the *Regulae philosophandi*; it
appears at the beginning of book 3 of the *Principia*.

Rule 4: In experimental philosophy we are to look upon propositions
inferred by general induction from phenomena as accurately or very
nearly true, notwithstanding any contrary hypotheses that may be
imagined, till such time as other phenomena occur by which they may
either be made more accurate, or liable to exceptions (1962: 400; in
Thayer 1953: 5).

How can hypotheses evade induction? They could, Newton
thought, be deduced wrongly "from a confutation of contrary
suppositions" (in Thayer 1953: 7). It was common practice in this
age to believe that there were X number of possible explanations
for a phenomenon and to declare all but one false or misguided,
leaving the remaining explanation as true. Pemberton mentions

that the "custom was to frame conjectures; and if upon comparing them with things, there appeared some kind of agreement,
though very imperfect, it was held sufficient" (1728: 4). Newton,
however, was working toward the greatest possible accuracy
and thus toward a method of substantiating hypotheses—a
*proof*, as Newton calls it (modern terminology prefers the terms
*verification* or *confirmation* of hypotheses). This is why Newton
defines a *phenomenon* as that which presents itself to the senses
and contrasts it with the occult.

   In addition, he argued, hypotheses should not be understood
"in so large a sense as to include the first principles or axioms"
that have been "deduced from phenomena and made general
by induction" (in Thayer 1953: 6). Newton, by the way, uses the
word *principle* not as we do today but to designate an ultimate
character or propensity derived from sense experience; principles are, for example, mass, gravity, and cohesion in bodies. The
upshot for this usage: his three laws of motion are not hypotheses but proven principles or axioms. The type of hypotheses he
argues against are wildly speculative ideas that are not deduced
from phenomena and therefore lack experimental proof. The
Rules of Reasoning are, in effect, concessions to the uncertainty
involved with doing natural philosophy as opposed to using
purely mathematical reasoning (Strong 1951: 93–94). In his
efforts to defend his work, Newton alters the meaning of *hypotheses* to mean "inadequately substantiated speculation"
(Schumpeter 1954b: 20). Yet his argument remains clear: the use
of hypotheses in the sense of conjectures or hunches to direct
inquiry or suggest new experiments is legitimate.[69] After all, he
makes abundant use of hypotheses in the *Principia*,[70] and as
Cohen notes, if we go by Newton's definition of hypotheses as
that which is not deduced from phenomena, "the speculations
in the *Opticks* are indeed hypotheses" (in Newton 1952: xxxv).[71]

   There are good reasons for examining the other Rules of
Reasoning, too. Myron Ashley argues that Newton intended the

---

69. See Blake et al. (1960) and Hanson (1970).
70. Florian Cajori lists the hypotheses made by Newton in the *Principia* and
discusses in detail the problem of hypotheses in Newton's work (in Newton
1962: 671–76).
71. Cohen lists the many ways Newton uses the word *hypothesis* in appendix
1 of his *Franklin and Newton* (1966). The meaning ranges from a system of the
world to the premise of a mathematical theorem.

four Rules of Reasoning in Philosophy to be observed when forming useful hypotheses (1903: 159); Pemberton designates them as "concessions" that natural philosophy must make to epistemological certainty (1728: 4). Finally, the four Rules of Reasoning that open book 3 of the second edition of the *Principia* originally appeared in the first edition as "hypotheses." What the four rules amount to, then, is a collection of rules of thumb for making generalizations.

Newton formulated Rule 1 of the Rules of Reasoning as follows:

We are to admit no more causes of natural things than such as are both true and sufficient to explain their appearances (1962: 398).

This is, essentially, Ockam's razor: do not introduce more entities into philosophy than are sufficient to explain the phenomena.

Rule 2 simply states that like effects are to be ascribed to the same causes.

Therefore to the same natural effects we must, as far as possible, assign the same causes (398).

Newton illustrates this principle by noting that respiration in humans and animals is brought about by the same means and that bodies fall to the earth in America and in Europe from the same principle.

Rule 3, closely related to Rule 4, reads:

The qualities of bodies, which admit neither intensification nor remission of degrees, and which are found to belong to all bodies within the reach of our experiments, are to be esteemed the universal qualities of all bodies whatsoever (398).

Newton provides a lengthy explanation for this rule, illustrating it with examples. Part of his explanation is worth reproducing:

[I]f it universally appears, by experiments and astronomical observations, that all bodies about the earth gravitate towards the earth, . . . that the moon likewise, according to the quantity of its matter, gravitates towards the earth; that, on the other hand, our sea gravitates towards the moon; and all the planets one towards another; and the comets in like manner towards the sun; we must, in consequence of this rule, universally allow that all bodies whatsoever are endowed with a principle of gravitation (399).

Obviously, this rule tells us how to put induction into practice.

## Newton's Scientific Personality

I have borrowed Westfall's expression "scientific personality" (1987) to explain Newton's science and practice in a broader framework. We have already discussed two facets of his scientific personality: his facility as a pure mathematician and his talent for quantitative physics. Next, we consider Newton's efforts to define the relationship between natural philosophy and Christianity, which consumed his time between 1670 and 1685, and take a closer look at the rational image of him that the Newtonians promoted.

One of the greatest obstacles to Newton research is the fact that his work is still being discovered and interpreted. Newton's voluminous manuscripts and notes on alchemy, for example, have only recently become an object of "the Newtonian industry," as the literature on Newton is known. Most of the manuscripts on alchemy and magic were salvaged by John Maynard Keynes, who bought them at the Lymington auction in 1936 and gave them to King's College. (Earlier, Cambridge had refused to accept the manuscripts from Lord Portsmouth on grounds that they were "of no scientific interest" (Golinski 1988: 148)). Another obstacle that creates confusion is the wide variety of vulgarized interpretations of his work by Newton's followers, all falling under the rubric *Newtonianism*. Among the most famous Newtonians are Benjamin Franklin, David Hume, Adam Smith, and Voltaire.

Today's Newtonian industry has shown how the common understanding of Newton and his work lacks depth. Newton, we know, enjoys the reputation of being the first of the moderns. "In the eighteenth century and since, Newton came to be thought of as the first and greatest of the modern age of scientists, a rationalist, one who taught us to think on the lines of cold and untinctured reason," wrote J. M. Keynes in his eulogy "Newton, the Man" (1973: 363). But Keynes goes on to challenge this view that has been so often propagated by the Newtonian industry.

Keynes was the first scientist to pay attention to Newton's alchemical manuscripts. His judgment that they were "wholly devoid of scientific value" can only be considered a prejudice of Keynes's age (Henry 1988: 142). Newton's interest in alchemy was considerable. Of the 1,752 books in Newton's library, John

Henry discloses that 369 were of a nonscientific nature and 170
dealt with alchemy (142); Newton's notes contain over a million
words about alchemical pursuits. Only since the 1970s have
historians really begun to investigate these manuscripts. To most
scientists their discovery was a gross embarrassment, for they
show that Newton obviously revered the works of what we
would today call magicians. Yet alchemy ostensibly provided
inspiration for his lasting scientific contributions.

Newton was also the author of a biblical chronology. Apparently he wanted to portray Israel as the source of all knowledge
and wisdom that had flowed into the ancient world (Rattansi
1988: 193). Equally important, Newton wanted to prove that his
scientific work was a rediscovery of the mystical philosophy of
the Jews, which had been passed on to the Egyptians and Greeks
and subsequently corrupted. In trying to prove these theories he
twisted both historical and astronomical evidence in a way that
is inconsistent with the methodological prescriptions set forth in
his works on physics and optics. Having reached the conclusion
in his youth that the wisdom of creation had been corrupted by
humanity, Newton abandoned his faith in the orthodox view of
the Trinity and refused to take the holy orders necessary at that
time to take up a chair at Cambridge; Isaac Barrow interceded
on his behalf and obtained a royal decree exempting him. But
Newton did believe in the second coming of Christ; in his view,
God had everything to do with science, for all activity presupposes a divinity. For Newton, universal gravity indicated the
omnipresence of God, just as vegetable (or chemical) action
supposed supervision by Christ, "God's viceroy" (Dobbs 1982:
528). In this way, his interests in alchemy and astronomy were
united by his religious convictions.

In addition to his unorthodox religious views and his alchemical and magical pursuits, some of Newton's character traits fly
in the face of the superrational image he later acquired. He will
never go down in serious historical works as a magnanimous
personality; he was so sensitive to criticism that he almost abandoned scientific research altogether after being attacked by
Robert Hooke (Whittaker in Newton 1952: lxvii). Newton was
also guilty of numerous "ignoble quarrels" (Keynes 1973: 364)
that can hardly be reconciled with the standards of intellectual
integrity attested to by his work in astronomy. For instance,

when Hooke (1635–1703) claimed credit for the concept of gravity, Newton threatened to suppress the publication of book 3 of the *Principia*. In fact, Hooke had correctly formulated the inverse square law of attraction, but he could not offer the proof. Newton ungraciously refused to acknowledge any assistance from Hooke and, in fact, went through the *Principia* to strike every reference to him. "Such was his fury that he refused either to publish his *Opticks* or to accept the presidency of the Royal Society until Hooke was dead" (Westfall 1976: 19)).

This was by no means an isolated case. When Leibniz asked the Royal Society to examine his claim to the invention of infinitesimal calculus, Newton wrote the chief findings for the Royal Society: the report implied that Leibniz had received information from Newton. When John Flamsteed refused to publish his catalogue of stars at Newton's request, Newton tried to force the publication. Flamsteed won a court ruling after a long, embittered struggle; eventually his assistants had the work published posthumously in the form he preferred. Once again Newton sought revenge by combing the *Principia* and removing all references to Flamsteed. The fact is that Newton was subject to uncontrolled rages throughout his life and was irrationally protective of his work: The superrational image is but a myth, and one that was greatly bolstered by Newtonianism.

## John Locke (1632–1704), Epistemological Uncertainty, and the "Historical, Plain Method"

In Locke's time, the late seventeenth century, "debates over scientific discoveries were of less importance than debates over scientific method" (Soles 1985: 339); and more was at issue than just a break with the ancients. Sergio Moravia concludes that Locke "became the source in enlightened Europe of five fundamental epistemological options": the refusal to privilege mathematics as a method, a pluralization of cognitive alternatives, the tendency away from the formal and deductive and toward the empirical and inductive, and the rehabilitation both of factual description and of sense observation. It is clear, comments Moravia, how greatly the social and moral sciences could benefit from the "epistemological liberation produced by the Lockean philosophy" (1980: 248). The classic statement of the Lockean philosophy is his *Essay concerning Human Understanding* (1690), the work that John Maynard Keynes lauds as the "first modern English book."[72]

No doubt the classical economists knew Locke as the first Newtonian moral philosopher. Because he did not understand the *Principia,* he asked Dutch physicist Christiaan Huygens whether Newton's mathematical calculations in the *Principia* were sound. Upon learning that they were, he fully embraced Newton's mechanics as the basis for science.[73] In the *Essay concerning Human Understanding* Locke adopts the corpuscular, mechanical view of the world held by his contemporaries: science is viewed as a system of universal necessary truths, and the physical world is made up of solid, hard particles connected by mechanical causation. Locke's interest in Newtonian science, adherence to the corpuscular view, stress on observation and experiment, and attack on the Scholastics all make him very much a child of his age. The *Essay concerning Human Understanding,* a book concerned with the theory of knowledge, has not always been regarded as a work in the philosophy of science; it has traditionally been viewed as a study in moral philosophy. Often adjudged "a mass of confusion and inconsistencies" (Soles 1985: 369), the work is only starting to be appreciated by philosophers of science. In contrast to the conventional view, Soles insists that "Locke did have a coherent, sophisticated epistemology and philosophy of science" (369).

Because many scholars have thought John Locke had only a superficial interest in natural philosophy and in the logic and methods of science, they have termed him a mere "smatterer in science, a learned philosopher perhaps, but someone on the fringe of the scientific activity of his day" (Axtell 1965: 235).[74] Several compelling facts speak against this view. First, Locke had a long, active association with the Royal Society of Lon-

---

72. Quoted in Gordon (1991: 78). I was unable to locate this quotation in Keynes's collected works.
73. Desaguliers tells the story this way: "The great Mr. Locke was the first who became a Newtonian Philosopher without the help of Geometry; for having asked Mr. Huygens, whether all the mathematical Propositions in Sir Isaac's *Principia* were true, and being told he might depend upon their Certainty; he took them for granted, and carefully examined the Reasonings and Corollaries drawn from them, became Master of all the Physics, and was convinc'd of the great Discoveries contain'd in that Book" (1763: viii).
74. Both Axtell (1965) and Laudan (1981) seek to explode this myth.

don—he was a member from 1668 until his death—and with many of its members. He was a good friend of both Robert Boyle and Isaac Newton and expended considerable energy in securing for the latter a lucrative post at the Royal Mint. Living in an age in which Bacon's empirical method had established itself among England's practicing scientists, Locke was active in the empirical movement. He was a member of the "Invisible College" or "Philosophical Club," a group of empiricists, including Boyle and Petty, that met privately to discuss matters of scientific interest and later became the Royal Society of London.

The second thing that speaks against Locke's marginal involvement in science is an unpublished treatise on natural philosophy, "The Elements of Natural Philosophy," which Locke composed, perhaps with the assistance of Sir Isaac Newton, for a pupil of his, the twelve-year-old son of Sir Francis and Lady Masham. We cannot be certain of this collaboration, but Axtell (1965) believes the weight of evidence points to it. It is plausible that Locke asked Newton to write a short, simple statement on the current status of physical and astronomical knowledge to aid him in tutoring his pupil, that Newton complied, and that Locke used it to compose the treatise.[75] One of the fragments left in Newton's handwriting appears to be a draft of this work, although no final version has ever been discovered. Nonetheless, the scope and framework of both the Newton fragment and Locke's treatise are, in Axtell's view, so close as to almost rule out any doubt.[76] Whether a collaborative effort or not, the existence of the treatise proves not only that Locke was familiar with the natural philosophy of his time, but also that this was a public fact, and one that strengthened his pedagogical standing with the English aristocracy.

Farr correctly characterizes Locke's *Essay concerning Human Understanding* as wavering "ambivalently between two competing methods of understanding: (1) the method of natural history;

---

75. The section headings of the "Elements of Natural Philosophy" are (1) Of Matter and Motion, (2) Of the Universe, and particularly of the Solar System, (3) Of the Air, Atmosphere, and Meteors, (4) Of Mountains, Springs, Rivers, and the Sea, (5) Of Minerals, Vegetables, and Animals, and (6) Of the five Senses of Man, and of his Understanding (Secord 1985: 132). In my view this organization is more characteristically Lockean than Newtonian. Apparently this treatise was prepared as a pamphlet and began circulating for use in instructing young men after 1750 (Secord 1985: 131).
76. Secord (1985) does not find Axtell's evidence convincing.

and (2) the hypothetical method" (1987: 52). The method of natural history was to produce observations and experience perceived in the real world; the hypothetical method, speculations about things that lie beyond the reach of humane senses—things we must necessarily conjecture about. Starting with the empirical stream of thought, Locke believes that our external knowledge of the world is based on experience and not, as in the Cartesian view, on innate ideas. Experience for Locke includes both *sensation,* which provides us with information about the external world, and *reflection,* which gives us a knowledge of our mind. The passage in the *Essay concerning Human Understanding* that won Locke his reputation for being an empiricist is found in book 2: "Let us then suppose the mind to be, as we say, white paper void of all characters, without any *ideas.* How comes it to be furnished? . . . To this I answer, in one word, from *experience*" (1965, II: i, §2).[77] John Yolton, however, warns that "the reader who approaches Locke with the conviction that the label of 'empiricist' fits him will be disappointed," for Locke's empiricism is broad in scope and does not exclude rationalism (in Locke 1965: xviii-xix). Locke, in fact, greatly admired Descartes's *Discourse on Method* and devoted much of book 4 of the *Essay concerning Human Understanding* to a defense of deduction. Equally important, the uncertainty of knowledge and realism play such a great role in Locke's work that he gave hypotheses a central place in his philosophy of science.

   To understand Locke, it is necessary to recognize that he uses the word *science* ambiguously to refer both to the empirical, theoretical investigations of nature, such as those undertaken by Newton, and to demonstrable knowledge, such as that of mathematics and logic. Like his contemporaries, Locke believed that certainty is the genuine mark of knowledge. Real knowledge must, then, be true and infallible like the truths of mathematics. But once we enter the physical world, the certain character of mathematical relations vanishes. Then probable knowledge, what he calls *judgment,* serves as a guide. Our ignorance makes forming judgments unavoidable: both the complexity of the universe and man's inability to acquire sensory evidence of

---

77. Where multiple editions of a work exist and the text is divided into sections, the parenthetical reference drops the reference to the page and refers instead to the book, chapter, and section, respectively.

atomic particles limit our knowledge. The degree of justification of knowledge is measured by the degree of probability that a proposition is true. The better the hypothesis conforms to observation and experience and to the testimony of others, the more justified one is in believing it.[78]

Locke questions how we can know whether the Newtonian world exists if it is not observable. "I deny not but a man, accustomed to rational and regular experiments, shall be able to see further into the nature of bodies and guess righter at their yet unknown properties than one that is a stranger to them; but yet, as I have said, this is but judgment and opinion, not knowledge and certainty" (1965, IV: xii, §10). One reason for uncertainty in science can, then, be attributed to the inadequacy of observation, which Locke, however, suggests can be improved through the use of more accurate instruments. In natural philosophy, when considering unobservable matter, "[e]xperience is that which in this part we must depend on," says Locke. "And it were to be wished that it were more improved" (IV: iii, §16). One method Locke suggests for improving it is acquiring knowledge through natural history, a topic to which I return below (IV: xii, §10).

In accord with his definition of real knowledge, Locke concludes that little of natural philosophy qualifies as knowledge: "[I]t is easy to perceive what a darkness we are involved in, how little it is of being and the things that are that we are capable to know" (IV: iii, §29). Because of the empirical nature of natural philosophy, it can at best yield probable results or a judgment that "we can have but an experimental knowledge of" (IV: iii, §29). For this reason, Locke suspects that "natural philosophy is not capable of being made a science" (IV: xii, §10) and warns the reader: "*Certainty* and *demonstration* are things we must not, in these matters, pretend to" (IV: iii, §26).

In spite of their uncertain epistemological status and Newton's famous strictures against them, hypotheses were not treated

---

78. Locke's theory of knowledge, Osler argues, "represents an effort to fill the epistemological void left by Boyle's and Newton's rejection of the Cartesian ideal of certainty in natural philosophy." She adds that "Locke's emphasis on certainty points to the intellectual crisis underlying his theory of knowledge. By insisting that knowledge and certainty are equivalent, he remained at one with the Aristotelian and Cartesian traditions which maintained the ideal of certainty as the standard for science and for all knowledge" (1970: 10, 16).

with aversion by Locke. For "hypotheses, if they are well made, are at least great helps to the memory and often direct us to new discoveries"; they also assist in explaining nature. But he warns us that "we should *not take up any one* [hypothesis] *too hastily*" until we have examined the particulars, made experiments, and found substantiation for the hypothesis. A hypothesis must never be confused with a principle, "an unquestionable truth," for a hypothesis "is really at best but a very doubtful conjecture" (IV: xii, §13).

Locke never defines the word *hypothesis*, but he seems to use it to mean a probable conjecture beyond the facts of observation. Nor does he designate exact criteria for evaluating hypotheses, although he does discuss the use of analogies (IV: xvi, §12) and develop a competitive method of judging hypotheses—a hypothesis is rejected when a more illuminating one is found to replace it. In a little known fragment on "Method," first published in 1829 by Peter King, Locke sets forth his ideas on the hypothetical method.[79]

The way to finde truth as far as we are able to reach it in this our darke & short sighted state is to pursue the hypothesis that seems to us to carry with it the most light & consistency as far as we can without raising objections or striking at those that come in our way till we have carried our present principle as far as it will goe & given what light & strength we can to all the parts of it. And when that is done then to take into our consideration any objections that lie against it but not soe as to pursue them as objections against the Systeme we had formerly erected but to consider upon what foundation they are bottomed & examine that in all its parts & then putting the two whole Systems togeather see which is liable to most exceptions & labours under the greatest difficulties (in Farr 1987: 70–71).

No wonder James Farr concludes that "Locke's wariness in matters of fact and hypothesis suggests a falsificationist message (to use the idiom of our time)" (67).

Having laid out the substance of Locke's philosophy of science, we can now examine the "historical, plain method" that he advocates in the *Essay concerning Human Understanding*.[80] A

---

79. The essay on method is appended to Farr's article (1987: 70–72).
80. The phrase "historical, plain method" first appears on the first page of the *Essay* (1965, I: i, §2) and is mentioned again in the following passages: (II: xi, §15); (IV: xii, §10); and (IV: xvi, §11).

number of scholars have argued that this method is simply an extension of his understanding of the method of medicine and biology current in his day (Romanell 1991: 476; Givner 1991: 433). But it is also the method of Baconian natural science (Wood 1991). Locke unfortunately never explained what he meant by the "historical, plain method." It is, however, clear that he thought it was the only effective method for acquiring human knowledge. It is also clear that Locke is offering the "historical, plain method" as an alternative to the metaphysical indulgences and speculation of Descartes and Hobbes, who, he believed, had succumbed to fanciful thinking. Although Locke admired Descartes in some ways, it was not for his philosophy of science. To Locke and many of his contemporaries, Cartesian principles were merely hypotheses—fanciful deductions that beg the facts (Schankula 1991: 391). In Locke's words: "When mathematical men will build systems upon fancy, and not upon demonstration, they are as liable to mistakes as others" (in Schankula 1991: 393).

The point of the "historical, plain method," then, was to restrict oneself to the facts determined through the use of observation and the classification of the phenomena of nature as is practiced in natural history (Romanell 1991: 480). The word *historical* refers to the observational, descriptive element of his method and is used interchangeably with *natural history* (Romanell 1991: 480, 478). What for Bacon was a preliminary step to science becomes for Locke a primary way of understanding matters of fact. He surely saw the "historical, plain method" as the method of Robert Boyle and the Royal Society of London (Schankula 1991: 393). *Plain* refers to the practical or useful and is used in contrast with the speculative or fanciful. Locke, we recall, was writing to help men of practical affairs act more usefully and rationally. But his method originated in ancient medicine, where observation, history (classification of illnesses known to physicians), and analogy were the basic tools of doctors (Romanell 1991: 484). Knowing medicine and its method best, Locke advocated the method he knew to be most effective: the direct method of observation, fact collection and classification, and analogy—the practical tools of medicine and biology in his age (Givner 1991: 433, 443).

Medicine and biological science at that time did not rest on principles of motion, as did Newton's knowledge of the physical world; the greater part of their constituent material fell into descriptive science. Although Locke admired Newton, he did not understand Newtonian mathematics or see how general principles could be built into an axiomatic system. David Givner points out that, for Locke, general principles were generalizations from particulars; unaware of the significance of the manipulation of mathematical symbols—which he thought represented mathematical ideas—he believed mathematics had the same purpose as natural history (1991: 437). It is worth quoting Givner at length on this point. "He did not believe in a theoretical science in which the role of experience is to verify an elaborate theoretical structure erected from broad assumptions and mathematical deductions. Instead Locke supposed that the program for a general scientific knowledge of the world consisted of making known, by direct observation, the facts close at hand. Through this gradual piecemeal process man would accumulate an ever growing description of things which would serve as a practical guide to the perceptible world" (432). As I mentioned earlier, Locke also did not believe that medical knowledge could be systematized according to general principles based on unobservable things.

This, in a nutshell, is Locke's "historical, plain method." It is, moreover, the method that would have a great impact on the economics of the classical age. The *Essay*'s "historical, plain method" would, in many ways, influence Adam Smith more deeply than Locke's economic science, in which he collects so many of the bold assumptions of his age that it leaves the reader with the impression of being at odds with his more carefully formulated general epistemological prescriptions. Locke was convinced that everything *natural* is right or good and believed that natural laws could only be known by reasoning deductively from the nature of man and God. Natural law, the will of God, is a body of rules conforming to rational nature. In order to show that rules of moral obligation could be derived from nature (i.e., human nature), ethics had to be demonstrable. And the demonstrability of moral principles, thought Locke, is analogous to the demonstrability of mathematical principles: while in mathematics reasoning starts with properties of figures and numbers, in ethics it begins with the idea of man as a rational creature (Locke 1954: 54). He therefore concludes that mathematics and morality are cognate disciplines because both are capable of demonstration.[81]

For Locke, the laws of human virtue and vice are like the laws that govern the movements of planets. In terms of political economy's development as a science, "a body of fundamental laws was roughly equivalent to the importance for chemistry of Boyle's law and for physics of Newton's laws of motion" (Letwin 1963: 178). Locke believed he could, and had, established economic laws. While the laws Locke developed may well have lacked the mathematical precision of Boyle's or Newton's, they were bolder in assuming that humans act in accordance with laws and that economic relations are similar to natural phenomena. "Some tincture of this assumption has lingered in the work of economic theorists ever since," William Letwin tells us; "but more important is the fact that Locke first invested economic theory with the substance, in the form of his laws, that marked it off as a self-sufficient science" (1963: 178).

## David Hume (1711–1776): Pioneer in Moral Philosophy

### The Science of Man
Hume, the man who characterized merchants as "one of the most useful races of men" (1955: 52), is most famous for his views on induction, which I treat in chapter 4. In this section I consider his view of science (which is not the same as his theory of induction) and his attempt to erect a science of man.

Like his friend Smith, Hume was an Enlightenment thinker living in a time when social science was emerging as a discipline in the form of moral philosophy. Hume considered himself the founder of the science of human nature as an experimental (i.e., Newtonian) science. All that ethics, politics, and political economy needed to become a part of moral philosophy was a sound foundation to build upon. When humans know enough, surmised Hume, they will be able to form a complete system of philosophy, both natural and moral. In developing a "science of

---

81. Locke could have gotten this idea from Hobbes, Grotius, Spinoza, or Culverwel.

man" Hume understood his task as extending the scientific method—that is, what he took to be Newton's scientific method, the *experimental method*—to the study of human nature. Hence, his *Treatise of Human Nature, Being an Attempt to Introduce the Experimental Method of Reasoning into Moral Subjects,* whose appearance (in three volumes in 1759) marked the beginning of intense debate in Scotland over the problems of moral philosophy (Rendall 1978: 96).

In the *Treatise of Human Nature* (1739), his first and ultimately most famous book, Hume set forth his theory of science straight away.[82] He divides moral philosophy into four areas of inquiry: logic, morals, criticism (aesthetics), and politics. Like Bacon and Descartes before him, Hume sees the necessity of constructing a new foundation for a completely new science: "In pretending therefore to explain the principles of human nature, we in effect propose a compleat system of the sciences, built on a foundation almost entirely new, and the only one upon which they can stand with any security" (1896: xx).

Although his work is marked by an emphasis on experience and experiment, generalization, laws of nature derived from phenomena, and a suspicion of hypotheses—all evidence of Newton's influence —Paul Russell (1985) argues that the *Treatise of Human Nature* was modeled after Hobbes's *Human Nature,* which was first published in 1640 as a separate treatise and only later became the first part of the *Elements of Law.* There is good reason to believe that Hume did indeed pattern his work after Hobbes's. In addition to the obvious fact that the two works share the same title, Russell notes that Hume was familiar with Hobbes's writings and acknowledged that the plan of the *Treatise* was not original (56). Furthermore, the two works have three methodological principles in common: human nature is considered to be similar in all men; moral and political philosophy are thought to benefit from the methods of natural philosophy; and moral philosophy starts with the study of human nature (62). Acknowledging his debt to Hobbes without risking a charge of Hobbism would, however, have been impossible; and the last

---

82. In Hume's view, the *Enquiry concerning Human Understanding* (1748) was a superior treatise designed to supersede the *Treatise.*

thing Hume needed was to be accused of Hobbism.[83] As it was, we know that after Hume had been invited to take up the chair of ethics and pneumatical philosophy at Edinburgh, he was unjustly charged with six philosophical sins: universal skepticism, advocating principles leading to atheism, erring concerning the nature and existence of God, erring concerning God as the first cause, denying the immateriality of the soul, and "sapping the foundations of morality." His opponents won; later he was turned down for a second position as well.[84]

To understand a thinker like Hume, we need to know what he is arguing against. A prominent feature of Hume's work is his opposition to a philosophical view that has often been awkwardly labeled *rationality* or *rationalism*.[85] In his day it boiled down to an antagonism toward using mathematical deduction— often called *demonstrative reasoning*—as the model for explaining the operation of human reason. Hume was reacting against the strong ties between science and religion and against the ideas of the Cambridge Platonists, who believed that ethics rested on certain absolute, self-evident truths like the axioms of geometry. In Hume's opinion, their views invited superstition and error, for knowledge justified by deduction from a priori principles could not necessarily be trusted. He offers instead a view that appeals to experience as a method of substantiating our "beliefs" or "matters of fact."

[W]e can only expect success, by following the experimental method, and deducing general maxims from a comparison of particular instances. The other scientific method, where a general abstract principle

---

83. Locke, by the way, was charged with Hobbism (atheism) by critics in Oxford. Being put in a category with deists, unitarians, or materialists in that age was tantamount to being labeled an atheist.

84. See Norton (1968: 163ff.) for a discussion of Hume's defense in his *Letter from a Gentleman*, a last effort to win over both the authorities and the public to his appointment to the chair of ethics and pneumatical philosophy at Edinburgh. Apparently the charge of "sapping the foundations of morality" rested on Hume's assertion that moral propositions are not of the same eternal, unchanging nature as mathematical principles.

   Even though the charges were ridiculous, Hume was so controversial a figure in his day that Adam Smith was reprimanded for reading the *Treatise* while at Oxford (Stephen 1898: 3).

85. The label is awkward because Hume is not opposed to using deduction or, for that matter, any nonempirical, common-sense form of reasoning.

is first established, and is afterwards branched out into a variety of inferences and conclusions, may be more perfect in itself, but suits less the imperfection of human nature, and is a common source of illusion and mistake in this as well as in other subjects. Men are now cured of their passion for hypotheses and systems in natural philosophy, and will hearken to no arguments but those which are derived from experience (1975: 174–75).

The latter remark is, of course, a reference to Descartes's systems.

By the *experimental method* Hume means the analysis of objects within our direct experience and with which we experiment. He uses the word *experimental* to mean almost the same thing as *empirical* and contrasts it with *speculation*. What he had in mind was a collection of observations, the consultation of factual evidence apparent to the senses, to serve as a reliable basis for generalization to a principle. Hume presumably calls his philosophy *experimental* for the same reason that Newton, according to Maclaurin, labelled his philosophy *experimental*: "He [Newton] used to call his philosophy *experimental philosophy,* intimating, by the name, the essential difference there is betwixt it and those systems that are the product of genius and invention only" (in Newton 1952: lxviii). Newton was alluding to Descartes and his infamous theory of vortices, and it is likely that Hume, too, had him in mind in this passage: "When a philosopher has once laid hold of a favorite principle, which perhaps accounts for many natural effects, he extends the same principle over the whole creation, and reduces to it every phaenomenon, though by the most violent and absurd reasoning" (1875: 213–14).[86] Against rash generalization, Hume emphasized that "all general maxims in politics ought to be established with great caution; and that irregular and extraordinary appearances are frequently discovered in the moral, as well as the physical world"—a point that is at least as Baconian as it is Newtonian in emphasis (1875: 374).

Hume's view of science turns in part on his definition of knowledge, in which he adopts the distinction between certain knowledge and belief so dominant in this age. We can be certain, he asserts, of only a few things: mathematical relationships or

---

86. Hume never attacks Descartes openly, but he obviously does not think his philosophical system has much virtue, for Descartes's name is never mentioned in his multi-volume *History of England.*

demonstrative reasoning. Thus, from geometry, algebra, and arithmetic—all of which deal with relations and proportions—we obtain genuine knowledge. But the rest of our understanding has to do with "matters of fact" or "moral reasoning," areas of inquiry that can yield only probable knowledge.[87] Although the upshot is that the knowledge we gain in moral and natural philosophy can never be certain, Hume argues that moral philosophy—despite its epistemological uncertainty—towers over all other subjects: "All these [areas in moral philosophy] form the most considerable branches of science. Mathematics and natural philosophy, which only remain, are not half so valuable" (1875: 187).

Hume's empiricism "proposes to anatomize human nature in a regular manner, and promises to draw no conclusions but where he is authorized by experience" (1965: 6–7). The way Hume sees it, only a fool could dispute the authority of experience. For him, empirical science means the discovery that things behave in a certain way. An apprehension of the inner nature of substances is impossible because experience does not reveal to us its ultimate connections. He denies that arguments from experience can be deduced in nature. According to Hume, we discover the world, we do not demonstrate it. All reasoning on matters of fact is based on cause and effect, which is discoverable only by experience. Thus, Hume closes his *Enquiry concerning Human Understanding* with the following message: "If we take in our hand any volume; of divinity or school metaphysics, for instance; let us ask, *Does it contain any abstract reasoning concerning quantity or number?* No. *Does it contain any experimental reasoning concerning matter of fact and existence?* No. Commit it then to the flames: for it can contain nothing but sophistry and illusion" (1975: 165).

John Passmore notes that "Newton, rather than Bacon, was Hume's master" (1980: 43). Nicholas Capaldi dubs Hume "the Newtonian philosopher" for being "the first philosopher to understand fully, to appreciate, and to articulate the philosophical implications of Newtonian physics" (1975: 50) and provides perhaps the most detailed analysis of how Hume builds a

---

87. "All reasonings may be divided into two kinds, namely, demonstrative reasoning, or that concerning relations of ideas, and moral reasoning, or that concerning matter of fact and existence" (Hume 1975: 35).

Newtonian program in moral philosophy (65–69). In the first step, Hume identifies objects of analysis which are observable and on which experiments can be conducted. For Hume, the basic unit of analysis is perceptions (all the material provided by the senses: feelings, sounds, smells, visual information, etc.). Second, experiments are to be conducted on objects of observation taken from human life so that a general principle can be arrived at.[88] Third, a general principle connecting the relations between units, analogous to Newton's principle of attraction, is determined. For Hume, this principle is the principle of association.[89] The fourth and final stage entails extending the general principle to other phenomena (an application of Newton's Fourth Rule of Reasoning, the method of synthesis). Although he does not employ the Newtonian terminology, Hume was the first to apply Newton's methods of analysis and synthesis to the moral sciences. Later it would become a standard methodological tool of many of the British classical economists.

As enthusiastic as Hume is about Newton's method, he recognizes its limits for the science of man. Unlike many of his Scottish contemporaries, Hume was quite circumspect about the successes to be expected from introducing the experimental method into moral philosophy. Because mental units are difficult to isolate, he recognizes that experiments are more troublesome in moral philosophy than they are in natural philosophy:

> Moral philosophy has, indeed, this peculiar disadvantage, which is not found in natural [philosophy], that in collecting its experiments, it cannot make them purposely, with premeditation, and after such a manner as to satisfy itself concerning every particular difficulty which may arise. . . . We must therefore glean up our experiments in this science from a cautious observation of human life, and take them as they appear in the common course of the world, by men's behaviour in company, in affairs, and in their pleasures. Where experiments of this kind are judiciously collected and compared, we may hope to establish on them a science, which will not be inferior in certainty, and

---

88. A discussion of the Scottish experiments is included in chapter 3 in the section entitled "Natural History as Fact Collecting."

89. In Hume's view the principle of association was his greatest achievement. "Thro' this whole book," Hume summarized in his *Abstract of the Treatise on Human Nature*, "there are great pretensions to new discoveries in philosophy; but if any thing can intitle the author [Hume] to so glorious a name as that of an *inventor*, 'tis the use he makes of the principle of the association of ideas, which enters into most of his philosophy" (1965: 31).

will be much superior in utility to any other of human comprehensiveness (1896: xxii-xxiii).

Hume's views of what science can achieve are modest.[90] "The most perfect philosophy of the natural kind only staves off our ignorance a little longer: as perhaps the most perfect philosophy of the moral or metaphysical kind serves only to discover larger portions of it," Hume tells us (1975: 31). He does not believe that science can arrive at absolutely certain results; no method can protect scientists from error. Moreover, we can never arrive at ultimate principles. Just as deductive systems do not guarantee scientific validity,[91] Hume realizes his experimental method is also far from perfect.[92] "Thus the observation of human blindness and weakness is the result of philosophy," he concludes, "and meets us at every turn, in spite of our endeavors to elude or avoid it" (31). For these reasons, much of Hume's effort is focused on the problem of sifting through evidence and devising ways to estimate the relative strength of evidence, a topic I pick up in chapter 4 in setting forth Hume's problem of induction.

### Hume and Newton
Numerous scholars have assessed Newton's influence on Hume and examined the question of Hume's knowledge and interpretation of Newton.[93] Many have concluded that Hume had little interest in the science of his day or in Newton. The reasons for reaching this conclusion generally rest on the belief that Hume neither made use of mathematics nor acknowledged its value for the experimental method. According to James Force, modern scholars have been led to such a view because they are held captive by the narrow confines of twentieth-century perceptions of science. It seems to me, first, that modern scholars incorrectly assessed Hume's relationship with Newton and science, as Force

---

90. The fact that Hume was *not* a radical skeptic will be taken up in chapter 4 on the theory of induction.

91. "Nor is geometry, when taken into the assistance of natural philosophy, ever able to remedy this defect [of human ignorance and infallibility], or lead us into the knowledge of ultimate causes, by all that accuracy of reasoning for which it is so justly celebrated" (Hume 1975: 31).

92. "Though experience be our only guide in reasoning concerning matters of fact; it must be acknowledged, that this guide is not altogether infallible, but in some cases is apt to lead us into errors" (Hume 1975: 110).

93. Consider, for instance, Barfoot (1990), Force (1987), and Capaldi (1975).

rightly argues; and, second, that closer scrutiny of this issue is called for because it sheds light on the relationship between Adam Smith and Isaac Newton (which I explore in chapter 5). Because Smith's intellectual debt to Hume is undisputed, the results here are important for understanding Smith.

It has not been difficult for Hume scholars to find evidence to support the view that Hume's knowledge of Newton was superficial. For instance, there is Hume's Baconian interpretation of Newton. But, as Barfoot notes, this was typical even of Newton scholars of the day, and, most notably, of fellow natural philosophers who knew and worked with Newton: "Hume's insistence upon the role of empirical experience and facts in scientific discovery, together with the somewhat casual amalgamation of Newton's method with Bacon's, can be found in Pemberton and MacLaurin" (1990: 161).[94] In addition, Newton apparently approved their versions of Newtonianism in spite of deviations from his methods.[95]

There is, furthermore, the fact that Hume misinterprets Newton. He so eulogizes experience and fears that rash speculation could corrupt science, Hume scholars claim, that his common sense is overcome by a contempt for hypotheses that, as we see in the following passage, far surpasses Newton's own: "And tho' we must endeavor to render all our principles as universal as possible, by tracing up our experiments to the utmost, and explaining all effects from the simplest and fewest causes, 'tis still certain we cannot go beyond experience; and any hypothesis, that pretends to discover the ultimate original qualities of human nature, ought at first to be rejected as presumptuous and chimerical" (Hume 1896: xxi). Hume scholars claim that this

---

94. The third edition of the *Principia* was edited by Pemberton. Maclaurin, to borrow Dugald Stewart's characterization, was "one of the most illustrious of Newton's followers" (*Works* 3: 273). In his *View of Sir Isaac Newton's Philosophy*, Pemberton outlines Bacon's philosophy by bringing out the parallels with Newton's method (1728: 5–10). The connection between Bacon and Newton, in Pemberton's view, is the element of caution in deriving principles: "the only method, that can afford us any prospect of success in this difficult work, is to make our enquiries with the utmost caution, and by very slow degrees" (4).
95. Pemberton's *View of Sir Isaac Newton's Philosophy* (1728), stresses Cohen, was written "with Newton peering over his shoulder," and with Newton's full approval (1966: 210).

attitude toward hypotheses is problematic for several reasons. First, Newton did not mean to reject all hypotheses with his maxim *hypotheses non fingo,* but to caution against taking seriously hypotheses unsubstantiated by the results of experiment. Ayer puts the matter this way: "What Newton presumably meant by his disclaimer of hypotheses at the beginning of his *Principia* . . . was that he advanced no propositions for which he lacked experimental evidence. What Hume apparently took him to have meant was that he abstained from any generalisation that was not directly founded upon observed instances" (1980: 25). Yet it seems to me that this passage from Hume has been misinterpreted. He is not rejecting all hypotheses lacking a base in observation, but only those pretending to discover ultimate principles, the possibility of which he strictly denies.

Finally, it is obvious that some of Hume's applications of Newtonian ideas do stray far from the original intention. For instance, in a letter in 1751 to his cousin, Mrs. Dysart, about the marriage of his 42-year-old brother, John Hume of Ninewells, Hume comments that his older brother "has engag'd himself without being able to compute exactly the consequences. But what Arithmetic will serve to fix the proportion betwixt good & bad Wives, & rate the different classes of each? Sir Isaac Newton himself, who cou'd measure the courses of the Planets, and weigh the Earth as in a pair of scales, even he had not Algebra enough to reduce that amiable Part of our species to a just equation: and they are the only heavenly bodies, whose orbits are as yet uncertain" (1932, I: 158–59). No doubt this was written in jest; yet it is exactly the kind of unscientific remark that would ruffle the feathers of many good twentieth-century scientists.

Nonetheless, dismissing the seriousness of Hume's intent based on his misinterpretations or amusing applications is grossly unfair. It does not matter that Hume "writes nothing of conic sections or the lunar apogee" or makes no use of geometry or calculus. Like many of his contemporaries, especially Adam Smith, "Hume often speaks with the vulgar while he thinks with the learned" (Force 1987: 178). He followed the maxim, "Be a philosopher; but amidst all your philosophy, be still a man," a prescription on style entreating the philosopher to express himself so that the "man of the world" can understand him (in

Raynor 1984: 64).[96] Moreover, Hume's interest in science cannot be separated from his interest in epistemology or religion and is, as Force points out, "precisely what one ought to expect from an eighteenth-century man of letters curious about all intellectual topics of contemporary importance but whose special project is to define the limits of human enquiry and banish from it any sort of theology, natural or revealed. The fact that so many of Hume's arguments rely on examples traceable to sources which we today should characterize as literary, theological, or deistic, and not as 'scientific,' tells us more about science in our day than it does about science in Hume's time when religion was an integral part of the scientific enterprise" (1987: 188). In that completely interdisciplinary world, all men of letters kept abreast of the latest scientific developments, a fact confirmed by a perusal of the periodicals of the day, such as the *Gentleman's Magazine* (see Appendix I).

Thus, in spite of the fact that Hume and Newton's methodological positions diverge, the claim that Hume was not interested in Newton or in the science of his day does not withstand close scrutiny. Quite to the contrary, there appears to be strong evidence for Hume's direct knowledge of Newton's science, for it is certain that he had at least a basic understanding of the *Principia*. For instance, in the introduction to his *Treatise*, Hume makes use of Newton's famous Rules of Reasoning. Although I think it is safe to say that Hume, like Locke before him, did not care about the mathematical details of the mechanical propositions in the *Principia*, no one would dispute his familiarity with the prefaces, definitions, and axioms of the *Principia*, the General Scholium, the Rules of Reasoning from book 3, and Cote's famous preface to the second edition (Force 1987: 202, n. 27).

There is also a wealth of evidence underscoring Hume's interest in science in general. As a student, he was a member of the Physiological Library, a class library founded in 1724 for students and gentlemen by Robert Steuart, professor of natural philosophy at Edinburgh. After bringing this fact to light, Barfoot shows that Hume was very familiar with the natural phi-

---

96. Hume makes the same point when he praises Smith's style in his "Abstract of the *Theory of Moral Sentiments*": "Though he [Smith] penetrates into the depths of philosophy, he still talks like a man of the world" (appended to Raynor 1984: 78).

losophy tradition (1990).[97] Force offers in Hume's defense his awareness of recent scientific developments in astronomy, optics, psychology, geology, microscopy, cosmogony, and electricity (Force 1987: 191). To this we can add political economy, for he knew both Smith and Steuart and their works, the two great treatises in political economy of eighteenth-century Britain. In addition, Hume was elected joint secretary of the Philosophical Society of Edinburgh in 1751 when it was expanded and reorganized.[98] Under its auspices, he edited two volumes of essays on medicine, astronomy, optics, meteorology, physiology, and biology and corresponded with Benjamin Franklin about the latter's essay on lightning rods (Force 1987: 195).[99]

Hume mentions Newton by name numerous times[100] and draws on his terminology; but "by introducing the 'experimental method of reasoning' into moral philosophy, Hume was doing more than simply jumping on a rhetorical bandwagon" (Barfoot 1990: 167). He marshalls Newton's Rules of Reasoning to illuminate the limits of knowledge in his science of man. Newton's celebrated Rules of Reasoning, Hume thinks, are fully capable of being adapted to the science of man, as this passage from the *Inquiry concerning the Principles of Morals* attests: "It is entirely agreeable to the rules of philosophy, and even of common reason; where any principle has been found to have great force and energy in one instance, to ascribe to it like energy in all similar instances" (1975: 204). Here Hume is referring to Rule 2, but Rule 4 plays an important role in Hume's work as well. Force concludes, rightly I think, that Hume's understanding comes from a direct reading of the *Principia* (1987: 185).[101]

---

97. Barfoot concludes that "Hume's familiarity with mathematics and mathematical natural philosophy is now in urgent need of attention. . . . [I]ts significance is more profound than most Hume scholars have previously recognized" (1990: 190).

98. Smith, by the way, was a member.

99. Hume's letter to Franklin, written in his capacity as secretary of the Philosophical Society and dated 10 May 1762, concerns the publication of a paper on electricity that Franklin had submitted to the society (1954: 66).

100. Force lists all eleven of Hume's direct references to Newton (1987: 169–78).

101. There are at least two other possible reasons that could bring us to this conclusion. Hume was very much a scholar and would probably not have resorted to secondary materials. In addition, because he had to withstand rather heavy criticism, he would have been compelled to proceed with great caution.

Hume clearly sees in Newton a fellow skeptic, and he seems to draw this conclusion from a reading of Newton's Rules of Reasoning. He writes in the *Treatise:*

As long as we confine our speculations to *the appearances* of objects to our senses, without entering into disquisitions concerning their real nature and operations, we are safe from all difficulties, and can never be embarrass'd by any question. . . . If we carry our enquiry beyond the appearances of objects to the senses, I am afraid, that most of our conclusions will be full of scepticism and uncertainty. . . . If *the Newtonian* philosophy be rightly understood, it will be found to mean no more. . . . Nothing is more suitable to that philosophy, than a modest scepticism to a certain degree, and a fair confession of ignorance in subjects, that exceed all human capacity (1896: 638–39).

Thus, Hume interprets Newton as agreeing with him that generalizations can be made so long as the philosopher accepts two restrictions: that such reasoning is fallible and that it has the status of a hypothesis and is thus subject to revision in the light of the test of experience.

Force's strongest argument for Hume's direct knowledge of Newton's work is his interest in Newton's design argument (1987: 183). The design argument was first appended as the General Scholium to the second edition of the *Principia* at Cote's request; accusations that Newton was an atheist, especially from Leibniz and Bishop Berkeley, prompted its inclusion. In the design argument, Hume saw that Newton followed Rule 2, but failed to heed the caution he had set forth in Rule 4, the rule on induction. Force offers convincing support for the view that Hume could not have taken this argument from a popular edition of the *Principia*, for most editions did not deal with Newton's Fourth Rule of Reasoning, which first appeared in the third edition in 1726.[102] Force observes that Hume alone saw the

102. According to Force, John Keill's *An Introduction to Natural Philosophy* (1720) and David Gregory's *Elements of Astronomy, physical and geometrical translated* (1715) were based on the first and second editions of the *Principia* (1987: 185–86). Although Chamber's article on "Newtonian Philosophy" in the *Cyclopaedia* was probably known to Hume, it does not mention the Rules. John Clarke's and Henry Pemberton's commentaries provide brief summaries of Rule 4, but not in connection with the problem of induction. Even Colin Maclaurin's *Account of Sir Isaac Newton's Philosophy* (1748) fails to mention the Rules of Reasoning. In view of the large number of works in print on Newtonian science, it is, however, impossible to determine exactly what works Hume

consequences of Rule 4 for Newton's design argument—and that Hume was justified in thinking he knew more than Newton's disciples and even Newton himself (186). He concludes: "Just as Hume's interest in Newton's thought is a vital and serious one, it seems to me that his interest in science in general is also quite serious given his goal of completely destroying the unique synthesis of science and religion which existed in the first half of the eighteenth century" (187).[103] Hume was, after all, the only one of his age to provide arguments for the secularization of the Royal Society that took place after 1741 under the leadership of Martin Folkes.[104]

Before leaving my discussion of Hume it would be instructive to ask what he wanted to achieve by using Newton's philosophy as a prototype for his science of man. Barfoot's answer is worth noting: "Hume expected that the application of the latter [the practice of experimental natural philosophy] to moral subjects would reveal new and surprising truths on a par with those discovered in hydrostatics. As long as the science of human nature based its experiments on what he described as 'a cautious observation of human life', he anticipated it would be at least as certain as, and actually much more useful than, any other science" (1990: 167).[105] For Hume, it is chiefly the method of the *Opticks*, but also the Rules of Reasoning, that constitute Newton's experimental method. Because he is interested in the

---

read. Force mentions the two foremost Newton scholars, I. B. Cohen and A. Koyré, once thought of writing a history of the commentaries on the *Principia* but quickly abandoned the project when they realized that it would require a book of 1,500 to 2,400 pages of small type (1987: 185).

103. "One of Hume's most basic purposes in erecting his new 'science of man' is to attack this synthesis [of science and religion] as it exists and wherever it exists" (Force 1987: 191).

104. On this issue Force points out that "Hume is the only writer in the eighteenth century to mount careful attacks upon all the separate elements of the 'first' Royal Society's elaborate synthesis of general and special providence" (1984: 534). Within the Royal Society secularization apparently became established "more through ridicule and mockery than as a result of explicitly argued tracts and pamphlets" (528).

105. Note Hume's remark in "A Discussion on the Passions": "It is sufficient for my purpose, if I have made it appear that, in the production and conduct of the passions, there is a certain regular mechanism, which is susceptible of as accurate a disquisition, as the laws of motion, optics, hydrostatics, or any part of natural philosophy" (1854, 4: 226).

hypothetical character of science, he does not draw on the mathematics, the tightly deductive system, or even the *Principia*'s method of prediction and strict testing. Nor is his system mechanical: Hume recognizes that the processes of the mind are adaptive, not mechanical, in nature.

By Hume's interpretation, Newton's method served two chief purposes. In keeping with Enlightenment thought, it "served as a critical instrument for the exposure of humbug, prejudice, and intellectual pretension" (Guerlac 1965: 318). It served further as a vehicle for penetrating the hidden mechanisms of human nature. Hume considers the main causal principles discovered by natural philosophers to be elasticity, gravity, cohesion of parts, and communication of motion by impulse (1975: 30). Applying Newton's second Rule of Reasoning, which he construes as "like causes produce like effects," Hume explains:

It is universally acknowledged that there is a great uniformity among the actions of men, in all nations and ages, and that human nature remains still the same, in its principles and operations. The same motives always produce the same actions: The same events follow from the same causes. Ambition, avarice, self-love, vanity, friendship, generosity, public spirit: these passions, mixed in various degrees, and distributed through society, have been, from the beginning of the world, and still are, the source of all the actions and enterprises, which have ever been observed among mankind (1975: 83).

Once uniformity in human nature is established, principles can be established: "general principles, if just and sound, must always prevail in the general course of things . . . and it is the chief business of philosophers to regard the general course of things" (1955: 4). But reasoning in moral philosophy can surpass that of natural philosophy, according to Hume, "because we not only observe, that men *always* seek society, but can also explain the principles, on which this universal propensity is founded" (1896: 402). The union of the sexes, he points out, is every bit as certain as mechanical attraction; so is the care children receive from parents and the assimilation of families into society. What moral philosophy has that natural philosophy does not have is empirical *and* moral significance, a point I take up again in the discussion of induction in chapter 4.

## Dugald Stewart (1753–1828) and Scottish Philosophy of Science

Dugald Stewart, "easily the foremost academic philosopher in Britain during the whole Revolutionary and Napoleonic period" (Randall 1962, 2: 524), knew Adam Smith, learned political economy from Adam Ferguson, and held the chair in moral philosophy in Edinburgh from the latter's death in 1785 until 1810. Stewart was one of the Common Sense philosophers and one of the first great interpreters of Smith's *Wealth of Nations*.[106] James McCosh says of his influence: "In his classes of moral philosophy and of political economy, he had under him a greater body of young men who afterwards distinguished themselves, than any other teacher that I can think of" (1990: 283). Among his students were Sir Walter Scott, Francis Jeffrey, John Ramsay McCulloch, Thomas Chalmers, Lord Brougham, Francis Horner, Thomas Brown, Sydney Smith, Lord Palmerston, Lord John Russell, Archibald Allison, Lord Webb Seymour, Henry Cockburn, Macvey Napier, and the senior Mill—as Randall remarks, "the whole Edinburgh liberal galaxy of the Reform agitation era" (1962, 2: 524). Although he was characterized by Wilhelm Hasbach as the "founder of every mistaken methodology," recent studies show that the impact of Stewart on his age has been greatly underestimated and misunderstood.[107]

Like Hume and the Scottish natural historians, Stewart's view of science starts with the study of human nature. He learned Newtonian physics in his classes on natural philosophy and "caught an enthusiastic affection for the inductive method and for Bacon" (McCosh 1990: 278). He believes that natural philosophy becomes scientific when it concentrates on the discovery of

---

106. Besides Stewart, the Scottish Common Sense school consisted of Thomas Reid (1710–1796) and Thomas Brown (1778–1819). Some writers, e.g., Olson (1975), also include William Hamilton (1788–1856). Reid is usually considered the founder of the school; Olson (27) designates James Beattie (1735–1802) as cofounder. Common Sense philosophy was an outgrowth of the discussions of the Philosophical Society of Aberdeen (also called the Wise Club), which met twice monthly from 1758 to 1773. It arose in response to the philosophical writings of Hume, in particular to the skepticism and atheism they professed to find in them. Still, as Olson remarks, they were "as much the philosophical disciples of David Hume as they were his religious enemies" (28).

107. "Der Begründer jener irrtümlichen Methodologie ist meines Wissens der schottische Philosoph Dugald Stewart" (Hasbach 1904: 315).

laws by observation and experiment and that science advances
by bringing uniformities under laws of higher generality. Notably, Stewart is perhaps the first Scottish philosopher to make a
clear statement defending the necessity of using both empiricism
and general principles:

Nothing, indeed, can be more absurd than to contrast, as is commonly
done, experience with theory, as if they stood in opposition to each
other. Without theory (or, in other words, without general principles
inferred from a sagacious comparison of a variety of phenomena)
experience is a blind and useless guide; while, on the other hand, a
legitimate theory (and the same observation may be extended to hypothetical theories . . . ) necessarily presupposes a knowledge of connected and well ascertained facts, more comprehensive by far than any
mere empiric is likely to possess (*Works*, 3: 329).

His *Elements of the Philosophy of the Human Mind* is a defense of
the application of general principles to politics.

Stewart's father was a mathematician in the geometrical mode,
and the junior Stewart followed him, educationally speaking,
sometimes even substituting for his father at the university
(McCosh 1990: 276). "From his own father, and through his own
academical teaching," McCosh tells us, Stewart "acquired a taste
for the geometrical method, so well fitted to give clearness and
coherency to thought, and to teach caution in deduction" (1990:
277–78). Yet, because of his training in geometry, Stewart's assertions about scientific achievements at times surpass a healthy
optimism. Consider, for example, his proposition that moral and
physical science can obtain the certainty of mathematics: "it
appears that it might be possible, by devising a set of arbitrary
definitions, to form a science which, although conversant about
moral, political, or physical ideas, should yet be as certain as
geometry" (*Works*, 3: 115).[108]

Stewart, again in Scottish tradition, warned against a careless
use of speculative hypotheses and analogies in science. But he
parts company with many of the Scottish Common Sense philosophers by arguing for the importance of hypotheses. In his
*Elements,* he dedicates a section to the "Use and Abuse of
Hypotheses in Philosophical Inquiries" (*Works*, 3: 298–316).

108. Similar ideas are expressed by the elder Mill.

Newton's views on hypotheses, he insists, should not be taken literally.[109] Reversing a long philosophical tradition of dismissing the role of hypothesis in science, Stewart approves of the creative uses of hypotheses, stressing "that most discoveries have been made" by using hypotheses (3: 301). Essentially the same goes for analogies: used carefully, they suggest and stimulate—but they must not be confused with theories. A hypothesis is verified if it predicts unknown phenomena; and usually Stewart treats a verified hypothesis as a theory. In contrast with Reid, Stewart thinks the simplicity of hypotheses is worth striving for.

In addition to a bold new stance on hypotheses, Stewart introduces two further novelties that distinguish his ideas about the philosophy of science from the rest of the Scottish school. It appears that no one has noticed that Stewart can be ranked as a precursor of Karl Popper, although he clearly recognized the importance of learning from error: "Nor is it solely by the erroneous results of his *own* hypotheses, that the philosopher is assisted in the investigation of truth," he writes, adding that "[s]imilar lights are often to be collected from the errors of his predecessors" (*Works,* 3: 306). Up to that time, no moral scientist had recognized prediction's usefulness for science. With Stewart this changes:

The ultimate object of philosophical inquiry is the same which every man of plain understanding proposes to himself, when he remarks the events which fall under his observation, with a view to the future regulation of his conduct. The more knowledge of this kind we acquire, the better can we accommodate our plans to the established order of things, and avail ourselves of natural Powers and Agents for accomplishing our purposes (2: 6).

A failure to appreciate prediction as a goal of science is one of his criticisms of Adam Smith, a point to which I return in chapter 5.[110]

---

109. "But the language of this great man, when he happens to touch upon logical questions, must not always be too literally interpreted" (Stewart, *Works,* 3: 299).
110. As far as I can determine, it was Comte who first made prediction the ultimate measure of science. The moral philosophers were clever enough to see that all scientists are not astronomers.

### Sir John F. W. Herschel (1792–1871): Model Philosopher

Herschel's contributions to the philosophy of science are only now coming to light, although he was "England's most famous scientist from 1830 to about 1860" (Cannon 1967: 491) and doubtless the most influential natural scientist of his age.[111] An astronomer, physicist, chemist, and philosopher, Herschel strongly influenced John Stuart Mill, William Stanley Jevons, and William Whewell. Jevons and James Clerk Maxwell were his chief followers. The friendship between Herschel and William Whewell was closer than the famous Malthus-Ricardo relationship.[112] So illustrious was Herschel in his lifetime that he was regarded as "the personification of natural philosophy" (Charpa 1987: 124). Addressing the Royal Society in 1833, His Royal Highness the Duke of Sussex praised Herschel above all others as "such a model of an accomplished philosopher, as can rarely be found beyond the regions of fiction" (in Cannon 1961: 217–18). All this makes his relative obscurity today all the more bewildering.

Herschel's *Preliminary Discourse on the Study of Natural Philosophy*, first published in 1830, quickly earned the reputation of a "minor classic" (Cannon 1961: 230). In it, Herschel lays out his philosophy of science.[113] As Cannon explains, it also served as "a starting point for his philosophic contemporaries, the more radical (post-Kantian) Whewell and the more conservative (Humean) Mill" (1967: 491). Charles Darwin, Michael Faraday, and James Clerk Maxwell all claimed that the *Discourse* helped them to their success. In economics, John Stuart Mill and William Stanley Jevons borrowed generously from Herschel's work. Mill, for instance, quoted Herschel at length in the second edition of his *System of Logic*, which he had revised after Herschel supplied

---

111. Cannon (1961) documents just how influential Herschel was. Herschel was knighted for his accomplishments in 1831 and made a baronet in 1838.

112. Herschel and Whewell's friendship began in their student days at Cambridge, where they met at the Sunday "philosophical breakfasts" they both attended. After Herschel left Cambridge, they kept in contact through a lengthy correspondence (preserved at the Royal Society at London and the Wren Library at Trinity College). Each reviewed the other's works; Whewell dedicated his *History of the Inductive Sciences* to Herschel. When the friendship came to an end in 1866 at Whewell's death, Herschel wrote the obituary.

113. Unfortunately, there are no modern editions of Herschel's works. Because the editions of the *Discourse* are so numerous, parenthetical references to it are to the section number.

detailed criticisms of the first edition. Both the feedback from Herschel and the transfer of Herschel's comments and ideas entitle Mill's *System of Logic* to be considered "a descendent of Herschel's *Discourse*" (Cannon 1961: 220).

Because he worked in the tradition of Bacon and Newton, Herschel is deemed to be closer to the Scottish philosophers descending from Hume than to his contemporaries.[114] He placed great stock in Bacon's views: the title page of his *Preliminary Discourse* displays a likeness of Bacon, and the book can be regarded as an attempt to update Bacon's theory of induction.[115] The similarities to the Scottish philosophers go even further. Herschel develops a logic of induction (which I discuss in detail in chapter four) and sees the scientist in the chemist's role. His philosophy of mathematics is also in the Scottish tradition. Richard Olson has concluded that "the range of agreement between Herschel and the Common Sense school on both epistemological issues and methodological questions warrants placing Herschel squarely within the Common Sense tradition" (1975: 269–70). The similarities are so striking that "[a]fter the publication and widespread dissemination of Herschel's work, it is next to impossible to judge from most scientific works whether methodological ideas were directly adopted from the Scottish tradition or whether they were more closely connected with Herschel's *Discourse*" (270), a point to keep in mind when we explore John Stuart Mill's philosophy of science.

For all his praise for Bacon, Herschel redefines science in a way that is often incompatible with Bacon's system. Like Dugald Stewart, Herschel emphasizes the fruitfulness and suggestiveness of hypotheses and advocates forming bold hypotheses and verifying hypotheses. By the 1830s, Newton's strictures on hypotheses had completely lost their bite among natural philosophers: Herschel recalled that his father, the famous astronomer William Herschel, emphasized how greatly Newton's methodological prescriptions had gone awry by reminding him that the rule of thumb in science was actually *hypotheses fingo* (in Wilson

---

114. "In his emphasis on generalizations and their induction from particular phenomena, Herschel continued in the tradition started by Bacon and given almost exclusive emphasis by the Common Sense philosophers Reid and Gregory" (Olson 1975: 265).
115. See Herschel's comments on the latter issue in his *Discourse* (1831: 114, §105).

1974: 85–86, n. 38). Herschel also insists that science must use both the inductive and deductive method: "it is very important to observe," he writes in his *Discourse* "that the successful process of scientific enquiry demands continually the alternative use of both the *inductive* and *deductive* method" (1831: 174–75, §184).

Herschel praises no one more highly than Newton, whose mathematical skills, he insists, brought science to maturity (1831: 271–72, §30). Newton's influence can be found in Herschel's advocacy of the hypothetical-deductive method, in his preoccupation with *vera causae*,[116] and in the development of his own rules of philosophy—although, all this, as Blake and associates recognize, can be found in Bacon, albeit in more primitive form (1960: 156). With Whewell, who shared Herschel's enthusiasm for Newton, Herschel was still fighting Newton's battle with the Cartesians. Both made negative remarks about Descartes, including attacks on his personal character, even blaming Newton's exaggerated position on hypotheses on Descartes.[117] Finally, like Newton, both Herschel and Whewell interspersed theological considerations throughout their writings.

Herschel had only a peripheral interest in political economy and mentions it only once in his *Discourse,* at the end of the first section, where he discusses the effects of advances in natural philosophy on other sciences. Like most Cambridge thinkers of this era, Herschel believed that adopting the scientific method in social science would produce a scientific approach to legislation and political economy. In the passage below, the dissenting voices of the age also make themselves heard.

The successful results of our experiments and reasonings in natural philosophy, and the incalculable advantages which experience, system-

---

116. Both Herschel and Whewell believed true causes, *vera causae*, existed and could be discovered. Wilson explains this as an outgrowth of the optimistic, progressive times in which they were living: "Given the state of science as Whewell and Herschel saw it in the 1830s, they perhaps could scarcely do other than champion true causes. . . . Overwhelmingly impressive accomplishments in astronomy and optics had made the theme of true causes (with respect to both their actual existence in the external and the possibility of accurate knowledge of them) a brute fact of scientific life—a fact which any satisfactory system or philosophy of science would have to recognize" (1974: 87).
117. On Herschel and Whewell's treatment of Descartes, see Wilson (1974: 88). Their interpretation of Newton's position on hypotheses would never have been so excessive had they realized that *hypotheses non fingo* referred only to gravitation.

atically consulted and dispassionately reasoned on, has conferred in matters purely physical, tend of necessity to impress something of the well weighed and progressive character of science on the more complicated conduct of our social and moral relations. It is thus that legislation and politics become gradually regarded as experimental sciences. . . . Political economy, at least, is found to have sound principles, founded in the moral and physical nature of man, which, however lost sight of in particular measures—however even temporarily controverted and borne down by clamour—have yet a stronger and stronger testimony borne to them in each succeeding generation, by which they must, sooner or later, prevail (Herschel 1831: 72–73, §65).

The source of knowledge, according to Herschel, is experience, either through observation or experimentation. He indicates, following Hume, that experience separates mathematics from natural philosophy. But even "the axioms of geometry themselves may be regarded as in some sort an appeal to experience, not corporeal, but mental," Herschel argues (1831: 95, §86). He briefly discusses prejudices of opinion and the senses in an exposition smacking of Bacon's idols before defining science as the study of phenomena governed by laws. To have laws, we must have uniformity in phenomena. Finding ever broader generalizations is the task of science. For Herschel, the word *law* designates general facts as opposed to particular facts. As Blake and associates note, Herschel, Hume, and Mill never distinguish clearly between the notions of *cause* and *law:* "On this account, many of the statements in which he [Herschel] uses the terms have the sort of obscurity confusion breeds" (1960: 181). For instance, Herschel sometimes uses the word *axiom* as a synonym for a general proposition that explains phenomena, and other times to mean a general fact or even a law of nature. In the *Discourse* he uses the term *cause* in at least four ways. When used to refer to simple phenomena that have been analyzed as component parts of more complex phenomena—or, more importantly, as a "proximate cause" to designate a phenomenon antecedent to an effect (i.e., the invariable antecedent of its effect)—the term *cause* takes on its greatest significance.[118]

Herschel's philosophy of science focuses on discovery rather than the justification of induction. In Herschel's view, the major

---

118. On Herschel's usage of the word *cause*, see Blake et al. (1960: 164ff.) and Cannon (1967: 491) and (1961: 221 ff.).

aim of scientific inquiry is to analyze complex phenomena into simpler ones for which "proximate causes" may be discovered. "We must go to nature itself, and be guided by the same kind of rule as the chemist in his analysis, who accounts every ingredient an *element* till it can be decompounded and resolved into others. So, in natural philosophy, we must account every phenomenon an elementary or simple one till we can analyse it, and show that it is the result of others, which in their turn become elementary" (1831: 92, §83). He does not, however, believe there are general rules for analyzing unknown phenomena into simpler components. "But, it will now be asked, how we are to proceed to analyse a composite phenomenon into simpler ones, and whether any general rules can be given for this important process? We answer, None; any more than . . . general rules can be laid down by the chemist for the analysis of substances of which all the ingredients are unknown. Such rules, could they be discovered, would include the whole of natural science; but we are very far, indeed, from being able to propound them" (1831: 96–97, §88).

"Dismissing . . . as beyond our reach, the enquiry into causes," Herschel points out that "we must be content at present to concentrate our attention on the laws which prevail among phenomena, and which seem to be their immediate results" (1831: 91, §83). Much of part 2 of his *Discourse* involves the problem of finding the laws of nature, which for Herschel play "the same part in natural philosophy that axioms do in geometry" (1831: 95, §86). The business of science is, however, not just to formulate general laws of force and matter, but also to explain arbitrary features of nature (for example, sunspots), what J. S. Mill was later to refer to as "counteracting causes." Instead of iron rules, Herschel offers his famous "nine rules of philosophizing" to make the search for causes easier (152–59, §146–162).[119] Because they are lengthy, the rules below appear in abridged form.

Rule 1 reduces to the method of elimination; Rule 2, to the method of agreement.

---

119. Blake and associates (1960) and Charpa (1987: 141) speak of *ten* rules, arbitrarily adding §162, an elaboration of Rule 9, as the tenth rule.

1st, That if in our group of facts there be one in which any assigned peculiarity, or attendant circumstance, is wanting or opposite, such peculiarity cannot be the cause we seek.

2d, That any circumstance in which all the facts without exception agree, *may* be the cause in question, or, if not, at least a collateral effect of the same cause: if there be but one such point of agreement, this possibility becomes a certainty; and, on the other hand, if there be more than one, they may be concurrent causes.

Rule 3 emphasizes the fruitfulness of analogies, while the 4th makes the point that both positive and negative instances can be instructive in the search for causes.

3d, That we are not to deny the existence of a cause in favour of which we have a unanimous agreement of strong analogies, though it may not be apparent how such a cause can produce the effect, or even though it may be difficult to conceive its existence under the circumstances of the case; in such cases we should rather appeal to experience when possible, than decide *a priori* against the cause, and try whether it can be made apparent. . . .

4th, That contrary or opposing facts are equally instructive for the discovery of causes with favourable ones. . . .

Rules 5, 7, and 8 deal with the degree of intensity of phenomena as a determinant of cause and effect. In Rule 6 Herschel argues that we must allow for counteracting causes.

5th, That causes will very frequently become obvious, by a mere arrangement of our facts in the order of intensity in which some peculiar quality subsists; though not of necessity, because counteracting or modifying causes may be at the same time in action. . . .

6th, That such counteracting or modifying causes may subsist unperceived, and annul the effects of the cause we seek, in instances which, but for their action, would have come into our class of favourable facts; and that, therefore, exceptions may often be made to disappear by removing or allowing for such counteracting causes. . . .

7th, If we can either find produced by nature, or produce designedly for ourselves, two instances which agree *exactly* in all but one particular, and differ in that one, its influence in producing the phenomenon, if it have any, *must* thereby be rendered sensible. If that particular be present in one instance and wanting altogether in the other, the production or non-production of the phenomenon will decide whether it be or be not the only cause: still more evidently, if it be present *contrariwise* in the two cases, and the effect be thereby reversed. But if its total presence or absence only produces a change in the *degree* or intensity of the phenomenon, we can then only conclude that it acts as a concurrent cause or condition with some other to be sought elsewhere. In nature, it is comparatively rare to find instances pointedly differing in one circumstance and agreeing in every other; but when we call experiment to our aid, it is easy to produce them; and this is, in fact, the grand application of *experiments of enquiry* in physical researches. They become more valuable, and their results clearer, in proportion as they possess this quality (of agreeing exactly in all their circumstances but one), since the question put to nature becomes thereby more pointed, and its answer more decisive.

8th, If we cannot obtain a complete negative or opposition of the circumstance whose influence we would ascertain, we must endeavour to find cases where it varies considerably in degree. . . .

That subduction, a method of calculating deviations from theory by isolating first the effect of a known cause and then studying the remaining phenomenon to discover the secondary cause, should be used to simplify complicated phenomena is the thrust of Rule 9.

9th, Complicated phenomena, in which several causes concurring, opposing, or quite independent of each other, operate at once, so as to produce a compound effect, may be simplified by subducting the effect of all the known causes, as well as the nature of the case permits, either by deductive reasoning or by appeal to experience, and thus leaving, as it were, a *residual phenomenon* to be explained. It is by this process, in fact, that science, in its present advanced state, is chiefly promoted. Most of the phenomena which nature presents are very complicated; and when the effects of all known causes are estimated with exactness, and subducted, the residual facts are constantly appearing in the form of phenomena altogether new, and leading to the most important conclusions. . . .

Blake and associates regard these rules as Herschel's "greatest contribution" to the philosophy of science since in the rules and remarks accompanying them are to be found "for the first time both distinctly enunciated and amply illustrated, the famous four methods of agreement, difference, concomitant variations, and residues" (1960: 181). Scholars have attributed these four methods to John Stuart Mill, who, however, rightly credited Herschel with their first clear formulation and refined and popularized them in his *System of Logic* (Mill, *Works*, 7: 414).[120] While

120. According to Mill, the *Discourse* is "a work replete with happily-selected exemplifications of inductive processes from almost every department of

Herschel's rules of philosophizing involve the *discovery* of causal connection, the *proof* of causal connection is left to his theory of induction (verification by deduction and confronting predictions with facts), which is taken up in chapter 4.

### William Whewell (1794–1866), Gentleman of Science

Herschel's good friend William Whewell, a scientist and philosopher at Trinity College, Cambridge, and for a time Master of the College, was "the very model of a gentleman of science" (Morrell and Thackray 1982: 425). Although he founded no school, Whewell wielded considerable influence at Cambridge and in the British Association for the Advancement of Science (BAAS), where Whewell served as vice president three times (1832, 1835, and 1837), president once in 1841, and president of Section A three times and of Section B once.[121] He coined the words *scientist*[122] and *physicist* and established the notion of a hierarchy of sciences with physics at the top that we know today.

Whewell suffered the same historical fate as Herschel: in both cases an illustrious career was eclipsed by J. S. Mill's success as a philosopher. For years Whewell's name was known only in connection with the arguments J. S. Mill advanced against him in his *System of Logic;* Whewell's philosophy of science is, nonetheless, undeniably modern,[123] and many twentieth-century scholars look upon him as the better historian and philosopher of science than Mill.[124] One of the first philosophers to recognize the value of his philosophy of science was Charles Sanders Pierce; only recently have other philosophers begun to show an interest in Whewell's work. The same goes for his economics,

---

physical science, and in which alone, of all books which I have met with, the four methods of induction are distinctly recognised, though not so clearly characterized and defined, nor their correlation so fully shown, as has appeared to me desirable" (*Works*, 7: 414).

121. The BAAS played a central role in Victorian culture and is discussed in greater detail in chapter 3. See also Morrell and Thackray (1982).

122. The word *scientist,* by the way, was coined to refer exclusively to those who attended the festive meetings of the BAAS.

123. He is so modern that we find in his works concepts such as *theory-laden* and *paradigms* (see Charpa 1987: 123).

124. On his reputation vis-à-vis Mill, see, for instance, Ryan's comments (1974: 59).

which, as Cochrane laments, "has been consistently neglected" (1970: 430).

Whewell's theory of knowledge has been characterized as "the most conspicuous example, up to his time, of an attempt to base a detailed and concrete philosophy of science upon essentially Kantian epistemological premises" (Blake et al. 1960: 217). From Kant Whewell borrowed the idea that science involves both subjective and objective empirical elements. One fundamental thesis of his theory of knowledge is that all knowledge is characterized by the antithesis of two elements. As two examples of this antithesis, Whewell cites induction and deduction and theory and facts. In German philosophy, he reminds us, the antithesis is between subjectivity and objectivity. This break from traditional British empiricism probably explains, in part, why the merits of Whewell's philosophy were originally neglected.

The central thesis of his philosophy of science is that "science develops by becoming a more and more comprehensive system of laws that are both universal and necessary and that are, nevertheless, in some sense the result of induction" (Butts in Whewell 1968: 4). Whewell's two principal works are the *History of the Inductive Sciences, From the Earliest to the Present Time* (3 vols., 1837) and the *Philosophy of the Inductive Sciences* (1840).[125] But, starting with the third edition, the latter work was published as three separate titles: the *Novum organum renovatum* (1858), the *History of Scientific Ideas* (2 vols., 1858), and *On the Philosophy of Discovery* (1860). In these works, Whewell's theory of method attains its fullest expression.

In the 1830s "a re-evaluation of Bacon was under way," and Whewell had a strong hand in this turn of events (Morrell and Thackray 1982: 272). The distinguishing feature of the Cambridge group of philosopher-scientists was a commitment to the inductive method. The BAAS had originally embraced Bacon as its guiding spirit; but with Whewell's rise to ascendancy in the Cambridge literati, naive induction—the collection and recording of data—came increasingly under fire. Although still hailed as a prophet of science, Bacon was quickly losing ground to Newton as his weaknesses as a practitioner of science were becoming apparent. Newton, thought Whewell, had succeeded precisely because he had not followed Bacon's methods. Whe-

---

125. J. S. Mill, we remember, published his *System of Logic* in 1843.

well's goal, then, was to update, extend, and qualify Baconian science in light of Newton's accomplishments. With respect to political economy, however, Whewell stayed in the Baconian camp, insisting that a large body of economic facts had to be collected and evaluated before deductive economic theory could be established.[126] Two points struck Whewell as particularly important for a new methodological creed. First, facts alone were not valuable in science: they become knowledge only when connected together by theory. Consequently, empirical work was to be guided by theoretical views. Second, mathematics was necessary for the discovery of physical principles. In the 1830s and 1840s Whewell's views on science became well established at the BAAS.[127]

Sciences, in fact, could be ranked according to how well they joined facts to theory. As far as Whewell was concerned, only one science, physical astronomy, had transformed knowledge into certain theory. In an address to the BAAS, Whewell stated that astronomy is "not only the queen of the sciences, but, in a stricter sense of the term, the only perfect science" (in Wilson 1974: 84). Expressed in modern jargon, the remaining sciences were *immature*. A measure of the level of maturity of a science, in Whewell's view, corresponds closely to the order of its acceptance as a section of the BAAS. In declining order of importance, the hierarchy took this shape:

A: mathematics and physical sciences
B: chemistry and mineralogy
C: geology and geography
D: natural history (zoology and botany)
F: statistics.

---

126. "The most profitable and philosophical speculations of Political Economy are . . . those which are employed not in reasoning *from* principles, but *to* them: in extracting from a wide and patient survey of facts the laws according to which circumstances and conditions determine the progress of wealth, and the fortunes of men. Such laws will necessarily at first, and probably always, be too limited and too dependent on moral and social elements, to become the basis of mathematical calculation: and I am perfectly ready to admit, that the discovery of such laws, and the investigation of their consequences, is an employment of far higher philosophical dignity and importance than any office to which the Mathematician can aspire" (Whewell 1831: 43–44).
127. "The Association's edicts on proper science came increasingly from Trinity College, Cambridge" (Morrell and Thackray 1982: 267).

The sections for medicine and mechanical sciences were ignored in Whewell's hierarchy of science. Section F, of course, later became the section for economics. Not only was his hierarchy accepted without challenge by his contemporaries, it became natural to assume that all sciences should try to approach the level of knowledge attained by those in Section A. Whewell, then, ushered in the idea of a hierarchy of sciences as we still know it today.

He was also interested in and took part in the debates in economic methodology, frequently taking a stance against many of the classical political economists. The major points of divergence revolved around two interrelated points: his position on induction and mathematics. Whewell led the attack against "the deductivist school of political economy"—the Ricardians—and often preached the advantages of using mathematics to aid scientific inquiry. In 1833 he was the first economist to develop a mathematical model of Ricardian theory.[128] His mathematical contributions to economics are contained in four papers that were read before the Cambridge Philosophical Society and published in the *Transactions of the Cambridge Philosophical Society* (1829, 1831, 1850a, and 1850b). In them, Whewell dressed Ricardo's economics in mathematics to make three basic points. First, he showed that Ricardo's conclusions, and thus his principles, were false.[129] Then, he took pains to demonstrate that Ricardo's deductions were incorrect and point out that Ricardo disregarded "disturbing causes." Whewell's attack on Ricardian theory was often grounded in the charge that it was insufficiently supported by empirical evidence to be considered established. In short, Whewell formulates Ricardo's principles mathematically, finds contradictions, and then concludes that Ricardo needs to go back to the first stage, fact collecting.[130]

128. Henderson mentions that a group formed around Whewell at Cambridge with an interest in mathematicizing political economy; it included Dionysius Lardner, Sir John William Lubbock, Edward Rogers, Col. T. Peronet Thompson, and John Edward Tozer (1985: 406).
129. In one of Whewell's rare tactful comments about Ricardian principles, he explained that "to trace their consequences may be one of the most obvious modes of verifying or correcting them" (1831: 3).
130. Whewell, for example, went to great lengths to prove that Ricardo's deductive system was indefensible and his argument that a tax levied on produce of land would always fall on the consumer was simply fallacious. By using progressively more realistic assumptions, Whewell showed that the tax would fall on the landlord (1829).

Whewell, joined by Richard Jones, advocated the development of a body of economic theory based on the inductive approach (an approach, according to the Cambridge group, that was diametrically opposed to the reigning Ricardian method).

That Whewell was a full supporter of the use of mathematics in economics is made clear in the introduction to the first of his four papers in the *Transactions*. There he states that his aim is "to present in a mathematical form some of the doctrines which have been delivered as part of the science of Political Economy" (1829: 1). In the second paper read to the Cambridge Philosophical Society he elaborates on the importance of expressing ideas in mathematics: "I have already . . . observed that when our object is to deduce the results of a few precise and universal principles, mathematical processes offer to us both the readiest and safest method; since by them we can most easily overcome all the difficulties and perplexities which may occur in consequence of any complexity in the line of deduction, and are secure from any risk of vitiating the course of our reasoning by tacit assumptions or unsteady applications of our original principles" (1831: 1–2).

Yet, before facts are collected, he cautions: "Any attempt to make this subject at present a branch of Mathematics, could only lead to a neglect or perversion of facts, and to a course of trifling speculations, barren distinctions, and useless logomachies" (1831: 43). Only after the collection of facts reaches a certain stage, reasons Whewell, can mathematics be used with success to construct quantitative concepts and to verify inductively derived principles. Because mathematics "is the logic of quantity," it will "necessarily, sooner or later, become the instrument of all sciences where quantity is the subject treated, and deductive reasoning the process employed," concludes Whewell (1831: 43).

In Whewell's opinion, three areas of natural science were not yet mature enough to profit from the use of mathematics: terrestrial magnetism, meteorology, and tidology. The benefits of mathematics for political economy, however, were indisputable. "[S]ome parts of this science of Political Economy, may be presented in a more systematic and connected form, and I would add, more simply and clearly, by the use of mathematical language than without such help; and that moreover to those accustomed to this language, they may thus be rendered far more intelligible and accessible than they are without it" (1829: 1).

Thus, the reason for introducing mathematics into political economy in the 1830s had less to do with the science's progress as measured by its success in gathering facts than with a perceived affinity with mechanics.[131] As Whewell sees it, mathematization would make the discipline "more clear, compendious, and manageable" than the approaches taken by Smith or Ricardo (1831: 2).

Whewell was, however, perspicacious enough to warn of the limitations of a tool like mathematics, especially the always fashionable dress-it-up-like-science trick: "There is perhaps in some persons a propensity to believe that any subject, when clothed in a mathematical shape, acquires something of mathematical demonstrative character; and that by applying mathematics to assumed principles of knowledge, we in some measure create a science. I must beg leave very distinctly to repudiate all pretensions of this kind" (1850a: 1).

Similarly, Whewell recognized that the problems of method in the social sciences surpassed those in the natural sciences: "I think that by attempting at present to include the Moral sciences in the same formulae with the Physical, we open far more controversies than we close." The key, he insists, is "that in the moral as in the physical sciences, the first step towards showing how truth is to be discovered, is to study some portion of it which is assented to so as to be beyond controversy." Imitating other sciences is not the solution; like J. S. Mill he defends the view of the separate nature of each science. "Each science has for its basis a different class of Ideas; and the steps which constitute the progress of one science can never be made by employing the Ideas of another kind of science" (1968: 266, 116).

When assessing Whewell's failure to establish political economy as a mathematical discipline, we need to keep in mind that this fledgling science was not one of Whewell's primary interests. He was, after all, intellectually committed to what he called an inductive philosophy of science and to the natural sciences. Well ahead of his time, Whewell with his plea for using mathematics was not understood by the political economists. As we

---

131. "It appears I think that the sciences of Mechanics and Political Economy are so far analogous, that something of the same advantage may be looked for from the application of mathematics in the case of Political Economy" (Whewell 1829: 5).

will see in chapter 6, Malthus admitted that Whewell's mathematics—not particularly sophisticated by today's standards—were above him. Whewell was painfully aware of the language gap, for "[t]he quality of mathematics taught in the British universities had deteriorated to the point that it required a major effort by Whewell, Herschel, Peacock, and Babbage to upgrade the subject during the 1820s" (Henderson 1985: 426). The deficiency in teaching mathematics caused them to form a pact to introduce French mathematics into the English system as a replacement of Newton's fluxions (calculus). "It was not until the early 1830s," explains Henderson, "that Whewell felt prepared to defend the quality of mathematics at Cambridge" (426). And by then, a philosophical tradition in political economy was firmly entrenched. No wonder, then, that mathematics did not catch on.

Other areas separating Whewell's thought from that of the classical mainstream are worth brief mention. His denial of fixed laws of human nature, for instance, put him at odds with the classical school; he espoused instead the view that human behavior is formed by cultural mores and tradition.[132] He also accused the Mills of abusing science by pretending to deduce rigorous conclusions from axioms of political economy. A final point of contention is Whewell's objection to applying the equilibrium analogy to economics. In its stead, he suggested adopting the analogy of the dynamics of waves, when analyzing, for instance, fluctuations in national wealth (see Wise/Smith 1989: 396).

---

132. On this issue Whewell appears to be a precursor of the American institutionalists.

*Newcastle upon Tyne*, 1739
HYMN *to* SCIENCE.

O *Vita Philosophia Dux!* O *Virtutis inda-*
*gatrix, expultrixq; Vitiorum.—Tu Urbes*
*peperisti ; tu inventrix Legum, tu magistra*
*Morum & Disciplinæ fuisti : Ad te confu-*
*gimus, a te Opem petimus.* CIC. *Tusc. Qu.*

SCIENCE! thou fair effusive ray
From the great source of mental Day,
Free, generous, and refin'd !
Descend with all thy treasures fraught,
Illumine each bewilder'd thought,
And bless my lab'ring mind.

But first with thy resistless light,
Disperse those phantoms from my sight,
Those mimic shades of thee ;
The scholiast's learning, sophist's cant,
The visionary bigot's rant,
The monk's philosophy.

O ! let thy powerful charms impart
The patient head, the candid heart,
Devoted to thy sway ;
Which no weak passions e'er mislead,
Which still with dauntless steps proceed
Where Reason points the way.

Give me to learn each secret cause ;
Let number's, figure's, motion's laws
Reveal'd before me stand ;
These to great Nature's scenes apply,
And round the globe, and thro' the sky,
Disclose her working hand.

Next, to thy nobler search resign'd,
The busy, restless, human mind
Thro' ev'ry maze pursue ;
Detect Perception where it lies,
Catch the ideas as they rise,
And all their changes view.

Say from what simple springs began
The vast, ambitious thoughts of man,
Which range beyond controul;
Which seek Eternity to trace,
Dive thro' th' infinity of space,
And strain to grasp THE WHOLE.

Her secret stores let Memory tell,
Bid Fancy quit her fairy cell,
In all her colours drest ;
While prompt her sallies to controul,
Reason, the judge, recalls the soul
To Truth's severest test.

Then launch thro' Being's wide extent ;
Let the fair scale, with just ascent,
And cautious steps, be trod ;
And from the dead, corporeal mass,
Thro' each progressive order pass
To Instinct, Reason, GOD.

There, *Science!* veil thy daring eye ;
Nor dive too deep, nor soar too high,
In that divine abyss ;
To Faith content thy beams to lend,
Her hopes t' assure, her steps befriend,
And light her way to bliss.

Then downwards take thy flight agen,
Mix with the policies of men,
And social nature's ties :
The plan, the genius of each state,
Its interest and its pow'rs relate,
Its fortunes and its rise.

Thro' private life pursue thy course,
Trace every action to its source,
And means and motives weigh :
Put tempers, passions in the scale,
Mark what degrees in each prevail,
And fix the doubtful sway.

That last, best effort of thy skill,
To form the life, and rule the will,
Propitious pow'r ! impart :
Teach me to cool my passion's fires,
Make me the judge of my desires,
The master of my heart.

Raise me above the vulgar's breath,
Pursuit of fortune, fear of death,
And all in life that's mean.
Still true to reason be my plan,
Still let my action speak the man,
Thro' every various scene.

Hail ! queen of manners, light of truth ;
Hail ! charm of age, and guide of youth ;
Sweet refuge of distress :
In business, thou ! exact, polite ;
Thou giv'st Retirement its delight,
Prosperity its grace.

Of wealth, pow'r, freedom, thou ! the cause;
Foundress of order, cities, laws,
Of arts inventress, thou !
Without thee what were human kind ?
How vast their wants, their thoughts how
Their joys how mean ! how few ! [blind!

Sun of the soul ! thy beams unveil !
Let others spread the daring sail,
On Fortune's faithless sea ;
While undeluded, happier I
From the vain tumult timely fly,
And sit in peace with Thee.

*To a young Gentleman.* WINTER *improv'd.*

PHœbon, the Winters shiv'ring reign !
With snowy mountains heaps the plain,
And binds the rolling sea ;
But soon the sun's enliv'ning beam
Shall glance upon the yielding stream,
And melt the snows away.

But oh ! when hoary Age has shed
His silver triumphs o'er our head,
'Tis vain for mortal man
To try, if Art can take the snow,
And the rough wrinkle off his brow,
And stretch his narrow span.

Soon as the sultry summer's fled,
The Autumn triumphs in its stead,
And winter's chilling sway
Succeeds the next ; but soon the spring,
Advancing on a *Zephyr's* wing,
Appears in green array.

**Figure 2**
"Hymn to Science" in *The Gentleman's Magazine* (volume IX, 1739, p. 544)

# 3

# Science in Eighteenth- and Nineteenth-Century Britain

Eighteenth-century developments are crucial to an understanding of the history of social science, especially economics, for in this era moral philosophy, the direct intellectual forebear of political economy, emerged and the foundations of statistics and econometrics were laid.[1] But this was the age of science in general. By the late eighteenth century the Scottish universities had gained a reputation for being the best for science in Europe and the English-speaking world.[2] All men of letters were interested in science. Odes were written to science, that "sun of the soul," which—as the anonymous author of the poem in figure 2 asserts—would disperse phantoms, the Scholastic's learning, the sophist's cant, the bigot's rant, and the monk's philosophy.[3] So popular and important was science to this age that, at some time in his life, Adam Smith belonged to three Glasgow philosophical clubs—the Political Economy Club, the Literary Society, and Mr. Robin Simson's Club (also called the Anderson Club); four Edinburgh groups—the Philosophical Society, the Select

1. The foundations of *mathematical* statistics, however, were laid between 1890 and 1930. Moral philosophy is, by the way, also the intellectual forebear of psychology, sociology, and political science.
2. Shortly before the Americans declared independence from Britain, Benjamin Franklin claimed that the University of Edinburgh possessed "a set of as truly great men, Professors of the Several Branches of Knowledge, as have ever appeared in any Age or country." By the end of the century Thomas Jefferson was convinced that, in terms of science, "no place in the world can pretend to a competition with Edinburgh" (in Morrell 1971: 159).
3. In nearly every volume of the *Gentleman's Magazine* science wins encomiums. Cowley's "Ode to the Royal Society" was published with Thomas Sprat's *History of the Royal Society*. One of the most distinguished women scientists of the nineteenth century, Mary Somerville, was even honored for understanding astronomy with a sonnet by William Whewell (Cannon 1961: 231–32).

Society, the Poker Club (whose purpose was to liven up Scottish culture, not to play poker), and the Oyster Club; and two London clubs—the Royal Society and the London Literary Club, dubbed The Club (Dankert 1974: 25). Moreover, most of the major figures of this age saw themselves as founders of some science: David Hume of moral philosophy, Thomas Hobbes of civil philosophy, Adam Smith of political economy, Robert Malthus (and other Cambridge scientists) of moral statistics, Adolphe Quetelet of "social physics," the Ricardians of analytical political economy, and J. S. Mill of the science of ethology.

All this suggests that understanding the concept of science in this era is imperative. Because our interpretation of science is always conditioned by current views on science, it should come as no surprise to learn that most of the mistakes contemporary historians make when they write about eighteenth- and nineteenth-century methodological issues are rooted in a wrong-minded conception of science. It is always dangerous to try to detach philosophers' thought from their time and circumstances; in this chapter, I, therefore, intend to provide background information that places the concepts and values of those of past ages in their proper historical setting.

## The Emergence of Moral Philosophy

The term *moral philosophy* has an anachronistic ring to the modern economist's ear; it conjures up the two areas of inquiry that generations of economists have believed economics should steer clear of—ethics and philosophy. Yet as late as the 1890s, economists such as Arthur C. Pigou (1877–1959) were still learning economics in a faculty of history and moral science. It was Alfred Marshall who, before retiring in 1908, finally won the battle to establish economics as an independent subject of study at Cambridge—against the will of the faculty.[4] Even at the end of the 1930s John M. Keynes was still insisting that the discipline of economics must be considered a moral science.[5]

Whereas the seventeenth century had been dominated by physics, the eighteenth was absorbed in the science of man. One

---

4. When Cecil Pigou succeeded him, it was to a chair in economics.
5. "I want to emphasize strongly the point about economics being a moral science," wrote Keynes to Harrod on 16 July 1938 (1973: 300).

thing stands out about the era of the birth of social science, and in particular, of economics: it had a distinctly Scottish character about it, as did the general intellectual climate of the eighteenth century. Political economy is very much a Scotch science, making Scottish views on science and epistemology central to this chapter. We will see, in fact, that several strong Scottish threads—views on mathematics, the employment of a "Newtonian method," and the conscious extension of methods of natural philosophy to social science—weave their way through the methodological fabric of the classical era.

**The Idea of Science**
This was an age so intensely interdisciplinary that Isaac Newton penned essays on economics and Smith composed a history of astronomy—and both achieved recognition in the minor area of expertise.[6] "[T]he inclination of men to gain an acquaintance with the operations of nature; which disposition to enquire after the causes of things is so general," Henry Pemberton tells us, "that all men of letters, I believe, find themselves influenced by it" (1728: 2–3). Implicit in most discussions of the eighteenth and nineteenth centuries was an assumption that all knowledge was a part of one system. At the time of the British classical economists, it would never have occurred to them to offer a discussion of methods of moral philosophy distinct from those of natural philosophy.

It is an astounding fact that historians of science rarely explain natural and moral philosophy, even though they are the forerunners of modern science and were distinct enterprises in themselves. In the seventeenth century no distinction was made

---

6. Most historians of economic thought are familiar with Smith's "History of Astronomy," which is discussed in chapter 5. Newton's work on economics, on the other hand, is rather obscure; he wrote on economic topics after taking up his position as Master of the Royal Mint in March 1696, where his papers were not published or made accessible to the broader public. Most of his papers from his years at the Mint are now at the English Public Record Office (*Mint Papers* 19.1.–5). The bulk of the advice Newton gave the government—mostly in the form of memoranda—centered on monetary policy and reflected, to a great extent, the informed mercantilist policies of his day (Westfall 1980: 618–19). Although his economic papers have never been published in their entirety, a few reports have been collected by S. Dana Horton (in Newton 1887). Shirras and Craig cite several other sources in which various reports have been reprinted (1945: 218).

between the terms *science* and *philosophy;* one term stemmed from Latin, the other from Greek, and both referred to systematic inquiry. An inquiry into the material world of nature was called natural philosophy; into the workings of the mind, mental philosophy; and into human action, moral philosophy. Although the word *science* is old—meaning general knowledge and carrying the negative connotation of an "ignoble Americanism" in England as late as 1890[7]—we forget how modern the term *scientist,* first coined by Whewell in 1833, is.[8] At approximately the same time, the expression *social science* first came into common usage and the philosophy of science emerged as a distinct area of discourse. Although J. S. Mill is often credited with being the first to use the term *social science* (Senn 1958), the expression was already established in the English and French languages by the time Mill was writing about social science in 1836 (Iggers 1959). Charles Fourier, for instance, had used the term *science sociale* in 1808, Jean Sismondi in 1827. The history of the concept is even older, reaching back at least to Smith and Hume's understanding of moral philosophy.

I have said that doing science, or philosophy, in the eighteenth century meant systematic inquiry. What exactly did this entail? For the Scots, science was a body of coherent knowledge organized around a few simple principles of explanation. But it must be understood that the words *philosophy* and *science* were used much more loosely than they are today: philosophical principles could be applied to virtually any serious undertaking—farming, literature, history, gardening, cooking, navigation, child-rearing, bathing, and more. By far, the Scots preferred to speak of philosophy rather than science, for they believed that philosophy was anchored firmly in hard facts and freed from theological considerations. From a practical perspective, philosophical activity meant classifying observations under a known principle of explanation. Science, they observed, begins with an

---

7. Gordon (1991: 114) cites H. L. Mencken's *The American Language* as the source for this.

8. At a Cambridge meeting of the British Association for the Advancement of Science (BAAS) in 1833, Samuel Taylor Coleridge's idea that the clergy should take the lead in the enterprise of knowledge was well received. When, in response, Coleridge spontaneously forbade members of the BAAS to call themselves philosophers, Whewell reportedly coined the word *scientist* on the spot (Morrell/Thackray 1982: 20).

assumption of regularity in nature. Once a regularity was determined, it was considered to be valid for all phenomena of the same type or class.

Nearly every important contributor to the Scottish science of man acknowledged the influence of the writings of Francis Bacon, Isaac Newton, and John Locke. Perhaps the most important strand of Enlightenment thinking in Scotland during its intellectual apex in the eighteenth century was the reception of Newton's ideas. Before 1660, natural philosophy in Scotland was based largely upon scholastic works such as Aristotle's *Acroamatic Physics* (E. Forbes 1983: 33). In the 1670s and 1680s René Descartes's *Discourse on Method* dominated philosophical streams of thought in Scotland. Descartes's influence waned in the 1690s as interest turned to Locke.[9] By the turn of the century Newton had captured the Scottish imagination; by 1710 the Newtonian philosophy was in London "generally received among Persons of all Ranks and Professions, and even the Ladies, by the Help of Experiments," wrote one of Newton's important early interpreters (Desaguliers, 1763: ix).[10] Scottish intellectuals reaching adulthood between 1710 and 1730 were fascinated by Newton and natural law theory (Emerson 1990: 25); Newtonian physics was taught at Scottish universities during Adam Smith's lifetime. "St. Andrews, Edinburgh, and Aberdeen all appointed Newtonians as Professors of Mathematics between 1668 and 1725" (Chitnis 1986: 9). David Gregory (1661–1708), a mathematician at Edinburgh and later at Oxford, was the first to teach the *Principia* in Britain. Popular versions of Newton's philosophy were made available by the "ablest early Newtonians" (Strong 1957: 54), namely, Newton's most famous expounder in Scotland, Colin Maclaurin (1698–1746), a

---

9. "Carmichael's Glasgow lectures of 1704 are thoroughly anti-Cartesian, and many other regents were distrustful by this time of the implications of Descartes' method (e.g. mind-body dualism)" (E. Forbes 1983: 32). See also Shepherd (1982).

10. "By the beginning of the eighteenth century, Newtonian ideas on all aspects of natural philosophy had been adopted unreservedly by most regents in Edinburgh, Aberdeen, and St. Andrews—Glasgow remaining more conservative in this, as indeed in logic, metaphysics, and ethics teaching as well. If Newton's theories of movement, gravity, and light were not taught, it was because they were too difficult for the students and the regent to understand, and not because they were regarded with disfavour" (E. Forbes 1983: 34).

mathematician, member of the Royal Society, and Newton's associate;[11] John Keill (1671–1721), the first mathematician to teach Newtonian principles at Oxford;[12] J. T. Desaguliers (1683–1744), a natural philosopher held in great esteem by Newton and the demonstrator and curator of the Royal Society;[13] the Dutch scientist W. J. s'Gravesande (1688–1742);[14] William Whiston (1667–1752), Newton's successor at Cambridge, who was later banished from the university on charges of religious heterodoxy;[15] Henry Pemberton (1694–1771), who edited the third edition of Newton's *Principia*;[16] and John Clarke (1682–1757), a distinguished Cambridge mathematician.[17]

Underestimating Newton's importance for this era would be great folly, for all of the eighteenth- and nineteenth-century thinkers treated in this work were influenced by him, and several of them, including Hume and Smith, have been dubbed "Newtonian philosophers."[18] During the Scottish Enlightenment, Roger Emerson tells us, "the obligation to make a new study of the mind was very great, for, as Bacon had shown, all that was known related to the mind of man. . . . If minds were to be understood as well as matter, that deficiency had to be made good" (1990: 24). Francis Hutcheson, David Hume, and Adam Smith were only three of a much larger group who set out to found a science of man by using Newtonian methods.[19] Locke, it was thought, embodied the Newtonian procedure most perfectly (Bryson 1968: 18).

Since the classical political economists discussed in part 2 of this volume take Isaac Newton's achievements as a starting point

---

11. See his *Account of Sir Isaac Newton's Philosophy* (1748). Maclaurin owed his position at the University of Edinburgh to Newton, who gave him a strong recommendation and promised to contribute 20 pounds a year towards his stipend (Platts 1893: 196).
12. Author of *Introduction to Natural Philosophy* (1720).
13. Consider his *System of Experimental Philosophy Proved by Mechanicks* (1719).
14. Author of *Mathematical Elements of Natural Philosophy* (1721).
15. Notable for his *Sir Isaac Newton's Mathematick Philosophy More Easily Demonstrated* (1972). There was a trial concerning Whiston's alleged unorthodox religious views, but the proceedings were eventually dropped.
16. Known for *A View of Sir Isaac Newton's Philosophy* (1728).
17. Author of *Sir Isaac Newton's Principles of Natural Philosophy* (1730).
18. Millar, for instance, argued that Montesquieu was the Bacon of moral philosophy; Smith, the Newton (in Stewart 1980: 275 n. 4).
19. Others include George Turnbull, John Pringle, David Fordyce, Archibald Campbell, and Alexander Gerard—all friends of Hume and Smith.

for moral philosophy and political economy, Newton's use of the term *natural philosophy* is central to understanding the birth of modern social science. Although his philosophy of science and methodology have been given separate consideration in the foregoing chapter, it is worth stressing the breadth of his philosophy, which ranges from physics to the soul. Not only was the scope of his philosophy broader than that of today's science, its goals, inspiration, and outlook were completely different, for they had to do with God.[20] Religion clearly motivated Newton (and many of his contemporaries) to develop a system of natural philosophy to counter the atheism he believed to be inherent in Descartes's system (Cunningham 1991: 383). Perhaps the most notable fact about natural philosophy in this age was its subordinate stature with respect to moral philosophy. Natural philosophy was not the queen of the sciences but "subservient to purposes of a higher kind," its chief value lying in its ability to furnish "a sure foundation for natural religion and moral philosophy" (Maclaurin 1971: 3).

Newtonian science, the Scots thought, was characterized by its empiricism and a parsimony and simplicity of organizing principles. They held Newton to be the patron of the empirical method. Because the *Principia* (1687) was abstruse and difficult even for the educated, many scholars turned to the *Opticks* (1701) for their understanding of Newton and came away with the one-sided impression that Newton's methodology was experimental. Thus, depending on who was doing the interpreting, the stress on each element of Newton's mathematical-deductive experimental method was uneven. The Scots tended to associate Newton's method with the hypothetico-experimental tradition of the *Opticks*, rather than the mathematico-deductive (but also empirical) tradition of the *Principia*. Hume, for instance, subtitles his *Treatise of Human Nature* "An Attempt to Introduce the Experimental Method of Reasoning into Moral Subjects" and by *experimental* means Newton's hypothetico-experimental method—the interpretation of the Newtonian method generally accepted in this period (Rendall 1978: 21). This

---

20. "To describe the *phenomena* of nature, to explain their causes, to trace the relations and dependencies of those causes, and to enquire into the whole constitution of the universe, is the business of natural philosophy," wrote Colin Maclaurin in 1748 (1971: 3).

interpretation, however, completely ignores the mathematico-deductive substance of the *Principia*, as Maclaurin notes: "Experiments and observations, 'tis true, could not alone have carried him [Newton] far in tracing the causes from their effects, and explaining the effects from their causes: a sublime geometry was his guide in this nice and difficult enquiry" (1971: 8).[21] Later, Jeremy Bentham and James Mill would embrace the deductive side by advocating what they called Euclid's "geometrical method."

Like natural philosophy, moral philosophy was broader and had different bases of emphasis than today's social science. It only roughly corresponds to today's disciplines of social science and ethics and is best explained—in juxtaposition with natural philosophy, the study of physical phenomena—as the study of all human activities. In the first edition of the *Encyclopaedia Britannica*, published in Edinburgh in 1771 in three volumes,[22] moral philosophy is defined as "the science of MANNERS or DUTY; which it traces from man's nature and condition, and shews to terminate in his happiness" (Fordyce 1771: 270). Although moral philosophy is an art, Fordyce adds that it is "likewise called a science, as it deduces those rules from the principles and connexions of our nature, and proves that the observance of them is productive of our happiness" (270). We find Dugald Stewart expounding a similar view at the end of the era of moral philosophy: "The object of Moral Philosophy is to ascertain the general rules of a wise and virtuous conduct in life" (*Works*, 2: 11).

As the works of the classical economists, and those of Adam Smith in particular, so clearly show, the moral philosophers were convinced that natural philosophy had found the key to understanding and explaining not only natural but also social phenomena. So impressive were the accomplishments of Newtonian

---

21. Maclaurin continues on this subject: "We may, at length, rest satisfied, that in natural philosophy, truth is to be discovered by experiment and observation, with the aid of geometry, only; and that it is necessary first to proceed by the method of *analysis*, before we presume to deliver any system *synthetically*" (1971: 90–91).

22. The *Encyclopaedia Britannica* continued to be published in Edinburgh through the tenth edition (1902), after which editorial management moved to Cambridge.

physics that the eighteenth-century philosophers, including the founders of political economy, never questioned the suitability of transferring Newton's methods to moral philosophy. After all, as they saw it, philosophy, science, social science, and ethics were all the same kind of activity. Only later did social scientists begin to question whether the social sciences should be a branch of the natural sciences, that is, whether social science is really similar to, or even derivable from, physical science. Yet in defending the use of a common method, these eighteenth-century thinkers did not fail to see substantive differences between moral and natural philosophy. And, in spite of their overt acknowledgment of the intention to imitate natural philosophy, the practices of moral philosophers and political economists bear only a superficial resemblance to the practices of natural philosophers, "for they employed different conceptual and analytic tools when they employed the same terms to describe natural systems" (Wise/Smith 1989: 291).[23]

The classical era, then, was distinguished by the absence of a natural intellectual barrier between natural philosophy, logic, ethics, and moral philosophy. The methods of physics and chemistry were widely admired and imitated by the moral philosophers; and, as historians of science are just now realizing, almost all moral philosophers were interested in natural philosophy (Emerson 1990: 32–33). By 1720 "experimental philosophy" was established at Scottish universities (Emerson 1990: 22); both Hume and Smith showed an active interest and attained some competence in it.[24] We should also not neglect the moral philosophers' interest in method as a means of divorcing morals from religion: "Empirical methods," Emerson points out, "allowed for the autonomous and discrete study of societies, man, and his mind, or of physics, chemistry, and any number of other specialties" (1990: 35).

---

23. Wise/Smith continue by stressing "the notion of a shared model as an abstraction. Sharing a model did not imply anything like the same meaning or the same development in the two areas" (1989: 291).
24. Adam Smith's knowledge of natural science is discussed in chapter 5 of this volume; Hume's competence in that area is examined in chapter 2. The point of Barfoot's (1990) article is to show that Hume was a member of the Physiological Library and that scholars have neglected Hume's competence in natural science. E. Forbes (1983) defends a similar claim.

## The Science of Man

### The Scottish Way to Study Mankind

For the Scots, moral philosophy was the foundation of the study of human beings in society. Starting with Locke and Hume and culminating in the thought of the Scottish natural historians, the Common Sense philosophers, and John Stuart Mill, the study of society meant the study of human nature. An understanding of the activities of the human mind, they thought, was the first step to learning; all Scottish students were, accordingly, required to take a two- or three-year sequence of courses entitled, alternatively, "humanities, rhetoric, and logic" or "moral philosophy" (Olson 1975: 13). An understanding of the human mind was viewed as a foundation for all disciplines—even mathematics. David Hume's *Treatise of Human Nature* is the *locus classicus* of this view: "'Tis evident, that all the sciences have a relation, greater or less, to human nature. . . . Even *Mathematics, Natural Philosophy, and Natural Religion,* are in some measure dependent on the science of Man; since they lie under the cognizance of men, and are judged of by their powers and faculties" (1896: xix).

The Scottish literati had a decidedly philosophical bent and were dedicated to a broad, liberal education.[25] The highest compliment a Scottish scholar could receive was that he commanded a knowledge of wide-ranging subjects. To advance a liberal education and develop one's intellectual powers was the purpose of studying moral philosophy. Almost all scholars, and especially mathematicians, had an interest in the foundations of their subject. In Scotland, where professors were paid by the number of students they drew in, lecturers also laid a pronounced emphasis on how a lecture was delivered. Consequently, rhetoric, in their view, played a major role in the development of science.[26]

---

25. This philosophy of education is, by the way, the backbone of the American liberal arts system. Today, however, specialization is considered to foster scientific development and is often cited as the reason for the international superiority of American graduate education in economics (Sargeant 1963).

26. The Scots placed such a strong emphasis on style and language because they did not want to be thought of as provincial compared with the Londoners and Parisians. There was even a movement to eradicate Scotticisms, the Scotch idioms the Scots mistakenly took for English expressions (Berry, 1974). A list

I have mentioned that Scottish universities accepted very early Newton's achievements as superior to the rival Cartesian philosophy and that Smith's good friend Hume believed he was following Newton in creating a science of man. Like most of his fellow moral philosophers, Hume thought it was worth a try to make all sciences as rigorous as Newtonian physics: "'tis at least worth while to try if the science of *man* will not admit of the same accuracy which several parts of natural philosophy are found susceptible of. There seems to be all the reason in the world to imagine that it may be carried to the greatest degree of exactness" (Hume 1965: 6).[27] Newton's optimism in the *Opticks* about the potential development of moral philosophy was picked up and intensified by the Scottish philosophers: His almost nonchalant comment that "the bounds of Moral Philosophy" would be "enlarged" if natural philosophy were to be perfected became the motto of the science-of-man movement. George Turnbull even placed the quotation on the title page of his *Principles of Moral Philosophy* (see figure 3).

In both Newton and Smith's day, science was assumed to be intrinsically linked to values. Just as the Royal Society of London was established in 1662 to foster natural philosophy and improve the material condition of man (Merton 1970), political economy was founded to promote human happiness through the correct implementation of its principles (Chitnis 1986: 25). After Newton had found order and harmony in the physical universe by discovering the laws that govern its movements, philosophers reasoned that disorder must be man-made and could be averted by studying human nature and ascertaining the natural laws or connecting principles that govern society. The existence of guiding social principles was taken for granted; the search for them became a primary goal. The scholars of this age were convinced that immutable laws such as those reigning in the physical universe existed in society and in mental states of human beings. A conviction prevailed that a general law of the social world could be found in the chaos of society that

of Scotticisms can be found in Hume (1854, 1: cxi-cxv). It is interesting that many of the Scotticisms endured and now qualify as proper English (e.g., the Scottish "in the long run" for the English "at long run").
27. Hume's statement comes from his *Abstract of a Treatise on Human Nature,* originally written in 1740 as a review of his own book (1965).

THE

# PRINCIPLES

OF

MORAL PHILOSOPHY.

AN

# ENQUIRY

Into the wise and good

# GOVERNMENT

OF THE

# MORAL WORLD.

IN WHICH

The Continuance of GOOD ADMINISTRA-
TION, and of DUE CARE about VIRTUE,
for ever, is inferred from prefent Order in all
Things, in that Part chiefly where VIRTUE
is concerned.

By GEORGE TURNBULL, *L. L. D.*

*And if* NATURAL PHILOSOPHY, *in all its Parts, by
purfuing this Method, fhall at length be perfected, the
Bounds of* MORAL PHILOSOPHY *will alfo be enlarged.*
NEWTON's Opt. B. III.
*Account for Moral, as for Nat'ral Things.*
Effay on Man, Ep. I.

*L O N D O N:*
Printed for the AUTHOR, and Sold by A. MILLAR,
at *Buchanan's* Head, over againft St. *Clement's* Church,
in the *Strand.*   MDCCXL.

**Figure 3**
Title page of George Turnbull's *Principles of Moral Philosophy* with Newton
quotation as it appeared in 1740 (Hildesheim, Georg Olms Verlag, 1976)

would demonstrate how individual behavior could serve the well-being of all. Accumulating a knowledge of social laws, the Scots thought, would present humankind with the key to multiplying the happiness of the individuals in society.[28] "Ethics, thus, was the final arbiter in matters of social organization and behavior; the authors were, after all, moral philosophers, and values had to be emphasized" (Bryson 1968: 25).

The primary goal of the Scots was a sound basis for the study of human life. Several assumptions underlay the Scots' science of man. To start with, they believed there were irreducible human elements, an analogue to chemical elements, and that these smallest, basic components followed laws. The discovery of these elements, would, then, allow the philosopher to abstract certain, predictable qualities from the variety and complexity of human life. The uniformity of human nature was taken for granted; human nature, they believed, could be understood just as well as other phenomena.[29] By studying human nature, philosophers could identify key customs and institutions on which to build a science of man. Finding that humans share the same feelings, inclinations, and emotions, the Scots abstracted from these common elements to identify the organizing principles of the science of man. The "truths" of human nature were assumed to be universal and known to the earliest peoples. Once these basic common elements—certain characteristics of human nature—were determined, human development could then be

---

28. Consider Hume's statement: "The greatness of a state, and the happiness of its subjects, how independent soever they may be supposed in some respects, are commonly allowed to be inseparable with regard to commerce" (1955: 5).

29. No one says this better than Hume: "It is universally acknowledged that there is a great uniformity among the actions of men, in all nations and ages, and that human nature remains still the same, in its principles and operations. The same motives always produce the same actions: The same events follow from the same causes. Ambition, avarice, self-love, vanity, friendship, generosity, public spirit: these passions, mixed in various degrees, and distributed through society, have been, from the beginning of the world, and still are, the source of all the actions and enterprises, which have ever been observed among mankind. . . . Mankind are so much the same, in all times and places, that history informs us of nothing new or strange in this particular. Its chief use is only to discover the constant and universal principles of human nature, by showing men in all varieties of circumstances and situations, and furnishing us with materials from which we may form our observations and become acquainted with the regular springs of human action and behavior" (1975: 83).

traced through time through the use of a stage theory, the
backbone of natural history. Change, they thought, was natural,
slow, and predictable. All of the Scots were enamored of the
idea of progress—but not to such an extent as to ignore its
undesirable side effects.

The Scots proposed to arrive at a knowledge of human nature
by using empirical methods in the spirit of Bacon and Newton.
As mentioned, their approach to psychology was atomistic; one
need only break up the object of study into its component parts
and consider the parts in relationship to one another. General
principles, or laws of nature, were to be inferred from experience
(observation and experiments). With certain principles of human
nature established, predictable outcomes, conduct, and behavior
could be deduced as typical or natural. Thus, we have Smith,
for example, finding a natural order of things, contending that
philosophy is "the science of the connecting principles of nature," and defining as the philosopher's task the determination of properties shared universally by the phenomena under
observation (1980c: 45). What the Scots were doing, however,
was not psychology, but the philosophy of the mind.[30] They
were interested in answering such questions as, What are the
sources of knowledge? and What guarantees the validity of
knowledge?—themes that I explore later in this chapter when I
examine natural history. Before turning to natural history, however, Scottish attitudes toward mathematics and history deserve
elaboration.

**On the role of mathematics and history.** By modern standards,
the Scots had a peculiar attitude toward both mathematics and
history that needs special consideration. Mathematics, mechanism, and motion all preoccupied the Scots' minds in this era.
Certainly their general attitude toward mathematics was not
only prudent but well balanced. They did not underestimate the
importance of mathematics; on the contrary, they shared "a
passion for mathematics and mathematical tools usable in the
pursuit of science" (Bryson 1968: 21). Nor did their optimism
overstep the boundaries of common sense: they did not equate

---

30. The word *psychology* also came into use at the end of the eighteenth
century. The discipline of sociology was also born in this age, although in a
bit different form as the "science of society."

a subject's scientific value with the amount of mathematics it contained, recognizing that in such disciplines as biology and tidology mathematics played a negligible role. In like manner, they saw that science could not be measured by the amount of experimentation supporting it, for neither geology nor paleontology were experimental sciences.

The peculiarity of their position on mathematics has two facets. First, the Scots accorded geometry a pre-eminent position to the detriment of, for instance, calculus or algebra. Even though a number of Scottish mathematicians and natural philosophers believed that analytical techniques were more powerful tools than geometrical methods, until the Analytic Society was established at Cambridge in the 1820s, mathematics in Great Britain was chiefly directed at geometrical methods. In Scotland geometry held its position of prominence into the 1890s.[31]

The second distinctive feature is rooted in the Scots' conception of geometry. According to Olson, the Scottish philosophers considered three approaches to the nature of mathematics. The first was prominent before the Common Sense era and held that mathematical ideas were divorced from the physical world; thus, there was no need for empirical substantiation. The second approach, scantily represented, was that mathematical ideas do need empirical validation. The third and most commonly held view was that mathematical ideas were grounded in experience in the sense that suggestions for mathematical relations derive from sense data (Olson 1971: 31–33); the process of abstraction, however, was believed to free mathematical reasoning from the necessity of empirical validation. The third approach is, in fact, Hume's position: "Geometry assists us in the application of this law [of motion], by giving us the just dimensions of all the parts and figures which can enter into any species of machine; but still the discovery of the law itself is owing merely to experience, and all the abstract reasonings in the world could never lead us one step towards the knowledge of it" (1975: 31).

---

31. "Most students [at Scottish universities] received an elementary, philosophically-based, mathematical education which tended to favour geometrical over algebraical approaches. Only advanced students could expect to ascend to the heights of sophistication displayed in Newton's *Principia,* and be initiated in the mysteries of fluxions" (Barfoot 1990: 154). See also Olson (1971) on the issue of mathematics at Scottish universities.

What is more important, because the steps of reasoning in a geometrical argument are carefully set forth and considered, geometry was viewed by the Scottish philosophers as a tool for improving the intellect. Algebra, in comparison, was opaque because symbols were substituted for the process of reasoning. For this reason Descartes's use of algebraic symbols was thought to disguise and conceal the operations of the mind and, thus, the process of reasoning (Olson 1971: 42). The epistemological doctrines of Thomas Reid and Dugald Stewart consequently "provided a significant obstacle to the acceptance of analytical methods by Scottish mathematicians" (30).

This did not, however, stop the Scots from experimenting with mathematics, including algebra. Francis Hutcheson, Hume and Smith's celebrated teacher, applied mathematical analysis to morality in the first (1725), second (1726), and third (1729) editions of his *Inquiry into the Original of Our Ideas of Beauty and Virtue* (1990a).[32] He begins his formulation of mathematized moral theory by stating the moral "propositions" or "axioms," terms he uses interchangeably, in algebraical form. In the first equation, Hutcheson equates the "moral Importance of any Character, or the Quantity of publick Good produc'd by him" with the "compound Ratio of his Benevolence and Abilitys" (1990a: 168). With the use of the variables

$M$ = the moral impact of the agent's action on the public,

$B$  = the benevolence of the agent, and

$A$  = the ability of the agent,

Hutcheson obtains Axiom 1: $M = B \times A$ (1990a: 168).

In Axiom 2, Hutcheson compares the virtue of two agents: "When, in comparing the *Virtue* of two Actions, the *Abilitys* of the *Agents* are equal, the *Benevolence* is as the *Moment* of *publick Good*, produc'd by them in like circumstances: or $B = M \times 1$." Axiom 3 states the relationship that exists when two agents have equal benevolence and thus the moment of public good is equal to the ability: $M = A \times 1$. Axiom 4 is derived through a simple manipulation of Axiom 1: $B = M/A$. What this is supposed to mean, in Hutcheson's words, is that agents' benevolence "is

---

32. Only the first edition included the following phrase in its subtitle: "With an Attempt to Introduce a Mathematical Calculation in Subjects of Morality."

always *directly* as the *Moment of Good* produc'd in like Circumstances, and *inversely* as their *Ability*" (1990a: 168–69).

Hutcheson continues to explore more complicated relationships with further axioms that include evil and malice as variables and allow him to reach the conclusion that an agent who does not benefit personally from an action that brings with it a moral public good is, *ceteris paribus*, more benevolent than one who does benefit. What Hutcheson was after was an exact measure of benevolence (B), self-love (S), and hatred or malice (H)—concepts that are not directly observable or quantifiable. He must have been aware of the difficulties imposed by such an attempt, for he claimed that his application of mathematics to moral subjects appears "at first *extravagant* and *wild*"—ostensibly too extravagant and wild to include in the fourth and subsequent editions of the *Inquiry*, i.e., from 1738 on (1990a: 177). In the later editions, he simply dropped this section without making any other changes in his line of reasoning. Why Hutcheson deleted the section and lost faith in a mathematical formulation is explained in the preface to the fourth edition of the *Inquiry*: "[S]ome Mathematical Expressions are left out, which, upon second Thoughts, appear'd useless, and were disagreeable to some Readers" (ix). For some, the failed venture into moral algebra was a direct invitation to poke fun at Hutcheson. Richard Griffith, for instance, wrote that Hutcheson "plus's and minus's you to heaven and hell, by algebraic equations—so that none but an expert mathematician can ever be able to settle his accounts with St. Peter" (in Brooks/Aalto 1981: 354). Certainly many of Hutcheson's contemporaries objected to his venture into moral algebra. Some critics accused him of relying too much on reason;[33] Thomas Reid rejected his attempt to quantify the unquantifiable. Although Hutcheson's two most distinguished students, Hume and Smith, did not follow Hutcheson, his work did find imitators, albeit only epigones.[34] No doubt plain old

---

33. If their criticisms were the reason for the change, assert Brooks and Aalto, Hutcheson should have rewritten the exposition in this section of the *Inquiry* (1981: 349ff.).

34. Brooks and Aalto cite as two examples Archibald Campbell (1691–1756) and an anonymous work (1981: 351–52). Later William Stanley Jevons (1879) listed Hutcheson's *Inquiry* (1720) as the first item in his appendix "List of Mathematico-Economic Books, Memoirs, and other published writings."

common sense and a climate of opinion that preferred observations of the world to abstractions from it forced Hutcheson to see how "useless" his numbers were.[35]

It was not in mathematics but in history that the Scots rooted their science, for studying history and past societies would provide the all-important facts necessary to construct a science of man. In this age, history was born as a scientific, or in keeping with the usage of the age, philosophical discipline. The eighteenth-century thinkers had a great interest in history, and more particularly in the "philosophy of history," to borrow Voltaire's term.[36] Not by accident did Hume write to his friend William Strahan: "I believe this is the historical Age and this the historical nation" (1932, 2: 230). In Hume and Smith's lifetime, history was treated as a branch of literature and regarded as a fledgling field that, in their hands, would blossom into a scientific discipline. Voltaire, for example, opens his article in the *Gentleman's Magazine* with the contention that "the same thing may shortly happen, with respect to the manner of writing History, which has happened in *Natural Philosophy*; where new Systems have exploded the antient Ones. We may discover the Genius of Mankind by considering the Particulars which form the Basis of Physics" (1744: 420).

---

35. The attempt to formulate moral and social issues in mathematical terms was, however, to repeat itself. In the 1980s, the nomination of the Harvard political scientist Samuel Huntington to the National Academy of Sciences (NAS) was based in part on his *Political Order in Changing Societies*, in which he claims to reduce his most important message to three mathematical equations: social mobilization/economic development = social frustration; social frustration/mobility opportunities = political participation; and political participation/political institutionalization = political instability. When he heard about the nomination, the famous mathematician Serge Lang, an NAS member, launched a campaign against it and exposed Huntington's use of mathematics as humbug. In spite of a great ruckus—in which numerous social scientists, most notably economic Nobel laureate Herbert Simon, took Huntington's side—and two further nominations that came to a vote in 1986 and 1987, Huntington failed to get the necessary votes for election. For a summary of the affair see the dialogue between Koblitz and Simon in the *Mathematical Intelligencer* (1988).

36. Voltaire used the expression as the title of the first part of his *Essai sur les moeurs et l'esprit des nations*. By *philosophy of history* he sometimes meant an examination of facts recorded and views entertained in past histories of man; more usually, however, the focus was on interpreting the customs, practices, and moral, aesthetic, and religious views of ancient civilizations (Rosenthal 1955: 151).

Because history delivered the raw material from which generalizations were deduced, history and philosophy were inseparable. History was to be more than a chronicle of facts; it was to serve a didactic function—usually by demonstrating the superiority of the age. To be philosophical it had to seek the causes underlying historical events; that is, it had to explain, not just describe.[37] Precisely because history had not yet been written "philosophically," Hume set out to write the first scientific history of England.[38]

In order to understand eighteenth-century science, one must recognize that the mission of history, according to the Scots, was inextricably entwined with the philosophical.[39] To be philosophical, history had to be abstract: its purpose was to expose and illuminate the principles of recurrence and uniformity of phenomena.[40] Hume, as we know, was interested in determining the extent to which the past is composed of arbitrary events rather than of recurring causes. In Hume's words, "the study of history confirms the reasonings of true philosophy" (1846: 562), for the facts of history are evidence and support for principles. History was the collection of facts and circumstances, which, upon examination, forms a regular chain of causes and effects, to employ the popular expression of the day. What history meant to the Scots is perhaps best summed up as "philosophy teaching by examples" (Bryson 1968: 79). The favored genre of history, however, was not social or political history, but natural history, to which we now turn.

## Natural History

**The historiographical background.** The Scots' methodological approach to the science of man has been variously called *natural, philosophical, conjectural, hypothetical,* or *theoretical history.* The eighteenth century was pre-eminently the age of natural

37. No one in this age equalled Montesquieu in the search for determinist trends shaping history (Carrithers 1986: 64).
38. It is often forgotten that Hume was a renowned historian in his day; his *History of England* remained a classic and standard history for nearly a century until Mill and Macaulay challenged his position (see Norton 1965: xxxii).
39. *Logic,* for instance, is defined in the first edition of the *Encyclopaedia Britannica* as "the science or history of the human mind" ("Logic," 1771: 984).
40. Today history is not considered to be a science precisely because it is concerned with particular events rather than regularities.

history—originally the methodological tool of natural philosophers—for moral philosophy was believed to be rooted in the natural history of man. The Scots adopted the idea from both Bacon and the French, whose *histoires naturelles* were very popular. "None of the sciences indeed seem to be cultivated in France with more eagerness than natural history," wrote Adam Smith in 1756 (1980b: 248). On the Continent, Montesquieu, Rousseau, Buffon, and others provided the stimulus for the historical researches of the Scots. In Britain, the Scots found support in the methods of Bacon and the Royal Society.

And how popular natural history must have been! Smith owned a copy of *Histoire naturelle, générale et particulière*, a fifteen-volume work on natural history edited by Georges Buffon and Louis Daubenton; John Hunter's *Natural History of Human Teeth*; Lord Kames's (Henry Home's) *Essays on the Principles of Morality and Natural Religion*; David Hume's *Dialogues concerning Natural Religion*; and Voltaire's *Philosophie de l'histoire*. Smith thought the *Histoire naturelle* important enough to review it in his famous letter to the *Edinburgh Review* in 1756 (1980b). It is known that the Scots were avid readers of Buffon's *Histoire naturelle* and that it, like Newton's work, was reduced to a popular juvenile's edition that featured moralized descriptions of members of the animal kingdom (Secord 1985: 130).[41] The works of both Buffon and the Swede Linnaeus were viewed by the Scots as important sources of empirical data on human nature (P. Wood 1989: 89).

Bacon coined the term *natural history*, and Smith, Hume, and the French did not deviate significantly from his usage. The fact that the term enjoyed wide currency in Smith's day is just one reason why *natural history* is the more appropriate appellation for this genre of history. In addition, the name underscores the Scots' idea that notions of human nature should be based solely on the historical record. The term *philosophical history* is also apt to the extent that this kind of history was meant to be scientific; natural histories were requisite to philosophizing, serving to link intimately history and philosophy. For similar reasons *theoretical history* is also a suitable term. In Bacon's system, the collection

---

41. Newton's physics had gone to the nursery as early as 1761 with the publication of Tom Telescope's *Newtonian System of Philosophy, adapted to the capacities of young gentlemen and ladies*. And thus Isaac Newton took his place alongside "Goody Two-Shoes" and "Wog-Log the Giant" (Secord 1985: 127).

of data—that is, natural history—delivered the material from which the natural historian would deduce or infer the connecting principles of a moral system of the world. In other words, data collection (natural history in the first sense) makes possible theorizing (natural history in the second sense).

The term *conjectural history* is, however, ill suited to capturing the essence of this type of history, being inappropriate both in purpose and breadth. Dugald Stewart coined the term—now the standard designation for this type of history—and generalized it to the entire group of Scottish philosophers.[42] In Stewart's view, conjectural history found its purest expression in the works of Adam Smith. Stewart rightly explains the motivation behind the Scots' interest in natural history as a way to explain man's origins (1980: 292). The problem this poses is obvious: history can deliver little information about people living in primitive times, for no records exist. Lacking direct evidence, the Scottish philosophers supplied conjectures about what might have happened under natural conditions.[43]

If, however, Stewart used *conjectural history* to imply that the Scots were going beyond the evidence, i.e., the historical record, he was wrong. Unfortunately, the natural history of the mind has been largely ignored by scholars (P. Wood 1989: 90); we are also in dire need of a comparative study of each major figure's use of the term *natural history.* What is certain is that Smith and Hume would have objected to a criticism of having gone beyond the evidence. If philosophers were to know anything, both agreed, facts were required. Where they lacked direct evidence of our human ancestors, they resorted not to completely unsubstantiated guesses, but to a different kind of evidence, namely, the examination of existing primitive peoples. In his letter to the *Edinburgh Review,* Smith criticizes Buffon's use of natural history for being tenuous: it "is almost entirely hypothetical; and with regard to the causes of generation such, that it is scarce possible to form any very determinate idea of it" (1980b: 248). It is

---

42. "To this species of philosophical investigation, which has no appropriated name in our language, I shall take the liberty of giving the title of *Theoretical* or *Conjectural History;* an expression which coincides pretty nearly in its meaning with that of *Natural History,* as employed by Mr. Hume, and with what some French writers have called *Histoire Raisonée*" (Stewart 1980: 293).

43. Apparently, these hunches were not called *hypotheses* because of Newton's pronouncement against them.

unlikely that Smith would commit the very errors that he criticized in others.

The problematic breadth of the label has been noticed by P. B. Wood, who complains that the common scholarly practice of grouping together without qualification the histories of Hume, Robertson, Smith, Kames, Dunbar, Millar, Monboddo, and Ferguson under the rubric *conjectural history* to describe the writings of the Scottish school is "arguably misconceived" (1989: 113–14). He illustrates the problem by mentioning that Andrew Skinner's explanation of the word *natural* to mean inevitable progress, which is valid for Smith, nonetheless does not coincide with Millar's view of human progress (1967: 45). Hume's *History of England*, Robertson's *History of Scotland*, Kames's *Historical Law Tracts*, and Millar's *History of the English Government* are other examples of deviations from natural history, for they are written as narrative histories (Höpfl 1978: 21). Consequently, Stewart's sweeping generalization needs to be qualified, a project that will present challenges for future generations of Enlightenment scholars.

Smith, on the other hand, gives us clear clues of what he means by *natural history*. For instance, in his letter to the *Edinburgh Review* mentioned above, he makes the following comment: "Perspicuous description and just arrangement constitute a great part of the merit of a natural historian," while noting with approbation that the natural histories of the French "either seem to add something to the public stock of observations . . . or arrange in a better order, the observations that have already been made" (1980b: 248–49). Natural history for Smith, then, coincides closely with Bacon's vision of fact collection and classification. Natural history, however, is not limited to the collection and arrangement of a stock of information. When the Scots spoke of natural history, they included the stage—called *induction* by Bacon—that deals with the formation of laws and theory; natural history therefore also supplied the "links" and "chains"—to borrow the terminology of the period—from which a coherent system emerges.

**Natural history as fact collecting.** While Smith's comment on natural history focused on the collection and arrangement of facts and observations, Bacon's facts of natural history, we recall, included experiments. The Scots followed Bacon's lead, while introducing their own peculiar approach to experimentation. Like Bacon, they viewed the foundation of science as experiment and observation, but infused both terms with a new meaning by basing them on psychology and introspection—that is, on a method of "self-consciousness" (McCosh 1990: 4).

The goal of the Scottish philosophers was to establish a science of the mind based solely on observation and the facts of experience. This, explains James McCosh, the last major figure of the Scottish Enlightenment, meant relying on psychological "experiments" that entailed "a survey of the thoughts and feelings of others so far as he [i.e., the moral philosopher] can gather them from their deeds and from their words; from the acts of mankind generally, and of individual men, women, and children; from universal language as the expression of human cogitation and sentiment; and from the commerce we hold with our fellow-men by conversation, by writing, or by books" (1990: 5–6). Such "experiments" allowed them to collect specimens of all the varieties of human nature. Because of the historical nature of their material and the "mysteries in the mind of man," Scottish philosophers did not claim to have "discovered all truth," but only to have "discovered and settled some truth" (11). It was this element of natural history that provoked William Cobbett's famous comment that the Scottish philosophers were metaphysians, mere "feelosophers."[44] Indeed, in the 1830s John Rae, a fellow Scot who emigrated to Canada, labeled Smith's method unscientific because of its alleged metaphysical nature (1834).

**Natural history as theory formation.** Natural history seems to be an extension of ancient Greek thought. When explaining a phenomenon the Greeks posed the questions: Of what is it composed? and How did it originate? The Scots were interested in both questions, but the answer to the latter lies at the heart

---

44. In *Rural Rides* Cobbett claims, "I have now discovered the true ground of all the errors of the Scotch *feelosophers* with regard to population, and with regard to poor laws" (1957: 296). The explanation for their errors is stated succinctly: "The two countries are about as different as any two things of the same nature can be; that which applies to one does not at all apply to the other."

of natural history as a theoretical tool.[45] The approach was, as
Frederick Teggart sums up, "a most serious effort to lay the
foundations for a strictly scientific approach to the study of
man" (1977: 92). The Scots were acutely aware that their system
of moral philosophy had to have a firm base; natural history
offered its own particular method of guaranteeing the scientific
validity of its results—tracing a process in stages, starting with
a primitive or, in Smith's words, "early and rude state" and
progressing to a civilized or polished state. Natural history as a
history of progress concentrated on the study of the effects of
institutional, legal, and politico-economic conditions on human
progress. The analogy borrowed by the Scots in developing their
natural history was physiology, which is fitting because it traces
the course of development of an organism from embryo to death.

Natural history imposed two conditions to guarantee the
scientific validity of its results. First, it required that the starting
point of social inquiry be grounded in experience so that the
fanciful hypotheses Newton had warned against would be
avoided. That knowledge must be induced from principles holding in all times and places was the second condition. Natural
history, therefore, had little to do with reconstructing the past.
Its aim was, rather, to trace the history of society back to its most
basic, universal components or principles and then to demonstrate both how a few connecting principles were capable of
rendering the chaos of the human world intelligible and how
policy could be erected on these principles.

The first step in natural history was to determine which simple psychological element of human nature was the earliest,
most basic element. The Scottish philosophers supposed that a
common set of psychological properties were operating in human beings at all times, which in turn allowed them to conclude
that ancient barbarous peoples could be compared with living
American Indians.[46] Savages, in effect, became the evidence of

---

45. The answer to the first question lies at the heart of the eighteenth-century
fascination with the method of analysis, to be explored in greater detail later
in this chapter.

46. The idea that human nature is uniform through time was new in this age.
Until then, a reference to "the people" had always meant the aristocracy. But
when Smith speaks of the nation, he means a nation with all its inhabitants.
This is just one example that underscores the democratic nature of the Scottish
Enlightenment.

human origins. The recognition of similarities between contemporary primitive peoples and human's savage ancestors became known as the comparative method (Burrow 1966: 11).[47] The Scottish philosophers wrote as if the first stage actually reached back to primitive times—an assumption that was merely "artistic license," Höpfl reminds us, since both ancient and living peoples were thought to be in the "early and rude" stage (1978: 24). Hence Smith's references to the American Indians and juxtapositions of the Scottish Highlands with the Lowlands and Scotland with England. Höpfl also comments that the Scots were attempting to avoid Rousseau's mistake of assuming an original state of nature that could not be proved (1978). Unfortunately, their first stage is no more sound than Rousseau's: "They simply converted the traditional state of nature into a postulated first stage in a postulated progress of an ideal society" (26).

Once man's initial condition was determined and they were satisfied that the scientific foundation rested on sound empirical legs, the Scots viewed the task of natural history as depicting the "chains and mechanisms" of progress, a smooth process by which humanity advanced to a civilized or polished state, although movement from one stage to the next did not necessarily entail an improvement in conditions.[48] The purpose of scientific inquiry was to determine the natural or normal course of things. The word *natural*, by the way, was juxtaposed with *miraculous* or *artificial*.[49] To explain human institutions over time, the Scots developed a stage theory and used the comparative method. While the stage theory showed how humans progressed from primitive to more polished societies, the comparative method involved contrasting a cultural trait in one epoch with the same trait in another. The method of comparison was "a sort of middle-road between observation and abstract formalization. Those who compare know that reality is made up of discontinuous and

---

47. The term *comparative method* can probably be attributed to Montesquieu.
48. By identifying ideal states in his works, Smith could trace the course of progress. But progress in the *Wealth of Nations* was not necessarily linear: it could be thwarted by human behavior inconsistent with social welfare, e.g., rapacious merchants, monopolists, prejudices of the public, etc. Cole (1958), Evensky (1989), and Heilbroner (1973) discuss limiting influences on economic progress.
49. In Hume's words: "Natural may be opposed, either to what is *unnatural*, *miraculous*, or *artificial*" (1975: 307 n. 2).

individual data, which are not, however, completely unrelated
among themselves and, indeed, are susceptible to being juxtaposed and connected" (Moravia 1980: 250). Thus, when Smith
contrasts rude and civilized societies he employs them not
merely as illustrative examples, but "to drive his point home
'scientifically'" (D. Forbes 1954: 647).[50]

Stage theory was not new. It had been used by Rousseau and
Condorcet and probably originated with Turgot, who in 1750
formulated a scheme of cultural stages in terms of progress: the
hunting stage, pastoral life, agriculture, and the introduction of
government.[51] Much of the material Smith incorporated into the
*Wealth of Nations* shows how and why society evolved through
four similar stages—hunting, pasturage, agriculture, and commerce. The task of natural history, then, consisted primarily in
gaining an understanding of and not of obtaining control over
the social phenomena (Höpfl 1978: 39).

Change was thought to be slow, natural, progressive, and
leading towards perfection. Because progress was natural and
anticipated, it was not the conditions under which progress
takes place but the obstacles hindering a natural course of development that became the Scots' focus. The study of the improvement of society thus consisted in investigating the causes
that had hitherto impeded the progress of mankind toward
happiness and then examining the effects of the total or partial
removal of those causes (Teggart 1977: 89). The Scots' acceptance
of the idea of the beneficent character of "unintended consequences" was at the bottom of their view that unintended results
of human actions would propel society to an ideal end stage—
the civilized or polished stage. The invisible hand that promotes
the interests of society "without intending it, without knowing

50. The same goes for the stages in science outlined in his "History of Astronomy." The comparative method, which Burrow defines as "the recognition of
similarities between the practices and beliefs of contemporary primitive or
barbaric peoples and those recorded in the past history of civilization," is a
distinguishing characteristic of all of Smith's works (1966: 11). Smith traced the
origins of man, society, punishment, jurisprudence, and other human institutions from their rudest to their more refined stages.
51. See Turgot's *Plan de deux discours sur l'histoire universelle.* Teggart, however,
argues that Turgot got the idea from Bossuet's *Discours sur l'histoire universelle*
(1681), a history of mankind in 12 stages (1977: 97). Condorcet used a ten-phase
scheme in his *Esquisse d'un tableau historique des progrès de l'esprit humain* (the
first four stages correspond to Smith's four stages). See Meek (1971).

it" is, of course, an outgrowth of this idea (Smith 1976b: 185).
The concept of progress was thus "a metaphysic, a scientific
credo, a value judgment, a philosophy of history" (Bryson 1968:
243).

The Scots explained human conduct through a narrow range
of motives serving as "springs of action," to draw on the terminology of the age (Höpfl 1978: 34). It was based on motives,
passions, and interests and not on a postulate of rational calculation (35). These motives were not to be understood as valid
for all times, stages, or human endeavors. This point is made by
Hume as follows. "We must not, however, expect that this uniformity of human actions should be carried to such a length as
that all men, in the same circumstances, will always act precisely
in the same manner, without making any allowance for the
diversity of characters, prejudices, and opinions. Such a uniformity in every particular, is found in no part of nature. On the
contrary, from observing the variety of conduct in different men,
we are enabled to form a greater variety of maxims, which still
suppose a degree of uniformity and regularity" (1975: 85). In
other words, Hume and Smith's psychology causes them to see
sameness and not differences in cultures, but does not bind them
dogmatically to this approach.

Although the Scots saw their own philosophy and methods
as breaking away from Cartesian rationalism, the Cartesian and
Scottish epistemologies still have certain things in common.
Cartesian philosophy assumes stability, regularity, permanence,
an established order in the universe, and the immutability of the
laws of nature. Descartes was interpreted as believing that science meant, essentially, reducing phenomena logically to geometric axioms. The Scots believed they had parted ways with
Descartes by denying that reason is a spring of human action;
instead, they assumed that the base and beginning of science
was empirical in nature—sensation and sentiments. In practice,
however, the Scots were as concerned with natural laws as
Descartes was, although by *law*, they often meant habits and
custom—sometimes even divine will or command—instead of
regularities.[52] Despite the Scots' insistence on a radical departure

---

52. There is a "constant interplay between the concepts of law as a generalized
description of what takes place normally, and law as an expression of will and
command [of the deity]," explains Bryson (1968: 24). See chapter 5 on Smith's
methods for further discussion of the concepts *law* and *natural*.

from the Cartesian tradition, they did not hold that experience alone could disclose the laws of human nature. As Bryson notes, "there would not have been so much concern with natural laws had it not been for Descartes, who had retaken for the modern world the position that there is order and uniformity in the universe on which men can count" (1968: 24).

## The Method of Analysis and Synthesis

Capturing Newton's methods of *analysis* and *synthesis* was central to the approach of most moral philosophers. This joint method has a long history; it began with the ancients, in particular, Euclid and Archimedes, and continued through the Middle Ages.[53] It was called *resolution* and *composition* (from the Latin *resolutiva* and *compositiva*) until about 1600, after which *analytica* and *synthetica* were the preferred usages. In his new science, for instance, Galileo advocated the joint use of the methods of resolution and composition in his new science, the methodological approach adopted by most seventeenth-century scientists. After the publication of Galileo's works, this joint method became quite universal; and the writings of one of its most notable exponents, the theologian Hugo Grotius (1586–1645), had a considerable influence in the seventeenth and eighteenth centuries.[54] Whereas Descartes used the term *resolution* in juxtaposition to *synthesis* and *composition*, Newton made the change to *analysis* and *synthesis*, at times retaining *composition* as a synonym for *synthesis*.[55]

Strangely enough, Newton, who admired Greek geometry, identifies his method of experiment with the analytical method. He thinks of *geometrical analysis* as an analysis of figures; *analysis* for Newton implies the study of interdependencies between a number of quantities, some known, others unknown. What is important to grasp, Jaako Hintikka and Unto Remes explain, is how Newton extends the concept of *analysis* to experiments.

---

53. See Hintikka and Remes, chapter 9, "On the Significance of the Method of Analysis in Early Modern Science" (1974).

54. Adam Smith, for instance, was familiar with Grotius's writings and praised his work on natural jurisprudence in *The Theory of Moral Sentiments* for being "perhaps at this day the most complete work that has yet been given on this subject" (1976b: 342).

55. See Randall (1940) and Schouls (1980).

"Newton was trying to analyse an experimental situation in the same way as a Greek geometer like Pappus was trying to analyse a figure in the sense of trying to establish the interrelations of its several parts" (1974: 106). This method may not be construed as the analysis of deductive connections, warn Hintikka and Remes: Newton's method is difficult to force into terminology of the contemporary philosophy of science (107). Given this framework, Newton's strictures against hypotheses become clearer: The hypotheses he rejects are "assumptions which are not generalized from the results of an analysis of the interrelations of the different factors of a suitable experimental setup or a comparable situation" (109). Thus, Hintikka and Remus conclude, Newton's method differs from the hypothetico-deductive method because not just any hypothesis having testable deductive consequences is necessarily acceptable; only those "deduced from the phenomena" are scientific hypotheses and theories (110).

In the hands of Colin Maclaurin in 1748, the method of analysis consisted of the following procedure: begin with phenomena, investigate the powers and causes operating in nature, and then proceed from particular causes to more general ones until the final argument is generalized. The method of analysis is followed by synthesis: by descending from the causes "in a contrary order" we are able to "explain all the phaenomena that are their consequences, and prove our explications" (1971: 9). The method of analysis must always proceed the method of synthesis. Only by adhering to this joint method, Maclaurin urges, can we be sure that our principles are "not mere dream and illusion" (9). It is worth stressing that many Scots believed they had found in this method an infallible tool;[56] Newton's methodological position, we recall, is not so sanguine.

For the Scottish moral philosophers, the method of analysis answered the first question the Greeks had posed when confronted with unknown phenomena: Of what is it composed? The answer drew on an analogy with chemistry. The chemist seeks to isolate chemical elements, then considers their relationship to one another, and subsequently determines the processes of chemical change.

---

56. Hume comes to mind as the major exception.

In the first edition of the *Encyclopaedia Britannica*, David Fordyce observed in his article on moral philosophy that an adherence to the scientific method meant that "we must inspect his [man's] constitution, take every part to pieces, examine their mutual relations one to another, and the common effort or tendency of the whole" (1771: 270). In the *Encyclopedia* article on logic, the method of analysis is described this way: After assembling "our whole stock of knowledge relating to any subject; and after a general survey of things," we begin by examining it "separately and by parts" ("Logic," 1771: 1002). Remarking that analysis and synthesis are best understood when illustrated by examples, the author first explains what is meant by the method of analysis:

[L]et us suppose any machine, for instance a watch, presented to us, whose structure and composition we are as yet unacquainted with, but want if possible to discover. The manner of proceeding in this case is, by taking the whole to pieces, and examining the parts separately one after another. . . . By this means we gradually trace out the inward make and composition of the whole, and come at length to discern, how parts of such a form, and so put together, as we found in unravelling and taking them asunder, constitute that particular machine called a watch, and contribute to all the several motions and phaenomena observable in it (1002).

The author calls this method the "analytick method" or "the method of resolution" because it "traces things backward to their source, and *resolves* knowledge into its first and original principles" (1003).

After accomplishing this, the author explains that "we can take things the contrary way, and, beginning with the parts, so dispose and connect them, as their several uses and structures require, until at length we arrive at the whole itself, from the unravelling of which these parts resulted" (1002). The "synthetick method" or the "method of composition" is so named because we "proceed by gathering together the several scattered parts of knowledge, and *combining* them into one whole system, in such manner, that the understanding is enabled distinctly to follow truth through all her different stages and gradations" (1003). Synthesis, unlike analysis, is "well accommodated to the purposes of evidence and conviction"; since we begin "with intuitive truths, and advance by regular deductions from them, every step of the procedure brings evidence and conviction along with it" (1003).[57]

The method of analysis viewed as an analogy with chemistry was carried through the classical era of economics, from Smith to Mill, and perhaps culminated in James Mill's *Analysis of the Phenomena of the Human Mind*, whose final edition in 1869 was edited by John Stuart Mill. In the preface to this work, the senior Mill explains that "chemical analysis" is the process by which "one analyses substances into simpler substances" (1869: vii). Through this process of analysis, "of which the Newtonian generalization is the most perfect type," the "order of the phenomena was resolved into a more general law" and "laws into simpler laws" (vi-vii). Mill's predilection for the method of analysis is the reason for choosing the title; the title of his textbook *Elements of Political Economy* (1821) was, undoubtedly, also inspired by the chemical method of analysis that dissects nature into its constituent elements.[58]

## The Clock Metaphor

As we saw in the section above, taking a clockwork apart to understand how it works was a commonly used illustration of the method of analysis. The scientific temperament and methodological idiosyncrasies of this age are captured in the changing attitudes toward the clockwork metaphor.[59] Enjoying a long history as a model of society, the watch or clock became the symbol of the eighteenth century. The first mechanical clock had appeared shortly before 1300 A.D. and was greeted "with an almost religious veneration" (Mayr 1986: 120). In the beginning, the clock image was associated almost exclusively with positive attributes. Enchanted with its harmony and orderliness, Europe-

---

57. Cohen also discusses the importance of the analytic and synthetic methods for the eighteenth century (1966: 184–94).

58. The same goes for Marches Cesare's *Elementi di Economia Pubblica* (1821), Josiah Tucker's *Elements of Commerce, and Theory of Taxes* (1755), Thomas Mortimer's *Elements of Commerce, Politics, and Finance* (1774), Forbonnais's *Éléments du commerce* (1754), and Richard Heathfield's *Elements of a Plan for the Liquidation of the Public Debt of the United Kingdom* (1820), to mention only those titles listed in McCulloch's bibliography of works on political economy (1845).

59. In English the clock or watch, in French *le montre* or *l'horloge*, in German *die Uhr*—all were regarded as automatons.

ans soon likened the world to a clockwork and subsequently deduced that nature obeys similar laws of mechanics—an assumption that forms part of the new science. Philosophers, it was thought, should approach nature like a clockmaker, who disassembles its many parts to discover the malfunction.

Both a destructive and a constructive element was implied in the employment of the clock metaphor. The mechanical philosophy indicated a deliberate break with Scholastic philosophy, metaphysical speculation, and the long-standing custom of associating nature with magic (Mayr 1986: 55). The constructive element was the clock metaphor's compatibility with the method of analysis, whose "method of uncovering the secrets of nature was that of the clockmaker; to find out how an unfamiliar clock worked or why a broken clock did not, the clockmaker would take it apart" (84). Disassembling a clockwork thus became an illustration of the process of analysis.

In Britain the metaphor flourished in the second half of the seventeenth century; it was popularized in natural philosophy by the writings of Descartes, who saw in mechanics the key to nature. "[T]he hallmark of the new philosophy was the claim that it analyzed the phenomena of nature as though they were actions of machinery" (Mayr 1986: 56). Attracted by the fact that the cause-and-effect relationship of a machine could be expressed easily in mathematics, Descartes associated mechanical properties with a machinelike character; in his view, even animals were machinelike. Since clockmaking was the first industry to put the theoretical discoveries in physics to practical use, clocks came to symbolize the achievements of classical mechanics. Samuel Clarke (1675–1729), G. W. Leibniz (1646–1716), and Robert Boyle (1627–1691) all repeatedly used the model of a clock to illustrate their ideas. For Leibniz the world was a perfect clock controlled partly by the mechanism and partly by the intervention of the overseer, God (Freudenthal 1982: 106–7). The clock metaphor was widely applied—even though Newton never used it and it did not apply to and is inconsistent with his views.[60] An interesting application appears in 1753 in *The Gen-*

---

60. Newton's interpreters, however, did employ the clock metaphor. Consider John Clarke's explanation of Newton's system of the world: "If therefore we would thoroughly understand the material System of the World, and see how it is held together, and what Laws of Motion the several Parts of it are subject

*tleman's Magazine,* a journal that kept abreast of the latest developments in horology, in an article on "the new principle" of equilibrium featuring diagrams that bear a striking resemblance to those used by modern economists to explain supply and demand or IS-LM analysis ("Regulation of Watches," 1753).

The clock metaphors "idealized the qualities of regularity, order, and harmony" and was widely applied—to planetary systems, the human body, and the body politic (Mayr 1986: 119). In using it, the world was typified by a mechanism, thus discrediting magic and promoting rationality. "For several centuries, the clock's most important function was perhaps to serve as an instrument of popular education and, indeed, indoctrination. To progress-minded Europeans of the Renaissance, the clock embodied the best things the future could bring: an end to magic and superstition, rationality in thought, and order in public life (120–21). Otto Mayr notes, further, that the clock image was used to illustrate similarities of structure, especially to introduce the concept of a system as "an integrated assembly of numerous, dynamically interacting parts" (119). Accordingly, the clockwork became "a metaphor for the flawless working together of a complex combination of parts" (117). In the political realm, it illustrated the advantages of an authoritarian, centralized structure in society. An enlightened form of absolutism, for instance, was characterized as a mechanical theory of government.[61]

The word *mechanical* was used in diverse ways and applied to the universe, the world order, the state, and more. For some philosophers, the world really was a machine; for others, mechanical analogies were merely abstract concepts or even figures of speech used to express complexity not easily grasped by the human mind. Mayr argues that Voltaire's use of clock imagery often puts him in the latter category, suggesting that Voltaire is wrongly classified as a mechanist (1986: 77–78). By the time Adam Smith was making references to engines, machines,

---

to, we must do by it as we do by an artificial complicated Machine, take it to pieces, and examine well the Matter of which the several Parts are composed, and try by what Rules and Measures they are proportioned and adjusted to each other" (1972: 101).

61. Not to be neglected is Voltaire's famous comment: *l'horloge implique l'horloger,* the clockwork implies the clockmaker.

springs, and wheels,[62] they were, according to Mayr, "neither analogies nor metaphors, for they no longer suggested any specific mechanical device; rather they were shopworn figures of speech chosen precisely for their ambiguousness" (1986: 106).[63]

That the clockwork concept lacked realism as a mechanical model of the universe became more and more obvious as time went on and it underwent refinement.[64] "Speculation about natural phenomena became self-critical and cautious, favoring empirical evidence over the free roaming of the imagination" (Mayr 1986: 59). The clock metaphor also found itself increasingly in conflict with certain goals of the new science: "Generally, in the quest for truth about the physical nature, preference was given to empirical evidence; explanations were to be based on objective, verifiable observation. Speculation, deductions from a priori hypotheses, and reasoning by analogy were discredited" (61).

The demise of the clockwork analogy was sealed by the rise of liberalism and its new conception of order. Once free will was illustrated by emphasizing the distinction between man and machines, freedom and liberty of choice were viewed as antithetical to mechanism. More and more often the concept *mechanical* was used in opposition to *liberal* (Mayr 1986: 125). Well suited to liberal goals was the concept of self-regulating systems, which philosopher-economists from Smith to Marx saw as inherent in nature. For Smith, order comes about not through the workings of a centralized government but through the hidden workings of self-interest. As Mayr clearly notes, the invisible hand represented the "quality of self-regulation" (175). In the end, the clock metaphor slowly succumbed to the invisible hand

---

62. Smith, for example, describes self-interest as the "mainspring" of social activity.

63. When Mayr, however, goes on to say that these "shopworn figures of speech" referred to "subjects for which the writer lacked affection"—figures of speech that "were neither capable of nor meant for clearly defining, to say nothing of shaping, any ideas that were important to the writer"—he goes decidedly too far. When Smith spoke of systems as "little machines" and self-interest as the "mainspring" of social activity, it is impossible to miss the affection he had for such figures of speech and the importance they assumed in his framework of analysis. (See chapter 5 below.)

64. Mayr, citing Johannes Kepler, says that the clock metaphor started to lose popularity with natural philosophers as early as the beginning of the seventeenth century (1986: 60).

and the balance concept. Balance or equilibrium soon came to be perceived as a highly desirable state or condition. "It is likely, Mayr suggests, "that the fascination with self-regulating systems which took hold in Britain around the turn of the eighteenth century had its origins in the widespread popularity of the balance image" (148). I return to the balance concept in the next section on popular instruction of economics and in the discussion of Malthus, who made it the core of his method.

## Social Engineering and the Diffusion of Economic Knowledge

If the eighteenth century was distinguished by its glorification of science, the nineteenth was marked by a insatiable hunger for information. The first third of the nineteenth century was characterized by a flurry of industrial activity, accompanied by a hunger for knowledge that extended to the lower and middle British classes, women, and children, and subsequently by an explosion in media to bring these ideas to the people. The century saw the democratization of British life and an increasing demand for public education. Suddenly elevated to the status of a cure-all for the whole spectrum of society's ills, social science "seemed to promise to heal the breach between the natural world, over which man seemed progressively to be gaining the mastery, both practical and intellectual, and the puzzling, untidy, disturbing world of human affairs" (Burrow 1966: 106). Social engineering was born; and the knowledge social engineers acquired was to be based not on decree, custom, superstition, or fancy, but on facts and logical reasoning. The confidence in the ability of social science to provide solutions to social problems was at times utterly overwhelming: Harriet Martineau, for instance, was said to have wept with joy while translating the works of Auguste Comte.[65] As might be expected, the natural system of Newtonian physics remained the prototype approach to problem-solving in social science.

Education in political economy in the early classical era was still, of necessity, almost always self-education, for political

---

65. Burrow describes this reaction as "a feat of sensibility which only those who have read Comte at length can fully appreciate" (1966: 107 n. 1).

economists were only gradually acquiring professional status. The 1820s and 1830s saw the establishment of university chairs in political economy and its popularization. Malthus was the "pioneer of academic economics in England" (Spiegel 1991: 290), but it was Nassau Senior who, in 1824, was appointed to the first chair in political economy at a British university (Oxford). In 1828 a chair in political economy was established at Cambridge University, followed by one each in Dublin and Edinburgh.[66] In Smith's day economists were academics, but when the Political Economy Club of London was founded with thirty members in 1821, Malthus was the only academic in a group consisting primarily of businessmen and politicians.

**The Proliferation of Journals**
The great increase in persons interested in "polite culture" meant an enlarged audience for periodicals.[67] In the first third of the nineteenth century, new outlets for the writings of economists appeared and boomed: the *Edinburgh Review* was founded in 1802, followed by the *Quarterly Review* in 1809, *Blackwood's Edinburgh Magazine* in 1817, and the *Westminster Review* in 1824.[68] Throughout the nineteenth century, most of the articles in all four journals were anonymous.

The *Edinburgh Review* was founded by Whig sympathizers Sydney Smith, Francis Jeffrey, and Francis Horner and was the journal that placed the heaviest emphasis on economics.[69] Its significance in this period is suggested by the fact that, except for Ricardo, almost every important figure in British economics

66. In 1805 Malthus took up a chair at the newly founded East India College in Haileybury, not a real college but a school for boys who intended to enter civil service at the East India Company. See Say's discussion of academic developments in political economy across Europe (1971: lii).
67. In the eighteenth century the word *polite* "usually denoted a complex of ideas which included graceful or tasteful expression; the ability to please, entertain and divert; the capacity to promote sociability and evident utility. Scientific work which resulted in the presentation of clear, well-written essays to gatherings of men intent upon bettering the conditions in which they lived was as polite an occupation as was the writing of verse or the composition of political essays or literary history" (Emerson 1988: 364).
68. On the founding and development of these journals see Frank Fetter (1953, 1958, 1960, and 1962).
69. Horner, by the way, was chair of the Bullion Committee, which I discuss later in chapter 6.

from Smith to J. S. Mill contributed to it.[70] It took a stand for reform and viewed political economy as essential for developing policies leading to national prosperity and an increase in public welfare. A mouthpiece of laissez-faire doctrine, the *Review* urged that a change in the economic, political, and social structure could come about only by letting market forces operate freely. In the years between 1818 and 1837, its editor, John R. McCulloch, monopolized the journal and used it to promote Ricardian doctrines. Although the journal did not cease publication until 1928, after 1817 it was no longer the focus of economic issues.

The founding of the *Quarterly Review* seven years after the *Edinburgh Review* was motivated by a desire to counteract the influence of the latter, whose leaning was not appreciated in several quarters of the kingdom. No one more clearly embodied this sentiment than William Cobbett, who swore that he would welcome the day when "the Scotch political economy is blown to the devil, and the *Edinburgh Review* and Adam Smith along with it" (1957: 92).[71] Unlike the *Edinburgh Review*, the *Quarterly Review*'s focus was on literary criticism; but the raging controversies of the day—e.g., the corn trade, East India trade, poor relief, and the policies of the Bank of England—finally forced it to carry numerous articles on economic issues. Its founders were Tories and its position was conservative; the editors published

---

70. In spite of this, Fetter notes that Sraffa's edition of Ricardo's complete works contains sixty-five references to the *Review* (1953: 232).

71. For readers unacquainted with his reputation and place in the history of ideas, William Cobbett (1762–1835) was one of England's most famous radicals. His *Rural Rides* (1830), from which the quotation is taken, is the journal account of his journeys through England in the 1820s and early 1830s. (The full title of the work is *Rural Rides in the Counties of Surrey, Kent, Sussex, Hants, Berks, Oxford, Bucks, Wilts, Somerset, Gloucester, Hereford, Salop, Worcester, Stafford, Leicester, Hertford, Essex, Suffolk, Norfolk, Cambridge, Huntington, Nottingham, Lincoln, York, Lancaster, Durham, and Northumberland, in the Years 1821, 1822, 1823, 1825, 1826, 1829, 1830, and 1832, with Economical and Political Observations Relative to Matters Applicable to, and Illustrated by, the State of Those Counties Respectively*.) The changes Cobbett saw in his home county—the growth of cities and industries especially—greatly troubled him, prompting travels throughout England to discover the true state of affairs and, subsequently, the publication of his findings and proposed remedies. Cobbett fought what he called national corruption, including among other things the use of paper money (he called it "rag money" and opposed Pitt's resort to it to finance the war in 1797), the national debt, patronages and sinecures, the economic power of the Jews, and the use of machinery.

only articles in line with Tory views, that is, only those in
defense of the status quo who expressed precious little sympathy for either political economists or laissez-faire doctrine.[72] The
journal opposed reform of Parliament and the Church, assumed
the dominance of the landed aristocracy, and, in keeping with
the belief that the classes should be kept in their place, tolerated
discrimination against Dissenters, Catholics, and Jews (Fetter
1958: 48). After the 1850s the *Quarterly Review* ceased to be a
significant journal of economic ideas.

*Blackwood's Edinburgh Magazine,* founded in 1817 by a group
of Scottish Tories contemptuous of political economy and political economists, also published articles on economic affairs in
response to prevailing interest. As supporters of the established
order, its contributors came out in favor of maintaining tariffs
and government expenditures and suspending the gold standard (which would, they thought, augment employment by
stimulating demand). Favoring the aristocracy and opposing
absenteeism, they valued agriculture over industry and did not
try to conceal their feelings of Scottish (as opposed to English)
superiority (Fetter 1960).

In 1824 the *Westminster Review* was founded by Jeremy Bentham (1748–1832) to challenge the aristocratic bias of the other
journals and promote the philosophy and policies of the Utili-
tarians and Philosophical Radicals. Its founding editors were
John Bowing and Henry Southern, but it changed owners, and
subsequently names, many times.[73] Until the 1840s it spread the
belief that the laws of political economy could provide the
correct guide to promote human welfare. Pushing for social
change, the journal was always concerned with the welfare of
mankind; it came out for abolishing the privileges of monopoly
and aristocracy, establishing a more equitable tax system, and
guaranteeing the free interplay of economic forces; it, in addi-

72. Fetter relates that the editors commissioned an article from James Mill, but
rejected it when they found his ideas unpalatable (1958: 49).
73. With a change of ownership in the mid-1830s it became the *London and
Westminster Review,* reverting to the original name in 1840. Four years later it
changed ownership and names again to become the *Westminster and Foreign
Quarterly Review.* In 1851 it changed hands yet again and reverted to its original
name.

tion, supported the gold standard and free trade and warned against the dangers of stimulating the economy through government intervention. Essentially, it was Ricardian in outlook. From 1824 to 1829 its articles in economics focused on an attack of both the Corn Laws and the idea that public expenditure could improve production or augment employment. Its most distinguished years are said to have coincided with J. S. Mill's tenure as editor, that is, from 1834 to 1840 (Fetter 1962: 577). The journal discontinued publication in 1914; but the last article on economics was, in fact, written by J. S. Mill, for after 1840 the *Westminster Review* declined as a forum of economic opinion.

**The Role of Instruction**
The spread of information in the early nineteenth century was not limited to journals or to the intellectual world. Sciences were abounding and the consensus was that political economists had reached fundamental truths. John McCulloch, for example, wrote in his typically impassioned style in 1824: "[T]he errors of which Political Economy was formerly infected have now nearly disappeared, and a very few observations will suffice to show that it really admits of as much certainty in its conclusions as any science founded on fact and experiment can possibly do" (in Marsh 1977: 116). McCulloch's sentiments were fully in tune with the times; the Malthus-Ricardo era was manifestly enthusiastic. A. Tyrrell rightly describes it as an "age for practising the art of converting conjecture into certainty, . . . a time when the study of the physical sciences was fashionable [and thus] the tendency to expect other branches of learning to yield scientific laws was persistent" (1969: 152). Spreading the science of political economy to the common man, it was thought, would contribute to the enlightenment of humankind. The principal motive for promoting educational instruction in economics, however, was its use in controlling society.[74] The rationale behind this development was tied to the political implications of the equilibrium concept.

In 1826 the Society for the Diffusion of Useful Knowledge was founded, but its members showed little interest in providing

---

74. On this see Marsh (1977) and Tyrrell (1969).

politico-economic instruction.[75] Since the benefits reaped from moral and natural philosophy were believed to lead to a progressively improved moral and material state of affairs, doing science and teaching its principles were deemed a service to the British empire. In fact, political economy was accorded reverential status; it was believed that especially the workers and the young could benefit from knowledge of the new discipline.

But first suitable textbooks had to be written. The principles of political economy developed by Smith, Malthus, and Ricardo were considered truisms that any worker—or even woman or child—could understand. Richard Whately is perhaps the most significant figure involved in bringing political economy to children, although Jane Marcet was the celebrated expositor of political economy for children (Marsh 1977: 116). In her most influential work in economics, *Conversations in Political Economy, in which the Elements of that Science are familiarly explained* (1816), the science is explained to a child named Caroline. James Mill also tried his hand at simplifying the principles of political economy with his *Elements of Political Economy* (1821). His aim, stated in the preface, was "to compose a schoolbook of Political Economy" (1821: iii).[76] That he believed his work would have a powerful impact on society is apparent, for he adds: "I am myself persuaded, that nothing more is necessary for understanding every part of the book, than to read it with attention—such a degree of attention as persons of either sex, of ordinary understanding, are capable of bestowing" (iii). Political economy suddenly became suitable subject matter for the instruction of children because it was regarded as an established, unchallengeable body of knowledge governed by natural laws whose "truths" were not open to debate. In short, its principles were the stuff optimally suited for rote memory.

---

75. The British Association for the Advancement of Science (BAAS) was founded in 1831 and followed by numerous statistical societies, discussed in detail in the final section of this chapter. The BAAS, one of whose main functions was the education of the common man, was distinctly liberal in its political and religious views. Members were typically Whigs who ranged from moderate conservatives like William Whewell, on the right, to Herschel, who represented a center position, to philosophical radicals like John Stuart Mill on the left (Wise/Smith 1989: 267).

76. And further, "to detach the essential principles of the science from all extraneous topics, to state the propositions clearly and in their logical order, and to subjoin its demonstration to each" (1821: iii).

But political motivations also lay behind the pedagogical movement. Before 1830 natural philosophy and economics shared a model of natural systems as economies. Originally all educated persons drew on the analogy of the economy of the solar system; but eventually all economies of nature carried implicit analogies with the political world. "Everyone read political economy, while only some read astronomy, or geology" (Wise/Smith 1989: 266). As a consequence of the general public's broad interest in the economy of nature, a common language centering on notions of natural laws, natural states, variations, and optimum conditions was developed. Central to this dialogue among a wide spectrum of the population was the concept of *balance*.[77] A balanced order, or equilibrium, was juxtaposed with unbalanced chaos and almost always associated with rationality and the rule of natural law. As Wise/Smith explain, "critical to the Enlightenment faith in rational order was the belief that natural states are eternally stable states. This belief in turn assumed a model of how nature produces stability. Stability seemed to require balance, 'well weighed' reason" (1968: 268). Natural states were important because they were generally thought of as in equilibrium, usually an equilibrium brought about by counterbalancing tendencies of two or more forces. Thus, the concept of equilibrium was bound to that of an optimum.[78] Balance was a particularly French theme: Wise and Smith discuss the contributions of Lavoisier, Laplace, Condillac, Lagrange, and Condorcet in detail (268 ff.).

In no time at all, the equilibrium concept and the statics that had originated in natural philosophy were applied to the class structure of society: poor governance posed a threat to the equilibrium between classes, which, they believed, could, in turn, lead to revolution or upheaval. McCulloch argued that uprisings of the manufacturing population could be prevented by instructing working men in political economy; the instruction would guide them away from strikes and violence, thus safeguarding the stability of society (Tyrrell 1969: 155). Most educated persons of the era deplored trade unionism and the violence with which it was associated. Writings on political

---

77. According to Wise and Smith, the emphasis shifted from balance and equilibrium to evolution and temporal dynamics after the 1830s (1989: 392).
78. With J. M. Keynes the equilibrium concept was clearly dissociated from the idea of an optimum.

economy were thus marked, on the one hand, by the "fear of an increasingly unruly population of working poor" and, on the other, by an "optimism about a scientific solution" (Wise/Smith 1989: 285).[79] While one group—Jane Marcet, Harriet Martineau, and, to some extent, T. R. Malthus—was popularizing doctrines of natural harmony, others, most notably Ricardo, Mill, and Marx, regarded conflict and antagonism as inherent in the market. Keeping the poor in their place was the overriding theme of the popularizers' work.

Serious theoretical pedagogy soon failed, however, and was replaced by packaged entertainment for the common man—amusing tales with strong edifying, moralistic overtones. Harriet Martineau's short novels illustrating the principles of Malthusian and Ricardian economics led all other works in educating the masses on political economy.[80] Most members of the working class, however, viewed the popularizers of orthodox political economy, such as McCulloch, with suspicion, holding them for employers' spokesmen who believed that workers could never be made to labor too long or too hard (Tyrrell 1969: 165). By the end of economics' classical period, both adult and secondary education in political economy had proved themselves failures as effective control or stabilizing mechanisms. As the truisms of political economy became suspect and the subject more complex and less policy oriented, economics instruction for children and ordinary men and women was abandoned.[81]

## The Birth of Econometrics

### Political Arithmetic
The final stream of eighteenth- and nineteenth-century science important to the rise of political economy as a science is the birth

---

79. Malthus's population theory, with its balance between the forces of procreation on the one hand and starvation and misery on the other, is a case in point. Both Condorcet and Laplace believed that algebra and probability calculus should be used to establish equilibrium conditions for the "social statics."

80. Harriet Martineau's most famous work, her *Illustrations of Political Economy*, was a bestseller that originally appeared as twenty-five stories on a monthly basis and was subsequently published in nine volumes between 1832 and 1834.

81. "It is significant," Marsh explains, "that political economy as a school subject was abandoned or modified as the academic study of the subject was becoming more complex. The truisms of the classical system used as propa-

of economic statistics. Histories of econometrics, especially its infant state, are rare.[82] Yet this age was rich in statistical developments. Political arithmetic predates classical economics and is bound up with the emergence of statistics as a new field of knowledge in seventeenth-century England. Although Gottfried Achenwall (1719–1792) coined the word *Statistik* and is often dubbed the "father of statistics," the early German usage, following the Italian root, *statista*, the statesman, focused on a theory of the state, statecraft, and constitutional history. The work Achenwall and Hermann Conring (1606–1681) performed amounted to nothing more than a collection of descriptive, nonnumerical facts about the state that has nothing to do with today's statistics.

Statistics in the modern sense emerged in its incipient state as *political arithmetic.* Although Sir William Petty (1623–1687) coined the word, he was not, strictly speaking, the inventor of the English school of political arithmetic. It was a joint effort with Petty's friend John Graunt (1620–1674), whose careful estimates of London's population provided the method and stimulus for the political arithmetic movement. Neither Petty nor Graunt, however, used the word *statistics,* which was first brought into the English language by a Scotsman, Sir John Sinclair (1754–1835), at the close of the eighteenth century.[83]

Several circumstances favored the emergence of political arithmetic in seventeenth-century England. The most important factor was the spirit of the age. Baconian optimism—a general interest in experimental science and a pursuit of knowledge for knowledge's sake—was in the air. It was the age of panometry; measurement knew no limits. In addition, there was a real demand for concrete data. The political arithmeticians were interested in quantifying demographic matters and questions of the state to produce reliable comparisons of England's wealth

---

ganda were no longer certain, and as the subject became more academic and specialized in the course of the 'marginal revolution' from the 1870s, the popularisers lost ground" (1977: 118). If that didn't cast the fatal blow, the vituperation of Alfred Marshall, who despised the popularizing movement, surely must have.
82. Mary Morgan's *History of Econometric Ideas* (1990), for instance, starts with Jevons. On the early history of econometrics, see the sources listed in the bibliography as well as Schumpeter (1954b: 209–215) and Letwin (1963, ch. 5).
83. Sinclair is known for his impressive 21-volume *Statistical Account of Scotland* (1791–1799).

and power with that of her two arch rivals, Holland and France. Underlying the movement was a quest to promote sound, well-informed state policy. Without numbers, it was thought, policy is poorly informed. Moreover, the information numbers provide could both help to control the population and augment tax revenues.

In the middle of the seventeenth century, after the last major outbreak of the plague, the English Parliament passed a law requiring every parish to register every birth and burial; by the end of the century the age at death was also being recorded. At this time changes were also made in the tax system to provide, for the first time, data on the number of houses, acres of land, number of livestock, and consumption of certain foods. Finally, a series of navigation acts provided for the gathering of more reliable data on trade. Such were the data—though scanty and perilously deficient by today's standards—at hand for the first statisticians.[84]

Out of this environment emerged the first monograph on vital statistics and the first extensive set of statistical inferences drawn from mortality records: the *Natural and Political Observations on the London Bills of Mortality* (1662) by the London merchant John Graunt. Graunt, who was not a political economist, must be considered the real founder of statistics, the first demographer, and a cofounder of political arithmetic.[85] The *Observations on the London Bills of Mortality*, his only book, went through five editions in his lifetime.[86] Upon publication Graunt sent complimentary copies to the Royal Society, which responded a month later by making him a fellow. Although only a shopkeeper, he was recommended for membership by King Charles II himself,[87]

---

84. There is some disagreement about how much data was available and how good they were. While economists usually emphasize the dearth of data, Hacking argues that "plenty of data were already in existence" at the time Political Arithmetic was emerging as a movement (1975: 102).

85. See Pearson for the details of the confusion surrounding the founding of statistics (1978: 4ff.). Petty was sometimes mistakenly taken for the author of the *Observations on the London Bills*, which explains why it was published in 1899 with Petty's works.

Hacking points out that many people hit on the idea of probability independently around 1660 (1975: 11).

86. The fifth edition appeared in 1676, two years after Graunt's death. Changes in the five editions were minimal except for some appendices.

87. The Royal Society's founder and patron.

with the additional instruction to Society fellows to admit any other such tradesmen as could be found without any further ado (Pearson 1978: 12).

Graunt used the death returns from the London Bills of Mortality and data from parish records to calculate the first estimates of the total population for London and England. In his *Observations on the London Bills of Mortality,* he investigated numerous demographic relationships that we now take for granted: male and female population trends, death rates by age and location, fertility in town and countryside, immigration and its effects on population, incidence of fatal and new diseases, infant mortality, fatalities caused by epidemics, and life expectancy. The results encouraged Graunt to believe that, on average, social phenomena are regular and predictable—the assumption that became the foundation stone of statistical and actuarial science. Once Graunt had demonstrated the value of statistics for England, other countries followed; Paris started keeping tabulations in 1667, a year after Petty reviewed Graunt's book in the *Journal des sçavans* (Hacking 1975: 102). Graunt's figures were sound enough to lead to the establishment of life insurance and to encourage others to use his methods.

The regularities occurring in statistical phenomena is one of the chief ideas of his book. Unfortunately, it also leads him to draw conclusions that are too bold. From a list of christenings and burials of a single county parish, for example, he deduces figures for the whole population of London. In addition, because Dissenters and Catholics were not counted, christenings did not adequately reflect the birth rate. Nonetheless, Graunt's estimates were made with care and provided the stimulus that led to the emergence of political arithmetic as a movement. Petty, Edmond Halley, William Derham, Abraham de Moivre, and others later used the bills of mortality to arrive at estimates of population and vital statistics.

Sir William Petty, a disciple and intimate friend of Hobbes, introduced the term political arithmetic in 1674 when applying statistics to national wealth. His interest in measurement derived from his study of medicine; once again the analogy to physiology played a notable role in shaping early views on the science of economics. In his *Political Anatomy of Ireland* Petty comments on the "judicious Parallel" made by Bacon between "the Body

Natural, and Body Politick" and compares the method of political arithmetic to the scalpel of a surgeon (1899: 129).[88]

Although Petty speaks of Bacon with great respect, he is just
as much an exponent of Hobbes's method as of Bacon's (Bevan
1894: 85–86). He advocated a rigorous method of investigation
and an increase in scientific experiments. Petty himself carried
out technological experiments in agriculture, navigation, and
land carriage (1899: 249–50). He also proposed plans for getting
better, more exact data and supported the state collection of
information on trade, commerce, and agriculture. While these
goals underscore a Baconian emphasis on method, he nonetheless follows Hobbes in giving mathematical proof or quantification the highest place in science and in viewing certainty as the
aim of all investigation.

Petty also played a major role in founding the Royal Society
(which was patterned after the French Academy of Science, but
had a stronger orientation towards natural science); he was one
of the promoters for changing the name of the London Philosophical Club, or Invisible College, as it was sometimes also
called, to the Royal Society. At its meetings he never tired of
reminding members to avoid indefinite generalizations.[89] In his
opinion, political arithmetic was the next best thing to experimentation because it yields precise results. "The Method I take
to do this, is not yet very usual; for instead of using only
comparative and superlative Words, and intellectual Arguments,
I have taken the course (as a Specimen of the Political Arithmetick I have long aimed at) to express my self in Terms of
*Number, Weight,* or *Measure;* to use only Arguments of Sense, and
to consider only such Causes, as have visible Foundations in
Nature" (1899: 244).

The concept of national income was perhaps first formulated
in the seventeenth century by Petty, who used it to denote the
flow of goods and services. He defined the income of the people
as the "Annual Proceed of the Stock, or Wealth of Nations"
(1899: 108). Estimates of the current national income of England

---

88. Europeans already had a long history of likening the state to the human
body (consider, e.g., Plato's *Laws* and Aristotle's *Politics*).
89. It is reported that at one meeting of the Royal Society someone used the
expression "considerably bigger," to which Petty objected that only expressions denoting number, weight, or measure may be used (Hull in Petty 1899:
lxiv).

appeared in his *Verbum sapienta*, written in 1665 and published in 1691, and again seven years later in his *Political Arithmetick*, written in 1671–1672 but published posthumously in 1690. Although he formulates a concept of national income, he does not go on to develop a theory of income determination or pursue measuring changes in income.

Petty's estimates were motivated by two objectives. First, he wanted to prove that England could raise more revenues from taxes more equitably, the point of both his *Verbum sapienta* and his *Treatise of Taxes and Contributions* (1662). Second, he was bent on disproving the widespread view that England had been ruined by foreign wars and revolution and could no longer compete on an economic basis with France or Holland, the purpose of his *Political Arithmetick*.[90] In his conclusions, Petty showed that an English tax rate of ten percent would raise the revenues the nation needed and refuted, point for point, the prevailing pessimistic notions about the deteriorating state of England's economic and political power.

The only mathematical device that Petty uses in his political arithmetic is basic arithmetic; the only statistical device employed is the simple average, already an established concept by that time.[91] While his works contain no graphical representation, there are some basic tables (e.g., 1899: 458, 464). What, however, makes Petty one in spirit with twentieth-century econometricians is his conviction that statistical investigation is the best substitute for experimentation available to economists. In his preface to the *Political Anatomy of Ireland*, the substitution is literal, for he turns Ireland into a social scientist's guinea pig: "As Students in Medicine, practice their inquiries upon cheap and common Animals, and such whose actions they are best acquainted with, and where there is the least confusion and perplexure of Parts; I have chosen Ireland as such a Political Animal" (1899: 129).

Yet, as precise as Petty's numbers might have seemed, they left much to be desired. Their inadequacy did not elude him, for he once remarked: "I hope that no man takes what I say about

---

90. Three famous advocates of such views were Sir Josiah Child, Thomas Papillon, and Roger Coke. Petty was especially interested in discrediting Coke's views.

91. Letwin tells us that the concept *average*, or *medium*, was well known in Petty's day (1963: 137).

the living and dyeing of men for a mathematical demonstration" (1899: lxviii).[92] But the point is, as Letwin pithily notes, that "Petty's way with numbers . . . was utterly cavalier. The facts, whatever they were, always had a congenial way of upholding Petty's conclusions" (1963: 134). Equally noteworthy is Charles Hull's observation that Graunt's *Observations upon the Bills of Mortality* is, from a statistical perspective, superior to Petty's statistics because "Graunt uses his numerical data as a basis for conclusions, declining to go beyond them" (in Petty, 1899: lxxv). Moreover, "Graunt's book has the advantage of priority and the greater advantage of dealing with a body of statistical data sufficiently extended and complete to warrant some confidence in deductions properly made from it. Petty's materials, on the other hand, were highly defective" (lxvi).

Indeed, Petty's unreliable methods became as famous as the theme of his *Political Arithmetick*. The most notorious example deals with his calculation of the population of London and England. By comparing "superfluous and spare Oxen, Sheep, Butter and Beef," he finds that one-third more were exported in 1664 than in 1641 and thus concludes that the population had grown by one-third in that period (Petty 1899: 149). To calculate the population of London, he multiplied the number of burials by thirty or, alternately, the number of houses by six or eight, assuming six and one-third persons per family. Then, by multiplying London's population by eight, he arrived at a figure for England's total population (1899: 459ff.). As we can see, when data were scarce, Petty simply improvised. As far as he was concerned, the assumption that the population increases at the same ratio at all times is unproblematic. Charles Davenant criticized Petty, in addition, for manipulating the data with the intent of flattering the King (1698: 6).

Petty's successor, Gregory King (1648–1712), was conspicuous for his meticulous way of performing calculations and drawing conclusions. His chief statistical work, *Natural and Political Observations and Conclusions upon the State and Condition of England*

---

92. Petty was a practical man, not a scholar. In his *Treatise of Ireland* (1687) he lays out his expectations of Political Arithmetic: "I know these are not so perfect Demonstrations as are required in pure Mathematicks; but they are such as our Superiors may work with, as well as Wheelwrights and Clockmakers do work without the Quadrature of a Circle" (1899: 611).

*1696,* is the best account of the population and wealth of England available at the close of the century. He has better estimates than Petty both because of the availability of somewhat improved data and his more scientific spirit. Although his calculations of average income are only informed guesses, King's estimates of England's annual income and expenditure for 1688 were, in fact, remarkable (see the excerpt from his statistics in figure 4). His work brought seventeenth-century political arithmetic to the zenith of its reliability—where it would remain for at least a decade. Moreover, he not only constructed an annual series of estimates,[93] he projected series into the future—thus earning the distinction of being the first pioneer econometrician in the tradition of modern, twentieth-century econometrics.

Although Charles Davenant (1656–1714) went on to plead for better data from official sources and to expound the value of statistics, no reliable estimates of national income were published during the first half of the eighteenth century. Paul Studenski refers to the years from 1700 to 1770 as the "period of neglect of Political Arithmetic" (1958: 40). "Indeed there was a signal lack of the spirit of careful and impartial enquiry that distinguished several writers at the end of the seventeenth century," observes Phyllis Deane. After King a series of pamphleteers simply adorned their arguments with a smattering of Petty or King's calculations, producing works that were, as Deane aptly describes them, "mainly distinguished by their extremely inaccurate use of figures." One example serves to capture the tenor of the age: One self-professed "political chemist," a certain Andrew Hooke, actually expounded the following advice on the use of statistics: "[L]et it be observed that when the nature of any subject does not admit of positive Proofs or where such Proofs are not come-at-able, high Probabilities are always allowed to supply their Place" (1956: 13, 14).

It was this intellectual climate that triggered Adam Smith's famous statement, "I have no great faith in political arithmetick" (1976a: 534); evaluated in its proper setting, this simply means that Smith "did not credit numbers arrived at by a process of guessing and fiddling" (Letwin 1963: 140). Soon thereafter

---

93. Yearly estimates of English income were first made in the second quarter of the twentieth century (Spengler 1961: 142).

The Annual Income, & Expence of the Nation as it stood
An.° 1688.

That the Yearly Income of the Nation a.°
   1688 Was ...................... 43,500,000 Sterlg.
That the Yearly Expence of the Nation
   Was ......................... 41,700,000
That then the Yearly Increase of wealth
   was ......................... 1,800,000
That the Yearly Rent of the Lands were
   about ....................... 10,000,000
   of the Burgage or Houseing about.... 2,000,000
   of all other Heriditaments about...... 1,000,000

                                  In all 13,000,000
That the yearly Produce of Trade arts &
   Labour was ab.ᵗ................. 30,500,000

                                  In all 43,500,000
That the Number of Inhabited Houses
   being about ................... 1,300,000
   The Number of Families about...... 1,360,000
   And the Number of People about..... 5,500,000
   The People answer to 4¼ ℗ House, & 4 ℗ Family.
That the Yearly Estates or Income of the several Families
   answer

|  | £ | s. | d. |  |
|---|---|---|---|---|
| In common To about............ | 32 | .. | .. | ℗ Family |
| And about ..................... | 7 | 18 | .. | ℗ head |

That the yearly expense of the Nation
   is about ..................... 7  11  4 ℗ head
   And the yearly Increase about...... ..  6  8 ℗ head
That the whole Value of the Kingdom    £
   in Gen.ˡˡ is about............... 650,000,000 Stlg.

**Figure 4**
An example of Gregory King's statistics from *Natural and Political Observations and Conclusions upon the State and Condition of England* (1696), in *Two Tracts* (Baltimore: The Johns Hopkins Press, 1936, p. 30)

political arithmetic as a school of thought fell into oblivion. Certainly the surplus of quacks predetermined its demise; but in the first part of the eighteenth century its failure can also be attributed to a lack of official statistics. No population or occupational data were available; data on national income and expenditure were incomplete; and trade figures actually became less reliable as the century progressed. Trade statistics, the most reliable data, were available from the beginning of the century, but were still problematic.[94]

After the eighteenth century, political arithmetic no longer received an entry in the *Encyclopaedia Britannica*. Statistical data improved toward the very end of the eighteenth century, as official sources poured forth more data, enabling John Playfair (1748–1819), "the inventor of lineal arithmetic," to graph economic trends (Deane 1956: 17). By 1800, political arithmetic may have ceased to exist as a movement, but the idea of econometrics—the use of statistics to back up economic arguments—had set down deep roots.

**The Statistical Societies**
The statistics movement organized and consolidated in early nineteenth-century Britain, when the collection of statistical data on topics of social relevance, especially crime, education, and religion was known as *moral statistics*.[95] While the government had a special stake in the collection of such data, a general interest in social statistics was stimulated by a growing awareness of the need to provide evidence in support of social reform; to document concretely, and so understand, the great social changes taking place; and to collect and analyze economic data to refute Ricardo and his "deductivist school" of political economy (which included the senior Mill and Bentham).[96] The animus directed at Ricardo and his followers rightly implies that the nineteenth-century statistical movement emanated from Cambridge, where Whewell and Babbage played significant roles.

---

94. The dearth of data is cited by everyone. See, e.g., Deane (1956) and Spiegel (1991: 142).
95. For more on the history of moral statistics, see Cullen (1975, ch. 5).
96. Goldman claims the motivating force for forming the statistical societies was a contempt for Ricardian methods (1983: 594, 599).

There was a great burst of activity in the 1830s. As early as 1801 the first official census had been organized in response to manpower needs during the Napoleonic Wars. But the first four decennial censuses were deemed unsatisfactory, even at the time, because the information had been gathered by the Church. After 1831, when the British Association for the Advancement of Science (BAAS) was founded, all types of sciences and their associations suddenly began sprouting up like mushrooms in a moist, warm climate. The first statistical society, the Manchester Royal Society, was founded in 1833, the same year that a statistical section, Section F (today also the economics section) was added to the British Association. A year later the Statistical Society of London (later the Royal Statistical Society) was formed. In 1832 a statistical office, the Board of Trade, was set up, and in 1837 the General Register Office was created to collect vital statistics and supervise the census. The enthusiasm for statistics reached its heights in the 1830s and 1840s (Hilts 1973: 211).

The introduction of statistical techniques in the social sciences, according to Victor Hilts (1973: 207), "one of the most important methodological innovations of nineteenth-century science," was due in great part to the efforts of the Belgian mathematician and astronomer Adolphe Quetelet (1796–1874) and the English scientist Sir Francis Galton (1822–1911). In his *Sur l'homme et le développement de ses facultés, ou essai de physique sociale* (1836), Quetelet creates the new science of social statistics called "social physics" (*physique sociale*), which enjoyed a warm reception in the 1830s.[97] His statistics, as can be seen in the excerpt from his book (in figure 5), were far more advanced than anything the British had to offer at the time. At the roots of Quetelet's theory was a focus on regularities, mainly averages; he made the idea of the average concrete, employing the concept of the "average man" (*l'homme moyen*) to dispense with the problem of individual irregularities. In other words, the social body rather than particular individuals became the object of his research. As he saw it, the average is a mean that is analyzable, whereas devia-

---

97. The English translation, *A Treatise on Man and the Development of His Faculties*, first appeared in 1842.

tions from the mean are accidental in nature and thus not capable of being analyzed.

Francis Galton recognized the error in this reasoning. While studying heredity, he saw that the law of error was a limiting case of the more general law of distribution.[98] Deviations from the mean were not accidents and could be found to be correlated. "By approaching statistics with an awareness of individual differences and through the problem of hereditary variation, Galton was led into those studies which eventually resulted in his discovery of the correlation coefficient and thus to the beginning of modern mathematical statistics as used in the social sciences" (Hilts 1973: 230). Hilts explains further that Quetelet's social physics, an attempt to apply the mathematical methods used by astronomers to the social arena, highlighted the difficulties of developing statistical methods for the social sciences and biology when the particular problems of the new sciences were not taken into account (230).

The venture into social statistics was not always welcomed by the public. With the BAAS supporting a plethora of projects, so many new "sciences" were vying to gain legitimation from the institution Charles Dickens dubbed the "Mudfog Association for the Advancement of Everything" that the British press derided it as "the British Ass" (Morrell/Thackray 1982: xix).[99] Moreover, due to its overt connections with economic, social, and political problems, statistics was a sensitive subject.

In such an environment, it is little wonder that the statistical section's entry into the BAAS was eventually unconstitutional. Section F was very much the work of Robert Malthus (who died shortly after the Statistical Society of London was founded),

---

98. Galton's first published work on the importance of heredity for human ability and character appeared in 1865, six years after the publication of Darwin's *Origins of the Species* (see Galton 1869).

99. To give the reader a taste of its multifarious interests, the BAAS supported projects on anthropological and astronomical reductions, cerebral physiology, fossil ichthyology, mining records, physical optics, railway constants, tidology (study of tides), vital statistics, and zoological nomenclature (Morrell/Thackray 1982: xix). Not all petitioners, however, had their "science" accepted into the BAAS. Music, literature, and other humanities were turned down, as was phrenology, a science that purported to determine human character and mental ability by studying the shape of the skull (Morrell/Thackray 1982: 276ff.).

| AGE. | TABLE DE MORTALITÉ DE LA BELGIQUE | | | | TABLE GÉNÉRALE. VILLES ET CAMPAGNES. |
| --- | --- | --- | --- | --- | --- |
| | POUR LES VILL. | | POUR LES CAMP. | | |
| | HOMMES. | FEMMES. | HOMMES. | FEMMES. | HOMMES ET FEMMES. |
| NAISSANC. | 10000 | 10000 | 10000 | 10000 | 100000 |
| 1 mois. | 8840 | 9129 | 8926 | 9209 | 90396 |
| 2 | 8550 | 8916 | 8664 | 8988 | 87936 |
| 3 | 8361 | 8760 | 8470 | 8829 | 86175 |
| 4 | 8195 | 8641 | 8314 | 8694 | 84720 |
| 5 | 8069 | 8540 | 8187 | 8587 | 83571 |
| 6 | 7981 | 8437 | 8078 | 8490 | 82526 |
| 1 an. | 7426 | 7932 | 7575 | 8001 | 77528 |
| 18 mois. | 6954 | 7500 | 7173 | 7603 | 73367 |
| 2 ans. | 6626 | 7179 | 6920 | 7326 | 70536 |
| 3 | 6194 | 6761 | 6537 | 6931 | 66531 |
| 4 | 5911 | 6477 | 6326 | 6691 | 64102 |
| 5 | 5738 | 6295 | 6169 | 6528 | 62448 |
| 6 | 5621 | 6176 | 6038 | 6395 | 61166 |
| 7 | 5547 | 6095 | 5939 | 6299 | 60249 |
| 8 | 5481 | 6026 | 5862 | 6215 | 59487 |
| 9 | 5424 | 5966 | 5792 | 6147 | 58829 |
| 10 | 5384 | 5916 | 5734 | 6082 | 58258 |
| 11 | 5352 | 5873 | 5683 | 6018 | 57749 |
| 12 | 5323 | 5838 | 5634 | 5960 | 57289 |
| 13 | 5298 | 5807 | 5589 | 5908 | 56871 |
| 14 | 5271 | 5771 | 5546 | 5862 | 56467 |
| 15 | 5241 | 5732 | 5502 | 5796 | 56028 |
| 16 | 5209 | 5689 | 5456 | 5725 | 55570 |
| 17 | 5171 | 5645 | 5408 | 5668 | 55087 |
| 18 | 5131 | 5600 | 5357 | 5608 | 54575 |
| 19 | 5087 | 5551 | 5302 | 5546 | 54030 |
| 20 | 5038 | 5500 | 5242 | 5484 | 53450 |
| 21 | 4978 | 5445 | 5178 | 5421 | 52810 |
| 22 | 4908 | 5387 | 5109 | 5356 | 52172 |

**Figure 5**
Mortality table for Belgium by age (up to age 104) and by town and country.
Adolphe Quetelet, *Sur l'homme et le développement de ses facultés* (Bruxelles,
Louis Hauman et comp., 1836, pp. 170–71)

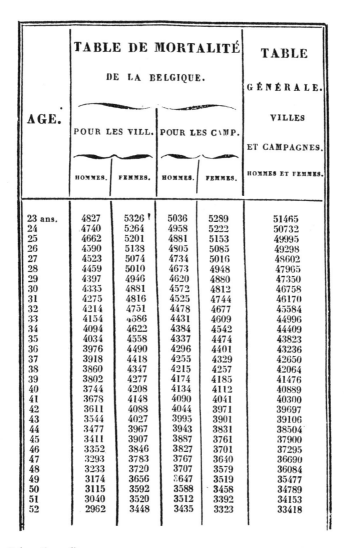

| AGE. | TABLE DE MORTALITÉ DE LA BELGIQUE. | | | | TABLE GÉNÉRALE. VILLES ET CAMPAGNES. |
|---|---|---|---|---|---|
| | POUR LES VILL. | | POUR LES CAMP. | | |
| | HOMMES. | FEMMES. | HOMMES. | FEMMES. | HOMMES ET FEMMES. |
| 23 ans. | 4827 | 5326 | 5036 | 5289 | 51465 |
| 24 | 4740 | 5264 | 4958 | 5222 | 50732 |
| 25 | 4662 | 5201 | 4881 | 5153 | 49995 |
| 26 | 4590 | 5138 | 4805 | 5085 | 49298 |
| 27 | 4523 | 5074 | 4734 | 5016 | 48602 |
| 28 | 4459 | 5010 | 4673 | 4948 | 47965 |
| 29 | 4397 | 4946 | 4620 | 4880 | 47350 |
| 30 | 4335 | 4881 | 4572 | 4812 | 46758 |
| 31 | 4275 | 4816 | 4525 | 4744 | 46170 |
| 32 | 4214 | 4751 | 4478 | 4677 | 45584 |
| 33 | 4154 | 4686 | 4431 | 4609 | 44996 |
| 34 | 4094 | 4622 | 4384 | 4542 | 44409 |
| 35 | 4034 | 4558 | 4337 | 4474 | 43823 |
| 36 | 3976 | 4490 | 4296 | 4401 | 43236 |
| 37 | 3918 | 4418 | 4255 | 4329 | 42650 |
| 38 | 3860 | 4347 | 4215 | 4257 | 42064 |
| 39 | 3802 | 4277 | 4174 | 4185 | 41476 |
| 40 | 3744 | 4208 | 4134 | 4112 | 40889 |
| 41 | 3678 | 4148 | 4090 | 4041 | 40300 |
| 42 | 3611 | 4088 | 4044 | 3971 | 39697 |
| 43 | 3544 | 4027 | 3995 | 3901 | 39106 |
| 44 | 3477 | 3967 | 3943 | 3831 | 38504 |
| 45 | 3411 | 3907 | 3887 | 3761 | 37900 |
| 46 | 3352 | 3846 | 3827 | 3701 | 37295 |
| 47 | 3293 | 3783 | 3767 | 3640 | 36690 |
| 48 | 3233 | 3720 | 3707 | 3579 | 36084 |
| 49 | 3174 | 3656 | 3647 | 3519 | 35477 |
| 50 | 3115 | 3592 | 3588 | 3458 | 34789 |
| 51 | 3040 | 3520 | 3512 | 3392 | 34153 |
| 52 | 2962 | 3448 | 3435 | 3323 | 33418 |

**Figure 5** (continued)

Adolphe Quetelet, Richard Jones, Charles Babbage, Adam Sedgwick, and, behind the scenes, William Whewell.[100] On the 26th
of June 1833, after Quetelet had presented his work on suicide
and crime, Babbage spontaneously established the section without going through the BAAS General Committee. The next day
he simply submitted the section to the President, Adam Sedgwick, as a fait accompli. Unhappy about the circumstances leading to the creation of the section, he nonetheless did nothing to
undo it; Sedgwick did, however, feel compelled to advise the
members that science is distinguished by measurement and
calculation and that statistics were only appropriate in the form
of facts and numbers that could function as "raw material to
political economy and political philosophy" (Morrell/Thackray
1982: 291). With Jones chairing the committee, the BAAS held
that Section F's scope would be limited, in Jones's words, to
"facts capable of being expressed by numbers" (Cullen 1975:
82–83). Consequently, higher generalizations so common to the
theories of the day were forbidden.

In the case of statistics, then, facts were not to be related to
theories—to prevent users from questioning the social order.
This decision, as Jack Morrell and Arnold Thackray so aptly
note, stood in direct conflict with the official BAAS methodology
of the 1830s and 1840s, which, it so happened, was Whewell's
position on method. So it was that the gentlemen of science
"adopted the convenient, if inconsistent, fiction that statistical
facts were value-free, pure, and noncontroversial. BAAS statisticians were simply to produce the quantitative data from which
in the indefinite future some statistical Kepler might induce the
true laws of political economy. Statisticians were to register
what existed, and not to suggest what ought to exist by providing remedies for dire social problems" (Morrell/Thackray 1982:
292). At the heart of the problem was Whewell and colleagues'
insistence that scientists distance themselves from political issues on grounds that science at the British Association was to

---

100. Babbage was Lucasian professor of mathematics at Cambridge; Quetelet
was at the Belgian Royal Observatory and had been invited to the founding
meetings by Whewell; Jones, who had graduated from Cambridge in 1816,
had just taken up a chair in political economy at King's College, London; and
Sedgwick, then BAAS President, was professor of geology and Whewell's
colleage at Trinity College.

be "a 'neutral' court of appeal, a well-spring of authority and power, an objective and impersonal means to good and desirable ends, a tangible object of public pride, and an instrument of the common weal" (Morrell/Thackray 1982: 33).

In spite of this, most members of the early statistical societies were politically active and very willing to pledge their names for the cause. But getting members to do the dirty work of gathering, sifting, and organizing the statistics and compiling reports was another matter. While the Statistical Society of London did not meet expectations,[101] it survived, publishing some useful work and a few surveys. By the end of the nineteenth century statistics as a discipline and an empirical arm of political economy was established and the BAAS strictures on the methodological limits of social science were not swallowed whole: "The uncomfortable reality remained . . . that in social questions facts and values were forever interlocked: the statistics Section existed as the political dog beneath the Baconian skin of the Association's professed ideology of science" (Morrell/Thackray 1982: 296).

---

101. By the end of the 1830s, the founding group began to view the statistical societies as a failure and had almost abandoned the project. Malthus died in 1834; Quetelet resided in Brussels; and Whewell as Master of Trinity and Jones in Malthus's old chair at Haileybury were both too busy for the societies. These and other problems are mentioned in the Statistical Society of London's first publication (R. Robertson, 1838).

# 4  A Short History of Induction

It was from induction, claimed the thinkers in classical political economy, that they derived the ultimate source of knowledge of their world, making the concept critical not only to their age, but also to the development of economics in general. The concept of induction is, in fact, so significant that I have placed it within the wider historical tradition of classical induction. Extending the sketch beyond the nineteenth century to the present state of the discussion has two major advantages.[1] It shows how David Hume's problem of induction has come full circle in the twentieth century, and—just as important—it highlights the slippery quality of the word *induction*, which was commonly used well into the nineteenth century not in contrast with deduction or the hypothetico-deductive method, but as a synonym for it.[2] If nothing else, this historical sketch demonstrates how changes in the meaning of the word *induction* have served to obstruct understanding.

*Induction* as we use the word today often refers to a technical term of logic. Frequently it designates any nondeductive procedure that attempts to justify the acceptance of a conclusion. Others, Karl Popper included, use it to stand for a particular way in which some philosophers, notably Francis Bacon and J. S. Mill, try to justify their findings. According to this view, scientific laws and theories are justified through the use of an

---

1. Due to space considerations, my examination of induction can only be a sketch. To my knowledge, there are no general histories of induction as used either in natural or social science. This introductory section owes much to de Haan (1982) and Nagel (1958).
2. The hypothetico-deductive method involves proposing hypotheses and testing their acceptability or falsity by determining whether their logical consequences are consistent with the data.

argument whose premises are singular statements of observation and experiment. Advocates of Popperian science juxtapose what they call Bacon-Millian induction with the opposing view that scientists arrive at laws and theories by the hypothetico-deductive method, that is, by testing hypotheses or, in Popper's words, by a process of "conjectures and refutations." A study of the history of the induction concept reveals both how old the hypothetico-deductive method is and how closely the latter has been associated with scientific investigation by induction. In other words, it becomes very difficult to talk about induction without also talking about deduction and the role of hypotheses in science. This is the message of both William Whewell's and J. S. Mill's work.

Today we usually associate induction with reasoning from the particular to the general or with the inference of laws from observations; deduction is the antithetical process, the drawing of particular truths from a general truth. Whereas induction is the method of empirical science, deduction is a purely logical process. Historically, however, there have been two ways of viewing induction, and this distinction is crucial for an understanding of eighteenth- and nineteenth-century science.[3] Induction has been viewed both in a broad sense as the process of scientific inquiry and in a restrictive sense as a method of weighing evidence for a particular generalization or conclusion.

In the first case, induction is the method or methods of reasoning employed in establishing general laws and propositions about individual occurrences on the basis of specific observational evidence. Such a process is used, for instance, to predict tomorrow's weather based on meteorological data or to determine the inflation rate based on price comparisons of a basket of goods. The question the investigator is asking is How can evidence be obtained? or What steps do we take in handling a question scientifically? Induction understood broadly as a process of general steps taken in scientific inquiry can involve the following issues:

---

3. The concept of induction or inductive inference is old and can be traced back to ancient Greece. Aristotle first used the word in no less than three ways to mean the passage from the individual or particular to the universal, the enumeration of all instances, and the abstraction by intuition of a general truth by considering a particular case. It is the first definition that forms the basis for much modern discussion.

1. recognizing the problem,

2. cooking up a hypothesis to solve the problem,

3. deriving deductive consequences of the hypothesis,

4. collecting evidence for and against some of the deductions by confronting them with data of observation and other well-established propositions,

5. accepting, modifying, or rejecting the hypothesis in light of the evidence in step four (Nagel 1958: 71).

It may also include questions of logic or considerations of psychological factors that affect science. The point to be made here is that induction in this sense is not antithetical to deduction, the derivation of deductive consequences of hypotheses being an integral feature of almost all scientific inquiry.

Only when two qualifying statements are added—that the premises of deductive arguments logically imply their conclusion (making them absolute evidence of it) and the premises of inductive arguments do not necessitate the conclusion (making the conclusions probable)—do we arrive at the contemporary definition of induction as antithetical to deduction. Then the question raised by the investigator becomes, Is the conclusion or generalization adequately supported by the body of evidence? or, How do we know that something that is true of a certain number of members of one class will also be true of unknown members of the same class? In struggling to answer this question, scientists have sought to formulate principles that enable them to evaluate evidence and, in turn, to justify these principles. This type of induction is usually called *ampliative induction,* in accordance with C. S. Peirce's usage, because the conclusion is "amplified" beyond the premises: it may entail inferences from the past to the future, from a sample to a population, or from data to a hypothesis. The problem ampliative induction obviously poses is one of extrapolation: it necessarily goes beyond its premises—either by drawing a conclusion from the observed to the unobserved or from an inference to the future—making the generalization or conclusion only probable. J. S. Mill tried to get around this problem by maintaining that we make inferences from particulars to particulars and, thus, do not need laws. It is, nonetheless, impossible to ignore the fact that science does rely, if only tacitly, on laws.

Two other types of induction need to be mentioned briefly.
When *recursive* or *mathematical induction* is used in mathematics
to determine propositions of unrestrained universality (the sum
of series), extrapolation does not create a problem. In the case of
*summative* or *perfect induction* (called *induction by simple enumeration* by Mill), the generalization is based on an exhaustive enumeration of its instances. Two examples illustrate this type of
induction: All planets move in orbit around the sun; and, All U.S.
presidents have been white men. Because summative induction
is valid for restricted universal statements—that is, for the case
where all members of a class are known—it is trivial. Philosophers of the scientific revolution viewed summative induction
as a type of deduction precisely because it yields no new information (de Haan 1982: 729). Neither the recursive nor the summative variety of induction has much use in establishing universal
propositions in science—for the propositions of science are both
unrestricted and incapable of complete reduction to mathematical relations—and will therefore not concern us further.

## Bacon's Theory of Induction

Because Bacon and Newton were the two chief exponents of
scientific method in the eighteenth and nineteenth centuries, the
way they used the term *induction* is particularly worthy of close
attention. Francis Bacon made the first serious attempt to formulate the methods of the natural sciences; to him we owe the
first systematic account of induction by elimination. The *locus
classicus* of his work on induction is to be found in the *Novum
organum*. There, Bacon specifies two ways of philosophizing
about nature. The first way, then very much in vogue, was to
move rashly from particulars to general principles. The second
method, not yet tried at that time, was to derive principles by a
gradual process from experience until general axioms are
reached—induction.[4] The correct way to discover the truth, ac-

---

4. "For hitherto the proceeding has been to fly at once from the sense and
particulars up to the most general propositions. . . . Now my plan is to proceed
regularly and gradually from one axiom to another, so that the most general
are not reached till the last" (Bacon 1858: 25). In his *Philosophy and Discovery*
(1860) William Whewell appraised Bacon's chief methodological tenet—to
proceed gradually from the facts to broader and broader generalizations—as
his greatest contribution.

cording to Bacon, "derives axioms from the senses and particulars, rising by a gradual and unbroken ascent, so that it arrives at the most general axioms last of all" (1858: 50). Experience must be duly sifted and digested before general principles can be deduced. Since the object of inquiry—determining the forms or laws of matter—becomes less and less entangled the closer it gets to "simple natures," Bacon argues that science moves from the complicated to the simple. General principles so discovered suggest experiments and even more general principles. Each principle must be subjected to particulars for verification to show that it is operative in nature. Bacon's method, "though hard to practice, is easy to explain": its purpose is "to establish progressive stages of certainty" (40).

Bacon's is not a simple theory of induction. He straightforwardly rejects simple enumeration as "a puerile thing" and as a method erroneously expounded by Aristotle and the Schoolmen (1858: 25).[5] He recognizes the problem that a number of favorable instances cannot establish generalizations as true. Enumeration of particulars without a consideration of contradictory instances is, in his view, mere conjecture; only eliminative induction can arrive at certain laws.[6] The merits of the method of elimination—of discovering contradictory as opposed to positive evidence—are repeatedly lauded by Bacon: "Now what the sciences stand in need of is a form of induction which shall analyse experience and take it to pieces, and by a due process of exclusion and rejection lead to an inevitable conclusion" (25). In designing such a process, Bacon was the first to formulate the principles of agreement and difference later taken up by Herschel and made popular by J. S. Mill. The eliminative aspect, combined with the belief that knowledge is cumulative and should be used for practical ends, seems to be every bit as

---

5. "For the induction which proceeds by simple enumeration is childish; its conclusions are precarious, and exposed to peril from a contradictory instance; and it generally decides on too small a number of facts, and on those only which are at hand" (1858: 97).
6. Mill contends that it "was, above all, by pointing out the insufficiency of this rude and loose conception of Induction [simple enumeration], that Bacon merited the title so generally awarded to him, of Founder of the Inductive Philosophy" (*Works*, 7: 313).

suggestive of Popper as Bacon's theory of the idols.[7] This, then, is Bacon's theory of induction in a nutshell.

Yet this greatly compressed representation of induction conceals the actual process Bacon envisioned. In fact, Bacon and his followers always had at least two processes in mind when they used the word *induction:* (1) a process of investigation and of collecting facts, including observation and experimentation and (2) a process of deducing an inference from these facts, that is, of generalizing from particulars to a class. The task of collecting and ordering facts is fulfilled by Bacon's "Natural and Experimental History" and must precede the formation of laws.

### Natural History
His "Natural and Experimental History" consists of "the primary material of philosophy and the stuff and subject-matter of true induction" (1858: 254). An interpretation of nature depends upon its existence; without it, induction would be useless. The "primary material of philosophy" is essentially a grand collection of observations and experiments. Relying on induction could correct the old philosophy, which had been based "on too narrow a foundation of experiment and natural history" and had resulted in decisions based on "too few cases" (63). Because inchoate empirical science in Bacon's age was in such a primitive state, he drew up a catalogue of all of the natural histories that needed to be assembled (see the excerpt from the complete catalogue in figure 6). No great intellect was needed to accumulate a large stock of data, he thought, but it would require cooperation and much effort (251–52). Science needed artisans and craftsmen to fill the dearth in data.[8] All data that make up a natural history "should be sifted diligently and severely before they are received," and "special care is to be taken that it [the stock of data] be of a wide range" (255). Several additional things could be added to the natural history. Questions that

---

7. Quinton calls Bacon "the most confident, explicit and influential of the first exponents of the idea of progress" (1980: 29). He, Hattaway (1978), and Urbach (1982) see a precursor of Popper in Bacon; the thesis is most systematically and eloquently developed by Urbach.

8. "But then only will there be good ground of hope for the further advance of knowledge, when there shall be received and gathered together into natural history a variety of experiments, which are of no use in themselves, but simply serve to discover causes and axioms" (Bacon 1858: 95).

come to mind should be recorded "to provoke and stimulate further inquiry." The manner in which the experiment was conducted should be recorded as well so that "men may be free to judge for themselves whether this information obtained from that experiment be truthworthy or fallacious" (261–62). For similar reasons, doubts about statements or facts should be registered, as should any general observations.[9] A brief summary of received opinions on the subject may also be appended to the history.

Bacon was aware of the weaknesses of the senses but did not see them as an insurmountable problem: the use of instruments or aids would sharpen the senses. For Bacon, the data used in inductions are not just simple observations but facts gathered from experimentation under controlled conditions. He was decidedly against the experimental practice of his contemporaries: "the manner of making experiments which men now use is blind and stupid" because they experimented carelessly, without trying to find true causes and axioms (1858: 70). "[W]e have as yet had either none or very weak ones [experimental practices]; no search has been made to collect a store of particular observations sufficient either in number, or in kind, or in certainty, to inform the understanding, or in any way adequate. . . . Nothing duly investigated, nothing verified, nothing counted, weighed, or measured, is to be found in natural history: and what in observation is loose and vague, is in information deceptive and treacherous" (1858: 94). The point is that "the whole edifice tumbles" if axioms and generalizations "be improperly and overhastily abstracted from facts" (24). Bacon was reacting against the commonplace view that the mind is denigrated by doing the dirty work of performing experiments. He argued that experiments bearing directly on a particular problem or piece of work—*experimenta fructifera* (experiments of fruit)—are of less scientific value than those performed to discover causes and axioms—*experimenta lucifera*—or experiments of light.

---

9. In another passage, Bacon writes: "The registering and proposing of doubts has a double use: first it guards philosophy against errors . . . secondly, doubts once registered are so many suckers or sponges which continually draw and attract increase of knowledge; whence it comes that things which, if doubts had not preceded, would have been passed by lightly without observation, are through the suggestion of doubts attentively and carefully observed" (1858: 357–58).

# CATALOGUE
## OF
# PARTICULAR HISTORIES
### BY TITLES.

1. History of the Heavenly Bodies; or Astronomical History.
2. History of the Configuration of the Heaven and the parts thereof towards the Earth and the parts thereof; or Cosmographical History.
3. History of Comets.
4. History of Fiery Meteors.
5. History of Lightnings, Thunderbolts, Thunders, and Coruscations.
6. History of Winds and Sudden Blasts and Undulations of the Air.
7. History of Rainbows.
8. History of Clouds, as they are seen above.
9. History of the Blue Expanse, of Twilight, of Mock-Suns, Mock-Moons, Haloes, various colours of the Sun; and of every variety in the aspect of the heavens caused by the medium.
10. History of Showers, Ordinary, Stormy, and Prodigious; also of Waterspouts (as they are called); and the like.
11. History of Hail, Snow, Frost, Hoar-frost, Fog, Dew, and the like.
12. History of all other things that fall or descend from above, and that are generated in the upper region.
13. History of Sounds in the upper region (if there be any), besides Thunder.
14. History of Air as a whole, or in the Configuration of the World.

15. History of the Seasons or Temperatures of the Year, as well according to the variations of Regions as according to accidents of Times and periods of Years; of Floods, Heats, Droughts, and the like.
16. History of Earth and Sea; of the Shape and Compass of them, and their Configurations compared with each other; and of their broadening or narrowing; of Islands in the Sea; of Gulfs of the Sea, and Salt Lakes within the Land; Isthmuses and Promontories.
17. History of the Motions (if any be) of the Globe of Earth and Sea; and of the Experiments from which such motions may be collected.
18. History of the greater Motions and Perturbations in Earth and Sea; Earthquakes, Tremblings and Yawnings of the Earth, Islands newly appearing; Floating Islands; Breakings off of Land by entrance of the Sea, Encroachments and Inundations and contrariwise Recessions of the Sea; Eruptions of Fire from the Earth; Sudden Eruptions of Waters from the Earth; and the like.
19. Natural History of Geography; of Mountains, Vallies, Woods, Plains, Sands, Marshes, Lakes, Rivers, Torrents, Springs, and every variety of their course, and the like; leaving apart Nations, Provinces, Cities, and such like matters pertaining to Civil life.
20. History of Ebbs and Flows of the Sea; Currents, Undulations, and other Motions of the Sea.
21. History of the other Accidents of the Sea; its Saltness, its various Colours, its Depth; also of Rocks, Mountains and Vallies under the Sea, and the like.

*Next come Histories of the Greater Masses.*

22. History of Flame and of things Ignited.
23. History of Air, in Substance, not in the Configuration of the World.
24. History of Water, in Substance, not in the Configuration of the World.
25. History of Earth and the diversity thereof, in Substance, not in the Configuration of the World.

*Next come Histories of Species.*

26. History of perfect Metals, Gold, Silver; and of the Mines,

Veins, Marcasites of the same; also of the Working in the Mines.
27. History of Quicksilver.
28. History of Fossils; as Vitriol, Sulphur, &c.
29. History of Gems; as the Diamond, the Ruby, &c.
30. History of Stones; as Marble, Touchstone, Flint, &c.
31. History of the Magnet.
32. History of Miscellaneous Bodies, which are neither entirely Fossil nor Vegetable; as Salts, Amber, Ambergris, &c.
33. Chemical History of Metals and Minerals.
34. History of Plants, Trees, Shrubs, Herbs; and of their parts, Roots, Stalks, Wood, Leaves, Flowers, Fruits, Seeds, Gums, &c.
35. Chemical History of Vegetables.
36. History of Fishes, and the Parts and Generation of them.
37. History of Birds, and the Parts and Generation of them.
38. History of Quadrupeds, and the Parts and Generation of them.
39. History of Serpents, Worms, Flies, and other insects; and of the Parts and Generation of them.
40. Chemical History of the things which are taken by Animals.

*Next come Histories of Man.*

41. History of the Figure and External Limbs of Man, his Stature, Frame, Countenance and Features; and of the variety of the same according to Races and Climates, or other smaller differences.
42. Physiognomical History of the same.
43. Anatomical History, or of the Internal Members of Man; and of the variety of them, as it is found in the Natural Frame and Structure, and not merely as regards Diseases and Accidents out of the course of Nature.
44. History of the parts of Uniform Structure in Man; as Flesh, Bones, Membranes, &c.
45. History of Humours in Man; Blood, Bile, Seed, &c.
46. History of Excrements; Spittle, Urine, Sweats, Stools, Hair of the Head, Hairs of the Body, Whitlows, Nails, and the like.
47. History of Faculties; Attraction, Digestion, Retention, Expulsion, Sanguification, Assimilation of Aliment into

CATALOGUE OF

the members, conversion of Blood and Flower of Blood into Spirit, &c.

48. History of Natural and Involuntary Motions; as Motion of the Heart, the Pulses, Sneezing, Lungs, Erection, &c.
49. History of Motions partly Natural and partly Violent; as of Respiration, Cough, Urine, Stool, &c.
50. History of Voluntary Motions; as of the Instruments of Articulation of Words; Motions of the Eyes, Tongue, Jaws, Hands, Fingers; of Swallowing, &c.
51. History of Sleep and Dreams.
52. History of different habits of Body — Fat, Lean; of the Complexions (as they call them), &c.
53. History of the Generation of Man.
54. History of Conception, Vivification, Gestation in the Womb, Birth, &c.
55. History of the Food of Man; and of all things Eatable and Drinkable; and of all Diet; and of the variety of the same according to nations and smaller differences.
56. History of the Growth and Increase of the Body, in the whole and in its parts.
57. History of the Course of Age; Infancy, Boyhood, Youth, Old Age; of Length and Shortness of Life, and the like, according to nations and lesser differences.
58. History of Life and Death.
59. History Medicinal of Diseases, and the Symptoms and Signs of them.
60. History Medicinal of the Treatment and Remedies and Cures of Diseases.
61. History Medicinal of those things which preserve the Body and the Health.
62. History Medicinal of those things which relate to the Form and Complexion of the Body.
63. History Medicinal of those things which alter the Body, and pertain to Alterative Regimen.
64. History of Drugs.
65. History of Surgery.
66. Chemical History of Medicines.
67. History of Vision, and of things Visible.
68. History of Painting, Sculpture, Modelling, &c.
69. History of Hearing and Sound.

PARTICULAR HISTORIES.

70. History of Music.
71. History of Smell and Smells.
72. History of Taste and Tastes.
73. History of Touch, and the objects of Touch.
74. History of Venus, as a species of Touch.
75. History of Bodily Pains, as species of Touch.
76. History of Pleasure and Pain in general.
77. History of the Affections; as Anger, Love, Shame, &c.
78. History of the Intellectual Faculties; Reflexion, Imagination, Discourse, Memory, &c.
79. History of Natural Divinations.
80. History of Diagnostics, or Secret Natural Judgments.
81. History of Cookery, and the arts thereto belonging, as of the Butcher, Poulterer, &c.
82. History of Baking, and the Making of Bread, and the arts thereto belonging, as of the Miller, &c.
83. History of Wine.
84. History of the Cellar and of different kinds of Drink.
85. History of Sweetmeats and Confections.
86. History of Honey.
87. History of Sugar.
88. History of the Dairy.
89. History of Baths and Ointments.
90. Miscellaneous History concerning the care of the body,— as of Barbers, Perfumers, &c.
91. History of the working of Gold, and the arts thereto belonging.
92. History of the manufactures of Wool, and the arts thereto belonging.
93. History of the manufactures of Silk, and the arts thereto belonging.
94. History of manufactures of Flax, Hemp, Cotton, Hair, and other kinds of Thread, and the arts thereto belonging.
95. History of manufactures of Feathers.
96. History of Weaving, and the arts thereto belonging.
97. History of Dyeing.
98. History of Leather-making, Tanning, and the arts thereto belonging.
99. History of Ticking and Feathers.
100. History of working in Iron.

CATALOGUE OF PARTICULAR HISTORIES.

101. History of Stone-cutting.
102. History of the making of Bricks and Tiles.
103. History of Pottery.
104. History of Cements, &c.
105. History of working in Wood.
106. History of working in Lead.
107. History of Glass and all vitreous substances, and of Glass-making.
108. History of Architecture generally.
109. History of Waggons, Chariots, Litters, &c.
110. History of Printing, of Books, of Writing, of Sealing; of Ink, Pen, Paper, Parchment, &c.
111. History of Wax.
112. History of Basket-making.
113. History of Mat-making, and of manufactures of Straw, Rushes, and the like.
114. History of Washing, Scouring, &c.
115. History of Agriculture, Pasturage, Culture of Woods, &c.
116. History of Gardening.
117. History of Fishing.
118. History of Hunting and Fowling.
119. History of the Art of War, and of the arts thereto belonging, as Armoury, Bow-making, Arrow-making, Musketry, Ordnance, Cross-bows, Machines, &c.
120. History of the Art of Navigation, and of the crafts and arts thereto belonging.
121. History of Athletics and Human Exercise of all kinds.
122. History of Horsemanship.
123. History of Games of all kinds.
124. History of Jugglers and Mountebanks.
125. Miscellaneous History of various Artificial Materials,— as Enamel, Porcelain, various Cements, &c.
126. History of Salts.
127. Miscellaneous History of various Machines and Motions.
128. Miscellaneous History of Common Experiments which have not grown into an Art.

*Histories must also be written of Pure Mathematics; though they are rather observations than experiments.*

129. History of the Natures and Powers of Numbers.
130. History of the Natures and Powers of Figures.

**Figure 6**
Francis Bacon's list of planned natural histories. Francis Bacon, *The Great Instauration and the New Organon*. Vol. 4: The Works of Francis Bacon (London: Longman and Co., 1858, pp. 265–70).

### The Formation of Axioms

The store of information made available by a natural history, says Bacon, "may suffice for the formation of true axioms" (1858: 254). Induction to axioms is described by Bacon this way:

> In establishing axioms, another form of induction must be devised than has hitherto been employed; and it must be used for proving and discovering not first principles (as they are called) only, but also the lesser axioms, and the middle, and indeed all. . . . But the induction which is to be available for the discovery and demonstration of sciences and arts, must analyse nature by proper rejections and exclusions; and then, after a sufficient number of negatives, come to a conclusion on the affirmative instances (1858: 97).

As the passage below indicates, Bacon's inductive process is dynamic. General principles, just discovered, will at some time be swallowed by even more general principles or axioms.

> But in establishing axioms by this kind of induction, we must also examine and try whether the axiom so established be framed to the measure of those particulars only from which it is derived, or whether it be larger and wider. And if it be larger and wider, we must observe whether by indicating to us new particulars it confirm that wideness and largeness as by a collateral security; that we may not either stick fast in things already known, or loosely grasp at shadows and abstract forms; not at things solid and realised in matter. And when this process shall have come into use, then at least shall we see the dawn of a solid hope [for the advancement of science] (98).

In spite of Bacon's optimism, a number of obstacles thwarted Bacon's theory of induction, perhaps the worst being the youthful state of science. Bacon's exposition on induction, which is reminiscent of Descartes's description of the state of science, could not be supported by detailed experiment and observation because his proposed method of natural history had not yet built up a wealth of empirical information. When, in the second book of the *Novum organum,* Bacon applies his methodological principles by using tables and exclusions, he inevitably encounters problems with incomplete tables and ambiguous observation terms (Blake et al. 1960: 71). The unfortunate result was that Bacon got so caught up in the fact-collecting stage of science that, in practicing science, his efforts were so consumed in the gathering, ordering, and classifying of natural phenomena that he never got to the point to be able to deduce general principles (Rossi 1973: 175).

Second, special difficulties raised by induction first emerged after Hume had aired his criticisms. Bacon believed that every event had a cause that was simple enough to be discovered and recorded. In other words, he ignored the possibility that causes might be difficult or even impossible to discover.[10] In short, explains Anthony Quinton, "Bacon's theory of forms assumes away in advance the main difficulties that beset induction when it is conceived as a method of acquiring certain knowledge" (1980: 63).

**Bacon and Hypotheses**
The standard interpretation of Bacon's theory of induction rests on a view that he believed absolute truth in science would result by applying a mechanical method, a view for which support can be found.[11] Most philosophers attribute this position to Bacon and condemn it, but appreciate Bacon's emphasis on

---

10. Mill, on the other hand, improves on Bacon by recognizing two possible ways in which causes can be troublesome: the case of complex causes (a combination of causal factors working together to elicit an effect) and a plurality of causes (which Mill, however, thinks is not intractable because he is convinced it will be possible to find a common element). For more on this problem, see chapter 7.

11. As a distinguished proponent of the standard view, Hesse's summary conclusion of Bacon's contribution to methodology is worth citing in full.

[M]any things may be said in criticism of Bacon's method: he made little first-hand contribution to science by means of it, and his successors did not use it; he underestimated the place of hypothesis and of mathematics in scientific theories; he claimed a mechanical certainty for the method which is quite unjustified; and he failed to see the difficulties involved in introducing hidden entities and processes into science. On the other hand, it must be put to his credit that he encouraged detailed and methodical experimentation; he saw clearly the need to look for negative instances or refuting experiments in relation to all positive or confirmatory instances; he visualized a structure of scientific laws which is formally not unlike that of subsequent hypothetical-deductive systems; his tables of discovery constituted a method of systematic analogy which assisted the development of theoretical models; his influence in introducing mechanical hypotheses into seventeenth-century science can be compared with that of Descartes and Gassendi; and yet finally he did not allow the attractions of mechanism to blind him to the difficulties of pure atomism" (1964: 152).

experimentation. It is, however, important to caution that the inconsistencies in Bacon's works, added to the fact that he never finished *The Great Instauration*, cause "any reading of the philosopher's work . . . to be conjectural" (Urbach 1982: 113). But a view that Bacon opposed the hypothetico-deductive method pulls the mechanical interpretation out of context. Although Bacon does at times seem to advocate a mechanical procedure with his theory of induction, his theory of *anticipations* and endorsement of *interpretation* reveal not a mechanical method, but one that foreshadows the hypothetico-deductive method.

Numerous scholars have noted that hypotheses play a role in Baconian science. Michael Hattaway, for example, acknowledges that Bacon works mostly by analogies (1978: 184). Urbach shows how Bacon's method of *interpretation*, the preferred method, corresponds to Popper's method of conjectures and refutations, while the method of *anticipation*, which Bacon rejects, amounts to the dogmatic protection of (ad hoc) hypotheses (1982: 116–17).[12] A careful reading of Bacon reveals an opposition, not to hypotheses per se but to the dogmatic defense of speculations, especially those against which contrary evidence has accrued. In the following passage, Bacon uses the expression *new particulars* for what we would today call *novel facts.* "The axioms now in use, having been suggested by a scanty and manipular experience and a few particulars of most general occurrence, are made for the most part just large enough to fit and take these in: and therefore it is no wonder if they do not lead to new particulars. And if some opposite instance, not observed or not known before, chance to come in the way, the axiom is rescued and preserved by some frivolous distinction; whereas the truer course would be to correct the axiom itself" (1858: 51). Peter Urbach suggests that Bacon's idols are "psychological proclivities towards the method of anticipation," merely ad hoc theories whose removal "would produce not an empty mind, but a critical one" (1982: 119). In his view, then, Bacon is advocating

---

12. "The conclusions of human reason as ordinarily applied in matter of nature, I call for the sake of distinction *Anticipations of Nature* (as a thing rash or premature). That reason which is elicited from facts by a just and methodical process, I call *Interpretation of Nature*." Bacon adds that "no great progress [will] ever be made in science by means of anticipations" (1858: 51).

the method of testing hypotheses through a process of conducting new experiments on them.[13]

Although Urbach labels Bacon a falsificationist, Bacon did not
emphasize the use of hypotheses in science (although it is easy
to see that he assumes it) or build a theory of science around it.
As Hattaway explains, the notion of hypotheses in Bacon was
not "developed as a result of logical thinking about science but
in a context of thinking of new worlds, of the heavens and the
*terrae incognitae* of the explorers, and of worlds opened by linguistic creation" (1978: 184). What Urbach does convincingly is
explode the myth that Bacon's and Popper's philosophies of
science are poles. Bacon's frequent references to an infallible
method can perhaps be explained by the fact that he was trying
to sell his new theory to the king. After all, as Urbach interestingly notes, "Karl Popper's writings . . . show a remarkably
similar tension between his characteristic thesis that universal
theories are neither proved nor probabilified by evidence and
his frequently advanced claim that corroborated theories are
epistemologically meritorious and worth seeking out and relying upon in practical action" (1982: 130).

## A Closer Look at Newton's Third Step

After Bacon, perhaps the most noteworthy claim for induction
came from Isaac Newton. We have already mentioned the fact
that Newton labeled one part of his method, the third step,
inductive. It, nevertheless, has nothing to do with induction by
enumeration or by elimination. Although he never defines the
term, Newton uses *induction* in several key passages of both the
*Principia* and *Opticks*. In Rule 4 of his famous Rules of Reasoning
Newton, we recall, argued for this approach: "In experimental
philosophy we are to look upon propositions inferred by general
induction from phenomena as accurately or very nearly true"
(1962: 400). And in Query 31 of the *Opticks*, we find Newton

---

13. "But my course and method . . . is this,—not to extract works from works
or experiments from experiments (as an empiric), but from works and experiments to extract causes and axioms, and again from those causes and axioms
new works and experiments, as a legitimate interpreter of nature" (Bacon 1858:
104). Note that Bacon uses *axiom* loosely, sometimes to mean hypotheses,
sometimes laws or theories, and that the word *empiric* meant quack in his day.

expressing the view that "although the arguing from Experiments and Observations by Induction be no Demonstration of general Conclusions; yet it is the best way of arguing which the Nature of Things admits of, and must be looked upon as so much the stronger, by how much the Induction is more general" (1952: 404). This sounds much like Newton's Third Rule of Reasoning: "For since the qualities of bodies are only known to us by experiments, we are to hold for universal all such as universally agree with experiments" (1962: 398). Whereas there is no doubt that by *induction* Newton sometimes means drawing conclusions from experiments and observations, by *induction from experience* he often means deduction from phenomena (Passmore 1980: 51).[14]

We recall that induction, the third step of Newton's method, is a generalization of experimental results, and not an application of the generalization to other cases to test its adequacy, which is synthesis, the fourth step of his method. There is a sense—albeit a restricted one—in which Newton's inductive method is a kind of method of discovery with Baconian overtones. The apple tree anecdote used to illustrate the law of gravity, popularized by both Voltaire and Newton (Jacquette 1990: 661), is one such example of his attitude toward inductive generalization: it exemplifies the Second Rule of Reasoning, which specifies that effects of the same kind known to have the same properties have the same causes. The "descent of stones in *Europe* and in *America*" is one example that Newton offers to illustrate Rule 2 (1962: 398).

It is, however, the anti-Baconian aspect of Newton's theory of induction that is dominant. Although Newton indicates that induction is stronger "by how much the Induction is more general," he does not mean that the scientist collects as many positive instances as humanly possible to substantiate a theory or hypothesis. What he had in mind instead was a single, well-contrived experiment to answer a specific question. This position put Newton in direct opposition to Bacon and fellow Royal Society member Robert Boyle, "the father of chemistry," who advocated hundreds of trials before generalizing. It was, then,

---

14. Here Newton follows Descartes, who also uses *induction* and *deduction* interchangeably, as we saw in chapter 2.

Newton who gave the concept *crucial experiment* its modern meaning: "Newton thus appears more anti-inductivist than inductivist, especially as the role of the crucial experiment apparently must have been for him, not the elimination of competing hypotheses, but the very formation of the law to be 'rendered general by induction'" (Hintikka/Remes 1974: 111). Newton's interpreters, by the way, did not feel obliged to follow Newton on this point. Thus, we find Henry Pemberton interpreting Rule 4 of Newton's "System of the World" exactly as Boyle, rather than Newton, would have it: "The only caution here required is, that the observations and experiments, we argue upon, be numerous enough, and that due regard be paid to all objections, that occur, as the Lord BACON very judiciously directs" (1728: 25).[15]

## The Myth of Causality and Its Consequences

### Hume and Skepticism

The history of science, observes D. C. Stove, is filled with makers and breakers: Newton was a grandiose maker; Hume, the most famous breaker of all time (1977: 189). Indeed, once Hume wrote on the existence of God, arguments from is to ought, universal causation, and induction, these topics would never again be the same.

Before going into the details of Hume's theory of induction, we need to dispose of the issue of Hume's skepticism. It involves more than just the issue of whether Hume was really a radical skeptic. Some Hume specialists, swimming against the general intellectual current, even assert that Hume was not a skeptic at all.[16] Stove stresses that the specialists are wrong (1977), and the evidence supports him. It is hard to ignore the fact that Hume's skeptical views were met with hostility in his lifetime. His reputation as a skeptic prevented him from being named to the chair of ethics and pneumatical philosophy at Edinburgh University

---

15. Pemberton illustrates the rule with an example comparing two phenomena, gravity and the impenetrability of bodies, and concludes that "this rule will more strongly hold in this case . . . because there will *more instances* be had of bodies gravitating, than of their being impenetrable [emphasis added]" (1728: 26).

16. This position is held most notably by Norman Kemp Smith in his *Philosophy of David Hume* (1966).

in 1744 and the chair in logic at Glasgow University in 1751. But on this issue we can take Hume at his word: "[T]he philosophy contain'd in this book is very sceptical," he wrote in the *Abstract of a Treatise of Human Nature,* his own review of the book, "and tends to give us a notion of the imperfections and narrow limits of human understanding" (1965: 24).

The question of the degree of intensity of Hume's skepticism remains. N. Scott Arnold (1983), Robert Butts (1959), David Norton (1968), and numerous others argue forcefully that Hume does not embrace radical or total skepticism. It is certainly true that he does not deny the existence of causal connections or the necessity of having to infer from factual evidence. Hume himself termed his skepticism modest. In the *Letter from a Gentleman,* Hume's reply to those who opposed his appointment to a university chair, he is quoted as saying his skepticism is "*Modesty* then, and *Humility,* with regard to the operation of our natural Faculties" (in Norton 1968: 164). Before forming a final judgment, we need to take a closer look at Hume's theory of causation.

## Hume's Theory of Causation
David Hume is given the distinction of having first formulated the problem of induction: Under which conditions is induction rationally justified? His answer to the problem of induction, in a nutshell, is that there is only a succession of events and no reason to believe that what is observed will hold for the unobserved. Hume's point is very simple and has often been illustrated this way: No matter how many black ravens we encounter, we can never infer from these findings that all ravens are black, or even that the next raven we encounter will be black. Hume sees that the inductive justification of induction is circular: inferring the future success of the inductive method from past successes invokes the very principle whose justification is sought, and so we enter the "Humean circle."[17] Justification of

---

17. In Hume's words: "When a man says, *I have found, in all past instances, such sensible qualities conjoined with such secret powers:* And when he says, *Similar sensible qualities will always be conjoined with similar secret powers,* he is not guilty of a tautology, nor are these propositions in any respect the same. You say that one proposition is an inference from the other. But you must confess that the inference is not intuitive; neither is it demonstrative. Of what nature is it, then? To say it is experimental, is begging the question. For all inferences from experience suppose, as their foundation, that the future will resemble the past, and that similar powers will be conjoined with similar sensible qualities. If

induction by deductive argument also fails because the conclusion goes beyond what is contained in the theory's premises. Thus Hume is forced to conclude that inductive inference cannot be given a rational foundation.

Hume's view of induction, established after the publication of his *Enquiry concerning Human Understanding* in 1748, jeopardized the validity of the "inductive" inferences that held up Newton's system. Contemporaries believed that if Hume was right, Newton's science rested on an edifice that was not rational. Indeed, it is difficult to ignore Hume's conclusions, for a satisfactory account of induction is required in order to formulate a theory of causality, to generalize scientific laws, and to predict.

Taking a closer look at the problem of induction, we find that Hume never uses the word *induction*,[18] although he recognizes that the validity of generalizations depends on the uniformity of nature and explains both how uniformity must be formulated in order to warrant generalizations and how it cannot be obtainable from experience (Blake et al. 1960: 152). All reasoning concerning matter of fact, according to Hume, is founded on the relation of cause and effect, for "we can never infer the existence of one object from another, unless they be connected together, either mediately or immediately. In order therefore to understand these reasonings, we must be perfectly acquainted with the idea of a cause; and in order to [do] that, must look about us to find something that is the cause of another" (Hume 1965: 11).[19]

---

there be any suspicion that the course of nature may change, and that the past may be no rule for the future, all experience becomes useless, and can give rise to no inference or conclusion" (1975: 37–38).

18. This is unexpected, for both Bacon and Newton before him used the term. Perhaps Hume noted variances in its meaning, or wished to distance himself from the inductive position taken by other Scottish philosophers of the day (see next section).

19. I am relying heavily here on Hume's *Abstract of a Treatise of Human Nature* (1740), which, Keynes and Sraffa tell us, he originally intended to offer as an anonymous review to the periodical *History of the Works of the Learned*. When, by the summer of 1739, six months after his *Treatise of Human Nature* had appeared, it still had not received a review, Hume was so distressed that he felt compelled to write his own review. In his autobiography, he remarks that the *Treatise* "fell *dead-born from the press,* without reaching such distinction as even to excite a murmur among the zealots" (n.d.: 4). Shortly before Hume planned to send off the *Abstract,* an extensive review appeared in the November/December issue of the same journal. And so it was that the 32-page abstract was published in 1740 as a separate pamphlet, "An Abstract of a Book Lately Published; entitled A Treatise of Human Nature, Etc."

The thing Hume finds is a billiard ball, which, upon hitting a second ball, represents "as perfect an instance of the relation of cause and effect as any which we know, either by sensation or reflection" (1965: 11). His point is that anyone can see that the same cause always produces the same effect. Cautioning that "no inference from cause to effect amounts to a demonstration," he adds: "It follows, then, that all reasonings concerning cause and effect, are founded on experience, and that all reasonings from experience are founded on the supposition, that the course of nature will continue uniformly the same. We conclude, that like causes, in like circumstances, will always produce like effects" (1965: 14–15). Hume declares that this is "the case when both the cause and the effect are present to the senses" (13) and then notes that we should consider using the past record as a guide to the future.

Since the course of nature is not uniform, he argues, it is not possible to prove "by any *probable* arguments, that the future must be conformable to the past" (1965: 15). We can only establish a resemblance between the past and future. What makes us believe that the future is conformable to the past is custom or habit. "When I see a billiard-ball moving towards another, my mind is immediately carry'd by habit to the usual effect, and anticipates my sight by conceiving the second ball in motion." But, Hume cautions, "[t]here is nothing in these objects, abstractly considered, and independent of experience, which leads me to form any such conclusion" (16). He concludes that it is not "reason, which is the guide of life, but custom" that is the "standard of our future judgments" (22).[20]

Hume's answer, then, to how anticipations of the future (predictions) are related to past experience is that regularities give rise to a habit of expectation. The next question is: Why should we prefer one prediction to another? Hume responds that we do so because it accords with past regularity. Nelson Goodman

---

20. Elsewhere he puts it this way: "No matter of fact can be proved but from its cause or its effect. Nothing can be known to be the cause of another but by experience. We can give no reason for extending to the future our experience in the past; but are entirely determined by custom, when we conceive an effect to follow from its usual cause. But we also believe an effect to follow, as well as conceive it . . . Belief, therefore, in all matters of fact arises only from custom, and is an idea conceived in a peculiar *manner*" (1965: 19).

notes that critics of Hume's account point out that tracing origins is not the same thing as establishing validity (1973: 60). The real question for them is how prediction is justified; but A. J. Ayer objects, claiming that justification does not square with Hume's purpose. "What we want and cannot obtain, except by circular argument, is a justification for our actual interpretation of the lessons of the past; a justification for adhering to a special corpus of beliefs. That we cannot obtain it is an insight which we owe to Hume" (1980: 74).

Although Hume proves that there is no necessary connection between events, he does not conclude there is no reason to trust inference from factual evidence.[21] He believes we can find laws, as this passage from his *Abstract* reveals. "If, in examining several phaenomena, we find that they resolve themselves into one common principle, and can trace this principle into another, we shall at last arrive at those few simple principles, on which all the rest depend. And tho' we can never arrive at the ultimate principles, 'tis a satisfaction to go as far as our faculties will allow us" (1965: 6). On the other hand, there is no reason to put all factual reasoning on the same footing, or to take the liberty of extrapolating from the past to the future any way we wish, for in that case there would be no reason to advocate the experimental method (Ayer 1980: 70).

There is no escaping the Humean circle: the problem of causality, as formulated, is unsolvable. Yet the need to evaluate the impact of experimental results remains. We need to be able to answer the question, How strong is the evidence? Many scholars, including Hume and Bacon, thought that a sufficiently large number of confirming instances constituted evidential grounds for the likelihood of a theory's truth, especially where no or only a few negative instances were found. While Boyle and Hooke, for instance, emphasized that the test of a hypothesis was its forecasting ability, they also defended the view that the more confirming instances that are found, the more probable is the hypothesis.

Because gaining reliable knowledge in natural and moral philosophy is difficult, much of Hume's effort is devoted to the

---

21. "What he neither proved nor even sought to prove was that the consequence is that the beliefs should be abandoned" (Ayer 1980: 74).

problem of sifting through evidence, in particular, to determining how we can estimate the relative strength of evidence and
know which evidence is reliable.[22] In the section of the *Enquiry
concerning Human Understanding* entitled "Of Miracles," Hume
writes: "Though experience be our only guide in reasoning
concerning matters of fact; it must be acknowledged, that this
guide is not altogether infallible, but in some cases is apt to lead
us into errors" (1975: 110). His answer to this problem and
advice to the scientist is lengthy but well worth noting:

A wise man . . . proportions his belief to the evidence. In such conclusions as are founded on an infallible experience, he expects the event
with the last degree of assurance, and regards his past experience as
a full *proof* of the future existence of that event. In other cases, he
proceeds with more caution: He weighs the opposite experiments: He
considers which side is supported by the greater number of experiments: to that side he inclines, with doubt and hesitation; and when
at last he fixes his judgement, the evidence exceeds not what we
properly call *probability*. All probability, then, supposes an opposition
of experiments and observations, where the one side is found to
overbalance the other, and to produce a degree of evidence, propor-
tional to the superiority. A hundred instances or experiments on one
side, and fifty on another, afford a doubtful expectation of any event;
though a hundred uniform experiments, with only one that is contradictory, reasonably beget a pretty strong degree of assurance. In all
cases, we must balance the opposite experiments, where they are
opposite, and deduct the smaller number from the greater, in order to
know the exact force of the superior evidence (1975: 110–11).

Hume gives a similar answer to the same question in his "Of
the Rise and Progress of the Arts and Sciences"; in essence, it is
a rule for using inductive procedures. "The distinguishing between chance and causes must depend upon every particular
man's sagacity, in considering every particular incident. But, if
I were to assign any general rule to help us in applying this
distinction, it would be the following, *What depends upon a few
persons is, in a great measure, to be ascribed to chance, or secret and
unknown causes: What arises from a great number, may often be
accounted for by determinate and known causes* (1875: 175).

22. Butts formulates the point this way: "Hume was not interested in marking
off precisely types of statements [as analytic from synthetic statements], but
in discovering the kinds of evidence permissible for any kinds of statements
whatever" (1959: 415).

## "Plebian Induction" and Induction to Theories

Laudan (1981) notes that there is more to Hume's problem of induction than this. He rightly observes that it has been fashionable, since Keynes and Peirce, to subsume everything not falling under deductive inference under induction, a practice that blurs distinctions between various types of ampliative inference. To shed light on the situation, he draws a useful distinction between two types of induction, *plebian induction*, which he unfortunately attributes to Hume, and *aristocratic induction*, or induction to theories.

Laudan (1981: 73) formulates the problem of plebian induction this way:

Given a universal empirical generalization and a certain number of positive instances of it, to what degree do the latter constitute evidence for the warranted assertion of the former? (1981: 73).

With plebian induction we know that all positive instances of a general statement are true because they are observable. For Laudan plebian induction is Humean because most of Hume's illustrations of induction deal with observable events, objects, and processes, such as the sun's rising tomorrow (75). I return to Laudan's interpretation of Hume after discussing the second type of induction.

Induction to theories, on the other hand, involves testing a theoretical statement that contains terms with no direct connection to observables (hence, theoretical statements may have confirming instances but not positive confirming instances). Laudan formulates the problem of induction to theories this way:

Given a theory, and a certain number of confirming instances of it, to what degree do the latter constitute evidence for the warranted assertion of the former?" (1981: 74).

Induction to theories involves drawing conclusions about the truth status of a theoretical statement on the strength of its known confirming instances.[23] The problem that arises is this: true conclusions can be drawn from false premises. In other words, a number of confirming instances cannot establish the truth of a theory.

---

23. Note that Lauden uses *positive instances* to denote observable supporting instances, *confirming instances* to indicate nonobservables.

It is clear that the philosophical issues posed by the two types
of induction are different. The problems plebian induction poses
are quite trivial. If nature were uniform, we would have a
solution to plebian induction. Not so with induction to theories,
for it makes a claim about processes that is not directly testable.
With induction to theories, all confirming instances of a theoretical statement could be true even when the statement is false.
The problem induction to theories poses is that experience cannot discriminate between competing theories that are observa-
tionally equivalent. This problem had a long tradition before
Hume, arising in the astronomy of the Middle Ages and Renaissance after multiple hypotheses describing the motions of
planets came into existence. By the sixteenth and seventeenth
centuries, argues Laudan, the skeptical approach to induction to
theories had moved out of astronomy into "a general critique of
the role of empirical science in authenticating theoretical claims"
(1981: 82).[24]

I have chosen to elaborate on Laudan's interpretation of
Hume's theory of causation both for its faults and its virtues.
Paying particular attention to the two types of induction is
crucial because induction has generated so much confusion.
Laudan's chief message—the mistakenness of the view that plebian induction is archetypal in science—is well worth emphasizing. "We have rejected . . . plebian epistemology, in large
measure because it offers an impoverished account of scientific
knowledge; yet we have retained his [i.e., Hume's] formulation
of the inductive problem, refusing to face up to the equal injus-
tice it does to an understanding of scientific inference," concludes Laudan (1981: 83).

We now turn to Laudan's interpretation of Hume. Limiting
theoretical statements to only those terms that refer to observables, says Laudan, "is a little embarrassing for Hume, or at least
it ought to have been, since most of the best known theories of
Hume's day—including those of Newton, Descartes, Boerhaave,
Huygens, and Boyle—did not consist primarily of statements
which could be said to have positive instances. These theories
involved numerous statements about various unobservable en-

24. Laudan refutes Hacking's claim that Hume was the first to formulate the
skeptical problem of induction and that before 1660 there was no concept of
inductive evidence (1975, ch. 19).

tities—atoms, subtle fluids, imperceptible forces, and the like" (1981: 75). Laudan attributes Hume's supposed use of plebian induction and his neglect of induction to theories by "his almost unparalleled ignorance of the science of his time" (1981: 83). As we learned in chapter 2, this prejudice of modern scholarship has been soundly discredited.

On several issues in the history of philosophy Laudan unfortunately goes very wrong. Many of the misunderstandings surrounding Hume's theory of causality rest on exegetical problems specific to both Hume's and Smith's writings. While the individual arguments of both authors are easy to understand, grasping the way in which they bear on each other can be highly problematic. Hume is certainly interested in the nonobservable mechanisms of the physical world: this interest is most notably reflected in his preoccupation with Newton's design argument (see Force 1987). After all, the principles of human nature, the object of Hume's science, are unobservable, but may "be discovered by careful conjectures, which at the same time go beyond observation *and* are based on it; and simplicity can be a goal for science because science dares to go beyond the limits of simple induction" (Montiero 1981: 341–42).

It would be unfair not to note that numerous passages in Hume's writings do appear to confirm Laudan's view that he is interested only in observables. Yet this interpretation goes completely against the temper of the times, for the principal function of the eighteenth-century philosopher, Henry Guerlac reminds us, was "to suggest plausible mechanisms . . . of the 'secret motions of things'" (1965: 322). And indeed, that was what both Hume and Smith were doing. "We are placed in this world, as in a great theatre, where the true springs and causes of every event are entirely concealed from us," writes Hume in *The Natural History of Religion* (1976: 33). Montiero's depiction of Humean science is lengthy but captures its true flavor:

Human beings (and also animals) have an instinct which causes them to expect in the future the same regularities they have experienced in the past. These regularities are composed of observable objects or events, which are commonly called causes and effects. But these observable regularities are produced by unobservable mechanisms, and it is with these that science is primarily concerned. They are the unknown causes of all phenomena; they are concealed, unattainable by the senses, and are not possible of inductive inference; but they are not entirely unknowable. Men are sometimes able to frame hypotheses concerning them, by which these causes may be said, in some degree, to be discovered. These hypotheses are always explanatory conjectures: they aim at accounting for the visible phenomena and are partly based on observation of these phenomena. Their explanatory power is what gives them plausibility in our eyes (1981: 342).[25]

Laudan is, nevertheless, right about Hume's preoccupation with observables for several reasons.[26] First, he was interested in illuminating the most basic, simplest inductive processes—not the higher processes—in order to convince readers to be skeptical of ultimate causal connections. If at the most basic, simplest level there is no necessary causal connection between events, then it cannot be otherwise at higher levels. Such an approach, I might add, is to be expected, for it is fully in keeping with the Scottish method of natural history. Second, Hume's purpose was to purge causal conceptions of their rationalism, not to provide a logic of natural science. Third, Hume was a moral philosopher and, as Livingston so forcefully argues, "[i]t is a favorite theme of Hume's that the moral world, being the result of human feeling and opinion, can be understood by men without the need to posit the existence of exotic theoretical entities such as light waves and gravitational forces" (1984: 198).

This last point needs to be explained, for when Hume extends his theory of causality to moral philosophy, he gives it a small twist. Moral philosophy has an advantage over natural philosophy, he contends, because it has an additional mode of making the data intelligible. In the *Treatise of Human Nature,* Hume argues that moral philosophers explain human action in a way not available to natural philosophers. "We must certainly allow, that the cohesion of the parts of matter arises from natural and necessary principles, whatever difficulty we may find in explaining them: And for a like reason we must allow, that human society is founded on like principles; and our reason in the latter

---

25. Montiero, however, incorrectly interprets Hume's theory of causation (as opposed to his theory of science, which he correctly interprets) as requiring that causes and effects, like the famous billiard balls, be observable.

26. In this section, I am greatly indebted to Livingston (1984), who explains Hume's views on causality in natural and moral philosophy in chapters 6 and 7 of his *Hume's Philosophy on Common Life,* which, by the way, seems to be, by far, the best interpretation of Hume's theory of science available.

case, is better than even that in the former; because we not only observe, that men *always* seek society, but can also explain the principles, on which this universal propensity is founded" (1896: 401–2). Hume's message is this: The assumption that "men always seek society" is a regularity (a moral force of attraction) explainable by men's psychological and physiological needs; it is a regularity rendered more intelligible than Newton's principle that "bodies attract as the inverse square of their distance" (a physical force of attraction), for the former is capable of being apprehended not only empirically but also morally (Livingston 1984: 194).

Finally, Laudan misses the point that Hume's theory of causality ends in philosophical theism. "The whole frame of nature bespeaks an intelligent author," says Hume, "and no rational enquirer can, after serious reflexion, suspend his belief a moment with regard to the primary principles of genuine Theism and Religion" (1967: 25). Thus, Hume adopts pure theism and accepts the argument from design. But whereas Newton, Boyle, and others believed scientific reasoning could provide grounds for belief in a supreme intelligence, Hume asserted that the belief in a supreme intelligent author provides grounds for scientific thinking (Livingston 1984: 178). For Hume, "God as revealed in the presuppositions of science and in the argument from design is simply the ultimate cause of all order in the universe" (180). We grasp the idea of divine power in much the same way as we comprehend gravity—not by direct experience but by events that support or falsify a hypothesis about it (181).

In time, Hume's problem of induction would eventually be displaced by the problem of how to substantiate a hypothesis, which is known in the literature of the twentieth century as the problem of confirmation. Instead of asking how to justify induction, scientists increasingly turned to the issue of how to identify "confirmable" and "nonconfirmable" hypotheses. Realizing that not all positive instances of a generalization lend it support, philosophers sought to discover when positive instances provide grounds for predicting other such instances. This part of the history of induction is far too intricate a subject to be dealt with in any detail here. Although I return to it in the section on probability, the reader is directed to Goodman (1973) and

Salmon (1973) for a fuller history of the movement. I now revisit the Scottish moral philosophers, who, unfortunately, did little to clarify induction as Newton and Hume had left it.

## Induction in the Hands of the Scots

The Scots—and thinkers in the Scottish tradition, such as Herschel and Mill, were no exceptions—loved to call their method inductive while relying, in practice, on a combination of induction and deduction. McCosh gives the Scottish school credit for "being the first, avowedly and knowingly, to follow the inductive method, and to employ it systematically in psychological investigation" (1990: 3). The Scottish philosophers of the eighteenth century were convinced that their method of induction, which proceeds by observation and experiment, distinguished the school from all previous generations. Other philosophies and inquiries, they thought, "were conducted in the dogmatic, or deductive, or analytic manner, explaining phenomena by assumed principles, or bringing facts to support theories" (2). In their view, the dogmatic spirit had first been banished from natural philosophy in the sixteenth century by Bacon, and then by Newton and the Royal Society of London. Bacon and Newton, above all, were their heroes.

One of the clearest definitions of induction is given by David Fordyce in his article in the first edition of the *Encyclopaedia Britannica* on moral philosophy. In his view, induction is the binding element between moral and natural philosophy.

Moral Philosophy has this in common with Natural Philosophy, that it appeals to nature or fact; depends on observation; and builds its reasoning on plain uncontroverted experiments, or upon the fullest induction of particulars of which the subject will admit. We must observe, in both these sciences, how nature is affected, and what her conduct is in such and such circumstances. Or, in other words, we must collect the appearances of nature in any given instance; trace these to some general principles, or laws of operation; and then apply these principles or laws to the explaining of other phenomena (1771, 3: 270).

Here we encounter a conflation of several scientific processes very similar to those that we found in Bacon. There is a reference to a collection of facts, to experimentation, to the assembly of the "fullest" number of positive instances, to an inference from the facts to general principles, and to broader generalization. Induction in this passage is obviously being used in the sense of the general process or main steps of scientific inquiry. The conflation of numerous scientific operations is, we will see, but one factor at the bottom of the confusion with the Scottish position.

George Turnbull (1698–1748), writes McCosh, "was the first metaphysician of the Scottish . . . school to announce unambiguously and categorically that we ought to proceed in the method of induction in investigating the human mind" (1990: 99). Turnbull, for whom induction was broadly termed "a method of investigation," recognized that experiments were made in natural philosophy and that philosophers reasoned from those experiments (1976: 2). As Turnbull sees it, reasoning from experiments has the same relation to moral philosophy that mathematical truths have to natural philosophy: moral philosophy is a mixed science of observation and reasoning from principles known by experience (McCosh 1990: 100). Once facts are extracted from experience, thought Turnbull, we can reason deductively from them. McCosh, however, comments that this is really a method similar to J. S. Mill's deductive method, which, we will see, is both inductive and deductive (100).[27] By using this method, an established order and reliable general laws can be discovered that will demonstrate divine wisdom and the progressiveness of knowledge. An outgrowth of this belief was Turnbull's view that language is built on facts and universal feelings and thus expresses universal sentiments among man.

The eighteenth-century Scottish philosophers saw their first task as preparing a natural history and tables (on, for example, fear, anger, virtue, modesty, and other sentiments) to serve the infant science of moral philosophy, just as Bacon's tables had served as the foundation of natural philosophy. They repeatedly cited Bacon's view on the unity of method, along with the closing remark in Newton's *Opticks* that moral philosophy will "be enlarged" by natural philosophy's continuing perfection.

---

27. John Stuart Mill's Scottish heritage may well be the reason for his confusing and confused views on induction and deduction (which I analyze in part 2).

Thomas Hobbes, on the other hand, is the butt of much criticism because he did not follow his friend Bacon, while John Locke is praised for proceeding by observation but reprimanded for not acknowledging it. Although some philosophers had interpreted René Descartes as proceeding by the method of induction, notes McCosh, the Scots were convinced that he did not arrive at laws by gradual generalization (1990: 3). Instead, the heart of Descartes's method, as far as they were concerned, was a geometric plan, a "joint dogmatic and deductive method" (3).

The object of Scottish Enlightenment science was the human mind, and the human mind was to be studied exclusively by the method of observation and experimentation. Although the Scottish philosophers said they conducted experiments, they used the word *experiment,* as I mentioned earlier, as a technical term unrelated to its usual meaning. "Self-consciousness" or "introspection" was the instrument of observation and the basis for experimentation. Bacon, the Scots thought, had no understanding of the way observation should be carried out (McCosh 1990: 4); and, in fact, Bacon does not say anything about the correct method of experimentation. *Self-consciousness, inward experience,* and *internal sense* were all expressions used by the Scots to mean introspection or inner reflection and to designate their method of experimentation. This tool, they felt, guaranteed their results as scientific and allowed them to conclude that certain human traits were timeless and uniform and thus could be anticipated or predicted.

The Scottish philosophers believed that a science of human nature could be erected not by looking into the soul of man, but by surveying human thoughts and feelings and actions and comprehending language as an expression of human sentiment. Human actions and language were proof that principles of the mind exist. They "professed to draw all the laws of mental philosophy—indeed, their whole systems—from the observations of consciousness" (McCosh 1990: 4). Only through introspection, they thought, could man understand the mind and its various operations; knowledge acquired by any other manner "must ever be regarded as subordinate and subsidiary" (5). Theory meant referring particular operations to general principles or referring particular effects to the causes from which they proceed. Verification of theories was a relatively simple process: it meant widening the field of observation (Bryson 1968: 17).

What Adam Smith has to say about induction is worth careful consideration here, for his views illustrate a mixing of the process of investigation with the process of inferring from particulars that was typical in this age. In the *Theory of Moral Sentiments,* Smith explains how general principles are formed.

The general maxims of morality are formed, like all other general maxims, from experience and induction. We observe in a great variety of particular cases what pleases or displeases our moral faculties, what these approve or disprove of, and, by induction from this experience, we establish those general rules. But induction is always regarded as one of the operations of reason. From reason, therefore, we are very properly said to derive all those general maxims and ideas (1976b: 319).

Although he does not provide us with a definition of induction, Smith appears to use the word to mean both generalization from particulars and from universal or a priori principles. In the passage above Smith starts by describing a process of reasoning from something known—individual instances—to something unknown—a class or whole. The problem is the word *reason:* from reason we can deduce a generalized conclusion from particular instances (induction as we use the term today) or we can deduce particulars from general or universal principles (deduction in its modern sense). Although in this passage Smith refers to induction from particulars, he no doubt proceeds in both directions when constructing a philosophical system: once the psychological principles are established, he goes on to deduce facts from them. It was this ambivalence, by the way, that allowed a debate on the "true nature" of the method of *The Wealth of Nations*—deductive or inductive?—to rage for literally generations.[28]

A few lines later Smith tells us that general principles are, nonetheless, the result not of reason but of experience.

28. A century after *The Wealth of Nations* appeared, Ingram bemoaned the unresolved state of the situation: "There have been great differences of opinion as to the method of economic inquiry pursued by Adam Smith. Mr. Lowe insists that his method was deductive—that he had the unique merit of having raised the study of a branch of human transactions to the dignity of a deductive science. At the same celebration at which this opinion was put forward, Professor Thorold Rogers expressed his surprise that anyone should entertain such a view. It seemed to him clear that Adam Smith was pre-eminently an inductive philosopher" (1962: 62). Buckle's position (1861) falls at the extreme end of the spectrum, with those claiming Smith's method was deductive.

These first perceptions, as well as all other experiments upon which any general rules are founded, cannot be the object of reason, but of immediate sense and feeling. It is by finding in a vast variety of instances that one tenor of conduct constantly pleases in a certain manner, and that another as constantly displeases the mind, that we form the general rules of morality (1976b: 320).

In this passage Smith is describing an act of discovery and a process of investigation rather than a process of deducing a generalized conclusion from the facts. The process of investigation is empirical in nature and prior to the process of deducing an inference from the facts, but both processes would be dubbed inductive today. It is, however, not difficult to see how the casual reader could be tempted to set these passages against one another as proof of contradiction. The problem is, as Vincent Bevilacqua aptly puts it, that "Smith maintains with the rationalists that there are propensities of the mind prior to experience, but rejects any such propensities which are beyond observation. He holds with the empiricists . . . that the nature of the mind can be determined only by observation, but holds in opposition connatural propensities (like sympathy) implanted exclusive of experience" (1965: 49).

This, then, is the manifest illogic that permeates the Scottish position on induction. McCosh had caught the major contradiction by 1875: The Scottish philosophers believed observations of consciousness would lay bare general principles reached prior to and independent of experience, at the same time insisting that a science of the mind can be constructed solely on observation from facts of experience (1990: 4–7).[29] Maintaining this contradiction allowed them to believe their school superior to both empiricism and dogmatic a priori speculation. But the contradiction could exist because they used the term *observation* ambiguously to refer to both sensory experience and introspection as a mental operation.

Besides the fact that the word *induction* was being used to mean the general process of scientific investigation, there are several other possible reasons why the Scots (Hume is an exception) called their method inductive when it was really both

---

29. To quote McCosh once more, "men of ability in Scotland have commonly been more distinguished by their tendency to inward reflection than inclination to sensuous observation" (1990: 8).

inductive and deductive. The confusion is easier to understand if we keep in mind that until their time the words *infer* and *deduce* were used as synonyms and *inference* (whether inductive or deductive) seems to have been equated with induction.[30] Moreover, their mentors, Bacon and Newton, both used the word *induction* ambiguously. By induction from phenomena Newton usually meant deduction. As far as I can determine, it was Richard Whately, who, in 1826, first saw clearly that the word *induction* was being employed confusingly to designate sometimes "the process of *investigation* and of collecting facts" and at other times "the deducing of an inference *from* those facts" (1988: 208). At any rate, we should regard as exaggeration Henry Buckle's assertion (1861) that the stronghold of theologians over seventeenth-century Scotland explains the Scots' claim of adopting induction to the exclusion of deduction.[31]

## Induction's Heyday: Herschel, Mill, and Whewell

Inductive reasoning for Herschel means examining all the particular cases, piecing together the results of observation, and generalizing from them (1831: 198, §210). In his view, induction ensures not mathematical, but practical, certainty. Herschel distinguishes between two levels of induction: one that yields lower laws of generality (what we today would call empirical laws based on observables) and a second that entails the formation of theories or laws of higher generality (in today's jargon theoretical laws involving nonobservables). He puts it this way: "[W]hen we have amassed a great store of such *general facts*, they become the objects of another and higher species of classification, and are themselves included in laws which, as they dispose of groups, not individuals, have a far superior degree of generality, till at length, by continuing the process, we arrive at *axioms* of the highest degree of generality of which science is capable. This process is what we mean by induction" (1831: 102, §94/95).

---

30. The third edition of the *Encyclopaedia Britannica* gives the definition of *induction* in logic and rhetoric as "a consequence drawn from several propositions or principles first laid down"—in other words, deduction ("Induction," 1797: 218).

31. Smith's dislike of deductive systems was a reaction to the systems of Descartes, Hobbes, and others and not just to the Church.

Deferring to Newton, Herschel assumes that mathematics will be used to discover laws of higher generality (1831: 199, §211). "What we have then in Herschel," observes Richard Blackwell, "is a conception of science as a pyramid of laws of phenomena, which express proximate causes only, and which grows by inductive accretion"—a modern definition of induction (1974: 201).

Inductive reasoning is, however, not the only way to arrive at laws. Herschel names two other possibilities for doing so: by forming "bold hypotheses" or using processes that combine induction and bold hypotheses (1831: 198–99, §210). I have already mentioned Herschel's stance favoring the use of both inductive and deductive methods of inquiry as complementary processes. He, in fact, often calls deduction "inverse induction" (174, §184). Induction and deduction "may be said to go hand in hand, the one verifying the conclusions deduced by the other; and the combination of experiment and theory, which may thus be brought to bear in such cases, forms an engine of discovery infinitely more powerful than either taken separately" (181, §189).

Herschel finds hypotheses fruitful in several ways. First, they are useful in discovering laws and making novel predictions. "Hypotheses, with respect to theories, are what presumed proximate causes are with respect to particular inductions: they afford us motives for searching into analogies; grounds of citation to bring before us all the cases which seem to bear upon them, for examination. A well imagined hypothesis, if it have been suggested by a fair inductive consideration of general laws, can hardly fail at least of enabling us to generalize a step farther, and group together several such laws under a more universal expression" (1831: 196, §208). Second, they are a necessary part of the verification process, that is, of checking hypotheses. When we have two rival theories, Bacon's *instantia crucis*[32] or crucial instances become useful in the verification process: "When two theories run parallel to each other, and each explains a great many facts in common with the other, any experiment which affords a crucial instance to decide between them, or by which one or other must fall, is of great importance" (206, §218).[33] The

---

32. Mill prefers the term *experimentum crucis.*
33. Consider also Herschel's comment that crucial instances afford "the readiest and securest means of eliminating extraneous causes, and deciding between rival hypotheses" (1831: 186, §196).

verification process is described more elaborately in this passage.

> Whenever, therefore, we think we have been led by induction to the knowledge of the proximate cause of a phenomenon or of a law of nature, our next business is to examine deliberately and *seriatim* all the cases we have collected of its occurrence, in order to satisfy ourselves that they are explicable by our cause, or fairly included in the expression of our law: and in case any exception occurs, it must be carefully noted and set aside for re-examination at a more advanced period, when, possibly, the cause of exception may appear, and the exception itself, by allowing for the effect of that cause, be brought over to the side of our induction; but should exceptions prove numerous and various in their features, our faith in the conclusion will be proportionally shaken, and at all events its importance lessened by the destruction of its universality (165, §172).

Herschel, like Hume, deems results satisfactory when an adequate number of supporting instances have been obtained: "But how, it may be asked, are we to ascertain *by* observation, data more precise than observation itself? How are we to conclude the value of that which we do not see, with greater certainty than that of quantities which we actually see and measure? It is the number of observations which may be brought to bear on the determination of data that enables us to do this" (215, §227). In this way Herschel manages to combine harmoniously the inductive and hypothetico-deductive methods (Charpa 1987: 145).

With John Stuart Mill, induction takes on its mature form. His chief account of induction is in his *System of Logic* (vols. 7 and 8 of his *Collected Works*), where various conflicting definitions of induction can be found. "Induction is the process by which we conclude that what is true of certain individuals of a class is true of the whole class, or that what is true at certain times will be true in similar circumstances at all times," writes Mill (*Works*, 7: 288). It is also "Generalization from Experience" (7: 306), or alternatively, "the operation of discovering and proving general propositions" (7: 284). *The System of Logic* does not, however, provide us with a logic of discovery, as the last definition would suggest. Mill's aim is, rather, to establish general factual propositions and formulate a set of abstract rules similar to the rules of syllogism—rules that can be used to establish and test inductive inferences. In the same passage, Mill argues that "the process of indirectly ascertaining individual facts . . . is as truly inductive as that by which we establish general truths." Because "generals are but collections of particulars" (7: 284), the process by which we arrive at general propositions is also inductive: "We shall fall into no error, then, if in treating of Induction, we limit our attention to the establishment of general propositions. The principles and rules of Induction as directed to this end, are the principles and rules of all Induction; and the logic of Science is the universal Logic, applicable to all inquiries in which man can engage" (7: 287).

Because for Mill, "[a]ll inference is from particulars to particulars," deduction reduces to induction (*Works*, 7: 193). It must, for Mill wants to exclude deductive syllogism as a legitimate way of establishing general propositions. Hence, to prove that the Duke of Wellington is mortal we do not deduce it from "all men are mortal" but from "the mortality of John, Thomas, and others" (187). That is, all evidence must be drawn from past particulars. "We have thus obtained what we were seeking, an universal type of the reasoning process. We find it resolvable in all cases into the following elements: Certain individuals have a given attribute; an individual or individuals resemble the former in certain other attributes; therefore they resemble them also in the given attribute" (202). This "is the reason why Mill can and does indiscriminately define induction both as an inference from the particular to the particular and from the particular to the general, which would be inconsistent on most all other interpretations of the status of universals" (Blackwell 1974: 203).[34]

Let's pause and sum up Mill's position. For Mill, science starts with sensory evidence, that is, with observation. From sensory evidence generalizations take shape; in other words, a theory emerges from the facts. Induction, then, is the method of science. Mill, whose motive for ascertaining the method of science was

---

34. Writes Passmore: "Experience, he had learnt from Hartley and from Bentham, is always of particular phenomena; we do not directly experience general connexions. If, then, universal propositions assert general connexions, and if, furthermore, such propositions . . . form the point of departure in all scientific thinking, it would seem to follow that science is not wholly empirical. This argument, indeed, was the great standby of intuitionists in their battle against empiricism. If, on the other hand, all reasoning is from particulars to particulars, if universal propositions are convenient devices, forming no essential part of scientific inference, then, Mill thought, empiricism has a complete answer to its critics" (1957: 21).

to apply it to social problems, saw rightly that deduction was not the method of scientific discovery. He realized that "the process of deduction as such only uncovers, brings out into the open, makes explicit, information that is already present in the axioms or premises from which the process of deduction started. The process of deduction reveals nothing to us except what the infirmity of our own minds has so far concealed from us" (Medawar 1964: 42).

That is not, however, Mill's last word on induction. Perhaps Mill's fullest discussion of induction can be found in this passage.

Although, therefore, all processes of thought in which the ultimate premises are particulars, whether we conclude from particulars to a general formula, or from particulars to other particulars according to that formula, are equally Induction; we shall yet, conformably to usage, consider the name Induction as more peculiarly belonging to the process of establishing the general proposition, and the remaining operation, which is substantially that of interpreting the general proposition, we shall call by its usual name, Deduction. And we shall consider every process by which anything is inferred respecting an unobserved case, as consisting of an Induction followed by a Deduction (*Works*, 7: 203).

Mill devotes a chapter of the *System of Logic* to the deductive method, which he recommends for cases in which direct methods of observation and experiment cannot be used—for instance, for social phenomena. The deductive "mode of investigation . . . consists of three operations: the first, one of direct induction; the second, of ratiocination; the third, of verification" (7: 454).[35]

The first step has already been discussed. He defines the second step, ratiocination, as "reasoning from a general law to a particular case" (*Works*, 7: 459). Verification, the final step,

---

35. His reason for making induction a component process of deduction is in some measure explained by this comment: "The opposition is not between the terms Deductive and Inductive, but between Deductive and Experimental. A science is experimental, in proportion as every new case, which presents any peculiar features, stands in need of a new set of observations and experiments—a fresh induction. It is deductive, in proportion as it can draw conclusions, respecting cases of a new kind, by processes which bring those cases under old inductions; by ascertaining that cases which cannot be observed to have the requisite marks, have, however, marks of those marks" (*Works*, 7: 219).

involves testing "general conclusions arrived at by deduction" by checking to see whether they "accord with the results of direct observation wherever it can be had" (460). Mill concludes that it is "[t]o the Deductive Method, thus characterized in its three constituent parts, Induction, Ratiocination, and Verification, [that] the human mind is indebted for its most conspicuous triumphs in the investigation of nature," since "[t]o it we owe all the theories by which vast and complicated phenomena are embraced under a few simple laws" (462). This conclusion prompts Britton's wry remark: "It is the great achievement of John Stuart Mill to have found logic deductive and to have left it both inductive and deductive" (1969: 147). What Britton nevertheless fails to see is that Mill recognized that scientific method intrinsically involves both the inductive and deductive methods. In effect, Mill employs *deduction* instead of *induction* to refer to scientific inquiry in a broad sense.[36]

Two chapters later Mill admits that science can start with a hypothesis rather than observation (*Works*, 7: ch. xiv, §4). Hypotheses are crucial because "nearly everything which is now theory was once hypothesis" (496). "The hypothesis, by suggesting observations and experiments, puts us on the road to that independent evidence if it be really attainable; and till it be attained, the hypothesis ought only to count for a more or less plausible conjecture" (496). When Mill accepts that the first step of science is the formation of a hypothesis, his deductive method approaches that of Newton, Herschel, and Whewell. "The net import of Mill's discussion of the 'Deductive Method'," explain Ralph Blake and associates, is "an acknowledgement of the superiority of the method that *Whewell* calls induction, to that which *Mill* calls induction" (1960: 231).

Thus we come to Whewell, who also formulates a systematic theory of induction in terms of the so-called Newtonian method of hypothesis-deduction-verification (Blake et al. 1960: 217). By the late nineteenth century, Mill's theory of induction had won

---

36. One can well understand Blaug's comment that "the sudden support for deductive methods after hundreds of pages extolling inductive ones . . . is well calculated to leave the reader utterly confused about Mill's final views on the philosophy of the social sciences" (1992: 64). Yet Mill's position, when examined carefully, is really today's hypothetico-deductive method. (A useful summary of Mill's views on induction, deduction, and scientific method in general appears in chapter 7 below.)

such acceptance that it eclipsed Herschel and Whewell's theories. This is unfortunate, for Whewell's theory of science is in many ways modern, although no one today would label his theory of science induction. He radically transformed the traditional meaning of induction, leaving behind induction by enumeration and Bacon's eliminative induction. Induction instead represents a "conjectural process whereby we introduce a new conception, not immediately given 'in' the available evidence, which 'colligates' that evidence, while going beyond it in both generality and degree of abstraction" (Laudan 1981: 164).[37]

According to Whewell, Bacon's theory of induction needed to be taken up anew because the inductive sciences had progressed since Bacon wrote the *Novum organum:* hence Whewell writes the *Novum organum renovatum* (1858). In Whewell's view, "[a]ll our knowledge of nature is obtained by Induction" and the only way to understand scientific method is to examine it at work in history (1968: 140). Whewell characterizes science as a historically developing process whose results at any time are incomplete. Yet, in spite of the evolutionary nature of science, scientists do take some propositions as established. Anyone studying history, claims Whewell, will see that induction is *not* the generalizing argument advanced by logicians such as Mill: practicing scientists do not reason by virtue of its form, but instead test and try hypotheses until their hunches yield results. Consequently, the focus is less on form than on sound results. Ultimately, then, Whewell has two theories of induction: a hypothetico-deductivist account of the justification of scientific results and a theory of inductive logic as a tool to generate rules by which theories are rejected or accepted (Butts 1977: 54).

In Whewell's philosophy, science means interpreting—not describing or cataloguing—nature. Science involves conceptualization: we impose a form or idea over the facts, or *colligate* the facts.[38] Induction, stresses Whewell, is not a generalization of facts but their *colligation,* that is, an intelligible connection of facts yielding a new idea. The act of colligation is not just recognizing similarity; it also involves the ability to see phenomena

---

37. That induction came to mean deduction and even the hypothetico-deductive method shows that the concept did not evolve semantically but adapted itself to the perceived process of science.

38. "We shall speak of the two processes by which we arrive at science, as *the Explication of Conceptions* and the *Colligation of Facts*" (Whewell 1968: 105).

in a new light and includes lower generalizations.[39] Whewell's concept of colligation is central to induction. Not every colligation is true or correct; some generalizations are false. The purpose of inductive logic is to weed out false generalizations, leaving correct colligations as valid inductions.

The essential problem, then, is to show how we distinguish between valid and invalid colligations. Whewell introduces three tests of hypotheses: adequacy (hypotheses should be able to explain phenomena observed); the capacity to predict undisputed facts; and the capacity to predict novel facts.[40] "The truth of tentative hypotheses must be tested by their application to facts. The discoverer must be ready, carefully to try his hypotheses in this manner, and to reject them if they will not bear the test, in spite of indolence and vanity," advises Whewell (1968: 130). In terms of predictions, he distinguishes between two levels of testing. At the first level, successful predictions of similar facts or phenomena are made. The second level, however, requires the explanation of novel facts, what Whewell calls a *consilience of inductions*. This occurs when a hypothesis introduced to explain one class of phenomena is seen to explain a different class of phenomena.[41] Often two laws become consilient when a more general theory subsumes them. In short, "the concept of consilience is the touchstone of Whewell's logic of induction" (Butts 1977: 62).

The concept of consilience elevates the role of hypotheses in science and separates Whewell's methodology from Mill's. "A maxim which it may be useful to recollect is this,—that *hypotheses may often be of service to science, when they involve a certain*

---

39. "An Induction is not the mere sum of the Facts which are colligated. The Facts are not only brought together, but seen in a new point of view" (Whewell 1968: 139). And in a similar vein: "The general law is not the mere sum of the particular laws. It is, as I have already said, their amount *in a new point of view*" (298).

40. "It is a test of true theories not only to account for, but to predict phenomena" (1968: 138).

41. "We have here spoken of the prediction of facts *of the same kind* as those from which our rule was collected. But the evidence in favour of our induction is of a much higher and more forcible character when it enables us to explain and determine cases of a *kind different* from those which were contemplated in the formation of our hypothesis. The instances in which this has occurred, indeed, impress us with a conviction that the truth of hypothesis is certain. No accident could give rise to such an extraordinary coincidence" (1968: 153).

*portion of incompleteness, and even of errour"* (1968: 149). When
Mill complains about Whewell's laxness in treating hypotheses,
he "is *not* objecting to the method of conjecture, but to Whewell's
(supposed) failure to deal adequately with conditions of verification" (Jacobs 1991: 83). In fact, although Whewell talks about
testing, he is more interested in showing how science benefits
from the use of hypotheses that may be wrong (Butts 1977: 56).

   Progress in science for Whewell means "successive generalization." In his *Philosophy of the Inductive Sciences,* Whewell argues that science progresses from empirical generalizations of
observations to more and more comprehensive generalizations.
He invents the "Inductive Table" to show how elementary scientific facts are linked by lower hypotheses and laws to a unifying
theory (1968: 160–77).[42] Simplicity plays a role in this process,
for the more facts a hypothesis colligates, the simpler it is.
Laudan notes the similarity between the concept of a consilience
of inductions and Karl Popper's requirements for the growth of
knowledge—that the theory be independently testable, make
novel predictions, and pass severe tests. "Popper's major 'discovery' of the 1950s was a reformulation of the problem of
consilience," Laudan concludes (1981: 176).

   A consilience impresses us that a hypothesis is true. Yet in
spite of Whewell's claim that the history of science shows that
consilient hypotheses always turn out to be valid,[43] a consilience
as a test of truth or certainty "fails to do the required epistemological job" (Butts 1977: 64). Mill saw that consilience did not
guarantee the truth of a theory, arguing that innumerable tests
cannot guarantee that the next prediction will not be false.
Whewell met Mill's criticism on two grounds: first, that such a
successful hypothesis cannot go wrong; and second, that history
supports him. Laudan's conclusion is worth quoting in full:
"Precisely when and how a hypothesis reaches that threshold of
confirmation (or severe testing) when it warrants acceptance is
as intractable a problem for modern confirmation theorists as it

---

42. "The Tables, as we have presented them, exhibit the course by which we
pass from Particular to General through various gradations, and so to the most
general. They display the order of *discovery*" (1968: 165).
43. "I believe the history of science offers no example in which a theory
supported by such consiliences, had been afterwards proved to be false" (1968:
295).

was for Whewell. Like him, they tend to identify that threshold with a successful consilience, or, like Popper, they deny that any such belief-threshold exists. But their justifications for doing so seem no more clear-cut than Whewell's, in spite of the impressive array of formal tools of analysis which they have brought to bear on the problem" (1981: 176–77).

Induction for Whewell consequently involves far more than modern usage suggests: it is scientific discovery, hypothesis formation, deduction, and a "logic of confirmation." It encompasses the imposition of new ideas on data, consilience, simplicity, and successive generalization. *Induction*, as Whewell uses it, also includes deductive processes, for deduction justifies inductive hunches and "confirms" the steps of induction, elevating verification to an important part of the inductive process.[44]

Two final points about Whewell's concept of induction are worth considering. First, Whewell concludes with Mill that induction in the social sciences will be more difficult than in natural science. "I am quite ready to admit that in Mental and Social Science, we are much less likely than in Physical Science, to obtain new truths by any process which can be distinctively termed *Induction;* and that in those sciences, what may be called *Deductions* from principles of thought and action of which we are already conscious, or to which we assent when they are felicitously picked out of our thoughts and put into words, must have a large share; and I may add, that this observation of Mr. Mill appears to me to be important, and, in its present connexion, new (1968: 303–4). Second, as Henderson aptly notes, Whewell's inductive methodology never caught on in economics because it clashed with the established economics tradition: "[T]he classical school of economists judged the validity of their hypotheses by appealing to the underlying assumptions rather than relying on predictions" (1985: 407).

## Jevons and the Decline of Induction

In the thirty years between the publication of Mill's *System of Logic* and William Stanley Jevon's *Principles of Science*, formal

---

44. "The process of scientific discovery is cautious and rigorous, not by abstaining from hypotheses, but by rigorously comparing hypotheses with facts, and by resolutely rejecting all which the comparison does not confirm" (1968: 138).

logic made great advances, especially, but not only, at the hands of George Boole. Jevons wed induction to probability theory in an effort to challenge Mill's concept of induction—which Jevons was highly critical of not just because he believed it was not borne out by the history of science. Above all, Jevons objected to Mill's claims that induction brings certitude, that induction is inference from particulars to particulars, and that induction is more important than deduction.

Mill's fundamental mistake, in Jevon's opinion, was his belief in the possibility of discovering causes in the sense of necessary and sufficient conditions. Jevons shows that this is too much to expect of science, which can never go beyond hypotheses that are only probable in nature. Jevons compares the scientist to a person confronted with an urn containing a number of balls. Drawing balls from the urn, the scientist notes regularities (the number of white and black balls), constructs all possible hypotheses compatible with the regularity, and computes their probabilities. The calculations then reveal the hypothesis with the greatest probability—the one the scientist should adopt. Jevons knows that this hypothesis could still be false, but believes it is the best we can do.[45]

Jevons does not believe science involves a method of induction distinct from deduction. Turning Mill on his head, Jevons claims induction is inverse deduction.[46] Forming hypotheses is central to Jevon's theory of science. In taking this stance, he declares himself to be a true enemy of Baconian science and even argues that no one followed Bacon's method. According to Jevons, both Bacon and Mill fail to understand the nature of evidence. Science does not induce from particulars, but formulates hypotheses and deduces evidence from the hypotheses— "inverse deduction." Alluding to Mill, Jevons expresses the view that all reasoning including induction reduces to deduction. Induction consists in anticipating nature, that is, in forming hypotheses about the laws in operation and observing whether phenomena follow from the laws postulated. Deduction involves: (1) framing a hypothesis about the character of a law;

---

45. Blake and associates (1960) analyze the technical development of Jevon's probability theory.
46. In his *Principles of Science*, Jevons says that "induction is really the inverse process of deduction," from which it follows that "all reasoning is founded on the principles of deduction" (1874, 1: 14).

(2) deducing consequences from the law; and (3) observing whether the consequences agree with the facts—a clear formulation of the hypothetico-deductive method. Jevons objects strongly to what he takes to be Mill's lack of both an appreciation for the role of hypothesizing in science and an awareness of the fact that discovery follows no rules of logic. Jevons does not, however, go as far as Popper and reject induction altogether.

Richard Blackwell concludes that Jevons was right to claim that theories are not derived from induction and that induction plays a less important role in science than Mill attributes to it. Nonetheless, he notes, Jevons, too, had his excesses: "[T]he inductivist model has an extraordinary weakness in explaining the origin of scientific theories. Contrary to Jevons, it seems to be true that at least some of the lower level empirical laws of science are established by inductive procedures, whether the latter are logically sound or not. But the jump to theories which involve nonobservables is the Achilles heel of inductivist model[s]" (1974: 211–12).

## The New Approach to Induction: Probability Theory

Another approach aimed at saving induction from skepticism takes as its point of departure Hume's conclusion that sensory evidence cannot render a generalization or prediction certain. It is grounded in the belief that evidence can be associated with a degree of probability and, further, that its probability would increase with increasing evidence according to the rules of mathematical probability calculus. By this view, the question, How can induction be justified? was essentially transformed into, When are we entitled to assert that a generalization is highly probable? The first persons to treat induction this way were Thomas Bayes (1702–1761) and Richard Price (1723–1791). After Bayes's death, Price brought his work to the attention of the Royal Society. Bayesianism, the name given to the view that induction can be explained by probability theory, arose in response to the problems raised by Hume's skepticism.

If probability calculus was to explain induction and confirmation as Bayesians desired, it first had to acquire an epistemological foundation that would allow it to be understood as a degree of knowledge or belief. The two chief epistemological positions to emerge have been logical and subjective interpretations, both of which have problems. Bertrand Russell (1872–1970) and G. E. Moore (1873–1958) first developed the logical interpretation, which was, in turn, refined substantially by John M. Keynes (1883–1946) and Rudolf Carnap (1891–1970). To get around the problem that the hypothesis "All ravens are black" does not follow logically from, or entail, the evidence "All ravens observed so far have been black," Keynes and others attempted to extend deduction to inductive or probability logic by arguing that the evidence *partially entails* the hypothesis to degree $p$. This theory of probability is called logical because it focuses on the degree of rational belief.

The Bayesian thesis is normally formulated as a claim that the degree of confirmation ($c$) of a hypothesis ($h$), given evidence ($e$) and background knowledge ($b$), satisfies the standard axiom of the mathematical calculus of probability:

$$c(h,e \ \& \ b) = p(h,e).$$

In other words, confirmation is a probability function, where $p(h,b)$ is known as the prior probability (in the sense of prior to collecting evidence $e$ conditional on background information $b$) and $p(h,e \ \& \ b)$ is known as the posterior probability.

The Bayesian approach is made plausible by the idea that evidence that makes a hypothesis more probable is close in meaning to the idea that evidence $e$ confirms a hypothesis and is formulated in precise mathematical terms. Because probability theory is based on a study of games of chance and random phenomena, questions about its adequacy for weighing evidence in natural or social science arise—questions that are still being explored today.

The subjective interpretation of probability was developed by Frank Ramsey (1903–1930) and Bruno De Finetti (1906– ). In contrast to the logical view that, given evidence $e$, all rational people will have the same degree of rational belief in a prediction $x$, the subjective position assumes that there will be varying degrees of belief in $x$. They develop a way of measuring degrees of belief that satisfies the axiom of probability by basing the measure of belief on bets and by imposing rationality constraints that satisfy the standard axiom of probability. The problem with subjective probability is that its power of explaining confirmation is clearly limited.[47]

All of these efforts in probability theory have greatly increased our understanding of induction, especially with respect to mathematical-statistical techniques. While it is obvious that these developments assume the soundness of inductive inference, not all philosophers accept this assumption. Thus, the final section of this sketch of the history of induction is dedicated to a brief exposition on what Popper calls "the myth of induction."

## Karl Popper: Induction as Myth

The gravity of Hume's conclusions has led other philosophers, most notably Karl Popper, to conclude that induction does not exist and plays no role in science whatsoever. Popper found Mill wrong on numerous accounts. The starting point of scientific discovery, he insists, is not neutral observation; we normally start with a problem, or perhaps a theory or a criticism of a theory. Second, the formulation of theory and demonstration or proof are two separate things, which Mill mistakenly conflates, for instance, when he defines induction as "the operation of discovering and proving general propositions." Popper believes that Mill was right in seeing that discovery and proof are the same in the process of deduction, for instance, when deducing a theorem from geometrical axioms. In that case, the theorem is the discovery (although it is hidden in the axioms) and the process of deduction is proof of the discovery because it is logically correct. But scientific discovery, the formulation of a scientific theory, is not an inductive process, as Mill claims. In science, discovery and proof are separate. In order to generalize, a scientist needs more information than merely the sum of statements upon which a generalization is founded. Popper, however, goes a step beyond Jevons and completely rejects induction.

For Popper hypotheses and their testing are central to science. From a hypothesis one can deduce certain consequences (make predictions about what will or will not be the case). If predic-

---

47. On this issue see Gillies (1988: 188–204).

tions are wrong, hypotheses can be discarded or modified. If a prediction is fulfilled, the hypothesis has withstood a trial or test. This is the hypothetico-deductive interpretation of science, which Popper has convinced us is the correct way of viewing science.

The problem with Popper is that he attempts to demonstrate that science is an entirely deductive enterprise by emphasizing eliminative methods—his famous theory of falsification (which includes statistical hypothesis-testing). But Popper, seeing that we need to know more than that a test disproves our theory, discovers that induction creeps back into his proposed completely deductive approach. Ayer puts the problem this way: "there would seem to be no point in testing hypotheses unless their passing the test was thought to enhance their credibility: but that it does so enhance it is an inductive assumption" (1980: 73). The lesson: Induction cannot be banished from science.[48]

Pierre Duhem gave us two additional reasons for suspecting falsification of theories. Crucial experiments or observations do not exist in practice, and hypotheses cannot be tested in isolation. It can be added that forming a hypothesis is informed guesswork and not a logic as Popper's *Logic of Discovery* suggests. There simply is no rigorous way of devising hypotheses.

And so today's theories of induction are still steeped in controversy. Goodman's conclusion would bring a smile to David Hume's face: "The vast amount of effort expended on the problem of induction in modern times has thus altered our afflictions but hardly relieved them" (1973: 81).

---

48. See Redman for a more detailed discussion of the reappearance of induction in Popper's theory of science (1991, ch. 4, esp. 32–33).

# II  Classical Economic Methodology

# 5    Adam Smith and His "Newtonian Method"

The proposition that Adam Smith (1723–1790) and Isaac Newton (1642–1727) have something in common would strike most economists and historians of science as remote. Yet, Smith did invoke the "Newtonian method" in some of his more obscure works, and most economists and historians seem to have accepted the view that Smith's method was Newtonian. Mark Blaug, for instance, argues that the economist's two major works, *The Theory of Moral Sentiments* and *The Wealth of Nations,* "must be regarded as deliberate attempts by Smith to apply this Newtonian method first to ethics and then to economics" (1992: 52). Henry Bittermann indicates that Smith's "procedure was an application of the techniques of Newtonian experimentalism to the question of morals" (1940: 504).[1] Andrew Skinner writes that "Smith made much of the Newtonian 'method' of argument," adding that there is no doubt that Smith's economics "was originally conceived in the image of Newtonian physics" (1974: 182; 1979: 110).[2] Norriss Hetherington sets forth the thesis that "Adam Smith's efforts to discover the general laws of economics were directly inspired and shaped by the example of Newton's success in discovering the natural laws of motion" (1983: 497). These few examples are not exhaustive but serve to show how widespread is the belief that Smith applied the Newtonian method to economics.

---

1. The Bitterman essay also appears in the Wood collection; the respective citation is J. Wood (1984, 1: 197).
2. The 1979 article is reprinted in the Wood collection; see J. Wood (1984, 1: 739).

**The Tie to Newton**

What is meant by the term *Newtonian*, however, is problematic, for it suggests at least three meanings. First, it may simply echo the words Newton used to designate his method. No doubt Smith at times uses the term this way; it, however, reveals nothing about the content of the term. *Newtonian* could, on the other hand, indicate that Smith was consciously employing Newton's method. This interpretation, which is not as uncommon as one would think, is a gross error because Smith instead adapts and shapes to his needs what he takes to be Newton's method. Finally, the word *Newtonian* could refer to one of the methods used by Newton's many followers, the Newtonians. This last interpretation is correct. Smith's writings belong to the literature designated as *Newtonianism*, that is, the writings of Newton's followers who adopted his work "for many different, even contradictory, purposes—not only in eighteenth-century culture, but also in our time" (Cantor 1988: 220). The purpose of this section, then, is to consider Smith's "Newtonian method" in light of the method Newton used.

The famous passage on the Newtonian method—one of Smith's clearest pronouncements on methodology—appears in his *Lectures on Rhetoric and Belles Lettres*. In this passage, which is reported to have been a part of his 1762–63 lectures, Smith contrasts the Newtonian with the Aristotelian method.

In the same way in Natural Philosophy or any other Science of that Sort we may either like Aristotle go over the Different branches in the order they happen to cast up to us, giving a principle commonly a new one for every phaenomenon; or in the manner of Sir Isaac Newton we may lay down certain principles known or proved in the beginning, from whence we account for the severall Phenomena, connecting all together by the same Chain.—This latter which we may call the Newtonian method is undoubtedly the most Philosophical, and in every science whether of Moralls or Naturall philosophy etc., is vastly more ingenious and for that reason more engaging than the other. It gives us a pleasure to see the phaenomena which we reckoned the most unaccountable all deduced from some principle (commonly a wellknown one) and all united in one chain, far superior to what we feel from the unconnected method where everything is accounted for by itself without any reference to the others (1983: 145–46).[3]

---

3. The orthographical inconsistencies in this passage are true to the original manuscript; similar variations occur throughout his writings. Skinner explains

Although this passage indicates that Smith embraced a unity-of-science approach, his position stems from the fact that philosophy, social science, and natural science were all regarded as the same type of activity in his day; it does not mean that Smith invites the wholesale appropriation of the method of physical science. He was aware that moral and natural philosophy require somewhat different approaches, an issue to which I return several times in this chapter. The second point to be noted is the theme that runs through all of Smith's pronouncements on method: the argument for using a few familiar or well-known guiding principles from which phenomena can be deduced and concatenated in a way that is pleasing to the mind. It is this "connectedness"—the formation of a system or theory complex around a few basic universal principles—that Smith interprets as Newtonian. Finally, the passage makes evident that the primary object of philosophy is to satisfy a psychological need—our desire for coherence and organization.

Smith also refers to Newton, albeit indirectly, in a passage of *The Theory of Moral Sentiments* (1759) that I discussed in chapter 4. In a tone unmistakably reminiscent of Baconian interpretations of Newton's Fourth Rule of Reasoning, Smith writes: "The general maxims of morality are formed, like all other general maxims, from *experience and induction*. We observe in a great variety of particular cases what pleases or displeases our moral faculties . . . and *by induction from this experience, we establish those general rules* [emphasis added]" (1976b: 319). Here, Smith's "induction from experience" corresponds to Newton's "induction from phenomena," which, as noted in chapter 2, often meant deduction from phenomena. In so far as the label *induction* goes, this methodological position corresponds to the third step of Newton's method. The major difference, however, can be found in Newton and Smith's differing views on the way the "induction from phenomena" is to be carried out. Newton, we recall, never subscribed to a consideration of "a great variety of particular cases," preferring to let the results of a cleverly conceived crucial experiment guide him. Smith, however, seems to have

---

their existence by the fact that no less than three separate amanuenses were involved in preparing Smith's manuscripts (1993). Three amanuenses notwithstanding, orthographical inconsistencies were typical of the age; a short perusal of Hume's works or the early volumes of the *Gentleman's Magazine* makes this abundantly clear.

taken his view of induction from a popular version of Newton's philosophy. John Clarke's interpretation of Newton's Fourth Rule of Reasoning in *Sir Isaac Newton's Principles of Natural Philosophy* (1730) appears to come closest to Smith's position: "TRUE Philosophy must be built upon Experiments, and those Experiments must be so many and so plain, that we cannot be deceived in them, but may argue universally from them, and apply them in all Cases and Circumstances whatsoever; for this is the only possible Way of coming at the Truth in these Things: Hypotheses are endless, and every Imagination of any ingenious Person may produce a new One; but the real Nature and Constitution of Things is Matter of Fact, and may be come at by constant Observations and repeated Trials" (1972: 100). Clearly, what Smith calls induction is more Baconian than Newtonian in nature: the number of instances legitimates generalizations—a point to which I return below.

Today's scholar can only speculate about Smith's first-hand familiarity with and depth of understanding of the *Principia* and *Opticks*. We know that Smith owned a copy of both works; a copy of Newton's *Method of Fluxions* and *Arithmetica* can also be found in his library (Mizuta 1967: 123; Yanaihara 1951: 84). One thing we can be certain of is Smith's exposure to Newton through the works of Hume and Voltaire. No doubt Hume's, if not also Voltaire's, influence was greater than Newton's.[4] Smith must have been familiar with Voltaire's *Éléments de la philosophie de Newton*, for he owned a copy and was influenced by it when writing the section on Newton's physics in his "History of Astronomy" (1980c: 90).[5] Like Voltaire, he interpreted Newton

---

4. Cremaschi concurs, describing Smith's method as "Humeo-Newtonian" and arguing that the "methodological attitude underlying Adam Smith's economic works is . . . an application of the program of a 'Moral Newtonianism' stated in Hume's *Treatise*" (1981: 125). In Patten's view, too, "the work of Adam Smith follows so closely after that of Hume that it may be called part of the same scheme;" but it must be added that Smith molds Hume's thought to his own purposes (1899: 226).

Voltaire's influence should not be underestimated, for Smith regarded him as "the most universal genius perhaps which France has ever produced" and met him during his two-year stay in France (1980c: 254). According to Stephen, when, in a conversation someone was referred to as a 'Voltaire', Smith emphatically replied: "Sir, there has been but one Voltaire" (1898: 6).

5. Smith owned Voltaire's *Oeuvres complètes*, of which the *Éléments* was a part (Mizuta 1967: 150).

as placing particular emphasis on not going beyond the facts (Voltaire 1992: 55). Other popular versions of Newtonian philosophy that probably slipped through his hands are Colin Maclaurin's *Account of Sir Isaac Newton's Philosophy* (1748),[6] Pemberton's *View of Sir Isaac Newton's Philosophy* (1728),[7] and Clarke's *Sir Isaac Newton's Principles* (1730).

Smith certainly used the *Principia* as an analogy for finding laws of motion of the social world,[8] although the *Opticks* was decisive in building a theoretical corpus. No doubt Smith's interpretation of Newton rested primarily on the latter work.[9] Speaking for this interpretation is his pronounced emphasis on observation and experience, as well as his association with Benjamin Franklin, whose understanding of Newton's philosophy is known to have been limited to the *Opticks*.[10] Franklin's contemporaries considered him to be one of the foremost experimental scientists of the age (Cohen 1966: 7); and, although unable to understand the *Principia*, he was still regarded as a Newtonian.[11] Smith is known to have met with Franklin on several occasions to discuss chapters of *The Wealth of Nations* in detail (Carey 1928: ch. 6). Also noteworthy is Smith's decision not to use the word *principles* in the title, a practice that

---

6. It would be difficult to imagine Smith passing up a work by Scotland's foremost scientist; and, in fact, he mentions Maclaurin in his account of Newton in the "History of Astronomy" (1980c: 90).

7. Pemberton's book made Newton's ideas particularly accessible to men of letters unequipped with the mathematical training to digest them first-hand. His exposition of Newton's thought was highly praised by Voltaire (1992: 36).

8. Keep in mind Newton's aim as stated in the preface to the *Principia*: "from the phenomena of motions to investigate the forces of nature, and then from these forces to demonstrate the other phenomena" (1962: xvii-xviii).

9. His friend Thomas Pownall—an administrator of the American colonies and later governor of the Massachusetts Bay Colony—nonetheless thought that Smith had relied chiefly on the *Principia* as his model. "I do really think, that your book . . . might become an institute, containing the *principia* of those laws of motion, by which the system of the human community is framed and doth act, AN INSTITUTE of *political economy*," he wrote Smith (in Smith 1987: 375).

10. See Cohen (1966: 10). Smith's private library contained a copy of *Experiments and Observations on Electricity*, a collection of Franklin's letters and observations concerning his experiments on electricity that was first published in 1751 and went through five editions. Franklin, who was well known and received in Britain, was elected a fellow of the Royal Society in 1756.

11. Cohen also notes that Franklin had read the *Opticks*, was an intimate of Henry Pemberton, and was familiar with the popular versions of Newton's work by Pemberton, Boerhaave, 's Gravesande, and Desaguliers (1966: 8–10).

enjoyed a vogue after Newton's *Principia* met with resounding success.[12]

Attempts to isolate and systematize the various strains of Newtonianism—especially those that deal with the social sciences—are, unfortunately, rare.[13] To highlight similarities and differences between Smith's and Newton's approaches I adopt in this chapter a scheme similar to the one developed in chapter two to illustrate Newton's method. Like Newton, Smith wants to create a "system of the world," but his is to serve as a counterpart for the social world.[14] In doing so, he assumes d'Holbach's theory of motion[15] and Hume's science of man. As he sees it, the foundation of a system of the social world is laid in human nature; human propensities, which Smith believes are constant over time, serve a theoretical function in Smith's system similar to the properties of physical matter in Newton's system. Having established this foundation, it is possible to summarize Smith's method in the following steps:

1. abstract and isolate social (including economic) motivations and processes;

2. examine the interdependencies between the component parts;

3. generalize the relationships discovered to all similar situations (establish principles via induction, the process of deducing an inference from the facts);

---

12. Newton's *Principia* spawned a slew of *Principles* in political economy. Ricardo (1817), Malthus (1820), J. R. McCulloch (1825), G. Poulett Scrope (1836), H. C. Carey (1837–40), and J. S. Mill (1848), to name a few, all wrote monographs entitled *Principles of Political Economy*.
13. Schofield (1978) tries to provide a taxonomy of the various Newtonianisms. Most taxonomies of Newtonianism focus on natural philosophy, with an occasional digression on Voltaire. See also Buchdahl (1961), Cohen (1966), Guerlac (1968 and 1965), M. Jacob (1974), Secord (1985), Schaffer (1988), and Shepherd (1982).
14. "Adam Smith undoubtedly started with the purpose of giving to the world a complete social philosophy" (Bonar 1893: 149).
15. Smith owned a copy of d'Holbach's *Système de la nature*, which was originally published under the pseudonym Mirabeau (Mizuta 1967: 103). In the work, d'Holbach sets forth a theory of motion not influenced by Newton. For Smith and d'Holbach, all of the phenomena of nature, including people, are in motion. The continual action and reaction of humans results in a series of causes and effects whose laws are unknown, but can be determined. French officials, by the way, ordered the work to be burned publicly for reviving the materialistic system of Epicurus and Lucretius (Guerlac 1958: 19–20).

4. draw inferences from the general or universal principles (deduction) to form a system, illustrate the theory, and show and explain the effects of the workings of the principle on social institutions.[16]

Step 1 corresponds roughly to Newton's first step: divide the object into its most basic parts and factors and analyze it. In Smith's system, the basic component or element is the individual. Step 2 is reminiscent of Newton's second step, the difference being the nonmathematical nature of the interdependencies of economic phenomena in Smith's system. Self-interest emerges as an explanatory principle like gravitation in Newton's system. The idea of self-interest as moral gravitation, by the way, did not originate with Smith, but was widespread in his time.[17] Steps 1 and 2 of Newton's method, we remember, jointly constitute the method of analysis. Smith, unfortunately, does not use the word *analysis*—perhaps why Gideon Freudenthal claims that Smith neglects the method of analysis and resorts solely to synthesis (1981: 135).[18] It is, however, worth noting that Smith's contemporaries interpreted him as following the method of analysis—analysis to the Scots being Newtonian generalization, that is, the process by which the order of the phenomena is resolved into general laws. In his celebrated letter to Smith in 1776, Thomas Pownall praises Smith for using the methods of analysis and synthesis. On the issue of analysis he says, "[Y]ou have, I find, by a truly philosophic and patient analysis,

---

16. There is evidence to support the view that the Scots saw their method—like Bacon saw his—as proceeding in a series of steps (Cantor 1971: 72).
17. Myers points out that Lord Bolingbroke, Soame Jenyns, and Peter Paxton (1983, ch. 6) used this analogy. Also noteworthy is d'Holbach, who in his *System of Nature* uses *self-love* as a synonym for *self-gravitation* and argues that "self-gravitation, then, is clearly a necessary disposition in men, and in all other beings; which, by a variety of means, contributes to the preservation of the existence they have received, as long as nothing deranges the order of their machine, or its primitive tendency" (1971: 44).
18. I find no substantiation for this view. Cremaschi, correctly reading both the methods of analysis and synthesis into Smith's approach, argues that analysis is "a collection of observations on human behavior at different times and places, on which a few general maxims concerning human conduct in economic affairs could be based" (1988: 10). The fact that the scheme I use for analyzing Newton and Smith's methods is somewhat arbitrary (neither man methodically dissected the methods they used) needs to be underscored here. In the next section we will see that Smith's employment of the machine analogy adds support to the view that he did indeed employ the method of analysis.

endeavored to investigate *analitically* those principles, by which nature first moves and then conducts the operations of man in the individual, and in community" (in Smith 1987: 337–76).

In step 3, the interrelationships discovered are generalized (and substantiated) by extending the principle to ever more cases. We have already noted the strong Baconian character of this step. It is doubtful that Smith was aware of his deviation from Newton on this point: after all, Newton had called this step induction, the method for which Bacon was famous. In any case, a new solution had to be discovered, as moral philosophers could not resort to the use of crucial experiments. No doubt the factual information packed into *The Wealth of Nations,* whether Smith's own observations, historical material, or observation reports of others, served to give Smith's hypotheses or theories strength and credibility: "The purpose of Smith's historical investigations . . . was to acquire the data necessary to back up or refute a generalization" (Raphael 1985: 105).[19] As mentioned in chapter 4, Smith was against "loose and vague" observation and "improperly and overhastily abstracted" generalizations. Yet even in Smith's lifetime, this step in Smith's method led to objections. Consider, for example, Dugald Stewart's complaint that Smith was "misled by too great a desire of generalizing his principles," but nonetheless "had the merit of directing the attention of philosophers to a view of human nature which had formerly in a great measure escaped their notice" (in Smith 1980a: 290).

Step 4 in Newton's philosophy is synthesis, deductive applications of the general laws to substantiate given facts and predict novel facts. Synthesis in this sense plays no role in Smith's philosophy, which is focused instead on drawing inferences from the connecting principles (deduction), forming a system, illustrating the theory, and explaining the effects of the principles on institutions.[20] Pownall describes Smith's use of synthesis

---

19. The great bulk of the facts presented in the *Wealth of Nations* is "used by Smith not as data from which to draw generalizations, but as examples of a theory already advanced," points out Bryson (1968: 86).
20. Stewart criticizes Smith's neglect of prediction. In his view, order "is not the *leading* object of that plan of inductive investigation which was recommended by Bacon, and which has been so skilfully pursued by Newton." All

this way. "And then, next, by applications of these principles to fact, experience, and the institutions of men, you have endeavored to deduce *synthetically*, by the most precise and measured steps of demonstration, those important doctrines of practice, which your very scientifick and learned book offers to the consideration of the world of business" (in Smith 1987: 337). Smith was, as Ferguson notes, "concerned not so much in summarizing the more or less common stock of knowledge of that day, or of adducing new facts, as he was in the inter-relation and interpretation of facts and the portrayal of a new perspective," the system of natural liberty (1950: 59). Consequently, the conclusions of Smith's philosophy are not subject to tests or legitimated by reference to mathematical calculation or experiment in Newton's sense.[21]

In this short introduction I have tried, as far as possible, to bare and dissect Smith's method and illuminate its similarities with Newton's method. Obviously, there are radical differences between Smith's "Newtonian method" and Newton's method. It is to an analysis of these differences that I now turn.

## Departures from Newtonian Method

### Smith and the Use of Mathematics
With or without an intimate knowledge of the *Principia*, Smith knows that Newton's system is mathematical and gains its precision from the ability to quantify the interrelationships within the system. Newton's system, Smith observes in his essay on astronomy, is the best known to man precisely because it "ascertains the time, the place, the quantity, the duration of each individual phaenomenon, to be exactly such as, by observation, they have been determined to be" (1980c: 104). On the other hand, the only calculations in *The Wealth of Nations* are simple

---

systems, says Stewart, "both please the imagination and assist the memory, by introducing order and arrangement among facts, which had the appearance before of being altogether unconnected and isolated." But a system also "furnishes the means of ascertaining, by synthetic reasoning, those [facts] which we have no access to examine by direct observation" (*Works*, 3: 251).

21. Ferguson, however, tells us that Smith "endeavored to check his deductions by means of personal observation and historical research" (1950: 59). Such measures, however, surely cannot be considered an exact counterpart to testing in the Newtonian system.

arithmetic, usually averages. It is obvious that Smith's method bears little similarity to Newton's mathematical way, and this, I propose, was fully intentional.

Smith's nonmathematical approach cannot, however, be attributed to either an ignorance of or a disinclination for mathematics.[22] In his biography of Smith, Stewart recounts the anecdote that a fellow student of Smith's at Glasgow University recalled Smith's favorite pursuits as mathematics and natural philosophy (in Smith 1980a: 270–71). Certainly Smith's personal library was well stocked with works on mathematics. According to the official list of books owned by Smith and drawn up in 1781, shelves four and five of his personal library alone contained Maclaurin's *Algebra*, Simpson's *Algebra*, Robins's *Mathematical Tracts*, Barrow's *Lectiones Opticae & Geometricae*, the *Discorsi et dimonstrazioni mathematiche*, Gregory's *Arithmeticae et algebra compendium* and *Practical Geometry*, Wright's *Elements of Trigonometry*, Merville's *Lexicon de mathematiques*, Trail's *Algebra*, Malcolm's *Arithmetic*, and Saunderson's *Elements of Algebra* (Yanaihara 1951: 84–85). Nor was his collection lacking in works that deal with applications of mathematics to astronomy. Smith owned Jean Sylvain Bailly's *Astronomie ancienne*, *Astronomiae moderne*, and *Astronomie indienne*, James Ferguson's *Astronomy*, David Gregory's *Astronomiae physicae et geometricae elementa* and *Catopricae et dioptricae sphaericae elementa*, John Keill's *Introductio ad verum astronomiam* and the English translation (*Introduction to Natural Philosophy*), Johann Heinrich Lambert's *Système du monde*, Manlius's *Astronomica* (1739), Pierre Louis Moreau de Maupertius's *Figure of the Earth* (1738), John Playfair's *Astronomy of the Brahmins* (1786), and the works by Newton already mentioned (Mizuta 1967).[23] I would not, however, go so far as to

22. C. Clark, considering Smith's position on the use of mathematics in moral philosophy, asserts that he "seemed to be quite hostile to its use in political economy" (1988: 63). To support his view that Smith had a low opinion of political arithmetic he offers Smith's famous statement, "I have no great faith in political arithmetick." As we shall see in a later section on Smith's attitude toward political arithmetic, this statement indicates not an aversion to either mathematics or statistics per se, but to the use of unreliable statistics.
23. The books that comprise Smith's personal collection have been the object of three monographs: James Bonar's *Catalogue of the Library of Adam Smith* (1932, 2nd ed.), Tadao Yanaihara's *Full and Detailed Catalogue of Books Which Belonged to Adam Smith* (1951), and Hiroshi Mizuta's *Adam Smith's Library* (1967). The bibliographical information provided by these three works is incomplete and

suggest that Smith understood Newton's "fluxions," which presented an insurmountable obstacle to even the most learned of that age.[24]

The fact of the matter is that Smith was not against mathematics at all; he did not use it because he saw no purpose for it in this system. The aim of all philosophers, in his view, is to connect diverse phenomena in a way pleasing to the mind by the least number of connecting principles. The principle of gravity admitted of mathematical quantification; the principle of self-interest, however, did not, as he had surely learned from his teacher Francis Hutcheson's futile, if not downright embarrassing, attempts to formulate a moral algebra. There are, in addition, several other reasons that would have made a mathematical approach lack appeal to Smith. First, he was a man who preferred facts to reason. He associated mathematics, abstraction, highly developed systems, and logic, "the science of the general principles of good and bad reasoning," with the fanciful, a priori Cartesian systems (Smith 1976a: 770). In this age "the dangers as well as the delights of purely deductive reasoning were widely recognized" (Campbell and Skinner in Smith 1976a: 3). To Smith the "fanciful," "ingenius," and "elegant" but "fallacious" Cartesian systems embodied a greatly oversimplified explanation for phenomena that Smith insisted were more complex.[25] The social scientist, he believed, was obliged to hold more closely to the messy facts and resist giving in to coherence and elegance.[26] Thus, William Stanley Jevons's much quoted

uneven (hence the absence of publication dates and forenames). I am, however, uncertain whether a comprehensive work that conforms to modern bibliographical standards is feasible.

24. "Adam Smith did not appreciate the difference between the value of a variable, and the rate of change in the value, and his economics theory suffers for it," says Worland (1976: 254). To be fair, Smith was looking for changes, but his preoccupation was with social change and improvement as society passes from the rude to a polished state, changes that do not admit of mathematical manipulation.

25. This was a widespread view in his day. Desaguliers explains that the Cartesians, "who taking a few Principles for granted, without examining their Reality or Consistence with each other, fancied they could solve all Appearances mechanically by Matter and Motion; and, in their smattering Way, pretended to demonstrate such things, as perhaps Cartesius himself never believ'd" (1763: v).

26. Evidence in support of this statement is set out later in this chapter in the section on the difference between social and physical phenomena.

remark that Smith's theory was essentially mathematical more readily reflects Jevons's own ability to conceptualize Smith's contributions in mathematical form than it does any true aspect of Smith's method (1965: 200).

Second, Smith was not interested in optimization problems, "which offer an irresistible invitation to mathematical treatment" (Spiegel 1976: 487). He never used the word *equilibrium*, which the Physiocrats had already introduced into the language of political economy, although the idea of balance is clearly present in this writings.[27] Thus, the many modern interpretations of Smith's theory that mathematize and axiomatize his theory are not Smith at all but a transformation of Smith.[28]

The final point has already been discussed in chapter 3: the Scots' particular views on mathematics. Both calculus—or fluxions as they called it—and algebra were suspect because the steps of reasoning were concealed by symbols and long chains of reasoning. Geometry, which Newton also used, was the preferred form of mathematics. Sir James Steuart, Smith's contemporary, sums up the tenor of the age this way: "Long steps in political reasoning lead to error;" but shorter steps of reasoning allow us to draw conclusions while keeping "experience and matter of fact before our eyes" (1966: 19; 1967, 2: 121). Smith does in fact make use of abstraction, but not in true-to-Newton mathematical style. He abstracts from the real world to determine a typical—what he terms *natural*—representation of the facts.[29]

## Smith and Mechanism

The bulk of scholarly opinion mistakenly adheres not only to the view that Smith was against mathematics, but also to the

---

27. The idea of equilibrium was common in this age and is conspicuous in the writings of Hume as well (Vickers 1957).
28. Recktenwald (1978) discusses many of the "transformers."
29. "These ordinary or average rates may be called the natural rates of wages, profit, and rent, at the time and place in which they commonly prevail.
   When the price of any commodity is neither more nor less than what is sufficient to pay the rent of the land, the wages of the labour, and the profits of the stock employed in raising, preparing, and bringing it to market, according to their natural rates, the commodity is then sold for what may be called its natural price" (Smith 1976a: 72).

idea that his economics is mechanical.[30] According to the mechanical interpretation, the orderliness of nature is understood in mechanism, and social phenomena are all bound together by a cause and effect relationship that only needs to be discovered. Smith, it is said, conceived the economic system as a machine whose parts interact to keep it coherent and stable. Individuals are the "atoms" of the social world; these "atoms" act according to universal (human) propensities with which they are endowed. Equilibrium is obtained by the interplay of forces, with self-interest working like gravity as the underlying force stabilizing the system.

Certainly there is evidence for this view. Smith makes explicit use of Newtonian terminology: market prices "gravitate,"[31] and he talks of "centers of repose" and "motion." There are as well abundant references to machines. In Smith's day, however, making generous use of rhetorical devices, especially by drawing on concepts from Newton's classical mechanics, was very much in vogue, Hume's work being a second case in point. The role of analogy, as we see later, takes on considerable significance in Smith's science. Although "an overall analogy between the physical and the moral was exploited by Smith in creating the main theoretical elements of his economic theory," the use of analogy nevertheless does not suffice to make Smith's system mechanical (Cremaschi 1988: 9). We see this more clearly in the next section, where the machine analogy is examined in some detail.

Stephen Worland shows that Smith's theory falls short of fulfilling the formal requirements of a mechanical system because it does not provide an explanation of subprocesses (1976: 254). His technical analysis, however, is unnecessary, for Smith's method is adaptive and evolutionary. In *The Wealth of Nations* he is interested in tracing the natural progress of opulence and in showing how, through a continuous process of adaptation, an ideal (polished) state is approached. Economic reality is a process—a complicated one whose complex facets

---

30. Consider, for example, the numerous references by Black to the mechanical nature of Smith's thought (1963: 90, 93, 124, 175, 186, 188, 190, 192, 198, 199, 200). The major objectors to this view, besides myself, are Cremaschi and Lindgren (1969: 899, 909, 910).

31. For example, "[t]he natural price, therefore, is, as it were, the central price, to which the prices of all commodities are continually gravitating" (1976a: 75).

need to be captured by the system. At the heart of this process is a four-stage theory that makes the stage of development, and with it the form of government, dependent on the mode of subsistence. Within this evolutionary framework institutions evolve as the unintended results of human action.

Considered from today's viewpoint, Smith's advocacy of the "Newtonian method" is most unfortunate, for it easily leads modern readers to the mistaken conclusion that Smith favored a mathematico-deductive, mechanical method—in direct conflict with the intention, purpose, and substance of his work.[32]

## The Significance of the Essay "The History of Astronomy"

The only other place where we find Smith explicitly discussing methods in science is in his essay "The Principles Which Lead and Direct Philosophical Enquiries; Illustrated by the History of Astronomy" (hereafter referred to as "The History of Astronomy"). Published posthumously in 1799 as one of three essays on philosophical topics, it was written when Smith was a young man, around 1750. Joseph Schumpeter refers to the essay as "the pearl of the collection" and adds, "Nobody, I venture to say, can have an adequate idea of Smith's intellectual stature who does not know these essays" (1954b: 182). D. D. Raphael argues in the same vein that "Smith's long essay 'The History of Astronomy', in *Essays on Philosophical Subjects,* deserves to rank with *The Wealth of Nations* and *The Moral Sentiments* as the work of an outstanding mind" (1985: 107).

W. P. D. Wightman suggests that Smith develops in the "History of Astronomy" not a methodological view but a "history of the idea of the 'philosophy of science'" (in Smith 1980a: 14). Although it is true that Smith is writing as a historian of science in this essay, his historical approach is methodologically significant. John Rae rightly objects to the suggestion that Smith is presenting solely a history of philosophy; what he is doing, according to Rae, is illustrating "the *universal* motives of philosophical researches" (1834: 332). The significance of the essay

---

32. The evidence Mayr (1971) presents for Smith's conscious use of a feedback system is unconvincing for similar reasons. Reading into Smith the idea of modern feedback loops is analogous to Jevons's ability to dress Smith's theory in mathematical form: both views ignore the rhetorical nature of Smith's use of the terminology of Newtonian mechanics and so distort his intentions.

lies in Smith's application of the philosophy of science developed there to the construction of a moral theory and an economic system.

The essay is divided into four parts, with the first two dedicated to the role of the sentiments surprise and wonder. Smith then traces the "origins of philosophy" and closes with "The History of Astronomy," the lengthiest section. In typical Scottish style, Smith first notes that science, like the economic world, develops in stages.[33] Once law and order have been established, man's wonder and imagination—his powers of curiosity—are aroused. "Wonder, therefore, and not any expectation of advantage from its discoveries, is the first principle which prompts mankind to the study of Philosophy . . ." (Smith 1980c: 51).[34] Psychological principles, or laws of the mind, govern scientific endeavor. "It is evident that the mind takes pleasure in observing the resemblances that are discoverable betwixt different objects," remarks Smith (37). Thus, "surprise," a harrowing feeling, occurs when the mind perceives a "singular appearance," a phenomenon having no similarity with other phenomena. The sense of "wonder," a feeling of a "gap between objects," causes disutility because it arouses uncertainty and anxious curiosity. "Imagination" tries to fill the gap by discovering a similarity or explanation.[35]

---

33. His famous four stages of economic development are hunting, pasturage, agriculture, and commerce (see Meek 1971).

34. According to Raphael, Smith's view that philosophy or science begins in wonder can be traced to Plato (1985: 108). Certainly it can be found in Descartes, who in his *Passions of the Soul* (1649) talks of astonishment—"an excess of wonder"—and wonder, which "makes us disposed to acquire scientific knowledge" and which is both positive and negative (1985: 354–55).

35. *Wonder* was used two ways by Smith, to indicate both intellectual dissatisfaction, as in this context, and awe and admiration for something beautiful (see, e.g., 1980a: 56). The latter usage allows Mark Blaug to argue in the first edition of his *Methodology of Economics* that "Smith credited the origin of science in the essay on astronomy, not to men's idle curiosity or the impulse to master nature, but to the simple desire to maximize 'wonder, surprise, and admiration'" (1980: 57). In the second edition, Blaug changes the word *maximize* to *assuage* (1992: 53). The latter word choice is better because *wonder* and *surprise* in Smith's system are normally negative attributes that cause disutility. Smith did not talk in terms of maximization or minimization, viewing the economic process, as Malthus later did, as more of a balancing act. If we nevertheless insist on squeezing Smith into the modern theoretical mold, we can conceive the process of scientific discovery as approximating the modern idea of maximizing (the pleasure of) understanding and minimizing the disutility associated with gaps in explanation.

For Smith, then, scientific inquiry "is an effort to introduce order and harmony into appearances" by using principles that connect phenomena in a chain-like fashion (Lindgren 1973: 8). The principles of the mind are essentially Hume's science of human nature: "At the heart of Smith's explanation [of the psychological development of science] is an account of the functions of the imagination, which comes straight out of Hume but is adapted from Hume's theory of our belief in a persisting external world and is used instead to show how scientific theory builds a framework to fit on to observed phenomena" (Raphael 1985: 109). In brief, Smith takes Hume as his starting point: the science of man constructed by Hume is for him established beyond doubt.[36]

Smith continues by suggesting that the process of theorizing is best illustrated with the use of the analogy to a machine.

Systems in many respects resemble machines. A machine is a little system, created to perform, as well as to connect together, in reality, those different movements and effects which the artist has occasion for. A system is an imaginary machine invented to connect together in the fancy those different movements and effects which are already in reality performed. The machines that are first invented to perform any particular movement are always the most complex, and succeeding artists generally discover that, with fewer wheels, with fewer principles of motion, than had originally been employed, the same effects may be more easily produced. The first systems, in the same manner, are always the most complex, and a particular connecting chain, or principle, is generally thought necessary to unite every two seemingly disjointed appearances: but it often happens, that one great connecting principle is afterwards found to be sufficient to bind together all the discordant phaenomena that occur in a whole species of things (1980c: 66).

Explanation by way of an analogy such as a machine can in fact become "the great hinge upon which every thing turned," insists Smith (47).[37] Three components of a philosophy of science re-

36. Interestingly, the main thesis in the essay on astronomy also appears to be an elaboration of Hutcheson's view in *A Short Introduction to Moral Philosophy* (1947) that to discover "some natural connexion or order" among the "confused combination of jarring principles" and "to shew how all these parts are to be ranged in order" represents "the main business of Moral Philosophy" (1990b: 36).
37. Later in this same essay Smith nevertheless cautions that the use of analogy—"that passion for discovering proportions and resemblances betwixt the different parts of nature"—could be, as it was in Kepler's case, "excessive"

appear in this passage: a theory connects together isolated phenomena; the paucity of first principles necessary to explain a complex world is an aesthetic virtue; and theories become simpler in time.[38] Incidentally, the view that the economy resembles a machine is an idea that is not lost on today's economist. Consider, for example, Wassily Leontief's comment that "[t]he economy of a modern industrial nation . . . must be visualized as a complicated system of interrelated processes" (1966: 188–89). This view is, however, unlike Smith's, quantitative in nature: "the economic system can be viewed as a gigantic computing machine which tirelessly grinds out the solutions of an unending stream of quantitative problems" (237).

The reason for employing machines as an analogy for philosophical systems—it demonstrates how society, like a machine, can be taken apart and explained and shows how it is governed by laws—is not immediately apparent in the above passage. Smith's friend, David Hume, perhaps put this point more clearly when he penned this passage.

Look round the World: Contemplate the Whole and every Part of it: You will find it to be nothing but one great Machine, subdivided into an infinite Number of lesser Machines, which again admit of Subdivisions, to a degree beyond what human Senses and Faculties can trace and explain. All these various Machines, and even their most minute Parts, are adjusted to each other with an Accuracy, which ravishes into Admiration all Men, who have ever contemplated them. The curious adapting of Means to Ends, throughout all Nature, resembles exactly, tho it much exceeds, the Productions of human Contrivance; of human Design, Thought, Wisdom, and Intelligence (1976: 161–62).

For Smith, the preoccupation with parts stems from a desire for greater accuracy and the search, not for final causes, but for efficient causes. Smith and his contemporaries reasoned that the

---

(1980c: 84). Still, the analogy to systems and machines appears repeatedly in Smith's works; human society, the universe, power, and politics are all compared to machines.

38. This last point is made again in Smith's "Considerations concerning the First Formation of Languages": "All machines are generally, when first invented, extremely complex in their principles, and there is often a particular principle of motion for every particular movement which it is intended they should perform. Succeeding improvers observe, that one principle may be so applied as to produce several of those movements; and thus the machine becomes gradually more and more simple, and produces its effects with fewer wheels, and fewer principles of motion" (1983: 223).

movement of a wheel in a watch could be described more precisely than the reason for the watch's existence; by the same reasoning, human sentiments could be studied with greater precision than broader issues on the meaning of human beings (Myers 1983: 104). In short, "Smith is more interested in the operations of parts than in ultimate purposes, because parts have an immediacy that purposes can never have" (104).[39]

Smith goes on to describe the four major systems of natural science that history had known up to that time; he takes the Greek scholar Eudoxus as his starting point and focuses on the systems of Copernicus, Kepler, and Galileo, and the culmination point, Newtonian physics. He analyzes "how far each of them was fitted to soothe the imagination" and how one system was replaced by another (1980c: 46). Surprising for scholars today, the truth content of the systems is ignored, for the analyses are performed "without regarding their absurdity or probability, their agreement or inconsistency with truth and reality" (46). Instead, three criteria determine the replacement of an old system: An old system is made obsolete when (1) a new system can connect phenomena that the preceding one could not; (2) it can build a chain by using fewer or more familiar principles; or (3) it connects a wider domain of phenomena (Cremaschi 1989: 86).

Smith's predilection for aesthetics as a yardstick for appraising theories—he argues that a theory should soothe the mind—may startle us, but it has striking similarities to the contemporary philosophy of science. Compare, for instance, Smith's appeals to aesthetics, system, and realism to Stephen Toulmin's concluding insight in *Foresight and Understanding: An Enquiry into the Aims of Science,* a work dealing exclusively with physics: "The mainspring of science is the conviction that *by honest, imaginative enquiry we can build up a system of ideas about Nature which has some legitimate claim to 'reality'.* That being so, we can never make less than a three-fold demand of science: its explanatory techniques must be not only (in Copernicus' words) 'consistent with the numerical records'; they must also be acceptable—for the time being, at any rate—as 'absolute' and *'pleasing to the mind'* [emphasis added]" (1961: 115).

---

39. "Smith has read enough sweeping sermons outlining the grand and glorious purposes of society and of creation," explains Myers. "He now wants to investigate the inner workings of man and society to see how these workings conspire to produce the grand designs alluded to" (1983: 104–5).

Smith assumes that each new philosophical system brings progress.[40] While the creation of a system soothes the imagination, eventually, according to Smith, anomalies are observed that conflict with the system, embarrassing philosophers' sense of imagination. As imagination seeks to explain the gap, a new system evolves, once again soothing the imagination until new anomalies arise. Descartes's theory of vortexes and Newton's theory of gravitation, for example, were two systems competing with the Copernican system. The advantage of Newton's system over Descartes's is the ability of the principle of gravitation to explain planetary motions. Newton's system is, in general, superior because its "parts are all more strictly connected together, than those of any other philosophical hypothesis" (Smith 1980c: 104). Nowhere does Smith state that Newton's system is the final or best system of all times; like the others, it is a mere hypothesis. Implied, then, is a view that no system is ever fully complete, that there is no absolute knowledge.

Although no system of natural philosophy (roughly corresponding to a present-day theory in physics or a model in economics) is complete, Smith observes, it serves "to introduce order into this chaos of jarring and discordant appearances, to allay this tumult of the imagination, and to restore it, when it surveys the great revolutions of the universe, to that tone of tranquillity and composure, which is both most agreeable in itself, and most suitable to its nature" (1980c: 45–46). That all systems or theories are ideal—"mere inventions of the imagination"—is clear from the closing passage on Newton's system in which Smith cautions us to keep in mind that we are theorizing and thus dealing with abstractions from reality: "And even we, while we have been endeavoring to represent all philosophical systems as mere inventions of the imagination, to connect together the otherwise disjointed and discordant phaenomena of nature, have insensibly been drawn in, to make use of language expressing the connecting principles of this one, as if they were the real chains which Nature makes use of to bind together her several operations" (105). In other words, the best theory may "introduce order in the chaos" and "soothe the imagination,"

---

40. Progress need not be linear, and unenlightened periods in the history of science can occur, caused, often, by human weaknesses. By *progressive* Smith usually means, as is clear from the passage on machines above, that fewer "connecting principles" are utilized in the explanation.

but it does not rank as a true representation of reality. Unfortunately, after this point the essay is unfinished. Smith left behind some notes and memoranda indicating that the final section on Newton was insufficient and in need of augmentation.

Before summing up the significance of this essay, Smith's reservations about science need to be mentioned. Up to now, we have seen how science progresses within Smith's system. But what hinders science? In this essay Smith names several hindrances, all reminiscent of Bacon's idols. The first is the ignorance of learned men. In the age of Seneca, he tells us, all mathematicians and astronomers were held in "supercilious and ignorant contempt" by the "professed instructors of mankind" (1980c: 65). A second negative influence is an exaggerated respect for authority. After the reign of Antoninus, "the great reputation which the earlier philosophers had acquired, so imposed upon the imaginations of mankind, that they seem to have despaired of ever equalling their renown" (67). He adds that no one would have dared to invent a new system for fear of insulting the memory of their much revered predecessors. The "prejudices of sense, confirmed by education" represent the third hindrance (76). Smith illustrates its power by reference to the resistance met by the view that the earth rotates and is not stationary—a prejudice supported by the feeling that the earth is at rest and not in motion. The final hindrance he points to is an exaggerated attachment to a particular system. Alluding to Cartesian philosophy, Smith argues that the great opposition to Newton's system exhibited by Descartes's followers "did not arise from any difficulty which mankind naturally felt in conceiving gravity as an original and primary mover in the constitution of the universe." Rather, "it was the attachment the world had conceived for this [i.e., the Cartesian] account of things, which indisposed them to that of Sir Isaac Newton" (1980c: 104).

We have seen that "The History of Astronomy" employs a history of stages to depict how natural philosophy arose and progressed. In the essay, Smith emphasizes the importance of using a system with the least possible number of the most familiar connecting principles to explain natural phenomena. The essay provides its readers with a psychological, generally progressive explanation of the scientific discovery of natural phenomena: the process of theory building is one in which the imagination restlessly gropes for an order and coherence ever more soothing to the mind and in which successive theories improve our knowledge by using fewer chains or more familiar principles to connect phenomena. But, because theories or systems are ideal representations of nature, Smith warns us not to forget that they deviate from reality and are incomplete. He acknowledges, in addition, that the growth of science is often hindered by human failures and shortcomings.

Blaug mentions that Smith's essay "went entirely unnoticed by the English classical economists that came after him" (1992: 53). This is not strictly true: John Rae, at least, was familiar with the work, and J. S. Mill knew Rae's book (1834, ch. 15).[41] Blaug's assertion that the essay "exerted no influence whatsoever on nineteenth-century philosophy of science" is, however, mistaken, for the methodological prescriptions in the essay are carried over into Smith's moral philosophy—his system of social science, political economy, and ethics. And Smith's moral philosophy, we know, had a major impact on later thought.

## Tying Up Odds and Ends: Other Clues to Smith's Method

Smith's works and correspondence contain a paucity of methodological commentary, forcing one to delve deeply into his work to puzzle out the facets of his method and methodology. In the first section of this chapter, I reduced Smith's method to four steps and showed why Smith's philosophy is not mathematical or mechanical. We have also seen how important familiar connecting principles, simplicity, aesthetics, and analogy are for Smith. The fact that since the publication of *The Wealth of Nations* his method has been invoked by countless economists on behalf of quite conflicting views warrants revisiting orthodox opinion and combing Smith's works for hidden strands of method. Smith, like Hume, has the habit of setting up numerous subarguments, all valid in themselves—a complex of "lesser systems," to employ Hume's metaphor. The problem lies in understanding how the pieces form the whole.[42] This

---

41. Mill praises Rae's work in his *Principles of Political Economy* (*Works*, 2: 162).
42. Campbell and Skinner say the same thing in their introduction to *The Wealth of Nations* (Smith 1976a: 57). Letwin observes that an "apparent lack of clarity on the surface . . . was the cost of extraordinary richness and intricacy in Smith's analytic system" (1963: 227).

methodological idiosyncracy is one reason for the occurrence of such wide divergences in the interpretations of Smith's work and a justification for the ensuing discussion.

## Smith's Eclecticism Revisited

If we consider judgments passed on Smith's methodology by some of the great names in economics, we will find near una-nimity on the view that Smith was an eclectic. Thomas Sowell, for instance, characterizes Smith's method as an "eclectic" mix-ture of empirical, institutional, historical, philosophical, rhetori-cal, and other elements (1974: 112). John Neville Keynes's comment that Smith "rejected no method of inquiry that could in any way assist him in investigating the phenomena of wealth" also captures this methodological stance (1973: 10). In a similar vein, T. W. Hutchison concludes that "Smith was methodologi-cally comprehensive. Though sharing much of the intellectual confidence of his age, he realised that significant or useful social and philosophical truth, including economic truth, was always a *very* scarce commodity. . . . So the student of society, or of the economy, cannot afford to overlook *any* method by which some grain or crumb of truth, however insubstantial and fragmentary, may be picked up" (1990: 86). There is much that speaks for Smith's advocacy of a pluralism of methods—in particular his way of extracting information by using every imaginable method and his understanding that different problems call for the use of different methods.[43]

His eclecticism, however, has doubtless made it easy for economists since Smith to find support in his work for any method whatsoever. The scholar confronts a difficult choice, for Smith's methodology may not be equated with a free-for-all. It would be folly to neglect the fact that Smith, like Hume, advo-cated and held to a specific method, one he called Newtonian and obviously believed was the proper mode of scientific in-quiry. Indeed, we have already shown that we can be more

---

43. This methodological approach has once again become the fashion in eco-nomic methodology. The return to pluralism came as a reaction to the overly restrictive methodologies of logical positivism and falsification. See Caldwell (1982), Deane (1983), and Redman (1991). Smith's eclecticism, of course, is broadly related, but does not exactly conform, to that of the twentieth-century economists above.

specific about Smith's method than simply labeling it eclectic or, for that matter, pluralistic.

## The Difference Between Social and Physical Phenomena

We can understand the method Smith actually used and his reason for labeling it Newtonian only by placing it in the wider context of both the Scottish philosophical tradition and the literature on Newtonianism. The Scots' optimistic pronouncements about using the natural sciences as a model for social science were no doubt overly confident. Thus, even though their rhetoric supported a transfer, *en masse,* of methods from the natural to the social sciences, in practice they observed a marked distinction between the approaches to social and natural phenomena. Indeed, it is clear in the following passage from *The Theory of Moral Sentiments* that Smith himself drew a fundamental distinction between the study of physical and social phenomena: "A system of natural philosophy may appear very plausible, and be for a long time very generally received in the world, and yet have no foundation in nature, nor any sort of resemblance to the truth . . . But it is otherwise with systems of moral philosophy, and an author who pretends to account for the origin of our moral sentiments, cannot deceive us so grossly, nor depart so very far from all resemblance to the truth" (1976b: 313–14). In this passage Smith differentiates moral from natural philosophy in two primary ways: first, moral philosophers have greater accountability to the public; and, second, moral philosophers must adhere to a higher level of theoretical realism than natural philosophers. Precisely because "it is otherwise with systems of moral philosophy," Smith's "Newtonian method" had to be shaped and readapted to social phenomena in a way that stripped away the exact mathematical-deductive character of the method Newton actually used.

## Smith and Specialization

We have already learned that Scottish education in the eighteenth century was broadly based and manifestly interdisciplinary. And so, too, was Smith's approach to science. Support for this assertion can be found in the contents of Smith's personal library. The books he owned cover a broad spectrum of topics in philosophy, politics, language, literature, history, mathematics, astronomy, biography, geography, religion, art, political economy, ethics, and more. (Actually, the works in political economy are only a small fraction of the total collection.) Smith's lectures and publications, which dwelt on moral philosophy, rhetoric, political economy, jurisprudence, economic history, and the history and philosophy of science, also reveal that he was not an economic specialist. Quite to the contrary, he was a man who, like Bacon, made all areas of human knowledge his intellectual domain—"a general practitioner," to borrow Clyde Dankert's characterization (1974: 224). The consequence of this intellectual maneuverability was that his writings reflect "a vast panorama of human society," making it, with all its historical detail, almost "a moving picture of society" (225).

To today's reader it may, however, appear that Smith supports greater and greater academic specialization. He does consider specialization to be a positive phenomenon, and in his day, it indisputably was. "Philosophy itself," he says, "becomes a separate trade and in time like all others subdivided into various provinces: we have a mechanical, a chymicall, an astronomicall, a metaphysicall, a theologicall, and an ethical philosopher. This division improves it as well as all other trades. The philosophers, having each there [sic] peculiar business, do more work upon the whole and in each branch than formerly" (1978: 347).[44] Smith goes on to explain that this division of labor "is not however the effect of any human policy, but is the necessary consequence of a naturall disposition altogether peculiar to men, viz. the disposition to truck, barter, and exchange" (347). In an age in which philosophers, natural scientists, and social scientists all did essentially the same thing, Smith could not have dreamed of how far specialization in science in general and political economy in particular would go. He was unable to foresee the negative side,

---

44. Consider this complementary passage in the *Wealth of Nations*: "In the progress of society, philosophy or speculation becomes, like every other employment, the principal or sole trade and occupation of a particular class of citizens. Like every other employment too, it is subdivided into a great number of different branches, each of which affords occupation to a peculiar tribe or class of philosophers; and this subdivision of employment in philosophy, as well as in every other business, improves dexterity, and saves time. Each individual becomes more expert in his own peculiar branch, more work is done upon the whole, and the quantity of science is considerably increased by it" (1976a: 21–22).

for the notion of *Fachidiotie*—the specialist with blinders or the economist who is only an economist—lay far in the future. The point is, it was impossible for Smith to approach political economy with anything other than a wide-angle view broad enough to include all of social science and ethics.

### The Golden Mean as Method

Although Smith nowhere states that he is following the golden mean, it is implicit in his method.[45] Without using the word *equilibrium*, Smith plays on the ideas of moderation and balance. He sees that the economy will be in balance when goods are sold at their natural price and factors in their employment are paid at the natural rate. The economy is in a state of balance because "there can be no tendency to move resources within or between employments" (Skinner 1987: 365). Today equilibrium should not be treated as a desideratum; it is an analytic concept, a fiction (Machlup 1963: 59–60). For Smith, however, balance is undoubtedly a desired state of affairs: it is linked with the order that can best satisfy human needs. Smith is a meliorist for whom values are a necessary part of philosophy; he associates the idea of balance with fairness—a fair or natural price brought about by competition, to name one example. The idea of a natural balance of sentiments is also manifest in Smith's writings, with the "impartial spectator" serving as a kind of "arbiter among the sentiments" (Evensky 1987: 452).[46] The impartial spectator, says James Bonar, "is clearly a reminiscence of Aristotle's prudent man who knows where to place the mean" (1893: 166).

Smith's moderate approach is also evident in his recognition that there are two sides to each argument and his endeavors to seek out a middle path. We have already mentioned several cases in which his moderation shines through. For example, he finds analogy a useful tool, while he, at the same time, recognizes that it can be abused.[47] He is cautious about rationality,

---

45. J. J. Burke (1978) argues that Hume, too, is a man of moderation who tries to follow the golden mean and recommend policies of moderation.
46. Shaftesbury, before Smith, had argued that a natural balance among the passions would direct human actions onto a moderate course.
47. This is also, by the way, the case when Smith evaluates Quesnay's system of political economy. He thinks Quesnay went wrong in applying the analogy of human health to the body politic because it does not fit the facts of politics (1976a: 674).

but does not deny it a place in science, as we saw in chapter 4. Several other examples of his moderation are worth noting. Although Smith opposes Descartes's "fanciful" and "fallacious" system, he admits that it is "ingenious and elegant" and that "it had the same superiority over the Peripatetic system, which the Newtonian philosophy has over it" (1980c: 244). Smith advocates a policy of allowing the economy to pursue the natural course of things, yet clearly recognizes flaws in the natural order.[48] He is in favor of commerce, but admits that "some inconveniences" arise from a "commercial spirit."[49] We see in later sections that Smith knows that all desires can have excesses: the desire for personal advancement can become blind ambition, just as self-interest can become selfishness. In the system of natural liberty both are tempered by sympathy.

This moderate strand in the methodological chain would find followers: the idea of balance as method was precisely formulated by Robert Malthus as the "doctrine of proportions." The desire to present both sides of the issue is one reason, by the way, why Smith's methodology can be used to support conflicting views: scholars finding evidence for one side of the view simply assume that they know all Smith has to say on the subject. It is also a reason why Smith is often unjustly criticized for being inconsistent. In the next chapter we will see that the same problems of interpretation have hampered an understanding of Malthus's methodological position.

## The Legitimation of Science in Smith's System

Although overlapping occurs when we try to break Smith's method into clearly distinct parts, his method of social inquiry

---

48. Viner catalogs the flaws Smith sees in the natural economic order (in J. Clark et al. 1966: 134–36). Alone in *The Wealth of Nations*, Smith sees, for example, that employers and employees have the potential to conflict over wages; that the latter have a weakness in bargaining power; that merchants and manufacturers want high profits while the public wants to buy at low prices; and that private interests will oppose the complete freedom of trade (1976a: 84, 114–15, 471).

49. He names three inconveniences in his *Lectures on Jurisprudence*. He observes that the worker whose "whole attention is bestowed on the 17th part of a pin or the 80th part of a button" becomes "exceedingly stupid." Another problem is that "education is neglected." Finally, the commercial spirit "sinks the courage of mankind, and tends to extinguish martial spirit" (1978: 539, 540).

emerges in sharper focus when we consider how Smith legitimates science. In this section we see that the use of connecting
principles, the idea of a system, natural history, an appealing
and appropriate use of rhetoric, and the prudent implementation of statistics make political economy scientific.

## Connecting Principles

**Principles that form a system of uniform causal relations.**  The
idea of *philosophy* suggests to Smith the existence of a natural
order, a cause of order as opposed to irregularity in human
actions. This is, by the way, also the significance of his "invisible
hand" and such similar expressions as "invisible Power," "a
chain of invisible objects," "invisible causes," "invisible chains,"
and "invisible beings."[50] In every case it is the philosopher's
duty to discover and explain the workings of these hidden
mechanisms of natural order, a task that cannot be accomplished
without connecting principles.

In the "History of Astronomy" Smith speaks of principles, not
of laws: philosophy is "the science of the connecting principles
of nature." While Smith often means by *principles* general truths,
he also uses it, as Cremaschi aptly notes, to refer both to theoretical entities—such as the gravitation of prices or self-interest
—and to the laws according to which they act (1988: 13). Smith
notes again and again the beauty of systems distinguished by a
paucity of principles—even in *The Wealth of Nations,* where he
comments that the "beauty of a systematical arrangement of
different observations connected by a few common principles,
was first seen in the rude essays of those antient times towards
a system of natural philosophy" (1976a: 768–69). In *The Theory
of Moral Sentiments,* he tells us, "the propensity to account for
all appearances from as few principles as possible" is a propensity "which philosophers in particular are apt to cultivate with
a peculiar fondness" (1976b: 299). A good system has neither too

---

50. The *invisible hand* takes on multifarious meanings in Smith's writings: it
represents divine beneficence, a state of balance in a competitive market, a
literary embellishment, harmony, the mutual advantage of free exchange, and
a concept of natural order. See Dankert's attempts at an informal taxonomy
(1974: 268–70). The expression *invisible hand* occurs only three times in Smith's
writings: once in *The Wealth of Nations,* once in *The Theory of Moral Sentiments,*
and once in "The History of Astronomy" (1976a: 456, 184, 49).

many nor too few principles and utilizes principles that are familiar. "[N]o system, how well soever in other respects supported, has ever been able to gain any general credit on the world, whose connecting principles were not such as were familiar to all mankind" (1980c: 46). Smith was convinced that his connecting principles—for example, sympathy and self-interest—were so well known and familiar that, like the workings of gravity, anyone could see that they exist.[51]

The two chief connecting principles of human nature are commercial ambition and sympathy. Self-interest is the familiar connecting principle in the commercial world and sympathy the familiar bond of connection between phenomena in the moral world. Unlike sympathy, self-interest is motivational in nature. Individuals are motivated by self-love, "the desire of bettering our condition, a desire which . . . comes with us from the womb, and never leaves us till we go into the grave" (Smith 1976a: 341). The principle of self-interest is illustrated in one of the most famous passages of *The Wealth of Nations:* "It is not from the benevolence of the butcher, the brewer, or the baker, that we expect our dinner, but from their regard to their own interest." (1976a: 26–27). Everything in *The Wealth of Nations* depends on self-interest: because of self-interest people exchange goods with each other and accumulate capital, which leads to an unintentional improvement of the human condition. The "propensity to truck, barter and exchange one thing for another" explains the division of labor and the transition from the early and rude state of society to commercial society (25). Unlike twentieth-century usage, Smith's *self-interest* is not rooted in a concept of rationality. He did not believe that reason should be the primary guide of human destiny; in *The Theory of Moral Sentiments* he asserts that nature implants a consciousness in the human breast that is wiser than reason, for nature intends the good of the species and endows people with social sentiments (1976b: 80).

Smith opens the *Theory of Moral Sentiments* with this sentence: "How selfish soever man may be supposed, there are evidently some principles in his nature, which interest him in the fortune

---

51. Unlike Newton's adversaries, the Scottish philosophers were convinced that no explanation for gravity need be found; by the same token, the principles of human nature needed no explanation other than that they are so familiar that no rational person would dare to doubt their existence.

of others, and render their happiness necessary to him, though he derives nothing from it except the pleasure of seeing it" (1976b: 10). Instead of serving as a motive of moral action, sympathy explains the origin and nature of moral judgment. Smith uses sympathy to explain two types of moral judgment: the judgment of the propriety of an action (whether it is right or wrong) and a judgment about an action's merit (whether it deserves praise or blame). Because people usually seek approval and shy away from disapproval, the approbation and disapprobation they receive from other people tend to function as controlling devices, which subsequently induce conformity of behavior. In this way sympathy creates social bonds and becomes a "socializing agent," a sort of "cement of society" (Raphael 1985: 31).

**Principles as moral axioms: the role of Nature and God.** Connecting principles in Smith's system are tied to values and embedded in the moral structure of the system. Perhaps the most conspicuous value in Smith's system is social progress.[52] The propensity to truck, barter, and exchange becomes the "engine of progress" in *The Wealth of Nations* and makes the idea of progress central to Smith's economics (Spiegel 1976: 482). The desire for betterment is an impulse that sets society in motion. People are driven to creativity, which, in turn, becomes a tool of advancement. They are thus led "to cultivate the ground, to build houses, to found cities and commonwealths, and to invent and improve all the sciences and arts, which ennoble and embellish human life" (Smith, 1976b: 183). In all Smith's works the goals of order and the improvement of the human lot go hand in hand.

Smith's works abound as well in veiled values. The connecting principles double as moral axioms, the link being (1) that both causal laws and the principle of design are grounded in the belief that all causes have an order and operate in a pattern in a dependable way; and (2) that human beings are subject to this order. Thus, not only principles or causal laws but also moral

---

52. "The idea of the progress of society can be described as the historical frame of reference of *The Wealth of Nations*—a fact that seems to have been ignored in the long debate as to how far Smith's method is really deductive or empirical" (D. Forbes 1954: 648).

maxims of nature—"those general rules which our moral faculties observe in approving or condemning whatever sentiment or
action is subjected to their examination"—control the course of
events (Smith 1976b: 165). Moral maxims "have a much greater
resemblance to what are properly called laws, those rules which
the sovereign lays down to direct the conduct of his subjects"
(165–66). Moral maxims that are just and knowable to humans
exist (and are dubbed "natural" because they are characteristic
of human nature). As Hutcheson explains, civil laws were
thought to confirm the laws of nature (1990b: 325). For Smith,
all principles are beneficent, as are established physical laws.
Principles as moral maxims control the natural course of things
while also representing "the precepts of Nature" that people
should discover and follow. The upshot of this value system is
the idea of an ideal social order ordained by nature and the view
that only a society created in accordance with these precepts will
allow things to take their natural course.[53] At work throughout
his thought is an interplay of varying concepts of order: order
in the physical universe, social order, divine order, order
through man-made laws. In explaining moral actions—how
moral judgments are made and why they exist—Smith and his
contemporaries were trying to help people live more morally.
The insight that "there is certainly much truth in the proposition that 'the desire for better men, rather than for larger national incomes, was a main theme of the classical economics'"
is particularly pertinent to Smith's methodological position
(Hutchison 1964: 132).

And so it was that political economy in the eighteenth century
was caught up inextricably in a labyrinthine interweaving of
scientific and ethical ideas—of the theory of natural laws of the
economic process and the theory of a legal structure ordained
by "Nature" as the one in which the economic process would
best promote the general welfare. The writings of the era refer
frequently to a cosmic "Nature" as a "lawgiver," an idea obvi-

---

53. Raphael argues that Smith "made his own signal contribution to it [natural
law theory] by interpreting normative or prescriptive law as arising from
scientific laws of nature. That is to say, Smith treated general principles telling
us how we ought to behave as being the result of general truths about the
way people do in fact behave" (1985: 74).

ously originating in physical science, where a harmonious order in the physical universe had been discovered that was maintained by nature through the laws of physics. Thus we find Smith remarking that the rules that "the governing principles of human nature . . . prescribe are to be regarded as the commands and laws of the Deity" and "are calculated to promote the same great end, the order of the world, and the perfection and happiness of human nature" (1976b: 165, 168).[54] In other words, "the divine Being, . . . contrived and conducted the immense machine of the universe, so as at all times to produce the greatest possible quantity of happiness" (236). By acting according to "the dictates of our moral faculties," we pursue the most effective means of promoting human happiness, "and may therefore be said, in some sense, to co-operate with the Deity, and to advance as far as in our power the plan of Providence" (166).[55] Nevertheless, this reference to God, says D. D. Raphael, "is not a piece of theology." Instead, Smith is drawing "on the familiar heritage of religious language simply in order to make his readers appreciate the remarkable character of the phenomena" (1985: 72).

Because the order of nature is providential, the free market that reflects natural order also reflects the workings of providence. In this way the spheres of morality, theology, jurisprudence, and economics became hostages to nature, so to speak. To Smith and his contemporaries the word *natural* conveys the idea of following nature, which is contrary to existing conditions: a natural society is one that is not artificial.[56] The concept is related to the state of nature postulated by Jean-Jacques Rousseau—that in the state of nature people were uncorrupted and free. Smith often slips into a use of *natural* that refers to instinct

54. And again: "those important rules of morality are the commands and laws of the Deity" (Smith 1976b: 163).
55. We recall that Newton and his colleagues were interested in theological questions. The goal of the early Royal Society (1662–1741) was to "illustrate the providential glory of God manifested in the works of His Creation" (Force 1984: 517). According to Force, the early members of the Royal Society sought to institutionalize the design argument demonstrating God's general providence, at the same time noting that God also made acts of special providence, such as intervention in the orderly operation of the machine of nature (520).
56. Puro (1992) analyzes the use of *natural* in the *Wealth of Nations* and finds eight distinct uses of the term.

or custom, whether rational or irrational. Nature is not to be equated with reason, which Smith trusts less than people's natural instincts and propensities to achieve a natural order. Nature works through natural propensities of human nature, in accordance with the doctrine of unintentional spontaneity, to produce beneficence. Smith no doubt agreed with Hume's view that "[r]eason is, and ought only to be, the slave of the passions, and can never pretend to any other office than to serve and obey them" (1896: 415). Overton Taylor adds that "Smith's references to the purposes of Nature, the 'guiding hand,' etc., were not substitutes for scientific explanations of social phenomena but an appendage to them" (1955: 91).

**Laying the Adam Smith problem to rest.** The existence of two primary connecting principles—sympathy and self-interest—in two separate works invited a consideration of their relationship. During the nineteenth century a number of Smith scholars found in Smith's two chief works two seemingly irreconcilable guiding principles: the controversy over the compatibility of these two works that raged in the literature has became known as the Adam Smith problem. It was the product of Continental (primarily German) commentary on Smith. As D. D. Raphael and Alec Macfie stress in their introduction to *The Theory of Moral Sentiments*, this "was a pseudo-problem based on ignorance and misunderstanding" (Smith 1976b: 20).[57]

The unifying idea underlying all of Smith's work is the "natural system of liberty." Within this system, the sympathy of *The Theory of Moral Sentiments* may not be equated with altruism; similarly, the self-interest of *The Wealth of Nations* does not represent unbridled rapacity. An idea of balance comes into play, which supports the underpinnings of an enlightened legal order. Smith was dealing with two parts of a single subject: the sympathetic and self-interested sides of human nature. Their

---

57. The inconsistency some economists find in Smith seems to be traceable to a neglect or half-hearted reading of *The Theory of Moral Sentiments*. There is also the problem, noted by Bonar, that Smith is more verbal about the limitations of his principles in that work than he is in *The Wealth of Nations*: "In the first place, he recognizes that the desire of advancement has more forms than one, and the desire of wealth is only one out of many alternative objects of ambition. The great admiration felt for the rich and powerful may become a source of corruption in a State" (1893: 163).

interaction is worth consideration, for—instead of being inconsistent with one another, as is so often assumed—they act on each other to induce cooperative behavior. In *The Theory of Moral Sentiments*, sympathy, the cement of human society, is responsible for forming social attitudes (through approbation and disapprobation). Smith acknowledges that everyone pursues his or her own interests; we do not rely on others' benevolence to provide our dinner, but on our mutual dependence, a byproduct of the division of labor.[58] This fundamental interdependence of economic agents—the idea of I'll buy your shoes and you'll purchase my grain—underscores the need for cooperation.

I have come across no better explanation of the interdependence of the two major connecting principles than Taylor's. It might, however, be useful to add that Smith seems always to have in mind the idea of a balance brought about by the interplay of opposing forces—that is, of sympathy and self-interest.

In one work we have a theory of the way in which 'sympathetic transfers of feeling' set limits to the assertion of individual interests and promote social harmony: partly by creating moral sentiments in the minds of individuals which directly modify their conduct, and partly by causing society to evolve a legal system which expresses the moral sentiments common to the mass of mankind, and imposes restraints which not every individual would always impose upon himself. In the other work we have a theory of the way in which individual interests, thus limited, themselves promote economic adjustment and harmony. The two treatises therefore give us complementary halves of Smith's social philosophy (Taylor 1955: 93).

In *The Wealth of Nations,* adds Taylor, competition serves as a restraining force to limit unfair self-interest by making it necessary for individuals to treat everyone with whom they deal as they would their competitors. Competition, thus, could only function in a system of natural liberty, that is, in "a society whose legal system, and whose current and effective standards of business morality, were products of the effective working of the force of sympathy. It was the moral sentiments engendered by sympathy which dictated the system of natural liberty as the just legal system" (1955: 97).

---

58. Myers, too, notes that "the division of labor arises from a desire to serve one's self-interest but in such a way as to engage the self-interest of others" (1983: 13).

### The Idea of a System of Social Philosophy

If we reflect on the development of Smith's writings, it seems logical for Smith to write first a historical treatise on the great astronomical systems of the universe, outlining the systems that, historically, had given order to natural phenomena. Then, having familiarized himself with the guiding principles and systems of the natural world, he turned to *The Theory of Moral Sentiments*, a work on human nature fitting the Scottish academic mold and representing the foundation of a system of the social world.[59] In this work Smith shows how sympathy is a guiding principle of society, or socializing agent, that creates social bonds. Self-interest is also present, but stands in the background. With the advent of the Industrial Revolution, it is no wonder that Smith's interests finally turned to political economy. In *The Wealth of Nations*, he delineates the nature and workings of a subsystem of the social world, the commercial world, in which self-interest at work in a free market economy promotes order and happiness. Since justice is the main pillar holding up society (1976b: 86), Smith's lectures on jurisprudence round out the system by illuminating the institutional considerations necessary for maintaining a well-functioning system of natural liberty.

By now it is clear that the nature of Smith's system of social philosophy is quite different from that of a system of natural philosophy.[60] There is also little room for doubt that Smith believed the systematization of knowledge and use of familiar assumptions about human behavior to build a coherent body of intellectual thought justified his claim to use of the "Newtonian method." That may seem a trivial matter to us today, but

---

59. This becomes all the more plausible in light of the later argument advanced by Playfair, a fellow Scot, that the best way to promote science is through a thorough knowledge of the methods of inductive investigation, an acquaintance with practical discovery, and a study of the sciences in which the rules of philosophizing have been most successful (Cantor 1971: 78).

60. Considerable confusion has arisen from an unfortunate choice of words perpetrated less by Smith than by his followers. The terms *system* and *analytic* have frequently been used to describe his achievements, although they offer a wide choice of interpretations, ranging from an approach treatable by methods of algebra and calculus (Newton's concept of a system) to the breaking down of a whole into its component parts or constituent elements so that it becomes easier to comprehend (Smith's usage and one, as we have seen, traceable to the Greeks). Such divergent usage clearly underscores how different Smith's and Newton's analytic powers and systems were.

"mastering the unwieldy material that flowed from many sources and . . . subjecting it, with a strong hand, to the rule of a small number of coherent principles" underlies Smith's claim as the founder of economics (Schumpeter 1954b: 185). J. Ralph Lindgren maintains, in the same vein, that *The Wealth of Nations* must be considered "a milestone in the history of thought, mainly because it managed to systematize an unwieldy mass of economic opinion according to those popular beliefs of Smith's day" (1969: 897).[61]

Although the idea of a system—a compendious body of thought organized in a coherent way—is central to Smith's method, it can be pushed too far. I have mentioned the fact that Smith always recognized two sides to every argument. The passage in which he warns against being enticed by systems of social philosophy that are too simple is worth quoting in its entirety.

The man of system . . . is apt to be very wise in his own conceit; and is often so enamoured with the supposed beauty of his own ideal plan of government, that he cannot suffer the smallest deviation from any part of it. He goes on to establish it completely and in all its parts, without any regard either to the great interests, or to the strong prejudices which may oppose it. He seems to imagine that he can arrange the different members of a great society with as much ease as the hand arranges the different pieces upon a chess-board. He does not consider that the pieces upon the chess-board have no other principle of motion besides that which the hand impresses upon them; but that, in the great chess-board of human society, every single piece has a principle of motion of its own, altogether different from that which the legislature might chuse to impress upon it (1976b: 233–34).[62]

This is, of course, a plea to allow the system of natural liberty to proceed along its natural course. It represents yet another example of Smith's sensitivity to the complexity of the subject matter, a complexity incompatible with a mechanical viewpoint.

61. In spite of Smith's accomplishments, Hume appears to have believed that the system in *The Theory of Moral Sentiments* was a failure (Raynor 1984: 58–59).
62. Nine years before him, Sir James Steuart had made the same point in almost the same way. Steuart warned against the limitations of the French *systèmes* that "are no more than a chain of contingent consequences, drawn from a few fundamental maxims, adopted, perhaps, rashly. Such systems are mere conceits. . . ." (1966: 8).

Chapter 5

**Rhetoric**
We have already mentioned that Smith and his contemporaries
in the Scottish philosophical tradition placed a significant emphasis on style and language, in part because they did not want
such centers of culture as London and Paris to look down on
them as provincial. A movement was even launched to eradicate
"Scotchisms," the idioms many Scots mistakenly took for English expressions (see Berry 1974). The Society of Arts aspired to
teach the Scots to write English "and incurred ridicule, which
probably led to its extinction in 1765," comments Leslie Stephen
(1898: 5). Henry Home, after 1752 Lord Kames, hoped to make
Scotland a country of distinguished writers and speakers of
good English. It was he who, knowing of Smith's six-year stay
at Oxford, proposed that Smith deliver lectures on rhetoric and
*belles lettres* at the University of Edinburgh. By the time Smith
was delivering those lectures, a movement to reform rhetoric
was well under way. Robert Boyle, Thomas Sprat, and John
Locke before him were all critics of the old rhetoric; it was
their reforms that Smith was dedicated to (Howell 1975: 15,
16, 20).[63]

To Smith, rhetoric is the general theory of all branches of
literature: the historical, using the narrative method; the poetical;
the didactic, using the scientific method; and the orational. After
Shaftesbury there was a strong tendency towards the aesthetic;
it appealed not to reason but to sentiments and the imagination.
Moral beauty was perceived as analogous to the aesthetic appeal
of a piece of art (Bevilacqua 1965: 46). Thus, James Becker rightly
suggests that "Smith looked at the world much in the manner
of the great artists of the 17th century, wanting to construct a
true image of nature, with language replacing paint and brush
as the essential medium" (1961: 16).[64]

In Smith's hands, rhetoric became "the theoretical instrument
for the communication of ideas" and "the study of the structure

---

63. Some scholars have noted the influence of Ramus but have not, to date,
developed these arguments at length (Howell 1975: 32; Bevilacqua 1965: 52).
64. The respective citation to the Wood collection is J. Wood (1984, 1: 314).
Nine years before *The Wealth of Nations* appeared, Sir James Steuart described
his task as a political economist this way: "My work resembles the formation
of the pure colours for painting, it is the artist's business to mix them: all I can
pretend to, is to reason consequentially from suppositions" (1966: 201). Smith
and Steuart certainly disagree on many fundamental issues of political economy, but method is not one of them.

and function of all the discourses which ideas produce as they seek passage from person to person and from age to age" (Howell 1975: 21). The new rhetoric was distinguished by its broadly communicative, as opposed to narrowly persuasive, character; it sought to teach the eloquence of plainness, distinctness, and perspicuity while adopting the method of direct proofs (42). The golden mean is applied here as well: Smith opposes fuzzy expression as much as he does language that makes overly fine distinctions that do not exist in reality.

Wightman (1975) argues that Smith believed in the progress of knowledge through successive refinements in the language used to describe nature. In other words, Smith attributed to rhetoric a major role in the development of science, making rhetoric methodologically significant. Some scholars (e.g., Bevilacqua, 1964) even go so far as to argue that Smith's mode of investigation was rhetorical. Although we can be sure that he considered the style of presentation to be related to the substance of the argument, rhetoric is not *the method* of science in Smith's system; it is, rather, one device that serves to legitimate and improve science.

The influence of rhetoric on Smith is primarily manifested in his thought in two ways. First, there is the use and popularization of Newtonian and mechanical concepts, a device commonplace in that era. In eighteenth- and nineteenth-century Scotland, ideas from physics were introduced into moral philosophy, altered, and then reintroduced into physics (Olson 1975, ch. 1). As a consequence, Smith could say he was applying the "Newtonian method" even though he had, in fact, radically modified the Newtonian concepts he drew on. "According to Smith's reconstruction of the Newtonian discovery in *The History of Astronomy*, theory building is a process by which a term is taken out of the one discourse (gravity as a phenomenon of the sphere of the "sublunar"); it is partially modified in its meaning; and it is finally fitted into another discourse (the theory of the heavenly motions) so that another system is produced. In this new system the modified element is ranked alongside the preexisting elements of the second field of discourse" (Cremaschi 1981: 127). In superimposing Newtonian concepts on an entirely different area of discourse—quite a radical feat—Smith is "not aware of the fact that this procedure is bound to modify to an extent the meanings of the preexisting elements as well" (127).

The second way that rhetoric affected Smith's methodological position was a preference for a demotic style, a method of expression that could be understood by the common man. This element can also be found in Hume's writings and was incorporated, we recall, into the list of methodological prescriptions drawn up in Sprat's *History of the Royal Society*. Smith wrote for the general public, and thus as Schumpeter tells us, "never moved above the heads of even the dullest readers"(1954b: 185). This style, however, should not be attributed to the author's insipidness, as the tone of Schumpeter's comment might suggest, but to the democratic spirit of Enlightenment Scotland. It was probably also a response to his audience, for, as Steven Shapin points out, in eighteenth-century Scotland, scientists' audiences were reliant on the patronage, approval, and support of the nonprofessional sector of society (1974: 99).

**Natural History**
Smith's use of natural history is another factor legitimating his science of political economy—one with many facets. It stemmed from a perceived need to study human life in its social, economic, and historical nature and setting. Natural history validates its conclusions through various paths: through tracing origins and determining basic, universal elements; through the study of existing histories; through drawing up and compiling a natural history of mankind, a storehouse of facts; through the use of the comparative method; through grounding results in the facts; through the use of such basic tools as "experiments," observations, and appeals to common sense; and through the depiction of the chains and mechanisms of a natural course of progress.

As I mentioned in chapter 3, to guarantee the scientific validity of its results, natural history required that knowledge be induced from principles holding in all times and places. Hence, the principle "from which publick and national, as well as private opulence is originally derived" is the "uniform, constant, and uninterrupted effort of every man to better his condition" (Smith 1976a: 343). That this stipulation really did legitimate Smith's science can be gleaned from the reception given his publications. Writing to Smith in 1759, Edmund Burke noted: "A theory like yours founded on the Nature of man, which is always the same, will last, when those that are founded on his [i.e., man's] opinions, which are always changing, will and must be forgotten" (in Smith, 1987: 46).

Smith's aim was to trace the history of society back to its most basic, universal components and principles (the method of analysis, step 1 of the four-step method) and then to demonstrate how these few connecting principles are capable of rendering the chaos of the human world intelligible and subsequently how they could erect a policy on these principles (step 4). The first task is to break up the object of study into individual components, which entails "considering one particular end and motive of human life in detachment from the rest, and afterwards replacing it in its context" (Bonar 1893: 178). For Smith the basic element is the individual. In the words of Walter Bagehot, Smith "wanted to begin with the origin of the [mental] faculties of each man and then build up that man, just as he wished to arrive at the origin of human society and then build up society" (1891, 3: 282).

In searching for the origins of mankind and society, Smith looked to the experience of former times to furnish general principles that could be used to guide policy. To determine man's original condition, for which scanty or no evidence existed, he turned both to existing primitive peoples and to written history.[65] Raphael notes that Smith's "favoured method of finding his feet in a subject was to study its history and then, after critical examination of earlier theories, to make his own contribution by improving upon them" (1985: 105). Studying natives was the ideal way to begin a history of the natural course of progress from a rude to polished state because they were believed to live in the oldest, most simple (and thus most scientific) state in a natural order governed by natural laws. The comparative method, or "the illumination of the past by the exotic present," as J. W. Burrow vividly describes it, not only allowed Smith to explain progress by natural causes, it gave him the means to study conditions of man in all societies (1966: 12).

---

65. The *Systema naturae* by the Swede Carl Linnaeus and Lafitau's *Histories des découvertes et conquestes* are, for example, two works owned by Smith that investigate primitive peoples. Franklin (n.d.), whom Smith greatly admired, also published on the American Indians. On the Scots' fascination with Indians, see Emerson (1979).

The Scots thought that language was perhaps the best way to trace the origins of people because, in their view, the institution of language was highly invariable through time. And so it is that the purest form of natural history in Smith's works is to be found in his essay on language, which he published in 1767 as an appendix to *The Theory of Moral Sentiments*. In his "Considerations concerning the First Formation of Languages," he posits an encounter between two savages who have no language and asks how language would arise. He proceeds by breaking words down into their component parts or elements (the method of analysis) and then examining the natural features of human phenomena and progress, which, he admits, do not always coincide with historical facts. His conclusion is significant for the philosophy of science: he argues that the greater the degree of abstraction in a linguistic structure, the later in time it must have been developed. In other words, abstraction becomes a sign of progress. Stephen Land, who considers the essay in great detail, finds that two main notions stand out in this essay: the idea "that the human intellect has developed through time according to certain discoverable principles, and that the development of language is conditioned by the developing human mind" (1977: 689).

Besides tracing origins, the second demand natural history makes on the scientific validity of its results is that the starting point of social inquiry be grounded in experience—observations, facts, and "experiments." Thus, we find Smith explaining in *The Theory of Moral Sentiments* that general maxims are formed from experience and induction (1976b: 319). What Smith was attempting to create was a Baconian "natural history of man," but he outdoes Bacon. To explain human conduct a natural history of human nature—a collection of specimens of all the varieties of human nature—had to be developed. For this purpose information was collected about the "springs of action," a range of motives, or "passions" as the Scots called them: ambition, self-love, vanity, generosity, fellow feeling, public spirit, etc. Smith and his fellow natural historians asserted that only through "observations of consciousness" can we learn "what our perceptions, and judgments, and feelings, and wishes, and resolves, and moral appreciations are, not by the senses or the microscope, not by chemical analysis, or the estimation of the vital forces, but solely through our inward experience revealed by consciousness" (McCosh 1990: 5). Once he had obtained a knowledge of the human mind by sifting through the facts of this natural history, Smith deduced connecting principles. The method of introspection was designed to overcome the inability of performing experiments in the science of man. Although no social scientist today would profess to making such "mental experiments," the use of psychological assumptions—what introspection amounted to—began with Smith and has an established place in economics.[66]

"Experiments," observations, history, and comparative sociology are the sources from which Smith draws evidence for the hypotheses and premises he postulates. The business of philosophers, according to Smith, is "not to do any thing, but to observe every thing" (1976a: 21). Philosophers are to cull out the facts and not indulge in idle speculation. These facts are to be grounded in everyday experience that can be taken in by anyone.[67] Stewart puts it this way. "The premises, it is perfectly obvious, from which these conclusions are deduced, are neither hypothetical assumptions, nor metaphysical abstractions. They are practical maxims of good sense, approved by the experience of men in all ages of the world; and of which, if we wish for any additional confirmations, we have only to retire within our bosoms, or to open our eyes on what is passing around us" (Works, 3: 333).

Hume praises Smith's method in his review of The Theory of Moral Sentiments: "[A]fter accounting for every part of his theory, by the abstract principles of human nature, he illustrates his argument every moment by appeals to common sense and experience" (in Raynor 1984: 78–79). That is also Marshall's message when he states that "Adam Smith seldom attempted to prove anything by detailed induction or history. The data of his proofs were chiefly facts that are within everyone's knowledge, facts physical, mental, and moral. But he illustrated his proofs by curious and instructive facts; he thus gave them life and force,

---

66. In some ways Smith's method was actually more scientific than that of today's economist. Whereas today's economist simply makes assumptions that they feel are suitable, Smith's "mental experiments" were an attempt to give the reader assumptions that were more than just fancies plucked from the air.
67. In Smith's words, the chain of truths is connected together by a "fact . . . the reality of which we have daily experience" (1980c: 105).

and made his readers feel that they were dealing with problems
of the real world, and not with abstractions" (in J. N. Keynes
1973: 232, n. 1). That this was indeed Smith's intention is confirmed in a passage in the letter Smith wrote to the editors of
the *Edinburgh Review*. In it he praises Buffon's system for being
"explained in an agreeable, copious, and natural eloquence" and
for having been "supported and connected . . . with many singular and curious observations and experiments of his own"
(1980b: 248). Thus, when Smith traces the different progress of
opulence in various nations or digresses into lengthy historical
detail, he is demonstrating that his principles and results are
grounded in everyday facts and are "agreeable to experience"
(1980c: 100).[68]

That Smith believed a particular method needed to be used
to write good history, and that some methods were unsuitable,
is indisputable. Skinner reminds us that Smith placed Thucydides well above Herodotus as a historian because the principal
aim of Thucydides's method in *The Peloponnesian War* was to sift
evidence with the purpose of culling history from myth and
legend (1967: 33–34).[69] If we consider life in Scotland by the late
eighteenth century, we can better understand the trend that
Smith opposed: the inhabitants of the Highlands were quite
barbarous; even the best educated among them still entertained
superstitious beliefs. Smith not only uses history, by and large,
in a responsible way, the emphasis he placed on history as
evidence and illustrations for his hypotheses and premises complements the current trend in the philosophy of science that has
rediscovered the importance of the history of science for the

---

68. This facet of Smith's method has been poorly understood, even by the
economists of the classical era. Jean-Baptiste Say comments in his *Treatise on
Political Economy*: "Dr. Smith's long digressions, have, moreover, with great
propriety, been much censured. An historical account of a particular law or
institution as a collection of facts, is in itself, doubtless, highly interesting; but
in a work devoted to the support and illustration of general principles, particular facts not exclusively applicable to these ends, can only unnecessarily
overload the attention" (1971: xliii–xliv).
69. "History continued in the same state as Herodotus left it till Thucydides
undertook a history of the Peloponesian war. His design was different from
that of former historians, and was that which is the proper design of historicall
writing. He tells us that he undertook that work . . . by recording in the truest
manner the various incidents of that war and the causes that produced it. . . .
In this design he has succeeded perhaps better than any preceding or succeeding writer" (Smith 1983: 106).

philosophy of science. Contemporary philosophers of science have learned that they, not unlike Smith before them, can "use history to provide an empirical base for their statements, or at least to find examples in the real world of science . . . which may illustrate a thesis of their own or confute a thesis of their opponents" (I. B. Cohen 1977: 349).

Smith's final task for natural history is to depict the "chains and mechanisms" of the natural course of progress, which could deviate from the actual course of things. Within this framework, barbarians are placed in the context of development and progress; the result is a history of human development in stages that depict a progression from rudeness to refinement.[70] The assumption that people seek improvement allowed the movement to the refined state to be an "unintended consequence" of human action.[71] Smith next provides a genetic account of social institutions: the way in which they are molded by (1) the economic base of society and (2) their peculiar circumstances. The resulting theory of institutions is rooted in universal principles of human nature, but Smith does not so strongly embrace a principle of the uniformity of human propensities that the four-stage theory comes into conflict with it. His historical illustrations are employed to show how a particular society proceeded according to the natural order of things or, given the existence of an arbitrary policy, how the natural order was inverted. Precisely because of impediments to the system of natural liberty, progress in *The Wealth of Nations* is not necessarily linear: it can be thwarted by human behavior that is inconsistent with social welfare (e.g., rapacious merchants, monopolists, prejudices of the public, or by accident).[72]

It was Stewart, we recall, who dubbed Smith's type of history *conjectural history*. We are now in a position to see why the

---

70. Bagehot recounts colorfully that Smith showed "how, from being a savage, man rose to be a Scotchman" (1891, 3: 277).

71. There is almost universal agreement that "[n]o part of Smith's message has proved more durable and influential than his doctrine of nonpurposive social foundation" (Spiegel 1976: 492). Surely nothing in *The Wealth of Nations* has caught the fancy of the modern economist more than the idea that exchange and free enterprise occur spontaneously without conscious control or design. The concept of unconscious or unplanned spontaneity is especially favored by the Austrians; see, e.g., Hayek (1986: 143).

72. Cole (1958), Evensky (1989), and Heilbroner (1973) examine limiting influences on economic progress adduced in *The Wealth of Nations*.

adjective *conjectural* "is misleading if taken (as it has been by some) to imply that Smith invented some of his data and called the result history" (Raphael 1985: 106). And it has been interpreted this way all too often. The most extreme exponent of this view is Philip Mirowski (1982), who insists that Smith was an "indifferent empiricist" who made up a story where he lacked evidence; who did not test his theories and was not skeptical of facts; who failed to be methodologically comprehensive; who applied methodological standards that have no counterparts today; and, last, who cared little about substantiating the predictions he made (1982: 196–98). No doubt one could complain that "the four stages theory of the history of society reaches its hypothesis of historical sequence on the basis of rather scanty evidence" (Raphael 1985: 106) and that his theory of language is speculative. There is, however, precious little else that is speculative or conjectural in Smith's historical accounts, and there is certainly nothing conjectural about Smith's history of astronomy. Quite to the contrary, it is "theoretical history . . . because it draws on the history of science as evidence for a philosophy of science" (106–107).[73] In short, Smith's "way with evidence was generally far from cavalier" (Höpfl 1978: 40). A failure to appreciate this doubtless stems from a failure to understand Scottish methods and aims.[74]

**Political Arithmetic**
In Smith's day, *political arithmetic,* not the term statistics, was current English. In chapter 3, I have already sketched the history of political arithmetic and found that statistics in Smith's lifetime were very primitive. Few reliable data for guaranteeing the soundness of theories were at hand for Smith's use.[75] Of the statistical information available to Smith, the data on trade were

---

73. "Smith deals far more with actual than with hypothetical history" (J. Clark et al. 1966: 71).

74. In this section I have not attempted to assess the accuracy of Smith's facts and statistics. On this issue, see Hooker (1964–66), Klein (1992), Rashid (1992), and Rubin (1959). Such an assessment would be difficult indeed because it would be necessary to take into consideration the many ways in which Smith uses facts, not to mention his frequent efforts to depict the natural course of things, which, he knows, conflicts with historical facts.

75. See Bagehot (1891, 3: 286) on the availability of statistical information in the eighteenth century.

superior to those on population and agronomy (Hooker 1964). Demographic statistics were so lacking that "Smith could resort to nothing as reliable as Gregory King's estimates for the later seventeenth [century]" (23).[76] What is more, few eighteenth-century thinkers seem to have had an interest in exploiting the data that were available (1965: 51). When, in this climate, Smith remarks, "I have no great faith in political arithmetic," he is not condemning the wholesale use of statistics, but only the irresponsible use of unreliable statistics (1976a: 534). Stewart summed up the problem perfectly when he complained, "instead of appealing to political arithmetic as a check on the conclusions of political economy, it would often be more reasonable to have recourse to political economy as a check on the extravagances of political arithmetic" (*Works*, 3: 332).

Smith's complaints about unreliable statistics are not limited to the methods of the political arithmeticians. He also raises questions about data collection. "Heavy duties being imposed upon almost all goods imported, our merchant importers smuggle as much, and make entry of as little as they can. Our merchant exporters, on the contrary, make entry of more than they export; sometimes out of vanity, and to pass for great dealers in goods which pay no duty; and sometimes to gain a bounty or a drawback. Our exports, in consequence of these different frauds, appear upon the customhouse books greatly to overbalance our imports; to the unspeakable comfort of those politicians who measure the national prosperity by what they call the balance of trade" (Smith 1976a: 883). In this passage we can perceive a plea for more accurate data collection, not a jab at political arithmetic. This is but one example that reflects Smith's positive attitude toward a responsible use of statistics and his negative attitude toward the existing state of statistics. The same spirit is captured in a letter to George Chalmers, in which Smith praises Alexander Webster, author of *An Account of the Number of People in Scotland in the Year 1755*, as being "of all the men I have ever known, the most skilful in Political Arithmetic" (1987: 288). Smith goes on to recount a conversation he had with Webster shortly before the latter's death. Webster was worried that he

---

76. The first British national census was held in 1801, although Alexander Webster took a census of Scotland in 1755.

had underestimated his figures on the population of Scotland;
upon reconsideration, he thought, the figure needed to be revised upwards from 1,250,000 to 1,500,000. Smith concludes his
letter with this statement: "You know that I have little faith in
Political Arithmetic and this story does not contribute to mend
my opinion of it" (288).

Several other references to political arithmetic hint at Smith's
positive attitude toward their use. Although William Petty is not
mentioned in his works, Smith speaks of him respectfully in a
letter to Lord Shelburne (1987: 32).[77] Gregory King is mentioned
twice in *The Wealth of Nations,* first as a man "whose skill in
political arithmetick is so much extolled by Doctor Davenant"
and then as "a man famous for his knowledge in matters of this
kind," i.e., in matters of political arithmetic (1976a: 95, 215).[78]
Since in both cases he goes on to cite King's calculations, the
statements must be taken as positive.[79] Finally, although Smith
does not cite Charles Smith by name, he does borrow calculations from his 1766 publication, *Three Tracts on the Corn Trade and
Corn Laws* (Smith 1976a: 217, note 25).

Although Petty's works were not among them, Smith owned
several books on political arithmetic.[80] What is more, he made
generous use of statistics in *The Wealth of Nations:* he stressed the
use of averages and appended to book I a lengthy table on the
prices of wheat from 1202 to 1764 (1976a: 267–75). To compile
the tables Smith combined information from three sources: for
1223–1597 Smith draws on Bishop Fleetwood's *Chronicum precio-*

77. Not mentioning another writer in a publication was often a sign, in that
age, that the author of the publication did not care for the neglected author's
work.
78. The reference is to King's *State and Condition of England* and Davenant's
*Political and Commercial Works,* in which excerpts of King's work were reprinted.
79. Although Spiegel says Smith mentions King with "condescension," I find
no support for this assertion (1976: 488). In that age, writers seldom drew
attention to authors whose views they opposed or rejected. Consider, for
instance, that Hume never mentions Descartes in his *History of England* and
that Smith never mentions Steuart in *The Wealth of Nations.* It is more likely
that Smith drew attention to King because he was one of the few political
arithmeticians to produce reliable figures.
80. He owned William Heberden's *Collection of the Yearly Bills of Mortality, from
1657 to 1758 inclusive* (1759)—which, incidentally, Dr. Heberden (1710–1801)
designated as the sixth edition of Graunt's *Bills of Mortality*—as well as Arthur
Young's *Political Arithmetic,* Davenant's *Political and Commercial Works,* and
Charles Smith's *Three Tracts on the Corn Trade and Corn Laws.*

*sum* (1707); for 1598–1601, on accounts from Eton College; and from 1602 onward, on Smith's *Three Tracts on the Corn Trade*. The table shows the price of wheat per quarter, the annual average, and the annual average in current pounds. Smith was particularly interested in documenting long-run trends and often remarks on the reliability of the data. The price of corn drew interest in this age because economic investigators correlated it with the cost of living. According to John Hooker, however, "the samples remained much too narrow to authenticate regional or national generalization" (1964: 24).

A final point. It is difficult to portray Smith as a great opponent of statistics when he himself develops several statistical concepts. In *The Wealth of Nations,* for instance, we find a rough idea of GNP: "The whole annual produce of the land and labour of every country, or what comes to the same thing, the whole price of that annual produce, naturally divides itself . . . into three parts—the rent of the land, the wage of labour, and the profits of stock" (1976a: 265). He also approximates today's concept of national income. "The gross revenue of all the inhabitants of a great country, comprehends the whole annual produce of their land and labour; the neat revenue, what remains free to them after deducting the expense of maintaining; first, their fixed; and secondly, their circulating capital (286).

When we view him in this light, we are forced to conclude that Smith was not against statistics any more than he was against mathematics. What he opposes is the use of unreliable data. And, unlike his position on mathematics, his attitude toward statistics clearly suggests that he believes they can be employed as a useful tool in political economy.

### Lessons for Today's Economist

We have seen that Smith's generous use of Newton's terminology and appeal to the Newtonian method veiled his true methods and methodology.[81] The differences notwithstanding, the two approaches do have general features in common. Smith starts, for instance, with an idealized view of human nature; Newton, with an idealized view of nature. Both are convinced

---

81. No doubt the Smithian counterparts to Newtonian concepts could have been developed without recourse to Newton's ideas.

that they have found only "partial glimpses of truth" rather than boast absolute certainty (McCosh 1990: 10). Both were interested in bringing order to the object of their study; and both found the methods of analysis and synthesis valuable while reserving the right to mold them to their own particular needs.[82] Besides being a source of optimism about science in general, the Newtonian impact on Smith's methodology can be summed up cursorily this way: Newton no doubt was to Smith what alchemy was to Newton—a very rich source of inspiration. Newton's philosophy was an aid to understanding, an analogy, a heuristic device. Because these features are so broad, those who persist today in labeling Smith's method Newtonian and mean by it a conformance to Newton's method are being deceptive, for doing so would continue to invite mistaken interpretations such as the highly mathematical, deductive, mechanical "transformations" of Smith's economics.

It should also be clear that Smith's methodology is really a complex of subsystems. Experiment, reason, history, natural history (as both the collection of data and the process of generalizing to laws), a generalist's perspective, the golden mean, connecting principles, moral axioms, natural laws, the idea of system and fairness, rhetoric, and statistics all play a part. Because an attempt to reduce this system complex to simple methodological rules has great dangers, what follows should be viewed as a collection of rules of thumb, or perhaps as some general steps that Smith would have endorsed when using a "philosophical approach":[83]

• Learn the history of the subject and build a natural history of the subject matter if it is not already available.

• Abstract and isolate motivations and processes (through observation, introspection, analogy).

---

82. On the personal level, too, there are several similarities. Both lost their fathers shortly before their births and were consequently very attached to their mothers. Neither married. Both made efforts to guarantee their title to originality, although Newton's defenses, unlike Smith's, were neurotic and unscrupulous. For an insight into Smith's personality, see A. Dow (1984). Finally, both enjoyed public success while they were still living—highly unusual at that time. One scholar, Rashid (1982), has challenged the received view that *The Wealth of Nations* was an instant success.

83. Such an approach, it seems to me, was what the Scots had in mind.

• Examine the interdependencies among the component parts.

• Generalize the relationships to similar situations, that is, form general principles (through observation and introspection and by sifting through the natural history and accumulating as many positive instances as possible).

• Form a system by drawing inferences from the general principles (deduction).

• Illustrate the theory with the facts of natural history, with any available reliable statistics, and with observations from daily life.

• Explain the effects and workings of the principles on social institutions (in part by using natural history).

• Adopt a pellucid writing style: "Be a philosopher," to employ Hume's maxim, "but amidst all your philosophy, be still a man" (in Raynor 1984: 64).

• Base the system on common sense and "put before us the arguments on both sides of the question in their true light, giving each its proper degree of influence, and . . . perswade no farther than the arguments themselves appear convincing" (Smith 1983: 62).

The interconnectedness of the methodological subsystems makes it difficult to isolate components or formulate steps of his method. Any attempt to pull out any one component of Smith's methodology and elevate it to "Smith's method" would be to misunderstand his intentions.[84]

Are any facets of Smith's methodology relevant for today's economist? Because his predilection for rhetoric and analogy has been misunderstood, an interesting, in certain ways unmistakably modern, yet non-Newtonian[85] methodological approach has gone unappreciated while the narrow, technical, mathematical elements that Smith indirectly supported by labeling his method Newtonian have become increasingly exaggerated in the course of the twentieth century. While in the short run the rhetorical element of his philosophy probably aided its popularity (quite

---

84. Consider, for example, Buckle's (1861) proposition that Smith's method is purely deductive and the many other arguments that it is primarily inductive, empirical, rhetorical, etc.

85. By *non-Newtonian*, I, of course, mean not conforming to Newton's methods.

unexpectedly considering the prolixity of *The Wealth of Nations*), in the long run it has generated gross misunderstandings.[86] Clearly, invocation of the Newtonian method and unity-of-science view, as well as the numerous analogies to machines and systems, have left behind a less than enlightened legacy in economics. The "forcing of the broad ideas of the eighteenth century into the narrow categories of modern economics," Myers explains, has caused Smith's ideas to be "separated from their philosophical sources, shorn of their humane features, in order to make them fit the narrow confines of modern economics." The consequence is that "those parts of Smith's economics providing connections with his moral philosophy were largely ignored and Smith became, by later interpretation, the father of the highly deductive science of modern economics in spite of his warnings against abstract methods" (1983: 111).

Misunderstood by later generations, Smith's rhetoric in fact encourages misinterpretations he would never have approved of, especially the wholesale adoption of the physics analogy by nineteenth- and twentieth-century economists without any discernible reflection about its suitability. Smith, who carefully tailored his "moral physics" to fit the social sciences, would certainly regret some of today's trends in economics: for instance, that economics supposedly no longer has anything to do with values, that mathematics has become the chief mode of communication in economic theory, and that fundamentals and assumptions are no longer firmly anchored in familiar principles of human nature.[87] No doubt Smith would also regret an ever-encroaching specialization and its consequences: that economics is no longer written for the general public, often loses sight of

---

86. The emphasis on rhetoric should be mentioned with respect to its current methodological counterpart in economics: the rhetorical studies of Donald McCloskey and Arjo Klamer (see Redman 1989, ch. 16). Smith, McCloskey, and Klamer all stress how economists use rhetorical tools to construct convincing arguments. But McCloskey (1985) goes much further, suggesting that rhetoric be substituted for methodology. Moreover, the main thrust of their message—that positivism (what they call modernism) has done economics wrong—has nothing to do with Smith.

87. To provide one example, some economists contend that involuntary unemployment does not exist; in their view, unemployment essentially becomes a preference for leisure. Bergmann (1987) attacks this and similar assumptions of these new classical models for their conspicuous lack of realism and pragmatism.

the more general conceptual picture, and has completely dissolved its ties with the other social sciences and ethics.

Today's economics, in fact, comes closer to using Newton's approach than Smith's did: his system neither strived for logical consistency nor boasted a fancy axiomatic foundation.[88] Although we can safely bid adieu to Smith's psychological method of introspection, as Claus Horst Recktenwald rightly recognizes, we still need Smith's intuitive approach because mathematical economics "by itself . . . is not enough for a meaningful and useful economic and political theory or even for revealing the 'objective truth.' No amount of mathematical technicality, however refined, can . . . ever replace this inexplicable intuition [of Smith's]. This intellectual activity is in my view by far the most vital part of our science" (1978: 120).

I conclude, then, that the richness of Smith's method lies not in the beauty of a precise mathematical theory or in a system like Newton's, but in its *wide social emphasis:* the special stress on the psychological underpinnings and sociological aspects of political economy, the striving for breadth of understanding and an overall grasp of the economy rather than specialized knowledge, and the view of political economy as an interdisciplinary pursuit entrenched in the moral, political, historical, psychological, and philosophical.[89] Other merits of his "Scottish approach" are its *methodological modesty and realism*—that is, Smith's rejection of absolute truth, his understanding that the economy and its "truths" evolve, and his emphasis on the limits of theoretical knowledge and on human failings. A final virtue is Smith's *practical insight:* his concern with current policy matters and the insistence that the science be grounded in facts (including historical facts). Whereas the method of comparative statics implicit in *The Wealth of Nations* is still alive in economics today, the Scottish approach is rapidly being relegated to history, even though, as several authors have recognized, it actually

88. Reconstructions of Smith's ideas that assume that he moves from clearly stated premises to their logical consequences both distort and miss the intention of his thought.

89. Macfie notes that each of the major figures of the Scottish Enlightenment gave his work "a special slant towards his own special interest: Hutcheson towards morals, Hume towards metaphysical scepticism and also history, Ferguson towards sociology and Smith towards economics" (in Mair 1990: 3).

*complements* today's analytic approach.[90] In fact, there would probably be no better antidote to the narrowness of economics's current methods than a greater appreciation of and revival of the Scottish approach in association with today's analytical, theoretical approach.[91]

---

90. Cf. Macfie (1955), S. Dow (1987), and Mair (1990).

91. A revival of the Scottish approach (in conjunction with and not replacing the current approach) would counteract today's excessive concentration on highly specialized subtopics, the preoccupation with only a part and the consequent loss of the broader picture, and the tendency towards refinement of theory per se (i.e., refinements not created in response to problems in the economy).

# 6          Malthus and Ricardo: Opposing or Complementary Methods?

It has long been believed that Robert Malthus and David Ricardo espoused opposing methods and methodologies and, more important, that only one of them was right. That is a myth, for a closer look at the literature reveals that they come closer to concurring on the basic issues than has been generally contended. Furthermore, on many points of disagreement one economist's method supplied what the other's lacked; instead of being mutually exclusive, the methods advocated by Malthus and Ricardo are, in many ways, complementary.[1]

Discovering Malthus's and Ricardo's real views on method and theory presents no minor exegetical problem. What they really meant and which methods they used and adhered to in practice has been a subject of lively discussion ever since their views were published in the first third of the nineteenth century. It is unfortunate that the answer to these questions is strongly correlated with fluctuations in their images. A look at how their reputations have changed over time is, thus, the first task of this chapter. Next, we will glean further clues about their methodological leanings by considering their educations and scientific temperaments. Finally, I will examine their dialogue on methodology, paying particular attention to their differences, before advancing final conclusions.

## Malleable Scientific Reputations

It is probably safe to say that there have rarely been two more controversial figures in the history of economic thought than

---

1. For this reason, and because Malthus and Ricardo carried on a dialogue with one another on questions of theory and method, it seems most sensible to treat them both in one chapter.

Malthus and Ricardo. In the age of classical economics, Malthus was damned for his "scurrilous" population theory and the policy conclusions opposing alms for the poor he deduced from it. To this day he remains poorly understood, while Ricardo, who was made an instant hero and prophet of the new political economy by John R. McCulloch and James Mill, was later vilified by many for what Schumpeter dubbed "the Ricardian Vice".[2] Indeed both men have become ensnared in a maze of myths and clichés. Ricardo has been characterized as logical, deductive, and clear-headed; he became known for theory that is starkly simplified and fully stripped of sociological, philosophical, or historical underpinnings. He supposedly focused solely on the long run and made generous use of the *ceteris paribus* assumption. Malthus, on the other hand, has been pegged as illogical, inconsistent, fuzzy-minded, but realistic—a thinker with an empirical, historical bent. He is said to have preferred the short run to the long run, to have emphasized facts, and to have insisted on testing theories against experience.

Like all stereotypes, there is an element of truth in both characterizations. Nonetheless, there is, in addition to the stereotypes, an amazing string of conflicting, contradictory opinions about the two men and their rightful place in the history of economic thought—judgments unsurpassed in their extreme nature and in the endorsement they have received from economic luminaries. Because the authoritative sway of these commentators continues to exert a distorting influence on our view of the history of economic thought, we need to look carefully at a sample of these interpretations.

It took no time for the contradictions and extreme views to be aired. After the appearance of Ricardo's *On the Principles of Political Economy and Taxation* in 1817, William Cobbett assessed

---

2. It is impossible to escape the conclusion that Malthus's work has been misunderstood because of a lack of close reading of primary texts. Bonar made this point in 1885: "When an author becomes an authority, he too often ceases to be read, and his doctrines, like current coin, are worn by use till they lose the clear image and superscription of the issuer. In this way an author's name may come to suggest, not his own book, but the current version of his doctrines. Malthus becomes Malthusianism—Darwin, Darwinism; and if Adam Smith's name were more flexible he too would become an epithet. *As it is, Adam Smith has left a book which "every one praises and nobody reads," Malthus a book which no one reads and all abuse* [emphasis added]" (2–3).

it as "a heap of rubbishy paragraphs" (in Checkland 1985: 69). McCulloch, that man who was less critical of Ricardo's ideas than Ricardo was himself, on the other hand, praised it so effusively that Ricardo was prompted to respond: "The praise indeed is far beyond my merits, and would perhaps have really told more if the writer had mixed with it an objection here and there" (Works, 7: 282). Certainly contemporary opinion viewed Ricardo as the winner of the rivalry between Malthusian and Ricardian economics, and it seems fair to say that, on balance, McCulloch's judgment has tended to prevail.[3]

As is well documented, during Malthus's lifetime the tide of opinion ran against "the best-abused man of the age" (Bonar 1885: 1). In spite of J. S. Mill's well-known generosity—lavished even upon his critics—Mill clearly did not favor Malthus's economic contributions: "For if Mr. Malthus excels in any thing, it is not certainly in smoothing the road to knowledge; and if any truths are contained in the works to which we have alluded, they must be of the number of those truths which lie hidden in the bottom of the well" (Works, 4: 28).[4] Walter Bagehot criticized Malthus in 1888 in a similar vein: "[T]here is a mist of speculation over his facts and a vapour of fact over his ideas" (1891, 5: 399).[5] Joseph Schumpeter comments quite rightly that "Marx poured on him vitriolic wrath [while] Keynes glorified him" (1954b: 480). Karl Marx's treatment of Malthus is, in fact, filled with hate and scorn: "We have seen how childishly weak, trivial, and meaningless Malthus is when, basing himself on the weak side of Adam Smith, he tries to put forward a counter-theory in opposition to that formulated by Ricardo on the basis of the

---

3. This is true even though Ricardian economics has at times gone out of style, as for instance, between the world wars (see Lewinski (1919)). It has suffered, most notably, at the hands of W. S. Jevons (1879), J. M. Keynes (1972), and Joseph Schumpeter (1954b).
4. Later in the same article, a review of Malthus's then anonymous article "Political Economy" in the Quarterly Review (vol. 30, 1834), J. S. Mill writes: "When it has been our fate to peruse any of Mr. Malthus's lucubrations on the more intricate subjects of political economy, we have remarked, that although they are in general sufficiently obscure, yet if there is one part of them which is more obscure than another, it is where he attempts anything like explanation or illustration" (Works, 4: 34).
5. Mitchell warns the reader that Bagehot's judgment is "a dictum of a mind temperamentally akin to Ricardo's and therefore temperamentally unfitted to do full justice to a mind like Malthus's" (1967: 275, n. 28).

strong side of Adam Smith. One could hardly imagine a more comical exhibition of impotence than Malthus's work on value" (in Meek 1953: 158). He also accuses Malthus of plagiarism and cautions that Malthus's work sprang from envy of Ricardo (116, 119, 121). Yet in an oft-cited passage in the second edition of his *Theory of Political Economy*, William Stanley Jevons argues that "that able but wrong-minded man, David Ricardo, shunted the car of Economic science on to a wrong line" and praises Malthus for "his complete appreciation of the mathematical nature of economic questions" (1879: lvii, xxix).[6] So it was that Jevons's age ushered in the first major change in public temper.

Although John Maynard Keynes glorified Malthus, he left behind an inconsistent legacy, insisting that "Ricardo's was the greatest mind that found economics worthy of its powers" (in Harrod 1952: 467). Yet he openly concedes that "the almost total obliteration of Malthus's line of approach and the complete domination of Ricardo's for a period of a hundred years has been a disaster to the progress of economics," adding a few pages later: "If only Malthus, instead of Ricardo, had been the parent stem from which nineteenth-century economics proceeded, what a much wiser and richer place the world would be to-day!" (1972: 98, 100–101). Last but not least, Keynes designates Malthus one of the most important precursors of his own economics (1972: 71–108).

Schumpeter accuses Ricardo of having "infected his followers with the Ricardian Vice, that is, with the habit of establishing simple relations between aggregates that then acquire a spurious halo of causal importance, whereas all the really important (and, unfortunately, complicated) things are being bundled away in or behind these aggregates" (1954b: 668).[7] He goes on to add

---

6. Jevons concludes that "the only hope of attaining a true system of Economics is to fling aside, once and for ever, the mazy and preposterous assumptions of the Ricardian School" (1879: xlix).

7. The most famous passage on the "Ricardian Vice" is somewhat more precise. There Schumpeter argues that Ricardo's "interest was in the clear-cut result of direct, practical significance. In order to get this he cut that general system to pieces, bundled up as large parts of it as possible, and put them in cold storage—so that as many things as possible should be frozen and 'given.' He then piled one simplifying assumption upon another until, having really settled everything by these assumptions, he was left with only a few aggregative variables between which, given these assumptions, he set up simple one-way relations so that, in the end the desired results emerged almost as tautologies" (1954b: 472–3).

that Keynes, who claimed Malthus had anticipated his ideas, actually uses the same method as Ricardo, since both were intent on deriving answers to policy questions. "Keynes was Ricardo's peer in the highest sense of the phrase. But he was Ricardo's peer also in that his work is a striking example of what we have called above the Ricardian Vice" (1171).[8] Although Malthus's reputation up to Schumpeter's time was more marred than lustrous, Schumpeter recognizes that "[t]he man who realized that some economic problems are like the problems 'de maximis et minimis in fluxions' (calculus) was no dunce" (1954b: 481).

But Ricardo's supporters were not wholly uncritical of their master. To cite a famous example, Ricardo's abstract thinking, in particular his rationale for abandoning the Corn Laws, prompted a fellow M.P. to muse aloud in Parliament: "Where has the Honourable Member (Mr. Ricardo) been? Has he just descended from some other planet?" (Ricardo, *Works*, 5: 56, 85). And a surprising judgment came from Alfred Marshall, one of Ricardo's champions, when he attributed the "faults and virtues of Ricardo's mind" to his "Semitic origin," his faults being "excessively abstract reasonings," his virtues being his contributions to demand and supply theory (1925: 153).[9]

The same traits, however, have invoked the most generous eulogies of Ricardo. Like so many others, George Stigler views the two economists not as complementary thinkers but as opponents; thus he impugns Malthus's lack of analytical ability while extolling Ricardo's logic. "Malthus had one wondrous gift, the intuition to bring to an explicit level deep problems of economic life. . . . And he had one great weakness—he could

---

8. Consider another passage in Schumpeter: "The similarity between the aims and methods of those two eminent men, Keynes and Ricardo, is indeed striking, though it will not impress those who look primarily for the advice a writer tenders. Of course, there is a world between Keynes and Ricardo in this respect, and Keynes's views on economic policy bear much more resemblance to Malthus's. But I am speaking of Ricardo's and Keynes's methods of securing the clear-cut result. On this point they were brothers in the spirit" (1954b: 473, n. 3).
9. The claims Marshall made for Ricardo's Jewish heritage were made five years earlier by Bagehot (1880: 152–53). It is worth noting that, although Marshall enthusiastically praises Ricardo's contributions to modern marginalist theory, Ricardo himself remarked in his *Principles:* "The opinion that the price of commodities depends solely on the proportion of supply to demand, or demand to supply, has become almost an axiom in political economy, and has been the source of much error in that science" (*Works*, 1: 382).

not reason well. He could not construct a theory that was consistent with either itself or the facts of the world." Stigler comes to the amazing conclusion that the "triumph of Ricardo over Malthus cannot be regretted by the modern economist: it is more important that good logic win over bad than that good insight win over poor" (1985: 111, 118).

We can see today, with the advantage of hindsight, that Schumpeter evaluated the situation equitably when he said: "Both the vituperation and the eulogy are readily seen to be due to prejudice" (1954b: 481). After examining the trendiness of the judgments passed on the accomplishments and intentions of these two men, we can understand why Wesley Mitchell tells us that "Ricardo is a notoriously difficult writer to represent fairly" (1967: 307); why Mark Blaug asserts that "[w]ith the possible exception of Karl Marx, no great economist of the past has received so many divergent and even contradictory interpretations as David Ricardo" (1985: 3); and why J. S. Nicholson summarizes Malthus's position with the statement that "[n]o economist of the first rank has been so utterly misrepresented" (in Bonar 1926: 676). Unfortunately, these extreme views from illustrious sources have left their mark on the history of economic theory and, in all fairness, must be taken with a hefty grain of salt. Only after being recognized for their extreme quality will they lose their distorting grip on history.

In 1957 H. M. Robertson identified "the Ricardo problem" as the "general problem of the position of Ricardo in the history of economic thought" (171).[10] It is no credit to historians of economic thought that this problem, accompanied by the far less acknowledged "Malthus problem," persists. One explanation for its persistence could be that the overstated, extreme opinions about the rightful place of Malthus and Ricardo in the history of economic thought have been, at least, matched by the clashing interpretations of their theoretical accomplishments.

Research on Malthus's and Ricardo's theoretical contributions has understandably fluctuated as new findings became available. The publication of Piero Sraffa's eleven-volume edition of *The Works and Correspondence of David Ricardo* (1951–73) has provided additional information on both economists. The edition

10. The respective citation to the Wood collection is J. Wood (1985, 1: 180).

includes Ricardo's published and unpublished writings, as well as his correspondence, parliamentary speeches, biographical material, and an introduction to the edition that is now deemed a classic. It is doubtful whether the future will yield many more new facts about Ricardo's life and writings.

Not so for Malthus. Malthus's diary of his travels to continental Europe in 1799, kept to record evidence for or against his population theory, was discovered in the twentieth century, edited by Patricia James, and published in 1966.[11] Another new discovery is a set of lecture notes taken by one of Malthus's students, Inverarity, at Haileybury in the late 1820s (see Pullen 1981b). In addition, in 1973 Neil De Marchi and R. P. Sturges published for the first time three letters from Malthus to William Whewell that provide a clearer insight into his methodological position. Until 1986 research on Malthus was impeded by the fact that his collected works had not yet appeared and that copies of some of his works—for instance the first edition of his *Essay on Population*—were very rare. Since his works were first collected in 1986, the *Essay on the Principles of Population* and *Principles of Political Economy* have appeared in *variorum* editions (Malthus 1989a & 1989b) so that we can more easily assess his changes of mind—a special problem, for as T. W. Hutchison has noted, "over his long career, Malthus changed his ideas without explicitly recognising or recording his changes" (1978: 150). Due to an active "Malthus industry," details about Malthus's life and his contributions are still being uncovered and interpreted.

Since 1950 there has been a tendency to appreciate Malthus as an economist-philosopher and not just as the author of the *Essay on Population*. Much of the new work demonstrates that Malthus's views were not as extreme as scholars once believed. As early as 1945, Joseph Spengler showed that Malthus was not opposed to population growth in itself but was interested in achieving the optimum population level.[12] Thanks to John Pullen, we also recognize today that Malthus was neither as pro-landlord nor as dismal as once suggested (in Rashid 1988:

---

11. James is also the author of the most recent Malthus biography, *'Population' Malthus: His Life and Times* (1979).
12. Although Spengler's article is now a classic whose thesis remains unchallenged, we still encounter all too often the myth that Malthus was against population growth.

88); nor was he the staunch defender of agriculture or opponent of manufacturing that many historians have made him out to be (Gilbert 1980). There is also a growing appreciation of Malthus's emphasis on both supply and demand as an anticipation of Marshall's synthesis. This trend toward understanding the whole Malthus is gaining momentum; even his theological views and their relationship to his economics are being explored.[13]

The question of whether Malthus was Keynes's precursor has also generated a copious literature providing glaringly conflicting answers. Most writers find that Keynes was too generous to Malthus. Yet R. D. C. Black makes a valid point when he remarks that the question "'Was Malthus an anticipator of Keynes?' seems to have received almost every possible answer." Although we can never settle this issue decisively—the answer is a matter of judgment—Black's conclusion is disturbing: "We seem to be in danger of reaching a position where Malthus can be 'all things to all men'"—a position that "can only partly be attributed to that lack of clarity and precision in his writings which has sometimes been remarked" (1967: 59, 247).[14]

Turning to Ricardo, we find that there are still several unsettled issues involved with his theory. They center primarily on his value and distribution theory and, particularly, on the controversy over his role as a precursor of the Jevons-Walras-Marshall tradition or, alternatively, as a natural child of Marx. Many economists view classical economics as branching into two clearly opposing streams of thought: (1) the Jevons-Walras-Marshall tributary of general equilibrium analysis derived from Smith and the Physiocrats and (2) the Ricardo-Marx-Sraffa tributary founded on a "social surplus" approach in which the creation and distribution of output is the primary focus of economic analysis. In the latter, distribution is more important than pricing, while economic variables are causally determined; the real wage is predetermined and acts as a starting point for the analysis. A reaction to the view that Ricardo is a part of the

---

13. See, for instance, Harvey-Phillips (1984), Pullen (1981a), and Waterman (1991a and 1991b).

14. The respective citation in the Wood collection is J. Wood (1986, 1: 244, 247). Besides Black's, a sample of the literature on the Malthus-Keynes relationship includes Blaug (1958); Corry (1959); Guthrie (1984); Hollander (1962); J. M. Keynes (1973); Lambert (1986); O'Leary (1940); Paglin (1961); and Robbins (1967).

Marxian stream of thought—in particular to the intellectual tradition characteristic of Piero Sraffa's landmark work, *Production of Commodities by Means of Commodities* (1960) and the further elaborations set forth in the works of Michael Kalecki, Joan Robinson, and Nicholas Kaldor—ignited the controversy over Ricardo's true lineage.

Alfred Marshall first argued that Ricardo's value and distribution theory accords him a place among the neoclassicals. Later, Samuel Hollander (1979) took up this theme in a polemic against Sraffian economics (labeled *neo-Ricardianism* by the Cambridge economists). Ricardo's labor theory of value—or, more precisely, its changes over successive editions of his *Principles*, its empirical versus analytical nature, and the role of the "invariable standard of value"—took a central position in this dispute. In addition, Ricardo's position on supply and demand has become a criterion by which his place in the history of economic thought is measured. Amazingly, a full spectrum of views has emerged on the latter issue: Ricardo completely ignored the role of demand, had an implicit theory of demand, and worked fully within a supply-and-demand framework (see Peach 1988: 121 ff.). Hollander's efforts (1979) to demonstrate Ricardo's ties to neoclassical theory rank as perhaps the most extreme response to Sraffian economics.

Blaug correctly argues against the attempts to treat Ricardo as a thinker who matches up to twentieth-century neoclassical standards. "This tendency frequently results in the creation of a purely wished-for Ricardo whose ingenuity of analytical reasoning is capable of making even a modern reader gasp in admiration. At moments like these, the history of economic thought ceases to have anything to do with the actual past and becomes a kind of social science fiction. Indeed, it is difficult to peruse some of the more extravagant of these imaginative readings of Ricardo (such as Samuel Hollander's) without bursting out in laughter" (in Peach 1988: 134).[15] Certainly both Sraffian economics and the efforts to disprove the Sraffian interpretation have

---

15. The purpose of Hollander's *Economics of David Ricardo* (1979) is to refute Sraffa's position. The work is a polemic in which the modern elements in Ricardo's thought are exaggerated. The problem seems to be that Hollander "floodlights material which was only of collateral importance to Ricardo. . . . The resulting image is a David Ricardo who never existed" (Peach 1988: 125). On Hollander's Ricardo see also Blaug (1985), Moss (1979), Roncaglia (1982), and Stigler (1981).

generated distortions in the history of economic thought. Interpretations of Ricardo are now so diverse and conflicting that it would be easy to conclude from a study of the literature that history must be relative—something different to each person who reads Ricardo.

To come to this conclusion, however, would be gross error. No one should doubt that there are ambiguities in and exegetical problems involved with Ricardo's works. After all, Ricardo himself claimed that no more than twenty-five people in England understood his book; he modestly attributed the misunderstandings to his lack of literary skills (in Mitchell 1967: 302). Nevertheless, Ricardian economics is entrenched firmly in real facts. We can, for instance, say with assurance that Ricardo departs from Smith in method and substance, "virtually reducing economics to comparisons of steady-state equilibria" (Blaug in Peach 1988: 133). At the same time, we can admit with equal confidence the aspects of Ricardian economics that have much in common with Sraffa and Marx—to mention one good example, the focus on the determination of the rate of profit. Thus, Blaug can argue compellingly that "it is perfectly correct to characterize Ricardo and Marx as outliers, not in the sense that they followed a surplus approach to economic problems, but rather that they minimized the role of demand and adopted a cost-oriented analysis of the problems of value and distribution" (133). Despite the marginal features of his theory, Ricardo's theory of comparative cost clearly belongs to mainstream neoclassical thought. It is important to recognize, in this context, that many of the distortions of classical economic thought have sprung from ideological preference or polemical design and can be dispelled if the classical writers' goals and methods of social inquiry are kept in mind.[16]

**Education and Accomplishments**

No one should underestimate the influence of Malthus's and Ricardo's education and professional interests on their approaches to political economy. Their conceptions of political

16. On dispelling the distortions of both Sraffian economics and Hollander's interpretation of Ricardo's economics, see especially Hutchison (1994) and Peach (1993).

economy, the questions they formulated, and their purpose were very much a function of that background.

### Robert Malthus (1766–1834)

Thomas Robert Malthus, known always as Robert Malthus, was born 13 February 1766 in the county of Surrey, England, as the son of an independently wealthy father who was acquainted with David Hume, corresponded with Voltaire, and acted as the literary executor of Jean-Jacques Rousseau. Not surprisingly, Malthus received a rigorous, if somewhat eccentric, private education.[17] In 1784 he entered Jesus College at Cambridge University, where he studied, chiefly, mathematics and the classics. In his first year at Cambridge, Malthus wrote home that he was learning mechanics, Maclaurin, Newton, and Keill's *Physics* (James 1979: 25). He owned a well-worn copy of the third edition of Newton's *Principia* (the Pemberton edition) and complained to his father that "we have had no lectures of any consequence in algebra and fluxions, and yet a man would find himself very deficient in going through the branches of natural philosophy and Newton's *Principia,* without a decent knowledge of both" (29). In 1788 he graduated from this course of study with honors as "ninth wrangler" in the mathematical tripos. Because he studied mathematics, we might assume that Malthus would subsequently develop a taste for the abstract. And so he did: His theory of population was based on geometrical and arithmetical ratios.[18] Even so, the lack of training in "fluxions" that he so regretted later resurfaced in his correspondence on methodological matters with Whewell.

The taste for things mathematical, however, was balanced with a penchant for the practical that would distinguish his economic writings to the end of his life. In 1786, while still at

---

17. Malthus's tutors were unusual characters. By far the dullest, his first teacher was the Reverend Richard Graves, an author of a satiric novel on the Methodists. Malthus was later sent to the Dissenting Academy at Warrington, which had been established for the sons of Protestant dissenters. Finally, in 1783, he became the private student of Gilbert Wakefield, a Unitarian minister who had been imprisoned for his radical political views (in particular, for his belief that the British lower class would have nothing to lose from an invasion of the armies of the French Revolution).

18. "The idea for the ratios must have been acquired by Malthus at Cambridge University where he read mathematics for his degree" (Hartwick 1988: 357). See also Lloyd (1969: 23).

university, Malthus reassured his father: "I am by no means however inclined to get forward without wishing to see the use and application of what I read, on the contrary am rather re-mark'd in College for talking of what actually exists in nature or may be put to real practical use" (in Pullen 1987: 281).

In the classical era, political economy was usually a self-taught hobby. Malthus's chief vocation was the clergy. In 1789 he was ordained deacon and presented with a stipendiary curacy at Okewood Chapel (spelled Oakwood during Malthus's lifetime) in Surrey. He married in 1804 at the age of 38 and a year later became the first person in England to become a professor of political economy, taking up an appointment as "Professor of History and Political Economy" at the East India College in Haileybury.[19] Known to his pupils as "Pop," Malthus based his economic lectures on an exegetical study of Smith's *Wealth of Nations*.[20] He considered himself to be a follower of Smith and regarded the "new political economy" of David Ricardo, James Mill, and J. R. McCulloch as an unwelcome departure from Smithian orthodoxy.[21]

Malthus's first published work, *An Essay on the Principle of Population as It Affects the Future Improvement of Society*, appeared anonymously in 1798 when he was 32. In it he develops the thesis that "population, when unchecked, goes on doubling itself every twenty five years, or increases in a geometrical ratio," while the growth of the means of subsistence "is evidently arithmetical" (*Works*, 1: 12). The *Essay on Population* did not remain anonymous for long, for the first edition was polemical in nature and provoked controversy. The central thesis, well known even to the layman, is that population tends to outstrip food supply in the long run if not checked by misery, vice, or self-restraint. Malthus grounded his *Essay in Population* in two

---

19. His original title was "Professor of General History, Politics, Commerce, and Finance" before being shortened. East India College, a new school (by formal definition not a college) was established at Haileybury near London by the East India Company as a training school for its employees. Malthus held the position until his death in 1834.

20. If the notes left behind by one of his students, Inverarity, provide us with a representative sample of his teaching methods, Malthus required that his students answer hundreds of questions on *The Wealth of Nations*. See Pullen (1981b).

21. Malthus's contributions to the *Quarterly Review* in 1823 and 1824 point out the differences between his and Smith's views, on the one hand, and those of the Ricardians, on the other.

assumptions—that food is necessary for sustaining life and that, after the desire for food, the passion of the sexes is "the most powerful and general of our desires"—and then deduced the consequences from them (*Works*, 3: 468). So rigid was the deductive structure of the first edition that his critics chided him for being too deductive a thinker. Thereafter Malthus made a conscious effort to be more moderate and to give the role of empirical evidence much more weight in his work.

Often neglected in discussions of Malthus's first essay on population theory is his goal—a goal with strong methodological implications: He set out chiefly to refute William Godwin's notions about the perfectibility of mankind, which he rejected as mere unsubstantiated conjectures. In the opening pages of the first edition of the *Essay on Population*, he reveals his intent in colorful metaphor:

> In entering upon the argument I must premise that I put out of the question, at present, all mere conjectures; that is, all suppositions, the probable realization of which cannot be inferred upon any just philosophical grounds. A writer may tell me that he thinks man will ultimately become an ostrich. I cannot properly contradict him. But before he can expect to bring any reasonable person over to his opinion, he ought to show, that the necks of mankind have been gradually elongating; that the lips have grown harder, and more prominent; that the legs and feet are daily altering their shape; and that the hair is beginning to change into stubs of feathers (*Works*, 1: 8).

Ultimately, Malthus's aim in the *Essay on Population* "was to create a scientific basis for predicting the future state of mankind, in opposition to the speculations of utopian writers" (Weir 1987: 290). There are two things to note about this goal. First, Malthus was very much a man of his times in trying to avoid speculative hypotheses. Second, he was probably the first economist to make prediction an aim of economics.

The *Essay on Population* went through six editions in Malthus's lifetime. In 1803 a much enlarged second edition, bearing a new subtitle—*An Essay on the Principle of Population, or a View of Its Past and Present Effects on Human Happiness*—was published in response to criticisms of the first edition.[22] It was virtually a new work—almost four times as long as the first edition, clearly more scholarly, and packed with empirical facts gathered from books

---

22. The title of the second edition was retained through the four subsequent editions of the *Essay on Population*.

and observations made during his visits to northern continental Europe in 1799 and to France and Switzerland in 1802. In the second edition, Malthus tells us that he "endeavored to soften some of the harshest conclusions of the first *Essay*" (*Works*, 2: iii). He also lays far greater stress on the preventive check to population growth, "moral restraint," meaning deferring marriage until a husband is financially capable of supporting a wife and six children (which Malthus considered to be the normal family size).[23]

Malthus's work has often been interpreted as inhumane and opposing population growth, a view that lacks justification. He was not against population growth; he was for ascertaining an *optimum* population level—one that is in balance with the food supply level. The *Essay on Population* also invites the related criticism that its thesis is trite: "It is a truism that the number of people who can live in any place cannot exceed the number of people who can gain subsistence there" (Gide and Rist 1960: 140). For Malthus, however, the problem was one of obtaining a balance between food and population and is, therefore, not trite. In an appendix to the third through sixth editions of the *Essay on Population* Malthus expressly observes that it would be "an utter misconception of my argument to infer that I am an enemy to population. I am only an enemy to vice and misery, and consequently to that unfavourable proportion between population and food, which produces these evils" (*Works*, 3: 578). We recall, moreover, that David Ricardo, John Stuart Mill, and Knut Wicksell, among other political economists, took Malthus's principle of population as the basis for their own economics. The population principle also seems to be the only one developed by a social scientist to have greatly influenced the natural sciences: Darwin acknowledged that reading Malthus's *Essay* inspired the theory of natural selection for which he became renowned.[24]

---

23. Contrary to popular views, the first edition of his *Essay on Population* does dwell upon moral restraint. (See, for instance, *Works*, 1: 26–28). Vice and misery are, however, prominent themes. Malthus must have been speaking in part from personal experience, for he put off his own marriage for financial reasons until he was 38.

24. See Vorzimmer (1969). Malthus's influence on Darwin is mentioned by Darwin in his autobiography (1974: 71). Darwin also critically discusses Malthus's calculations on population in *The Descent of Man* (1936: 428–29).

The *Essay on Population* was followed by numerous pamphlets that aimed at influencing policy on the Poor Laws, which he attacked for stimulating population growth among the poor. In the pamphlet "An Investigation of the Cause of the Present High Price of Provisions," Malthus argued that high food prices were caused by too generous payments to the poor, a stance that brought him in direct conflict with reigning public opinion. A further source of friction was his belief that celibacy was a solution to poverty; because of their early marriages and large families, he argued, the poor "are themselves the cause of their own poverty" (*Works*, 3: 485).

In 1811 Malthus took a stand on the bullion controversy, concurring with Ricardo and the *Bullion Report of a Select Committee of the House of Commons* that an excess of bank notes contributed to the rise in the price of bullion in 1810 and 1811. To this cause he, however, added a second: the high demand for currency.[25] Malthus's "aversion to a reductionist causality which would ignore all causes but one" is characteristic of his general methodological position (Pullen 1987: 283). It was his publications on the bullion controversy that brought Malthus and Ricardo together. In June of 1811 Malthus introduced himself to Ricardo; a warm intellectual partnership, accompanied by an extensive correspondence, ensued.

In 1814 and 1815 Malthus entered the controversy over the Corn Laws and the question of rents. Unlike Ricardo, Malthus supported the Corn Laws because he believed protection would help Britain meet its food requirements. In so doing he made an exception to the principle of free trade that both he and Ricardo advocated. His argument for keeping prices high, however, caused people to believe that he was a mere apologist for the landlords. Nevertheless, the pamphlets on the Corn Laws entitle Malthus—with Ricardo, Anderson, and West—to be seen as a codiscoverer of the differential fertility theory of rent.

The *Principles of Political Economy Considered with a View to Their Practical Application*, perhaps Malthus's greatest work, was published in 1820. The treatise that prompted J. M. Keynes to lavish praise on Malthus is more than just a response to

---

25. On the multiple causes of the depreciation of paper currency, see Malthus's summary review of the pamphlets on the bullion controversy in the *Edinburgh Review* (1811: esp. 343).

Ricardo's "new political economy" as set forth in the latter's *Principles of Political Economy and Taxation*.[26] Malthus's work is distinguished by its key contributions to supply and demand theory, discussion of national income accounting, theory of gluts or general depressions, and theory of effective demand. His analysis of the problems involved with defining national income is so impressive that Salim Rashid believes he should be considered the first methodologist of national income accounting (1981: 68). Unlike his *Essay on Population*, which stresses the inadequacy of supply, Malthus's *Principles* focuses on the inadequacy of demand. Malthus believed that while the supply of goods would constantly increase because of technological progress, consumers, having fixed tastes, would be satiated in the short run and the result would be stagnation. As a relief measure he suggested stimulating effective demand: the "unproductive consumers" or service sector—those who consume without adding to market supply—could take up the slack. Another solution he proposed was the creation of wants through public works programs.

In 1827 his last work, *Definitions of Political Economy*, a volume on semantics, appeared. In it, Malthus designates four rules for defining and applying terms in political economy. Only in recent times has this volume received attention for its methodological merits.[27] From 1820 to the end of his life Malthus prepared the second edition of his *Principles*, which appeared posthumously in 1836. No one knows with certainty who the editor of the second edition was; Pullen believes it was John Cazenove (1987: 285). At any rate, we should be aware that Malthus alone was not responsible for the changes between the first and second editions.

### David Ricardo (1772–1823)

David Ricardo was born six years before Malthus and died eleven years before him at the age of 51. His career in political economy commenced at age 38 and lasted only fourteen years.

Unlike Malthus, Ricardo was not university educated. His father, a Sephardic Jew who emigrated from Amsterdam to

---

26. Ricardo replied by writing a 220-plus page response to Malthus that was later published as *Notes on Malthus*.

27. Machlup, for instance, praises it in the opening pages of his *Essays on Economic Semantics* (1963).

London, sent his 11-year-old son back to Amsterdam to learn Hebrew and prepare for his bar mitzvah 2 years later. When he was 14 he joined his father at his stock brokerage firm, where he learned the business and worked until he married, at age 21, his neighbor's daughter, a Quaker. The marriage led to an estrangement with his family and to Ricardo's setting up his own brokerage business in 1793. By 1810 Ricardo had amassed a fortune, which he invested in land; by 1814 he was able to retire to the life of a country gentleman while only in his early forties.[28] Thereafter, he dedicated his time to political economy, other intellectual hobbies, and, in the final years of his life, politics as a member of Parliament. When the Political Economy Club was founded in 1821, he and Malthus were among the original twenty-one founding members.[29]

Ricardo first became interested in political economy after reading a copy of *The Wealth of Nations* at age 27. It was, however, the urgency of current events—Britain's departure from the gold standard and the economic problems brought on by the Napoleonic Wars—that whetted his interest. As Bagehot aptly observed in 1880, "[t]he peculiar circumstances of his time also conducted Ricardo to the task for which his mind was most fit. He did not go to Political Economy—Political Economy, so to say, came to him." (153). Political economy soon became the "favorite topic" among his various pastimes, which also included mathematics, chemistry, geology, and minerology.[30]

The currency question drew Ricardo into the world of political economy and preoccupied his mind between 1809 and 1819. The Bank of England had discontinued the practice of redeeming

28. At his death, Ricardo's estate encompassed more than 6,000 acres worth £275,000. He made his fortune by manipulating the markets in government securities, which fluctuated wildly during the Napoleonic Wars, consequently helping many to their fortunes.
29. Ricardo is sometimes mistakenly taken for the founder of the Political Economy Club, an idea that may well be an outgrowth of the famous economic breakfasts and dinners he held after his retirement from the London stock exchange. Although its founding was a group effort (see Henderson, 1983), Spiegel identifies Thomas Tooke as the "moving force behind the founding of the Political Economy Club" (1991: 351).
30. Although lacking a formal education, Ricardo obviously enjoyed well-rounded intellectual interests and was active in the various scientific movements of the day. He was one of the founding members of the British Geological Society in 1808, had his own laboratory, and maintained a mineral collection.

bank notes in gold in 1797, with the consequence that English currency diverged from the value of gold. In his first contribution to economics, a pamphlet entitled *The High Price of Bullion; A Proof of the Depreciation of Bank Notes* (1810), Ricardo analyzes the rise in the price of bullion and the falling exchange rate. He attributes fluctuations in the value in money to a surplus of bank notes in circulation rather than to a rise in the value of gold—one of the explanations being offered by the opposing group of antibullionists.[31] His argument and policy conclusions hang on a narrow quantity theory of money that makes monetary expansion alone responsible for the wartime inflation. "The remedy which I propose for all the evils in our currency, is that the Bank should gradually decrease the amount of their notes in circulation until they shall have rendered the remainder of equal value with the coins they represent, or, in other words, till the prices of gold and silver bullion shall be brought down to their mint price" (*Works*, 3: 94).

Although historians commonly insist that his pamphlet induced the English government to appoint a parliamentary committee, the Bullion Committee, to examine the issue and, that, moreover, Ricardo drafted the committee's findings, there is no evidence that he played a greater role in the bullion controversy than any other bullionist of the time.[32] The committee's findings, the *Bullion Report*, did, however, reflect the basic principles of Ricardo's treatise, thus boosting his credibility as an economist. His views were reaffirmed when the Bank Acts of 1822 and 1844 put bullionist principles into practice. Contrary to popular opinion, however, the major result of Ricardo's pamphlet was that it brought him into contact with Malthus and James Mill.

Another outcome of the *Price of Bullion* was that it touched off a methodological dispute with Charles Bosanquet, a merchant and self-professed champion of the practical man.[33] In his *Prac-*

31. Ricardo read Hume, Locke, Smith, Steuart and even Isaac Newton's works on money before summoning up the confidence to publish the pamphlet.
32. "The strength of the legend about Ricardo and the Bullion Report is in part the result of an anachronism, which attributes to the young stockbroker of 1810 the influence and prestige of the famous economist of later years" (Fetter 1942: 657). See also Daugherty (1942/1943), Sayers (1953), and Viner (1937).
33. Bosanquet (1769–1850) was governor of the South Sea Company and one of the directors of the Bank of England.

*tical Observations on the Report of the Bullion Committee,* Bosanquet attacked *The High Price of Bullion* and the *Bullion Report* for being mere theory unsupported by facts. Ricardo answered in 1811 with his *Reply to Mr. Bosanquet's Practical Observations,* where he demonstrates that his work adhered to both theory and fact and soundly refutes Bosanquet's "facts" (*Works,* 3: 154–256). In his *Practical Observations,* Bosanquet had cited a table of the exchange rates between London, Paris, and Hamburg that demonstrated, in his view, that the high price of bullion in England could be explained by differences in foreign exchange rates. Ricardo shows that if Bosanquet's table figures were correct, a broker could have made an annual profit on his capital of more than 100 percent over a four-year period by shipping gold from Hamburg to Paris. He sums up the situation this way. "For any man to compare the account of the Hamburgh exchange, and of the Parisian, and not to see that the accounts were incorrect, that the facts could not be so stated, is very like a man who is all for fact and nothing for theory. Such men can hardly ever sift their facts. They are credulous, and necessarily so, because they have no standard of reference" (*Works,* 3: 181). Most economists since take the position that Ricardo's reply to Bosanquet was "completely victorious" (Stephen 1896: 94).[34]

Unfortunately, the story is not as black and white as either Ricardo or Bosanquet would have wished.[35] R. S. Sayers (1953) has shown that Ricardo's solution to the bullion controversy was unsophisticated and deficient in its simple quantity-theory-of-money explanation of currency depreciation. Jacob Viner finds little brilliance in Ricardo's exposition; he summarizes Ricardo's contributions to the bullion controversy by pointing out that "Ricardo made but few additions to the analysis of his predecessors, and . . . on some important points he committed errors from which some of the earlier supporters of the bullionist position had been free. But the comprehensiveness and the force and skill of his exposition and the assurance and rigor of his reasoning made him at once the leading expositor of the

---

34. In his bibliographical essay on the literature of political economy McCulloch writes that "Mr. Ricardo met Mr. Bosanquet on his own grounds, and overthrew him with his own weapons" (1845: 174).
35. Mitchell's *Types of Economic Theory* (1967), otherwise a very reliable source, greatly exaggerates Ricardo's merits in the Bosanquet challenge.

bullionist position. It was largely through Ricardo's writings, moreover, that the bullionist doctrines exercised their influence on the subsequent century of monetary controversy" (1937: 122).[36]

The next issue to catch Ricardo's attention was the question of protection for agriculture—the Corn Law controversy—which was intimately related to Ricardo's celebrated rent theory. Ricardo was again motivated by practical interests. Rent was a burning issue of the day: high rents and high prices constituted the most important phenomenon in the economic history of England towards the end of the eighteenth and the beginning of the nineteenth centuries (Gide and Rist 1960: 160). Up to 1794, the highest price paid for corn had been 60 shillings per quarter. By 1796 it had risen to 92 shillings; by 1801, to 177 shillings. In the period from 1810 to 1813 the price had stabilized at about 106 shillings (160).

Ricardo defines rent as the compensation "paid to the landlord for the use of the original and indestructible powers of the soil" (*Works*, 1: 67). Both Malthus and Ricardo consider rent a differential surplus; but whereas Malthus believes rent is due to the bounty of nature, Ricardo attributes it to the outcome of the niggardliness of nature. Since high rents signal diminished profits and high profits are the cause of progress, Ricardo believed that the trend of the rate of profits was the most significant factor of production for measuring economic progress. For him, rent first appears when the pressure of population causes land of inferior quality to be cultivated.[37] Ricardo could therefore conclude: "The labour of nature is paid, not because she does much, but because she does little. In proportion as she

36. The arguments of the bullionists and antibullionists still find their echoes in contemporary economic theory; the issues have never been fully resolved. For a discussion of problems with Ricardo's position and the significance of both positions for us today see Laidler (1991), Chipman (1984), and the sources in note 32.

37. Assuming, for the sake of illustration, that first-class lands yield a bushel of grain after 10 hours of work and corn is selling for 10 shillings the bushel, and that furthermore, the population increases, causing land of second-class quality to come under cultivation, then a bushel of corn will require 15 hours of labor and the price, correspondingly, will rise to 15 shillings. Landowners of first-class plots thus receive a surplus value (i.e., rent) of 5 shillings per bushel. This principle is extended further as the population grows and forces land of a lower quality into cultivation (Gide and Rist 1960: 159).

becomes niggardly in her gifts, she exacts a greater price for her work" (*Works*, 1: 76n.). Ricardo's theory has been attacked because "the hierarchy of lands has simply been invented for the purpose of illustrating the theory. But what Ricardo has really done is to put in scientific language what every peasant knows—what has been handed down to him from father to son in unbroken succession, namely, that all land is not equally fertile" (Gide and Rist 1960: 160).

In his 1815 pamphlet *An Essay on the Influence of a Low Price of Corn on the Profits of Stock; Showing the Inexpediency of Restrictions on Importation* (usually referred to as the *Essay on Profits*), Ricardo demonstrates that rising corn prices draw capital into marginally poorer lands, causing the landlords' earnings to rise and the farmers' profits to fall. Reasoning that a rise in corn prices causes wages to rise and profits to fall, which in turn dampens accumulation, Ricardo takes the easy step to the conclusion "that the interest of the landlord is always opposed to the interest of every other class of the community" (*Works*, 4: 21; 8: 182).[38] This anti-landlord stance alone probably did more to split Ricardo's audience into champions and enemies of his theory than any other issue.

Ricardo's theories of free trade, wages, and profit are logical extensions of his theory of rents. While Malthus takes the protectionists' side on the issue of the Corn Laws, Ricardo argues that free trade will reverse the trend of corn prices, for it assures that foreign fields of richer soil will be cultivated rather than the less fertile British fields under a protected system. The price of corn will fall if free trade policies are followed, Ricardo argues, because inferior lands in England will lie fallow. There is impressive evidence of Ricardo's influence in the conclusion of the House of Commons commission appointed in 1813 to inquire about the price of corn: the committee members accepted Ricardo's reasoning that new lands could not produce corn for less than 80 shillings.

Ricardo's theory of wages is very simple: Whatever raises the wages of labor lowers the profits of stock. In other words, wages

---

38. In his *Principles*, Ricardo wrote: "The dealings between the landlord and the public are not like dealings in trade, whereby both the seller and buyer may equally be said to gain, but the loss is wholly on one side, and the gain wholly on the other. . . ." (*Works*, 1: 336).

can only rise at the expense of profits or vice versa. Thus when the population swells, the law of diminishing returns causes continuous rises in prices, which mean both rising prices and low wages for the workers. Ricardo's theory of wages has been attacked by many economists for its tautologous nature. Gide and Rist nonetheless defend it: "There can be no objection to Ricardo's method of stating the law. The whole thing is so evident that it is almost a truism. A cake is being shared between two persons. If one gets more than his due share is it not evident that the other must get less?" (1960: 175).

It is, then, not difficult to conjecture why Ricardo thought profits would tend toward a minimum. The cultivation of inferior lands means that the capitalists's share must fall because the costs of higher wages, which are inversely related to profits, could not be passed on to consumers. When the wage can no longer absorb higher labor costs and the capitalist is just receiving a return for his efforts and no more, the incentive to accumulate capital is arrested. Population growth comes to a standstill; no new lands are cultivated; the economy stagnates. Gide and Rist remark that "there is a delicate piece of irony in the thought that the tendency of profits towards a minimum should have been first noted by this great representative of capitalism" (1960: 176).

If Ricardo had never met James Mill, it is likely that he would never have written a book. The story that Mill goaded Ricardo into writing a monograph is well known. "For as you are already the best *thinker* on political economy," Mill wrote Ricardo, "I am resolved you shall also be the best writer" (in Ricardo, *Works*, 6: 340).[39] *On the Principles of Political Economy and Taxation* was published in April 1817, followed by a second and third edition in 1819 and 1821. Mill's influence did not stop there: he also encouraged Ricardo to embark upon a political career. Ricardo bought a seat in the House of Commons and in 1819 became the member from Portarlington.

Ricardo's *Principles* is a loosely connected collection of essays; written hastily within the course of a year, it unsurprisingly lacks organization. In spite of this, the work immediately

---

39. Mill added, in the same letter: "You must not tell Mrs. Ricardo how I am thus acting the pedagogue over you. She will think (what I think myself) that my impudence truly is not small" (Ricardo *Works*, 6: 340).

brought Ricardo prominence. The "principle problem in Political Economy" is clearly stated in the preface: "to determine the laws which regulate this distribution . . . respecting the natural course of rent, profits, and wages" (*Works*, 1: 5). The changed focus toward the distribution of wealth and away from production opened up a new field of economic inquiry.

Because Ricardo wanted to compare the total value of the different distributive shares, the problem of value became important. It is worth stressing that Ricardo first discovered his "laws of distribution" and then tried to deduce a theory of value from them. He dedicates the first chapter of his book to the problem of value. Whereas Smith had claimed that labor is an unvarying measure of value, Ricardo knew that it is as variable as any other good. He suggests that gold be made the standard even though he is aware that an invariable standard of measure cannot be found.[40] This realization did not, however, stop him from searching for it or from revising the first chapter in subsequent editions of the *Principles.*

Given the advantage of hindsight, we can see that the pearl of the work is the chapter on foreign trade, where Ricardo sets forth the theory of comparative advantage. There he demonstrates that given free trade, a country will specialize in the production of those goods for which it possesses a comparative advantage in terms of real costs. Specialization benefits both countries involved. It is characteristic of Ricardo that the assumptions he makes are quite limiting: free trade takes place in two goods only and between two countries; labor costs are constant and reflect the real costs of labor for production; free competition exists.[41] Of all Ricardo's theories, the theory of comparative advantage has had the most enduring influence.

Between the first and third editions of the *Principles*, Ricardo's ideas about machinery changed. Originally, he held the effects of introducing machinery to be beneficial for all classes. After his change of mind, he asserted that the substitution of machinery for human labor is "very injurious to the interests of the class

---

40. "It must then be confessed that there is no such thing in nature as a perfect measure of value" (*Works*, 4: 404).
41. These assumptions allow Ricardo to claim that the supply prices of the two goods are proportionate to the labor costs of production. His results have, of course, been generalized.

of labourers" if the size of the wages fund is reduced (*Works*, 1: 388). This change of mind, in spite of McCulloch's pleadings not to publish a reversal of opinion, underscores Ricardo's strong sense of intellectual honesty and scientific responsibility.[42]

Ricardo wrote his *Notes on Malthus* in response to Malthus's *Principles of Political Economy* (1820), again, in great haste (in four months' time). Malthus read the commentary late in 1820; thereafter the notes vanished for a century. In 1919 Frank Ricardo, David Ricardo's great-grandson, found the manuscript at the former residence of the economist's eldest son.[43] The notes were published in 1928. They are a windfall for better understanding the differences in Ricardo's and Malthus's methodological positions, for the "quite different habits of mind, methods of analysis, and treatment of material of Malthus and Ricardo are thrown into the foreground" (Mason 1928: 695).[44]

Shortly before he died Ricardo again argued for free trade and against the Corn Laws in a pamphlet, *Protection to Agriculture* (1822). In two other pamphlets he voiced his reservations about the mismanagement of the Bank of England, especially the high profits reaped by the Bank. With his *Proposals for an Economic and Secure Currency* (1816) and *Plan for a National Bank* (1824) he returned to monetary concerns, arguing that the government, not the Bank of England, should have the right to issue money. "One would hardly expect the great champion of Liberal political economy to outline a banking system which could only operate through a State bank," comment Gide and Rist (1960: 181). He also pleaded for the monetary discipline associated with the gold standard.

---

42. Ricardo explains his change of mind in the chapter on machinery this way: "It is more incumbent on me to declare my opinion[s] on this question, because they have, on further reflection, undergone a considerable change; and although I am not aware that I have ever published any thing respecting machinery which it is necessary for me to retract, yet I have in other ways given my support to doctrines which I now think erroneous; it, therefore, becomes a duty in me to submit my present views to examination, with my reasons for entertaining them" (*Works*, 1: 386).

43. Ricardo wanted to publish the notes, but James Mill, McCulloch, and Trower were convinced that they would not find an audience. Ricardo probably laid them aside somewhere safe and out of the way, where they gathered dust for a century before being discovered.

44. For more on Ricardo's *Notes on Malthus*, see Diehl (1929); Bonar (1929); Mason (1928); and Hollander's introduction to the 1928 edition, edited by Hollander and Gregory (Ricardo 1928).

Ricardo died unexpectedly and suddenly of the complications of an ear infection in 1823. In his final letter to Malthus he wrote in "tender and almost prophetic parting" (Empson 1837: 499): "I should not like you more than I do if you agreed in opinion with me" (Works, 9: 382). Upon learning of Ricardo's death, Malthus declared: "I never loved any body out of my own family so much" (in Pullen 1987: 283). And so the intellectual partnership came abruptly and unexpectedly to an end.

## The Methodological Dialogue

### The False Deductive-Inductive Dichotomy

It is, as already mentioned at the beginning of this chapter, a commonplace that Malthus and Ricardo took virtually diametrically opposed approaches to political economy. The cliché, as formulated by J. M. Keynes, goes like this: "In economic discussions Ricardo was the abstract and *a priori* theorist, Malthus the inductive and intuitive investigator who hated to stray too far from what he could test by reference to the facts and his own intuitions" (1972: 95). In other words, Ricardo was the deductive, Malthus the inductive thinker. For a time Ricardo was even dubbed "the father of deductive method" (Rogers and Gonner 1926: 305); Whewell and Richard Jones clearly viewed Malthus as a fellow inductivist (Henderson 1990: 19).[45]

The inductive-deductive dichotomy does neither man's aims justice. Malthus was interested in forming a theoretical apparatus possessing universal validity, in maintaining semantical purity, and in delineating the limitations of theory and stressing the complexity of the subject matter. Ricardo, on the other hand, concentrated his efforts, foremost, on creating a logical structure that would enable him to derive fast policy conclusions consistent with his system. Yet the most serious argument against seeing a dichotomy between principles based on abstract assumptions and those based on factual premises (a very common

---

45. Whewell caricatures the deductive character of Ricardo's political economy in the following way: "[C]ertain definitions were adopted, as of universal application to all countries upon the face of the globe and all classes of society; and from these definitions, and a few corresponding axioms, was deduced a whole system of propositions, which were regarded as of demonstrated validity" (1859: x). This method Whewell then contrasts with the much preferred inductive method of Richard Jones.

way of viewing method in that era and the one that became the basis for the inductive-deductive distinction) is that such a dichotomy does not exist, as J. S. Mill would later show. Mill recognized that both empiricists and theorists use deductive reasoning and assumptions derived from observations of the real world. It is worth noting that an economic law can be a statement of empirical regularity or, as in Ricardo's case, a logical construct derived from definitions, premises, and deductions. Part of the confusion, it seems, thus centers on differing conceptions of a law.

The main consequence of this inductive-deductive dichotomy has been the generation of myths. The foremost of these is, of course, that Malthus did not proceed deductively and Ricardo had no interest in facts. Concerning Malthus, Schumpeter recognized long ago that Malthus shared with Ricardo a basic methodological position—one involving as its first step the formulation of principles—that has not been accorded adequate consideration. His remarks are worth producing in full.

It is certain that the basic views of the various authors differed as did their method of presentation. Nevertheless, nobody who knows their theory will doubt that as regards theoretical problems they all go substantially the same way. Malthus has often been represented as if he stood in opposition to Ricardo as concerns the method employed by them. This is quite unjustified, since Malthus appears to us more 'inductive' than Ricardo for two reasons only: Firstly, because he worked in a descriptive way in a non-theoretical field, that of population, in which, incidentally, he collected his material essentially in order to verify views which he had already adopted. Secondly, because his *Principles* state historical facts as well. Yet the essence of his thought process and the manner of his argumentation is just as 'theoretical,' though not as bold and precise as is the case with Ricardo (1954a: 81–82, n. 1).[46]

As we will see, a closer examination of the two men's approaches to economic problems confirms Schumpeter's thesis.

The second myth related to the false inductive-deductive dichotomy is the belief that Ricardo was not a man of the facts.

---

46. At the risk of belaboring the point, I would argue that it is fallacious to insist, as many authors have done, that Malthus's method was inductive and Ricardo's deductive. What the nineteenth-century authors should have said is this: Malthus put more emphasis on the empirical, Ricardo more on logical deduction as a means of validating theories.

He has, in fact, often been described as "a man writing in a cave" (Dunbar 1985: 474).[47] Anyone familiar with Malthus's frequent reproaches to Ricardo for not paying enough attention to the facts would think Ricardo never considered them. Yet, as his refutation of Bosanquet's "facts" demonstrated, Ricardo was intimately familiar with banking and brokerage practices. Although facts play a different, more restricted role in his theorizing than they do in Malthus's, Ricardo believes they shape his conclusions. In formulating bold hypotheses, he relied on general observation and his knowledge of the commercial world, that is, the London stock market. He builds his laws on the behavioral postulate that people are guided by their (pecuniary) interests. After determining peoples' interests, he simply deduces the logical consequences. In other words, Ricardo studies the conditions that determine a certain economic phenomenon (e.g., the rate of profits) and reasons from the facts that are within his experience and field of observation.[48]

Ricardo's restricted use of facts nevertheless attracted and earned criticism on three grounds. In the world of the stock exchange, the problems he encountered normally required analytical manipulation and resulted in minimal conflict between fact and theory. "But when Ricardo wrote his *Principles*, he boldly extended his method to treatment of problems in which there was a much wider margin of conflict between fact and theory"—a practice that, understandably, invited criticism from all sides (Mitchell 1967: 316).[49] Second, for Ricardo, empirical evidence illustrates and does not determine the conclusions he reaches; and thus he reaches a methodological position reminiscent of Hobbes's. Third, Ricardo was, generally speaking,

---

47. The respective citation to the Wood collection is J. Wood (1985, 1: 7).

48. "Bold generalizations are drawn directly from the facts of some concrete problems which attracted his [Ricardo's] attention in his immediate environment. It was the happy selection of the right features of English industrial life for study, and not the breadth of his studies, that made his theories so important, and gave him his fame as an economist" (Patten 1893: 346).

49. Moreover, Ricardo's analysis is, unlike Malthus's, poor on historical facts. Schumpeter has a point when he comments: "I do not think that Ricardo ever did much historical reading. . . . The trouble with him is akin to the trouble I have, in this respect, with my American students, who have plenty of historical material pushed down their throats. But it is to no purpose. They lack the historical *sense* that no amount of factual study can give. That is why it is so much easier to make theorists of them than economists" (1954b: 472, n. 2).

disinterested in checking his results against the facts.[50] "In this respect," wrote the French economist Jean-Baptiste Say, Ricardo resembled "a philosophical mechanician, who, from undoubted proofs drawn from the nature of the lever, would demonstrate the impossibility of the vaults daily executed by dancers on the stage" (1971: xlvii).

## Diverging Scientific Temperaments

**Ricardo the broker.** It should be mentioned that both Ricardo and Malthus possessed a scientific temper. Both of them were guided by a search for the truth, and both were equally capable of admitting error and of giving and taking criticism. Ricardo was often dismayed that many people did not understand his economics; he modestly placed the blame on his poor literary skills. According to Mitchell, Ricardo "followed unflinchingly wherever he thought his subtle mind led him. Thus, on occasion he could acknowledge difficulties in his analysis and even frankly make what were partial reversals of opinion, much to the chagrin of his most devoted disciples (1967: 378)."[51] Through most of his life Malthus had to struggle against the stream of Ricardian economics. In an era that demanded a rhetoric of scientific certainty and precision, both men thus demonstrated not only an independent scientific bent, but personal courage.

James Bonar notes that Ricardo in 1810 was the first economist to use the word *law* in the sense of a reliable, stable relationship between economic variables (1893: 196).[52] It was an unfortunate

---

50. Some scholars assert that Ricardo and his followers were opposed to confronting theory with facts; this is what is meant when they say Ricardians were opposed to falsification or verification. Ricardo was not, in fact, opposed to such procedures per se; he simply thought them unnecessary; if conclusions are correctly deduced from assumptions that he believed plausible, they had, in his view, to be true.

51. As mentioned earlier, Ricardo made a full turnabout on the issue of machinery and its effect on labor in the third edition of his *Principles,* even though his doing so brought down the wrath of fellow Ricardians. He complained to Malthus in 1821 that "McCulloch has specifically, and strongly, objected to my chapter on Machinery—he thinks I have ruined my book by admitting it, and have done a serious injury to the science, both by the opinions which I avow, and by the manner I have avowed them" (*Works,* 9: 14). For McCulloch's comments, see his letter to Ricardo dated 5 June 1821 (8: 381–82).

52. As far as I can see, earlier references to laws were to natural laws.

usage, Bonar informs us, because it connotes a greater certainty of tools and results than political economists could safely assume. As if to compensate for this overboldness, Ricardo frequently expresses his laws as statements of tendency: wages of labor *tend* to fall; the natural *tendency* of profits is to fall, and so on. Such tendency statements, which are common among the classical economists, may give the theory a more methodologically modest tenor, but they do not escape problems of ambiguity, for, as Richard Whately realized, the word *tendency* can refer to "the existence of a cause which, if *operating unimpeded,* would produce that result" or "the existence of such a state of things that that result *may be expected to take place*" (1966: 249–50).

Ricardo's distinctive way of approaching problems runs through all his works. He begins by searching for the underlying laws regulating the phenomena of his interest; on the currency issue, for example, he searches for "the laws that regulate the distribution of the precious metals throughout the world" (*Works*, 3: 65). He knows that the problem has to be greatly simplified and that this sometimes means theorizing on the basis of assumptions that significantly distort reality. After he formulates a broad generalization, his next step is the deduction of a policy statement. Ricardo's introduction of policy issues in the first paragraph of his *Essay on Profits* indicates the priority he gave them.[53]

Being accustomed to grasping financial relations as a broker, Ricardo was without a doubt gifted at thinking up useful hypotheses. To Ricardo, reasoning made the facts clear. He trusted his abstract general propositions and the policy prescriptions logically deduced from them because his system was consistent: if they were logically deduced, the conclusions were true. We have already mentioned his tendency to cite facts not to support his principles but to illustrate the workings of his laws (Mitchell 1967: 269). Another habit was his reasoning with the aid of hypothetical cases, with what he called "strong cases." We return to Ricardo's use of facts below when we examine Malthus's and Ricardo's differing approaches to theorizing.

---

53. "The consideration of those principles, together with those which regulate the profit of stock, have convinced me of the policy of leaving the importation of corn unrestricted by law" (*Works*, 4: 9).

Out of these practices emerged a narrow view of political economy. "With Ricardo economics took a major step toward abstract models, rigid and artificial definitions, syllogistic reasoning—and the direct application of the results to policy. The historical, the institutional, and the empirical faded into the background, and explicit social philosophy shrank to a few passing remarks. Comparative statics became the dominant—though usually implicit—approach" (Sowell 1974: 113). Phyllis Deane makes the important point that "Ricardo was the first specialist economist" (1978: 75). This, she rightly sees, involves both a positive and negative side: "[U]ndoubtedly he oversimplified the practical economic problems which he considered, by abstracting them from their social and political context. And it is arguable that he helped to narrow the scope and significance of economic thought by giving it a rationale for developing independently of the other social sciences" (75). Indeed, political economy had not yet built up a body of analytical principles and was not firmly delimited from neighboring disciplines; students of political economy needed principles to organize their thoughts, just as practitioners of the profession needed a common approach that would allow them to assess the discipline's progress. This narrow, exigent type of theorizing that aimed at extracting principles and putting them to use to deduce policy conclusions must surely count as a landmark in the history of the methodology of economics.

But its narrowness also entails shortcomings. Perhaps the most objectionable quality of Ricardo's method derives from the fact that he approached political economy as a broker does. His working on the London stock exchange required the ability to make quick decisions and assess the situation by reducing the problem to simple analytical relations that, nonetheless, did not deviate from reality so greatly that his calculations would go awry. After years of awe-inspiring success on the exchange, Ricardo was self-assured and fully at ease with this approach. For a political economist, however, this method can only lead to what might be termed, euphemistically, "brokers' myopia." A broker, after all, focuses chiefly on two variables in the economy: inflation and interest rates. Although adequate for someone working in the money market, such a perspective results in distortions when considering the economy, which includes a goods market and is affected by such other crucial variables as the unemployment rate, growth, the ability to export, consumer income, and so on.[54]

Unfortunately, in Ricardo's case, brokers' myopia was combined with a most uncompromising character. Although sincerely interested in Malthus's ideas on political economy, he was often so pleased with his own arguments that he found it unnecessary to amend them in the face of criticism. He admitted this failing in a letter to his friend Hutches Trower in 1818. "My discussions with Malthus have been innumerable, and in my eagerness to convince him that he was wrong, on some points on which we differed, I was led into a deeper consideration of many parts of the subject than I had before given them, and though I have failed to convince him, and may not have satisfied others, I have convinced myself; and think that I have a very consistent theory in my own mind" (*Works*, 7: 246).

But Ricardo's one-track mind sometimes also worked to the detriment of his theory. He was "one of those men who, though gifted with keen reasoning powers, nevertheless lack the ability to grasp the meaning of anyone whose mind follows a different train of thought" (St. Clair 1957: 186). He was at least superficially aware of this weakness, for he conceded the fault to Malthus in November 1820. "Knowing as I do how much we are influenced by taking a particular view of a subject, and how difficult it is to destroy a train of ideas which have long followed each other in the mind, I will not say I am right about the effects of unproductive demand, and therefore it is possible that five years hence I may think as you do on the subject, but at present I do not see the least probability of such a change for every renewed consideration of the question confirms me in the opinion which I have long held" (*Works*, 8: 311). In spite of Ricardo's acknowledgement, Malthus, would continue to complain to Ricardo in a letter he wrote to him in October 1821: "I am either most unfortunate in my explanations, or your mind is so entirely

---

54. Marx also noted this phenomenon: "Ricardo makes his primitive fisherman and primitive hunter into owners of commodities who immediately exchange their fish and game in proportion to the labour-time which is materialized in these exchange-values. On this occasion he slips into the anachronism of allowing the primitive fisherman and hunter to calculate the value of their implements in accordance with the annuity tables used on the London Stock Exchange in 1817" (1976: 169, n. 31).

prepossessed with your own views on the statement, which departs from them the degree of attention which is necessary to put you in possession of what is meant" (9: 90). Ricardo replied in turn: "It is certainly probable that the fault is with me, in not understanding the propositions you submit to me, and it may arise, as you say, from my being too much prepossessed in favour of my own views; but I do not plead guilty to the charge of not giving the requisite degree of attention to the propositions themselves" (9: 95).

Ricardo's tendency to a one-track mind is most clearly at work in two issues: his refusal to accept the possibility of a general depression and the tone of his *Notes on Malthus*. He could not admit the possibility of gluts because he defined production in his system as production for consumption in a doctrinaire and unyielding fashion.[55] All Malthus's proddings could not jar him out of his pre-capitalist preconceptions of simple commodity production in which money acts solely as a medium of exchange. The *Notes on Malthus* are filled with impatient comments about the position Malthus took in his *Principles*, "a book which on not a few, even of the technical questions of economic theory, occupies a position which in the light of the later knowledge seems sounder than his friend David Ricardo's *On the Principles of Political Economy and Taxation*" (Mitchell 1967: 259).[56]

**Malthus: proportions, principles, and statistics.** The fact of the matter is that Ricardo was more interested in results than in method. Consequently, it comes as no surprise to learn that Malthus was the better methodologist. He developed his own distinct position on methodology, "the doctrine of proportions," which, in a nutshell, meant identifying the extremes and then finding a middle way that he viewed as an optimum. To William

---

55. "Productions are always bought by productions, or by services; money is only the medium by which the exchange is effected. Too much of a particular commodity may be produced, of which there may be such a glut in the market, as not to repay the capital expended on it; but this cannot be the case with respect to all commodities" (*Works* 1: 291–92).

56. Consider, for example, the sharp tone of two of Ricardo's comments. To Malthus's statement that rents appear on land after a nation obtains a certain level of affluence, Ricardo responds with considerable irritation: "Who denies this?" On Malthus's contention that there can be gluts, Ricardo has this to say: "Mr. Malthus's peculiar theory is that supplies may be so abundant, that they may not find a market" (*Works* 2: 127, 240).

Empson, Malthus's doctrine of proportions is the central tenet running through all his writings (1837: 470). The essence of this idea is stated in his *Principles*.

It will be found, I believe, true that all the great results in political economy, respecting wealth, depend upon *proportions;* and it is from overlooking this most important truth, that so many errors have prevailed in the prediction of consequences; that nations have sometimes been enriched when it was expected that they would be impoverished, and impoverished when it was expected that they would be enriched; and that such contradictory opinions have occasionally prevailed respecting the most effective encouragements to the increase of wealth (*Works*, 6: 330).

Related to this doctrine is Malthus's oft-quoted comment that "[m]any of the questions both in morals and politics seem to be of the nature of the problems *de maximis* and *minimus* in fluxions; in which there is always a point where a certain effect is the greatest, while on either side of this point it gradually diminishes"—an obvious reference to calculus (*Works*, 7: 102). Malthus often said that we have to content ourselves with approximations in political economy where we are working with proportions, and added that "[a]ll general proportions however of every kind should be applied with considerable caution" (2: 196). Thus, toward the end of the *Principles*, we find Malthus explaining that his doctrine of proportions cannot deliver certain results because of the nature of the subject matter:

In reference to the main doctrine inculcated in the latter part of this work, namely, that the progress of wealth depends upon proportions, it will be objected, perhaps, that it necessarily opens the way to differences of opinion relating to these proportions, and thus throws a kind of uncertainty over the science of political economy which was not supposed to belong to it. If, however, the doctrine should be found, upon sufficient examination, to be true; if it adequately accounts for things as they are, and explains consistently why frequent mistakes have been made respecting the future, it will be allowed that such objectors are answered. We cannot make a science more certain by our wishes or opinions; but we may obviously make it much more uncertain in its application, by believing it to be what it is not (6: 344).

Malthus's doctrine of proportions is a temperate method. Even in his discussion of the costs and benefits of generalization and empiricism he advocates striking a balance: "Aware, however, of my liability to this error [of oversimplifying] on the one side, and to the error of not referring sufficiently to experience on the other, my aim will be to pursue, as far as I am able, a just mean between the two extremes, and to approach, as near as I can, to the great object of my research—the truth" (*Works*, 5: 17). The author of the *Essay on Population* has often been portrayed as an extreme thinker, but "any interpretation of Malthus that depicts him as an extreme necessitarian, or any other kind of extremist for that matter, has to overcome the evidence of his commitment to moderation and the golden mean as a methodological principle" (Collini et al. 1983: 72).

Malthus systematically applied the doctrine of proportions to his economic analysis. He found fault, for instance, with Smith's theory of saving because "the principle of saving, pushed to excess, would destroy the motive to production" (*Works*, 5: 9). He also applied the principle to the division of landed property: "There is here then a point as well as in the other instance, though we may not know how to place it, where the division of property is best suited to the actual circumstances of the society, and calculated to give the best stimulus to production and to the increase of wealth and population" (5: 10). He speaks too of a balance or the right proportion between consumption and accumulation; both the *Principles* and *Essay on Population* abound with other examples.[57]

Malthus held to the doctrine of proportions not only for economic but also for moral reasons (Pullen 1982: 284). Steeped in the Smithian tradition as he was, Malthus stipulated that political economy was a science closer to moral philosophy than mathematics. Pullen speculates that Malthus's mild personal temperament may also explain why he adhered to the doctrine of proportions (1982: 284); but although Ricardo, too, was known for a moderate, equanimous disposition, the scientific temperaments of the two men diverged sharply. Pullen mentions yet another reason that seems more plausible: "All economic problems appeared to him essentially as *problems not of scarcity or of choice, but of balance*. He believed that the theoretically correct solution to any economic problem would be the one that identified the optimum levels for the relevant determinants, and that the best economic policies would be those designed to attain the

---

57. Cf. also Malthus's *Works* (6: 326, 327, 344), (2: 196, 197, 251), and Pancoast (1943).

optimum levels [emphasis added]" (1982: 285). This explanation is particularly valid for Malthus's population theory, in which political economy is conceived as the balance of opposing forces; that is, population is regulated by balancing the need for subsistence with the passion between the sexes. Pullen concludes, rightly, that the doctrine of proportions should be considered a major contribution to the history of economic thought. "The view that in most if not all economic matters the best solution lies somewhere between two extremes is far from trite. It gives a new dimension to the methodology of economics. It directs the course of debate away from confrontations over extremes, and focuses attention on the crucial issue of delineating the middle ground and searching for the best balance between opposing tendencies. If this framework of analysis had been more widely accepted, much unnecessary controversy might have been avoided in the history of economics" (285).

A second reason for Malthus's adherence to this doctrine is that this framework of analysis was not novel; it reached back at least as far as Adam Smith. The idea of moderation or a golden mean that permeates his works is not just a relic from Smith; it is a part of Malthus's training as a clergyman at Cambridge—the theological *via media*, a modest stance about the possibility of obtaining theological knowledge. A. M. C. Waterman describes the epistemological stance on theology prevailing at Cambridge in Malthus's day this way: "The proper course is to affirm all that scripture clearly affirms, and where the scripture is doubtful or ambiguous to go on using the actual works and phrases without insisting on any exclusive interpretation" (1991a: 427). Moreover, the balance analogy was popular in science at the time and considered a highly desirable state of affairs. The question facing Malthus, then, was how to establish and maintain this condition in the practical realm. Generally speaking, the answer was that balance could be achieved by "purposeful, judicious action" (Mayr 1986: 155), exactly the idea manifested in Malthus's theory of moral constraint.

As mentioned earlier, the portrayal of Malthus as a purely inductive, antideductive thinker is a myth. Contrary to popular opinion, he knew facts could not replace theory and recognized the importance of and the need for general principles. This is clear from the title of chapter 9 of the second and later editions of the *Essay on Population,* "Of the necessity of general principles on the subject." He was acutely aware that the generalizations made in the first edition of the *Essay* were too sweeping and therefore remedied this defect in later editions. Moreover, in his letters to Whewell, the primary advocate of what was then called the inductive approach, Malthus defends Ricardo's abstract reasoning (De Marchi and Sturges 1973; Henderson 1990: 18–19). Shortly after the Political Economy Club had debated whether any of Ricardo's principles were correct and come to rather negative conclusions, Malthus wrote Whewell: "My apprehension at present is that the tide is setting too strong against him [Ricardo]" (in Henderson 1990: 21).[58] In other words, Malthus took a middle position between the Ricardians and the Cambridge inductivists (primarily Whewell and Jones). What I am getting at is this: It is wrong to assume, as most scholars of political economy do, that Ricardo alone deserves the title "founder of economics"[59] because he was the primary figure to contribute to modern economic analysis "abstract reasoning, proceeding from a few general principles that commend themselves to the reader as reasonable to a multitude of conclusions checked at points against everyday observation," or, for that matter, that it was "Ricardo more than anyone else who created the flavour of economic theory and analysis" (Arrow 1991: 77). The fact is that both Ricardo and Malthus made use of abstract reasoning and Ricardo did not regularly check his conclusions against everyday observation.

Malthus's firm belief that comprehensiveness should not be sacrificed to clarity has been interpreted ungenerously by his critics as inconsistency and indecision. Even his friend David Ricardo, for instance, complained to McCulloch after reading Malthus's *Principles:* "At present I feel a real difficulty, for I confess I do not very clearly perceive what Mr. Malthus system is" (*Works,* 8: 182). Although Ricardo was irritated by Malthus's efforts to incorporate greater complexity into the subject matter,

---

58. In January and April of 1831 the Political Economy Club twice debated Torrens's question "What improvements have been affected in the science of political economy since the publication of Mr. Ricardo's great work; and are there any of the principles first advanced in that work now acknowledged to be correct?" (Goldman 1983: 598).

59. On Ricardo as the founding father of economics, consider, *inter alia,* the comments of Stephen (1896: 96) and the *Economist* (1951: 502).

that is exactly the direction much of the literature of the post-classical era has taken.[60] Moreover, unlike Ricardo, Malthus was clearly interested in the limitations of economic knowledge, especially in identifying exceptions to and qualifications of generalizations.[61] Yet to his contemporaries, looking for certain knowledge, Malthus was merely an uncertain bungler. Consciously circumspect, he never trusted elaborate simplification, reasoning from single causes or unrealistic assumptions, or reason without recourse to facts. Observation inspired him, and once a theory was born he never ceased to test it against the facts. The stimulus for his work derived from much wider, more scholarly sources than Ricardo's did: from the study of economic classics, current events, and history, from his observations during travels, and from conversations with Ricardo and others.

We can briefly sum up Malthus's method of inquiry in three stages. His starting point, like Ricardo's, was the formulation of a general proposition, not empirical research. The second step was to collect and sort out the data to assess what support could be mustered for the proposition. Here Malthus relied on observations to validate his results. The third step was to determine whether his generalizations could be extended to other countries, that is, to investigate the proposition's international validity.

Malthus's method was not flawless, for problems arise from his less than scholarly use of statistics. First, his theoretical generalizations are not valid: population, when unchecked, was not doubling every twenty-five years and the means of subsistence were not growing arithmetically. At the time the *Essay on Population* was being hotly debated, Nassau Senior, for one, found that, historically, foodstuffs increased faster than population. The geometrical rate of population growth rests on American data; but, as Kingsley Davis notes, Malthus did not grasp the fact that if the population in the United States was doubling every twenty-five years and the standard of living had not declined, the means of subsistence must, inevitably, be doubling

---

60. The literature of the new classical macroeconomics must be considered a major exception to this generalization.

61. What Ricardo and Malthus called *generalizations*, economists now call *laws, theories,* or *models.* The earlier term was used to refer to both theoretical and empirical claims.

every twenty-five years too (1955: 550). There was also the problem of sorting out the effects of immigration and population growth through procreation (Godwin 1820: 121–23; Rashid 1987b: 26). John Sumner points out, however, that Malthus never tried to prove his geometric theory of population increase and arithmetic subsistence growth rate (1817: 377). Instead he concentrates on showing, first, that the population is limited by the means of subsistence and, second, that the checks that repress population are all resolvable into moral restraint, vice, and misery.[62] According to this interpretation, we would have to regard Malthus's theory of population as a conditional hypothesis or, as J. S. Mill saw it, a simple illustration.[63] Much speaks for this position, for Malthus viewed the increase of population and food as proportions and the geometrical and arithmetical ratios as average figures for the earth.[64] From this perspective, the geometrical and arithmetical ratios become a kind a rhetorical decoration.

Certainly Malthus drew on a wider range of statistical material than Smith did;[65] he culled evidence from every region of the world, every period of history, and every stage in society (Sumner 1817: 381). He was familiar with the life expectancy tables of Euler, Barton, Süssmilch, Milne, and others. He was a founding member of both the BAAS statistical section in 1833 and the London Royal Society a year later; his "pursuit of accurate statistics and their correct interpretation," explains

62. This is Malthus's explanation in the second and later editions of the *Essay* (*Works* 2: 20–21).
63. Even though he usually had little good to say about Malthus, Mill (*Works* 2: 353) defended him in his *Principles of Political Economy*: "Some [critics], for instance, have achieved an easy victory over a passing remark of Mr. Malthus, hazarded chiefly by way of illustration, that the increase of food may perhaps be assumed to take place in an arithmetical ratio, while population increases in a geometrical: when every candid reader knows that Mr. Malthus laid no stress on this unlucky attempt to give numerical precision to things which do not admit of it, and every person capable of reasoning must see that it is wholly superfluous to his argument."
64. On the increase of population and foodstuffs as proportions, see Malthus's *Works* (2: 196). He says this about ratios: "It may be fairly pronounced, therefore, that, considering the present average state of the earth, the means of subsistence, under circumstances the most favourable to human industry, could not possibly be made to increase faster than in an arithmetical ratio" (2: 12).
65. For a detailed analysis of Malthus's statistical data and methods, see Rubin (1960).

Patricia James, were "among the intellectual passions of his life" (1979: 114). Yet in spite of this, many of the facts Malthus marshalls to support his theory are either "distortions of the available evidence" or were known in his lifetime to be unreliable (Rashid 1987b: 22). In the preface to the second and later editions of the *Essay on Population*, Malthus tells us that in formulating the principle of population he relied on Hume, Wallace, Smith, and Dr. Price (*Works*, 2: i). Richard Price's statistics were known to be unreliable.[66] Even Sumner, who was not in the opposing camp,[67] found Malthus's statistics inadequate when he reviewed the fifth edition of the *Essay* (1817: 378). Malthus's inexcusable offense, however, was that he apparently misquoted and distorted the statistics he took from J. P. Süssmilch's *Göttliche Ordnung*. He used Süssmilch's table on the effects of the plague to find support for his theory that increased deaths would remove the pressure of the preventive check on the population, thus allowing marriages to rise. To be able to claim that marriages had doubled after the plague, Malthus used a figure for 1711 that was actually a total of the years between 1709 and 1711.[68] Salim Rashid also points to discrepancies between Malthus's diaries (1966) and his position in the *Essay on Population* (1987b: 31–32).[69]

Clearly, Malthus's use of facts needs greater attention from scholars of classical economics. Still, his careless choice of statistics and opportunistic appropriation of Süssmilch's data beg for explanation. Rashid argues that Malthus "knew that it was impossible to succeed in scientific controversy unless he tried to be both factual and mathematical" (1987b: 34). No doubt he was aware that mathematical and statistical terms have an imposing

---

66. One of the earliest criticisms of Price's statistics can be found in a published letter to Price from Arthur Young (1967: 322–31).
67. Sumner reviewed his *Essay* positively and shared many of Malthus's views on method. He argued in his review that the "axioms of political economy, like those of natural philosophy, can only result from experience and repeated observation" and concluded that "[s]ociety has no greater enemy than the man who would substitute theory for experience; and no sincerer friend than the man who appeals to experience to refute him" (1817: 369–70, 390).
68. See Rashid (1987b) for the details. Consider also Godwin (1820: book 2, ch. 1).
69. Stapleton (1983), unlike Rashid, finds that Malthus's population principle corresponds to what he saw happening around him as the curate of Oakwood shortly before the turn of the century.

air of accuracy about them. It is, however, worth pointing out that statistics were still in their infancy, that data were poor, and that political economists before Malthus had been rather uninterested in guaranteeing the accuracy or integrity of the data they used. Consequently, it would be patently unfair to apply today's standards to Malthus. It is also easy to forget how violent was the controversy that arose after Malthus published his essay on population and how long that controversy raged. Malthus had come under such heavy fire that he perhaps thought admitting an error or an inability to provide sufficient empirical support for his position would gravely endanger his theory. These are, of course, possible explanations and not excuses for Malthus's shortcomings.

As a final point, we might wonder why Ricardo and Malthus did not rely more on mathematical methods, which, by the early nineteenth century, had become "the badge of scientific maturity" (Goldman 1983: 602, n. 104). Malthus was, after all, trained as a mathematician and Ricardo was the stockbroker-dilettante political economist who insisted that political economy was closer to mathematics than to any other discipline. Yet most classical economists were wary of the use of mathematics because they believed computations could not be made with certainty. "There was no apparent consideration that mathematics might be used to contribute to *conceptual clarity* rather than to derive numerical predictions" (Sowell 1974: 117–18). Oddly enough, it was Malthus, not Ricardo, who suspected that mathematics, especially calculus, would be a suitable tool for solving problems in economics. In a lengthy passage in a letter to William Whewell, who had sent him his mathematical analysis of Ricardo's theory, Malthus not only suggested applying calculus to economic problems of optimum but also underscored the problems with data collection that were plaguing political economists of his day.

[M]athematical calculations may in some cases be introduced with advantage into the science of Political Economy particularly with a view to determine the different *degrees* in which certain objects are affected, under different hypotheses. The grand difficulty, however, with a view to practical utility, is the getting data to work upon, sufficiently near the truth; and such as can be stated distinctly in mathematical language. In many cases where one should wish to come to definite conclusions I should fear this was quite impracticable. I have long thought that there are many of the results in political economy which have some resemblance to the problems *de maximis et minimis,* such as the most favourable division of landed property, neither too great nor too small . . . . But I do not see how such propositions could be put into proper language for a fluxional solution, varying as the result must do with the fertility of soils and the productiveness of capitals (in De Marchi and Sturges 1973: 179–80).

I have mentioned that Malthus never learned much algebra or calculus, but that mathematics was one of his major areas of study at Cambridge.[70] Pullen's research (1986), however, reveals that Malthus had to acquire his knowledge of algebra and calculus through outside readings. When confronted with Whewell's mathematical attacks on Ricardo's theory, Malthus admitted that the mathematics Whewell employed in papers read at the Cambridge Philosophical Society was beyond his comprehension.[71]

We can now turn to the specific methodological differences between Malthus and Ricardo, which center on matters of scope, semantics, the role of realism, views on theorizing, and the conflict between fact and theory.

## Two Conceptions of Political Economy

**Scope and semantics.** Malthus opened the introduction to his *Principles* with this message:

It has been said, and perhaps with truth, that the conclusions of political economy partake more of the certainty of the stricter sciences than those of most of the other branches of human knowledge. Yet we should fall into a serious error if we were to suppose that any propositions, the practical results of which depend upon the agency of so variable a being as man, and the qualities of so variable a compound as the soil, can ever admit of the same kinds of proof, or lead to the same certain conclusions, as those which relate to figure and number.

---

70. According to Hartwick, Malthus's use of the word *ratios* instead of the usual term, *progressions,* "leaves the impression of a lack of facility with mathematics in general, a notion not contradicted by his other writings" (1988: 369). Darwin, by the way, followed Malthus's lead in using *ratios.*

71. He wrote to Whewell, "I am ashamed to say that, never having been very familiar with the present algebraic notation, and for a great many years having been quite unaccustomed to it, I cannot follow you as I could wish, without more attention and application than I can give to the subject in the midst of our College examinations" (in Pullen 1986: 144).

There are indeed in political economy great general principles, to which exceptions are of the most rare occurrence, and prominent landmarks which may almost always be depended upon as safe guides; but even these, when examined, will be found to resemble in most particulars the great general rules in morals and politics founded upon the known passions and propensities of human nature: and whether we advert to the qualities of man, or of the earth he is destined to cultivate, we shall be compelled to acknowledge, that *the science of political economy bears a nearer resemblance to the science of morals and politics than to that of mathematics* [emphasis added]" (*Works*, 5: 5).[72]

This passage was directed at Ricardo, who insisted political economy had a close affinity to mathematics, and is a view J. M. Keynes shared (1973: 297, 300). One reason for the difference of opinion on scope seems to be the conceptualization of the problem at hand: Ricardo's perspective was that of a broker or banker (narrow in scope), while Malthus's was that of a social scientist-philosopher (very broad in scope).

Another reason for the divergence of views on scope is rooted in their conflicting approaches to the object of political economy. Ricardo wrote to Malthus about this issue in October of 1820.

Political Economy you think is an enquiry into the nature and causes of wealth—I think it should rather be called an enquiry into the laws which determine the division of the produce of industry amongst the classes who concur in its formation. No law can be laid down respecting quantity, but a tolerably correct one can be laid down respecting proportions. Every day I am more satisfied that the former enquiry is vain and delusive, and the latter only the true objects of the science (*Works*, 8: 278–79).

A few weeks later Malthus replied:

With regard to your new definition of the objects of Political Economy, I own it appears to me very confined; and if it be just, I should say that political economy would be at once converted from a science which I have always considered as the most practically useful in the whole circle, into one which would merely serve to gratify curiosity. In the same manner when you reject the consideration of demand and supply in the price of commodities and refer only to the means of

72. Later in the *Principles* Malthus repeats this view: "Still it must be allowed that this very doctrine, and the main doctrines of the foregoing work, all tend to show, as was stated in the introduction, that the science of political economy bears a nearer resemblance to the sciences of morals and politics, than to the science of mathematics" (*Works* 6: 345). He makes the same point again on the first page of his *Definitions in Political Economy* (8: 5).

supply, you appear to me to look only at the half of your subject (in Ricardo, *Works*, 8: 286).

Again it is clear that Malthus was following Smith, while Ricardo was concentrating on the new problem of distribution. Robert Heilbroner sums up the situation this way: "For Malthus, the issue was the immensely important one of How Much Is There? For Ricardo it was the far more explosive question of Who Gets What? No wonder they disagreed so endlessly; they were talking about different things" (1969: 93).[73]

Later, in 1821, Ricardo wrote to James Mill that

Malthus has been staying with me for a few days—he returned to London a week ago. We had plenty of discussion. In all those cases where he has advanced one proposition in which he says he differs with you, Say and me, and has actually endeavored to prove another, which we should not dispute, he appears to me to hold the proposition which he does prove to be identical with the one not proved; the error therefore is in his language, he appears to me not to be aware of the import of the words which he uses—they convey a totally different meaning to his mind, and to mine. Another of his great mistakes is I think this; *Political Economy he says is not a strict science like the mathematics, and therefore he thinks he may use words in a vague way, sometimes attaching one meaning to them, sometimes another and quite different. No proposition can surely be more absurd* [emphasis added] (*Works*, 8: 331).

This is just another instance in which Ricardo and Malthus were clearly talking past one another.[74] In reality, Malthus was very interested in the proper use of words: Malthus brought out his book on semantics six years after Ricardo wrote this letter. Ricardo, in contrast, showed no genuine interest in semantics

73. Schumpeter puts it slightly differently: "Malthus, again returning to A. Smith and again anticipating A. Marshall, geared his apparatus to the analysis of the whole economic process. Hence he treated total output (Marshall's 'national dividend'), not, like Ricardo, as a datum, but as the chief variable to be explained. Therefore, Malthus should indeed . . . stand in the history of analysis not only as the author of a valid alternative to Ricardo's theory but as the sponsor (or rather as one of the sponsors) of the victorious one" (1954b: 483).
74. Pullen suggests that the charges (especially from Ricardians) that Malthus expressed inconsistent opinions rests on a misunderstanding of his doctrine of proportions: "His particular methodology led him to state the respective advantages of extreme and contradictory positions, not in an illogical attempt to sustain such positions simultaneously, but as a prelude to the delineation of a middle way." This is, again, a point in which Malthus and Smith concur (1982: 270).

whatsoever, a trait that is reflected in his writings. Mitchell remarks that Ricardo is a writer who is difficult to represent fairly because "as frequent misunderstandings by Malthus and other friends made him realize, his power of expression was no match for his power of discriminating ideas. He had a confusing way of using different terms for the same concept and the same term for different concepts, relying upon the context to supply the appropriate meaning. Worse yet, he sometimes got out a valid idea by making two contradictory statements, one of which should be subtracted from the other; as if one should say 'some men have red hair,' by announcing 'men have red hair,' and adding later 'most men do not' (1967: 307–308).[75] Ricardo's complaint about Malthus is all the more remarkable in that he had admitted to Trower in 1818: "Your suggestion of a copious chapter of clear and concise definitions would be of great use, but it requires a degree of precision and accuracy beyond what I could furnish" (*Works*, 7: 259).

Malthus's *Definitions in Political Economy* is the only book-length work devoted solely to semantics to appear during the classical period, although a preoccupation with problems of terminology was a common pastime among his contemporaries.[76] In this volume Malthus was primarily concerned to put an end to multiple uses of terminology, which, he was convinced, led to unnecessary differences of opinion among writers. In the first chapter, he therefore lays down four rules of definition and application of terms. First, the meaning of technical terms borrowed from everyday usage should correspond to their everyday usage, if possible. If this is not possible because finer distinctions are needed, the second rule comes into play: the next best authority is the definition advanced by the writer who first uses the term. By the third rule, if a term's name must be changed, the new term must constitute an improvement over the old one. Finally, this new definition should be consistent

---

75. Schumpeter's view parallels Mitchell's: "Ricardo's *Principles* are the most difficult book on economics ever written. It is difficult enough even to understand it, more difficult to interpret it and most difficult to estimate it properly" (1954a: 80).

76. Samuel Bailey's pamphlet "Observations on Certain Verbal Disputes in Political Economy" (in Bailey 1967), first published in 1821, also explores questions of terminology.

with related terms. Malthus then goes on to show how these commonsense rules were followed or violated by economists, including Smith, Say, Ricardo, James Mill, McCulloch, and Bailey. In the penultimate chapter, he offers definitions of sixty key terms in political economy; the final chapter offers a discussion of problems that arise upon application of the definitions. Pullen surmises that Sismondi's *De la richesse commerciale* (1803) probably inspired Malthus to publish a dictionary of definitions, and that the numerous accusations of abuse of economic terminology from his contemporaries probably provided the motivation (1989: liii).

For Malthus the scope of political economy was virtually unlimited. "The science of political economy is essentially practical, and applicable to the common business of human life," he wrote in the *Principles* (*Works*, 5: 11). Ricardo's view on scope was unquestionably narrower than Malthus's was—not only philosophically but historically. His economics applies only to England's emerging capitalist system, whereas Malthus took care to extend his generalizations to as many countries as possible. In his *Notes on Malthus*, Ricardo remarks on Malthus's discussions of Ireland, the Americas, India, China, and the like with considerable irritation: "But what have all these suppositions to do with England, the country of which I was particularly speaking?" (*Works*, 2: 346). The fact that Malthus proposed to develop generalizations possessing international validity meant that they would be difficult to establish and that the number of trends that could be sanctioned as valid generalizations would, inevitably, be reduced. Not recognizing that their goals were at odds, the two political economists once again talked past one another.

Ricardo supported one restriction on scope that has particular significance for us today. In the following passage he reminds Malthus: "It has been well said by M. Say that it is not the province of the Political Economist to advise:—he is to tell you how you may become rich, but he is not to advise you to prefer riches to indolence, or indolence to riches" (*Works*, 2: 338). Malthus the clergyman periodically lapsed into edifying tones; but, for him, as for Adam Smith before him, political economy was a subdivision of moral philosophy anyway.

**Realism of assumptions.** Perhaps the loudest objection to Ricardo's new political economy was evoked by his use of unrealistic assumptions. Since all scientific propositions and theories simplify and are therefore not realistic in the sense of conforming exactly to reality (i.e., are not descriptively complete), it is worth probing into the nature of Ricardo's assumptions and his opponents' criticisms.[77]

No doubt Ricardo's adoption of highly simplified assumptions caused Malthus many a headache. Malthus's complaints most often turn on the fact that the assumptions Ricardo built into his theories were not even approximately true of the phenomena to which the theory was applied. Malthus was wrong, however, to criticize every deviation from reality without considering Ricardo's intentions. Ricardo readily admitted that some of his assumptions were hypothetical or imaginary. A footnote in his *Essay on Profits*, for example, contains the following caveat: "It is scarcely necessary to observe, that the data on which this table is constructed are assumed, and are probably very far from the truth. They were fixed on as tending to illustrate the principle" (*Works*, 4: 15). As with most exercises in today's theory textbooks (which also have nothing to with the real world), Ricardo's hypothetical figures serve as pedagogical devices to illustrate the workings of a principle he regarded as true.

At other times Ricardo seems to be illustrating ideal cases, what he refers to as "strong cases." For instance, Malthus agrees with Ricardo that if land could be made so fertile that a tenth of the labor could support the population by cultivating a tenth of the surface, rents would be low for a while. Yet Malthus, seldom so unrestrained, loses patience with Ricardo's "fanciful suppositions": "[I]t is of no sort of use to *dwell upon,* and draw general inferences from suppositions which never can take place" (*Works*, 5: 159). It nonetheless seems that these extreme cases can be justified as pedagogical devices. In a letter to Malthus, Ricardo offers this explanation: "Our differences may in some respects, I think, be ascribed to your considering my book as more practical than I intended it to be. My object was to elucidate principles, and to do this I imagined strong cases that I

---

77. The exposition in this section owes much to Hausman's analysis (1989) of the Friedman assumptions controversy.

might shew the operation of those principles" (8: 184). Indeed, similar strong cases have made their way into the body of established economic doctrine: ideal cases—perfect competition and perfect information are two examples par excellence—are commonplace analytical tools in economics.

Yet Ricardo does not always leave it at that. He occasionally gets carried away while concentrating exclusively on the truth of his "laws" and the conclusions he deduced from them. Indeed, Ricardo was sometimes very impractical about developing his generalizations. For example, in 1814 he revealed to Malthus: "I am not sanguine about the principle, if true, being of any use; but that is another consideration;—its utility has nothing to do with its truth, and it is the latter only which I am at present anxious to establish" (*Works*, 6: 163). It was Ricardo who began the practice in economics of consciously using as analytical tools assumptions having no real basis. For example, in his discussions on value, which "depends not on abundance, but on the difficulty or facility of production," he makes the following point:

Corn, as well as gold, may from difficulty or facility of production, vary 10, 20, or 30 per cent., relatively to other things; why should we always say, that it is those other things which have varied, and not the corn? That commodity is alone invariable, which at all times requires the same sacrifice of toil and labour to produce it. *Of such a commodity we have no knowledge, but we may hypothetically argue and speak about it, as if we had;* and may improve our knowledge of the science, by shewing distinctly the absolute inapplicability of all the standards which have been hitherto adopted [emphasis added] (*Works*, 1: 273, 275).

What is more important, Ricardo admits that he is not fully acquainted with the economic institutional reality about which he nonetheless draws policy conclusions. In early 1823, he wrote his friend Wilmot Horton:

You know I am frequently reproached with being a theorist, and if those who so reproach me, mean that I am not conversant with the practical details of the subjects which have engaged my attention, they are right. The subject of the Poor-laws for instance is one intimately connected with the science of Political Economy, but nobody is so little acquainted with them, as forming a part of parish economy, as I am (*Works*, 11: xv).

We have seen, then, that *unrealistic* can mean (1) hypothetical, (2) ideal, (3) theoretical, (4) not closely approximating the
phenomena to which the theory is applied, and (5) abstract in
the sense of highly simplified. There is one further sense in
which Ricardo's opponents use the word: to specify his assumptions as difficult to understand. I have noted that unrealistic
assumptions sometimes serve a pedagogical purpose (as the first
three meanings suggest). It is, however, to Ricardo's discredit
that he seldom admitted the rigid, narrow character of his theory
and rarely stated qualifications; he simply was not methodologically self-conscious.[78] Where he is not merely illustrating the
workings of a principle or offering an ideal case, the use of
unrealistic assumptions invites methodological criticism.
Malthus had this to say about the use of assumptions that do
not closely approximate the phenomena to which the theory is
applied: "A writer may, to be sure, make any hypothesis he
pleases; but if he supposes what is not at all true practically, he
precludes himself from drawing any practical inferences from
his hypothesis" (in Ricardo, *Works*, 7: 122).

Certainly, with time, the rigidity of Ricardo's theoretical principles has led to their abandonment. Even the gem of his theoretical achievements, the theory of comparative advantage, has
come under fire precisely because its assumptions are loosing
significance to the modern economic world.[79] And there is a
very good argument for taking the realism of assumptions seriously. "For there is no good way to know what to try when a

78. According to Mitchell: "The only trouble . . . is that Ricardo as a rule did
not take any pains to warn his readers of what he was doing. Probably he
went ahead with this operation without thinking much about what he was
doing himself; until it was called to his attention he was quite unaware of it.
He was paying too high a compliment to the intelligence of his readers" (1967:
324). I think this aspect of Ricardo's theorizing is more properly ascribable to
brokers' myopia.

79. Consider Krugman's opening statements in his *Rethinking International
Trade:* "If one had to provide a concrete example of what the new trade theory
is about, it might be this: conventional trade theory views world trade as
taking place entirely in goods like wheat; new trade theory sees it as being
largely in goods like aircraft. Since a good part of world trade *is* in goods like
wheat, and since even trade in aircraft is subject to some of the same influences
that bear on trade in wheat, traditional theory has by no means been disposed
of completely. Yet the new theory introduces a whole set of new possibilities
and concerns" (1990: 1–2).

prediction fails or whether to employ a theory in a new application without judging one's assumptions. Without assessments of realism (approximate truth) of assumptions, the process of theory modification would be hopelessly inefficient and the application of theories to new circumstances nothing but arbitrary guesswork" (Hausman 1989: 121).

**Generalization: its beauty and its drawbacks.** "In discussions on the question of method the attack is always directed against Ricardo, who is charged with being the first to lead the science into the fruitless paths of abstraction" (Gide and Rist 1960: 153). Other noteworthy objectors are the members of the German and English historical schools and J. M. Keynes, who complains that "Ricardo offers us the supreme intellectual achievement, unattainable by weaker spirits, of adopting a hypothetical world remote from experience as though it were the world of experience and then living in it consistently. With most of his successors common sense cannot help breaking in—with injury to their logical consistency" (1973: 192). Schumpeter even invented a name for Ricardo's particular method: "the Ricardian Vice." Yet, as Gide and Rist rightly indicate, Ricardo's "defects are as interesting as his merits, and have been equally influential"—a useful clue as to the nature of Ricardo's theorizing (1960: 154). Indeed, that type of theorizing has both very great advantages and drawbacks.

I have already mentioned that Ricardo's initial approach to political economy is to formulate bold generalizations. "As an active participant in the money market one might have expected Ricardo to have based his argument on facts rather than on generalisations," Deane remarks (1978: 76). Ricardo, we have seen, did, however, base his argument on facts, although his way of doing so was very different from Malthus's. For Ricardo, basing theories on facts is not the reason theories acquire scientific character: generalizations are scientific when they are logically consistent and correctly deduced from plausible premises. It is a curious fact that the reason Malthus put great stock in empirical evidence is the same reason Ricardo and his followers gave for refusing to trust direct experience as a method of substantiating hypotheses: that is, because economic phenomena are too complex. "If I am too theoretical which I really believe is the case," Ricardo wrote to Malthus, "you *I* think are too practical. There are so many combinations,—so many operating causes in Political Economy, that there is great danger in appealing to experience in favor of a particular doctrine, unless we are sure that all the causes of variation are seen and their effects duly estimated" (*Works*, 6: 295). These differences in approaching methodology, both stemming from the view that the complex nature of economic phenomena requires the use of a particular method, were never resolved by the two economists: Malthus approved theories less on the basis of general analysis than upon particular evidence; the converse was true of Ricardo.[80] Neither, I might add, saw that a generalization could be either a statement of empirical regularity or a logical premise built on assumptions and deductions.

Yet the point of Malthus's criticism of Ricardo, made clear in the introduction to his *Principles,* is that Ricardo's theorizing involves hasty generalizations that have the potential to spoil the newly founded science: "The principal cause of error, and of the differences which prevail at present among the scientific writers on political economy, appears to me to be a precipitate attempt to simplify and generalize. While their more practical opponents draw too hasty inferences from a frequent appeal to partial facts, these writers run into a contrary extreme, and do not sufficiently try their theories by a reference to that enlarged and comprehensive experience which, on so complicated a subject, can alone establish their truth and utility" (*Works*, 5: 7). Malthus found four major reasons to support this point, each of which will be handled in turn. His reasoning, by the way, places Malthus clearly in the intellectual stream springing from Bacon and continuing in the strains of those Newtonians whose interpretation of Newton's Fourth Rule of Reasoning was Baconian.

In formulating his first complaint about Ricardo's use of generalizations Malthus admits, on the one hand, that generalization is "the desirable and legitimate object of genuine

---

80. Sowell neatly sums up the differences in classical perspectives this way: "To some a science was characterized by the precision and rigor of its *methods of analysis;* to others a science was distinguished by the *certainty of its results*" (1974: 117).

philosophy," while cautioning, on the other, that hasty generalization leads to "crude and premature theories" because haste
results in error (*Works*, 5: 7, 8). "Certain appearances, which are
merely co-existent and incidental, may be mistaken for causes;
and a theory formed upon this mistake will unite the double
disadvantage of being both complex and incorrect," warns
Malthus (16). Malthus's point taken, we can nonetheless detect
that Malthus and Ricardo were, to a certain extent, talking past
one another due to their differing goals. Ricardo, for instance,
admits that they have different time periods in mind: "It appears
to me that one great cause of our difference in opinion, on the
subjects which we have so often discussed, is that you have
always in your mind the immediate and temporary effects of
particular changes—whereas I put these immediate and temporary effects quite aside, and fix my whole attention on the
permanent state of things which will result from them. Perhaps
you estimate these temporary effects too highly, whilst I am too
much disposed to undervalue them. To manage the subject quite
right they should be carefully distinguished and mentioned,
and the due effects ascribed to each" (*Works*, 7: 120). At last
Ricardo recognizes brokers' myopia as a methodological ail-
ment! "By driving matters to their ultimate conclusion, by stressing the long run, and by making time-absorbing adjustments
appear to take place instantaneously, Ricardo at times expresses
thoughts that border on the paradoxical," observes Spiegel
(1991: 316).

Indeed, Ricardo's recourse to simplification sometimes knew
no bounds. Such is the case when Ricardo finds fault with
Malthus's statement that a smaller proportion of people was
employed in agriculture in England than in other countries on
the Continent: "This is very possible, and very satisfactory if
true, but we must not leave out of consideration the greater
number of horses and cattle employed on the land in England;
*they come under the denomination of labourers, for they are substituted
for them, and are supported by provisions like them* [emphasis
added]" (*Works*, 2: 335). When horses and cattle become workers, surely the simplification process has gone awry. One
must wonder whether Ricardo was not following in the foot-
steps of William Petty, whose estimate of human population, as

mentioned earlier, was based on the changes in the sheep, cattle, and oxen populations.[81]

In his second argument, Malthus observes that incautious theorizing creates an aura of unnatural certainty, which in turn "produces a still greater disinclination to allow of modifications, limitations, and exceptions to any rule or proposition." There is, he continues,

> no truth of which I feel a stronger conviction that there are many important propositions in political economy which absolutely require limitations and exceptions; and it may be confidently stated that the frequent combination of complicated causes, the action and reaction of cause and effect on each other, and the necessity of limitations and exceptions in a considerable number of important propositions, form the main difficulties of the science, and occasion those frequent mistakes which it must be allowed are made in the prediction of results (*Works*, 5: 8–9).

The exceedingly cautious Malthus, who had learned that hasty generalization could stir up controversy, worried that facts could eventually come to light that would refute Ricardo's "premature theories," thus discrediting the young science of political economy. But his reservations were rarely taken seriously by his contemporaries; the very preoccupation with the limitations of the science caused them to sneer at him. Nevertheless, Malthus's attitude makes very good sense in today's world: "To know what can be done, and how to do it, is beyond a doubt, the most valuable species of information. The next to it is, to know what cannot be done, and why we cannot do it" (5: 14). The zeitgeist Malthus confronted—narrow-minded and overly ambitious, intent on absolute results—did not appreciate his message.[82]

---

81. There is an almost uncanny similarity between Petty and Ricardo's approaches, which was also noticed by Bevan: "In both we see the results of a mathematically trained mind. They both aimed at applying the rigorous method of that science to the study of social phenomena. Both were men who had made great fortunes. In both their practical training had not been supplemented by the broadening influence of education. Petty, like Ricardo, regarded man solely as a labor unit. He, as well as Ricardo, is open to the reproach of dealing with human beings as if they were nothing more than algebraic symbols" (1894: 98). Both men were practical—not men of letters and not much for book learning. And both men were drawn into the world of economics with the wish to solve the hotly debated issues of the times.

82. Consider also Schumpeter's observation that Malthus "was throughout in the most unenviable position an economist can be in, namely, in the position of having to defend plain sense against another man's futile but clever pirouettes" (1954b: 483).

Ricardo, unfortunately, counted to those who did not appreciate Malthus's reservations. In a letter to Trower, he confided that "it is one of my complaints against him [Malthus] that he does not answer your principle but wishes to shew that you have taken your case so wide, that it could under no circumstances exist; but however limited might be your case, the same principle is involved, and it is that which should be answered" (*Works*, 8: 234–35).

Malthus's position is rooted in his approach to facts: often he uses them like an institutionalist economist or a historian. Hence, we find him arguing, "I really think that the progress of society consists of irregular movements, and that to omit the consideration of causes which for eight or ten years will give a great *stimulus* to production and population, or a great *check* to them, is to omit the causes of the wealth and poverty of nations—the grand object of all enquiries in Political Economy" (in Ricardo, *Works*, 7: 122) In addition, he objects to Ricardo's impractical bent and to his unwillingness to consider "disturbing circumstances." Occasionally, however, Malthus goes too far with this argument, almost insuring, with his facts that do not fit the trends, the impossibility of theorizing. Their correspondence indicates that Malthus once criticized Ricardo's assumption that the wage of labor is low on grounds that it was high in America. Unwilling to accept the criticism because he had actually borrowed the assumption from Malthus, Ricardo responded: "I was dealing with your case, and not with America," adding, "I think I *do* shew that your fact does not invalidate my theory which you say I am bound to do, and I do not assume a different fact than the one you refer to in order to refute you" (*Works*, 9: 99)

In his third criticism of Ricardo, Malthus argues that simplification "has induced you to ascribe to one cause phenomena that properly belong to two" (in Ricardo, *Works*, 6: 82). This "unwillingness to acknowledge the operation of more causes than one in the production of particular effects" leads to crude, premature theories (*Works*, 5: 8). The passing of time has bolstered Malthus's position on this issue: in the long run Ricardo's adherence to single causation in the bullion controversy was debunked as unsophisticated.

Malthus's fourth objection to the Ricardians's tendency to hasty generalization is this consequence: "an unwillingness to bring their theories to the test of experience" (*Works*, 5: 10). He rightly observes that Ricardo saw little purpose in comparing his theoretical results with the facts. The confrontation of theory with facts represents to Malthus a process akin to theory assessment resulting in the substantiation, modification, or rejection of a hypothesis. The following passage from Malthus's *Principles* underscores the common sense of empirical consistency. "I should be the last person to lay an undue stress upon isolated facts, or to think that a consistent theory, which would account for the great mass of phenomena observable, was immediately invalidated by a few discordant appearances, the reality and the bearings of which there might not have been an opportunity of fully examining. But certainly no theory can have any pretension to be accepted as correct, which is inconsistent with general experience. Such inconsistency appears to me at once a full and sufficient reason of its rejection" (*Works*, 5: 10). Malthus makes this point repeatedly: "The first business of philosophy is to account for things as they are; and till our theories will do this, they ought not to be the ground of any practical conclusion" (10). Ricardo is frequently reprimanded for not giving "sufficient weight to the facts" (Ricardo, *Works*, 6: 82). Every theory must stand the test of experience, Malthus insists, for "an untried theory cannot fairly be advanced as probable, much less as just, till all the arguments against it, have been maturely weighed, and clearly and consistently refuted" (*Works*, 1: 7).

Much of what Malthus has to say about testing has a Popperian ring to it. "The chemist of thirty years ago may be allowed to regret, that new discoveries in the science should disturb and confound his previous system and arrangements," Malthus tells us, "but he is not entitled to the rank of philosopher, if he does not give them up without a struggle, as soon as the experiments which refute them are fully established" (*Works*, 5: 8).[83] As Karl Popper would later do, Malthus cautions against the irrational defense of theories. But whereas Popper dwells on ridding science of ad hoc defenses of pet theories, Malthus, like Smith before him, criticizes scientists who spurn innovation on filiopietistic grounds.

---

83. Experiments to Malthus, as to Adam Smith, often amounted simply to observations.

There is another class of persons who set a very high value upon the received general rules of political economy, as of the most extensive practical use. They have seen the errors of the mercantile system refuted and replaced by a more philosophical and correct view of the subject; and having made themselves masters of the question so far, they seem to be satisfied with what they have got, and do not look with a favourable eye on new and further inquiries, particularly if they do not see at once clearly and distinctly to what beneficial effects they lead.

This indisposition to innovation, even in science, may possibly have its use, by tending to check crude and premature theories; but it is obvious that, if carried too far, it strikes at the root of all improvement (5: 13).

We know today that Popper's falsification theory is not tenable for many reasons, one of which is his mistaken attempt to base methodological rules on logic, as the title of his celebrated *Logic of Scientific Discovery* suggests.[84] Malthus, however, was not searching for absolute foundations for science. It is precisely his cautiousness and his distrust of absolute solutions that made him a good methodologist.

It seems to me that Malthus's four objections to the hasty generalizations of his Ricardian opponents are well taken. Mitchell's final assessment points to the crux of the problem posed by the extremely abstract theoretical nature of Ricardo's theory. "This is a limitation on the value of this method of work. It shows that in order to get a clear cut set of conclusions about economic problems, no matter how deeply and vitally the theorist is interested in the practical issues of the day as was Ricardo, he is forced, if he adopts this way of working, to build up the discussion as a whole into a series of very artificial problems. And, to repeat again, he arrives at conclusions which are logically valid only with reference to conditions contrary to the facts from which they are drawn" (1967: 324). This evaluation should not be construed, however, as a wholesale condemnation of Ricardo's theorizing, which Mitchell makes clear. "But if the theorist remembers what he has done all the time, if he does not forget the limitations set upon the validity of the conclusions he has drawn, he is in a secure logical position and, if he has the

---

84. Popper, of course, also argues compellingly against absolute foundations in science. There are inconsistent strands of thought in his writings, a point illuminated by Redman (1994, and to a lesser extent, 1991, pt. 1).

insight of Ricardo, he may arrive at results which are practically of considerable significance. The danger is that he will forget that he has drawn conclusions on the basis of certain conditions contrary to fact, and then he will begin to think of these conclusions elsewhere as if they applied to the world at large; this is a failing into which his followers commonly fell" (324). And this is also a failing that Adam Smith cautioned against and that must still be taken seriously today. Using any analytical model correctly requires that we never lose sight of the more general conceptual picture.

We know that Ricardo's theory and method went on to enjoy great popularity. If Malthus is actually the better methodologist, why did this happen? Mitchell offers a compelling explanation: "this type of theory, seemingly so abstract in character, was intensely practical in its age" (1967: 372).[85] Malthus, so preoccupied with Ricardo's excesses, was unaware that Ricardo's method often *had* to be used to get results. Not only was there a dearth of good statistical data, most people did not know how to use the statistics that were available. "If the investigator wanted to get real light upon the economic problems of most general consequence in the day," Mitchell argues, "he was practically forced to resort to Ricardo's method of thinking about how people would behave under certain conditions" (326).

Whereas this is an argument for the historical significance of Ricardo's method, it does not justify glorifying it for all posterity. Both men had blind spots; but Ricardo's were, nevertheless, by far less perceptive than Malthus's. We have learned that Ricardo's restrictive assumptions and one-way causation invite danger unless coupled with scrupulous honesty and awareness of the limitations imposed on the system. Ricardo's love of logical consistency can, as Mitchell aptly warns us, lead to a double standard of truth—observation for facts and logical consistency for theories. "This attitude impedes scientific progress,

---

85. Mitchell explains further: "The reason [why Ricardian economics attained such a prominent position] has to be found not in the sheer scientific merits of his work but in the practical usefulness of his analysis to the class which had, because of peculiar circumstances, the deepest interest in economic theory, and for the promotion of whose interests the Ricardian theory was perfectly adapted" (1967: 363).

because it excuses theorists from reconstructing their work when conclusions are out of line with facts" (1967: 328). Indeed, later developments would appear to confirm that economists' emphasis on logical consistency has led to testing theories for internal consistency at the expense of empirical consistency.[86]

A second problem arose as the abstraction Ricardo resorted to became synonymous with scientific theory and objectivity par excellence. We know that Ricardo revered the works of Sir Dudley North and that the measure of objectivity that North and his brother Roger endorsed was a set of deductive principles, or Euclid's "method of demonstration," to employ the terminology of that age.[87] The point is that using the "method of Euclid's proofs" was believed to guarantee objectivity, since "nobody would accuse Euclid of maintaining any of his theorems because they suited his self-interest. The only relevant critique is that the premises are false or inadequate or the chain of reasoning imperfect; failing this, the conclusions are binding, no matter what may be the character of the author" (Letwin 1963: 97). This linking of a particular method with a guarantee of objectivity is misleading and dangerous, but is, I fear, still a tacit assumption of many of today's economists and one reason why Ricardo continues to be unduly venerated.

It is noteworthy, in summing up, that Ricardo's approach to theory—virtually unknown to political economists in his day, yet by today's standards crude and unnecessarily simplified— was, as Mitchell notes, an indispensable and fruitful technique in that era. Modified and tempered to eliminate most of its extreme features, Ricardo's method approximates Malthus's. Even in their lifetimes, political economists were establishing a basic problem-solving framework that was a compromise of the Malthus-Ricardo position. Thus, in 1836, we find Senior asserting a representative middle position: that the "business of a

---

86. This was the message of the Nobel prize laureate Wassily Leontief in his presidential address to the American Economic Association in 1970. See Leontief (1971) and, more recently, (1992).
87. Ricardo writes to McCulloch that he "had no idea that any one entertained such correct opinions, as are expressed in his publication [North's *Discourses on Trade*, 1691] (*Works*, 9: 158). For some reason, the *Discourses upon Trade* disappeared from circulation or was suppressed and was rediscovered by James Mill in 1818 and reprinted in 1822.

Political Economist is neither to recommend nor to dissuade, but to state general principles, which it is fatal to neglect, but neither advisable, nor perhaps practicable, to use as the sole, or even the principal, guides in the actual conduct of affairs" (1951: 3).

## Significance and Legacy of the Malthus-Ricardo Dialogue

We have now examined two different scientific temperaments that reflect the training of the two economists—one stemming from a broker/banker's perspective and focusing on logical consistency and quick results; the other shaped by a scholar's and theologian's outlook and directed towards empirical consistency, careful formulation of generalizations, semantical meticulousness, and realism of assumptions. We can see that these methodological bents need not be mutually exclusive. Nonetheless, it should be clear that orthodox neoclassical economics has evolved more in accordance with Ricardo's design (especially if mathematical economics is viewed as Ricardo's intellectual offspring), while American institutionalism (particularly the Mitchell strain) more closely conforms to Malthus's methodological conception. Sadly enough, contemporary economics still tends to propagate an understanding of the two approaches as opposed methodological fronts.

Malthus's and Ricardo's varying emphases on methodological issues have modern counterparts. Economists do rely on observation (even if expectations and other variables cannot be observed), perform empirical tests, and revise findings along the lines Malthus prescribed.[88] His insistence on checking the facts provides economics with a connection to reality, a test (though not absolute) of its theories, and Schumpeterian "vision"—a successful merging of practical insight with economic intuition. "No man asked better questions [than Malthus], and very few have framed more incisive or illuminating answers," concludes E. A. Wrigley (1986: 63). Our "analytical effort," or the cooking up of hypotheses, reasons Schumpeter, "is of necessity preceded by a preanalytic cognitive act that supplies the raw material for the analytic effort" (1954b: 41). This vision or insight, so scorned

---

88. Recent evidence of this process is the observed failure of the Phillips curve.

by Stigler, is indispensable if economics is to evolve or tackle the new problems it is confronted with. In providing this insight, Malthus was following in Smith's tradition.

Malthus's broad historical bent, like Smith's before him, also provides economists with an overview or grasp of the general conceptual picture so often neglected by pure theorists. Considering other important goals such as understanding how the economy works or worked in the past need not compromise economists' chief goals—predicting the future course of the economy and stabilizing it. "Malthus proved to be a poor guide to the future; but, though events were to prove that the limitations which he regarded as ineluctable could be overcome, his understanding of the nature of the pre-industrial world makes him an excellent guide to the past" (Wrigley in Malthus, *Works*, 1: 17).

Assessing Ricardo's method and legacy is somewhat more difficult. Much of his methodological developments are merely of historical significance today. He lived in an era that desperately needed a common body of analytical principles and an acceptable, timely method of abstracting policy conclusions. Ricardo certainly deserves credit for providing them and for severing the science's ties to politics and philosophy, an achievement that subsequently allowed political economy to emerge as an autonomous discipline.

Yet, by today's standards, Ricardo's method has severe limitations and major defects. His one-sided stress on logical consistency and quick policy results may have been useful when the discipline had no fully developed body of principles at its disposal, but they seem superfluous now that the theoretical corpus exists. For, once an accepted theoretical apparatus exists, logical consistency takes on a secondary role to empirical consistency. Moreover, there are real errors involved with certain aspects of Ricardo's method. Whereas brokers' myopia only distorts analysis and policy conclusions, the assumption that theory—especially one aimed primarily at logical consistency—guarantees objectivity and detachment is, doubtless, misleading and downright dangerous.

Unfortunately, the excesses of Ricardo's method are still making their mark on economics. To be sure, many twentieth-century economists have carried his approach to greater extremes, often deriving their inspiration solely from purely theoretical concerns. The postwar generation of economists has dwelt heavily on refinements of the mathematical structure passed on from Keynes, Hicks, Samuelson, and others. While no one doubts the importance of establishing and refining a consistent, coherent system of theories, we recognize—though we do not always observe—the limits of working solely on a purely theoretical basis. Barbara Bergmann's summary statement of the Ricardian legacy captures the barrenness associated with the theoretical and methodological rigidity of modern Ricardian methods. "Most of what each economist believes to be true was arrived at by a method of research that predates econometrics, and predates mathematical economics as well—it is the method used by Ricardo['s followers]. Most of what we represent ourselves as knowing we have learned from a 'theory' derived from musing at length on the implications of a few of the facts we know about the economy" (1987: 192).[89]

It seems to me that the shortcomings of Ricardo's method underscore the value of Malthus's neglected methodological message for our current generation of economists, who have at hand a very sophisticated theoretical apparatus. I have already mentioned the elevated role empirical consistency takes on once a working body of theory exists. After a discipline reaches a mature stage, an inquiry into the limitations of theorizing and a consideration of semantic problems also become important and unavoidable, as do reassessments of underlying assumptions when tests fail. It is, therefore, lamentable that economists have failed to appreciate or heed Malthus's message.

I have just provided a historical assessment of the legacy of the Malthus-Ricardo dialogue that suggests that, for today's purposes, the best aspects of these two bents can serve as two essential sources of inspiration to suggest different problems and, sometimes, disparate solutions. The two approaches can be used in conjunction with one another, for they naturally com-

89. Bergmann is wrong to assume this is the method Ricardo actually used. Although admittedly weak on institutional aspects and suffering from a broker's perspective, Ricardo, as argued throughout this chapter, was still a man of the facts.

plement and correct one another. Malthus's insistence on referring back to the facts to check the theory corrects the Ricardian double standard of truth for facts and theories. While Ricardo's analytics cut through the facts to deliver an analysis of the problem and a policy conclusion, Malthus's empirical, historical approach immediately ferrets out new directions and problems. Never satisfied with a theory, Malthus always tried to knock down poor theories and improve accepted ones. The one emphasis reminds economists that they should be cautious and modest; the other encourages them to break through the complexity and dare to advance bold hypotheses. A stress on empirical consistency requires that we never lose sight of the general conceptual picture; concentrating on logical consistency and purely theoretical problems allows us to focus on specialized problems.

Malthus and Ricardo's relationship could have been a true intellectual partnership if they had not so often talked past one another. More than one scholar of classical economics has noted that their intense conversations and debates were often "a dialogue of the deaf" (Barucci and Roggi 1981: 390).[90] This lack of mutual understanding must be attributed, in part, to their differing educations and practical experience. Ricardo the broker had a limited knowledge of history and the world stretching far beyond the frontiers of England. It is thus easy to understand why he made no claims to universality and was uninterested in theoretical limitations that had nothing to do with England. Malthus the parson, on the other hand, was well travelled and educated in mathematics, classical philosophy, and Smith's political economy. Viewed from this perspective, his interest in establishing internationally valid economic principles and in marshalling international comparative evidence and historical data to document and check his theories seems natural.

Although this view has never been widely or loudly endorsed by the discipline, it seems to me that to function optimally, the two approaches should be trained to coexist peacefully in a single mind. Economists, who normally split into quantitative versus qualitative and mathematical versus empirical camps,

---

90. The French passage I took the liberty of translating reads: "[L]e dialogue théoretique qui fut le leur, de façon si intense, fut un dialogue de sourds."

rarely grasp the benefits of combining the two approaches.[91] Ricardo and Malthus shaped the discipline without having the sort of formal education that could provide them with the training to master and appreciate the tools and perspectives of both approaches. Today's economists, however, have no excuse for not inculcating proficiency in and appreciation of both approaches. A glance through the literature suggests that Ricardo is still often made the hero at Malthus's expense. Yet a failure to recognize that both men forged modern economics's methodological heritage could weaken the discipline's collective productive and analytical faculties, for economists need both consistent theories and reliable results, both an analytical framework and the acumen to deviate from it when necessary or modify it as the economy evolves and new problems arise.

---

91. Bronfenbrenner (1991) has offered one of the more recent arguments for increasing the ranks of economists trained in "the literary stream" to balance those from "the quantitative stream." Only J. M. Keynes seems to concur with my view. The master economist, says Keynes, "must be a mathematician, historian, statesman, philosopher—in some degree. He must understand symbols and speak in words. He must contemplate the particular in terms of the general, and touch abstract and concrete in the same flight of the thought. He must study the present in light of the past for the purposes of the future. No part of man's nature or his institutions must lie entirely outside his regard" (1972: 173–74).

# 7

# John Stuart Mill: Last of the Newtonians

John Stuart Mill laid out his views on method primarily in his *System of Logic,* which was conceived and written between 1830 and 1842, and the acclaimed essay "On the Definition of Political Economy; and on the Method of Investigation Proper to It," which he wrote between 1830 and 1831 and revised in 1833.[1] Interpreting Mill's economic methodology and philosophy of science is made difficult by a number of factors: several changes of mind, some of which produced almost mutually contradictory views; ambiguities that may never be resolved; and a plethora of special terminology that can be semantically demanding. Moreover, because the *System of Logic* and the essay on political economy were written at approximately the same time, a chronological approach will not serve our purposes here. I begin instead with Mill's views on natural philosophy, which serves as the roots of general science; proceed to social science, which, in Mill's hands, acquires its method from reflections on natural science; and go on to a consideration of political economy, a particular branch of social science.

## The Historical Setting: Interest in Philosophy of Science Awakened

Very early in his career, at the latest by 1831 when he was writing his essay on political economy, Mill had already reached the

---

1. The writing of the *System of Logic* commenced in 1830 but ground to a halt in 1832, when Mill realized that his background knowledge in natural science was deficient. After a five-year break and the publication of a key work by Whewell that provided the much needed information, Mill resumed writing in 1837. The *System of Logic* was completely rewritten between 1841 and 1842 and published in 1843.

conclusion that "the only thing that I believe I am really fit for, is the investigation of abstract truth, and the more abstract the better. If there is any science which I am capable of promoting, I think it is the science of science itself, the science of investigation—of method" (*Works*, 12: 78–79). It was probably the dispute between his father, James Mill, and Thomas Macaulay (1800–1859) that brought him to this conclusion; certainly it triggered Mill's interest in methodology and in formulating a reliable method of the social sciences. The awakening of Mill's interest in "the science of science" and his resolution of this dispute are the underlying motivations behind his famous essay "On the Definition of Political Economy" and, subsequently, the *System of Logic* (1843), which culminates in book 6, "On the Logic of the Moral Sciences."

### The Macaulay-Mill Debate on Method

In 1829 Macaulay launched an attack on the psychological assumptions and deductive method advocated by the senior Mill in his *Essay on Government*, which had first appeared in 1825. As far as Macaulay was concerned, James Mill had erred in rigidly deducing a theory from a single principle. For Mill, a scientific approach meant the simplicity he found in Newtonian science, that is, the explanation of a mass of facts and details by using one organizing principle. In short, his position was that of "an extreme upholder of the virtues of the deductive method, a critic of practical men who professed to be 'all for fact and nothing for theory'" (Winch 1987: 466). Macaulay pointed out that asserting restrictive, unrealistic assumptions about human nature and then deducing the whole science of politics from them was ridiculous. The senior Mill's rigidly deductive method was dubbed *geometrical* (after Euclid's method) by his son and *abstract* or *a priori* by others. Both Macaulay and the junior Mill recognized it as the method of the Benthamites and Hobbes; and both were convinced it was inappropriate for the social sciences.

In contrast, Macaulay, claiming to follow Bacon, advocated the method of induction, by which he meant studying the past to acquire facts and assemble evidence. In a series of articles, he argued that human beings are more complex than James Mill thought; Mill, he believed, had considered only one side of human nature and had uncritically accepted the Benthamite assumption that all human behavior turns on self-interest. Because of Macaulay's stress on fact finding, J. S. Mill later labeled Macaulay's method *chemical* and *experimental*.

The junior Mill thus found himself in the awkward and uncomfortable position of having to admit that his father was, in part, wrong and that Macaulay's attack had some merits. Indeed, Mill saw that his father's premises were too narrow, and, what was worse, that his father's attempts to defend his position were inadequate. (James Mill had simply dismissed Macaulay's objections as irrational.) In time, the younger Mill came to the conclusion that his father's method was faulty on far more serious grounds: the doctrine in the *Essay on Government* was not a scientific theory. As Mill saw it, however, Macaulay was also in error. While his father was wrong for adopting a deductive method and choosing pure geometry instead of natural philosophy as his model for moral philosophy, Macaulay's mistake was using the "purely experimental method of chemistry" and associating it with Bacon's method. The method Mill sought was thus a middle road between his father's stark abstraction and Macaulay's historical, Baconian method.[2]

Mill never doubted his father's main supposition that politics could become a science. The conflict over method, however, made him realize that what was needed was a whole new model for the social sciences. As he explains in his *Autobiography*, "If I am asked what system of political philosophy I substituted for that which, as a philosophy, I had abandoned, I answer, no system: only a conviction, that the true system was something much more complex and many sided than I had previously any idea of, and that its office was to supply, not a set of model institutions, but principles from which the institutions suitable to any given circumstances might be deduced" (*Works*, 1: 169). Of one thing he was already certain: "the methods of physical science . . . [are] the proper models for [the] political" (173). Thus, the way to develop a new model was to generalize the methods that had already brought results scientists regarded as proof.

And so it was that the conflict between Macaulay and James Mill led J. S. Mill to work out a whole new conception of social

2. Recall that I am using the term *Baconian* to refer to Bacon's followers.

science and, subsequently, to write "On the Definition of Political Economy" and the *System of Logic*. The essay was first published in the *Westminster Review* in 1836, about a month after his father had died. The rest of his early essays on political economy were not published in book form, as *Essays on Some Unsettled Questions of Political Economy*, until 1844, after his *System of Logic* had become a success. The essay on economic methodology provides a complete account of Mill's method of political economy, except for the theory of induction, ethology, and inverse deduction he developed later in book 6 of his *System of Logic*.

### Background to the *System of Logic*

Before he could develop a special logic of the moral sciences, a general logic of science had to be worked out. Thus, the first task awaiting Mill was to gain an understanding of natural science and its methods. As he had no understanding of the physical sciences and no time to study them, he had to wait five years after beginning the *System of Logic* to obtain the information needed to finish the sections on induction. With the publication of Whewell's *History of Inductive Sciences* in 1837, a "comprehensive and at the same time accurate view of the whole circle of physical science" was laid at his fingertips (*Works*, 1: 215).[3] Mill also read the first three volumes of Auguste Comte's *Cours de philosophie positive* in 1837 and 1838 and the final three volumes from 1839 to 1843, after which he rewrote book 6 of the *System of Logic*.[4] Later we will see Comte's influence manifested in Mill's inverse deductive method and theory of history.

Mill's principal reason for writing the *System of Logic* was to build a solid foundation for studying society and politics. His general methodological outlook is distinguished by several factors. The first of these is optimism: Mill believed in the rationality and progress of humankind and assumed that science was

---

3. Actually, Mill never gained more than a very basic understanding of the natural sciences. In a letter to William G. Ward in February of 1867, Mill admitted: "I am not a safe authority on matters of physical science" (*Works*, 16: 1241). Mill also said he appreciated Whewell's *Philosophy of the Inductive Sciences* because it was written by an antagonist (1: 215).
4. In the autumn of 1841 we find him recommending Comte's work to Alexander Bain as "very nearly the grandest work of this age" (*Works*, 13: 487).

a universal panacea for all worldly problems. A second aspect of Mill's method is its many-sidedness.[5] Following in the tradition of his Scottish forebear Adam Smith and the little respected Robert Malthus, Mill always finds at least two sides to an argument, an approach that can easily lead to confusion, especially when this methodological aspect is not always made explicit. Mill, however, tells us that he took the device of many-sidedness from Goethe, who equated *Vielseitigkeit* (many-sidedness) with *Objektivität* (objectivity) (*Works*, 1: 171).

Finally, like his contemporaries and the Scottish philosophers, Mill assumed he was living in a Newtonian world and saw in Newtonian science the paradigm of all science.[6] "The three laws of motion, and the law of gravitation," he writes, "are common, as far as human observation has yet extended, to all matter" (*Works*, 4: 315). In typically Scottish style, Mill approached developing a methodology by gaining a knowledge of the methods of the successful sciences, observing the extent of their applicability to phenomena in the social and moral areas of inquiry, and then attempting to formulate laws that control human affairs. If by Newtonianism we mean that the order of nature is suggested by Newtonian physics and astronomy and that the goal is to formulate secondary laws of a science of society derivable from the simplest primary laws of human nature, Mill must be deemed the last of the great Newtonians in the eighteenth-century tradition.[7] To Mill, Newtonian science meant, essentially, the abstract, deductive method of Newton.[8] Political economy, too, was Newtonian because of its deductive, abstract nature. The scientific method Mill defends and calls deductive is the hypothetico-deductive method.

We should also keep in mind that Mill, as an adherent of associationist psychology, sought to refute the intuitionists' view that necessary truths exist and can be known by direct intuition

---

5. Both Ryan and Bonar mention that Mill made an effort to view all questions from the opposing point of view (1987: 467; 1893: 238).
6. "When Newton . . . discovered the laws of the solar system, he created, for all posterity, the true idea of science" (*Works*, 21: 236).
7. Castell's very informative dissertation elaborates on this theme (1936: 87).
8. In the *System of Logic* Mill argues for "giving to every science as much of the character of a Deductive Science as possible" and credits Newton for turning astronomy into a deductive science (*Works*, 7: 218).

of the mind without testing by sense experience.[9] To counter this view, Mill argues that the world's truths are not self-evident but are rooted in experience; this is true even of mathematical propositions.[10] As Ernest Nagel explains: "The chief emphasis of the *Logic* is upon the final authority of experience as the general warrant for beliefs, and upon the necessity for verifying propositions by observation of facts if futile speculation is to be avoided" (1950: xxxii).

Mill's *System of Logic* is laid out in the following way. Books 1 and 2 present an empiricist theory of deductive inference; book 3 examines observation, description, abstraction, and classification; book 4 outlines the operations subsidiary to induction; and book 5 is dedicated to identifying fallacies. The *System of Logic* culminates in book 6 on the logic of the moral sciences—by which Mill meant the science of human nature and social science. Because the *System of Logic* went into eight editions during Mill's lifetime, we can be quite sure that the ideas he developed there reflect his mature views. Book 6, on the methods of social science, is our chief concern here. Before discussing his method of social science, however, we need to understand his theory of natural science.

## Mill's Analysis of the Methods of Natural Science

For Mill, there are two sorts of sciences, natural science and social, or moral, science. At the heart of the *System of Logic* is a search for the principles of social science and the method of establishing them. The questions he asks are Can there be a science of human nature, a social science? and How can we formulate and solve problems of society scientifically? Thus, natural science was important insofar as its methods could be applied to moral science. As Alburey Castell puts it, Mill originally conceived of the *System of Logic* as "a sort of organon of the social-moral sciences" (1936: 2). That makes book 6 central

---

9. James Mill and David Hartley were perhaps the two greatest exponents of the associationist psychology. Mill regarded Sir William Hamilton as the "chief pillar of the 'intuitional' philosophy" (Nagel 1950: xviii). See Mill's *Examination of Sir William Hamilton's Philosophy* (*Works*, 9).

10. Thomas explains why Mill's account of mathematics is the weakest point of the *System of Logic* (1985: 56).

to his methodology of social science. To understand it, we need to become familiar with a certain amount of Mill's special terminology.

Mill starts by describing nature and analyzing the two principal methods of natural science, induction and deduction. He assumes a natural order in which many uniformities exist— spring follows winter, the sun rises and sets, the earth rotates, etc.—and distinguishes between two types of uniformities: *uniformities of co-existence* (whenever A occurs, B also occurs) and *uniformities of succession* (A is always followed by B). In natural science, he notes, regularities exist upon which to base laws. What Mill calls *laws of nature* are laws that cannot be further reduced, whereas *derivative laws* are hypotheses expressing reducible uniformities.

Two phenomena confound the discovery of laws: the *plurality of causes* and the *intermixture of effects* (*Works*, 7: 434–53). A *conjunction of causes* occurs, Mill tells us, when an effect is caused by the joint action of two or more causes. It can be broken down further into two levels. When a *combination of causes*, or *heteropathic effect*, exists, the effect differs from one produced by causes operating successively. An illustration that Mill takes from chemistry makes clear what is meant: Two substances combine to produce a third substance whose properties are completely different from the original substances. A *composition of causes*, or *compound effect*, occurs when the effect is the same as if it had been produced by causes operating successively.

Mill observes that it is easier to predict a compound effect than a heteropathic effect. In his view, moral and social phenomena are of a compound nature and can therefore be investigated in a scientific manner. Some phenomena can be difficult to analyze, he adds, because they can arise from a plurality of causes, that is, from multifarious causes. Illustrations of this phenomenon abound in both natural and moral science: heat can be caused by the sun, by fire, by friction, or other causes; death can be caused by cancer, poison, starvation, or similar causes; inflation can be caused, inter alia, by printing money and by anticipating inflation. Finally, Mill notes that there are *progressive effects* in nature—cumulative effects rather like the economist's multiplier effect. The rate of reproduction, for instance, tends to be geometrical rather than arithmetical. In Mill's philosophy, progressive effects lead to laws of progress and bring about advancement.

The object of science for Mill is the establishment of true generalizations, which entails, in part, identifying methods that are capable of eliminating false claims. The determination of causes is, as it is in Herschel's philosophy of science, at the heart of Mill's philosophy of natural science.[11] The proposition that the course of nature is uniform is the "ultimate major premise of all inductions," Mill points out (*Works*, 7: 308). At this stage in the development of his thought, Mill asserts that all science stems from induction because induction "is mainly a process for finding the causes of effects" (1: 167). Accordingly, he sets out to establish an account of causal explanation and causal laws. To understand how he proposes to do so, it is necessary to revisit Mill's theory of induction.

Induction for Mill is the source of general propositions, the bearer of both falsehood and truth, and, therefore, of utmost importance to his philosophy of science. Logic, he insists, is not the science of belief or discovery but of proof. A method of obtaining accurate premises is needed because science can only be true if its premises are true. Because facts alone cannot bring us to the truth, he seeks the answer in logic. Mill praised the Schoolmen for recognizing that scientific procedure consists in ascertaining premises and deducing conclusions. This two-fold process is, in fact, what Mill means when he speaks of induction in his early works. It is the search for proof that prompts Mill to tackle the problem of induction, and, eventually, to strictly reject induction as a bearer of truth in science.

Mill believes all phenomena are governed by universal laws. Induction rests on the uniformity of nature; the scientist strives to formulate propositions about phenomena that are as reliable as the law of causation.[12] The problem is that generalizing from instances of a sequence of phenomena can produce wrong propositions. To help the investigator, Mill develops five canons of inductive inference—rules of experimental method whose

---

11. "The really scientific truths, then, are not these empirical laws, but the causal laws which explain them" (*Works*, 8: 862).

12. Mill clearly bases his views on scientific investigation on Hume's theory of causation. (His answer to Hume's problem of induction is, obviously, to assume the uniformity of nature.)

purpose is to aid in the discovery of the causes and effects of phenomena. Although he concedes that they are not fully reliable, he argues that the canons of induction listed below can yield fruitful results:

• The method of agreement (If B is always present in A, then B is the effect of A.)

• The method of difference (If A is removed and B disappears, then B is the effect of A.)

• The method of residues (If all other known causes are excluded, the remaining effect is the residue.)

• The method of concomitant variations (If every change in B is preceded by some change in A, then B is the effect of A.)

• The joint method of agreement and difference, a combination of the first two above.[13]

The second type of proof discussed by Mill is deductive and determined within an axiomatic system. Convinced that we can find genuine causal and empirical laws in social science, Mill associates induction with both types of proofs and connects them together in a deductive system. "Deduction [for Mill] is not a mode of reasoning opposed to induction, but the culmination of it," explains William Thomas (1985: 54). Hence, induction in this sense is not synonymous with the term we use today, but refers more broadly to all general methods of reasoning employed by scientists to establish general laws (as discussed in chapter 4). Mill later modifies his definition of induction to include the verification of hypotheses, which he termed the *direct deductive method*. His brief summary of this method appears in book 3 of the *System of Logic* on induction: "The mode of investigation which, from the proved inapplicability of direct methods of observation and experiment, remains to us as the main source of the knowledge we possess or can acquire respecting the conditions, and laws of recurrence, of the more complex phenomena, is called, in its most general expression, the Deductive Method; and consists of three operations: the first, one of direct induction; the second, of ratiocination; the third, of verification" (*Works*, 7: 454).

---

13. I am indebted to Mawatari (1982, I: 132) for a simplified presentation of the canons of induction.

Later in book 6, when Mill discusses social phenomena, he differentiates between two types of verification—direct verification by specific experience and indirect verification.

Given that nature is a system of regularities, the problem becomes one of discovering the regularities and expressing them as laws. Mill identifies three methods of detecting regularities used by natural scientists: (1) observation, which leads to empirical laws but not to higher laws; (2) experimental control, for which the five canons of induction apply; and (3) the "deductive method," which is to be used in the presence of conjunctive causes and complex effects. In the case of investigation by observation, regularities give rise to empirical laws, science at its lowest level; but observation alone "cannot prove causation," cautions Mill (*Works*, 7: 386). With experimental control, the investigator can fall back on the five canons of induction. The third method, "deduction"—meaning a combination of induction, ratiocination, and verification—must be used in the presence of a composition of causes. Mill perceives this method as the Newtonian method, a method used at the highest level that science can reach.

The final point that Mill drew from his investigation of the natural sciences is the distinction between *exact* and *inexact sciences*. In exact sciences, phenomena act according to laws and can be predicted with accuracy (*Works*, 8: 845–46). Astronomy, chemistry, and natural science are exact; meteorology, tidology, and the social sciences are inexact because they cannot predict with accuracy. The expression *exact* should not be taken at face value, for Mill does not mean to suggest that science can be absolute: "In matters of evidence, as in all other human things, we neither require, nor can we attain, the absolute. We must hold even our strongest convictions with an opening left in our minds for the reception of facts which contradict them; and only when we have taken this precaution, have we earned the right to act upon our convictions with complete confidence when no such contradiction appears" (7: 574).

The conclusions described in this section represent, in essence, the conclusions Mill drew from a detailed consideration of natural science. In the next step Mill applies this knowledge to social science—the task he set for himself in book 6 of the *System of Logic*.

## The Development of a Method of Social Science

In Mill's scheme, the moral sciences break down this way:

**The science of human nature**

- psychology
- ethology

**The science of society**

- general sociology
  - social statics
  - social dynamics

**Particular social sciences**

- political economy
- political ethology.

Mill opens his discussion of the method of the social sciences with this comment: "The backward state of the Moral Sciences can only be remedied by applying to them the methods of Physical Science, duly extended and generalised" (*Works*, 8: 833). So it is that Mill strengthened the conviction, still common today, that the social sciences had fallen behind the physical sciences, and that this sad state could be remedied by applying to them a generalized method of the natural sciences. In book 6, Mill sets out to show how the moral sciences can be constructed; to demonstrate their natural interrelations; to carve out subfields of inquiry such as political economy and ethology; and to assess the potential and limitations of moral science. He is interested in determining both methods of investigation (i.e., ways to arrive at reliable conclusions) and requisites of proof (i.e., methods of testing evidence) (Castell 1936: 57–58).

Mill believes that the operations of the human mind are governed by universal laws; his goal is the discovery and application of the laws governing human action. Reasoning that the foundation of all science is the law of universal causation, he takes the next logical step and considers these questions: "Are the actions of human beings, like all other natural events, subject to invariable laws? Does that constancy of causation, which is the foundation of every scientific theory of successive phenomena, really obtain among them?" (*Works*, 8: 835). He answers in the affirmative (897). By demonstrating that human nature is subject to causation, he proves that social science can exist.

Mill's philosophy of moral science operates on several levels. He employs both the idea of a general and specialized science and the notion of the individual and the whole. Moral science breaks down into the science of human nature and the science of society. Because social science is rooted in a conception of human nature resting on fundamental laws of the mind, the science of the individual man (the science of human nature) must, logically, precede the science of man in society (social science, sociology).[14] The laws of the science of human nature are derived from two sources: the principles of psychology—the science of the elementary laws of mind—and *ethology*—the science dealing with the formation of the character of a specific people or age (914). In psychology, uniformities are exhibited by our ideas, by laws of the mind. Much of what Mill has to say about psychological laws is drawn from his father's *Analysis of the Phenomena of the Human Mind*.[15] Every proposition of moral science must, in his view, be derivable from the laws of human nature.

The science of the individual is followed by the science of society, also called social science, which, Mill remarks, "by a convenient barbarism, has been termed Sociology" (*Works*, 8: 895). The fundamental problem of social science is to determine laws according to which successive *states of society* evolve. A *state of society* is the status of all the social phenomena of a particular society in a particular age: the degree of education and technology; the artistic, intellectual, and moral level of the culture; the state of the economy; the levels of wealth and welfare of the society; the common beliefs, institutions, and customs; the form of government; and any other factors that affect the status of the society. Social science can be further divided into *social statics* and *social dynamics*. *Social statics* is built on uniformities of coexistence and aims to detect the relationships among social phenomena in a particular social state. *Social dynamics*, which is

---

14. In Mill's philosophy, the term *sociology* is not coterminous with today's academic discipline but with social science in general.
15. In *A System of Logic*, Mill refers his readers to his father's book, where "the principal laws of association . . . are copiously exemplified, and with a masterly hand" (*Works*, 8: 852–53).

based on uniformities of succession, seeks to discover the laws by which one social state passes into another.

Just as the science of psychology is the basis for the science of human nature, Mill expected the science of ethology to become the foundation of sociology, the science of society. Ethology, which Mill planned but never managed to develop, "may be called the Exact Science of Human Nature." Its truths, Mill tells us, "are not, like the empirical laws which depend on them, approximate generalizations, but real laws" (*Works*, 8: 870). According to Mill, the "actions and feelings of human beings in the social state are, no doubt, entirely governed by psychological and ethological laws" (896). The "middle principles" of ethology, in Mill's system, were to bridge the wide gap between the abstract laws of psychology and actual human behavior (870). In contrast to psychology, which is principally a science of observation and experiment, ethology is deductive (870). Its advances, he thought, would reduce the number of laws of human nature.[16] Because all group phenomena are phenomena of individual human nature, he needs to show that the laws of social dynamics and social statics can be derived from ethology and psychology.

Mill admits that the complexity of social phenomena is problematic; in social science we cannot be sure we know all of the causes. Yet, in his view, these problems are manageable. After all, the exact science of astronomy in its early stages and tidology in its mature phase also had to deal with complex matter. Still, social phenomena are so complicated that Mill has to concede the impossibility of exact prediction in the social sciences. "There is, indeed, no hope that these laws [of social science], though our knowledge of them were as certain and as complete as it is in astronomy, would enable us to predict the history of society, like that of the celestial appearances, for thousands of years to come. But the difference of certainty is not in the laws themselves, it is in the data to which these laws are to be applied" (*Works*, 8: 877). It is the fallible data and "the extraordinary number and variety of the data or elements" that, as we will see, make political economy an inexact science (895).

---

16. "The more highly the science of ethology is cultivated, and the better the diversities of individual and national character are understood, the smaller, probably, will the number of propositions become, which it will be considered safe to build on as universal principles of human nature" (*Works*, 8: 906).

Mill nonetheless believes that by combining the power of deductive laws of human nature (which, incidentally, give the science of man its "genuinely scientific character") with empirical laws, "we can lay down general propositions which will be true in the main, and on which, with allowance for the degree of their probable inaccuracy, we may safely ground our expectations and our conduct" (*Works*, 8: 848, 846). In other words, for most practical purposes social science can be treated like the exact sciences.[17] "[I]t is evidently possible with regard to such effects, to make predictions which will *almost* always be verified, and general propositions which are almost always true. And whenever it is sufficient to know how the great majority of the human race, or of some nation or class of persons, will think, feel, and act, these propositions are equivalent to universal ones. For the purposes of political and social science this *is* sufficient" (847).

Mill makes the case that social phenomena are the effects of the actions of individuals. The agglomeration of causes in social science, he argues, can be handled like the various forces in physics: they can be summed up or subtracted from one another. By adding them up, the social scientist can build up a theory of social behavior. The ultimate unit in society is the individual, which, unlike a chemical atom, does not yield a totally different substance when combined. "The laws of the phenomena of society are, and can be, nothing but the laws of the actions and passions of human beings united together in the social state. Men, however, in a state of society, are still men; their actions and passions are obedient to the laws of individual nature. Men are not, when brought together, converted into another kind of substance, with different properties. . . . In social phenomena the Composition of Causes is the universal law" (*Works*, 8: 879). In today's jargon this is an argument for methodological individualism.[18]

---

17. In Mill's words, "an approximate generalization is, in social inquiries, for most practical purposes equivalent to an exact one." By "approximate generalization" Mill means a generalization "which is only probable" (*Works*, 8: 847). Mill makes similar comments elsewhere (e.g., 7: 603).

18. Mill's assumption of social atomism was challenged by the organic conception of social order. A close examination of his methodological individualism unfortunately goes beyond the scope of this book. Readers interested in this aspect of Mill's thought are encouraged to consult Mitchell, who touches on some of the problems with Mill's position (1967: 592–93).

Before discussing the appropriate method for social science, Mill summarizes his solution to the Macaulay-James Mill debate over method. He reviews three methods—the chemical method of Macaulay, the abstract or geometrical method of his father, and the physical or concrete deductive method that represents his own solution to the problem of developing a method for the social sciences. Before elaborating on the correct method, he advances several arguments against the first two methods. The chemical method, he says, is not applicable to social science for the same reason that the geometrical method adopted by Hobbes, Bentham, and his father fails: both neglect the fact that social phenomena are governed by the composition of causes (879). On the other hand, the chemical method is wrong because, as we have seen, humans in society have no properties other than those derived from the properties of the individual and thus are not converted into a new substance when brought together. Moreover, Mill believes that Macaulay inaccurately represented Bacon's method as consisting solely of experiment and fact gathering.[19] According to Mill, Lord Bacon advocated both what we today call inductive and deductive procedures, a correct assumption on Mill's part. Hence, in establishing the first two components of his method—in modern terminology, induction and deduction—Mill appeals to Bacon and the Schoolmen. By 1833 it had occurred to him that a third component, *verification*, should also be incorporated in his method. We recall that he deemed the geometrical method inappropriate because it attempts to deduce sociological laws from a single principle of human nature. The experimental method, on the other hand, was useless because experiments are ruled out in social inquiry. This brings Mill to the conclusion that social science is a deductive science for which the concrete deductive method is best suited. He explains that social science "is a deductive science; not, indeed, after the model of geometry, but after that of the more complex physical sciences. It infers the law of each effect

---

19. Mill's attack on Macaulay is difficult to follow, for he condemns Macaulay's "empiricism," while himself defending an empiricist view of science. Anschutz remarks that Mill often uses the word *empiricism* in a deprecatory sense to mean "miscellaneous information" as opposed to scientific knowledge (in Schneewind 1968: 55ff.). Readers investigating primary materials should not only keep this in mind, but also note that Mill frequently uses *metaphysical* as a synonym for *psychological*.

from the laws of causation on which the effect depends; not, however, from the law merely of one cause, as in the geometrical method; but considering all the causes which conjunctly influence the effect, and compounding their laws with one another" (*Works*, 8: 895).

The concrete deductive method, however, also has its limitations, for it is evident that social science "cannot be a science of positive predictions, but only of tendencies." Although we may very well be able to conclude "that a particular cause will operate in a certain manner unless counteracted," we can never know what the collective result of the many combined elements affecting social phenomena will be. In spite of this drawback, "knowledge insufficient for prediction may be most valuable for guidance." General propositions in social science are hence "in the strictest sense of the word, hypothetical" (*Works*, 8: 898, 900).

Mill notes further that the "first difficulty which meets us in the attempt to apply experimental methods for ascertaining the laws of social phenomena, is that we are without the means of making artificial experiments" (*Works*, 8: 881). The lack of the *experimentum crucis* made finding another method of verification imperative. Again drawing on successful methods from the natural sciences, Mill turns to verification by specific experience. Although collecting empirical laws from direct observation "is an important part of the process of sociological inquiry" because the social scientist is searching to find "what is common to large classes of observed facts," empirical laws "are never more than approximate generalizations" (908, 907). Whereas specific experience for Mill is useful in verification—theories should be confronted with the facts—it is nonetheless limited by the variety of conditions influencing factors involved with social phenomena. Thus, Mill is led to what he calls *indirect verification*.

Under Comte's influence Mill came to the conclusion that a second, indirect method of verification of social phenomena was possible. The course of human history cannot be deduced from laws of human nature alone; a method that did so would overlook the effects of progression, the cumulative changes in human nature and society. Because social phenomena can, in fact, be so complex, Mill reasoned, history takes on a pivotal role in social science and Comte's *inverse deductive* or *historical method* becomes applicable. What this means, in short, is the employment of historical methods to establish and verify laws of science. Once

the facts of history supply a basis for generalization, observed
uniformities can be formulated as empirical laws and confirmed
by known deductions from human nature—hence the appellation *inverse deduction*.[20] The term *inverse* is employed in reference
to physical science, where direct deductions from known laws
are verified by their confrontation with empirical generalizations. When employing the inverse deductive method, empirical
generalizations drawn from history suggest a law, which is then
verified by known deductions from psychological or ethological
laws of human nature. Castell adeptly sums up the relation
between the inverse and direct methods this way: "In the direct
method the deduction is verified. In the inverse method the
empirical generalization is verified" (1936: 73). Mill describes the
circumstances that convinced him that the method he chose was
the appropriate one for the moral sciences:

The conclusions of theory cannot be trusted, unless confirmed by
observation; nor those of observation, unless they can be affiliated to
theory, by deducing them from the laws of human nature, and from a
close analysis of the circumstances of the particular situation. It is the
accordance of these two kinds of evidence separately taken—the coincidence of *à priori* reasoning and specific experience—which forms the
only sufficient ground for the principles of any science so "immersed
in matter," dealing with such complex and concrete phenomena
(*Works*, 8: 874).

The methods of the social sciences, remarks A. J. Ayer, thus
involve "a double process of verification; the proof, so far as we
can achieve it, that our historical generalisations conform to the
laws of human nature, and once again the observational tests"
(in Mill 1987: 11).

Finally, we come to the restrictive branches or subdisciplines
of sociology. Political economy is one because it confines itself
to one class of circumstances: those concerned with the pursuit
of wealth. *Political ethology*, which aims at discovering causes
that determine the character belonging to a specific people or
age, is the other.[21]

---

20. "History accordingly does, when judiciously examined, afford Empirical
Laws of Society. And the problem of general sociology is to ascertain these,
and connect them with the laws of human nature, by deductions showing that
such were the derivative laws naturally to be expected as the consequences of
those ultimate ones" (*Works*, 8: 916).
21. Mill leaves political ethology, like ethology, undeveloped.

Before moving to political economy, let us sum up the strands of Mill's thought that underlie his conception of social science so far. The phenomena of human nature and society exhibit regularities that can be resolved into a few basic principles derivative of the elementary laws of human nature; these uniformities are detectable by the "deductive method" and must be considered in their totality or in the context of their mutual relations within society; the uniformities of social phenomena can be formulated as tendencies (Castell 1936: 89). Moreover, social science and its subdisciplines are hypothetical, which means that formulations of their laws hold only if counteracting circumstances do not interfere; and all social sciences are inexact because a composition of causes makes direct verification and prediction impossible.

## The Inexact Science of Political Economy

We know that by 1828 J. S. Mill was already convinced that the "deductive method" was the method of political economy.[22] In the essay "On the Definition of Political Economy," Mill begins by first demarcating science from the arts. Science cannot, he stresses, be "a collection of practical rules"—although "practical rules must be capable of being founded upon it"—because practical rules are the "results of science." Mill makes the following distinction: "Science is a collection of *truths*; art, a body of *rules*, or directions for conduct. The language of science is, This is, This is not; This does, or does not, happen. The language of art is, Do this; Avoid that. Science takes cognizance of a *phenomenon*, and endeavors to discover its *law*; art proposes to itself an *end*, and looks out for *means* to effect it." Smith, who is Mill's target, is criticized for confounding is with ought and science with art. The rules for increasing the wealth of nations are not science, concludes Mill, but "the results of science" (*Works*, 4: 312).

He then discusses the distinction between social or moral science and physical science. "The physical sciences are those which treat of the laws of matter, and of all complex phenomena in so far as dependent upon the laws of matter. The mental or moral sciences are those which treat of the laws of mind, and of

---

22. Mill's review of Whately's *Elements of Logic* (1828) attests to this fact (*Works*, 11: 3–35).

all complex phenomena in so far as dependent upon the laws of mind" (*Works*, 4: 317). Mill agrees with Dugald Stewart that "the first principles of all sciences belong to the philosophy of the human mind" (311). Taking an example from political economy, the production of corn by human labor, he argues that it is the result of a law of the mind, namely, "that man desires to possess subsistence, and consequently wills the necessary means of procuring it" (317). But laws of mind and matter, he warns, "are so dissimilar in their nature, that it would be contrary to all principles of rational arrangement to mix them up as part of the same study" (317).

Mill goes on to provide a complete definition of political economy as the "science which traces the laws of such of the phenomena of society as arise from the combined operations of mankind for the production of wealth, in so far as those phenomena are not modified by the pursuit of any other object" (*Works*, 4: 323). To Mill, political economy is an abstract science of control and prediction: "When an effect depends upon a concurrence of causes, those causes must be studied one at a time, and their laws separately investigated, if we wish, through the causes, to obtain the power of either predicting or controlling the effect" (322).

What method should the political economist then use? Mill wrote this essay in the 1830s and did not revise it after reading Comte and incorporating the inverse deductive method into the *System of Logic*. As a consequence, his use of technical jargon in the essay does not coincide with that of the *System of Logic*, though what he means is clear. The method we today call induction (arguing "wholly *upwards* from particular facts to a general conclusion" he terms the "*à posteriori* method" (*Works*, 4: 324). The *a priori* method—the method political economists should use—is "a mixed method of induction and ratiocination" involving "reasoning from an assumed hypothesis" (325).[23] Mill

---

23. Schumpeter complains rightly that Mill used the term *a priori* in a misleading way. In the essay Mill, does, however, admit he does not use it in contrast to *empirical*, as is usually the case (1954b: 537). In his "Inaugural Address to the University of St. Andrews" (1867), Mill had this to say: "All true political science is, in one sense of the phrase, *à priori*, being deduced from the tendencies of things, tendencies known either through our general experience of human nature, or as the result of an analysis of the course of history, considered as a progressive evolution. It requires, therefore, the union of induction and deduction" (*Works*, 21: 237).

concludes that "it is vain to hope that truth can be arrived at, either in Political Economy or in any other department of the social science, while we look at the facts in the concrete, clothed in all the complexity with which nature has surrounded them, and endeavor to elicit a general law by a process of induction from a comparison of details; there remains no other method than the *à priori* one, or that of 'abstract speculation'" (329). The a posteriori method, or the method of inferring causes from single observations or "specific experience," cannot deliver truth because it cannot be relied on to disentangle a composition of causes. Nonetheless, as we see later, Mill believes it can be a fruitful complement to the a priori method.

The a priori method is, of course, the "deductive method" of the *System of Logic*. "It reasons, and, as we contend, must necessarily reason, from assumptions, not from facts. It is built upon hypotheses, strictly analogous to those which, under the name of definitions, are the foundation of the other abstract sciences" (*Works*, 4: 325–26). The primary hypothesis upon which political economy rests begs for closer consideration and justification, he argues, for the model of economic man as the avaricious pursuer of wealth had already come under attack in Mill's time.[24] Just as geometry assumes an arbitrary definition of a line, political economy presupposes an arbitrary definition of man "as a being who invariably does that by which he may obtain the greatest amount of necessaries, conveniences, and luxuries, with the smallest quantity of labour and physical self-denial with which they can be obtained in the existing state of knowledge" (326). Political economy is a separate, abstract science that deals with one motive, the desire for wealth, and which, he explains, "reasons from *assumed* premises—from premises which might be totally without foundation in fact, and which are not pretended to be universally in accordance with it. The conclusions of Political Economy, consequently, like those of geometry, are only true, as the common phrase is, *in the abstract*; that is, they are only true under certain suppositions, in which none but general causes—causes common to the *whole class* of cases under consideration—are taken into account" (326). The assumption of

---

24. The objections to political economy in Mill's age are well summarized in a review of James Mill's *Elements* in the *Westminster Review* (Anon. 1824: 294–97).

economic man, in other words, is a necessary simplification: "Not that any political economist was ever so absurd as to suppose that mankind are really thus constituted, but because this is the mode in which science must necessarily proceed" (322). Some simplification must be made; economic man is the best because "of all hypotheses equally simple, [it] is the nearest to the truth" (323). The fact of the matter is, without it, we cannot have science, for "no *general* maxims could ever be laid down unless *some* of the circumstances of the particular case were left out of consideration" (327).

Mill goes on to mention that many physical sciences have the advantage of being able to conduct controlled experiments, a method unfortunately not open to political economists or other social scientists. The consequence is that "we can rarely obtain what Bacon has quaintly, but, not unaptly, termed an *experimentum crucis.*" In political economy the "multitude of the influencing circumstances, and our very scanty means of varying the experiment" preclude the formulation of a crucial experiment such as either Bacon or Newton had in mind (*Works,* 4: 328). Due to these drawbacks there is no alternative available to the political economist but the a priori method of "abstract speculation." Economists must thus fall back upon general reasoning based on simplified and, consequently, somewhat narrow and unrealistic definitions and assumptions.

Mill also indicates the necessity of taking into account the role of disturbing causes in political economy. The presence of such causes "constitutes the only uncertainty of Political Economy; and not of it alone, but of the moral sciences in general." He defines a disturbing cause as "an uncertainty inherent in the nature of those complex phenomena, and arising from the impossibility of being quite sure that all the circumstances of the particular case are known to us sufficiently in detail, and that our attention is not unduly diverted from any of them" (*Works,* 4: 330). Yet disturbing causes are not to be treated as mere conjectures. Comparing them to friction in mechanics, Mill asserts that disturbing causes, too, have their laws, whose effect, once discovered, should "be added to, or subtracted from, the effect of the general ones" (330). Disturbing causes in his view can be of two types. They may be causes not yet discovered by political economists and, therefore, attributable to circumstances that operate on human behavior through the principle of human nature that distinguishes political economy as a science—that is, the desire for wealth. Or they may be attributable to some other law of human nature, which means that they fall outside the scope of political economy. In the latter case, "the mere political economist, he who has studied no science but Political Economy, . . . will fail" (331).

As for the final step of scientific method, Mill argues that we should try to verify our theory by comparing the results of our theory with the facts, especially proven facts. Here the a posteriori method of Bacon, or induction, which is not "a means of discovering truth, but of verifying it" becomes useful. Explains Mill: "We cannot, therefore, too carefully endeavor to verify our theory, by comparing, in the particular cases to which we have access, the results which it would have led us to predict, with the most trustworthy accounts we can obtain of those which have been actually realized. The discrepancy between our anticipations and the actual fact is often the only circumstance which would have drawn our attention to some important disturbing cause which we had overlooked" (*Works*, 4: 332). The political economist is warned to neglect neither a comprehensive overview nor meticulous detail. When Mill wrote the essay, he had not yet read Comte, but the role of history was already on his mind.[25] It seems reasonable to conclude that what he says about the inverse deductive method also holds for political economy. This means that the method of political economy also draws on the inverse deductive method, which, in a nutshell, takes the following form:

1. An empirical generalization drawn from the facts of history suggests a law.

2. The generalization is checked to see if it conforms to the laws of human nature or ethology.

3. The generalization is evaluated on the basis of the results.

In a strange twist, Mill concludes the essay with the point that a practical social scientist uses two procedures—the analytical

---

25. In the essay, Mill admits that "the uses of history, and the spirit in which it ought to be studied, are subjects which have never yet had justice done them, and which involve considerations more multifarious than can be pertinently introduced in this place" (*Works*, 4: 333, n. 36).

and the synthetic methods—to arrive at the truth, apparently paying lip service to Newton's rules of philosophizing. First, the scientist analyzes the existing state of society by breaking it into its component parts, individuals (the method of analysis). "After referring to the experience of individual man to learn the *law* of each of those elements, that is, to learn what are its natural effects, and how much of the effect follows from so much of the cause when not counteracted by any other cause, there remains an operation of *synthesis;* to put all these effects together, and, from what they are separately, to collect what would be the effect of all the causes acting at once" (*Works*, 4: 336). Mill concludes that "[i]f these various operations could be correctly performed, the result would be prophecy; but, as they can be performed only with a certain approximation to correctness, mankind can never predict with absolute certainty, but only with a less or greater degree of probability" (336).

The framework of Mill's general theory of social science is thus equally valid for economic science. In a letter to John P. Nichol in 1834, Mill reveals how important this essay is to him: "I am ambitious that the essay, even if for that end it should remain unpublished for twenty years, should become classical and of authority" (*Works*, 12: 211). It seems safe to say that his wish has been fulfilled.

## Mill on Specific Methodological Issues in Political Economy

Up to this point my presentation of Mill's methodology has been exclusively interpretative and exegetical—an exposition that purposely follows the somewhat disjointed evolution of his ideas on the methods of science from a general theory of science to the more particular science of political economy. In this section, I examine several specific issues about the method of political economy in greater detail in the hope of adding depth to the structure of Mill's thought and sorting out some erroneous interpretations of Mill's theories of method.

### On the Inexact Nature of Economic Theory
Mill originally took Newtonian astronomy as the model for social science. But, he observes in the *System of Logic*, moral science "falls far short of the standard of exactness now realized

in Astronomy" (*Works*, 8: 846). In the *Principles of Political Economy* (1848), his last book, he reiterates that "[w]e must never forget that the truths of political economy are truths only in the rough: they have the certainty, but not the precision, of exact science" (*Works*, 2: 422). Political economy not only has to fall back on tendencies, its predictive powers are considerably weaker than astronomy's. We can "neither make positive predictions nor lay down universal propositions," for the generalizations on which political economists rely for prediction are only approximately true (8: 847). "The actions of individuals could not be predicted with scientific accuracy," but we can predict "with tolerable certainty" the collective conduct of the masses (846, 846). At the macroeconomic level we can "make predictions which will *almost* always be verified, and general propositions which are almost always true" (847). For the practical purposes of social inquiry this is sufficient and must be accepted; after all, if our knowledge of the economy and the science of political economy were perfect, "we should become prophets" (4: 332). For Mill, then, prediction in political economy is not a matter of exact measurement but of good judgment and skill.

For the Mill who was working out the methods of natural science, mathematical demonstration as used in physics, astronomy, and mechanics seemed a suitable method for use in science in general. But after he had contemplated the scope and methods of moral science, and thus also of political economy, his ideas evolved and underwent revision. Margaret Schabas claims that "Mill's more developed study of the scope and methods of political economy . . . conforms very closely to his conception of an ideal mathematical science." As she sees it, "political economy [to Mill] was not only a deductive science, but also, like classical physics, essentially abstract and hypothetical in character. Its methods were more akin to those of mechanics than of chemistry. Indeed, it was possible to start with a study of economic laws under the most ideal and simplistic conditions, such as perfect competition, and then introduce disturbing causes, in much the same way in which the physicist would gradually complicate the fundamental laws of mechanics with various frictions and asymmetries" (1990: 107–108). Certainly we can find evidence that Mill sought a method whose results were expected to approach the certainty of mathematics.[26] Yet her viewpoint ignores the evolution of his thought, especially the incorporation of history as the inverse deductive method of Comte, and ultimately supports, in my opinion, exactly the converse of his true mature position. Mill certainly did not regard political economy as a discipline closely related to ideal mathematical science. As early as 1829, he was complaining that French philosophers "deduce politics like mathematics from a set of axioms & definitions, forgetting that in mathematics there is no danger of partial views: a proposition is either true or it is not, & if it is true, we may safely apply it to every case which the proposition comprehends in its terms: but in politics & the social science, this is so far from being the case, that error seldom arises from our assuming premises which are not true, but generally from our overlooking other truths which limit, & modify the effect of the former" (*Works*, 12: 36). In this passage Mill is clearly expressing the view that political economy is far more complex than mathematics; it is subject both to human prejudice and to errors caused by a failure to take into account some of the many causes operating in moral science.

Nor is this type of statement an isolated example. In a letter to William T. Thornton in 1867, Mill praises Thornton's latest book for having the potential to bring about "the emancipation of political economy" (*Works*, 16: 1320). What did political economy need to be liberated from? As far as Mill was concerned, the laws of political economy, for instance the law of supply and demand, were being treated "as if they were laws of inanimate matter, not amenable to the will of the human beings from whose feelings, interests, and principles of action they proceed" (1320).[27] Schabas, I think, is right in assuming that Mill

---

26. Mill writes, for instance: "The facts of statistics, since they have been made a subject of careful recordation and study, have yielded conclusions, some of which have been very startling to persons not accustomed to regard moral actions as subject to uniform laws. The very events which in their own nature appear most capricious and uncertain, and which in any individual case no attainable degree of knowledge would enable us to foresee, occur, when considerable numbers are taken into account, *with a degree of regularity approaching to mathematical* [emphasis added]" (*Works*, 8: 932).
27. Keep in mind as well that Mill followed Dugald Stewart more closely than has often been realized, and that Stewart clearly argued that moral science could not be organized according to geometrical or mathematical methods. On the Scottish influences on Mill, see Corsi (1987).

considered mathematics in developing his theories of method for natural and social science. Precisely because it put an ideal, simplified case at his fingertips, it was an excellent starting point for theorizing.[28] She is, I believe, also correct in assuming that Mill takes as his starting point the simplest cases and then gradually raises the level of complexity by adding disturbing causes. But it would be wrong to infer from this that he settled on a mathematico-deductivist view, for that would be to ignore the evolution of his thought and his interest in both the fine details of scientific method and the broader epistemological picture, a point to which I return in a later section.

As a final note, I want to point out that Mill's understanding of the word *inexact* calls for closer scrutiny. By an "inexact science," Mill generally means that the backbone of political economy is a structure of statements of tendencies rather than universal generalizations. In a most instructive analysis, Hausman discusses four ways of interpreting *inexactness* (1992: 128–31). *Inexact* may mean (1) approximate, or true within a margin of error, (2) probabilistic or statistical in nature, (3) how things would be in the absence of disturbing causes, or (4) qualified with *ceteris paribus* clauses. It is usually the third and sometimes the fourth meanings that Mill had in mind. Most frequently he uses laws to state how things would be if certain conditions hold. At least once he uses a *ceteris paribus* statement; and, as Hausman notes, *ceteris paribus* is often consistent with much of what Mill says (133).

## On History and the Relativism of Economic Theory
John Stuart Mill never wrote a work of history. Yet he provides us with "a conception of the relation between history and the science of society which surely belongs to a very different intellectual world from that in which we commonly locate the Benthamites" (Burns 1976: 4). One could easily conclude that Mill is ambiguous about the status of historical generalizations in political economy, for the gap between the *System of Logic* and the essay on the definition of political economy was never closed. The younger Mill, we recall, scorned the role of history

---

28. Note that the use of this method, again, allies Mill with the Scottish stream of thought.

that Macaulay envisioned as the foundation of political economy. After reading Comte, however, the emphasis on history that Macaulay supported reappears in the *System of Logic* as the inverse deductive method. If we assume that Mill's most mature view appears in this book, we are forced to conclude that he came to believe that social theory had to be supplemented by historical and sociological considerations.[29] The greatest task of history, according to Mill, is to discover the laws of the development of society, which in turn allow us to understand the future state of society.[30] The implication, then, is that "Mill swung round to the conviction that 'all questions of political institutions are relative'; and this conviction . . . may suggest that however successfully Mill upheld the deductive method in political economy, he thereafter embraced the study of history as the royal road to wisdom in the larger science of politics. Yet here, too, he resists easy categorisation" (Collini et al. 1983: 143).[31]

Mill's historical perspective adds a relativist element to his work. Because the laws of political economy and political institutions are relative to time and place, true causes cannot be verified. "We can never, therefore, affirm with certainty that a cause which has a particular tendency in one people or in one age will have exactly the same tendency in another, without referring back to our premises, and performing over again for the second age or nation, that analysis of the whole of its influencing circumstances which we had already performed for the first. The deductive science of society will not lay down a

29. Burns arrives at the same interpretation of Mill's mature position: "The establishing of a deductive connection between the facts of history and the laws of ethology and psychology is the only way in which we can advance from superficial empiricism to scientific understanding" (1976: 8).
30. "The fundamental problem, therefore, of the social science, is to find the laws according to which any state of society produces the state which succeeds it and takes its place. This opens the great and vexed question of the progressiveness of man and society; an idea involved in every just conception of social phenomena as the subject of a science" (*Works*, 8: 912).
31. Mill has sometimes been criticized for holding a deterministic and historicist view (one needs only think of Karl Popper). Such views are based, for instance, on Mill's comment in chap. 11 of the *System of Logic* that "the collective series of social phenomena, in other words the course of history, is subject to general laws" (*Works*, 8: 931). To be fair, we should keep in mind that Mill always saw two sides to an issue, and the other side in this case is the relativist quality of economic theory.

theorem, asserting in an universal the effect of any cause; but will rather teach us how to frame the proper theorem for the circumstances of any given case" (*Works*, 8: 899–900). His own principles of political economy, Mill admits, are only valid for the Anglo-Saxon world. "In political economy for instance, empirical laws of human nature are tacitly assumed by English thinkers, which are calculated only for Great Britain and the United States. Among other things, an intensity of competition is constantly supposed, which, as a general mercantile fact, exists in no country in the world except those two" (906). Mill insists repeatedly on the need to grasp the historical relativism of economic principles, warning that "it has been a very common error of political economists to draw conclusions from the elements of one state of society, and apply them to other states in which many of the elements are not the same" (903).[32]

## On the Proper Role of the Economist

I have mentioned that Mill was as interested in the epistemological parts as in their relationship to the whole. In *A System of Logic* he regards the methodology of political economy as a part of the methodology of science in general; and, as he emphasizes in his autobiography, in the *Principles of Political Economy* he addresses issues in political economy in the broader context of the science of social philosophy (*Works*, 1: 257). On the one hand, he notes that political economy can be an independent branch of science because it depends "on one class of circumstances only," and on the other hand, "[f]or practical purposes, Political Economy is inseparably intertwined with many other branches of social philosophy" (*Works*, 8: 901; 2: xci). When, however, forced to choose between the details of economic theory and the big, practical questions, Mill chooses the latter. "I confess that I regard the purely abstract investigations of political economy . . . as of very minor importance compared with the great practical questions which the progress of democracy & the spread of Socialist opinions are pressing on, & for which both the governing and the governed classes are very far from being in a fit state of mental preparation" (*Works*, 14: 87). In fact, Mill does not

---

32. Although there is much Scottish about his views, on this point Mill seems to disregard the Scots' natural history perspective.

think that the economic theorist without a broader understanding of the social world can be effective: "[A] person is not
likely to be a good political economist who is nothing else," he
cautions in his essay, "Auguste Comte and Positivism" (*Works*,
10: 306).

There are, nonetheless, areas where, he thinks, the political
economist should not dare to tread. Mill follows Hume in de-
limiting the scope of political economy to questions of "is," as
opposed to "ought." He defines the proper role of the economist
this way. "A scientific observer or reasoner, merely as such, is
not an advisor for practice. His part is only to show that certain
consequences follow from certain causes, and that to obtain
certain ends, certain means are the most effectual. Whether the
ends themselves are such as ought to be pursued, and if so, in
what cases and to how great a length, it is no part of his business
as a cultivator of science to decide, and science alone will never
qualify him for the decision" (*Works*, 8: 950). We should not
suppose, however, that Mill means that the science of political
economy is value-free. "Mill was committed before all else to
the proposition that science and values are not radically distinct
spheres but that, on the contrary, rationality has a place in ethics
as in science" (Jones 1992: 308). The direct deductions of natural
science and the empirical generalizations of social science help
the investigator understand the human condition and find a way
to improve man's lot (Thomas 1985: 77).

## On Partiality and Objectivity

In a passage of the essay that seems to have been overlooked
by scholars of economics, Mill warns against the misleading
view that all conclusions ground out of correctly deduced theoretical propositions are true: "[T]he coherence, and neat concate-
nation of our philosophical systems, is more apt than we are
commonly aware to pass with us as evidence of their truth." In
a similar vein, he explains that an economist "may be an excellent professor of abstract science; for a person may be of great
use who points out correctly what effects will follow from certain combinations of possible circumstances, in whatever tract
of the extensive region of hypothetical cases those combinations
may be found. . . . If, however, he does no more than this, he
must rest contented to take no share in practical politics; to have

no opinion, or to hold it with extreme modesty, on the applications which should be made of his doctrines to existing circumstances (*Works*, 4: 332, 333). This—from today's perspective, remarkable—view implies that the economic theorist who is only an economic theorist should never venture into the areas of applied economics or policy questions.

Mill goes on to warn that, even with "all the precautions which have been indicated [i.e., being more than just an economist, knowing that correctly deduced conclusions of theory are not necessarily true or objective, etc.] there will still be some danger of falling into partial views." The only other thing we can do beyond that already mentioned "is to endeavor to be impartial critics of our own theories, and to free ourselves, as far as we are able, from that reluctance . . . to admit the reality or relevancy of any facts which they have not previously either taken into, or left a place open for in, their systems" (*Works*, 4: 336). Reduced to its simplest form, this means that economists need to confront their theories with reality and acquaint themselves with, and consider carefully, the arguments against them. The scientist "can do no more than satisfy himself that he has seen all that is visible to any other persons who have concerned themselves with the subject. For this purpose he must endeavor to place himself at their point of view, and strive earnestly to see the subject as they see it; nor give up the attempt until he has either added the appearance which is floating before them to his own stock of realities, or made out clearly that it is an optical deception" (337). No matter how alert the economist, objectivity is especially difficult in political economy. "There is . . . almost always room for a modest doubt as to our practical conclusions. Against false premises and unsound reasoning, a good mental discipline may effectually secure us; but against the danger of *overlooking* something, neither strength of understanding nor intellectual cultivation can be more than a very imperfect protection" (*Works*, 4: 337).

As a final point, we need to consider Mill's views on the "differences of principle" that exist among political economists. Usually these are due to "a difference in their conceptions of the philosophic method of the science," observes Mill. "The parties who differ are guided, either knowingly or unconsciously, by different views concerning the nature of the evidence appropriate to the subject" (*Works*, 4: 324). With this comment, Mill, unfortunately, also reduces to differing methodological positions the often heated disagreements that stem from economists' preconceived political beliefs and that have distinguished the history of the discipline from its very beginnings.

## On the Ricardian Tone of Mill's Methodology

Orthodox opinion has it that Mill's *Essays on Some Unsettled Questions in Political Economy* (written 1829–31) is essentially Ricardian in nature (Bonar 1893: 239) and that Ricardo and Mill held the same views on method.[33] This judgment probably originated from Mill's own comments on Ricardian economics. In a letter to John Austen about the *Principles of Political Economy*, he says, "I doubt if there will be a single opinion (on pure political economy) in the book, which may not be exhibited as a corollary from his [Ricardo's] doctrines" (*Works*, 13: 731). And in his autobiography, Mill reveals that "it was one of my father's main objects to make me apply to Smith's more superficial view of political economy, the superior lights of Ricardo" (*Works*, 1: 31).[34]

Still, I find little support for the view that Mill followed Ricardo on matters methodological. His aim in the *Principles*, Mill admitted, was to produce a work along the lines of the *Wealth of Nations*.[35] Joseph Schumpeter rightly refuses to include Mill in the Ricardian school specifically because he saw that the *Principles* is not Ricardian (1954b: 529). One may be tempted to resolve the seeming contradictions in Mill's approach by attributing them to a kind of schizophrenic Mill, who followed Smith

---

33. See, e.g., Hollander (1979 and 1985) and De Marchi (1970 and 1988: 149). Blaug, who also categorizes Mill as a Ricardian, nonetheless admits that "[w]ith respect to the purely abstract questions of political economy, however, Mill was not simply Ricardo's echo, as is so often suggested" (1958: 166).

34. Other scholars, it might be added, find Mill's method eclectic. Mawatari, for instance, finds considerable support for this view in the literature (1983, III: 33). It seems to me, however, that, as in the case of Adam Smith, this explanation of his methodology rests on a superficial understanding of his methodological position.

35. In 1847 Mill explained to Henry Chapman that his *Principles* "is a book to replace Adam Smith, that is, to attempt to do for political economy what A. S. did at the time when he wrote, to make a book which, while embodying all the abstract science in the completest form yet attained, incorporating all important improvements, should at the same time be essentially a book of applications exhibiting the principles of the science in the concrete" (*Works*, 13: 708).

in the *Principles,* but elsewhere followed Ricardo. After all, Mark Blaug remarks, the *Principles* and the *System of Logic* "might just as well have been written by two different authors" (1992: 65). Yet this misses the point: Mill insisted that social scientists operate on both a narrow and a broadly social-philosophical base. His works are not disjointed; they present two different aspects of the same plan. Even when working through narrow questions of method in the essay "On the Definition of Political Economy," Mill builds up a theory of political economy by first erecting a science of the individual and then a theory of society—clearly following in Adam Smith's philosophical tradition.

## Mill's Place in the History and Philosophy of Science

Mill has always been admired for his intolerance of obscurantism and casuistry; his love of clarity and devotion to reasoned analysis has won him the respect even of his opponents. But much more can be said in support of his theory of social science. Mill overturned the view that the phenomena of society cannot be handled in a scientific way. He showed, further, that all rational scientific inquiry means isolation and abstraction—a process of selecting one aspect from reality—while maintaining that the science of society encompasses more than political economy (Castell 1936: 89, 90). He reminded us that human nature is a function of its environment and that, as a consequence, the "laws" of political economy are relative.

    Mill has often been criticized for being fuzzy-minded—and certainly his terminology is anachronistic, idiosyncratic, and consequently confusing—but a patient reading of Mill will be rewarded, for Mill sets forth a modern philosophy of science—a variety of the hypothetico-deductive method. He clearly perceived that principles are based on abstract assumptions and factual premises; and he carved out a theory of method whose purpose was to both predict an occurrence of events and make recorded facts intelligible. Mill's philosophy of science, its associationist psychology excepted, is prescient and forward-looking: the notion of a law of nature and lawlike uniformities in general would hold a prominent place in the positivist philosophy of science. In addition, the methodological problems of social inquiry he analyzes "remain with us, the only radical development being the rise of powerful methods of data collection and statistical analysis" (Whitaker 1975: 1003).[36] His most important legacy, however, is that his theory of method is, essentially, the one to which most economists since have actually subscribed.[37]

---

36. The respective reference in the Wood collection is 1987 (1: 479).
37. Hausman concurs with this point, but argues that Mill's "deductive method" is not the hypothetico-deductive method (1992: 123, 124, 148).

# 8                Concluding Remarks

I began this investigation into the methodology of the classical economists with an in-depth survey of the body of philosophical thought that was passed down to the classical economists—the writings of such great figures in classical and eighteenth- and nineteenth-century methodology as Bacon, Descartes, Newton, Hobbes, Locke, Hume, Stewart, Herschel, and Whewell. After examining their ideas, I considered the development of classical economic methodology as represented by four great figures of the classical era—Smith, Malthus, Ricardo, and Mill. More than anything else, this investigation makes clear how rich this age was in methodological developments. I do not think it an exaggeration to say that debates on scientific method were just as important as the scientific discoveries themselves.

At the center of the debates on economic methodology were interpretations of the methods advocated by Newton and Bacon—the "Newtonian method," "induction," history, and the methods of analysis and synthesis. This was the age of the science of man and the science of human nature; almost all its great figures were polymaths who knew natural science and made it important by carefully considering its methods before developing methods suitable to social science. The classical economists did not, however, slip into scientism: as methods and concepts were transferred from one domain to the other, they were altered. Although these four great classical economists recognized political economy as an independent science, Smith, Malthus, and Mill also saw it as inextricable from the other social sciences and from ethics. Moreover, these three believed that no political economist could be useful or effective who did not have a knowledge of the other social sciences. In the beginning of the classical period, the moral sciences were considered loftier than the natural sciences; by the end, the converse view held sway, for Whewell had introduced the hierarchy of the sciences that we take for granted today. Then, with Mill, came the notion that the social sciences were backwards, but could catch up if the methods of the natural sciences were generalized and extended to them.

The period from Smith to Mill was the age in which history and the method of "induction" came into their own. As the classical era opened, Smith was following Locke in advocating a "historical, plain method," while adding a Scottish touch with his idiosyncratic ideas about introspection and experiment. As it closed, Mill was advocating history's use as a means of verifying theory and cautioning his readers that the historical element of economic laws makes them relative to time and place. Even induction had a historical component, although a wide range of scientific operations fell under the label *induction*. In spite of Smith's and Mill's claims to have modeled social science after Newtonian astronomy, it was a Baconian interpretation of Newtonian science that both claimed for their systems. In practice, Newton's induction diverged from the Baconian induction of Robert Boyle and the Royal Society that influenced the classical economists. For Newton, formulating a crucial experiment to answer a specific question—not gathering confirming instances to make an induction ever more general—was the point of induction. Smith and Malthus, on the other hand, were very concerned about adding to the stock of existing observations and arranging observations already made in better order; in so doing they were practicing Bacon's natural history of fact collection and classification.

The era generated no inconsiderable confusion concerning the use of inductive and deductive methods. Several factors contributed to this. The term *induction* was construed so broadly that it, in effect, subsumed all methods of reasoning employed by a scientist to establish general laws, including deduction, natural history, induction, analogy, and the popular methods of analysis and synthesis. Equally important was the overreaction to the Cartesian systems. So loudly did Smith, Malthus, and Mill warn of the illusive simplicity of deduction, the need for gradual

generalizations, and the dangers of Descartes's rash generalizations that a myth of an inductive-deductive dichotomy grew up
that still, unfortunately, finds supporters today. The issue of
inductive versus deductive methods cannot be summed up as
the difference between reasoning from particulars to a general
conclusion and abstracting from a general principle, for all the
classical economists supported their findings with theoretical
principles and empirical details. No matter what they said about
the methods they claimed to use or how fervently they objected
to the Cartesian method, the classical economists were every bit
as interested in deducing the laws from which a coherent system
emerges as Descartes was. Although the patron of the empirical
method was Newton, it was the empirical-hypothetical method
of the *Opticks*—not the mathematical, deductive method of the
*Principia*—that the classical economists knew and took as their
model. Due to the blurring of the terms *induction* and *deduction*,
the idea of a law was ambiguous; political economists construed
it to mean either a statement of empirical regularities or a logical
construct derived from definitions, premises, and deductions
without seeming to be conscious of the dual uses of the term.

Of the major figures in economics featured in this work, one,
Ricardo, stands out as a methodological exception in several
ways. Only he seems to have been unaffected by the strong
influence that Newton, Bacon, and history exercised over his
contemporaries. Lacking a university education and under the
tutelage of James Mill, he claimed to adhere to the geometrical
method of Euclid, Hobbes, North, and, especially, the elder Mill.
His method, nevertheless, appears to be the one he had grown
accustomed to using as a broker—hence the term *broker's myopia*
to indicate its shortcomings. A man who concerned himself
almost exclusively with quick policy results, logical consistency,
and questions of pure theory, Ricardo also stands alone in making a radical departure in defining the scope of political economy. John Stuart Mill does follow him to a certain extent,
moving away from the unity-of-science perspective we find in
Smith and Malthus to the view of political economy as a "separate science"—albeit one still unquestionably tied to moral philosophy. Unlike Ricardo, however, Smith, Malthus, and Mill
(who believed he was improving Ricardo's theory), all cautioned

against the deceptive simplicity of political economists' systems and political economists who were only theorists engaged in "abstract investigations."

During the classical period, the philosophy of the science of economics reached its most mature state in the hands of John Stuart Mill. Mill analyzed the existing varieties of scientific method and improved what he took to be the most appropriate method, adding the step of verification and making prediction an integral part of economic method. He adopted Hume's is-ought distinction (the scientist is to show what is as opposed to what ought to be)—a distinction still accepted by today's economist—and discriminated between the exact and inexact sciences. Political economy, he recognized, was inexact because its practitioners could not predict with great accuracy. As Mill uses it, the term *inexact* refers to disturbing causes that function like friction in mechanics and render direct verification and prediction in political economy impossible. Yet disturbing causes, by Mill's definition, have their own laws; once discovered, their influence could be subtracted from or added to the general laws. Of all the classical economists, Mill provides us with the most realistic appraisal of the relations between the natural and social sciences; he knows that political economy as a moral science falls short of the standard of exactness obtainable in astronomy. Even with the additional methodological armory Mill brings to political economy, his expectations of economic method are modest. He comes to the conclusion that maintaining objectivity in economics will be difficult, not least because economists often prefer to overlook arguments against their theories. In a similar vein, he sees prediction in political economy as necessarily imperfect, and, therefore, requiring good judgment. As Mill noted, economists would be prophets if their knowledge of political economy were perfect.

By the advent of marginalist economics, the classical economists had established political economy as a science. They had shown that economic phenomena, like natural phenomena, could be handled in a scientific way. Despite conceptual confusion, most of the methodological issues raised in the era of classical economics were not trivial; many of them are still unsettled today. The major breakthrough remaining for the next generation of economists was grasping the usefulness of calculus and other sophisticated mathematical tools for political economy. Whereas Malthus had surmised its utility for the discipline, it was Whewell who actually applied sophisticated mathematics to the theoretical economic analysis of his day—in vain, for his pathbreaking work had no impact on his contemporaries. It would thus remain for the marginalists to demonstrate the benefits of mathematics for the discipline and incorporate it into the public body of economic thought.

# Appendix: Science and *The Gentleman's Magazine*, 1731–1759

*The Gentleman's Magazine* was a London-based monthly periodical styled for the eighteenth-century man of letters.[1] I chose it as a representative source for information about science in this era for two reasons: it was the leading British magazine of its day, and David Hume, Adam Smith, Robert Malthus, David Ricardo, and J. S. Mill were undoubtedly familiar with it.[2] Hume and Smith probably read the periodical faithfully. Issues published between 1769 and 1777 were in Smith's personal library (Mizuta 1967: 113), and both men mentioned it in their personal correspondence.[3] Its popularity and significance is reflected in Hume's reaction to the magazine's decision to reprint one of his essays. Writing to his oldest and best friend, William Mure, in November 1742, Hume remarked that being published in *Gentleman's Magazine* was essentially the same as "having publish'd to all Britain my Sentiments on that Affair" (1932 1: 44; Force 1987: 210, n. 44).

To discover what kind of articles appeared on natural science and economics during the mid-eighteenth century, I surveyed the *Gentleman's Magazine* covering a time span of 29 years. Even the most casual perusal of the journal in these years confirms what an integral role science played in eighteenth-century society and how important natural philosophy was for moral

---

1. *The Gentleman's Magazine* was an institution in Britain for almost two centuries. Publication was finally discontinued in 1907.
2. As mentioned in chapter 3, the real boom in the founding of periodicals occurred later, during the first and second decades of the nineteenth century. *The Gentleman's Magazine* was the first journal of its kind, and it soon attracted competition: *London Magazine* started up its presses in 1732; and *Scots Magazine,* in 1739. Today we can only puzzle over the *Gentleman's Magazine*'s decision to ignore the publication of Smith's *Wealth of Nations*.
3. Consider, for instance, Smith (1987: 329) and Hume (1932, 1: 44).

philosophy, and vice versa. One must come away with the impression that the *polite culture*—the men of letters or the "gentlemen of science" as they were called in the eighteenth and nineteenth centuries—strived to keep abreast of the latest scientific developments in all areas of inquiry.

The time period chosen, from 1731 to 1759, is somewhat arbitrary, but well situated in the movement in which a science of man was developing.[4] 1731 was the year the *Gentleman's Magazine* began publication. Between that year and 1759, the long-lasting achievements of an era focused on working out a science of human nature were made. In January of 1739, Hume published his *Treatise of Human Nature;* over the next two decades *Essays, Moral and Political* (1741–42), *An Enquiry concerning Human Understanding* (1748), and *An Enquiry concerning the Principles of Morals* (1751) all appeared. Smith's *Theory of Moral Sentiments* was first published in 1759.[5]

The following list of titles for this time period includes only articles on natural science, medicine,[6] and economics.[7] In these

----

4. Unfortunately, only the volumes from 1731 to 1759 and from 1790 on were available. As I was primarily interested in the period in which the science of man was being developed—which ended, at the latest, with Smith's death in 1790—I deemed the later issues irrelevant.

5. *Gentleman's Magazine* announced the publication of Smith's work in the May 1759 issue with this unceremonious and uncommented notice: "The history of moral sentiments. By *Adam Smith*, professor of moral philosophy in the university of *Glasgow*, 6s Millar" (vol. 29: 230).

6. Medicine is important because the plague and other diseases spurred on the development of statistics, the forerunner of econometrics. A look at the article titles in the early period also underscores the influential role the plague played in the development of medicine. (Veterinary medicine has been omitted, although a copious supply of articles on this subject existed.) Medicine, by the way, was also influential in the general development of economics. In the era before Smith, some political economists were merchants, but just as many were trained as physicians. Sir William Petty, as I noted earlier, was able to practice as a physician. Nicholas Barbon (1637–1698) received a degree in medicine from the University of Utrecht in 1661; and François Quesnay (1694–1774), personal physician to Madame Pompadour, was inspired to write his *Tableau économique* by William Harvey's (1578–1657) discovery of the circulation of blood, made public in his *De motu cordis* in 1628. John Locke (1632–1704), also inspired by Harvey, studied medicine at Oxford.

7. Although compiled with care, this list only approximates comprehensiveness. Time constraints prevented me from considering all the letters to the editor (Sylvanus Urban), many of which had to do with natural science or economics but carried no running head at the top of the page—my rule of thumb for including articles in this appendix. Summaries of the *Philosophical*

years, most issues of the *Gentleman's Magazine* carried a section on these topics: selected proceedings and debates in parliament; essays on politics and foreign affairs; poetry and music; weekly essays (often on literature); letters to the editor; reviews and notices of new books; obituaries, births, marriages, bankruptcies, and promotions; stock prices; and foreign history. Each volume concluded with the annual index. After 1734 an annual "Supplement" and after 1742 the "Annual London General Bill of Christenings and Burials" appeared at the end of the year. Colored pictures and a section on recent weather conditions and its effect on disease became integral parts of each issue from 1752 on.

The breadth of article topics in the *Gentleman's Magazine* reflects how broadly the term *philosophical* was construed in this age. Today's reader can get a feel for the wide-ranging scope of things philosophical, or scientific, in this era by considering a small sampling of other subjects. In addition to the standard features mentioned above, readers encountered articles on the following topics: the language of animals, a cure for love sickness, arguments against cursing and swearing, an inquiry into the existence of heaven and hell, evidence supporting tendencies toward the degeneracy of the people of England, the geography of Peru to Tasmania, methods of indoor exercise, tips on child rearing, the art of deciphering, descriptions of animals from the rhinoceros to the seahorse, complaints about bad roads, a series of cures for bovine distemper, evidence of the infamous chicanery of attorneys, a method of preventing grave robbing, detection of a Methodist's hypocrisy, arguments for decreasing the wearing of hoop petticoats, methods of making spruce beer and the best ale, a "philosophical inquiry" into what love is, and the invention of shorthand.

The Scots did not recognize a hierarchy of sciences or harbor the same preconceptions about mature and immature sciences that we do today: virtually anything could be treated philosophically. This does not mean that the presentation was unsophisticated: the technical articles in the *Gentleman's Magazine* convey serious rather than dilettantish or popular science. It is easy to see that the periodical served as a forum for philosophy

---

*Transactions of the Royal Society of London* frequently appeared in the latter part of this period, but have generally not been included because they reflect a mishmash of all sciences.

and science; many topics became the source of a broader discussion that continued from issue to issue. It was a markedly tolerant, democratic forum: anyone—man, woman, or foreigner—with something reasonable to say was included. For instance, an article appearing in volume nine in 1739 on a "new Method for making Women as useful and as capable of maintaining themselves, as the Men are" was written by a woman. Interestingly, she argues that women should be encouraged to become merchants and sell goods bought and used by women so they would not have to resort to prostitution or be reduced to a life of begging if they did not marry or were widowed at a young age. An article on cattle-raising in 1755 and on the scarcity of corn in 1758 were both signed by "A Farmer."

Simple lists of virtually anything that could be listed were popular, for instance, ships captured by almost every European country; the clans and chiefs of Scotland; titles of English barons, sheriffs, and other aristocrats and government officials. The same goes for rules and regulations, for example, new regulations at Cambridge University, rules for using a divining rod, a rule for determining Easter, rules for vain writers, regulations of a poor house, new regulations of the navy, and rules for choosing a wife. The bulk of the subject matter pertained to (natural) history,[8] geography, biology/zoology, and reports of technological inventions or improvements (e.g., horology, the water engine, thermometer, barometer, wheel-carriage, weaving machine, filtering machine, windmill, air pump, fire engine, sea gauge, pyrometer, micrometer, sea chronometer, etc.).

Frequently, articles on scientific matters were accompanied by illustrations. Many authors on astronomical topics referred to Newton by name. Two articles penned by Newton appeared well after his death: the one in 1753 dealt with a topic in economics—a reprint of the value of foreign coins prepared during Newton's service at the Mint; the other concerned astronomical calculations and their significance for the ancient calendar

---

8. Writing during the height of the Scottish tradition of natural history in the mid-eighteenth century, authors often inquired into the origins of peoples, civilizations, and institutions. In this time period we find inquiries into the origin of the Romans, the European states, and even the violin, to name just a few examples.

(1755). Although there are references aplenty to Benjamin Franklin and electricity, the only article he wrote for the journal during this period (1755) bears on demographic considerations and is an abstract of his *Observations concerning the Increase of Mankind.* A glance below confirms how popular articles on natural philosophy became after 1737.[9] It also reveals that economics was dominated by the problem of the debt and raising taxes and the high price of corn and that natural science was most concerned with astronomical problems and experiments on electricity.

## Volume 1. 1731

*Science:* None

*Economics:* None

## Volume 2. 1732

*Science:* Eclipse of the Moon, 20 November 1732 (November): 1080

*Economics:* State of the National Debt (June): 818

## Volume 3. 1733

*Science:* None

*Economics:* State of the National Debt (June): 313

## Volume 4. 1734

*Science:* The Solar System (October): 565

*Economics:* National Debt, Navy Debt, Grants for 1734 (April): 209

## Volume 5. 1735

*Science:* None

*Economics:* None

---

9. The spurt in scientific articles is due more to the change in editorial management than to changing tastes. The English printer Edward Cave, who began publishing the *Gentleman's Magazine* in 1731, was joined by Dr. (Samuel) Johnson in 1738. In the Cave years, the periodical contained numerous reprints of articles and essays published elsewhere (which was the reason for calling it a magazine). After 1738 original material became the standard fare, and the periodical took on its own personality.

**Volume 6. 1736**

*Science:* Solutions to a Mathematical Problem (November): 655–56 and (December): 739

*Economics:* None

**Volume 7. 1737**

*Science:* The Mathematical Question further consider'd (January): 25–26; Schemes for the Discovery of the Longitude (February): 66–72 and (October): 615–16; Use of comparing Curves and Fluents, etc. (February): 77–81; Early Method of comparing Fluents, etc. (March): 151; Occultation of Aldebaran by the Moon (March): 157; Solutions to Mathematical Questions (May): 271–74 and (July): 439–40 and (August): 503–504 and (September): 549 and (November): 676; A new Method of finding the Sun's Parallax (July): 412–14; Center of the Great Orb nearer than suppos'd (August): 490; Inefficiencies in the vulgar Planetary System demonstrated (September): 547–48; Of the Parallax of the Sun, by Mr Facio (October): 611–14

*Economics:* Of reducing the National Debts to 3 per Cent (March): 171–76; Account of the National Debt (November): 671

**Volume 8. 1738**

*Science:* Of a new Astronomical Equation (January): 8–12; Occultation of Aldebran (February): 77 and (August): 437; On the Refraction of Light in the Moon's Atmosphere (March): 130–34; Errors from neglecting the Refraction of Light, etc. (April): 185–87; Of the Obliquity of the Ecliptick (May): 263–64; Moon's Dichotomy observ'd by Mr Facio (July): 352–54; Remedy for Poisonous Bites (August): 416–17; Length and Dimensions of the Earth, etc. (August): 424–26; Mr. Facio's Answer to some Objections [on the Parallax of Mars] (September): 481; Of the Parallax of Mars (October): 525; Of Mrs Stephen's Medicine for the Stone [gall stones] (October): 548–50 and (December): 661; Occultation by the Moon to the Star Aldebran (November): 592

*Economics:* Answer to the Annuity-Question (May): 237

**Volume 9. 1739**

*Science:* None

*Economics:* Running of Wool sinks the Price of Land (February): 93–94; A new Method for making Women as useful and as capable of maintaining themselves, as the Men are; and consequently preventing their becoming old Maids, or taking ill Courses (October): 525–26

## Volume 10. 1740

*Science:* An Account of Great Frosts (February): 77–78; Occultation of Jupiter by the Moon (September): 453–55 and (October): 517

*Economics:* Instructions for Cultivating Flax (February): 79–80; State of the Woollen Trade, etc. (October): 500–502 and (November): 549–52

## Volume 11. 1741

*Science:* Method of Curing a Consumption (January): 17–19; On the Epidemical Fever, 1741 (December): 655–56

*Economics:* Considerations upon the Embargo on Corn, etc. (December): 634–38

## Volume 12. 1742

*Science:* Elements of the Comet's Motion (April): 183; Nature of Curve Describ'd by the Moon (May): 264–65; Nature of the Curve describ'd by the Moon (July): 369–71 and (August): 433

*Economics:* Schemes for preventing the Exportation of Wool (February): 83–86 and (March): 147–49; Causes of the Declension of the Woollen Trade (February): 86–89; Enquiry about Publick Money (May): 265–67; State of the Publick Debts (June): 288–89

## Volume 13. 1743

*Science:* A New Theory of Comets (April): 193–95 and (May): 250–53 and (June): 315–18; Objections to Mr Yate's Theory of Comets (July): 361–64; Surprising Instances of the Effects of Musick in acute Fevers, and for the Cure of the Bite of the Tarantula (August): 422–24; Mercury's Transit over the Sun, Oct. 25, 1743 (August): 424–25; The Path of the Moon demonstrated (August): 471–72; Observation of Mercury's Transit, Oct. 25 (November): 583–84; Mr Yate on the Moon's Curve (December): 639;

Trigonometrical Calculation of the Moon's Curve (Supplement): 701–702

*Economics:* Scheme for preventing the Exportation of Wool (January): 32–34, 42–43 and (February): 79 and (June): 318–19 and (December): 657–58; Answer to the Observations on Sheep and Wool (October): 537–41

## Volume 14. 1744

*Science:* A new Theory of the Earth (February): 84–86 and (April): 201–202; The Theory of the Late Comet constructed by Mr Thomas Wright (March): 138; Calculation of a Lunar Eclipse on April 15, 1744 (March): 139; On the Virtues of Tar Water (April): 193–96; An Account of Comets (April): 203–204; A Problem concerning the Late Comet (May): 271; Mr Yate's new Theory of the Earth (August): 429–30; Hypothesis concerning Comet's Tails examined (August): 435–36; On the present State, etc. of Physic and Surgery (August): 442–43

*Economics:* Duties paid on Spirits, Beer and Ale for several Years (January): 2; State of the National Debt (May): 268–69

## Volume 15. 1745

*Science:* An effectual Cure for the Cholera (February): 91; Experiments on Electricity (April): 193–96; Mr Wright's Construction of the late Comet disproved (April): 201–202; Mr Yate's Theory of Comet's overturned (June): 301; A View of Dr. Mead's essay on poisons (June): 308–313; Cases concerning the Virtues of Tar-Water (June): 317–19; Mr Yate's Defence of his Theory, etc. (August): 417–18

*Economics:* Experiments on preparing and sowing Grain (January): 31–32; On Defects in the British computations of time, coin, weights, and measures (July): 377–79

## Volume 16. 1746

*Science:* Account of Mr Watson on Electricity (June): 291–92; Experiments on Electricity (July): 371–74; A Cure for the Stone in the Bladder (August): 422–23; Of the Cause of Electricity (October): 521–22; Further Essays on Electricity (November): 557–60

*Economics:* An Account of several methods to preserve Corn well by Ventilation (June): 315–18

## Volume 17. 1747

*Science:* Experiments on Electricity (January): 15–16; Experiments on Glass Tubes (February): 65; An Observation of the Moon's Eclipse, on Feb. 14, 1746–7 [sic] (February): 65–66; Of Experiments in Electricity (February): 81; Electrical Experiments proposed (March): 140–42; Electrical Problems answer'd (April): 183–84; Electricity whence, and how applicable (May): 225–26; Causes of sizy [sic] Blood (June): 271; Solar Eclipse calculated (July): 377; Dr Mead on inoculating the Small-pox (November): 526–28

*Economics:* On Taxes, and the Ways and Means for Raising Them (February): 72–73; Schemes for Popular and easy Taxes (December): 568–69

## Volume 18. 1748

*Science:* Objections to Mr Yate's Theory [of the Earth] with Mr Yate's Answer (March): 124–25; Virtues of Musk in Medicine (March): 131; Observations of a new Comet (April): 151–52 and 167; Observations on the Solar Eclipse (July): 313; Answers to a mathematical Question (July): 315; Of Saturn and Its Rings (August): 344; The Depth of the Atmosphere determined (October): 458–59; A Palsy cured by Electrising (November): 486–88

*Economics:* Queries on exporting Corn to France (January): 30–31; Debt, and Publick Credit (April): 170–72; A Scheme of the national Debt (June): 247; Causes of Decay of Trade in London (September): 408–12

## Volume 19. 1749

*Science:* The Solar Eclipse observed by M. Monnier (January): 13–16; Solution of a Paradox demonstrated—Instructor answer'd (July): 311; Electrical Experiments (August): 351–53; Odorous Bodies in Glasses electrified (October): 450–53; Eclipse of the Moon observed (November): 553–54

*Economics:* Utility of publick Debts (July): 315–17; An early Method for reducing the publick Debt (November): 485

**Volume 20. 1750**

*Science:* Multiplication by Indices (January): 25–26; Thermomet-rical Observations, with Remarks (February): 64–68; The Earth's Figure (February): 69–70; Lights in the Air [Aurora Borealis] (February): 78; To find the Longitude (February): 78; Methods of communicating magnetism (March): 100–102; A New Theory of Colours (March): 102–104; Bone how convey'd to the Bladder (March): 111–112; Meteor-Physics, Optics (March): 112–13; Lead in the Bladder (March): 125–26; Inoculating for the Small-Pox (April): 147–48; Moon's Eclipse (April): 153; A probable Cure for the Bite of a Mad Dog (May): 195 and (August): 354; Physicians Unsuccessful against the Flat Worm (May): 203–206; Precautions Requir'd in Inoculation (May): 206–208; Effects of Points in Elec-tricity (May): 208; A friendly caution against drinking tea, coffee, chocolate, etc., very hot (May): 208–209; Query about Light (May): 208–209; Properties ascribed to the Nerves controverted (June): 251–52; Invention of Longitude explained (June): 255–56; Animadversions on Remarks concerning Inoculation (June): 256–58; Lunar Eclipse (July): 304; Cures for Poison (August): 342–43; A fiery [sic] surprising Meteor (August): 344; Memoirs and Cases in Surgery (August): 348–51; An ocular Demonstra-tion of Euclid (August): 354–55; Rays of Light contain Matter (August): 355–56; Gautier's Objection to Newton's Theory re-futed (August): 363–64; Expeditious Methods in Arithmetic (September): 403–404; Calculations of an Eclipse (October): 246; Elliptical Orbit of the Earth explained (October): 450–51; New-tonian System of Colours vindicated (November): 504–505; Of the Electrick Shock (November): 508–510; Of Abbreviations in Multiplication and Division (November): 510; Inoculation for the Small-Pox defended (December): 531–32; Of the Electric Coper-nican System (December): 534–35; Curious Experiments in Elec-tricity (December): 537; Reply to Gautier—Astronomical Equations (December): 550–51; Observations of the great Lunar Eclipse (December): 555; Inoculation (December): 558–59; Lunar Observations (Supplement): 579; Catoptric Paradox answer'd (Supplement): 584; Of a Brush to Cleanse the Stomach (Supple-ment): 597

*Economics:* The Fairest Way taken to reduce the National Debt (February): 53–55; The National Debt no Cause of Concern (Feb-ruary): 73–75

## Volume 21. 1751

*Science:* Of the Electric Shock—Blood the least electric (January): 9; Use of Comets (January): 19–20; Never failing Recipe for the Cure of Mad Dogs (February): 58–59; Medicinal Effects from Electricity (February): 68–69; Height of a Meteor calculated (February); 78–79; Jupiter's Satellite (February): 82; Observations on Inoculation (March): 123–25; Meteor (March): 125; Cure by Electricity (April): 152; Inoculation fatal (April): 152; Inoculation compared (April): 158; Colour of electric Spark (April): 166–67; Calculations of a Lunar Eclipse (April): 177; Of the Medical Effects of Electricity (May): 209–211; Construction of an Astronomical Instrument (June): 271–72; Solution of an Astronomical Problem (June): 272–73; Meteorological Observations (July): 293; Geometrical Question (July): 296; Cancers cured by the Phytolacca [pokeweed] (July): 305–308; Remarks on Mr Wright's Theory [of the Universe] (July): 315; Pivati's Electrical Experiments fallacious (August): 349–51; Occult. of Jupiter—Parallaxes of Mars and Venus (August): 361; Symptoms of the Cholera Morbus, etc. (September): 398–99; Sore Throats (October): 440–41; Astronomical Problem solved (October): 449; Moon's Eclipse and Transit (October): 445; A remarkable case in Medicine (October): 468; Dr Wall's Method of treating the ulcerated Sore Throat (November): 497–501; Mathematical Question (November): 505; The Moon's Eclipse (November): 505–506; Occultation of Jupiter (November): 506–507; Electricity not transmissive of Odours through Glass (December): 540–41; Poisonous Qualities of the Bru Waters (December): 542–43; Salutory Effects of the Bark in the Measles (December): 543–44; Blindness cured by Electrification (Supplement): 579; Observation on Weather and Diseases in December (Supplement): 577–78; Medical Experiments in Electricity ineffectual (Supplement): 600–601

*Economics:* Arguments against reducing the legal Interest of Money (November): 494–96; Reasons against laying a Tax upon Money and for adjusting the Land Tax (December): 548–49; Proposal for the Employment of the Poor (December): 559–60

## Volume 22. 1752

*Science:* Cure for the Hiccough (January): 5 and (April): 174; Effects of warm Bathing in gouty Cases (January): 18–20; Remedies for the Bite of a mad Dog uncertain (January): 33–35;

Comment on Dr Wall's Medical Observations (February): 66–67; Diseases of the Virgin Islands, and Their Remedies (February): 73–75; Experiments on Medical Electricity (February): 76; Astronomical Lecture at Gresham College (March): 99–101; Queries concerning Inoculation [against smallpox] (March): 127; An Exact Representation of a very remarkable Meteor (March): 129; Success of the Bark in a deplorable Small-pox (May): 209–10; Small-Pox communicated by Adhesion (May): 217–20; Arguments for Inoculation fallacious (June): 255–56; Identity of electric and tonitruous Matter (June): 264–65; Dr Cameron's Remarks on the Small-pox (June): 268–70; The Phaenomen of the Aurora Borealis (June): 274–75; Cancers cured by Phytolacca [pokeweed] (July): 302; Investigation of a mathematical Problem (July): 309; The Practice of Inoculation justified (July): 313–14; Remarkable Cure by Electricity (August): 363–64; Causes of the Aurora Borealis (August): 371–72 and (December): 565–68 and (Supplement): 592; Against trusting to Nurses in the Small-pox: Small-pox too nice a Point to be trusted to Women (September): 402–405; To prevent Infection from Mad Dogs (September): 441; An Ague Cured by Electricity (October): 442; On Electricity in the Clouds (October): 450–52; Several medical Cases submitted to Dr Mead (October): 457–58; Medicines proper for Nervous, Hysteric, Epilectic Fits, etc. (November): 496; Succinct Account of Mr Colden's *Principles of Action in Matter* (November): 498–500 and (December): 570–71 and (Supplement): 589–90; Inoculation a slight operation, and may be performed by Nurses, etc. (November): 511–13; Electrical Experiments in Coal-Mines (November): 526–27; Mechanical Problem solved (November): 527; New Electrical Experiment (December): 561; Mr Walpole's Case in the Stone [gall stones] (December): 571–73; Of the Course of the Blood to the Heart (Supplement): 595–96

*Economics:* Reasonableness of laying a Tax on Money (January): 16; Of reducing the Starch Duty [duty on corn] (January): 31–32; The Landed Interest [landowners] over-taxed (August): 365–67; Bounty for Corn exported hurtful to Farmers (August): 358–59; Bounty on Corn exported very beneficial (September): 410–12; Good Roads introduce Wealth into a Country (December): 552–54; More on the Corn Bounty (December): 561–62 and (Supplement): 605–606 and 612

## Volume 23. 1753

*Science:* Path of the Earth (January): 4–5; New Thoughts on the form of Planets, etc. (January): 19–21; Succinct Account of Mr Colden's *Action in Matter*, continued (February): 65–66; Small-Pox communicated by Contact (March): 113–114; Moon's Eclipse—Mercury's Transit over the Sun (March): 138; Moon's Eclipse, April 17, 1753 (April): 157; Transit of the Moon, etc. at the Cape of Good Hope (April): 190 and (May): 237; Observations on Mercury's Transit (May): 211 and (June): 259 and (July): 308; Methods of Inoculation—Accidents from it (May): 216–18; Electric cure (May): 227–28 and (June): 268–69 and (August): 379; Heart's Motion from a Stimulus of the Blood (May): 230–31 and Occultation of Venus by the Moon (June); 280 and (July): 308; Venus's Parallax at the Cape of Good Hope in 1751 (June): 281; Case on the Hydrophobia [rabies] (July): 303–305; Hypothesis of the Earth's Configuration (July): 312–13; Reaumur's Experiments on Digestion (July): 326–28 and (August): 375–76 and (September): 401–403; Mar's Parallax at the Cape of Good Hope in 1751 (July): 324 and (August): 355; Cure for Hydrophobia (August): 368; Uses of Sea Water—How curable of the Scurvy (August): 380–81; Inoculation in New England (September): 414; Solar Eclipse calculated (September): 427–28 and (October): 453; Fatal Effect of Electricty (September): 430–32; Medicines for the Gout and Rheumatism (December): 579; Observations of the last Eclipse of the Sun (December): 580; Eclipses of Jupiter's Satellites (December): 600; Dr Young's Remedy for Dysenteries (Supplement): 604–607

*Economics:* Value of foreign Coins: Table of the Assays, Weights, and Values, of Foreign Silver and Gold Coins, made at the Mint. By Sir Isaac Newton (January): 6–8

## Volume 24. 1754

*Science:* Euler's General principles of Mechanics (January): 6–7; Observations on the Cold and Heat; with Tables (January): 58–59; Cure for the Bite of the Tarantula: Musick (February): 69–70; Electricity in Cats—Paradox solved (March): 112–13; Maclaurin on the Variation of the Obliquity of the Ecliptic (May): 219–20; Gout powder (June): 56; Of the Cause of Respiration in Infants

(June): 257–61; Of the Treatment of some remarkable scrophu-
lous Cases (June): 265–66; Occultation of Aldebran (June): 276;
Receipt [recipe] for curing Cancers (July): 216–17; Astronomical
Question (July): 330; Uncommon Tumour (August): 362–63; To
find the Moon's Parallax (October): 458–59; Mayer's new Tables
of the Sun and Moon (August): 374–76; Hale's Method to Stop
the Plague (December): 543–44; Emerson's mechanical Axioms
(December): 551

*Economics:* Scheme for Raising Money by a new Lottery (Supplement): 585–88

## Volume 25. 1755

*Science:* Sir Isaac Newton on [astronomical considerations of]
the Antient [sic] Year (January): 3–5; Extraordinary Alimentary
Powder (January): 7–8; Remarkable Case in Surgery (January):
12–13; Method of treating Patients in Cases of Vegetable Poisons
(January): 29–30; Occultation of Aldebran (January): 34; New
Experiments on human Blood (February); 66–68; Cures performed at Stockholm by Electricty (March): 111–112; Cure of the
Hydrophobia [rabies] (June): 245–46; Medical Experiments of
Electricity (July): 313–15; Electrical Question (September): 417–
18; Of a fiery Meteor seen in Holland, and on the Thames
(October): 461–62; Jupiter's Satellites (October): 465; Medical and
philosophical Observations [excerpted from the Philosophical
Transactions of the Royal Society] (November): 489–91; Astronomical, geographical, and physical Observations (November):
511–13; Error concerning the expected Comet corrected (Supplement): 584

*Economics:* Cattle not monopolized by Graziers (August): 365–
66; B. Franklin's Observations concerning the Increase of Mankind, peopling of Countries, etc. (November): 483–85

## Volume 26. 1756

*Science:* Hally and Newton on the Comet expected in 1758
(January): 24–27; Queries concerning [Franklin's system of] Elec-
tricity (January): 32–33; History of Northern Lights in England
(April): 164; Ball of Fire at Newington (May): 215; Gout in the
Stomach cured by Musk (May): 244; Precepts to determine the
Course of the Comet (September): 413; New Method of curing
the Hydrophobia (December): 567–69; Physical and astronomical

Observations (Supplement): 618–19; The Eclipses of Jupiter's Satellites (Supplement): 624

*Economics:* Means for lessening the high Price of Corn (Supplement): 622–23

## Volume 27. 1757

*Science:* Medical Observations by a Society of London Physicians (May): 222–25 and (June): 258–61 and (July): 296–99 and (August): 360–64 and (September): 397–99; Melville's Observations on Light and Colours (July): 314–15 and (August): 351–52 and (November): 501–503; Curious Accounts of the present Comet (September); 393–94; An Indian Remedy for Venereal Disease (September): 405–406; Singular Case of a Lady after the Small Pox (September): 415–17; Easy Cure for a Catarrhous Cough (December): 543–44; Impracticability of ascertaining the Longitude by the Moon (December): 545–46; Eclipses of Jupiter's Satellites for 1758 (Supplement): 603

*Economics:* Proposals to increase the Revenue, and improve the Roads (January): 18–19; On the Price of Wool (February): 59; Reasons for continuing the Bounty upon Corn (February): 71–73; Utility of a Tax upon Dogs (April): 159

## Volume 28. 1758

*Science:* Question in Surgery (January): 7; Eclipse of the Moon (January): 7; Comets not dangerous (February): 66–68; Account of Hooping Cough and its Cure (March): 121–22; Answer to F. Sidler on the Wholesomeness of Milk (March): 123–24; A Case of Surgery (April); 154; Further Observations on the Qualities of Milk (April): 173; New Comet observed (June): 252–53; Essay on the Cause of Faintings in the Scurvy (June): 255–56 and 257–58; Transit of Venus over the Sun in 1761 (August): 367–68; Interesting Query on Blood letting (August): 368–69; New Electrical Experiment and Cure (October): 467–68; Use of rectified spirits of Wine for removing some Disorders from Human Bodies (November): 511–12; Important Astronomical Discovery (November): 512–13; Of the Appearance of the predicted Comet (November): 526–27

*Economics:* Answer to some former Queries on Wool (February): 60–61; Produce of the Sinking Fund and Debt of the Navy

(August): 349; The Causes of the late Scarcity of Corn considered in a new Light (December): 564–66

## Volume 29. 1759

*Science:* Further Directions for the Preservation of Health (January): 4–5; Memoirs of the Royal Academy at Paris [on discoveries in medicine] (January): 23–25; Time of expected Comet's Perihelion calculated (February): 52–54; Eclipses of Jupiter's Satellites (February): 68; Modern [natural] Philosophy explained for the use of the Ladies (March): 127–28; Problem proposed to the Astronomers (April): 154; A useful Medicine prescribed and recommended (April): 174; Further Observations on the present Comet (May): 204; Some New Observations on Cometical Astronomy (May): 205–209; Efficacy of the Bark in a Delirium (June): 247–48; Remedy for the Hiccough (July): 303; Observations on the Measles (July): 308; Experiments to prove the Principles of Electricity (August): 364–67; Case of a spontaneous Hydrophobia [rabies] (September): 401–403; Inflammation of the Liver, its Cure (September): 413–14; History of the late Comet (November): 521–24; Cure for the Bite of Mad Dogs and Serpents (December): 580; Improvements in Optics (December): 580–83

*Economics:* Arguments in favour of the Dutch West-India Trade (January): 26–28; Proposal for supplying the scarcity of Silver Money (March): 122–25

# Selected Bibliography
# by Topic

## I. On the Philosophical Background

### Francis Bacon

Bacon, Francis. 1858. *The Great Instauration* and *The New Organon. The Works of Francis Bacon*, vol. 4. Collected and edited by James Spedding, Robert Leslie Ellis, and Douglas Denon Heath. London: Longman.

Bacon, Francis. 1857. *Philosophical Works*, parts 2 and 3. *The Works of Francis Bacon*, vol. 3. Collected and edited by James Spedding, Robert Leslie Ellis, and Douglas Denon Heath. London: Longman.

Blake, Ralph M., Curt J. Ducasse, and Edward H. Madden. 1960. "Francis Bacon's Philosophy of Science." In their *Theories of Scientific Method: The Renaissance Through the Nineteenth Century*, pp. 50–74. Seattle: University of Washington Press.

Broad, C. D. 1976 [1926]. *The Philosophy of Francis Bacon*. N.Y.: Octagon Books.

Hattaway, Michael. 1978. "Bacon and 'Knowledge Broken': Limits for Scientific Method." *Journal of the History of Ideas* 39, no. 2 (April-June): 183–97.

Hesse, Mary B. 1964. "Francis Bacon." In *A Critical History of Western Philosophy*, pp. 141–52. Edited by D. J. O'Connor. N.Y.: Free Press.

Jones, Richard Foster. 1975. *Ancients and Moderns: A Study of the Rise of the Scientific Movement in Seventeenth-Century England*, 2nd ed. Gloucester, Mass.: Peter Smith.

Macaulay, Thomas Babington. 1837. "Francis Bacon." *Edinburgh Review* 65 (July): 1–104.

Martin, Julian. 1993. "Francis Bacon, Authority, and the Moderns." In *The Rise of Modern Philosophy*, pp. 71–88. Edited by Tom Sorell. Oxford: Clarendon Press.

Martin, Julian. 1992. *Francis Bacon, the State, and the Reform of Natural Philosophy*. Cambridge: Cambridge University Press.

McRae, Robert. 1957. "The Unity of the Sciences: Bacon, Descartes, and Leibnitz." *Journal of the History of Ideas* 18, no. 1 (January): 27–48.

Napier, Macvey. 1818. "Remarks, Illustrative of the Scope and Influence of the Philosophical Writings of Lord Bacon." *Transactions of the Royal Society of Edinburgh* 8: 373–425.

Prior, Moody E. 1954. "Bacon's Man of Science." *Journal of the History of Ideas* 15, no. 3 (June): 348–70.

Quinton, Anthony. 1980. *Francis Bacon.* Oxford: Oxford University Press.

Rossi, Paola. 1973 [1968]. "Baconianism." In *Dictionary of the History of Ideas: Studies of Selected Pivotal Ideas,* pp. 172–79. Edited by Philip P. Wiener. N.Y.: Charles Scribner's Sons.

Urbach, Peter. 1982. "Francis Bacon as a Precursor to Popper." *British Journal for the Philosophy of Science* 33: 113–32.

Yeo, Richard. 1985. "An Idol of the Market-Place: Baconianism in Nineteenth Century Britain." *History of Science* 23, no. 3 (September): 251–98.

## René Descartes

Blake, Ralph M., Curt J. Ducasse, and Edward H. Madden. 1960. "The Role of Experience in Descartes's Theory of Method." In their *Theories of Scientific Method: The Renaissance Through the Nineteenth Century,* pp. 75–103. Seattle: University of Washington Press.

Clarke, Desmond M. 1991a. "The Concept of Experience in Descartes's Theory of Knowledge." In Moyal 1991b: 455–72.

Clarke, Desmond M. 1991b. "Descartes's Use of 'Demonstration' and 'Deduction.'" In Moyal 1991b: 237–47.

Clarke, Desmond M. 1982. *Descartes' Philosophy of Science.* Manchester: Manchester University Press.

Cottingham, John. 1993. "A New Start? Cartesian Metaphysics and the Emergence of Modern Philosophy." In *The Rise of Modern Philosophy,* pp. 145–66. Edited by Tom Sorell. Oxford: Clarendon Press.

Descartes, René. 1984/1985. *The Philosophical Writings of Descartes,* 2 vols. Translated by John Cottingham, Robert Stoothoff, and Dugald Murdoch. Cambridge: Cambridge University Press.

Garber, Daniel. 1993. "Descartes and Experiment in the *Discourse* and *Essays.*" In *Essays on the Philosophy and Science of René Descartes,* pp. 288–310. Edited by Stephen Voss. N.Y.: Oxford University Press.

Garber, Daniel, and Lesley Cohen. 1982. "A Point of Order: Analysis, Synthesis, and Descartes's *Principles.*" *Archiv für Geschichte der Philosophie* 64, Heft 2: 136–47.

Gewirtz, Alan. 1941. "Experience and the Non-Mathematical in the Cartesian Method." *Journal of the History of Ideas* 2, no. 2 (April): 183–210.

Moyal, Georges J. D. 1991a. "Descartes's Method: From Things to Ideas." In Moyal 1991b: 1–27.

Moyal, Georges J. D. ed. 1991b. *René Descartes: Critical Assessments*, 4 vols. London: Routledge.

Roth, Leon. 1937. *Descartes' Discourse on Method*. Oxford: Clarendon Press.

Schouls, Peter A. 1991. "Descartes and the Idea of Progress." In Moyal 1991b: 50–60.

Schouls, Peter A. 1980. *The Imposition of Method: A Study of Descartes and Locke*. Oxford: Clarendon Press.

Sorell, Tom. 1987. *Descartes*. Oxford: Oxford University Press.

Van De Pitte, Frederick P. 1991. "Descartes's *Mathesis Universalis*." In Moyal 1991b: 61–79.

Walting, J. L. 1964. "Descartes." In *A Critical History of Western Philosophy*, pp. 170–86. Edited by D. J. O'Connor. N.Y.: Free Press.

## John Herschel

Blake, Ralph M., Curt J. Ducasse, and Edward H. Madden. 1960. "John F. W. Herschel's Methods of Experimental Inquiry." In their *Theories of Scientific Method: The Renaissance Through the Nineteenth Century*, pp. 153–82. Seattle: University of Washington Press.

Cannon, Walter F. 1967. "Herschel, John." In *Encyclopedia of Philosophy*.

Cannon, Walter F. 1961. "John Herschel and the Idea of Science." *Journal of the History of Ideas* 22, no. 2 (April–June): 215–37.

Charpa, Ulrich. 1987. "John F. W. Herschels Methodologie der Erfahrungswissenschaft." *Philosophia Naturalis* 24: 121–48.

Good, Gregory. 1987. "John Herschel's Optical Researches and the Development of His Ideas on Method and Causality." *Studies in History and Philosophy of Science* 18, no. 1 (March): 1–41.

Herschel, J. F. W. 1831 [1830]. *A Preliminary Discourse on the Study of Natural Philosophy*. London: Longman, Rees, Orme, Brown, and Greene.

Wilson, David B. 1974. "Herschel and Whewell's Version of Newtonianism." *Journal of the History of Ideas* 35, no. 1 (January/March): 79–97.

## Thomas Hobbes

Blake, Ralph M., Curt J. Ducasse, and Edward H. Madden. 1960. "Thomas Hobbes and the Rationalistic Ideal." In their *Theories of Scientific Method: The Renaissance Through the Nineteenth Century*, pp. 105–118. Seattle: University of Washington Press.

Doyle, Phyllis. 1927. "The Contemporary Background of Hobbes' 'State of Nature.'" *Economica* 7, no. 21 (December): 336–55.

Flew, A. G. N. 1964. "Hobbes." In *A Critical History of Western Philosophy*, pp. 153–69. Edited by D. J. O'Connor. N.Y.: Free Press.

Hobbes, Thomas. 1839–1845. *The English Works of Thomas Hobbes,* 11 vols. Edited by Sir William Molesworth. London: John Bohn.

King, Preston, ed. 1993. *Thomas Hobbes: Critical Assessments,* 4 vols. London: Routledge.

Lubienski, Z. 1993. "Hobbes's Philosophy and Its Historical Background." In King 1993, 1: 1–16.

Missner, Marshall. 1977. "Hobbes's Method in *Leviathan.*" *Journal of the History of Ideas* 38, no. 4 (October-December): 607–21.

Peters, R. S. 1967. "Hobbes, Thomas." In *Encyclopedia of Philosophy.*

Prins, J. 1990. "Hobbes and the School of Padua: Two Incompatible Approaches of Science." *Archiv für Geschichte der Philosophie* 72, Heft 1: 26–46.

Raphael, D. D. 1977. *Hobbes: Moralist Politics.* London: George Allen and Unwin.

Röd, Wolfgang. 1970. *Geometrischer Geist und Naturrecht. Methodengeschichtliche Untersuchungen zur Staatsphilosophie im 17. und 18. Jahrhundert.* Bayrische Akademie der Wissenschaften, Abhandlungen neue Folge, Heft 70. München: Verlag der Bayrischen Akademie der Wissenschaften.

Sacksteder, William. 1980. "Hobbes: The Art of Geometricians." *Journal of the History of Philosophy* 18: 131–46.

Seifert, G. F. 1993. "The Philosophy of Hobbes: Text and Content and the Problem of Sedimentation." In King 1993, 1: 303–13.

Shapin, Steven, and Simon Schaffer. 1985. *Leviathan and the Air-Pump: Hobbes, Boyle, and the Experimental Life.* Including a translation of Thomas Hobbes, *Dialogus physicus de natura aeris* by Simon Schaffer. Princeton: Princeton University Press.

Skinner, Q. 1993. "Thomas Hobbes and the Nature of the Early Royal Society." In King 1993, 1: 159–83.

Talaska, Richard A. 1988. "Analytic and Synthetic Method According to Hobbes." *Journal of the History of Philosophy* 26: 206–37.

Tuck, Richard. 1989. *Hobbes.* Oxford: Oxford University Press.

Weinberger, J. 1975. "Hobbes's Doctrine of Method." *American Political Science Review* 69, no. 4 (December): 1336–53.

Zagorin, Perez. 1990. "Hobbes on Our Mind." *Journal of the History of Ideas* 51, no. 2 (April-June): 317–35.

## David Hume

Arnold, N. Scott. 1983. "Hume's Scepticism about Inductive Inference." *Journal of the History of Philosophy* 21: 31–55.

Ayer, A. J. 1980. *Hume.* Oxford: Oxford University Press.

Barfoot, Michael. 1990. "Hume and the Culture of Science in the Early Eighteenth Century." In *Studies in the Philosophy of the Scottish Enlightenment*, pp. 151–90. Edited by M. A. Stewart. Oxford: Clarendon Press.

Blake, Ralph M., Curt J. Ducasse, and Edward H. Madden. 1960. "David Hume on Causation." In their *Theories of Scientific Method: The Renaissance Through the Nineteenth Century*, pp. 145–52. Seattle: University of Washington Press.

Burke, John J., Jr. 1978. "Hume's *History of England:* Waking the English from a Dogmatic Slumber." In *Studies in Eighteenth-Century Culture* 7: 235–50. Edited by Roseann Runte. Madison: University of Wisconsin Press.

Butts, Robert E. 1959. "Hume's Scepticism." *Journal of the History of Ideas* 20, no. 3 (June-September): 413–19.

Capaldi, Nicholas. 1995. "Hume as Social Scientist." In Tweyman 1995, 6: 3–23.

Capaldi, Nicholas. 1975. *David Hume: The Newtonian Philosopher*. Boston: Twayne Publishers.

Flew, Anthony. 1964. "Hume." In *A Critical History of Western Philosophy*, pp. 253–74. Edited by D. J. O'Connor. N.Y.: Free Press.

Force, James E. 1987. "Hume's Interest in Newton and Science." *Hume Studies* 13, no. 2 (November): 166–216.

Force, James E. 1984. "Hume and the Relation of Science to Religion Among Certain Members of the Royal Society." *Journal of the History of Ideas* 45, no. 4 (October-December): 517–36.

Frazer, Catherine S. 1970. "Hume's Criticism and Defense of Analogical Argument." *Journal of the History of Philosophy* 8: 173–79.

Groarke, Leo, and Graham Solomon. 1991. "Some Sources for Hume's Account of Cause." *Journal of the History of Ideas* 52, no. 4 (October-December): 645–663.

Hume, David. 1975. *Enquiries concerning Human Understanding and concerning the Principles of Morals*, 3rd ed. Reprinted from the posthumous edition of 1777; edited by L. A. Selby-Bigge; text revised and notes by P. H. Nidditch. Oxford: Clarendon Press.

Hume, David. 1967. *The Natural History of Religion and Dialogues concerning Natural Religion*. Edited by A. Wayne Colver and John Valdmir Price. Oxford: Oxford University Press.

Hume, David. 1965 [1938]. *An Abstract of a Treatise of Human Nature, 1740*. With an introduction by J. M. Keynes and P. Sraffa. Hamden, Conn.: Archon Books.

Hume, David. 1955. *Writings on Economics*. Edited and introduced by Eugene Rotwein. Edinburgh: Nelson.

Hume, David. 1954. *New Letters of David Hume*. Edited by Raymond Klibansky and Ernest C. Mossner. Oxford: Clarendon Press.

Hume, David. 1932. *The Letters of David Hume*, 2 vols. Edited by J. Y. T. Greig. Oxford: Clarendon Press.

Hume, David. 1896 [1739]. *A Treatise of Human Nature*. Reprint of original edition in 3 volumes; edited by L. A. Selby-Bigge. Oxford: Clarendon Press.

Hume, David. 1875. *Essays Moral, Political, and Literary,* vol. 1. Edited by T. H. Green and T. H. Grose. London: Longmans, Green.

Hume, David. 1854. *The Philosophical Works of David Hume,* 4 vols. Boston: Little, Brown; Edinburgh: Adam and Charles Black.

Hume, David. n.d. *The History of England,* 5 vols. New edition, with the author's last corrections and improvements. To which is prefixed a short account of his life, written by himself. Philadelphia: Porter and Coates.

Kemp Smith, Norman. 1966. *Philosophy of David Hume.* London: Macmillan.

Livingston, Donald W. 1984. *Hume's Philosophy of Common Life.* Chicago: University of Chicago Press.

Montiero, J. P. 1981. "Hume's Conception of Science." *Journal of the History of Philosophy* 19: 327–42.

Norton, David Fate. 1968. "Hume's *A Letter from a Gentleman,* A Review Note." *Journal of the History of Philosophy* 6: 161–67.

Norton, David Fate. 1965. "History and Philosophy in Hume's Thought." In *David Hume: Philosophical Historian,* pp. xxxii-l. Edited by David Fate Norton and Richard H. Popkin. Indianapolis: Bobbs-Merrill.

Passmore, John. 1980 [1968]. *Hume's Intentions,* 3rd ed. London: Duckworth.

Raynor, David R. 1984. "Hume's Abstract of Adam Smith's *Theory of Moral Sentiments.*" *Journal of the History of Philosophy* 22: 50–79.

Russell, Paul. 1985. "Hume's *Treatise* and Hobbes's *The Elements of Law.*" *Journal of the History of Ideas* 46, no. 1 (January-March): 51–63.

Sabine, George H. 1906. "Hume's Contribution to the Historical Method." *Philosophical Review* 15, no. 1 (January): 17–38.

Stove, D. C. 1977. "Hume, Kemp Smith, and Carnap." *Australasian Journal of Philosophy* 55, no. 3 (December): 189–200.

Tweyman, Stanley, ed. 1995. *David Hume: Critical Assessments,* 4 vols. London: Routledge.

Velk, T., and A. R. Riggs. 1995. "David Hume's Practical Economics." In Tweyman 1995, 1: 193–200.

Vickers, Douglas. 1957. "Method and Analysis in David Hume's Economic Essays." *Economica* 24 (August): 225–34.

## John Locke

Ashcraft, Richard, ed. 1991. *John Locke: Critical Assessments,* 4. London and NY: Routledge.

Axtell, James L. 1965. "Locke, Newton, and the Elements of Natural Philosophy." *Pædagogica Europæa* 1: 235–45.

Farr, James. 1987. "The Way of Hypotheses: Locke on Method." *Journal of the History of Ideas* 48, no. 1 (January-March): 51–72.

Givner, David A. 1991. "Scientific Preconceptions in Locke's Philosophy of Language." In Ashcraft 1991, 4: 430–45.

Gregory, Joshua C. 1927. "Locke on Seventeenth-Century Science." *Science Progress* 21, no. 83 (January): 492–501.

Laudan, Larry. 1981. "John Locke on Hypotheses: Placing the *Essay* in the 'Scientific Tradition.'" In his *Science and Hypothesis: Historical Essays on Scientific Methodology*, pp. 59–71. Dordrecht: D. Reidel.

Locke, John. 1965 [1690]. *An Essay concerning Human Understanding*, 2 vols. Edited by John W. Yolton. London: Dent; N.Y.: Dutton.

Locke, John. 1954. *Essays on the Law of Nature*. Edited by W. von Leyden. Oxford: Oxford University Press.

Locke, John. 1872. "Essay on Interest and Value of Money." An appendix to J. R. McCulloch's *Principles of Political Economy*, pp. 220–360. London: A Murray.

O'Connor, D. J. 1964. "Locke." In *A Critical History of Western Philosophy*, pp. 204–52. Edited by D. J. O'Connor. N.Y.: Free Press.

Odegard, Douglas. 1991. "Locke as an Empiricist." In Ashcraft 1991, 4: 1–12.

Odegard, Douglas. 1965. "Locke's Epistemology and the Value of Experience." *Journal of the History of Ideas* 26, no. 3 (July-September): 417–23.

Osler, Margaret J. 1970. "John Locke and the Changing Ideal of Scientific Knowledge." *Journal of the History of Ideas* 31, no. 1 (January-March): 3–16.

Romanell, Patrick. 1991. "The Scientific and Medical Genealogy of Locke's 'Historical, Plain Method.'" In Ashcraft 1991 4: 476–510.

Shankula, H. A. S. 1991. "Locke, Descartes, and the Science of Nature." In Ashcraft 1991, 4: 374–96.

Schouls, Peter A. 1980. *The Imposition of Method: A Study of Descartes and Locke*. Oxford: Clarendon Press.

Soles, David E. 1985. "Locke's Empiricism and the Postulation of Unobservables." *Journal of the History of Philosophy* 23: 339–69.

Vaughn, Karen Iversen. 1980. *John Locke: Economist and Social Scientist*. Chicago: University of Chicago Press.

Wood, Neal. 1991. "The Baconian Character of Locke's *Essay*." In Ashcraft 1991, 4: 333–73.

Yolton, John W. 1955. "Locke and the Seventeenth-Century Logic of Ideas." *Journal of the History of Ideas* 16, no. 4 (October): 431–52.

## Isaac Newton

Blake, Ralph M., Curt J. Ducasse, Edward H. Madden. 1960. "Isaac Newton and the Hypothetico-Deductive Method." In their *Theories of Scientific Method: The Renaissance Through the Nineteenth Century*, pp. 119–43. Seattle: University of Washington Press.

Boas, Marie, and Rupert Hall. 1959. "Newton's 'Mechanical Principles.'" *Journal of the History of Ideas* 20, no. 2 (April): 167–78.

Borzeszkowski, Horst-Heino von, and Renate Wahsner. 1980. *Newton und Voltaire. Zur Begründung und Interpretation der klassischen Mechanik.* Berlin: Akademie-Verlag.

Brooke, John. 1988. "The God of Isaac Newton." In Fauvel et al. 1988: 168–83.

Buchdahl, Gerd. 1961. *The Image of Newton and Locke in the Age of Reason.* London: Sheed and Ward.

Cantor, Geoffrey. 1988. "Anti-Newton." In Fauvel et al. 1988: 203–22.

Cassirer, Ernst. 1943. "Newton und Leibniz." *Philosophical Review* 53: 366–91.

Clarke, John. 1972 [1730]. *A Demonstration of Some of the Principles of the Principal Sections of Sir Isaac Newton's Principles of Natural Philosophy.* With introduction to reprint edition by I. Bernard Cohen. N.Y.: Johnson Reprint Corporation.

Cohen, I. Bernard. 1985a. *The Birth of a New Physics.* N.Y.: Penguin Books.

Cohen, I. Bernard. 1985b. "The Newtonian Revolution." In his *Revolution in Science,* pp. 161–75. Cambridge: Belknap Press of Harvard University Press.

Cohen, I. Bernard. 1980. *The Newtonian Revolution.* Cambridge: Cambridge University Press.

Cohen, I. Bernard. 1959. "Newton in Light of Recent Scholarship." *Isis* 51: 489–514.

Cunningham, Andrew. 1991. "How the *Principia* Got Its Name; Or, Taking Natural Philosophy Seriously." *History of Science* 29 (December): 377–92.

Desaguliers, J. T. 1763. *A Course of Experimental Philosophy,* 3rd ed. London: Millar.

Dobbs, Betty Jo. 1982. "Newton's Alchemy and His Theory of Matter." *Isis* 73: 511–28.

Dobbs, Betty Jo. 1975. *The Foundation of Newton's Alchemy: or, "The Hunting of the Green Lyon."* Cambridge: Cambridge University Press.

Fauvel, John, Raymond Flood, Michael Shortland, and Robin Wilson, eds. 1988. *Let Newton Be!* Oxford: Oxford University Press.

Garrison, James W. 1987. "Newton and the Relation of Mathematics to Natural Philosophy." *Journal of the History of Ideas* 48, no. 4 (October-December): 609–27.

Gjertsen, Derek. 1988. "Newton's Success." In Fauvel et al. 1988: 23–42.

Golinski, Jan. 1988. "The Secret Life of an Alchemist." In Fauvel et al. 1988: 146–67.

Guerlac, Henry. 1968 [1958]. "Newton's Changing Reputation in the Eighteenth Century." In *Carl Becker's Heavenly City Revisited,* pp. 3–26. Edited by Raymond O. Rockwood. [Hamden, Conn]: Archon Books.

Guerlac, Henry. 1965. "Where the Statue Stood: Divergent Loyalties to Newton in the Eighteenth Century." In *Aspects of the Eighteenth Century,* pp. 317–34. Edited by Earl R. Wasserman. Baltimore: Johns Hopkins University Press.

Hakfoort, Caspar. 1988. "Newton's Optics: The Changing Spectrum of Science." In Fauvel et al. 1988: 81–100.

Hanson, Norwood R. 1970. "Hypotheses Fingo." In *The Methodological Heritage of Newton*, pp. 14–33. Edited by Robert E. Butts and John W. Davis. Oxford: Basil Blackwell.

Henry, John. 1988. "Newton, Matter, and Magic." In Fauvel et al. 1988: 127–68.

Hessen, B. 1971. "The Social and Economic Roots of Newton's 'Principia.'" In *Science at the Cross Roads*, 2nd ed., pp. 151–212. With new foreword by Joseph Needham and a new introduction by P. G. Werksey. London: Frank Cass.

Jacob, M. C. 1974. "Early Newtonianism." *History of Science* 12 (June): 142–46.

Jacquette, Dale. 1990. "Aesthetics and Natural Law in Newton's Methodology." *Journal of the History of Ideas* 51, no. 4 (October-December): 659–66.

Keynes, John Maynard. 1972. "Newton, the Man." *Essays in Biography. The Collected Writings of John Maynard Keynes*, vol. 10. London: Macmillan for The Royal Economic Society, pp. 363–74; also in *Newton Tercentenary Celebrations*, pp. 27–34. Cambridge: The Royal Society, 1947.

Koyré, Alexandre. 1965. *Newtonian Studies*. Chicago: University of Chicago Press.

Kubrin, David. 1967. "Newton and the Cyclical Cosmos: Providence and the Mechanics Philosophy." *Journal of the History of Ideas* 28, no. 1 (January-March): 325–46.

Laudan, Laurens L. 1970. "Thomas Reid and the Newtonian Turn of British Methodological Thought." In *The Methodological Heritage*, pp. 103–31. Edited by Robert E. Butts and John W. Davis. Oxford: Basil Blackwell.

Maclaurin, Colin. 1971 [1748]. *An Account of Sir Isaac Newton's Philosophical Discoveries*. Hildesheim: Georg Olms Verlag.

McNeil, Maureen. 1988. "Newton As National Hero." In Fauvel et al. 1988: 223–40.

Merton, Robert K. 1970. *Science, Technology and Society in Seventeenth Century England*. N.Y.: Howard Fertig.

Newton, Sir Isaac. 1962 [1686]. *Sir Isaac Newton's Mathematical Principles of Natural Philosophy and His System of the World* [*Principia*]. Trans. Andrew Motte, 1729; revised with appendix by Florian Cajori. 2 vols. Berkeley: University of California Press.

Newton, Sir Isaac. 1952 [1730]. *Opticks*, 4th ed. Foreword by Albert Einstein, introduction by Sir Edmund Whittaker, preface by I. B. Cohen, and analytical table of contents by Duane H. D. Rolleo. N.Y.: Dover.

Newton, Sir Isaac. 1887. "Monetary Reports (1701–1702) Signed by Sir Isaac Newton." From manuscripts found in the Tower Mint and the Public Record Office. In *The Silver Pound and England's Monetary Policy Since the Restoration*. S. Dana Horton, pp. 261–71. London: Macmillan.

Pemberton, Henry. 1728. *A View of Sir Isaac Newton's Philosophy*. London: S. Palmer.

Pepper, John. 1988. "Newton's Mathematical Work." In Fauvel et al. 1988: 63–80.

Rattansi, Piyo. 1988. "Newton and the Wisdom of the Ancients." In Fauvel et al. 1988: 184–201.

Roche, John. 1988. "Newton's *Principia*." In Fauvel et al. 1988: 43–62.

Rose, Hilary, and Steven Rose. 1976. "The Incorporation of Science." In *The Political Economy of Science: Ideology of/in the Natural Sciences*, pp. 14–31. Edited by Hilary Rose and Steven Rose. London: Macmillan.

Schaffer, Simon. 1988. "Newtonianism." In *The Companion to the History of Modern Science*, pp. 610–26. Edited by G. N. Cantor, J. R. R. Christie, M. J. S. Hodge, and R. C. Olby. Beckenham: Croom Helm.

Schaffer, Simon. 1984. "Newton at the Crossroads." *Radical Philosophy* 37 (Summer): 23–28.

Schneider, Ivo. 1988. *Isaac Newton*. München: C. H. Beck.

Secord, James A. 1985. "Newton in the Nursery: Tom Telescope and the Philosophy of Tops and Balls, 1761–1838." *History of Science* 23: 127–51.

Shapere, Dudley. 1967a. "Newton, Isaac." In *Encyclopedia of Philosophy*.

Shapere, Dudley. 1967b. "Newtonian Mechanics." In *Encyclopedia of Philosophy*.

Shepherd, Christine M. 1982. "Newtonianism in Scottish Universities in the Seventeenth Century." In *The Origins and Nature of the Scottish Enlightenment*, pp. 65–85. Edited by R. H. Campbell and Andrew S. Skinner. Edinburgh: John Donald Publishers.

Shirras, G. Findlay, and J. H. Craig. 1945. "Sir Isaac Newton and the Currency." *Economic Journal* 55 (June-September): 217–41.

Strong, E. W. 1957. "Newtonian Explications of Natural Philosophy." *Journal of the History of Ideas* 18, no. 1 (January): 49–83.

Strong, E. W. 1951. "Newton's 'Mathematical Way.'" *Journal of the History of Ideas* 12, no. 1 (January): 90–110.

Thayer, H. S., ed. 1953. *Newton's Philosophy of Nature: Selections from his Writings*. Introduction by John Herman Randall, Jr. N.Y.: Hafner Press.

Truesdell, C. 1960. "A Program Toward Rediscovering the Rational Mechanics of the Age of Reason." *Archive for the History of the Exact Sciences* 1: 3–36.

Wallis, Peter, and Ruth Wallis. 1977. *Newton and Newtoniania 1672–1975, A Bibliography*. Dawson: Folkestone.

Westfall, Richard S. 1987. "Newton's Scientific Personality." *Journal of the History of Ideas* 48, no. 4 (October-December): 551–70.

Westfall, Richard S. 1980. *Never at Rest: A Biography of Isaac Newton*. Cambridge: Cambridge University Press.

Westfall, Richard S. 1976a. "The Changing World of the Newtonian Industry." *Journal of the History of Ideas* 37, no. 1 (January-March): 175–84.

Westfall, Richard S. 1976b. "Newton, Sir Isaac." In *Encyclopedia Britannica.*

Whiteside, D. T. 1962. "The Expanding World of Newtonian Research." *History of Science* 1: 16–29.

Whiston, William. 1972 [1716]. *Sir Isaac Newton's Mathematick Philosophy More Easily Demonstrated.* With an introduction to reprint edition by I. Bernard Cohen. N.Y.: Johnson Reprint.

## Dugald Stewart

Collini, Stefan, Donald Winch, and John Burrow. 1983. "The System of the North: Dugald Stewart and His Pupils." In *That Noble Science of Politics: A Study in Nineteenth-Century Intellectual History*, pp. 23–61. Edited by Stefan Collini, Donald Winch, and John Burrow. Cambridge: Cambridge University Press.

Rashid, Salim. 1985. "Dugald Stewart, 'Baconian' Methodology, and Political Economy." *Journal of the History of Ideas* 46, no. 2 (April-June): 245–57.

Stewart, Dugald. 1854a. *The Collected Works of Dugald Stewart.* Edited by Sir William Hamilton. Edinburgh: Thomas Constable; London: Hamilton, Adams.

Stewart, Dugald. 1954b. *Dissertation: exhibiting the progress of Metaphysical, Ethical, and Political Philosophy since the Revival of Letters in Europe. The Collected Works of Dugald Stewart*, vol. 1.

Stewart, Dugald. 1954c. *Elements of the Philosophy of the Human Mind*, to which is prefixed, introduction and part first of the *Outline of Moral Philosophy. The Collected Works of Dugald Stewart*, vols. 2–4.

Stewart, Dugald. 1954d. *Lectures on Political Economy. The Collected Works of Dugald Stewart*, vols. 8–9.

## William Whewell

Blake, Ralph M., Curt J. Ducasse, and Edward H. Madden. 1960. "William Whewell's Philosophy of Scientific Discovery." In their *Theories of Scientific Method: The Renaissance Through the Nineteenth Century*, pp. 183–217. Seattle: University of Washington Press.

Butts, Robert E. 1977. "Whewell's Logic of Induction." In *Foundations of Scientific Method:* The Nineteenth Century, pp. 53–85. Edited by Ronald N. Giere and Richard S. Westfall. Bloomington: Indiana University Press.

Cochrane, James L. 1970. "The First Mathematical Ricardian Model." *History of Political Economy* 2, no. 2 (Fall): 419–31.

Henderson, James P. 1985. "The Whewell Group of Mathematical Economists." *Manchester School* 53, no. 4 (December): 404–31.

Laudan, Larry. 1981. "William Whewell on the Consilience of Inductions." In his *Science and Hypothesis: Historical Essays on Scientific Methodology*, pp. 163–180. Dordrecht, Boston, London: D. Reidel.

Whewell, William. 1971a. *Mathematical Exposition of Some Doctines of Political Economy*. Reprint of four lectures first published in the *Transactions of the Cambridge Philosophical Society*, 1829, 1831, 1850. N.Y.: Augustus M. Kelley.

Whewell, William. 1971b [1829]. "Mathematical Exposition of Some Doctrines of Political Economy." In Whewell 1971a.

Whewell, William. 1971c [1831]. "Mathematical Exposition of Some Doctrines of Political Economy." In Whewell 1971a.

Whewell, William. 1971d [1850a]. "Mathematical Exposition of Some Doctrines of Political Economy—Second Memoir." In Whewell 1971a.

Whewell, William. 1971e [1850b]. "Mathematical Exposition of Certain Doctrines of Political Economy—Third Memoir." In Whewell 1971a.

Whewell, William. 1968. *William Whewell's Theory of Scientific Method*. Edited by Robert E. Butts. Pittsburgh: University of Pittsburgh Press.

Wilson, David B. 1974. "Herschel and Whewell's Version of Newtonianism." *Journal of the History of Ideas* 35, no. 1 (January/March): 79–97.

## II.  Science in Eighteenth- and Nineteenth-Century Britain

### On British Classical Economists and Their Society

Anon. 1824. "Review of James Mill's *Elements of Political Economy*." *Westminster Review* 2 (October): 289–310.

Bagehot, Walter. 1891. *The Works of Walter Bagehot*, 5 vols. Edited by Forrest Morgan. Hartford, Conn.: The Travelers Insurance.

Bagehot, Walter. 1880. *Economic Studies*. Edited by Richard Holt Hutton. London: Longmans, Green.

Blaug, Mark. 1987. "Classical Economics." In *The New Palgrave: A Dictionary of Economics*, 4 vols. Edited by John Eatwell, Murray Milgate, and Peter Newman. London: Macmillan; N.Y.: Stockton Press; Tokyo: Maruzen.

Bonar, James. 1893. *Philosophy and Political Economy in Some of Their Historical Relations*. N.Y.: Macmillan; London: Swan Sonnenschein.

Bowley, Marion. 1967. *Nassau Senior and Classical Economics*. N.Y.: Octagon Books.

Burrow, J. W. 1966. *Evolution and Society: A Study in Victorian Social Theory*. Cambridge: Cambridge University Press.

Cairnes, John E. 1965 [1875]. *The Character and Logical Method of Political Economy*. N.Y.: Augustus M. Kelley.

Carey, Lewis J. 1928. *Franklin's Economic Views*. Garden City, N.J.: Doubleday, Doran.

Cobbett, William. 1957 [1912]. *Rural Rides*, 2 vols. Introduction by Asa Briggs. London: Dent; N.Y.: Dutton.

Collini, Stefan, Donald Winch, John Burrow, eds. 1983. "Particular Politics: Political Economy and the Historical Method." In *That Noble Science of Politics: A Study in Nineteenth-Century Intellectual History*, pp. 247–75. Cambridge: Cambridge University Press.

Deane, Phyllis. 1991. "The Role of History of Economic Thought." In *Companion to Contemporary Economic Thought*, pp. 25–48. Edited by David Greenaway, Michael Bleaney, and Ian M. T. Stewart. London: Routledge.

Deane, Phyllis. 1978. *The Evolution of Economic Ideas*. London: Cambridge University Press.

Fay, C. R. 1956. *Adam Smith and the Scotland of His Day*. Cambridge: Cambridge University Press.

Ferguson, John M. 1950. *Landmarks of Economic Thought*, 2nd ed. N.Y.: Longmans, Green.

Fetter, Frank W. 1962. "Economic Articles in the *Westminster Review* and Their Authors, 1824–51." *Journal of Political Economy* 6 (December): 576–96.

Fetter, Frank W. 1960. "The Economic Articles in *Blackwood's Edinburgh Magazine*, and Their Authors, 1817–1853," parts 1 and 2. *Scottish Journal of Political Economy* 7: 85–107 and 213–31.

Fetter, Frank W. 1958. "The Economic Articles in the *Quarterly Review* and Their Authors, 1809–52," parts 1 and 2. *Journal of Political Economy* 66, no. 1 (February): 47–64; 66, no. 2 (April): 154–70.

Fetter, Frank W. 1953. "The Authorship of Economic Articles in the *Edinburgh Review*, 1802–47." *Journal of Political Economy* 61, no. 3 (June): 232–59.

Gide, Charles, and Charles Rist. 1960. *A History of Economic Doctrines from the Time of the Physiocrats to the Present Day*, 2nd English ed. translated from the French by R. Richards with Ernest F. Row. London: George G. Harrap.

Grammp, Willam D. 1973. "Classical Economics and Its Moral Critics." *History of Political Economy* 5, no. 2 (Summer): 359–74.

Heilbroner, Robert L. 1967 [1951]. *The Worldly Philosophers: The Lives, Times, and Ideas of the Great Economic Thinkers*. N.Y.: Washington Square Press.

Hollander, Samuel. 1987. *Classical Economics*. Oxford: Basil Blackwell.

Hutchison, T. W. 1978. *On Revolutions and Progress in Economic Knowledge*. Cambridge: Cambridge University Press.

Hutchison, T. W. 1964. *'Positive' Economics and Policy Objectives*. London: George Allen and Unwin.

Hutchison, T. W. 1951. "Review of Lecture Notes on Types of Economic Theory: as delivered by Professor Wesley C. Mitchell." *Economic Journal* 61 (March): 123–30.

Jevons, William Stanley. 1965. *The Principles of Economics: A Fragment of a Treatise on the Industrial Mechanism of Society and Other Papers*. Preface by Henry Higgs. N.Y.: Augustus M. Kelley.

Jevons, William Stanley. 1890. *Pure Logic and Other Minor Works*. Edited by Robert Adamson and Harriet A. Jevons, preface by Professor Adamson. London: Macmillan.

Jevons, William Stanley. 1879. *The Theory of Political Economy*, 2nd ed. London: Macmillan.

Keynes, John Maynard. 1973. *The General Theory and After; part 2. Collected Writings of John Maynard Keynes*, vol. 14. London: Macmillan.

Keynes, John Maynard. 1972. *Essays in Biography. Collected Works of John Maynard Keynes*, vol. 10. London: Macmillan for the Royal Society.

Letwin, William. 1963. *The Origins of Scientific Economics: English Economic Thought, 1660–1776*. London: Methuen.

Marsh, Jeffrey H. 1977. "Economics Education in Schools in the Nineteenth Century: Social Control." *Economics: The Journal of the Economics Association* 13, pt. 4, no. 60 (Winter): 116–18.

McCulloch, J. R. 1845. *The Literature of Political Economy:* A Classified Catalogue of Select Publications in the Different Departments of That Science, with Historical, Critical, and Biographical Notices. London: Longman, Brown, Green, and Longmans.

Mill, James. 1869. *Analysis of the Phenomena of the Human Mind*, 2 vols. New edition, with notes by Alexander Bain, Andrew Findlater, and George Grote; edited with additional notes by John Stuart Mill. London: Longmans Green Reader and Dyer.

Mill, James. 1821. *Elements of Political Economy*. London: Baldwin, Cradock, and Jay.

Miller, William L. 1971. "Richard Jones: A Case Study in Methodology." *History of Political Economy* 3, no. 1 (Spring): 198–207.

Mitchell, Wesley C. 1967. *Types of Economic Theory from Mercantilism to Institutionalism*, vol. 1. Edited by Joseph Dorfman. N.Y.: Augustus M. Kelley.

O'Brien, D. P. 1988. "Classical Reassessments." In Thweatt 1988: 179–220; commentary by R. D. Collison Black, pp. 221–25.

O'Brien, D. P. 1975. *The Classical Economists*. London: Oxford University Press.

Patten, Simon N. 1899. *The Development of English Thought: A Study in the Economic Interpretation of History*. N.Y.: Macmillan.

Roll, Eric. 1938. *A History of Economic Thought*, rev. ed. London: Faber and Faber.

Say, Jean-Baptiste. 1971 [1880]. *A Treatise on Political Economy*. Translation of 4th ed., *Traité d'Économie Politique* (1819). N.Y.: Augustus M. Kelley.

Schumpeter, Joseph A. 1954a. *Economic Doctrine and Method: An Historical Sketch*. (Translation by R. Aris of the German *Epochen der Dogmen- und Methodengeschichte*, J. C. B. Mohr [Paul Siebeck], 1912). London: George Allen and Unwin.

Schumpeter, Joseph A. 1954b. *History of Economic Analysis*. Edited from manuscript by Elizabeth Boody Schumpeter. N.Y.: Oxford University Press.

Senior, Nassau W. 1951 [1836]. *An Outline of the Science of Political Economy.* N.Y.: Augustus M. Kelley.

Skinner, Andrew S. 1965. "Economics and the Problem of Method: An Eighteenth Century View." *Scottish Journal of Political Economy* 12, no. 3: (November): 267–80.

Sowell, Thomas. 1974. *Classical Economics Reconsidered.* Princeton: Princeton University Press.

Spiegel, Henry William. 1991. *The Growth of Economic Thought,* 3rd ed. Englewood Cliffs, N.J.: Prentice-Hall.

Starbatty, Joachim. 1985. *Die englischen Klassiker der Nationalökonomie. Lehre und Wirkung.* Darmstadt: Wissenschaftliche Buchgesellschaft.

Steuart, Sir James. 1967. *The Works, Political, Metaphysical, and Chronological of Sir James Steuart,* 6 vols. Adam Smith Library. N.Y.: Augustus M. Kelley.

Steuart, Sir James. 1966. *An Inquiry into the Principles of Political Economy.* Edited by A. S. Skinner. Edinburgh: Oliver and Boyd; Chicago: Chicago University Press.

Thweatt, William O., ed. 1988. *Classical Political Economy: A Survey of Recent Literature.* Boston: Kluwer Academic.

Thweatt, William O. 1976. "Review of Sowell's *Classical Economics Reconsidered.*" *History of Political Economy* 8, no. 4 (Winter): 575–78.

Torrens, Robert. 1821. *An Essay on the Production of Wealth.* London: Longman, Hurst, Rees, Orme, and Brown.

Tyrrell, A. 1969. "Political Economy, Whiggism and the Education of Working-Class Adults in Scotland 1817–40." *Scottish Historical Review* 48: 151–65.

Whately, Richard. 1966 [1832]. *Introductory Lectures on Political Economy,* 2nd ed. N.Y.: Augustus M. Kelley.

Winch, Donald. 1971. *The Emergence of Economics as a Science 1750–1870.* Fontana Economic History of Europe, vol. 3, sect. 9. London: Collins Clear-Type Press.

Wise, M. Norton, with Crosbie Smith. 1989/1990. "Work and Waste: Political Economy and Natural Philosophy in Nineteenth Century Britain," parts 1–3. *History of Science* 27 (1989): 263–301, 391–449; 28 (1990): 221–61.

## On Economic Methodology

Black, Robert. 1963. "A Comparison of Classical English Economic Thought with Newtonian Natural Philosophy." Ph.D. dissertation, University of California, Berkeley.

Blaug, Mark. 1992. *The Methodology of Economics Or How Economists Explain,* 2nd ed. Cambridge: Cambridge University Press [1st edition: 1980].

Caldwell, Bruce. 1982. *Beyond Positivism: Economic Methodology in the Twentieth Century.* London: Allen and Unwin.

Deane, Phyllis. 1983. "The Scope and Method of Economic Science." *Economic Journal* 93, no. 369 (March): 1–12.

Gordon, Scott. 1991. *The History and Philosophy of Social Science.* London: Routledge.

Hasbach, Wilhelm. 1904. "Mit welcher Methode wurden die Gesetze der theoretischen Nationalökonomie gefunden?" *Jahrbücher für Nationalökonomie und Statistik* 27: 289–317.

Hausman, Daniel M. 1989. "Economic Methodology in a Nutshell." *Journal of Economic Perspectives* 3, no. 2 (Spring): 115–27.

Hausman, Daniel M. 1984. *The Philosophy of Economics: An Anthology.* Cambridge: Cambridge University Press.

Hirsch, Abraham. 1978. "J. E. Cairnes' Methodology in Theory and Practice." *History of Political Economy* 10, no. 2 (Summer): 322–28.

Hollis, Martin. 1985. "The Emperor's Newest Clothes." *Economics and Philosophy* 1: 128–33.

Keynes, John Neville. 1973 [1917]. *The Scope and Method of Political Economy,* 4th ed. Clifton, N.J.: Augustus M. Kelley.

Knight, Frank. 1956. *On the History and Method of Economics.* Chicago: University of Chicago Press.

Lessnoff, Michael. 1988. "The Philosophy of the Social Sciences." In *An Encyclopedia of Philosophy,* pp. 784–806. Edited by G. H. R. Parkinson. London: Routledge.

Machlup, Fritz. 1963. "Equilibrium and Disequilibrium: Misplaced Concreteness and Disguised Politics." In his *Essays on Economic Semantics,* pp. 43–72. Edited by Merton H. Miller. Englewood Cliffs, N.J.: Prentice-Hall.

McCloskey, Donald N. 1985. "Sartorial Epistemology in Tatters: A Reply to Martin Hollis." *Economics and Philosophy* 1: 134–37.

McCloskey, Donald N. 1983. "The Rhetoric of Economics." *Journal of Economics* 21 (June): 481–517.

Redman, Deborah. 1994. "Karl Popper's Theory of Science and Econometrics: The Rise and Decline of Social Engineering." *Journal of Economic Issues* 28, no. 1 (March): 67–99.

Redman, Deborah A. 1991. *Economics and the Philosophy of Science.* N.Y.: Oxford University Press.

Redman, Deborah A. 1989. *Economic Methodology: A Bibliography with References to Works in the Philosophy of Science, 1860–1988.* N.Y.: Greenwood Press.

Schabas, Margaret. 1992. "Breaking Away: History of Economics as History of Science." *History of Political Economy* 24, no. 1 (Spring): 187–203.

Wagenführ, Horst. 1933. *Der Systemgedanke in der Nationalökonomie. Eine methodengeschichtliche Betrachtung.* Jena: Gustav Fischer.

## On the Origins of Statistics and Econometrics

Bevan, Wilson Lloyd. 1894. *Sir William Petty: A Study in English Literature.* Publications of the American Economic Association, vol. 9, no. 4.

Buck, Peter. 1977. "Seventeenth-Century Political Arithmetic: Civil Strife and Vital Statistics." *Isis* 68 (March): 67–84.

Cullen, M. J. 1975. *The Statistical Movement in Early Victorian Britain: The Foundations of Empirical Social Research.* Hassocks: Harvester Press; N.Y.: Barnes & Noble.

Davenant, Charles. 1698. *Discourses on the Publick Revenues, and on the Trade of England.* London: James Knapton.

Deane, Phyllis. 1987. "Political Arithmetic." In *The New Palgrave: A Dictionary of Economics,* 4 vols. Edited by John Eatwell, Murray Milgate, and Peter Newman. London: Macmillan, N.Y.; Stockton Press; Tokyo: Maruzen.

Deane, Phyllis. 1956. "The Implications of Early National Income Estimates for the Measurement of Long-Term Economic Growth in the United Kingdom." University of Cambridge Department of Applied Economics Reprint Series no. 109.

Endres, A. M. 1985. "The Functions of Numerical Data in the Writings of Graunt, Petty, and Davenant." *History of Political Economy* 17, no. 2 (Summer): 245–64.

Galton, Francis. 1869. *Hereditary Genius: An Inquiry into Its Laws and Consequences.* London: Macmillan.

Goldman, Lawrence. 1983. "The Origins of British 'Social Science': Political Economy, Natural Science and Statistics 1830–1835." *Historical Journal* 26, no. 3: 587–616.

Graunt, John. See Petty, William.

Hilts, Victor L. 1973. "Statistics and Social Science." In *Foundations of Scientific Method: The Nineteenth Century,* pp. 206–33. Edited by Ronald N. Giere and Richard S. Westfall. Bloomington: Indiana University Press.

King, Gregory. 1936. *Two Tracts.* Edited by George E. Barnett. Baltimore: Johns Hopkins University Press.

Ménard, Claude. 1980. "Three Forms of Resistance to Statistics: Say, Cournot, Walras." *History of Political Economy* 12, no. 4 (Winter): 524–41.

Pearson, E. S., ed. 1978. *The History of Statistics in the 17th and 18th Centuries Against the Changing Background of Intellectual, Scientific and Religious Thought.* Lectures of Karl Pearson at University College London, 1921–1937. London: Charles Griffen.

Petty, Sir William [and John Graunt]. 1899. *The Economic Writings of Sir William Petty Together with the Observations upon the Bills of Mortality* [by John Graunt], 2 vols. Edited by Charles Henry Hull. Cambridge: Cambridge University Press.

Porter, Theodore M. 1986. *The Rise of Statistical Thinking 1820–1900.* Princeton: Princeton University Press.

Quetelet, Adolphe. 1836. *Sur l'homme et le développement de ses facultés, ou essai de physique sociale*, 2 vols. Bruxelles: Louis Hauman.

Robertson, R. John. 1838. "Transactions of the Statistical Society of London." *Westminster Review* 29 (April): 45–72.

Spengler, Joseph J. 1961. "Quantification in Economics: Its History." In *Quantity and Quality*, pp. 129–211. Edited by Daniel Lerner. N.Y.: Free Press.

Studenski, Paul. 1958. *The Income of Nations. Theory, Measurement, and Analysis: Past and Present.* N.Y.: New York University Press.

Westergaard, Harald. 1969. *Contributions to the History of Statistics.* N.Y.: Augustus M. Kelley.

Young, Arthur. 1967 [1774]. *Political Arithmetic containing Observations on the Present State of Great Britain.* N.Y.: Augustus M. Kelley.

## On Science and the Philosophy of Science

Ashley, Myron Lucius. 1903. "The Nature of Hypothesis." In *Studies in Logical Theory*, pp. 143–83. Edited by John Dewey. Chicago: University of Chicago Press.

Atkinson, R. F. 1988. "The Philosophy of History." In *An Encyclopedia of Philosophy*, pp. 807–30. Edited by G. H. R. Parkinson. London: Routledge.

Blackwell, Richard J. 1974. "The Inductivist Model of Science: A Study in Nineteenth-Century Philosophy of Science." *Modern Schoolman* 51 (March): 197–212.

Blake, Ralph M., Curt J. Ducasse, and Edward Madden. 1960a. *Theories of Scientific Method: The Renaissance Through the Nineteenth Century.* Seattle: University of Washington Press.

Blake, Ralph M., Curt J. Ducasse, and Edward Madden. 1960b. "W. S. Jevons on Induction and Probability." In their *Theories of Scientific Method: The Renaissance Through the Nineteenth Century*, pp. 233–47. Seattle: University of Washington Press.

Brooks, G. P., and S. K. Aalto. 1981. "The Rise and Fall of Moral Algebra: Francis Hutcheson and the Mathematization of Psychology." *Journal of the History of the Behavioral Sciences* 17, no. 3 (July): 343–56.

Bryson, Gladys. 1968 [1945]. *Man and Society: The Scottish Inquiry of the Eighteenth Century.* N.Y.: Augustus M. Kelley.

Buchdahl, Gerd. 1969. *Metaphysics and the Philosophy of Science: The Classical Origins: Descartes to Kant.* Cambridge: MIT Press.

Burke, T. E. 1988. "Science as Conjecture and Refutation." In *An Encyclopedia of Philosophy*, pp. 205–24. Edited by G. H. R. Robinson. London: Routledge.

Cantor, G. N. 1971. "Henry Brougham and the Scottish Methodological Tradition." *Studies in History and Philosophy of Science* 2, no. 1: 69–89.

Carrithers, David. 1986. "Montesquieu's Philosophy of History." *Journal of the History of Ideas* 47, no. 1 (January-March): 61–80.

Chitnis, Ahand. 1986. *The Scottish Enlightenment and Early Victorian English Society*. London: Croom Helm.

Cohen, I. Bernard. 1966. *Franklin and Newton: An Inquiry into Speculative Newtonian Experimental Science and Franklin's Work in Electricity as an Example Thereof*. Memoirs of the American Philosophical Society, vol. 43. Cambridge: Harvard University Press.

De Haan, Richard. 1982. "Induction." In *Collier's Encyclopedia*.

"Editorial." 1993. *European Journal of the History of Economic Thought* 1, no. 1 (Autumn): 1–4.

Emerson, Roger L. 1990. "Science and Moral Philosophy in the Scottish Enlightenment." In *Studies in the Philosophy of the Scottish Enlightenment*, pp. 11–36. Edited by M. A. Stewart. Oxford: Clarendon Press.

Emerson, Roger L. 1988. "Science and the Origins and Concerns of the Scottish Enlightenment." *History of Science* 26: 335–66.

Emerson, Roger L. 1979. "American Indians, Frenchmen, and Scot Philosophers." In *Studies in Eighteenth-Century Culture* 9: 211–36. Edited by Roseann Runte. Madison: University of Wisconsin Press.

Foote, George A. 1954. "Science and Its Function in Early Nineteenth Century England." *Osiris* 11: 438–54.

Forbes, Duncan. 1982. "Natural Law and the Scottish Enlightenment." In *The Origins and Nature of the Scottish Enlightenment*, pp. 186–204. Edited by R. H. Campbell and Andrew S. Skinner. Edinburgh: John Donald Publishers.

Forbes, Eric G. 1983. "Philosophy and Science Teaching in the Seventeenth Century." In *Four Centuries Edinburgh University Life, 1583–1983*, pp. 28–37. Edited by Gordon Donaldson. Edinburgh: Edinburgh University Press.

Fordyce, David. 1771. "Moral Philosophy, or Morals." In *Encyclopedia Britannica*, 1st ed. Edinburgh.

Freudenthal, Gideon. 1982. *Atom und Individuum im Zeitalter Newtons. Zur Genese der mechanistischen Natur- und Sozialphilosophie*. Frankfurt am Main. Suhrkamp.

Gillies, Donald A. 1988. "Induction and Probability." In *An Encyclopedia of Philosophy*, pp. 179–204. Edited by G. H. R. Parkinson. London: Routledge.

Goodman, Nelson. 1973. *Fact, Fiction and Forecast*, 3rd ed. Indianapolis: Bobbs-Merrill.

Guerlac, Henry. 1958. "Three Eighteenth-Century Social Philosophers: Scientific Influences on Their Thought." *Daedalus* 87: 8–24.

Hacking, Ian. 1975. *The Emergence of Probability. A Philosophical Study of Early Ideas about Probability, Induction and Statistical Inference*. London: Cambridge University Press.

Hintikka, Jaakko, and Unto Remes. 1974. *The Method of Analysis: Its Geometrical Origin and Its General Significance*. Dordrecht: D. Reidl.

Höpfl, H. M. 1978. "From Savage to Scotsman: Conjectural History in the Scottish Enlightenment." *Journal of British Studies* 17: 19–40.

d'Holbach, Paul Henri Dietrich Baron. 1971 [1770]. *A System of Nature, and Her Laws: An Application to the Happiness of Man, Living in Society; contrasted with superstition and imaginery systems.* London: James Watson.

Humphreys, Paul W. 1987. "Induction." In *The New Palgrave: A Dictionary of Economics,* 4 vols. Edited by John Eatwell, Murray Milgate, and Peter Newman. London: Macmillan; N.Y.: Stockton Press; Tokyo: Maruzen.

Hutcheson, Francis. 1990a. *An Inquiry into the Original of Our Ideas of Beauty and Virtue. Collected Works of Francis Hutcheson,* vol. 1. Hildesheim: Georg Olms Verlag.

Hutcheson, Francis. 1990b [1747]. *A Short Introduction to Moral Philosophy. Collected Works of Francis Hutcheson,* Vol. 4. Hildesheim: Georg Olms Verlag.

"Induction." 1797. In *Encyclopedia Britannica,* 3rd. ed. Edinburgh.

Iggers, G. G. 1959. "Further Remarks About Early Use of the Term 'Social Science.'" *Journal of the History of Ideas* 20 (July-September): 433–36. Reprinted in J. Wood 1987, 4: 154–57.

Jacob, J. R. 1980. "Restoration Ideologies and the Royal Society." *History of Science* 18: 25–39.

Jevons, William Stanley. 1874. *The Principles of Science: A Treatise on Logic and Scientific Method,* 2 vols. London: Macmillan.

Keynes, John Maynard. 1973 [1921]. *A Treatise on Probability. Collected Writings of John Maynard Keynes,* vol. 8. London: Macmillan for the Royal Society.

Laudan, Laurens L. 1981. "The Clock Metaphor and Hypotheses: The Impact of Descartes on English Methodological Thought, 1650–1670." In his *Science and Hypothesis,* pp. 27–58. Dordrecht: D. Reidel.

Laudan, Laurens L. 1981. "Hume (and Hacking) on Induction." In his *Science and Hypothesis,* pp. 72–85. Dordrecht: D. Reidel.

"Logic." 1771. In *Encyclopedia Britannica,* 1st ed. Edinburgh.

Mayr, Ernst. 1990. "When Is Historiography Whiggish?" *Journal of the History of Ideas* 51, no. 2 (April-June): 301–309.

Mayr, Otto. 1986. *Authority, Liberty and Automatic Machinery in Early Modern Europe.* Baltimore: Johns Hopkins University Press.

McCosh, James. 1990 [1875]. *The Scottish Philosophy: Biographical, Expository, Critical, from Hutcheson to Hamilton.* Hildesheim: Georg Olms Verlags.

Medawar, P. B. 1964. "Is the Scientific Paper Fraudulent?" *Saturday Review* (August 1): 42–43.

Moravia, Sergio. 1980. "The Enlightenment and the Sciences of Man." *History of Science* 18: 247–68.

Morrell, J. B. 1971. "The University of Edinburgh in the Late Eighteenth Century: Its Scientific Eminence and Academic Structure." *Isis* 62, pt. 2, no. 212 (Summer): 158–71.

Morrell, Jack, and Arnold Thackray. 1982. *Gentlemen of Science: Early Years of the British Association for the Advancement of Science.* Oxford: Clarendon.

Nagel, Ernest. 1958. "Induction." In *Encyclopedia Americana.*

Norgate, G. Le Grys. 1895. "Pemberton, Henry." In *Dictionary of National Biography.* Edited by Sidney Lee. London: Smith, Elder.

Norton, David Fate. 1975. "George Turnbull and the Furniture of the Mind." *Journal of the History of Ideas* 35, no. 4 (October-December): 701–716.

O'Connor, D. J., ed. 1964. *A Critical History of Western Philosophy.* N.Y.: Free Press.

Olson, Richard. 1975. *Scottish Philosophy and British Physics 1750–1880: A Study in the Foundations of the Victorian Scientific Style.* Princeton: Princeton University Press.

Olson, Richard. 1971. "Scottish Philosophy and Mathematics 1750–1830." *Journal of the History of Ideas* 32, no. 1 (January-March): 29–44.

Ong, Walter J. 1958. *Ramus: Method, and the Decay of Dialogue.* Cambridge: Harvard University Press.

Palter, Robert. 1966. "Newton and the Inductive Method." In *The Annus Mirabilis of Sir Isaac Newton,* pp. 244–57. Edited by Robert Palter. Cambridge: MIT Press.

Platts, Charles. 1893. "Maclaurin, Colin." In *Dictionary of National Biography.* Edited by Sidney Lee. London: Smith, Elder.

Popkin, Richard H. 1987. "The Religious Background of Seventeenth-Century Philosophy." *Journal of the History of Philosophy* 25: 35–50.

Randall, John Hermann. 1962. *The Career of Philosophy,* 2 vols. N.Y.: Columbia University Press.

Randall, John Hermann. 1940. "The Development of Scientific Method in the School of Padua." *Journal of the History of Ideas* 1, no. 2 (April): 177–206.

"Regulation of Watches." 1753. *Gentleman's Magazine* 23 (November): 518–21.

Rendall, Jane. 1978. *The Origins of the Scottish Enlightenment.* London: Macmillan.

Risse, Wilhelm. 1970. "Der Wissenschaftsbegriff in England im 17. und 18. Jahrhundert." In *Der Wissenschaftsbegriff,* pp. 90–98. Edited by Alwin Diemer. Miesenheim am Glan: Hain Verlag.

Robertson, J. Charles. 1976. "A Bacon-Facing Generation: Scottish Philosophy in the Early Nineteenth Century." *Journal of the History of Philosophy* 14: 37–49.

Robinson, Daniel N. 1986. "The Scottish Enlightenment and Its Mixed Bequest." *Journal of the History of the Behavioral Sciences* 22, no. 2 (April): 171–77.

Rosenthal, Jerome. 1955. "Voltaire's Philosophy of History." *Journal of the History of Ideas* 16, no. 2 (April): 151–78.

Ruby, Jane E. 1986. "The Origins of Scientific 'Law.'" *Journal of the History of Ideas* 47, no. 3 (July-September): 341–59.

Salmon, Wesley C. 1973. "Confirmation." *Scientific American* (May): 75–83.

Schofield, Robert E. 1978. "An Evolutionary Taxonomy of Eighteenth-Century Newtonianisms." In *Studies in Eighteenth-Century Culture* 7: 175–92. Edited by Roseann Runte. Madison: University of Wisconsin Press.

Senn, P. R. 1958. "The Earliest Use of the Term 'Social Science.'" *Journal of the History of Ideas* 19 (October): 568–70. Reprinted in J. Wood 1987, 4: 84–86.

Shapin, Steven. 1974. "The Audience for Science in Eighteenth Century Edinburgh." *History of Science* 12 (June): 95–121.

Skinner, Andrew. 1967. "Natural History in the Age of Adam Smith." *Political Studies* 15, no. 1: 32–48.

Sprat, Thomas. 1959 [1667]. *History of the Royal Society,* edited by Jackson I. Cope and Harold Whitmore Jones. St. Louis: Washington University; London: Routledge and Kegan Paul.

Teggart, Frederick J. 1977 [1941]. *Theory and Processes of History.* A preface by Kenneth Bock. Berkeley: University of California Press.

Tiles, Mary. 1988. "Science and the World." In *An Encyclopedia of Philosophy,* pp. 225–48. Edited by G. H. R. Parkinson. London: Routledge.

Turnbull, George. 1976 [1740]. *The Principles of Moral Philosophy.* Hildesheim: Georg Olms Verlag.

Voltaire, François-Marie Arouet. 1992 [1741]. *Eléments de la philosophie de Newton. The Complete Works of Voltaire,* vol. 15. Critical edition by Robert L. Walters and W. H. Barber. Oxford: Alden Press.

Voltaire, François-Marie Arouet. 1744. "On Writing History." *Gentleman's Magazine* 14 (August): 420–21.

Webster, C. 1967. "The Origins of the Royal Society." *History of Science* 6: 106–28.

Whately, Richard. 1988 [1826]. *Elements of Logic.* Edited by Paola Dessì. Bologna: Cooperativa Libraria Universitaria Editrice Bologna.

Wise, M. Norton, with Crosbie Smith. 1989/1990. "Work and Waste: Political Economy and Natural Philosophy in Nineteenth Century Britain," parts 1–3. *History of Science* 27 (1989): 263–301, 391–449; 28 (1990): 221–61.

Wolf, Abraham. 1952. *A History of Science, Technology and Philosophy in the Eighteenth Century,* 2nd ed. revised by D. McKie. London: George Allen & Unwin.

Wood, John Cunningham, ed. 1987. *John Stuart Mill: Critical Assessments,* 4 vols. London: Croom Helm.

Wood, P. B. 1989. "The Natural History of Man in the Scottish Enlightenment." *History of Science* 27: 89–123.

## III. On the Methodology of Adam Smith

Ahmad, Syed. 1990. "Adam Smith's Four Invisible Hands." *History of Political Economy* 22, No. 1 (Spring): 137–44.

Becker, James F. 1961. "Adam Smith's Theory of Social Science." *Southern Economic Journal* 28, No. 1 (July): 13–21. Reprinted in Wood 1984, 1: 310–22.

Berry, Christopher J. 1974. "Adam Smith's *Considerations on Language*." *Journal of the History of Ideas* 35, no. 1 (January-March): 130–38.

Bevilacqua, Vincent M. 1965. "Adam Smith's Lectures on Rhetoric and Belles Lettres." *Studies in Scottish Literature* 3: 41–60.

Bevilacqua, Vincent M. 1964. "Adam Smith's *Rhetoric*: Continental Scholarship." *Quarterly Journal of Speech* 50, no. 4 (December 1964): 445–47.

Bittermann, Henry. 1940. "Adam Smith's Empiricism and the Law of Nature," parts 1 and 2. *Journal of Political Economy* 48 (August): 487–520, (October): 703–34. Reprinted in Wood 1984, 1: 190–235.

Bonar, James. 1932. *A Catalogue of the Library of Adam Smith*, 2nd ed. London: Macmillan.

Boulding, Kenneth E. 1971. "After Samuelson, Who Needs Adam Smith?" *History of Political Economy* 3, no. 3 (Fall): 225–337.

Buckle, Henry Thomas. 1861. *History of Civilization in England*, vol. 2. London: Parker, Son, and Bourn.

Campbell, R. H. 1982. "The Enlightenment and the Economy." In *The Origins and Nature of the Scottish Enlightenment*, pp. 8–25. Edited by R. H. Campbell and Andrew S. Skinner. Edinburgh: John Donald Publishers.

Campbell, R. H., and A. S. Skinner. 1982. *Adam Smith*. London: Croom Helm.

Campbell, T. D. 1971. *Adam Smith's Science of Morals*. London: George Allen and Unwin.

Clark, Charles M. A. 1988. "Natural Law Influences on Adam Smith." *Quaderni di Storia dell' Economia Politica* 6, no. 3: 60–86.

Clark, John Maurice, et al. 1966 [1928]. *Adam Smith, 1776–1926. Lectures to Commemorate the Sesquicentennial of the Publication of The Wealth of Nations*. N.Y.: Augustus M. Kelley.

Cleaver, K. C. 1989. "Adam Smith on Astronomy." *History of Science* 27: 211–18.

Cole, Arthur H. 1958. "Puzzles of the '*Wealth of Nations*.'" *Canadian Journal of Economics and Political Science* 24, no. 1 (February): 1–8.

Cremaschi, Sergio. 1989. "Adam Smith: Skeptical Newtonianism, Disenchanted Republicanism, and the Birth of Social Science." In *Knowledge and Politics: Case Studies in the Relationship Between Epistemology and Political Philosophy*, pp. 83–110. Edited by Marcelo Dascal and Ora Gruengard. Boulder, Colo.: Westview Press.

Cremaschi, Sergio. 1988. "The Newtonian Heritage in Eighteenth Century Political Economy." Paper read at Conference on After Newton: Science and Society in the First Industrial Revolution (1727–1850), 14–18 November, Madrid.

Cremaschi, Sergio. 1981. "Adam Smith, Newtonianism and Political Economy." *Manucrito* 5, no. 1: 117–34.

Cropsey, Joseph. 1957. *Polity and Economy: An Interpretation of the Principles of Adam Smith.* The Hague: Martinus Nijhoff.

Dankert, Clyde E. 1974. *Adam Smith: Man of Letters and Economist.* Hicksville, N.Y.: Exposition Press.

Dow, Alexander. 1984. "The Hauteur of Adam Smith: An Unpublished Letter from James Anderson of Monkshill." *Scottish Journal of Political Economy* 31, no. 3 (November): 284–85.

Dow, Sheila C. 1987. "The Scottish Political Economy Tradition." *Scottish Journal of Political Economy* 34, no. 4 (November): 335–48. Reprinted in Mair 1990: 19–32.

Endres, A. M. 1992. "Adam Smith's Treatment of Historical Evidence as Illustrated from the Theory of Investment Priorities." *Journal of European Economic History* 21, no. 2 (Fall): 217–49.

Endres, A. M. 1991. "Adam Smith's Rhetoric of Economics: An Illustration Using 'Smithian' Compositional Rules." *Scottish Journal of Political Economy* 38, no. 1 (February); 76–95.

Evensky, Jerry. 1989. "The Evolution of Adam Smith's Views on Political Economy." *History of Political Economy* 21, no. 1 (Spring): 123–45.

Evensky, Jerry. 1987. "The Two Voices of Adam Smith: Moral Philosopher and Social Critic." *History of Political Economy* 19, no. 3 (Fall): 447–68.

Foley, Vernard. 1976. *The Social Physics of Adam Smith.* West Layfayette, Ind.: Purdue University Press.

Forbes, Duncan. 1954. "'Scientific' Whiggism: Adam Smith and John Millar." *Cambridge Journal* 7: 643–70. Reprinted in Wood 1984, 1: 273–96.

Freudenthal, Gideon. 1981. "Adam Smith's Analytic-Synthetic Method and the 'System of Natural Liberty.'" *History of European Ideas* 2, no. 2: 135–54.

Franklin, Burt, and Francesco Cordasco. 1950. *Adam Smith, A Bibliographical Checklist: An International Record of Critical Writings and Scholarship Relating to Smith and Smithian Theory, 1876–1950.* N.Y.: B. Franklin.

Hasbach, Wilhelm. 1891. *Untersuchungen über Adam Smith und die Entwicklung der politischen Ökonomie.* Leipzig: Duncker und Humblot.

Heilbroner, Robert L. 1973. "The Paradox of Progress: Decline in *The Wealth of Nations.*" *Journal of the History of Ideas* 34, no. 2 (April-June): 243–62. Reprinted in Skinner and Wilson 1975: 524–39.

Hetherington, Norriss S. 1983. "Isaac Newton's Influence on Adam Smith's Natural Laws in Economics." *Journal of the History of Ideas* 44, no. 3 (July-September): 497–505.

Hollander, Jacob H. 1966a [1928]. "The Dawn of a Science." In Clark, et al. 1966: 1–21.

Hollander, Jacob H. 1966b [1928]. "The Founder of a School." In Clark, et al. 1966: 22–52.

Hollander, Samuel. 1977. "Adam Smith and the Self-Interest Axiom." *Journal of Law and Economics* 20, no. 1 (April): 133–52. Reprinted in Wood 1984, 1: 680–97.

Hollander, Samuel. 1976. "The Historical Dimension of the Wealth of Nations." In *Transcriptions of the Royal Society of Canada*, series 4, 14: 277–92. Ottawa: Royal Society of Canada.

Hooker, John J. 1964–1966. "The Statistical Milieu of Adam Smith," parts 1–3. *American Statistician* 18, no. 5 (December 1964): 22–24; 19, no. 2 (April 1965): 49–51; 20, no. 1 (February 1966): 29–31.

Howell, Wilbur Samuel. 1975. "Adam Smith's Lectures on Rhetoric: An Historical Assessment." In *Essays on Adam Smith*, pp. 11–43. Edited by Andrew S. Skinner and Thomas Wilson. Oxford: Clarendon Press.

Hutchison, T. W. 1990a. "Adam Smith and *The Wealth of Nations*." In Mair 1990: 81–102.

Hutchison, T. W. 1990b. "History and Political Economy in Scotland: Alternative 'Inquiries' and Scottish Ascendancy." In Mair 1990: 61–80.

Hutchison, T. W. 1990c. "Moral Philosophy and Political Economy in Scotland." In Mair 1990: 33–60.

Hutchison, T. W. 1988. *Before Adam Smith: The Emergence of Political Economy, 1662–1776*. Oxford: Basil Blackwell.

Kleer, Richard A. 1995. "Final Causes in Adam Smith's *Theory of Moral Sentiments*." *Journal of the History of Philosophy* 33 (April): 275–300.

Klein, Lawrence R. 1992. "Smith's Use of Data." In *Adam Smith's Legacy: His Place in the Development of Modern Economics*, pp. 15–28. Edited by Michael Fry. London: Routledge.

Lamb, Robert Boyden. 1974. "Adam Smith's System: Sympathy Not Self-Interest." *Journal of the History of Ideas* 35, no. 4 (October-December): 671–82.

Land, Stephen K. 1977. "Adam Smith's 'Considerations concerning the First Formation of Languages.'" *Journal of the History of Ideas* 38, no. 4 (October-December): 677–90.

Leontief, Wassily. 1992. "The Present State of Economic Science." In *Adam Smith's Legacy: His Place in the Development of Modern Economics*, pp. 141–45. London: Routledge.

Leslie, Cliffe Thomas Edward. 1879a. "On the Philosophical Method of Political Economy." In his *Essays in Political and Moral Philosophy*, pp. 216–42. Dublin: Hodges, Foster, and Figges; London: Longmans, Green.

Leslie, Cliffe Thomas Edward. 1879b. "The Political Economy of Adam Smith." In his *Essays in Political and Moral Philosophy*, pp. 148–66. Dublin: Hodges, Foster, and Figges; London: Longmans, Green.

Lightwood, Martha Bolar. 1984. *A Selected Bibliography of Significant Works about Adam Smith*. Philadelphia: University of Pennsylvania Press.

Lindgren, J. Ralph. 1986. "Review of Lightwood's *Selected Bibiliography of Significant Works about Adam Smith.*" *History of Political Economy* 18, no. 3 (Fall): 536.

Lindgren, J. Ralph. 1978. "Review of Foley's *The Social Physics of Adam Smith.*" *History of Political Economy* 10, no. 4 (Winter): 683–85.

Lindgren, J. Ralph. 1973. *The Social Philosophy of Adam Smith.* The Hague: Martinus Nijhoff.

Lindgren, J. Ralph. 1969. "Adam Smith's Theory of Inquiry." *Journal of Political Economy* 77, no. 6 (November-December): 897–915.

Llobera, Josep R. 1971. "The Enlightenment and Adam Smith's Conception of Science." In *Knowledge and Society: Studies in the Sociology of Culture Past and Present.* A Research Annual 3: 109–36. Edited by Robert A. Jones and Henrika Kublick.

Longuet-Higgins, H. Christopher. 1992. "'The History of Astronomy': A Twentieth-Century View." In *Adam Smith Reviewed,* pp. 79–92. Edited by Peter Jones and Andrew S. Skinner. Edinburgh: Edinburgh University Press.

Macfie, Alec. 1971. "The Invisible Hand of Jupiter." *Journal of the History of Ideas* 32, no. 4 (October-December): 595–99.

Macfie, Alec. 1955. "The Scottish Tradition in Economic Thought." *Scottish Journal of Political Economy* 2 (June): 81–103. Reprinted in Mair 1990: 1–18.

Mair, Douglas, ed. 1990. *The Scottish Contribution to Modern Economic Thought.* Aberdeen: Aberdeen University Press.

Mayr, Otto. 1971. "Adam Smith and the Concept of the Feedback System: Economic Thought and Technology in 18th-Century Britain." *Technology and Culture* 12: 1–22.

Meek, Ronald L. 1971. "Smith, Turgot, and the 'Four Stages' Theory." *History of Political Economy* 3, no. 1 (Spring): 9–27. Reprinted in Wood 1984, 1: 142–55.

Megill, A.D. 1975. "Theory and Experience in Adam Smith." *Journal of the History of Ideas* 36, no. 1 (January-March): 79–94.

Mirowski, Philip. 1988. "Physics and the 'Marginalist Revolution.'" In his *Against Mechanism: Protecting Economics from Science,* pp. 11–30. Totowa, N.J.: Rowman and Littlefield.

Mirowski, Philip. 1982. "Adam Smith, Empiricism, and the Rate of Profit in Eighteenth-century England." *History of Political Economy* 14, no. 2 (Summer): 178–98. Reprinted in his *Against Mechanism: Protecting Economics from Science,* ch. 11. Totowa, N.J.: Rowman & Littlefield, 1988.

Mizuta, Hiroshi. 1967. *Adam Smith's Library. A Supplement to Bonar's Catalogue with a Checklist of the Whole Library.* Cambridge: Cambridge University Press for the Royal Economic Society.

Morrow, Glenn R. 1973 [1923]. *The Ethical and Economic Theories of Adam Smith.* Clifton, N.J.: Augustus M. Kelley.

Morrow, Glenn R. 1927. "Adam Smith: Moralist and Philosopher." *Journal of Political Economy* 35, no. 3 (June): 321–42. Reprinted in Wood 1984, 1: 168–81.

Moscovici, Serge. 1956. "A propos de quelques travaux d'Adam Smith sur l'histoire et la philosophie des sciences." *Revue d'histoire des sciences* 9: 1–20.

Myers, Milton L. 1983. *The Soul of Modern Economic Man: Ideas of Self-Interest, Thomas Hobbes to Adam Smith.* Chicago: University of Chicago Press.

Myers, Milton L. 1975. "Adam Smith as Critic of Ideas." *Journal of the History of Ideas* 36, no. 2 (April-May): 281–96.

Pack, Spencer J. 1995. "Theological (and Hence Economic) Implications of Adam Smith's 'Principles which Lead and Direct Philosophical Enquiries.'" *History of Political Economy* 27, no. 2 (Summer): 289–307.

Pokorný, Dušan. 1978. "Smith and Walras: Two Theories of Science." *Canadian Journal of Economics* 11, no. 3 (August): 387–403.

Puro, Edward. 1992. "Uses of the Term 'Natural' in Adam Smith's *Wealth of Nations.*" In *Research in the History of Economic Thought and Methodology* 9: 73–86. Edited by Warren J. Samuels. Greenwich, Conn.: Jai Press Inc.

Rae, John. 1834. "Of the *Wealth of Nations* as a Branch of the Philosophy of Induction." In *Statement of Some New Principles on the Subject of Political Economy, exposing the fallacies of the system of free trade, and of some other doctrines maintained in the "Wealth of Nations"*, ch. 15. Boston: Hilliard, Gray.

Raphael, D. D. 1985. *Adam Smith.* Oxford: Oxford University Press.

Rashid, Salim. 1992. "The *Wealth of Nations* and Historical Facts." *Journal of the History of Economic Thought* 14 (Fall): 225–43.

Rashid, Salim. 1982. "Adam Smith's Rise to Fame: A Re-examination of the Evidence." *Eighteenth Century* 23 (Winter): 64–85.

Recktenwald, Horst Claus. 1978. "An Adam Smith Renaissance *anno* 1976? The Bicentenary Output—A Reappraisal of His Scholarship." *Journal of Economic Literature* 16, no. 1 (March): 56–83. Reprinted in Mair 1990: 103–34.

Redman, Deborah A. 1993. "Adam Smith and Isaac Newton." *Scottish Journal of Political Economy* 40, no. 2 (May): 210–30.

Rothschild, Emma. 1994. "Adam Smith and the Invisible Hand." *American Economic Association Papers and Proceedings* 84, no. 2 (May): 319–22.

Rubin, Ernest. 1959. "Statistics and Adam Smith." *American Statistician* 13, no. 2 (April): 23–24.

Skinner, Andrew S. 1993. Letter to author, 15 April.

Skinner, Andrew S. 1990. "The Shaping of Political Economy in the Enlightenment." *Scottish Journal of Political Economy* 37, no. 2 (May): 145–65.

Skinner, Andrew S. 1987. "Smith, Adam." In *The New Palgrave: A Dictionary of Economics*, 4 vols. Edited by John Eatwell, Murray Milgate, and Peter Newman. London: Macmillan; N.Y.: Stockton Press; Tokyo: Maruzen.

Skinner, Andrew S. 1983. "Adam Smith's Rhetoric and the Communication of Ideas." In *Methodological Controversy in Economics: Historical Essays*, pp. 71–88. Edited by A. W. Coats. Greenwich, Conn.: Jai Press.

Skinner, Andrew S. 1979a. "Adam Smith: An Aspect of Modern Economics?" *Scottish Journal of Political Economy* 26, no. 2 (June): 109–26. Reprinted in Wood 1984, 1: 460–77.

Skinner, Andrew S. 1979b. *A System of Social Science: Papers Relating to Adam Smith.* Oxford: Clarendon Press.

Skinner, Andrew S. 1976. "Adam Smith: The Development of a System." *Scottish Journal of Political Economy* 23, no. 2 (June): 111–32.

Skinner, Andrew S. 1975. "Adam Smith: An Economic Interpretation of History." In Skinner and Wilson 1975: 155–78.

Skinner, Andrew S. 1974. "Adam Smith, Science and the Role of the Imagination." In *Hume and the Enlightenment*, pp. 164–88. Edited by William B. Todd. Edinburgh: Edinburgh University Press.

Skinner, Andrew S. 1972. "Adam Smith: Philosophy and Science." *Scottish Journal of Political Economy* 19: 307–19.

Skinner, Andrew S. 1965. "Economics and History—The Scottish Enlightenment." *Scottish Journal of Political Economy* 12 (February): 1–22.

Skinner, Andrew S., and Thomas Wilson. 1975. *Essays on Adam Smith.* Oxford: Clarendon Press.

Smith, Adam. 1976–1987. *Glasgow Edition of the Works and Correspondence of Adam Smith,* 6 vols. Oxford: Clarendon Press.

Smith, Adam. 1987. *The Correspondence of Adam Smith,* 2nd ed. Edited by Ernest Campbell Mossner and Ian Simpson Ross. *Glasgow Edition of the Works and Correspondence of Adam Smith,* vol. 6.

Smith, Adam. 1983. *Lectures on Rhetoric and Belles Lettres.* Edited by J. A. Bryce and A. S. Skinner. *Glasgow Edition of the Works and Correspondence of Adam Smith,* vol. 4.

Smith, Adam. 1980a. *Essays on Philosophical Subjects.* Edited by W. P. D. Wightman and J. C. Bryce with Dugald Stewart's Account of Adam Smith edited by I. S. Ross. *Glasgow Edition of the Works and Correspondence of Adam Smith,* vol. 3.

Smith, Adam. 1980b [1756]. "Letter to the Edinburgh Review." In Smith 1980a: 242–54.

Smith, Adam. 1980c. "The Principles Which Lead and Direct Philosophical Enquiries; Illustrated by the History of Astronomy." In Smith 1980a: 33–105.

Smith, Adam. 1978. *Lectures on Jurisprudence.* Edited by R. L. Meek, D. D. Raphael, and P. G. Stein. *Glasgow Edition of the Works and Correspondence of Adam Smith,* vol. 5.

Smith, Adam. 1976a [1776]. *An Inquiry into the Nature and Causes of the Wealth of Nations.* Edited by R. H. Campbell, A. S. Skinner, and W. B. Todd. *Glasgow Edition of the Works and Correspondence of Adam Smith,* vol. 2.

Smith, Adam. 1976b [1759]. *The Theory of Moral Sentiments.* Edited by D. D. Raphael and A. L. Macfie. *Glasgow Edition of the Works and Correspondence of Adam Smith.*

Spiegel, Henry W. 1976. "Adam Smith's Heavenly City." *History of Political Economy* 8, no. 4 (Winter): 478–93.

Stephen, Leslie. 1898. "Smith, Adam." In *Dictionary of National Biography.* Edited by Sidney Lee. London: Smith, Elder.

Stewart, Dugald. 1980 [1794]. "Account of the Life and Writings of Adam Smith, LL.D." In Smith 1980a: 269–351.

Taylor, Overton H. 1960. "Adam Smith's Philosophy of Science and Theory of Social Psychology and Ethics." In his *History of Economic Thought*, ch. 3. N.Y.: McGraw-Hill.

Taylor, Overton H. 1955a. "Economics and the Idea of 'Jus naturale.'" In his *Economics and Liberalism: Collected Papers,* pp. 70–99. Cambridge: Harvard.

Taylor, Overton H. 1955b. "Economics and the Idea of Natural Laws." In his *Economics and Liberalism: Collected Papers,* pp. 37–69. Cambridge: Harvard University Press.

Taylor, W. L. 1965. *Francis Hutcheson and David Hume as Precursors of Adam Smith.* Durham, N.C.: Duke University Press.

Thomson, Herbert F. 1965. "Adam Smith's Philosophy of Science." *Quarterly Journal of Economics* (February): 212–33. Reprinted in Wood 1984, 1: 323–41.

Viner, Jacob. 1968. "Smith, Adam." In *International Encyclopedia of the Social Sciences.* Reprinted in Wood 1984, 1: 111–25.

West, Edwin G. 1988. "Developments in the Literature on Adam Smith: An Evaluative Survey." In *Classical Political Economy: A Survey of Recent Literature.* William O. Thweatt, ed. pp. 13–44; commentary by Donald Winch, pp. 45–52. Boston: Kluwer.

Wightman, W. P. D. 1975. "Adam Smith and the History of Ideas." In Skinner and Wilson 1975: 44–67.

Wood, John Cunningham, ed. 1994. *Adam Smith: Critical Assessments,* 2nd series, vols. 5–7. London: Routledge.

Wood, John Cunningham, ed. 1984. *Adam Smith: Critical Assessments,* 4 vols. London: Croom Helm.

Worland, Stephen T. 1976. "Mechanistic Analogy and Smith on Exchange." *Review of Social Economy* 34, no. 4: 245–58.

Yanaihara, Tadao. 1951. *A Full and Detailed Catalogue of Books Which Belonged to Adam Smith.* Tokyo: Iwanami Shoten.

Young, Jeffrey T. 1990. "David Hume and Adam Smith on Value Premises in Economics." *History of Political Economy* 22, no. 4 (Winter): 643–57.

## IV. On the Methods of David Ricardo and Thomas Malthus

Arrow, Kenneth. 1991. "Ricardo's Work as Viewed by Later Economists." *Journal of the History of Economic Thought* 13, no. 1 (Spring): 70–77.

Ashley, W. J. 1891. "The Rehabilitation of Ricardo." *Economic Journal* 1 (September): 474–89. Reprinted in Wood 1985, 2: 8–20.

Ashley, W. J. 1962. "A Survey of the Past History and Present Position of Political Economy, Report of the British Association for the Advancement of Science." In *Essays in Economic Method: Selected Papers Read to Section F of the British Association for the Advancement of Science, 1860–1913*, pp. 223–46. Edited by R. L. Smyth with introduction by T. W. Hutchison. London: Gerald Duckworth. Reprinted from *Economic Journal* (December 1907): 467–89.

Ausubel, Herman. 1952. "William Cobbett and Malthusianism." *Journal of the History of Ideas* 13, no. 2 (April): 250–56.

Barucci, Piero, and Piero Roggi. 1981. "Malthus, economiste smithien antiricardien." *Rivista Internazionale di Scienze Economiche e Commerciale* 28, no. 4 (April): 378–90.

Bell, S. 1907. "Ricardo and Marx." *Journal of Political Economy* 15 (February): 112–17. Reprinted in Wood 1985, 4: 20–24.

Bergmann, Barbara R. 1987. "'Measurement' or Finding Things Out in Economics." *Journal of Economic Education* 18, no. 2 (Spring): 191–201.

Black, R. D. C. 1967. "Parson Malthus, the General and the Captain." *Economic Journal* 77 (March): 59–74. Reprinted in Wood 1986, 1: 244–59.

Blaug, Mark. 1985. "What Ricardo Said and What Ricardo Meant." In *The Legacy of Ricardo*. Edited by Giovanni A. Caravale, pp. 3–10. N.Y.: Basil Blackwell.

Blaug, Mark. 1968a. "Malthus, Thomas Robert." In *International Encyclopedia of the Social Sciences*.

Blaug, Mark. 1968b. "Ricardo, David." In *International Encyclopedia of the Social Sciences*.

Blaug, Mark. 1958. *Ricardian Economics: A Historical Study*. Yale Studies in Economics, no. 8. New Haven: Yale University Press.

Blaug, Mark. 1956. "The Empirical Content of Ricardian Economics." *Journal of Political Economy* 14, no. 1 (February): 41–58. Reprinted in Wood 1, 1985: 157–77.

Bonar, James. 1929. "Ricardo on Malthus." *Economic Journal* 39 (June): 210–18. Reprinted in Wood 1985, 1: 61–67.

Bonar, James. 1926. "Malthus, Thomas Robert." In *Palgrave's Dictionary of Political Economy*, new ed. Edited by Henry Higgs. London: Macmillan.

Bonar, James. 1911. "Where Ricardo Succeeded and Where He Failed." *American Economic Association Papers and Proceedings* 1 (April): 85–96. Reprinted in Wood 1985, 1: 52–60.

Bonar, James. 1885. *Malthus and His Work*. London: George Allen and Unwin.

Borchers, Hinrich. 1929. *Das Abstraktionsproblem bei David Ricardo*. Jena: Gustav Fischer.

Boulding, K. E. 1955. "The Malthusian Model as a General System." *Social and Economic Studies* 4 (September): 195–205. Reprinted in Wood 1986, 3: 57–67.

Cannan, E. 1894. "Ricardo in Parliament," Parts I-II. *Economic Journal* (June): 249–61 and (September): 409–23. Reprinted in Wood 1985, 1: 19–41.

Carlson, Mathieu J. 1994. "The Epistemological Status of Ricardo's Labor Theory." *History of Political Economy* 26, no. 4 (Winter): 629–47.

Checkland, S. G. 1952. "David Ricardo." *Economic History Review* 114, no. 3: 372–75. Reprinted in Wood 1985, 1: 68–71.

Chipman, J. S. 1984. "Balance of Payments Theory." In *Economic Analysis in Historical Perspective*, pp. 186–217. Edited by J. Creedy and D. P. O'Brien. London: Butterworths.

Corry, B. A. 1959. "Malthus and Keynes—A Reconsideration." *Economic Journal* 49 (December): 717–24. Reprinted in Wood 1986, 4: 75–83.

Cremaschi, Sergio, and Marcelo Dascal. 1993. "Malthus and Ricardo on Economic Methodology." Unpublished paper.

Darwin, Charles. [1936]. *The Origin of Species* and *The Descent of Man*. N.Y.: Modern Library.

Darwin, Charles, and Thomas Henry Huxley. 1974. *Autobiographies*. Edited by Gavin de Beer. London: Oxford University Press.

Daugherty, Marion R. 1942/1943. "The Currency-Banking Controversy," Parts 1 and 2. *Southern Economic Journal* 9, no. 1 (October 1942): 140–55; 9, no. 3 (January 1943): 241–51.

Davis, Kingsley. 1955. "Malthus and the Theory of Population." In *The Language of Social Research*, pp. 540–53. Edited by Paul F. Lazarsfeld and Morris Rosenberg. N.Y.: Free Press; London: Collier-Macmillan.

De Marchi, Neil. 1970. "The Empirical Content and Longevity of Ricardian Economics." *Economica* 37, no. 147 (August): 257–76. Reprinted in Wood 1985, 1: 217–34.

De Marchi, Neil, and R. P. Sturges. 1973. "Malthus and Ricardo's Inductivist Critics: Four Letters to William Whewell." *Economica* 40 (November): 379–93. Reprinted in Wood 1986, 4: 175–89.

De Vivo, G. 1987. "Ricardo, David." In *The New Palgrave: A Dictionary of Economics*, 4 vols. Edited by John Eatwell, Murray Milgate und Peter Newman. London: Macmillan; N.Y.: Stockton Press; Tokyo: Maruzen.

Diehl, Karl. 1929. "Ricardos »Notes on Malthus«." *Zeitschrift für die gesamte Staatswissenschaft* 87: 52–68.

Dorfman, Robert. 1989. "Thomas Robert Malthus and David Ricardo." *Journal of Economic Perspectives* 3, no. 3 (Summer): 153–64.

Dunbar, C. 1887. "Ricardo's Use of Facts." *Quarterly Journal of Economics* 1 (July): 474–76. Reprinted in Wood 1985, 1: 7–9.

*The Economist.* 1951. "The Scholar's Ricardo." (September 1): 502.

Empson, William. 1837. "Life, Writings, and Character of Mr. Malthus." *Edinburgh Review* 64 (January): 469–506.

Fetter, F. W. 1942. "The Bullion Report Reexamined." *Quarterly Journal of Economics* 56 (August): 655–65. Reprinted in *Papers in English Monetary History*, pp. 66–75. Edited by T. S. Ashton and R. S. Sayers. Oxford: Clarendon Press, 1953.

Fetter, F. W. 1969. "The Rise and Decline of Ricardian Economics." *History of Political Economy* 1, no. 1 (Spring): 67–84.

Flew, A. 1957. "The Structure of Malthus' Population Theory." *Australian Journal of Philosophy* 35 (May): 1–20. Reprinted in Wood 1986, 2: 91–106.

Foxwell, H. S. 1907. "A Letter of Malthus to Ricardo." *Economic Journal* 17 (June): 272–76. Reprinted in Wood 1986, 4: 10–13.

Gilbert, Geoffrey. 1980. "Economic Growth and the Poor in Malthus's *Essay on Population*." *History of Political Economy* 12, no. 1 (Spring): 83–96.

Gillman, J. M. 1956. "Ricardo's Development as an Economist." *Science and Society* 20, no. 3: 193–226. Reprinted in Wood 1985, 1: 132–56.

Godwin, William. 1820. *Of Population: An Enquiry concerning the Power of Increase in the Numbers of Mankind being an answer to Mr. Malthus's essay on that subject.* London: Longman, Hurst, Rees, Orme and Brown.

Gonner, E. C. K. 1890. "Ricardo and His Critics." *Quarterly Journal of Economics* 4 (April): 276–90. Reprinted in Wood 1985, 1: 10–18.

Grammp, William D. 1974. "Malthus and His Contemporaries." *History of Political Economy* 6, no. 3 (Fall): 278–304. Reprinted in Wood 1986, 1: 18–40.

Guthrie, W. G. 1984. "Selective Rediscovery of Economic Ideas: What Keynes Found in Malthus." *Southern Economic Journal* 50, no. 3 (January): 771–80. Reprinted in Wood 1986, 1: 437–49.

Hartwick, John M. 1988. "Robert Wallace and Malthus and the Ratios." *History of Political Economy* 20, no. 3 (Fall): 357–79.

Harvey-Phillips, M. B. 1984. "'Malthus' Theodicy: the Intellectual Background of His Contribution to Political Economy." *History of Political Economy* 16, no. 4 (Winter): 591–608.

Harvey-Phillips, M. B. 1983. "T. R. Malthus on the 'Metaphysics of Political Economy': Ricardo's Critical Ally." In *Methodological Controversy in Economics: Historical Essays in Honor of T. W. Hutchison*, pp. 185–210. Edited by A. W. Coats. Greenwich, Conn.: Jai Press.

Heertje, Arnold. 1991. "Three Unpublished Letters by David Ricardo." *History of Political Economy* 23, no. 3 (Fall): 519–26.

Heinsohn, Gunnar, and Otto Steiger. 1983. "The Rationale Underlying Malthus's Theory of Population." In *Malthus Past and Present*, pp. 223–32. Edited by J. Dupâquier, A. Fauve-Chamoux, and E. Grebenik. London: Academic Press.

Henderson, James P. 1990. "Induction, Deduction and the Role of Mathematics: The Whewell Group vs. the Ricardian Economists." In *Research in the History of Economic Thought and Methodology: A Research Annual*, 7: 1–36. Edited by Warren J. Samuels. Greenwich, Conn.: Jai Press.

Henderson, James P. 1985. "The Whewell Group of Mathematical Economists." *Manchester School* 53, no. 4 (December): 404–31.

Henderson, James P. 1983. "The Oral Tradition in British Economics: Influential Economists in the Political Economy Club of London." *History of Political Economy* 15, no. 2 (Summer): 149–79.

Hicks, J. R. 1967. "Monetary Theory and History—An Attempt at Perspective." In his *Critical Essays in Monetary Theory*, pp. 155–72. Oxford: Clarendon Press.

Hollander, J. H. 1911. "The Work and Influence of Ricardo." *American Economic Association Papers and Proceedings* 1 (April): 71–84. Reprinted in Wood 1985, 1: 42–51.

Hollander, Samuel. 1979. *The Economics of David Ricardo*. Toronto: University of Toronto Press.

Hollander, Samuel. 1977. "Smith and Ricardo: Aspects of the Nineteenth-Century Legacy." *American Economic Association Papers and Proceedings* 67, no. 1 (February): 37–41.

Hollander, Samuel. 1962. "Malthus and Keynes: A Note." *Economic Journal* 72 (June): 355–60. Reprinted in Wood 1986, 1: 217–22.

Hutchison, T. W. 1994. "On the Interpretation and Misinterpretation of Economic Literature: The Preposterous Case of David Ricardo." In his *Uses and Abuses of Economics: Contentious Essays on History and Method*, pp. 84–106. London: Routledge.

Hutchison, T. W. 1987. "James Mill and Ricardian Economics: A Methodological Revolution?" In his *On Revolutions and Progress in Economic Knowledge*, pp. 26–57. London: Cambridge University Press.

Hutchison, T. W. 1953. "Ricardo's Correspondence." *Economica* 20 N.S. (August): 263–73. Reprinted in Wood 1985, 1: 86–95.

Hutchison, T. W. 1952. "Some Questions about Ricardo." *Economica* 19 (November): 415–32. Reprinted in Wood 1985, 1: 72–85.

James, Patricia. 1979. *'Population' Malthus: His Life and Times*. London: Routledge and Kegan Paul.

James, Patricia, ed. 1966. *The Travel Diaries of Thomas Robert Malthus*. Cambridge: Cambridge University Press.

Jeffrey, Francis. 1825. "Political Economy." *Edinburgh Review* 18 (November): 1–23. [Fetter (1953: 252) attributes this article to Jeffrey.]

Johnson, L. E. 1993. "Professor Arrow's Ricardo." *Journal of the History of Economic Thought* 15, no. 1 (Spring): 54–71.

Kanth, Rajani. 1992. "Political Economy and Policy: The Malthus-Ricardo Embroilment." In his *Capitalism and Social Theory: The Science of Black Holes*, pp. 103–22. Armonk, N.Y.: M. E. Sharpe.

Kegel, Charles H. 1958. "William Cobbett and Malthusianism." *Journal of the History of Ideas* 19, no. 3 (June): 348–62.

Keynes, John Maynard. 1973. *The General Theory of Employment, Interest and Money. The Collected Writings of John Maynard Keynes*, vol. 7. London: Macmillan.

Keynes, John Maynard. 1972. "Thomas Robert Malthus." In his *Essays in Biography*, pp. 71–108. *The Collected Writings of John Maynard Keynes*, vol. 10. London: Macmillan.

Kishimoto, S. 1950. "Malthus's Theories in Classical Economics." *Kyoto Economic Review* 20, no. 1 (April): 1–37. Reprinted in Wood 1986, 1: 146–74.

Laidler, David. 1991. "The Quantity Theory Is Always and Everywhere Controversial—Why?" *Economic Record* 67 (December): 289–305.

Lambert, P. 1986. "Lauderdale, Malthus and Keynes." In Wood 1986, 1: 223–43.

Levin, Samuel M. 1966. "Malthus and the Idea of Progress." *Journal of the History of Ideas* 27, no. 1 (January-March): 92–108.

Levy, David. 1978. "Some Normative Aspects of the Malthusian Controversy." *History of Political Economy* 10, no. 2 (Summer): 271–85.

Lewinski, J. St. 1919. "Das System David Ricardos." *Zeitschrift für die gesamte Staatswissenschaft* 74: 223–43.

Lifschitz, F. 1907. "Zur Methode der Wirtschaftswissenschaft bei D. Ricardo." *Jahrbücher für Nationalökonomie und Statistik* 33: 314–24.

Lloyd, Peter J. 1969. "Elementary Geometric/Arithmetic Series and Early Production Series." *Journal of Political Economy* 77: 21–34.

Malthus, Thomas R. 1989a. *An Essay on the Principle of Population,* 2 vols. 1803 edition, with variora of 1806, 1807, 1817, and 1826. Edited by Patricia James. Cambridge: Cambridge University Press for the Royal Economic Society.

Malthus, Thomas R. 1989b. *Principles of Political Economy.* Variorum edition edited by John Pullen. Cambridge: Cambridge University Press.

Malthus, Thomas R. 1986. *The Works of Thomas Robert Malthus.* Edited by E. A. Wrigley and David Souden. London: William Pickering.

Malthus, Thomas R. 1986 [1798]. *An Essay on the Principle of Population,* ed. with introduction and bibliography. *Works,* vol 1.

Malthus, Thomas R. 1986. *An Essay on the Principle of Population,* 6th ed. (1826) with variora from 2nd edition (1803). *Works,* vols. 2–3.

Malthus, Thomas R. 1986. *Essays on Population. Works,* vol. 4.

Malthus, Thomas R. 1986. *Principles of Political Economy,* 2nd ed. (1836) with variant readings from the first edition (1820). *Works,* vols. 5–6.

Malthus, Thomas R. 1986. *Essays on Political Economy. Works,* vol. 7.

Malthus, Thomas R. 1986 [1827]. *Definitions in Political Economy. Works,* vol. 8.

Malthus, Thomas R. 1811. "Depreciation of Paper Currency." *Edinburgh Review* 17 (February): 339–72.

Marcuzzo, Maria Cristina, and Annalisa Rosselli. 1991. *Ricardo and the Gold Standard: The Foundations of the International Monetary Order.* Transl. from the Italian by Joan Hall. Houndmills: Macmillan.

Mason, E. S. 1928. "Ricardo's Notes on Malthus." *Quarterly Journal of Economics* 42 (August): 684–96.

Meek, Ronald L., ed. 1953. *Marx and Engels on Malthus: Selections from the Writings of Marx and Engels Dealing with the Theories of Thomas Robert Malthus.* London: Lawrence and Wishart.

Mill, John Stuart. 1967 [1825]. "The Quarterly Review on Political Economy." In his *Essays on Economics and Society,* pp. 23–43. *Collected Works of John Stuart Mill,* vol. 4. London: Routledge & Kegan Paul; Toronto: University of Toronto Press, pp. 23–43. Reprinted from *Westminster Review* 3, no. 5 (January 1825): 213–32.

Mitchell, Wesley. 1950 [1939]. "Postulates and Preconceptions of Ricardian Economics." In his *Backward Art of Spending Money and Other Essays,* pp. 203–24. N.Y.: Augustus M. Kelly.

Moss, Laurence S. 1979. "Professor Hollander and Ricardian Economics." *Eastern Economic Journal* 5 (December): 501–12.

O'Brien, D. P. 1981. "Ricardian Economics and the Economics of David Ricardo." *Oxford Economic Papers,* n. s. 33, no. 3 (November): 352–86.

O'Driscoll, Gerald P. 1977. "The Ricardian Nonequivalence Theorem." *Journal of Political Economy* 85, no. 1 (February): 207–10.

O'Leary, James J. 1940. "Malthus and Keynes." *Journal of Political Economy* 50: 901–19. Reprinted in Wood 1986, 1: 90–104.

Paglin, Morton. 1961. *Malthus and Lauderdale: The Anti-Ricardian Tradition.* N.Y.: Augustus M. Kelley.

Pancoast, Omar. 1943. "Malthus Versus Ricardo: The Effects of Distribution on Production." *Political Science Quarterly* 58, no. 1 (March): 47–66.

Patten, S. N. 1893. "The Interpretation of Ricardo." *Quarterly Journal of Economics* 7 (April): 322–52. Reprinted in Wood 1985, 3: 15–33.

Patten, S. N. 1889. "Malthus and Ricardo." *American Economic Association Papers and Proceedings* 4, no. 5: 9–33.

Peach, Terry. 1993. *Interpreting Ricardo.* Cambridge: Cambridge University Press.

Peach, Terry. 1988. "David Ricardo: A Review of Some Interpretative Issues." In *Classical Political Economy: A Survey of Recent Literature,* William O. Thweatt, ed., pp. 103–31; commentary by Mark Blaug: 132–36. Boston: Kluwer.

Perlman, Morris. 1986. "The Bullionist Controversy Revisited." *Journal of Political Economy* 94, no. 4 (August): 745–62.

Pullen, John M. 1987a. "Lord Grenville's Manuscript Notes on Malthus." *History of Political Economy* 19, no. 2 (Summer): 217–37.

Pullen, John M. 1987b. "Malthus, Thomas Robert." In *The New Palgrave: A Dictionary of Economics*, 4 vols. Edited by John Eatwell, Murray Milgate, and Peter Newman. London: Macmillan; N.Y.: Stockton Press; and Tokyo: Maruzen.

Pullen, John M. 1987c. "Some New Information on the Rev. T. R. Malthus." *History of Political Economy* 19, no. 1 (Spring): 127–39.

Pullen, John M. 1986. "Correspondence Between Malthus and His Parents." *History of Political Economy* 18, no. 1 (Spring): 133–54.

Pullen, John M. 1982. "Malthus on the Doctrine of Proportions and the Concept of the Optimum." *Australian Economic Papers* 21, no. 39 (December): 270–85. Reprinted in Wood 1986, 1: 419–36.

Pullen, John M. 1981a. "Malthus' Theological Ideas and Their Influence on His Principle of Population." *History of Political Economy* 13, no. 1 (Spring): 39–54.

Pullen, John M. 1981b. "Notes from Malthus: The Inverarity Manuscript." *History of Political Economy* 13, no. 4 (Winter): 794–811. Reprinted in Wood 1986, 4: 290–305.

Ramana, D. V. 1957. "Ricardo's Environment." *Indian Journal of Economics* 38, no. 149 (October): 151–64. Reprinted in Wood 1985, 1: 196–208.

Rashid, Salim. 1988. "Recent Literature on Malthus." In *Classical Political Economy: A Survey of Recent Literature*. William O. Thweatt, ed., pp. 53–84; commentary by J. M. Pullen, pp. 85–101. Boston: Kluwer.

Rashid, Salim. 1987a. "Malthus and Classical Economics." In *The New Palgrave: A Dictionary of Economics*, 4 vols. Edited by John Eatwell, Murray Milgate, and Peter Newman. London: Macmillan; N.Y.: Stockton Press; and Tokyo: Maruzen.

Rashid, Salim. 1987b. "Malthus's *Essay on Population:* The Facts of 'Super-Growth' and the Rhetoric of Scientific Persuasion." *Journal of the History of the Behavioral Sciences* 23, no. 1 (January): 22–36.

Rashid, Salim. 1981. "Malthus' *Principles* and British Economic Thought, 1820–1835." *History of Political Economy* 13, no. 1 (Spring): 55–79.

Reich, M. 1980. "Empirical and Ideological Elements in the Decline of Ricardian Economics." *Review of Radical Political Economics* 12, no. 3 (Fall): 1–14. Reprinted in Wood 1985, 3: 650–71.

Ricardo, David. 1951–1973. *The Works and Correspondence of David Ricardo*, 11 vols. Edited by Piero Sraffa, with M. H. Dobb. Cambridge: Cambridge University Press for the Royal Economic Society.

Ricardo, David. 1953 [1899]. *On the Principles of Political Economy and Taxation*, 3rd ed. *Works*, vol. 1.

Ricardo, David. 1951 [written 1820; first published 1928]. *Notes on Malthus's Principles of Political Economy*. *Works*, vol. 2.

Ricardo, David. 1928. *Notes on Malthus's "Principles of Political Economy"*. Edited and with an introduction and notes by Jacob H. Hollander and T. E. Gregory. Baltimore: Johns Hopkins University Press; London: Oxford University Press.

Robbins, Lionel. 1967. "Malthus as an Economist." *Economic Journal* 77 (June): 257–61. Reprinted in Wood 1986, 1: 260–65.

Robertson, H. M. 1942. "Reflexions on Malthus and His Predecessors." *South African Journal of Economics* 10 (December): 295–306.

Robertson, H. M. 1957. "The Ricardo Problem." *South African Journal of Economics* 25 (September): 171–86. Reprinted in Wood 1985, 1: 180–95.

Robinson, Joan. 1978. "Keynes and Ricardo." *Journal of Post Keynesian Economics* 1, no. 1 (Fall): 12–18. Reprinted in Wood 1985, 4: 146–51.

Rogers, J. D., and E. C. K. Gonner. 1926. "Ricardo, David." In *Palgrave's Dictionary of Political Economy,* new ed. Edited by Henry Higgs. London: Macmillan.

Roncaglia, A. 1982. "Hollander's Ricardo." *Journal of Post Keynesian Economics* 4, no. 3 (Spring): 339–59. Reprinted in Wood 1985, 4: 174–90.

Roy, H. N. 1978. "Towards a Reappraisal of Malthus as an Analyst—An Overrated or an Underrated Economist?" *Indian Economic Journal* 26, no. 1 (July-September): 128–56. Reprinted in Wood 1986, 2: 156–69.

Rubin, Ernest. 1960. "The Quantitative Data and Methods of the Rev. T. R. Malthus." *American Statistician* 14, no. 1 (February): 28–31.

St. Clair, Oswald. 1957. *A Key to Ricardo.* London: Routledge.

St. Clair, Oswald. 1953. "David Ricardo: A Review Article." *South African Journal of Economics* 21 (September): 251–60. Reprinted in Wood 1985, 1: 96–105.

Sayers, R. S. 1953. "Ricardo's Views on Monetary Questions." *Quarterly Journal of Economics* 67 (February): 30–49. Reprinted in Wood 1985, 4: 53–68; and in *Papers in English Monetary History,* pp. 76–95, edited by T. S. Ashton and R. S. Sayers. Oxford: Clarendon Press, 1953.

Schmidt, Christian. 1983. "Malthus et la sémantique économique." *Revue d'économie politique* 93, no. 2 (1983): 248–69.

Semmel, Bernard. 1965. "Malthus: 'Physiocracy' and the Commercial System." *Economic History Review,* 2nd ser. 17, no. 3 (April): 522–35. Reprinted in Wood 1986, 4: 115–29.

Simons, Richard B. 1955. "T. R. Malthus on British Society." *Journal of the History of Ideas* 16, no. 1 (January): 60–75.

Spengler, J. J. 1966. "Was Malthus Right?" *Southern Economic Journal* 33, no. 1: 17–34. Reprinted in Wood 1986, 3: 142–63.

Spengler, J. J. 1945. "Malthus's Total Population Theory: A Restatement and Reappraisal." *Canadian Journal of Economics and Political Science* 11: 83–110; 234–64. Reprinted in Wood 1986, 2: 30–90.

Stapleton, Barry. 1983. "Malthus: The Local Evidence and the Principle of Population." In *Malthus Past and Present,* pp. 45–59. Edited by J. Dupâquier, A. Fauve-Chamoux, and E. Grebenik. London: Academic Press.

Starbatty, Joachim. 1992. "Theorie ohne Geschichte? Zur Rolle der Vergangenheit in der Nationalökonomie." *Saeculum: Jahrbuch für Universalgeschichte* 43, no. 1: 78–94.

Stephen, Leslie. 1896. "Ricardo, David." In *Dictionary of National Biography*. Edited by Sidney Lee. London: Smith, Elder.

Stephen, Leslie. 1893. "Malthus, Thomas Robert." In *Dictionary of National Biography*. Edited by Sidney Lee. London: Smith, Elder.

Stigler, G. J. 1981. "Review of Hollander's *Economics of David Ricardo*." *Journal of Economic Literature* 19, no. 1 (March): 100–2.

Stigler, G. J. 1953. "Sraffa's Ricardo." *American Economic Review* 43 (September): 586–99. Reprinted in Wood 1985, 1: 106–19.

Sumner, John Bird. 1817. "Malthus on Population." *Quarterly Review* 17 (July): 369–403.

Viner, Jacob. 1937. *Studies in the Theory of International Trade*. N.Y.: Harper & Brothers Publishers.

Vorzimmer, Peter. 1969. "Darwin, Malthus, and the Theory of Natural Selection." *Journal of the History of Ideas* 30, no. 4 (October-December): 527–42.

Waterman, A. M. C. 1991a. "A Cambridge 'Via Media' in Late Georgian Anglicanism." *Journal of Ecclesiastical History* 42, no. 3 (July): 419–36.

Waterman, A. M. C. 1991b. *Revolution, Economics and Religion: Christian Political Economy, 1798–1833*. Cambridge: Cambridge University Press.

Weir, D. R. 1987. "Malthus's Theory of Population." In *The New Palgrave: A Dictionary of Economics*, 4 vols. Edited by John Eatwell, Murray Milgate, and Peter Newman. London: Macmillan; N.Y.: Stockton Press; and Tokyo: Maruzen.

Whewell, William. 1859. "Prefatory Notice." In *Literary Remains, Consisting of Lectures and Tracts on Political Economy, of the Late Rev. Richard Jones*, pp. ix-xl. Edited by William Whewell. London: John Murray.

Winch, Donald. 1987. *Malthus*. Oxford: Oxford University Press.

Wood, John Cunningham, ed. 1994. *David Ricardo: Critical Assessments*, 2nd ser., vols. 5–7. London: Routledge.

Wood, John Cunningham, ed. 1986. *Thomas Robert Malthus: Critical Assessments*, 4 vols. London: Croom Helm.

Wood, John Cunningham, ed. 1985. *David Ricardo: Critical Assessments*, 4 vols. London: Croom Helm.

Wrigley, A. E. 1986. "Elegance and Experience: Malthus at the Bar of History." In *The State of Population Theory Forward from Malthus*, pp. 46–64. Edited by David Coleman und Roger Scholfield. Oxford: Basil Blackwell.

Würgler, Hans. 1957. *Malthus als Kritiker der Klassik*. Ein Beitrag zur Geschichte der klassischen Wirtschaftstheorie. Winturthur: Verlag P. G. Keller.

Zinke, G. W. 1942. "Six Letters from Malthus to Pierre Prévost." *Journal of Economic History* 21 (November): 174–89. Reprinted in Wood 1986, 4: 43–58.

## V. On the Methodology of John Stuart Mill

Adams, James Eli. 1992. "Philosophical Forgetfulness: John Stuart Mill's 'Nature.'" *Journal of the History of Ideas* 53, no. 3 (July-September): 437–54.

Annan, Noel. 1968. "John Stuart Mill." In Schneewind 1968: 22–45.

Anschutz, R. P. 1968. "The Logic of J. S. Mill." In Schneewind 1968: 46–83.

Anschutz, R. P. 1963 [1953]. *The Philosophy of J. S. Mill.* Oxford: Clarendon Press.

Bain, Alexander. 1882. *John Stuart Mill. A Criticism: with Personal Recollections.* London: Longmans, Green.

Balassa, Bela A. 1959. "John Stuart Mill and the Law of Markets." *Quarterly Journal of Economics* 73, no. 2 (May): 263–74.

Blake, Ralph M., Curt J. Ducasse, and Edward H. Madden. 1960. "John Stuart Mill's System of Logic." In *Theories of Scientific Method: The Renaissance Through the Nineteenth Century,* pp. 218–32. Seattle: University of Washington Press.

Blaug, Mark. 1956. "The Empirical Content of Ricardian Economics." *Journal of Political Economy* 64, no. 1 (February): 41–58. Reprinted in Wood 1985, 1: 157–77.

Bonar, J. 1911. "The Economics of John Stuart Mill." *Journal of Political Economy* 19 (November): 717–25. Reprinted in Wood 1987, 1: 22–28.

Britton, Karl. 1969. *John Stuart Mill,* 2nd ed. N.Y.: Dover.

Buchdahl, Gerd. 1971. "Inductivist Versus Deductivist Approaches in the Philosophy of Science as Illustrated by Some Controversies Between Whewell and Mill." *The Monist* 55 (July): 343–67.

Burns, J. H. 1976. "The Light of Reason: Philosophical History in the Two Mills." In *James and John Stuart Mill/Papers of the Centenary Conference,* pp. 3–20. Edited by John M. Robson and Michael Laine. Toronto: University of Toronto Press.

Burns, J. H. 1959. "J. S. Mill and the Term 'Social Science.'" *Journal of the History of Ideas* 20, no. 3 (June-September): 431–32.

Cartwright, Nancy. 1989. *Nature's Capacities and Their Measurement.* Oxford: Clarendon Press.

Castell, Alburey. 1936. "Mill's Logic of the Moral Sciences: A Study of the Impact of Newtonism on Early Nineteenth Century Social Thought." Ph.D. Dissertation, University of Chicago, 1931.

Collini, Stefan, Donald Winch, and John Burrows, eds. 1983. "The Tendencies of Things: John Stuart Mill and the Philosophical Method." In *That Noble Science of Politics: A Study in Nineteenth-Century Intellectual History,* pp. 126–59. Cambridge: Cambridge University Press.

Corsi, Pietro. 1987. "The Heritage of Dugald Stewart: Oxford Philosophy and the Method of Political Economy." *Nuncius* 2, no. 2: 89–144.

Courtney, W. L. 1879. *The Metaphysics of John Stuart Mill.* London: C. Kegan Paul.

Day, J. P. 1964. "John Stuart Mill." In *A Critical History of Western Philosophy,* pp. 339–64. Edited by D. J. O'Connor. N.Y.: Free Press.

De Marchi, Neil. 1988. "John Stuart Mill Interpretation Since Schumpeter." In *Classical Political Economy: A Survey of Recent Literature,* William O. Thweatt, ed., pp. 137–62; commentary by Samuel Hollander, pp. 163–77. Boston: Kluwer.

De Marchi, Neil. 1983. "The Case for James Mill." In *Methodological Controversy in Economics: Historical Essays in Honor of T. W. Hutchison,* pp. 155–84. Edited by A. W. Coats. Greenwich, Conn.: Jai Press.

De Marchi, Neil. 1972. "Mill and Cairnes and the Emergence of Marginalism in England." *History of Political Economy* 4, no. 2 (Summer): 344–63.

De Marchi, Neil. 1970. "The Empirical Content and Longevity of Ricardian Economics." *Economica* 37, no. 147 (August): 257–76. Reprinted in Wood 1985, 1: 217–34.

Douglas, Charles, ed. 1973 [1897]. *The Ethics of John Stuart Mill.* Edinburgh: William Blackwood and Sons.

Douglas, Charles, ed. 1973 [1895]. *J. S. Mill, A Study of His Philosophy.* Edinburgh: William Blackwood and Sons; Folcraft Library Editions reprint, 1973.

Duncan, Graem. 1973. *Marx and Mill: Two Views of Social Conflict and Social Harmony.* Cambridge: Cambridge University Press.

Edgeworth, F. Y. 1896. "Mill, John Stuart." In *Dictionary of Political Economy.* Edited by R. H. Inglis. London: Macmillan.

Ekelund, R. B., and E. S. Olsen. 1973. "Comte, Mill and Cairnes: The Positivist-Empiricist Interlude in Late Classical Economics." *Journal of Economic Issues* 7, no. 3 (September): 387–416. Reprinted in Wood 1987, 1: 443–69.

Fletcher, Ronald, ed. 1971. *John Stuart Mill: A Logical Critique of Sociology.* London: Thomas Nelson and Sons.

Forbes, Duncan. 1951. "James Mill and India." *Cambridge Journal* 5 (October): 19–53.

Hargreaves-Heap, and Martin Hollis. 1987. "Economic Man." In *The New Palgrave: A Dictionary of Economics,* 4 vols. Edited by John Eatwell, Murray Milgate, and Peter Newman. London: Macmillan; N.Y.: Stockton Press; Tokyo: Maruzen.

Hausman, Daniel. 1992. *The Inexact and Separate Science of Economics.* Cambridge: Cambridge University Press.

Hausman, Daniel. 1981. "John Stuart Mill's Philosophy of Economics." *Philosophy of Science* 48, no. 3 (September): 363–85.

Hirsch, Abraham. 1992. "John Stuart Mill on Verification and the Business of Science." *History of Political Economy* 24, no. 4 (Winter): 843–66.

Hollander, Jacob H. 1916. "Economic Theorizing and Scientific Progress." *American Economic Association Papers and Proceedings* 6 (March): 124–39.

Hollander, Samuel. 1987. "Mill, John Stuart, as Economic Theorist." In *The New Palgrave: A Dictionary of Economics*, 4 vols. Edited by John Eatwell, Murray Milgate, and Peter Newman. London: Macmillan; N.Y.: Stockton Press; Tokyo: Maruzen.

Hollander, Samuel. 1985. *The Economics of John Stuart Mill*, vol. 1. Toronto: University of Toronto Press.

Hollander, Samuel. 1983. "William Whewell and John Stuart Mill on the Methodology of Political Economy." *Studies in History and Philosophy of Science* 14, no. 2 (June): 127–68. Reprinted in Wood 1987, 1: 567–608.

Hutchison, T. W. 1952. "Review: Mill's Essays on Some Unsettled Questions of Political Economy." *Economica* 19 (February): 78–81.

Jackson, Reginald. 1968. "Mill's Treatment of Geometry—A Reply to Jevons." In Schneewind 1968: 84–110.

Jackson, Reginald. 1937/1938. "Mill's Joint Method," parts 1 and 2. *Mind* 46, no. 184 (October 1937): 417–36; 47, no. 185 (January 1938): 1–17.

Jacobs, Struan. 1991. "John Stuart Mill on Induction and Hypotheses." *Journal of the History of Philosophy* 29: 69–83.

Jones, H. S. 1992. "John Stuart Mill as Moralist." *Journal of the History of Ideas* 53, no. 2 (April-June): 287–308.

Kubitz, Oskar Alfred. 1932. *Development of John Stuart Mill's System of Logic*. In *Illinois Studies in the Social Sciences* 18, nos. 1–2: 1–310.

Laine, Michael. 1982. *Bibliography of Works on John Stuart Mill*. Toronto: University of Toronto Press.

Leary, David E. 1982. "The Fate and Influence of John Stuart Mill's Proposed Science of Ethology." *Journal of the History of Ideas* 43, no. 1 (January-March): 153–62.

Lewisohn, D. 1972. "Mill and Comte on the Methods of Science." *Journal of the History of Ideas* 33 (April-June): 315–24. Reprinted in Wood 1987, 4: 267–77.

Losee, John. 1983. "Whewell and Mill on the Relation Between Philosophy of Science and History of Science." *Studies in History and Philosophy of Science* 14, no. 2 (June): 113–26.

Mawatari, Shohken. 1982/1983. "J. S. Mill's Methodology of Political Economy," parts 1–4. In *Keizai Gaku*, Annual Report of the Economics Society, Tokyo University 44, no. 2 (October 1992): 125–43; 44, no. 3 (December 1982): 249–69; 45, no. 1 (June 1983): 33–54; 45, no. 2 (August 1983): 165–83.

McCosh, James. 1866. *An Examination of Mr. J. S. Mill's Philosophy, Being a Defence of Fundamental Truth*. London: Macmillan.

Mill, James. 1966. "Whether Political Economy Is Useful." In *James Mill: Selected Economic Writings*, pp. 371–82. Chicago: University of Chicago Press.

Mill, John Stuart. 1960–1991. *Collected Works of John Stuart Mill*. Toronto: University of Toronto Press; London: Routledge and Kegan Paul.

Mill, John Stuart. 1981. *Autobiography and Literary Essays*. Edited by John M. Robson and Jack Stillinger. *Collected Works*, vol. 1.

Mill, John Stuart. 1965 [1871]. *Principles of Political Economy with Some of Their Applications to Social Philosophy*, 7th ed. Edited by J. M. Robson. *Collected Works*, vols. 2–3.

Mill, John Stuart. 1967. *Essays on Economics and Society*. Edited by J. M. Robson. *Collected Works*, vols. 4–5.

Mill, John Stuart. 1965 [1843]. *A System of Logic Ratiocinative and Inductive Being a Connected View of the Principles of Evidence and the Methods of Scientific Investigation*. Edited by J. M. Robson and R. F. McRae. *Collected Works*, vol. 8.

Mill, John Stuart. 1979. *An Examination of Sir William Hamilton's Philosophy and of the Principal Philosophical Questions Discussed in His Writings*. Edited by J. M. Robson and Alan Ryan. *Collected Works*, vol. 9.

Mill, John Stuart. 1969. *Essays on Ethics, Religion and Society*. Edited by J. M. Robson. *Collected Works*, vol. 10.

Mill, John Stuart. 1963. *The Earlier Letters of John Stuart Mill, 1812–1848.* Edited by Francis E. Mineka. *Collected Works*, vols. 12–13.

Mill, John Stuart. 1972. *The Latter Letters of John Stuart Mill 1849–1873*. Edited by Francis E. Mineka and Dwight N. Lindley. *Collected Works*, vols. 14–17.

Mill, John Stuart. 1984. *Essays on Equality, Law, and Education*. Edited by John M. Robson. *Collected Works*, vol. 21.

Mill, John Stuart. 1986. *Newspaper Writings by John Stuart Mill*, December 1822-July 1831. Edited by Ann P. Robson and John M. Robson. *Collected Works*, vol. 22.

Mill, John Stuart. 1988. *Journals and Debating Speeches by John Stuart Mill*. Edited by John M. Robson. *Collected Works*, vol. 26.

Mill, John Stuart. 1987. *The Logic of the Moral Sciences*, with introduction by A. J. Ayer. La Salle, Ill.: Open Court; London: Duckworth, 1986.

Mill, John Stuart. 1909. *Principles of Political Economy*, 7th ed. Edited by W. J. Ashley. N.Y.: Longman, Green.

Mueller, Iris Wessel. 1956. *John Stuart Mill and French Thought*. Urbana: University of Illinois Press.

Nagel, Ernest, ed. 1950. *John Stuart Mill's Philosophy of Scientific Method*. N.Y.: Hafner Publishing.

Oakley, Allen. 1994. *Classical Economic Man*. Aldershot, Hants: Edward Elgar.

O'Brien, G. 1943. "J. S. Mill and J. E. Cairnes." *Economica* 10 (November): 273–85. Reprinted in Wood 1987, 1: 104–23.

Passmore, John. 1957. "John Stuart Mill and British Empiricism." In his *Hundred Years of Philosophy*, pp. 11–32. London: Gerald Duckworth.

Randall, J. H. 1965. "John Stuart Mill and the Working Out of Empiricism." *Journal of the History of Ideas* 26 (January-March): 59–88. Reprinted in Wood 1987, 1: 252–81.

Rashid, Salim. 1987. "Political Economy as Moral Philosophy: Dugald Stewart of Edinburgh." *Australian Economic Papers* 26, no. 48 (June): 145–56. Reprinted in *Pioneers in Economics*, vol. 7, pp. 108–119. Edited by Mark Blaug. Aldershot, Hants: Edward Elgar.

Rees, John C., und V. W. Bladen. 1968. "Mill, John Stuart." In *International Encyclopedia of the Social Sciences.*

Reichel, Hans. 1903/1904. "Darstellung und Kritik von J. St. Mills Theorie der induktiven Methode," parts 1–3. *Zeitschrift für Philosophie und philosophische Kritik* 122, Heft 2 (1903): 176–97; 123, Heft 1 (1904): 33–46; 123, Heft 2 (1904): 121–51.

Robbins, Lionel. 1970. *The Evolution of Modern Economic Theory and Other Papers on the History of Economic Thought.* London: Macmillan.

Robbins, Lionel. 1967. "Introduction to Mill's *Essays on Economics and Society.*" In *Mill's Collected Works,* vol. 4. Toronto: University of Toronto Press. Reprinted in Robbins 1970: 118–63.

Robbins, Lionel. 1966. "Mill's *Principles of Political Economy.*" *Economica* 33 (February): 92–94. Reprinted in Robbins 1970: 164–68.

Robbins, Lionel. 1954. "Packe on Mill." *Economica* 24 (August): 250–59. Reprinted in Robbins 1970: 97–117, as "The Life of John Stuart Mill."

Russell, Bertrand. 1968 [1951]. "John Stuart Mill." In Schneewind 1968: 1–21.

Ryan, Alan. 1987. "Mill, John Stuart." In *The New Palgrave: A Dictionary of Economics,* 4 vols. Edited by John Eatwell, Murray Milgate, and Peter Newman. London: Macmillan; N.Y.: Stockton Press: Tokyo: Maruzen.

Ryan, Alan. 1974. *J. S. Mill.* London: Routledge and Kegan Paul.

Schabas, Margaret. 1990. *A World Ruled by Number: William Stanley Jevons and the Rise of Mathematical Economics.* Princeton: Princeton University Press.

Schneewind, J. B., ed. 1968. *A Collection of Critical Essays.* Notre Dame, Ind.: University of Notre Dame Press.

Schwartz, Pedro. 1972. *The New Political Economy of J. S. Mill.* Translated from Spanish edition, 1968. London: Weidenfeld and Nicolson.

Semmel, Bernard. 1984. *John Stuart Mill and the Pursuit of Virtue.* New Haven: Yale University Press.

Skorupski, John. 1989. *John Stuart Mill.* London: Routledge.

Stephen, Leslie. 1894. "Mill, John Stuart." In *Dictionary of National Biography.* Edited by Sidney Lee. London: Smith, Elder.

Strong, E. W. 1955. "William Whewell and John Stuart Mill: Their Controversy about Scientific Knowledge." *Journal of the History of Ideas* 16 (April): 209–31. Reprinted in Wood 1987, 1: 182–202.

Thomas, William. 1985. *Mill.* Oxford: Oxford University Press.

Walsh, Harold T. 1962. "Whewell and Mill on Induction." *Philosophy of Science* 29, no. 3 (July): 279–84.

Whitaker, J. K. 1975. "John Stuart Mill's Methodology." *Journal of Political Economy* 83, no. 5 (October): 1033–49. Reprinted in Wood 1987, 1: 479–94.

Whitmore, Charles E. 1945. "Mill and Mathematics: An Historical Note." *Journal of the History of Ideas* 6, no. 1 (January): 109–112.

Wilson, Fred. 1991. "Mill and Comte on the Method of Introspection." *Journal of the History of the Behavioural Sciences* 27, no. 2 (April): 107–29.

Winch, Donald. 1987. "Mill, James." In *The New Palgrave: A Dictionary of Economics*, 4 vols. Edited by John Eatwell, Murray Milgate, and Peter Newman. London: Macmillan; N.Y.: Stockton; Tokyo: Maruzen.

Winch, Peter. 1958. *The Idea of a Social Science and Its Relation to Philosophy.* London: Routledge and Kegan Paul; N.Y.: Humanities Press.

Wood, John Cunningham, ed. 1987. *John Stuart Mill: Critical Assessments,* 4 vols. London: Croom Helm.

Wood, John Cunningham, ed. 1985. *David Ricardo: Critical Assessments,* 4 vols. London: Croom Helm.

# Sources Cited

Anonymous. 1824. "Mill's *Elements of Political Economy.*" *Westminster Review* 2 (October): 289–310.

Anschutz, R. P. 1968. "The Logic of J. S. Mill." In Schneewind 1968: 46–83.

Arnold, N. Scott. 1983. "Hume's Scepticism about Inductive Inference." *Journal of the History of Philosophy* 21: 31–55.

Arrow, Kenneth. 1991. "Ricardo's Work as Viewed by Later Economists." *Journal of the History of Economic Thought* 13, no. 1 (Spring): 70–77.

Ashcraft, Richard, ed. 1991. *John Locke: Critical Assessments,* vol. 4. London: Routledge.

Ashley, Myron Lucius. 1903. "The Nature of Hypothesis." In *Studies in Logical Theory,* ed. John Dewey, pp. 143–83. Chicago: University of Chicago Press.

Axtell, James L. 1965. "Locke, Newton, and the Elements of Natural Philosophy." *Pædagogica Europæa* 1: 235–45.

Ayer, A. J. 1980. *Hume.* Oxford: Oxford University Press.

Bacon, Francis. 1858. *The Great Instauration* and *The New Organon. The Works of Francis Bacon,* vol. 4, eds. James Spedding, Robert Leslie Ellis, and Douglas Denon Heath. London: Longman.

Bacon, Francis. 1857. *Philosophical Works,* parts 2 and 3. *The Works of Francis Bacon,* vol. 3, eds. James Spedding, Robert Leslie Ellis, and Douglas Denon Heath. London: Longman.

Bagehot, Walter. 1891. *The Works of Walter Bagehot,* 5 vols, ed. Forrest Morgan. Hartford, Conn.: Travelers Insurance.

Bagehot, Walter. 1880. *Economic Studies,* ed. Richard Holt Hutton. London: Longmans, Green.

Bailey, Samuel. 1967. "Observations on Certain Verbal Disputes in Political Economy." In his *Critical Dissertation on the Nature, Measure and Causes of Value.* Reprint of 5 pamphlets first published 1821–1826. N.Y.: Augustus M. Kelley.

Balassa, Bela A. 1959. "John Stuart Mill and the Law of Markets." *Quarterly Journal of Economics* 73, no. 2 (May): 263–74.

Barfoot, Michael. 1990. "Hume and the Culture of Science in the Early Eighteenth Century." In *Studies in the Philosophy of the Scottish Enlightenment*, ed. M. A. Stewart, pp. 151–90. Oxford: Clarendon Press.

Barucci, Piero, and Piero Roggi. 1981. "Malthus, economiste smithien antiricardien." *Rivista Internazionale di Scienze Economiche e Commerciale* 28, no. 4 (April): 378–90.

Becker, James F. 1961. "Adam Smith's Theory of Social Science." *Southern Economic Journal* 28, no. 1 (July): 13–21. Reprinted in J. Wood 1984, 1: 310–22.

Bergmann, Barbara R. 1987. "'Measurement' or Finding Things Out in Economics." *Journal of Economic Education* 18, no. 2 (Spring): 191–201.

Berry, Christopher J. 1974. "Adam Smith's *Considerations on Language*." *Journal of the History of Ideas* 35, no. 1 (January-March): 130–38.

Bevan, Wilson Lloyd. 1894. *Sir William Petty: A Study in English Literature.* Publications of the American Economic Association, vol. 9, no. 4.

Bevilacqua, Vincent M. 1965. "Adam Smith's Lectures on Rhetoric and Belles Lettres." *Studies in Scottish Literature* 3: 41–60.

Bittermann, Henry. 1940. "Adam Smith's Empiricism and the Law of Nature," parts 1 and 2. *Journal of Political Economy* 48 (August): 487–520; 48 (October): 703–34. Reprinted in J. Wood 1984, 1: 190–235.

Black, R. D. C. 1967. "Parson Malthus, the General and the Captain." *Economic Journal* 77 (March): 59–74. Reprinted in J. Wood 1986, 1: 244–59.

Black, Robert. 1963. "A Comparison of Classical English Economic Thought with Newtonian Natural Philosophy." Ph.D. dissertation, University of California, Berkeley.

Blackwell, Richard J. 1974. "The Inductivist Model of Science: A Study in Nineteenth-Century Philosophy of Science." *The Modern Schoolman* 51 (March): 197–212.

Blake, Ralph M., Curt J. Ducasse, and Edward H. Madden. 1960. *Theories of Scientific Method: The Renaissance Through the Nineteenth Century.* Seattle: University of Washington Press.

Blaug, Mark. 1992. *The Methodology of Economics or How Economists Explain.* 2nd ed. Cambridge: Cambridge University Press [1st edition: 1980].

Blaug, Mark. 1987. "Classical Economics." In *The New Palgrave: A Dictionary of Economics.* 4 vols., eds. John Eatwell, Murray Milgate, and Peter Newman. London: Macmillan.

Blaug, Mark. 1985. "What Ricardo Said and What Ricardo Meant." In *The Legacy of Ricardo*, ed. Giovanni A. Caravale, pp. 3–10. N.Y.: Basil Blackwell.

Blaug, Mark. 1958. *Ricardian Economics: A Historical Study.* Yale Studies in Economics, no. 8. New Haven: Yale University Press.

Boas, Marie, and Rupert Hall. 1959. "Newton's 'Mechanical Principles.'" *Journal of the History of Ideas* 20, no. 2 (April): 167–78.

Bonar, James. 1929. "Ricardo on Malthus." *Economic Journal* 39 (June): 210–18. Reprinted in J. Wood 1985, 1: 61–67.

Bonar, James. 1926. "Malthus, Thomas Robert." In *Palgrave's Dictionary of Political Economy,* new ed., ed. Henry Higgs. London: Macmillan.

Bonar, James. 1893. *Philosophy and Political Economy in Some of Their Historical Relations.* N.Y.: Macmillan.

Bonar, James. 1885. *Malthus and His Work.* London: George Allen and Unwin Ltd.

Borzeszkowski, Horst-Heino von, and Renate Wahsner. 1980. *Newton und Voltaire. Zur Begründung und Interpretation der klassischen Mechanik.* Berlin: Akademie-Verlag.

Boulding, Kenneth E. 1971. "After Samuelson, Who Needs Adam Smith?" *History of Political Economy* 3, no. 3 (Fall): 225–337.

Britton, Karl. 1969. *John Stuart Mill.* 2nd. ed. N.Y.: Dover Publications.

Bronfenbrenner, Martin. 1991. "Economics as Dentistry." *Southern Economic Journal* 57, no. 1 (January): 599–605.

Brooks, G. P., and S. K. Aalto. 1981. "The Rise and Fall of Moral Algebra: Francis Hutcheson and the Mathematization of Psychology." *Journal of the History of the Behavioral Sciences* 17, no. 3 (July): 343–56.

Bryson, Gladys. 1968 [1945]. *Man and Society: The Scottish Inquiry of the Eighteenth Century.* N.Y.: Augustus M. Kelley.

Buchdahl, Gerd. 1969. *Metaphysics and the Philosophy of Science: The Classical Origins: Descartes to Kant.* Cambridge: MIT Press.

Buchdahl, Gerd. 1961. *The Image of Newton and Locke in the Age of Reason.* London: Sheed and Ward.

Buckle, Henry Thomas. 1861. *History of Civilization in England,* vol. 2. London: Parker, Son, and Bourn.

Burke, John J., Jr. 1978. "Hume's *History of England:* Waking the English from a Dogmatic Slumber." In *Studies in Eighteenth-Century Culture,* vol. 7, ed. Roseann Runte, pp. 235–50. Madison: University of Wisconsin Press.

Burns, J. H. 1976. "The Light of Reason: Philosophical History in the Two Mills." In *James and John Stuart Mill/Papers of the Centenary Conference,* eds. John M. Robson and Michael Laine, pp. 3–20. Toronto: University of Toronto Press.

Burrow, J. W. 1966. *Evolution and Society: A Study in Victorian Social Theory.* Cambridge: Cambridge University Press.

Butts, Robert E. 1977. "Whewell's Logic of Induction." In *Foundations of Scientific Method:* The Nineteenth Century, eds. Ronald N. Giere and Richard S. Westfall, pp. 53–85. Bloomington: Indiana University Press.

Butts, Robert E. 1959. "Hume's Scepticism." *Journal of the History of Ideas* 20, no. 3 (June-September): 413–19.

Caldwell, Bruce. 1982. *Beyond Positivism: Economic Methodology in the Twentieth Century.* London: Allen and Unwin.

Cannon, Walter F. 1967. "Herschel, John." In *Encyclopedia of Philosophy.*

Cannon, Walter F. 1961. "John Herschel and the Idea of Science." *Journal of the History of Ideas* 22, no. 2 (April-June): 215–37.

Cantor, Geoffrey N. 1988. "Anti-Newton." In Fauvel et al. 1988: 203–222.

Cantor, Geoffrey N. 1971. "Henry Brougham and the Scottish Methodological Tradition." *Studies in History and Philosophy of Science* 2, no. 1: 69–89.

Capaldi, Nicholas. 1975. *David Hume: The Newtonian Philosopher*. Boston: Twayne Publishers.

Carey, Lewis J. 1928. *Franklin's Economic Views*. Garden City, N.J.: Doubleday, Doran.

Carrithers, David. 1986. "Montesquieu's Philosophy of History." *Journal of the History of Ideas* 47, no. 1 (January-March): 61–80.

Cassirer, Ernst. 1943. "Newton und Leibniz." *Philosophical Review* 53: 366–91.

Castell, Alburey. 1936. *Mill's Logic of the Moral Sciences: A Study of the Impact of Newtonism on Early Nineteenth Century Social Thought*. Chicago: University of Chicago Libraries Ph.D. Dissertation, University of Chicago, 1931.

Charpa, Ulrich. 1987. "John F. W. Herschels Methodologie der Erfahrungswissenschaft." *Philosophia Naturalis* 24: 121–48.

Checkland, S. G. 1985. "David Ricardo." In J. Wood 1985: 1: 68–71.

Chipman, J. S. 1984. "Balance of Payments Theory." In *Economic Analysis in Historical Perspective*, eds. J. Creedy and D. P. O'Brien, pp. 186–217. London: Butterworths.

Chitnis, Ahand. 1986. *The Scottish Enlightenment and Early Victorian English Society*. London: Croom Helm.

Clark, Charles M. A. 1988. "Natural Law Influences on Adam Smith." *Quaderni di Storia dell' Economia Politica* 6, no. 3: 60–86.

Clark, John Maurice, et al. 1966 [1928]. *Adam Smith, 1776–1926. Lectures to Commemorate the Sesquicentennial of the Publication of* The Wealth of Nations. N.Y.: Augustus M. Kelley.

Clarke, Desmond M. 1991a. "The Concept of Experience in Descartes's Theory of Knowledge." In Moyal 1991b: 455–72.

Clarke, Desmond M. 1991b. "Descartes's Use of 'Demonstration' and 'Deduction.'" In Moyal 1991b: 237–47.

Clarke, Desmond M. 1982. *Descartes' Philosophy of Science*. Manchester, England: Manchester University Press.

Clarke, John. 1972 [1730]. *A Demonstration of Some of the Principles of the Principal Sections of Sir Isaac Newton's Principles of Natural Philosophy*. Intro. by I. Bernard Cohen. N.Y.: Johnson Reprint.

Cobbett, William. 1957 [1912]. *Rural Rides*, 2 vols. Intro. by Asa Briggs. London: J. M. Dent & Sons.

Cochrane, James L. 1970. "The First Mathematical Ricardian Model." *History of Political Economy* 2, no. 2 (Fall): 419–31.

Cohen, I. Bernard. 1980. *The Newtonian Revolution*. Cambridge: Cambridge University Press.

Cohen, I. Bernard. 1977. "History and Philosophy of Science." In *The Structure of Scientific Theories*. 2nd ed., ed. Frederick Suppe, pp. 308–49. Urbana: University of Illinois Press.

Cohen, I. Bernard. 1966. *Franklin and Newton: An Inquiry into Speculative Newtonian Experimental Science and Franklin's Work in Electricity as an Example Thereof*. Memoirs of the American Philosophical Society, vol. 43. Cambridge: Harvard University Press.

Cole, Arthur H. 1958. "Puzzles of the '*Wealth of Nations*.'" *Canadian Journal of Economics and Political Science* 24, no. 1 (February): 1–8.

Collini, Stefan, Donald Winch, and John Burrow, eds. 1983. *That Noble Science of Politics: A Study in Nineteenth-Century Intellectual History*. Cambridge: Cambridge University Press.

Corry, B. A. 1959. "Malthus and Keynes—A Reconsideration." *Economic Journal* 49 (December): 717–24. Reprinted in J. Wood 1986, 4: 75–83.

Corsi, Pietro. 1987. "The Heritage of Dugald Stewart: Oxford Philosophy and the Method of Political Economy." *Nuncius* 2, no. 2: 89–144.

Cottingham, John. 1993. "A New Start? Cartesian Metaphysics and the Emergence of Modern Philosophy." In *The Rise of Modern Philosophy,* ed. Tom Sorell, pp. 145–66. Oxford: Clarendon Press.

Cremaschi, Sergio. 1989. "Adam Smith: Skeptical Newtonianism, Disenchanted Republicanism, and the Birth of Social Science." In *Knowledge and Politics: Case Studies in the Relationship Between Epistemology and Political Philosophy*, eds. Marcelo Dascal and Ora Gruengard, pp. 83–110. Boulder, Colorado: Westview Press.

Cremaschi, Sergio. 1988. "The Newtonian Heritage in Eighteenth Century Political Economy." Paper read at Conference on After Newton: Science and Society in the First Industrial Revolution (1727–1850), 14–18 November, Madrid.

Cremaschi, Sergio. 1981. "Adam Smith, Newtonianism and Political Economy." *Manucrito* 5, no. 1: 117–34.

Cullen, M. J. 1975. *The Statistical Movement in Early Victorian Britain: The Foundations of Empirical Social Research*. Hassocks: Harvester Press.

Cunningham, Andrew. 1991. "How the *Principia* Got Its Name; Or, Taking Natural Philosophy Seriously." *History of Science* 29 (December): 377–92.

Dankert, Clyde E. 1974. *Adam Smith: Man of Letters and Economist*. Hicksville, N.Y.: Exposition Press.

Darwin, Charles. [1936]. *The Origin of Species* and *The Descent of Man*. N.Y.: Modern Library.

Darwin, Charles, and Thomas Henry Huxley. 1974. *Autobiographies,* ed. Gavin de Beer. London: Oxford University Press.

Daugherty, Marion R. 1942/1943. "The Currency-Banking Controversy," parts 1 and 2. *Southern Economic Journal* 9, no. 1 (October 1942): 140–55; 9, no. 3 (January 1943): 241–51.

Davenant, Charles. 1698. *Discourses on the Publick Revenues, and on the Trade of England.* London: James Knapton.

Davis, Kingsley. 1955. "Malthus and the Theory of Population." In *The Language of Social Research,* eds. Paul F. Lazarsfeld and Morris Rosenberg, pp. 540–53. N.Y.: The Free Press.

Deane, Phyllis. 1983. "The Scope and Method of Economic Science." *Economic Journal* 93, no. 369 (March): 1–12.

Deane, Phyllis. 1978. *The Evolution of Economic Ideas.* London: Cambridge University Press.

Deane, Phyllis. 1956. "The Implications of Early National Income Estimates for the Measurement of Long-Term Economic Growth in the United Kingdom." University of Cambridge Department of Applied Economics Reprint Series, No. 109.

De Haan, Richard. 1982. "Induction." In *Collier's Encyclopedia.*

De Marchi, Neil. 1988. "John Stuart Mill Interpretation Since Schumpeter." In Thweatt 1988: 137–62; commentary by Samuel Hollander, pp. 163–77.

De Marchi, Neil. 1970. "The Empirical Content and Longevity of Ricardian Economics." *Economica* 37, no. 147 (August): 257–76. Reprinted in J. Wood 1985, 1: 217–34.

De Marchi, Neil and R. P. Sturges. 1973. "Malthus and Ricardo's Inductivist Critics: Four Letters to William Whewell." *Economica* 40 (November): 379–93. Reprinted in J. Wood 1986, 4: 175–89.

Desaguliers, J. T. 1763. *A Course of Experimental Philosophy,* 3rd ed. London: Millar.

Descartes, René. 1984/1985. *The Philosophical Writings of Descartes,* 2 vols, transl. John Cottingham, Robert Stoothoff, and Dugald Murdoch. Cambridge: Cambridge University Press.

Diehl, Karl. 1929. "Ricardos >Notes on Malthus<." *Zeitschrift für die gesamte Staatswissenschaft* 87: 52–68.

Dobbs, Betty Jo. 1982. "Newton's Alchemy and His Theory of Matter." *Isis* 73: 511–28.

Dow, Alexander. 1984. "The Hauteur of Adam Smith: An Unpublished Letter from James Anderson of Monkshill." *Scottish Journal of Political Economy* 31, no. 3 (November): 284–85.

Dow, Sheila C. 1987. "The Scottish Political Economy Tradition." *Scottish Journal of Political Economy* 34, no. 4 (November): 335–48. Reprinted in Mair 1990: 19–32.

Doyle, Phyllis. 1927. "The Contemporary Background of Hobbes' 'State of Nature.'" *Economica* 7, no. 21 (December): 336–55.

Dunbar, C. 1985. [1887]. "Ricardo's Use of Facts." *Quarterly Journal of Economics* 1 (July): 474–76. Reprinted in J. Wood 1985, 1: 7–9.

*The Economist.* 1951. "The Scholar's Ricardo." (September 1): 502.

"Editorial." 1993. *European Journal of the History of Economic Thought* 1, no. 1 (Autumn): 1–4.

Emerson, Roger L. 1990. "Science and Moral Philosophy in the Scottish Englightenment." In *Studies in the Philosophy of the Scottish Enlightenment*, ed. M. A. Stewart, pp. 11–36. Oxford: Clarendon Press.

Emerson, Roger L. 1988. "Science and the Origins and Concerns of the Scottish Enlightenment." *History of Science* 26: 335–66.

Emerson, Roger L. 1979. "American Indians, Frenchmen, and Scot Philosophers." In *Studies in Eighteenth-Century Culture*, vol. 99, ed. Roseann Runte, pp. 211–36. Madison: University of Wisconsin Press.

Empson, William. 1837. "Life, Writings, and Character of Mr. Malthus." *Edinburgh Review* 64 (January): 469–506.

Evensky, Jerry. 1989. "The Evolution of Adam Smith's Views on Political Economy." *History of Political Economy* 21, no. 1 (Spring): 123–45.

Evensky, Jerry. 1987. "The Two Voices of Adam Smith: Moral Philosopher and Social Critic." *History of Political Economy* 19, no. 3 (Fall): 447–68.

Farr, James. 1987. "The Way of Hypotheses: Locke on Method." *Journal of the History of Ideas* 48, no. 1 (January-March): 51–72.

Fauvel, John, Raymond Flood, Michael Shortland, and Robin Wilson, eds. 1988. *Let Newton Be!* Oxford: Oxford University Press.

Ferguson, John M. 1950. *Landmarks of Economic Thought.* 2nd ed. N.Y.: Longmans, Green.

Fetter, Frank W. 1962. "Economic Articles in the *Westminster Review* and Their Authors, 1824–51." *Journal of Political Economy* 6 (December): 576–96.

Fetter, Frank W. 1960. "The Economic Articles in *Blackwood's Edinburgh Magazine,* and Their Authors, 1817–1853," parts 1 and 2. *Scottish Journal of Political Economy* 7: 85–107; 213–31.

Fetter, Frank W. 1958. "The Economic Articles in the *Quarterly Review* and Their Authors, 1809–52," parts 1 and 2. *Journal of Political Economy* 66, no. 1 (February): 47–64; 66, no. 2 (April): 154–70.

Fetter, Frank W. 1953. "The Authorship of Economic Articles in the *Edinburgh Review,* 1802–47." *Journal of Political Economy* 61, no. 3 (June): 232–59.

Fetter, Frank W. 1942. "The Bullion Report Reexamined." *Quarterly Journal of Economics* 56 (August): 655–65. Reprinted in *Papers in English Monetary History.* eds. T. S. Ashton and R. S. Sayers, pp. 66–75. Oxford: Clarendon Press, 1953.

Forbes, Duncan. 1954. "'Scientific' Whiggism: Adam Smith and John Millar." *Cambridge Journal* 7: 643–70. Reprinted in J. Wood 1984, 1: 273–96.

Forbes, Eric G. 1983. "Philosophy and Science Teaching in the Seventeenth Century." In *Four Centuries Edinburgh University Life, 1583–1983,* ed. Gordon Donaldson, pp. 28–37. Edinburgh: Edinburgh University Press.

Force, James E. 1987. "Hume's Interest in Newton and Science." *Hume Studies* 13, no. 2 (November): 166–216.

Force, James E. 1984. "Hume and the Relation of Science to Religion Among Certain Members of the Royal Society." *Journal of the History of Ideas* 45, no. 4 (October-December): 517–36.

Fordyce, David. 1771. "Moral Philosophy, or Morals." In *Encyclopedia Britannica,* 1st ed. Edinburgh.

Franklin, Benjamin. n.d. "Remarks concerning the Savages of North America." In *The Works of Dr. Benjamin Franklin: consisting of Essays, Humorous, Moral, and Literary; with his Life, Written by Himself,* pp. 200–206. London: J. F. Dove.

Freudenthal, Gideon. 1982. *Atom und Individuum im Zeitalter Newtons. Zur Genese der mechanistischen Natur- und Sozialphilosophie.* Frankfurt am Main: Suhrkamp.

Freudenthal, Gideon. 1981. "Adam Smith's Analytic-Synthetic Method and the 'System of Natural Liberty.'" *History of European Ideas* 2, no. 2: 135–54.

Galton, Francis. 1869. *Hereditary Genius: An Inquiry into its Laws and Consequences.* London: Macmillan.

Garber, Daniel. 1993. "Descartes and Experiment in the *Discourse* and *Essays.*" In *Essays on the Philosophy and Science of René Descartes,* ed. Stephen Voss, pp. 288–310. N.Y.: Oxford University Press.

Gewirtz, Alan. 1941. "Experience and the Non-Mathematical in the Cartesian Method." *Journal of the History of Ideas* 2, no. 2 (April): 183–210.

Gide, Charles, and Charles Rist. 1960. *A History of Economic Doctrines from the Time of the Physiocrats to the Present Day.* 2nd English ed., transl. R. Richards and Ernest F. Row. London: George G. Harrap.

Gilbert, Geoffrey. 1980. "Economic Growth and the Poor in Malthus's *Essay on Population.*" *History of Political Economy* 12, no. 1 (Spring): 83–96.

Gillies, Donald A. 1988. "Induction and Probability." In *An Encyclopedia of Philosophy,* ed. G. H. R. Parkinson, pp. 179–204. London: Routledge.

Givner, David A. 1991. "Scientific Preconceptions in Locke's Philosophy of Language." In Ashcraft 1991, 4: 430–45.

Gjertsen, Derek. 1988. "Newton's Success." In Fauvel et al. 1988: 23–42.

Godwin, William. 1820. *Of Population: An Enquiry concerning the Power of Increase in the Numbers of Mankind being an answer to Mr. Malthus's essay on that subject.* London: Longman, Hurst, Rees, Orme and Brown.

Goldman, Lawrence. 1983. "The Origins of British 'Social Science': Political Economy, Natural Science and Statistics 1830–1835." *Historical Journal* 26, no. 3: 587–616.

Golinski, Jan. 1988. "The Secret Life of an Alchemist." In Fauvel et al. 1988: 146–67.

Goodman, Nelson. 1973. *Fact, Fiction* and *Forecast*, 3rd ed. Indianapolis: Bobbs-Merrill.

Graunt, John (see Petty)

Gordon, Scott. 1991. *The History and Philosophy of Social Science.* London and N.Y.: Routledge.

Guerlac, Henry. 1968 [1958]. "Newton's Changing Reputation in the Eighteenth Century." In *Carl Becker's Heavenly City Revisited*, ed. Raymond 0. Rockwood, pp. 3–26. [Hamden, Conn.]: Archon Books.

Guerlac, Henry. 1965. "Where the Statue Stood: Divergent Loyalties to Newton in the Eighteenth Century." In *Aspects of the Eighteenth Century*, ed. Earl R. Wasserman, pp. 317–34. Baltimore: Johns Hopkins University Press.

Guerlac, Henry. 1958. "Three Eighteenth-Century Social Philosophers: Scientific Influences on Their Thought." *Daedalus* 87: 8–24.

Guthrie, W. G. 1984. "Selective Rediscovery of Economic Ideas: What Keynes Found in Malthus." *Southern Economic Journal* 50, no. 3 (January): 771–80. Reprinted in J. Wood 1986, 1: 437–49.

Hacking, Ian. 1975. *The Emergence of Probability. A Philosophical Study of Early Ideas about Probability, Induction and Statistical Inference.* London: Cambridge University Press.

Hanson, Norwood R. 1970. "Hypotheses Fingo." In *The Methodological Heritage of Newton*, eds. Robert E. Butts and John W. Davis, pp. 12–33. Oxford: Basil Blackwell.

Harrod, R. F. 1952. *The Life of J. M. Keynes.* London: Macmillan.

Hartwick, John M. 1988. "Robert Wallace and Malthus and the Ratios." *History of Political Economy* 20, no. 3 (Fall): 357–79.

Harvey-Phillips, M. B. 1984. "'Malthus' Theodicy: the Intellectual Background of His Contribution to Political Economy." *History of Political Economy* 16, no. 4 (Winter): 591–608.

Hasbach, Wilhelm. 1904. "Mit welcher Methode wurden die Gesetze der theoretischen Nationalökonomie gefunden?" *Jahrbücher für Nationalökonomie und Statistik* 27: 289–317.

Hattaway, Michael. 1978. "Bacon and 'Knowledge Broken': Limits for Scientific Method." *Journal of the History of Ideas* 39, no. 2 (April-June): 183–97.

Hausman, Daniel M. 1992. *The Inexact and Separate Science of Economics.* Cambridge: Cambridge University Press.

Hausman, Daniel M. 1989. "Economic Methodology in a Nutshell." *Journal of Economic Perspectives* 3, no. 2 (Spring): 115–27.

Hayek, F. A. von. 1991. *The Trend of Economic Thinking*, eds. W. W. Bartley, III and Stephen Kresge. London: Routledge.

Hayek, F. A. von. 1986. "The Moral Imperative of the Market." In *The Unfinished Agenda*, ed. Martin J. Anderson, pp. 143–49. London: Institute of Economic Affairs.

Heilbroner, Robert L. 1973. "The Paradox of Progress: Decline in *The Wealth of Nations.*" *Journal of the History of Ideas* 34, no. 2 (April-June): 243–62. Reprinted in Skinner and Wilson 1975: 524–39.

Heilbroner, Robert L. 1969 [1953]. *The Worldly Philosophers: The Lives, Times, and Ideas of the Great Economic Thinkers.* N.Y.: Washington Square Press.

Henderson, James P. 1990. "Induction, Deduction and the Role of Mathematics: The Whewell Group vs. the Ricardian Economists." In *Research in the History of Economic Thought and Methodology: A Research Annual,* ed. Warren J. Samuels, vol. 7: 1–36. Greenwich, Conn: Jai Press Inc.

Henderson, James P. 1985. "The Whewell Group of Mathematical Economists." *Manchester School* 53, no. 4 (December): 404–31.

Henderson, James P. 1983. "The Oral Tradition in British Economics: Influential Economists in the Political Economy Club of London." *History of Political Economy* 15, no. 2 (Summer): 149–79.

Henry, John. 1988. "Newton, Matter, and Magic." In Fauvel et al. 1988: 127–68.

Herschel, J. F. W. 1831 [1830]. *A Preliminary Discourse on the Study of Natural Philosophy.* London: Longman, Rees, Orme, Brown, & Greene.

Hesse, Mary B. 1964. "Francis Bacon." In *A Critical History of Western Philosophy,* ed. D. J. O'Connor, pp. 141–52. N.Y.: Free Press.

Hetherington, Norriss S. 1983. "Isaac Newton's Influence on Adam Smith's Natural Laws in Economics." *Journal of the History of Ideas* 44, no. 3 (July-September): 497–505.

Hilts, Victor L. 1973. "Statistics and Social Science." In *Foundations of Scientific Method: The Nineteenth Century,* eds. Ronald N. Giere and Richard S. Westfall, pp. 206–33. Bloomington: Indiana University Press.

Hintikka, Jaakko, and Unto Remes. 1974. *The Method of Analysis: Its Geometrical Origin and Its General Significance.* Dordrecht: D. Reidl.

Hobbes, Thomas. 1839–1845. *The English Works of Thomas Hobbes,* 11 vols., ed. Sir William Molesworth. London: John Bohn.

Höpfl, H. M. 1978. "From Savage to Scotsman: Conjectural History in the Scottish Enlightenment." *Journal of British Studies* 17: 19–40.

d'Holbach, Paul Henri Dietrich, Baron. 1971 [1770]. *A System of Nature, and Her Laws: An Application to the Happiness of Man, Living in Society; contrasted with superstition and imaginery systems.* London: James Watson.

Hollander, Samuel. 1985. *The Economics of John Stuart Mill,* vol. 1: *Theory and Method.* Toronto: University of Toronto Press.

Hollander, Samuel. 1979. *The Economics of David Ricardo.* Toronto: University of Toronto Press.

Hollander, Samuel. 1962. "Malthus and Keynes: A Note." *Economic Journal* 72 (June): 355–60. Reprinted in J. Wood 1986, 1: 217–22.

Hooker, John J. 1964–1966. "The Statistical Milieu of Adam Smith: I, II, and III." *American Statistician* 18, no. 5 (December 1964): 22–24; 19, no. 2 (April 1965): 49–51; 20, no. 1 (February 1966): 29–31.

Howell, Wilbur Samuel. 1975. "Adam Smith's Lectures on Rhetoric: an Historical Assessment." In *Essays on Adam Smith*, eds. Andrew S. Skinner and Thomas Wilson, pp. 11–43. Oxford: Clarendon Press.

Hume, David. 1975. *Enquiries concerning Human Understanding and concerning the Principles of Morals*, 3rd ed. Reprinted from the posthumous edition of 1777, ed. L. A. Selby-Bigge. Oxford: Clarendon Press.

Hume, David. 1967. *The Natural History of Religion and Dialogues concerning Natural Religion*, eds. A. Wayne Colver and John Valdmir Price. Oxford: University Press.

Hume, David. 1965 [1938]. *An Abstract of a Treatise of Human Nature, 1740*, intro. by J. M. Keynes and P. Sraffa. Hamden, Conn.: Archon Books.

Hume, David. 1955. *Writings on Economics*, ed. Eugene Rotwein. Edinburgh: Nelson.

Hume, David. 1954. *New Letters of David Hume*, eds. Raymond Klibansky and Ernest C. Mossner. Oxford: Clarendon Press.

Hume, David. 1932. *The Letters of David Hume*, 2 vols, ed. J. Y. T. Greig. Oxford: Clarendon Press.

Hume, David. 1896 [1739]. *A Treatise of Human Nature*. Reprinted from orig. ed. in 3 vols., ed. by L. A. Selby-Bigge. Oxford: Clarendon Press.

Hume, David. 1875. *Essays Moral, Political, and Literary*, vol. 1, ed. with dissertations and notes by T. H. Green and T. H. Grose. London: Longmans, Green.

Hume, David. 1854. *The Philosophical Works of David Hume*, 4 vols. Boston: Little, Brown: Adam and Charles Black.

Hume, David. n.d. *The History of England*, 5 vols. New ed., with the author's last corrections and improvements. To which is prefixed a short account of his life, written by himself. Philadelphia: Porter and Coates.

Hutcheson, Francis. 1990a. *An Inquiry into the Original of our Ideas of Beauty and Virtue. Collected Works of Francis Hutcheson*, vol. 1. Hildesheim: Georg Olms Verlag.

Hutcheson, Francis. 1990b [1747]. *A Short Introduction to Moral Philosophy. Collected Works of Francis Hutcheson*, vol. 4, facsimile ed. Bernhard Fabian. Hildesheim: Georg Olms Verlag.

Hutchison, T. W. 1994. "On the Interpretation and Misinterpretation of Economic Literature: The Preposterous Case of David Ricardo." In his *Uses and Abuses of Economics: Contentious Essays on History and Method*, pp. 84–106. London: Routledge.

Hutchison, T. W. 1990. "Adam Smith and *The Wealth of Nations*." In Mair 1990: 81–102.

Hutchison, T. W. 1978. *On Revolutions and Progress in Economic Knowledge*. Cambridge: Cambridge University Press.

Hutchison, T. W. 1964. *'Positive' Economics and Policy Objectives*. London: George Allen and Unwin.

Iggers, G. G. 1959. "Further Remarks About Early Use of the Term 'Social Science.'" *Journal of the History of Ideas* 20 (July-September): 433–36. Reprinted in J. Wood 1987: 4: 154–57.

"Induction." 1797. In *Encyclopedia Britannica*, 3rd. ed. Edinburgh.

Ingram, J. K. 1962 [1878]. "The Present Position and Prospects of Political Economy." In *Essays in Economic Method: Selected Papers read to Section F of the British Association for the Advancement of Science, 1860–1913*, ed. R. L. Smyth, with intro. by T. W. Hutchison, pp. 41–72. London: Gerald Duckworth.

Jacob, J. R. 1980. "Restoration Ideologies and the Royal Society." *History of Science* 18: 25–39.

Jacob, M. C. 1974. "Early Newtonianism." *History of Science* 12 (June): 142–46.

Jacobs, Struan. 1991. "John Stuart Mill on Induction and Hypotheses." *Journal of the History of Philosophy* 29: 69–83.

Jacquette, Dale. 1990. "Aesthetics and Natural Law in Newton's Methodology." *Journal of the History of Ideas* 51, no. 4 (October-December): 659–66.

James, Patricia. 1979. *'Population' Malthus: His Life and Times*. London: Routledge and Kegan Paul.

Jevons, William Stanley. 1965. *The Principles of Economics: A Fragment of a Treatise on the Industrial Mechanism of Society and Other Papers*, preface by Henry Higgs. N.Y.: Augustus M. Kelley.

Jevons, William Stanley. 1879. *The Theory of Political Economy*, 2nd ed. London: Macmillan.

Jevons, William Stanley. 1874. *The Principles of Science: A Treatise on Logic and Scientific Method*, 2 vols. London: Macmillan.

Jones, H. S. 1992. "John Stuart Mill as Moralist." *Journal of the History of Ideas* 53, no. 2 (April-June): 287–308.

Kemp Smith, Norman. 1966. *Philosophy of David Hume*. London: Macmillan.

Keynes, John Maynard. 1973. *The General Theory and After. Collected Writings of John Maynard Keynes*, vol. 14. London: Macmillan.

Keynes, John Maynard. 1972. *Essays in Biography. Collected Writings of John Maynard Keynes*, vol. 10. London: Macmillan for the Royal Society.

Keynes, John Neville. 1973 [1917]. *The Scope and Method of Political Economy*, 4th ed. Clifton, N. J.: Augustus M. Kelley.

King, Gregory. 1936. *Two Tracts*, ed. with intro. by George E. Barnett. Baltimore: Johns Hopkins University Press.

King, Preston, ed. 1993. *Thomas Hobbes: Critical Assessments*, 4 vols. London: Routledge.

Klein, Lawrence R. 1992. "Smith's Use of Data." In *Adam Smith's Legacy: His Place in the Development of Modern Economics*, ed. by Michael Fry, pp. 15–28. London: Routledge.

Koblitz, Neal. 1988a. "Reply to Unclad Emperors." *Mathematical Intelligencer* 10, no. 1 (Winter): 14–16.

Koblitz, Neal. 1988b. "Simon Falls Off the Wall." *Mathematical Intelligencer* 10, no. 2 (Spring): 11–12.

Koblitz, Neal. 1988c. "A Tale of Three Equations; or The Emperors Have no Clothes." *Mathematical Intelligencer* 10, no. 1 (Winter): 4–10.

Koyré, Alexandre. 1965. *Newtonian Studies*. Chicago: University of Chicago Press.

Krugman, Paul. 1990. *Rethinking International Trade*. Cambridge: MIT Press.

Laidler, David. 1991. "The Quantity Theory Is Always and Everywhere Controversial—Why?" *Economic Record* 67, no. 1999 (December): 289–305.

Lambert, P. 1986. "Lauderdale, Malthus and Keynes." In J. Wood 1986, 1: 223–43.

Land, Stephen K. 1977. "Adam Smith's 'Considerations concerning the First Formation of Languages.'" *Journal of the History of Ideas* 38, no. 4 (October-December): 677–90.

Laudan, Larry. 1981. *Science and Hypothesis: Historical Essays on Scientific Methodology*. Dordrecht: D. Reidel.

Leontief, Wassily. 1992. "The Present State of Economic Science." In *Adam Smith's Legacy: His Place in the Development of Modern Economics*, ed. by Michael Fry, pp. 141–45. London: Routledge.

Leontief, Wassily. 1971. "Theoretical Assumptions and Nonobserved Facts." *American Economic Review* 61, no. 1 (March): 1–7.

Leontief, Wassily. 1966. *Essays in Economics: Theories and Theorizing*. N.Y.: Oxford University Press.

Letwin, William. 1963. *The Origins of Scientific Economics: English Economic Thought, 1660–1776*. London: Methuen.

Lewinski, J. St. 1919. "Das System David Ricardos." *Zeitschrift für die gesamte Staatswissenschaft* 74: 223–43.

Lindgren, J. Ralph. 1973. *The Social Philosophy of Adam Smith*. The Hague: Martinus Nijhoff.

Lindgren, J. Ralph. 1969. "Adam Smith's Theory of Inquiry." *Journal of Political Economy* 77, no. 6 (November-December): 897–915.

Livingston, Donald W. 1984. *Hume's Philosophy of Common Life*. Chicago: University of Chicago Press.

Lloyd, Peter J. 1969. "Elementary Geometric/Arithmetic Series and Early Production Series." *Journal of Political Economy* 77: 21–34.

Locke, John. 1965 [1690]. *An Essay concerning Human Understanding*, 2 vols, ed. John W. Yolton. London: Dent: Dutton.

Locke, John. 1954. *Essays on the Law of Nature*, ed. W. von Leyden. Oxford: Oxford University Press.

"Logic." 1771. In *Encyclopedia Britannica*, 1st ed. Edinburgh.

Macaulay, Thomas Babington. 1837. "Francis Bacon." *Edinburgh Review* 65 (July): 1–104.

Macfie, Alec. 1955. "The Scottish Tradition in Economic Thought." *Scottish Journal of Political Economy* 2 (June): 81–103. Reprinted in Mair 1990: 1–18.

Machlup, Fritz. 1963. *Essays on Economic Semantics*, ed. Merton H. Miller. Englewood Cliffs, N.J.: Prentice-Hall.

Maclaurin, Colin. 1971 [1748]. *An Account of Sir Isaac Newton's Philosophical Discoveries*. Hildesheim: Georg Olms Verlag.

Mair, Douglas, ed. 1990. *The Scottish Contribution to Modern Economic Thought*. Aberdeen: Aberdeen University Press.

Malthus, Thomas R. 1989a. *An Essay on the Principle of Population*, 2 vols, ed. Patricia James. 1803 ed. with variora of 1806, 1807, 1817, and 1826. Cambridge: Cambridge University Press for the Royal Economic Society.

Malthus, Thomas R. 1989b. *Principles of Political Economy*, variorum ed., ed. John Pullen. Cambridge: Cambridge University Press.

Malthus, Thomas R. 1986. *The Works of Thomas Robert Malthus*, ed. E. A. Wrigley and David Souden. London: William Pickering.

Malthus, Thomas R. 1966. *The Travel Diaries of Thomas Robert Malthus*, ed. Patricia James. Cambridge: Cambridge University Press.

Malthus, Thomas R. 1811. "Depreciation of Paper Currency." *Edinburgh Review* 17 (February): 339–72.

Marsh, Jeffrey H. 1977. "Economics Education in Schools in the Nineteenth Century: Social Control." *Economics: The Journal of the Economics Association* 13, pt. 4, no. 60 (Winter): 116–18.

Marshall, Alfred. 1925 [1885]. "The Present Position of Economics." In *Memorials of Alfred Marshall*, ed. A. C. Pigou, pp. 152–74. London: Macmillan.

Martin, Julian. 1993. "Francis Bacon, Authority, and the Moderns." In *The Rise of Modern Philosophy*, ed. Tom Sorell, pp. 71–88. Oxford: Clarendon Press.

Martin, Julian. 1992. *Francis Bacon, the State, and the Reform of Natural Philosophy.* Cambridge: Cambridge University Press.

Marx, Karl. 1976. *Capital: A Critique of Political Economy*. Intro. by Ernest Mandel, transl. Ben Fowkes. N.Y.: Vantage Books.

Mason, E. S. 1928. "Ricardo's Notes on Malthus." *Quarterly Journal of Economics* 42 (August): 684–96.

Mawatari, Shohken. 1982/1983. "J. S. Mill's Methodology of Political Economy," parts 1–4. In *The Keizai Gaku*, Annual Report of the Economics Society, Tokyo University 44, no. 2 (October 1992): 125–43; 44, no. 3 (December 1982): 249–69; 45, no. 1 (June 1983): 33–54; and 45, no. 2 (August 1983): 165–83.

Mayr, Otto. 1986. *Authority, Liberty and Automatic Machinery in Early Modern Europe*. Baltimore: Johns Hopkins University Press.

Mayr, Otto. 1971. "Adam Smith and the Concept of the Feedback System: Economic Thought and Technology in 18th-Century Britain." *Technology and Culture* 12: 1–22.

McCloskey, Donald N. 1985. "Sartorial Epistemology in Tatters: A Reply to Martin Hollis." *Economics and Philosophy* 1: 134–37.

McCosh, James. 1990 [1875]. *The Scottish Philosophy: Biographical, Expository, Critical, from Hutcheson to Hamilton.* Hildesheim: Georg Olms Verlag.

McCulloch, John R. 1845. *The Literature of Political Economy: A Classified Catalogue of Select Publications in the Different Departments of That Science, with Historical, Critical, and Biographical Notices.* London: Longman, Brown, Green, and Longmans.

McRae, Robert. 1957. "The Unity of the Sciences: Bacon, Descartes, and Leibnitz." *Journal of the History of Ideas* 18, no. 1 (January): 27–48.

Medawar, P. B. 1964. "Is the Scientific Paper Fraudulent?" *Saturday Review* (August 1): 42–43.

Meek, Ronald L. 1971. "Smith, Turgot, and the 'Four Stages' Theory." *History of Political Economy* 3, no. 1 (Spring): 9–27. Reprinted in J. Wood 1984, 1: 142–55.

Meek, Ronald L., ed. 1953. *Marx and Engels on Malthus: Selections from the Writings of Marx and Engels Dealing with the Theories of Thomas Robert Malthus.* London: Lawrence and Wishart.

Merton, Robert K. 1970. *Science, Technology and Society in Seventeenth Century England.* N.Y.: Howard Fertig.

Mill, James. 1869. *Analysis of the Phenomena of the Human Mind,* 2 vols., ed. John Stuart Mill. New ed. with notes by Alexander Bain, Andrew Findlater, and George Grote. London: Longmans Green Reader and Dyer.

Mill, James. 1821. *Elements of Political Economy.* London: Baldwin, Cradock, and Jay.

Mill, John Stuart. 1981–1991. *Collected Works of John Stuart Mill,* 33 vols. Toronto: University of Toronto Press.

Mirowski, Philip. 1982. "Adam Smith, Empiricism, and the Rate of Profit in Eighteenth-century England." *History of Political Economy* 14, no. 2 (Summer): 178–98. Reprinted in his *Against Mechanism: Protecting Economics from Science,* ch. 11. Totowa, N.J.: Rowman & Littlefield, 1988.

Mitchell, Wesley C. 1967. *Types of Economic Theory from Mercantilism to Institutionalism,* vol. 1, ed. Joseph Dorfman. N.Y.: Augustus M. Kelley.

Mizuta, Hiroshi. 1967. *Adam Smith's Library. A Supplement to Bonar's Catalogue with a Checklist of the Whole Library.* Cambridge: Cambridge University Press for the Royal Economic Society.

Montiero, J. P. 1981. "Hume's Conception of Science." *Journal of the History of Philosophy* 19: 327–42.

Moravia, Sergio. 1980. "The Enlightenment and the Sciences of Man." *History of Science* 18: 247–68.

Morgan, Mary S. 1990. *The History of Econometric Ideas*. Cambridge: Cambridge University Press.

Morrell, J. B. 1971. "The University of Edinburgh in the Late Eighteenth Century: Its Scientific Eminence and Academic Structure." *Isis* 62, pt. 2, no. 212 (Summer): 158–71.

Morrell, Jack, and Arnold Thackray. 1982. *Gentlemen of Science: Early Years of the British Association for the Advancement of Science*. Oxford: Clarendon.

Moss, Laurence S. 1979. "Professor Hollander and Ricardian Economics." *Eastern Economic Journal* 5 (December): 501–12.

Moyal, Georges J. D. 1991a. "Descartes's Method: From Things to Ideas." In Moyal 1991b: 1–27.

Moyal, Georges J. D., ed. 1991b. *René Descartes: Critical Assessments*, 4 vols. London: Routledge.

Myers, Milton L. 1983. *The Soul of Modern Economic Man: Ideas of Self-Interest, Thomas Hobbes to Adam Smith*. Chicago: University of Chicago Press.

Nagel, Ernest. 1958. "Induction." In *Encyclopedia Americana*.

Nagel, Ernest, ed. 1950. *John Stuart Mill's Philosophy of Scientific Method*. N.Y.: Hafner Publishing.

Napier, Macvey. 1818. "Remarks, illustrative of the Scope and Influence of the Philosophical Writings of Lord Bacon." *Transactions of the Royal Society of Edinburgh*, 8: 373–425.

Newton, Sir Isaac. 1962 [1686]. *Sir Isaac Newton's Mathematical Principles of Natural Philosophy and His System of the World* [*Principia*], 2 vols, trans. Andrew Motte, 1729. Revised with historical and explanatory appendix by Florian Cajori. Berkeley: University of California Press.

Newton, Sir Isaac. 1952 [1730]. *Opticks*, 4th ed., with foreword by Albert Einstein, intro. by Edmund Whittaker, preface by I. B. Cohen, and analytical table of contents by Duane H. D. Rolleo. N.Y.: Dover.

Newton, Isaac. 1887. "Monetary Reports (1701–1702) Signed by Sir Isaac Newton." Printed from manuscripts found in the Tower Mint and in the Public Record Office. In *The Silver Pound and England's Monetary Policy Since the Restoration*. S. Dana Horton, pp. 261–71. London: Macmillan.

Norton, David Fate. 1968. "Hume's A Letter from a Gentleman, A Review Note." *Journal of the History of Philosophy* 6: 161–67.

Norton, David Fate. 1965. "History and Philosophy in Hume's Thought." In *David Hume: Philosophical Historian*, eds. David Fate Norton and Richard H. Popkin, pp. xxxii-l. Indianapolis: Bobbs-Merrill.

O'Leary, James J. 1940. "Malthus and Keynes." *Journal of Political Economy* 50: 901–19. Reprinted in J. Wood 1986, 1: 90–104.

Olson, Richard. 1975. *Scottish Philosophy and British Physics 1750–1880: A Study in the Foundations of the Victorian Scientific Style*. Princeton: Princeton University Press.

Olson, Richard. 1971. "Scottish Philosophy and Mathematics 1750–1830." *Journal of the History of Ideas* 32, no. 1 (January-March): 29–44.

Ong, Walter J. 1958. *Ramus: Method, and the Decay of Dialogue.* Cambridge: Harvard University Press.

Osler, Margaret J. 1970. "John Locke and the Changing Ideal of Scientific Knowledge." *Journal of the History of Ideas* 31, no. 1 (January-March): 3–16.

Paglin, Morton. 1961. *Malthus and Lauderdale: The Anti-Ricardian Tradition.* N.Y.: Augustus M. Kelley.

Pancoast, Omar. 1943. "Malthus Versus Ricardo: The Effects of Distribution on Production." *Political Science Quarterly* 58, no. 1 (March): 47–66.

Passmore, John. 1980 [1968]. *Hume's Intentions,* 3rd ed. London: Duckworth.

Passmore, John. 1957. "John Stuart Mill and British Empiricism." In his *Hundred Years of Philosophy,* pp. 11–32. London: Gerald Duckworth.

Patten, Simon N. 1899. *The Development of English Thought: A Study in the Economic Interpretation of History.* N.Y.: Macmillan.

Patten, Simon N. 1893. "The Interpretation of Ricardo." *Quarterly Journal of Economics* 7 (April): 322–52. Reprinted in J. Wood 1985 3: 15–33.

Peach, Terry. 1993. *Interpreting Ricardo.* Cambridge: Cambridge University Press.

Peach, Terry. 1988. "David Ricardo: A Review of Some Interpretative Issues." In Thweatt 1988: 103–31; commentary by Mark Blaug, pp. 132–36.

Pearson, E. S., ed. 1978. *The History of Statistics in the 17th and 18th Centuries Against the Changing Background of Intellectual, Scientific and Religious Thought.* Lectures of Karl Pearson at University College London, 1921–1937. London: Charles Griffen.

Pemberton, Henry. 1728. *A View of Sir Isaac Newton's Philosophy.* London: S. Palmer.

Peters, R. S. 1967. "Hobbes, Thomas." In *Encyclopedia of Philosophy.*

Petty, Sir William [and John Graunt]. 1899. *The Economic Writings of Sir William Petty Together with the Observations upon the Bills of Mortality* [by John Graunt], 2 vols., ed. Charles Henry Hull. Cambridge: Cambridge University Press.

Platts, Charles. 1893. "Maclaurin, Colin." In *Dictionary of National Biography,* ed. Sidney Lee. London: Smith, Elder.

Popkin, Richard H. 1987. "The Religious Background of Seventeenth-Century Philosophy." *Journal of the History of Philosophy* 25: 35–50.

Prins, J. 1990. "Hobbes and the School of Padua: Two Incompatible Approaches of Science." *Archiv für Geschichte der Philosophie* 72, Heft 1: 26–46.

Prior, Moody E. 1954. "Bacon's Man of Science." *Journal of the History of Ideas* 15, no. 3 (June): 348–70.

Pullen, John M. 1989. "Introduction to Malthus's *Principles of Political Economy,*" variorum ed. Cambridge: Cambridge University Press.

Pullen, John M. 1987. "Malthus, Thomas Robert." In *The New Palgrave: A Dictionary of Economics*, 4 vols, eds. John Eatwell, Murray Milgate and Peter Newman. London: Macmillan.

Pullen, John M. 1986. "Correspondence Between Malthus and His Parents." *History of Political Economy* 18, no. 1 (Spring): 133–54.

Pullen, John M. 1982. "Malthus on the Doctrine of Proportions and the Concept of the Optimum." *Australian Economic Papers* 21, no. 39 (December): 270–85. Reprinted in J. Wood 1986, 1: 419–36.

Pullen, John M. 1981a. "Malthus' Theological Ideas and Their Influence on His Principle of Population." *History of Political Economy* 13, no. 1 (Spring): 39–54.

Pullen, John M. 1981b. "Notes from Malthus: The Inverarity Manuscript." *History of Political Economy* 13, no. 4 (Winter): 794–811. Reprinted in J. Wood 1986, 4: 290–305.

Puro, Edward. 1992. "Uses of the Term 'Natural' in Adam Smith's *Wealth of Nations*." In *Research in the History of Economic Thought and Methodology*, vol. 9, ed. Warren J. Samuels, pp. 73–83. Greenwich, Conn: Jai Press.

Quetelet, Adolphe. 1836. *Sur l'homme et le développement de ses facultés, ou essai de physique sociale*, 2 vols. Bruxelles: Louis Hauman.

Quinton, Anthony. 1980. *Francis Bacon*. Oxford: Oxford University Press.

Rae, John. 1834. "Of the *Wealth of Nations* as a Branch of the Philosophy of Induction." Ch. 15 of his *Statement of Some New Principles on the Subject of Political Economy, exposing the fallacies of the system of free trade, and of some other doctrines maintained in the "Wealth of Nations."* Boston: Hilliard, Gray.

Randall, John Hermann. 1962. *The Career of Philosophy*, 2 vols. N.Y.: Columbia University Press.

Randall, John Hermann. 1940. "The Development of Scientific Method in the School of Padua." *Journal of the History of Ideas* 1, no. 2 (April): 177–206.

Raphael, D. D. 1985. *Adam Smith*. Oxford: Oxford University Press.

Raphael, D. D. 1977. *Hobbes: Moralist Politics*. London: George Allen and Unwin.

Rashid, Salim. 1992. "The *Wealth of Nations* and Historical Facts." *Journal of the History of Economic Thought* 14 (Fall): 225–43.

Rashid, Salim. 1988. "Recent Literature on Malthus." In Thweatt 1988: 53–84; commentary by J. M. Pullen, pp. 85–101.

Rashid, Salim. 1987a. "Malthus and Classical Economics." In *The New Palgrave: A Dictionary of Economics*, 4 vols., eds. John Eatwell, Murray Milgate and Peter Newman. London: Macmillan.

Rashid, Salim. 1987b. "Malthus's *Essay on Population*: The Facts of 'Super-Growth' and the Rhetoric of Scientific Persuasion." *Journal of the History of the Behavioral Sciences* 23, no. 1 (January): 22–36.

Rashid, Salim. 1982. "Adam Smith's Rise to Fame: A Re-examination of the Evidence." *The Eighteenth Century* 23 (Winter): 64–85.

Rashid, Salim. 1981. "Malthus' *Principles* and British Economic Thought, 1820–1835." *History of Political Economy* 13, no. 1 (Spring): 55–79.

Rattansi, Piyo. 1988. "Newton and the Wisdom of the Ancients." In Fauvel et al., 1988, pp. 184–201.

Raynor, David R. 1984. "Hume's Abstract of Adam Smith's *Theory of Moral Sentiments.*" *Journal of the History of Philosophy* 22: 50–79.

Recktenwald, Horst Claus. 1978. "An Adam Smith Renaissance *anno* 1976? The Bicentenary Output—A Reappraisal of His Scholarship." *Journal of Economic Literature* 16, no. 1 (March): 56–83. Reprinted in Mair 1990: 103–34.

Redman, Deborah A. 1994. "Karl Popper's Theory of Science and Econometrics: The Rise and Decline of Social Engineering." *Journal of Economic Issues* 28, no. 1 (March): 67–99.

Redman, Deborah A. 1991. *Economics and the Philosophy of Science.* Oxford: Oxford University Press.

Redman, Deborah A. 1989. *Economic Methodology: A Bibliography with References to Works in the Philosophy of Science, 1860–1988.* N.Y.: Greenwood Press.

"Regulation of Watches." 1753. *Gentleman's Magazine* 23 (November): 518–21.

Rendall, Jane. 1978. *The Origins of the Scottish Enlightenment.* London: Macmillan.

Ricardo, David. 1951–1973. *The Works and Correspondence of David Ricardo,* 11 vols., ed. Piero Sraffa with M. H. Dobb. Cambridge: Cambridge University Press for the Royal Economic Society.

Ricardo, David. 1928. *Notes on Malthus's "Principles of Political Economy,"* eds. Jacob H. Hollander and T. E. Gregory. Baltimore: Johns Hopkins University Press.

Robbins, Lionel. 1967. "Malthus as an Economist." *Economic Journal* 77 (June): 257–61. Reprinted in J. Wood 1986, 1: 260–65.

Robertson, H. M. 1957. "The Ricardo Problem." *South African Journal of Economics* 25 (September): 171–86; Reprinted in J. Wood 1985, 1: 180–95.

Robertson, R. John. 1838. "Transactions of the Statistical Society." *Westminster Review* 29 (April): 45–72.

Röd, Wolfgang. 1970. *Geometrischer Geist und Naturrecht. Methodengeschichtliche Untersuchungen zur Staatsphilosophie im 17. und 18. Jahrhundert.* Bayrische Akademie der Wissenschaften, Abhandlungen neue Folge, Heft 70. München: Verlag der Bayrischen Akademie der Wissenschaften.

Rogers, J. D., and E. C. K. Gonner. 1926. "Ricardo, David." In *Palgrave's Dictionary of Political Economy,* new ed., ed. Henry Higgs. London: Macmillan.

Romanell, Patrick. 1991. "The Scientific and Medical Genealogy of Locke's 'Historical, Plain Method.'" In Ashcraft 1991, 4: 476–510.

Roncaglia, A. 1982. "Hollander's Ricardo." *Journal of Post Keynesian Economics* 4, no. 3 (Spring): 339–59. Reprinted in J. Wood 1985, 4: 174–90.

Rosenthal, Jerome. 1955. "Voltaire's Philosophy of History." *Journal of the History of Ideas* 16, no. 2 (April); 151–78.

Rossi, Paola. 1973 [1968]. "Baconianism." In *Dictionary of the History of Ideas: Studies of Selected Pivotal Ideas*, ed. Philip P. Wiener, pp. 172–79. N.Y.: Charles Scribner's Sons.

Roth, Leon. 1937. *Descartes' Discourse on Method.* Oxford: Clarendon Press.

Rubin, Ernest. 1960. "The Quantitative Data and Methods of the Rev. T. R. Malthus." *American Statistician* 14, no. 1 (February): 28–31.

Rubin, Ernest. 1959. "Statistics and Adam Smith." *American Statistician* 13, no. 2 (April): 23–24.

Russell, Paul. 1985. "Hume's *Treatise* and Hobbes's *The Elements of Law.*" *Journal of the History of Ideas* 46, no. 1 (January-March): 51–63.

Ryan, Alan. 1987. "Mill, John Stuart." In *The New Palgrave: A Dictionary of Economics*, 4 vols., eds. John Eatwell, Murray Milgate, and Peter Newman. London: Macmillan.

Ryan, Alan. 1974. *J. S. Mill.* London: Routledge and Kegan Paul.

St. Clair, Oswald. 1957. *A Key to Ricardo.* London: Routledge.

Salmon, Wesley C. 1973. "Confirmation." *Scientific American* (May): 75–83.

Sargeant, J. R. 1963. "Are American Economists Better?" *Oxford Economic Papers* n.s. 15, no. 1 (March): 1–7.

Say, Jean-Baptiste. 1971 [1880]. *A Treatise on Political Economy*, trans. of 4th ed., *Traité d'Économie Politique*, by C. R. Prinsep and Clement C. Biddle. N.Y.: Augustus M. Kelley.

Sayers, R. S. 1953. "Ricardo's Views on Monetary Questions." *Quarterly Journal of Economics* 67 (February): 30–49. Reprinted in J. Wood 1985, 4: 53–68; and *Papers in English Monetary History*, eds. T. S. Ashton and R. S. Sayers, pp. 76–95. Oxford: Clarendon Press, 1953.

Schabas, Margaret. 1992. "Breaking Away: History of Economics as History of Science." *History of Political Economy* 24, no. 1 (Spring): 187–203.

Schabas, Margaret. 1990. *A World Ruled by Number: William Stanley Jevons and the Rise of Mathematical Economics.* Princeton: Princeton University Press.

Schaffer, Simon. 1988. "Newtonianism." In *The Companion to the History of Modern Science*, eds. G. N. Cantor, J. R. R. Christie, M. J. S. Hodge, R. C. Olby, pp. 610–26. Beckenham: Croom Helm.

Schankula, H. A. S. 1991. "Locke, Descartes, and the Science of Nature." In Ashcraft 1991, 4: 374–96.

Schneewind, J. B., ed. 1968. *A Collection of Critical Essays.* Notre Dame, Ind.: University of Notre Dame Press.

Schofield, Robert E. 1978. "An Evolutionary Taxonomy of Eighteenth-Century Newtonianisms." In *Studies in Eighteenth-Century Culture*, vol. 7, ed. Roseann Runte, pp. 175–92. Madison: University of Wisconsin Press.

Schouls, Peter A. 1980. *The Imposition of Method: A Study of Descartes and Locke.* Oxford: Clarendon Press.

Schumpeter, Joseph A. 1954a. *Economic Doctrine and Method: An Historical Sketch,* transl. R. Aris. London: George Allen and Unwin Ltd. (*Epochen der Dogmen- und Methodengeschichte,* J. C. B. Mohr (Paul Siebeck), 1912).

Schumpeter, Joseph A. 1954b. *History of Economic Analysis,* ed. Elizabeth Boody Schumpeter. N.Y.: Oxford University Press.

Secord, James A. 1985. "Newton in the Nursery: Tom Telescope and the Philosophy of Tops and Balls, 1761–1838." *History of Science* 23: 127–51.

Seifert, G. F. 1993. "The Philosophy of Hobbes: Text and Content and the Problem of Sedimentation." In King 1993, 1: 303–13.

Senior, Nassau W. 1951 [1836]. *An Outline of the Science of Political Economy.* N.Y.: Augustus M. Kelley.

Senn, P. R. 1958. "The Earliest Use of the Term 'Social Science.'" *Journal of the History of Ideas* 19 (October): 568–70. Reprinted in J. Wood 1987, 4: 84–86.

Shapin, Steven. 1974. "The Audience for Science in Eighteenth Century Edinburgh." *History of Science* 12 (June): 95–121.

Shapin, Steven, and Simon Schaffer. 1985. *Leviathan and the Air-Pump: Hobbes, Boyle, and the Experimental Life,* with Schaffer's transl. of Hobbes's *Dialogus physicus de natura aeris.* Princeton: Princeton University Press.

Shepherd, Christine M. 1982. "Newtonianism in Scottish Universities in the Seventeenth Century." In *The Origins and Nature of the Scottish Enlightenment,* eds. R. H. Campbell and Andrew S. Skinner, pp. 65–85. Edinburgh: John Donald Publishers.

Shirras, G. Findlay, and J. H. Craig. 1945. "Sir Isaac Newton and the Currency." *Economic Journal* 55 (June-September): 217–41.

Simon, Herbert A. 1988a. "The Emperor Still Unclad." *Mathematical Intelligencer* 10, no. 2 (Spring): 10–11.

Simon, Herbert A. 1988b. "Final Reply to Koblitz." *Mathematical Intelligencer* 10, no. 2 (Spring): 12.

Simon, Herbert A. 1988c. "Unclad Emperors: A Case of Mistaken Identity." *Mathematical Intelligencer* 10, no. 1 (Winter): 11–14.

Skinner, Andrew S. 1993. Letter to author, 15 April.

Skinner, Andrew S. 1987. "Smith, Adam." In *The New Palgrave: A Dictionary of Economics,* 4 vols., eds. John Eatwell, Murray Milgate, and Peter Newman. London: Macmillan.

Skinner, Andrew S. 1979. "Adam Smith: An Aspect of Modern Economics?" *Scottish Journal of Political Economy* 26, no. 2 (June): 109–26. Reprinted in J. Wood 1984, 1: 460–77.

Skinner, Andrew S. 1974. "Adam Smith, Sciences and the Role of the Imagination." In *Hume and the Enlightenment,* ed. William B. Todd, pp. 164–88. Edinburgh: Edinburgh University Press.

Skinner, Andrew S. 1967. "Natural History in the Age of Adam Smith." *Political Studies* 15, no. 1: 32–48.

Skinner, Andrew S., and Thomas Wilson. 1975. *Essays on Adam Smith.* Oxford: Clarendon Press.

Skinner, Quentin. 1993. "Thomas Hobbes and the Nature of the Early Royal Society." In King 1993, 1: 159–83.

Smith, Adam. 1987. *The Correspondence of Adam Smith,* 2nd ed., eds. Ernest Campbell Mossner and Ian Simpson Ross. Glasgow edition, *The Works and Correspondence of Adam Smith,* vol. 6. Oxford: Clarendon Press.

Smith, Adam. 1983. *Lectures on Rhetoric and Belles Lettres,* eds. J. A. Bryce and A. S. Skinner. Glasgow edition, *The Works and Correspondence of Adam Smith,* vol. 4. Oxford: Clarendon Press.

Smith, Adam. 1980a. *Essays on Philosophical Subjects,* eds. W. P. D. Wightman and J. C. Bryce; with Dugald Stewart's Account of Adam Smith, ed. I. S. Ross. Glasgow edition, *The Works and Correspondence of Adam Smith,* vol. 3. Oxford: Clarendon Press.

Smith, Adam. 1980b [1756]. "Letter to the Edinburgh Review." In Smith 1980a: 242–54.

Smith, Adam. 1980c. "The Principles Which Lead and Direct Philosophical Enquiries; Illustrated by the History of Astronomy." In Smith 1980a: 33–105.

Smith, Adam. 1978. *Lectures on Jurisprudence,* eds. R. L. Meek, D. D. Raphael, and P. G. Stein. Glasgow edition, *The Works and Correspondence of Adam Smith,* vol. 5. Oxford: Clarendon Press.

Smith, Adam. 1976a [1776]. *An Inquiry into the Nature and Causes of the Wealth of Nations,* eds. R. H. Campbell, A. S. Skinner, and W. B. Todd. Glasgow edition, *The Works and Correspondence of Adam Smith,* vol. 2. Oxford: Clarendon Press.

Smith, Adam. 1976b [1759]. *The Theory of Moral Sentiments,* eds. D. D. Raphael and A. L. Macfie. Glasgow edition, *The Works and Correspondence of Adam Smith,* vol. 1. Oxford: Clarendon Press.

Soles, David E. 1985. "Locke's Empiricism and the Postulation of Unobservables." *Journal of the History of Philosophy* 23: 339–69.

Sorell, Tom. 1987. *Descartes.* Oxford: Oxford University Press.

Sowell, Thomas. 1974. *Classical Economics Reconsidered.* Princeton: Princeton University Press.

Spengler, Joseph J. 1961. "Quantification in Economics: Its History." In *Quantity and Quality,* ed. Daniel Lerner, pp. 129–211. N.Y.: The Free Press of Glencoe.

Spengler, Joseph J. 1945. "Malthus's Total Population Theory: A Restatement and Reappraisal." *Canadian Journal of Economics and Political Science* 11: 83–110 and 234–64. Reprinted in J. Wood 1986, 2: 30–90.

Spiegel, Henry William. 1991. *The Growth of Economic Thought,* 3rd ed. Englewood Cliffs, N.J.: Prentice-Hall.

Spiegel, Henry William. 1976. "Adam Smith's Heavenly City." *History of Political Economy* 8, no. 4 (Winter): 478–93.

Sprat, Thomas. 1959 [1667]. *History of the Royal Society*, eds. Jackson I. Cope and Harold Whitmore Jones. St. Louis: Washington University.

Stapleton, Barry. 1983. "Malthus: The Local Evidence and the Principle of Population." In *Malthus Past and Present*, eds. J. Dupâquier, A. Fauve-Chamoux, and E. Grebenik, pp. 45–59. London: Academic Press.

Stephen, Leslie. 1898. "Smith, Adam." In *Dictionary of National Biography*, ed. Sidney Lee. London: Smith, Elder.

Stephen, Leslie. 1896. "Ricardo, David." In *Dictionary of National Biography*, ed. Sidney Lee. London: Smith, Elder.

Steuart, Sir James. 1967. *The Works, Political, Metaphysical, and Chronological of Sir James Steuart*, 6 vols. The Adam Smith Library. N.Y.: Augustus M. Kelley.

Steuart, Sir James. 1966. *An Inquiry into the Principles of Political Economy*, edited and abridged by A. S. Skinner. Edinburgh: Oliver and Boyd.

Stewart, Dugald. 1980 [1794]. "Account of the Life and Writings of the Life of Adam Smith, LL.D." In Smith 1980a: 269–351.

Stewart, Dugald. 1854. *The Collected Works of Dugald Stewart*, 11 vols., ed. William Hamilton. Edinburgh: Thomas Constable.

Stigler, G. J. 1985. "Sraffa's Ricardo." In J. Wood 1985, 1: 106–19.

Stigler, G. J. 1981. "Review of Hollander's *Economics of David Ricardo*." *Journal of Economic Literature* 19, no. 1 (March): 100–2.

Stove, D. C. 1977. "Hume, Kemp Smith, and Carnap." *Australasian Journal of Philosophy* 55, no. 3 (December): 189–200.

Strong, E. W. 1957. "Newtonian Explications of Natural Philosophy." *Journal of the History of Ideas* 18, no. 1 (January): 49–83.

Strong, E. W. 1951. "Newton's 'Mathematical Way.'" *Journal of the History of Ideas* 12, no. 1 (January): 90–110.

Studenski, Paul. 1958. *The Income of Nations. Theory, Measurement, and Analysis: Past and Present*. N.Y.: New York University Press.

Sumner, John Bird. 1817. "Malthus on Population." *Quarterly Review* 17 (July): 369–403.

Taylor, Overton H. 1955. "Economics and the Idea of 'Jus naturale.'" In his *Economics and Liberalism: Collected Papers*, pp. 70–99. Cambridge: Harvard University Press.

Teggart, Frederick J. 1977 [1941]. *Theory and Processes of History*, preface by Kenneth Bock. Berkeley: University of California Press.

Thayer, H. S., ed. 1953. *Newton's Philosophy of Nature: Selections from his Writings*, intro. by John Herman Randall, Jr. N.Y.: Hafner Press.

Thomas, William. 1985. *Mill*. Oxford: Oxford University Press.

Thweatt, William O., ed. 1988. *Classical Political Economy: A Survey of Recent Literature*. Boston: Kluwer.

Toulmin, Stephen. 1961. *Foresight and Understanding: An Enquiry into the Aims of Science*. London: Hutcheson.

Tuck, Richard. 1989. *Hobbes*. Oxford: Oxford University Press.

Turnbull, George. 1976 [1740]. *The Principles of Moral Philosophy*. Hildesheim: Georg Olms Verlag.

Tyrrell, A. 1969. "Political Economy, Whiggism and the Education of Working-Class Adults in Scotland 1817–40." *Scottish Historical Review* 48: 151–65.

Urbach, Peter. 1982. "Francis Bacon as a Precursor to Popper." *British Journal for the Philosophy of Science* 33: 113–32.

Van De Pitte, Frederick P. 1991. "Descartes's *Mathesis Universalis*." In Moyal 1991b: 61–79.

Vickers, Douglas. 1957. "Method and Analysis in David Hume's Economic Essays." *Economica* 24 (August): 225–34.

Viner, Jacob. 1937. *Studies in the Theory of International Trade*. N.Y.: Harper & Brothers.

Voltaire, François-Marie Arouet. 1992 [1741]. *Eléments de la philosophie de Newton*. Critical edition by Robert L. Walters and W. H. Barber. *The Complete Works of Voltaire*, vol. 15. Oxford: Alden Press.

Voltaire, François-Marie Arouet. 1744. "On Writing History." *Gentleman's Magazine* 14 (August): 420–21.

Vorzimmer, Peter. 1969. "Darwin, Malthus, and the Theory of Natural Selection." *Journal of the History of Ideas* 30, no. 4 (October-December): 527–42.

Wagenführ, Horst. 1933. *Der Systemgedanke in der Nationalökonomie. Eine methodengeschichtliche Betrachtung*. Jena: Gustav Fischer.

Waterman, A. M. C. 1991a. "A Cambridge 'Via Media' in Late Georgian Anglicanism." *Journal of Eccelesiastical History* 42, no. 3 (July): 419–36.

Waterman, A. M. C. 1991b. *Revolution, Economics and Religion: Christian Political Economy, 1798–1833*. Cambridge: Cambridge University Press.

Webster, C. 1967. "The Origins of the Royal Society." *History of Science* 6: 106–28.

Weir, D. R. 1987. "Malthus's Theory of Population." In *The New Palgrave: A Dictionary of Economics*, 4 vols., eds. John Eatwell, Murray Milgate and Peter Newman. London: Macmillan.

Westfall, Richard S. 1987. "Newton's Scientific Personality." *Journal of the History of Ideas* 48, no. 4 (October-December): 551–70.

Westfall, Richard S. 1980. *Never at Rest: A Biography of Isaac Newton*. Cambridge: Cambridge University Press.

Westfall, Richard S. 1967. "Newton, Sir Isaac." In *Encyclopedia Britannica*.

Whately, Richard. 1988 [1826]. *Elements of Logic*, ed. Paola Dessì. Bologna: Cooperativa Libraria Universitaria Editrice Bologna.

Whately, Richard. 1966 [1832]. *Introductory Lectures on Political Economy*, 2nd ed. N.Y.: Augustus M. Kelley.

Whewell, William. 1971. *Mathematical Exposition of Some Doctines of Political Economy.* Reprint of four lectures first publ. in *Transactions of the Cambridge Philosophical Society,* 1929, 1831, 1850. N.Y.: Augustus M. Kelley.

Whewell, William. 1968. *William Whewell's Theory of Scientific Method,* ed. Robert E. Butts. Pittsburgh: University of Pittsburgh Press.

Whewell, William. 1859. "Prefatory Notice." In *Literary Remains, Consisting of Lectures and Tracts on Political Economy, of the Late Rev. Richard Jones,* ed. William Whewell, pp. ix-xl. London: John Murray.

Whewell, William. 1850a. "Mathematical Exposition of Some Doctrines of Political Economy—Second Memoir." In Whewell 1971.

Whewell, William. 1850b. "Mathematical Exposition of Certain Doctrines of Political Economy—Third Memoir." In Whewell 1971.

Whewell, William. 1831. "Mathematical Exposition of Some of the Leading Doctrines in Mr. Ricardo's 'Principles of Political Economy and Taxation.'" In Whewell 1971.

Whewell, William. 1829. "Mathematical Exposition of Some Doctrines of Political Economy." In Whewell 1971.

Whiston, William. 1972 [1716]. *Sir Isaac Newton's Mathematick Philosophy More Easily Demonstrated,* intro. by I. Bernard Cohen. N.Y.: Johnson Reprint Corporation.

Whitaker, J. K. 1975. "John Stuart Mill's Methodology." *Journal of Political Economy* 83, no. 5 (October): 1033–49. Reprinted in J. Wood 1987, 1: 479–94.

Wightman, W. P. D. 1975. "Adam Smith and the History of Ideas." In Skinner and Wilson 1975: 44–67.

Wilson, David B. 1974. "Herschel and Whewell's Version of Newtonianism." *Journal of the History of Ideas* 35, no. 1 (January/March): 79–97.

Winch, Donald. 1987. "Mill, James." In *The New Palgrave: A Dictionary of Economics,* 4 vols., eds. John Eatwell, Murray Milgate, and Peter Newman. London: Macmillan.

Wise, M. Norton, with Crosbie Smith. 1989/1990. "Work and Waste: Political Economy and Natural Philosophy in Nineteenth Century Britain," parts 1–3. *History of Science* 27 (1989): 263–301; 27 (1989): 391–449; 28 (1990): 221–61.

Wood, John Cunningham, ed. 1987. *John Stuart Mill: Critical Assessments,* 4 vols. London: Croom Helm.

Wood, John Cunningham, ed. 1986. *Thomas Robert Malthus: Critical Assessments,* 4 vols. London: Croom Helm.

Wood, John Cunningham, ed. 1985. *David Ricardo: Critical Assessments,* 4 vols. London: Croom Helm.

Wood, John Cunningham, ed. 1984. *Adam Smith: Critical Assessments,* 4 vols. London: Croom Helm.

Wood, Neal. 1991. "The Baconian Character of Locke's *Essay.*" In Ashcraft 1991, 4: 333–73.

Wood, P. B. 1989. "The Natural History of Man in the Scottish Enlightenment." *History of Science* 27: 89–123.

Worland, Stephen T. 1976. "Mechanistic Analogy and Smith on Exchange." *Review of Social Economy* 34, no. 4: 245–58.

Wrigley, A. E. 1986. "Elegance and Experience: Malthus at the Bar of History." In *The State of Population Theory Forward from Malthus,* eds. David Coleman und Roger Scholfield, pp. 46–64. Oxford: Basil Blackwell.

Yanaihara, Tadao. 1951. *A Full and Detailed Catalogue of Books Which Belonged to Adam Smith.* Tokyo: Iwanami Shoten.

Young, Arthur. 1967 [1774]. *Political Arithmetic; containing Observations on the Present State of Great Britain.* N.Y.: Augustus M. Kelley.

Zagorin, Perez. 1990. "Hobbes on Our Mind." *Journal of the History of Ideas* 51, no. 2 (April-June): 317–35.

# Author Index

Aalto, S. K., 117
Achenwall, Gottfried, 143
Allison, Archibald, 83
Anderson, James, 3n, 273
Archimedes, 128
Aristotle, 12, 13n, 22, 24, 48, 160n, 163, 231
  author of *Acroamatic Physics*, 105
  author of *Politics*, 146n88
Arnold, N. S., 174
Arrow, Kenneth, 294
Ashley, Myron, 57
Austen, John, 351
Axtell, James, 45, 62, 63
Ayer, A. J., 177, 203, 337

Babbage, Charles, 99, 151, 156
Bacon, Francis (Lord), 11–21
  attacks on received systems, 12–15
  author of *Instauratio Magna*, 12, 170
  author of *Novum organum*, 12, 13, 16
  criticisms of the method of, 168, 169
  doctrine of idols, 13–16, 170, 226
  Engels on, 21
  experiments and, 18
  Hayek on, 21
  Hume on, 18n17
  hypotheses and, 16
  induction (*see* Induction)
  influence of religion on, 10, 11, 12
  influence on Scottish philosophers, 114
  Mill on, 335, 341, 342, 356
  natural history (*see* Natural history)
  natural philosophy of, 15, 16

  negative methodological rules of, 12
  *philosophia prima* and, 15
  position on empiricism and rationalism, 13
  position on human sciences, 16
  position on mathematics, 16, 17
  position on systems, 17
  skepticism as a philosophy of knowledge, 14
  Stubbe on, 18
  three positive methodological rules, 16
  Whewell on, 94, 95
Bagehot, Walter, 245, 249n70, 250n75, 261, 263n9, 275
Bailey, Samuel, 302n76, 303
Bailly, Jean Sylvain, 216
Bain, Alexander, 324n4
Balassa, Bela, 6
Barbon, Nicholas, 362n6
Barfoot, Michael, 76, 79n97, 81, 115n31
Barrow, Isaac, 60
Barucci, Piero, 319
Bayes, Thomas, 200
Beattie, James, 83n
Becker, James, 242
Bentham, Jeremy, 20, 35, 108, 138, 151, 192n4, 346
  method of, 322
Bergmann, Barbara, 318
Berkeley, George (Biship), 35, 80
Berry, Christopher, 242
Bevilacqua, Vincent, 188, 242, 243
Bittermann, Henry, 207
Black, R. D. C., 266

position on scope of economics, 300
position on semantics, 301, 302
position on Corn Laws, 279
reputation of, 260–268
Say on, 286
Schumpeter on, 260, 262, 263, 284, 285n49, 301n73
scientific temperament of, 286
scope of economics and, 288
similarity with Keynes's approach, 263n8
similarity with Petty's approach, 309, 310
single causation of, 311
Sraffian economics and, 266–268
Stigler on, 263, 264
"strong cases" of, 287, 304
summary of method of, 315, 357
theory of rents of, 278, 279
theory of wages of, 278, 279
use of laws, 286, 287
use of mathematics, 298, 299, 301
Whewell on, 283n45
*See also* "Ricardo problem"
Ricardo, Frank, 282
Rist, Charles, 272, 278–280, 282, 307
Robbins, Lionel, 266n14
Robertson, H. M., 264
Robertson, R. John, 157n
Robertson, William, 122
Robinson, Joan, 267
Röd, Wolfgang, 36, 39
Rogers, Edward, 96n128
Rogers, J. D., 283
Rogers, Thorold, 187n
Roggi, Piero, 319
Romanell, Patrick, 67
Roncaglia, A., 267n
Rosenthal, Jerome, 118n36
Rossi, Paoli, 169
Roth, Leon, 25, 33n
Rousseau, Jean-Jacques, 120, 125, 126, 237, 269
Rubin, Ernest, 296
Russell, Bertrand, 201
Russell, John, 83
Russell, Paul, 70
Ryan, Alan, 93n124, 325n5

St. Clair, Oswald, 289
Salmon, Wesley, 184
Samuelson, Paul, 318

Say, Jean-Baptiste, 3n, 4, 136n66, 248n68, 286, 303
Sayers, R. S., 276n31, 277
Schabas, Margaret, 344, 345, 346
Schaffer, Simon, 41, 212n13
Schankula, H. A. S., 67
Schneewind, J. B., 335n
Schofield, Robert, 212n13
Schumpeter, Joseph, 57, 143n82, 261n3, 316, 339n, 351
characterization of Malthus, 261, 263, 284, 301n73, 310n82
characterization of Ricardo, 260, 262, 263, 284, 302, 307
view of Smith, 220, 241, 244
Scott, Walter, 83
Scrope, G. Poulett, 212n13
Secord, James, 63, 212n13
Sedgwick, Adam, 156
Senior, Nassau, 3n, 4, 136, 295, 315
Senn, P. R., 104
Seymour, Lord Webb, 83
Shaftesbury, Earl of, 231n46
Shapin, Steven, 41, 244
Shepherd, Christine, 105n9, 212n13
Simon, Herbert A., 118n35
Sinclair, John, 143
Sismondi, Jean de, 3n, 4, 104, 303
Skinner, Andrew, 122, 209n, 217, 227n42, 231, 248
Skinner, Q., 42n53
Smith, Adam, 133, 134, 218–220
alleged mechanical nature of thought of, 133, 134, 218–220
alleged metaphysical nature of his method, 123
alleged use of feedback systems, 220n
atomism of, 106
author of "History of Astronomy," 210, 220–227, 233, 243
author of *Lectures on Jurisprudence,* 232n49
author of *Lectures on Rhetoric and Belles Lettres,* 208
author of *Theory of Moral Sentiments,* 209, 220, 233, 234, 238–240, 241n61, 246, 247, 362
author of *The Wealth of Nations,* 211, 215, 219, 220, 232n48, 233–235, 238, 239, 241, 252, 253, 256, 257

# Subject Index